토마토
BASIC
RC

토마토 BASIC 전면 개정판
RC

지은이	NE능률 영어교육연구소, 이미영
선임 연구원	한윤희
연구원	이경화, 이은비, 이보영, 고은정
영문 교열	Danielle M. Josset, Julie A. Tofflemire
감수	YBM 어학원 종로센터 이미영 강사
디자인	디자인샐러드
일러스트	정민영
맥편집	김선희
영업	한기영, 이경구, 박인규, 정철교, 김남준, 이우현
마케팅	박혜선, 남경진, 이지원, 김여진

토마토 BASIC RC
전면 개정판을 내면서

2005년 첫 출간 이후 독자 여러분께 꾸준히 사랑받아, 토익 입문서 베스트셀러 선두 자리를 굳건히 지키고 있는 토마토 BASIC이 2018년 새롭게 **전면 개정판**을 출시합니다.

최근 토익은 빠른 시간 내에 많은 정보를 이해하고 문맥을 파악하는 능력을 요구하고 있습니다. 이런 변화 속에서 정답을 빨리 찾는 요령보다는, 진짜 영어 실력이 뒷받침되어야 목표 점수에 도달할 수 있게 되었습니다. 이렇게 여러분의 영어 실력을 탄탄히 다지도록 하는 것이 토마토 BASIC이 출간부터 지금까지 추구해온 학습법이자, 오랫동안 토익 입문서 베스트셀러 자리를 지키고 있는 힘이라고 생각합니다.

토마토 BASIC RC 전면 개정판은 토익의 핵심을 짚어주어 토익이 쉬워지는 토익 입문서입니다. 영어 기본기를 다질 수 있도록 문법과 독해 학습을 구성하면서, 토익 유형의 예문과 어휘를 사용하여 영어 기본기와 토익 목표 점수, 두 가지를 한 번에 공략할 수 있도록 기획되었습니다. 그리고 입문자 여러분의 효과적인 학습을 위해 토익에 꼭 필요한 내용만을 핵심 POINT로 담았습니다. 또한, 토익 유형 역시 꼼꼼하게 분석하여, 이에 맞게 문제풀이 전략과 다양한 실전 문제를 배치했습니다.

토익을 처음 시작하는 학습자, 영어를 오랜만에 공부하는 학습자라면 토익을 어떻게 공부해야 할지 막막한 것이 당연합니다. 토마토 BASIC은 이런 막막함을 마주하고 있는 학습자에게 목표한 토익 점수를 받을 수 있는 최단 경로를 제공하고자 합니다. 여러분 혼자서 가는 그 길이 외롭고 힘들지 않도록 토마토 BASIC이 항상 여러분을 응원합니다.

이 책의 목차

PART 7

이 책의 특장점

핵심을 정확하게 짚어주는 문법 학습

핵심 POINT
토익에 자주 출제되는 핵심 문법 내용을 뽑아 삽화와 함께 정리했다. 문법 학습 전후에 확인하면 학습 효과가 배가될 것이다.

쉽고 자세한 내용 설명
토익에서 중요하게 다루는 문법 내용을 쉽고 자세히 풀어 설명했다. 토익형 예문들로 기본적인 개념부터 확실히 다질 수 있다.

핵심 POINT 확인하기
학습 내용을 제대로 알고 있는지 확인하기 위해 실전 문제 전 연습 단계로 2지선다형 문제를 배치했다. 문제 풀기가 쉽지 않다면 '핵심 POINT 슬쩍 보기'를 참고하자.

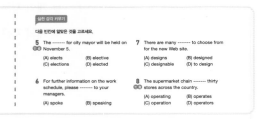

실전 감각 키우기
최신 기출 경향이 반영된 실전형 문제들을 통해 학습한 내용을 바로 적용해 볼 수 있게 했다. 시험에 자주 출제되는 유형은 빈출 아이콘으로 표시했다.

핵심 POINT 다시 보기
앞서 학습한 문법 내용의 핵심만 모아서 한 번 더 정리할 수 있다. 빈칸에 들어갈 알맞은 말을 적어보면서 확실히 이해했는지 확인해 보자.

주제별로 정리된 효과 만점 어휘와 패러프레이징

자주 출제되는 주요 어휘들을 주제별로 묶어서 정리했다. 표제어마다 의미, 파생어(파), 유의어(유), 반의어(반), 관련 어휘(관), 콜로케이션 정보를 같이 수록해서 깊이 있는 어휘 학습을 가능하게 했다. 해당 어휘는 별도의 단어장으로 인쇄해서 휴대할 수 있도록 www.nebooks.co.kr에서 무료로 다운로드 받을 수 있다.

PART 7 독해의 핵심인 패러프레이징의 다양한 예시와 문제가 실려 있어서 패러프레이징을 충분히 연습할 수 있다.

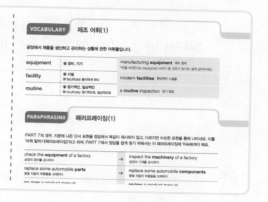

효율적인 문제 풀이를 도와주는 독해 전략

지문의 길이가 긴 PART 7을 효율적으로 풀 수 있도록 문제 유형별, 지문 유형별 문제 풀이 전략을 제시했다. 실전형 문제도 담아서 학습한 전략을 바로바로 적용하여 풀어볼 수 있다.

QR코드를 통해 어휘와 해설 제공

실전 모의고사에서 어휘를 바로 확인할 수 있도록 QR코드를 기획했다. 해설 역시 QR코드로 제공해서 해설지를 따로 챙기지 않아도 필요한 해설을 쉽게 확인할 수 있다.

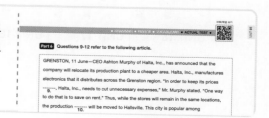

1주

Day 01 월 일	Day 02 월 일	Day 03 월 일	Day 04 월 일	Day 05 월 일	Day 06 월 일
WARM-UP UNIT 01	UNIT 02	UNIT 03	UNIT 04	UNIT 05	UNIT 06

2주

Day 07 월 일	Day 08 월 일	Day 09 월 일	Day 10 월 일	Day 11 월 일	Day 12 월 일
복습 WARM-UP UNIT 01~06	UNIT 07	UNIT 08	UNIT 09	UNIT 10	UNIT 11

3주

Day 13 월 일	Day 14 월 일	Day 15 월 일	Day 16 월 일	Day 17 월 일	Day 18 월 일
복습 UNIT 07~11	UNIT 12	UNIT 13	UNIT 14	UNIT 15	복습 UNIT 12~15

4주

Day 19 월 일	Day 20 월 일	Day 21 월 일	Day 22 월 일	Day 23 월 일	Day 24 월 일
UNIT 16	UNIT 17	UNIT 18	UNIT 19	UNIT 20	ACTUAL TEST

TOEIC은

Test **o**f **E**nglish for **I**nternational **C**ommunication의 약자로
영어가 모국어가 아닌 사람들을 대상으로 의사소통에 중점을 두고
일상 생활 또는 국제 업무에 필요한 실용 영어 능력을 평가하는 시험이다.

→ 시험 구성

구성	PART	내용		문항 수	시간	배점
Listening Comprehension	1	사진 묘사		6		
	2	질의 응답		25	100	45분	495점
	3	짧은 대화		39			
	4	짧은 담화		30			
Reading Comprehension	5	단문 공란 메우기 (문법/어휘)		30			
	6	장문 공란 메우기		16	100	75분	495점
	7	독해	단일 지문	29			
			이중 지문	10			
			삼중 지문	15			
Total		**7 Parts**		**200문항**	**120분**	**990점**

→ 접수 방법

TOEIC 접수는 한국 토익 위원회 사이트(www.toeic.co.kr)에서 온라인으로만 접수 가능하다.

→ 시험 준비물

신분증 규정 신분증만 가능
　　　　(주민등록증, 운전면허증, 기간 만료 전의 여권, 공무원증 등)
필기구 연필, 지우개 (컴퓨터용 사인펜이나 볼펜은 사용 금지)

→ 성적 확인

한국 토익 위원회 사이트에 안내된 일자에 인터넷 또는 ARS(060-800-0515)를 통해 성적이 발표된다. 성적표는 우편이나 온라인으로 발급받을 수 있으며, 우편 발급은 성적 발표 후 약 일주일이 소요되고, 온라인 발급은 성적 유효기간인 2년 안에 홈페이지에서 1회에 한해 무료로 출력할 수 있다.

PART **5**

단문 공란 메우기(30문항)

1 문제 유형

빈칸이 포함된 단문이 주어지고, 4개의 선택지 중에서 빈칸에 알맞은 것을 고르는 문제이다.

> Mattie White is going to lead a ------- on the new marketing policies this afternoon.
> **(A) workshop**
> (B) meaning
> (C) rule
> (D) model

2 시간 배분

Reading Comprehension을 푸는 데 주어진 시간은 총 75분이다.
PART 6와 PART 7에서 충분한 시간을 확보하려면 PART 5를 빨리 푸는 수밖에 없다. 그러므로 PART 5에서 12분을 넘기지 않도록 하자. 어려운 문제가 나오면 시간을 끌기보다 PART 6&7으로 넘어가는 것이 효과적이다.

3 출제 포인트

문법

특정한 문법 지식을 알고 있는지에 평가의 초점이 맞춰져 있다. 대명사, 전치사, 접속사처럼 하나의 문법 카테고리 내에서 문제가 출제되기도 하고, 시제와 태를 같이 묻는 문제처럼 복합적인 문법 내용을 묻기도 한다.

> Vegetables ------- they bought in the Roger's Supermarket are cheaper than others.
> **(A) that**
> (B) what
> (C) who
> (D) than

▶ '관계대명사'라는 문법 내용을 알아야 that을 정답으로 고를 수 있다. 이처럼 특정 문법 지식을 적용해야 하거나 특정 문법 지식에 구조나 어휘 지식을 복합적으로 묻기도 한다.

구조

문장 구조를 제대로 파악하고 있는지에 초점을 두고 있다. 빈칸에 들어갈 단어의 적절한 품사를 묻는 경우가 대부분으로, 선택지가 각기 다른 품사로 구성되어 있는 것이 특징이다.

> This morning, the manager called Ms. Gomez into his office and asked for her -------.
> (A) advise
> (B) advised
> (C) advisable
> **(D) advice**

▶ 선택지가 advise라는 동사와 다른 품사인 형용사, 명사로 이루어져 있다. 문장 구조를 빠르게 파악하면 해석 없이 해결할 수 있는 문제가 많으므로 구조 문제는 모든 문항을 맞춰야 한다.

어휘

다양한 어휘의 뜻을 얼마나 확실히 알고 있는지에 초점을 두고 있다. 개별 어휘의 기본 뜻은 물론, 2차 의미나 뉘앙스, 어법을 묻는 문제들도 출제된다.

> Send all the ------- in this company an e-mail about the construction plans.
> (A) jobs
> **(B) workers**
> (C) profits
> (D) tools

▶ 어휘 문제를 풀려면 기본적으로 문장 해석이 필요하지만 평소 자주 쓰이는 콜로케이션이나 어법을 알아두면 문제 푸는 시간을 절약할 수 있다. send는 〈send+간접 목적어+직접 목적어〉의 구조로 쓰이는 어휘이고, 간접 목적어는 사람이 쓰이는 경우가 많으니, 선택지에서 사람인 workers가 정답.

4 대비 전략

PART 5에서는 문법 지식을 갖추고 있는지 묻는 문제가 나오므로, 이에 대한 대비로 기본적인 문법 학습이 필요하다. 어휘 문제의 경우는 어휘의 의미를 통해 정답을 가려내는 문제뿐만 아니라 함께 자주 쓰이는 어휘나 어휘의 어법을 알아야 풀 수 있는 문제도 자주 나오므로, 해당 문제를 대비할 수 있도록 콜로케이션과 어법 등을 지속적으로 학습해야 한다.

PART 5 대비 전략은 문제를 빨리 풀어 PART 6와 PART 7을 위한 시간을 확보하는 것이다. 이를 위해 기본적인 내용 학습뿐만 아니라, 시간 단축을 목표로 하여 반복적으로 문제를 푸는 훈련도 해야 한다.

PART 6

장문 공란 메우기(16문항)

1 문제 유형

총 4개의 지문이 출제되고, 지문 하나당 4개의 문항이 딸려 있다. 각 문항은 PART 5 처럼 4개의 선택지 중 빈칸에 알맞은 것을 고르는 문제이다. PART 5처럼 문법, 구조, 어휘 지식을 묻지만, 지문 속에서 전체 맥락을 통해 정답을 골라야 하는 문제도 출제된다. PART 5와 달리, 빈칸에 적절한 문장을 고르는 문제도 출제되므로 글의 흐름을 파악하는 것이 중요하다.

Mr. Leonard Mosola
3508 West Road
Port Elizabeth
South Africa

Dear Mr. Mosola:

I am ------- to inform you that your membership with the Global Wildlife
        131.
Protection Agency has been fully processed. ------- . As such, you are
                                              132.
eligible to receive our monthly publication, *GWPA Concerns*, a quarterly
report on the ------- of our campaigns, and weekly e-mail updates
              133.
about ongoing environmental projects in your area. The membership fee
you have generously contributed entitles you to a 3-year membership
as ------- GWPA's rules and guidelines.
   134.

If you have any questions about your membership, or about the GWPA
organization, don't hesitate to contact us. Thank you so much for your
support!

Sincerely,

Ellen Fairchild
GWPA Membership Manager

---

131. **(A) delighted**
(B) delighting
(C) delightful
(D) delight

132. (A) Your application will take a week
to review.
(B) We advise you to renew your
membership.
**(C) GWPA welcomes you as a full
member!**
(D) We appreciate your interest and
generous donation.

133. (A) income
(B) brainstorming
(C) product
(D) progress

134. (A) specify
(B) specifying
(C) specified in
(D) specification of

2 시간 배분

16개의 문제를 8분 안에 해결하도록 하고 남은 시간을 PART 7에 쏟는 전략적인 시간 관리가 필요하다. 한 문제당 25-30초 내에 해결하도록 연습해야 한다.

3 출제 포인트

빈칸이 지문 중간에 들어가 있지만, 출제 포인트 및 선택지 구성은 PART 5와 같다. 그래서 빈칸이 있는 해당 문장만 봐도 해결되는 문제가 있는 반면, 문단으로 구성된 지문에서 출제되기 때문에 앞뒤 맥락을 통해 정답을 가려내야 하는 문제도 출제된다. 특히 PART 6에만 있는 '빈칸에 알맞은 문장을 고르는 유형'은 지문 전체의 구조나 문맥을 파악해야 정답을 가려낼 수 있다.

4 대비 전략

PART 5와 달리, 시제나 대명사 문제에서도 지문 전체의 문맥을 통해 답을 찾아야 하는 경우가 있다. 그래서 PART 6는 짧은 시간 안에 글의 흐름을 파악하여 문제에 접근하는 연습을 해야 한다. 글의 흐름을 자연스럽게 연결하기 위해 쓰이는 대명사, 접속사, 접속부사 등에 대해 익숙해지면 '빈칸에 알맞은 문장 고르기' 유형의 문제도 쉽게 풀 수 있다. 지문과 선택지가 분리된 형태라서, 글을 읽으면서 빈칸과 선택지를 빠르게 왔다 갔다 하며 보는 훈련도 필요하다.

PART 7

독해(54문항)

문제 유형

주어진 지문을 읽고 제시된 2-5개의 질문에 답하는 유형이다. 총 54문제가 출제되는데, 각 지문의 종류와 문항 수는 다음과 같다.

지문 종류	지문 수	지문 당 문항 수	전체 문항 수
단일 지문	10개	2-4문항	29
이중 지문	2개	5문항	10
삼중 지문	3개	5문항	15

To: All marketing staff
From: Charles Lane, Head of Marketing
Date: November 28

On Tuesday, December 10, the marketing department of Seatech Corporation will be holding its annual staff workshop in the second floor conference room. All marketing staff members except temporary part-time workers are expected to attend. The main purpose of this workshop will be to review the results of this year's marketing campaign. The final version of agenda will be circulated in a memorandum one week prior to the workshop.

The following are tentatively scheduled topics:
1. Internet marketing: Results and prospects
2. Marketing strategies in a global economy
3. Interdepartmental cooperation
4. Spreadsheet presentation

147. For whom is the December 10 program scheduled?
　　(A) Temporary workers
　　(B) Marketing staff members
　　(C) Marketing executives
　　(D) Staff from all departments

2 시간 배분

수험자들이 시간 부족을 가장 많이 호소하는 부분이 바로 PART 7이다. 긴 지문을 읽고 풀어야 해서 소요되는 시간도 길기 때문이다. 54문제를 풀려면 55분 정도는 확보되어야 하니 미리 시간 배분 연습을 하자.

3 출제 포인트

지문 종류

① 단일 지문: 이메일, 편지, 공지, 메모, 광고, 기사, 설명서 등 다양한 유형의 지문이 등장한다. 실제 생활에 많이 이용되는 문자 메시지나 온라인 채팅과 같은 대화체 지문도 나오므로 구어체에도 익숙해져야 한다.
② 이중 지문: 공지나 메모에 대한 문의, 편지나 이메일에 대한 답신, 공지문과 청구 내역 등 서로 연관된 지문들이 등장한다.
③ 삼중 지문: 광고를 보고 주문을 했는데 주문이 잘못되어 항의하는 이메일을 보내는 내용이 '광고-주문서-이메일'로 나오는 것과 같이, 서로 연관성 있는 세 개의 지문이 등장한다. 세 개의 지문이라고 해서 복잡하다고 생각하지 말고 두 개의 지문 형태와 마찬가지라고 생각해야 한다. 지문의 전체 길이는 두 개의 지문과 유사하므로 겁먹을 필요는 없다.

문제 유형

주로 일반적인 정보(글의 주제, 목적, 출처 등)와 구체적인 정보를 묻는 문제로 나뉜다. 대부분 한 지문당 일반적인 정보를 묻는 문제는 하나만 출제되고 나머지는 모두 구체적인 정보를 묻는 문제가 나온다. 구체적인 정보를 묻는 문제 유형 중 '화자의 의도를 묻는 유형'과 '문장의 적절한 위치를 찾는 유형'과 같은 특수한 유형은 각각 문제를 푸는 훈련이 필요하다.

패러프레이징

패러프레이징이란 어떤 내용을 반복해야 할 때 다른 말로 바꾸어 표현하는 것이다. 토익에서는 지문에 등장하는 표현을 질문이나 선택지에서 다르게 표현하여 출제된다. 이렇게 패러프레이징하는 이유는 내용을 제대로 이해했는지를 평가하기 위해서이다.

4 대비 전략

PART 7은 긴 지문으로 이루어져 입문자들에게는 더 어렵고 힘들게 느껴지는 부분이다. 단기간에 점수를 올리기 힘들기 때문에 가장 험난한 파트로 여겨지는데, 토익 시험은 독해 비중이 높아서 목표 점수를 얻으려면 독해를 등한시할 수 없다. 가장 중요한 것은 문장을 읽는데 막힘이 없도록 어휘와 독해 실력을 확보하는 것이다. 시간이 걸리더라도 꾸준히 독해량을 늘리며 훈련하는 것이 필요하다. 이에 더해, 평소 토익에 자주 출제되는 지문의 유형과 상황을 알아둔다면 지문을 파악하기가 훨씬 수월해질 것이다.

WARM UP

토익 리딩 기초 문법편

Reading Comprehension

영어를 공부하는 데 있어 가장 기본이 되는 것은 의미의 최소 단위인 '단어'입니다. 문장 안에서 단어는 일정한 쓰임이나 특징을 갖는데, 비슷한 쓰임이나 특징을 갖는 단어들끼리 분류한 것을 '품사'라고 합니다. 영어에는 모두 8가지의 '품사'가 있으며, 다양한 품사의 단어들이 모여 '구'나 '절'을 이룹니다. 또한, '구'나 '절'이 5가지의 일정한 순서로 배열되어 하나의 문장을 이루는데, 이를 '5문형'이라고 합니다.

본격적으로 토익 문장을 접하기에 앞서, 이들 기본 요소를 하나씩 짚어 볼까요? 처음부터 모두 외우려 하지 말고, '아~ 이런 특징이 있구나!' 정도로만 이해하고 넘어가면 됩니다.

품사는 단어를 기능, 형태, 쓰임에 따라 나눈 말의 종류입니다. 품사를 아는 것이 문법을 파악하는 기본입니다.

1 사물의 이름, 명사

명사란 사람, 동물, 사물, 장소 등의 '이름'이라고 이해하면 됩니다.

지금 공부하고 있는 'book', 손에 쥐고 있는 'pen', 시험 때 이용하는 'library' 와 'coffee', 미래의 'hope'와 'dream' 등이 모두 명사입니다.

그런데 영어의 명사는 셀 수 있는 명사(가산 명사)와 셀 수 없는 명사(불가산 명사)로 구분되고, 셀 수 있는 명사인 경우, 하나일 때(단수)와 둘 이상일 때(복수)의 형태가 달라진다는 특징이 있습니다.

위의 명사들 중에서 book, pen, library는 셀 수 있는 명사, coffee는 셀 수 없는 명사, hope, dream은 상황에 따라 셀 수 있는 명사 혹은 셀 수 없는 명사로 쓰입니다. 그리고 셀 수 있는 명사인 book, pen, library는 두 개 이상일 때 books, pens, libraries와 같이 형태를 바꿔 복수형으로 써야 해요.

그런데 이러한 가산·불가산 개념은 명사 앞에 쓰이는 단어에도 영향을 줍니다. 예를 들어, a book은 맞지만 a water는 틀리고, many pens라고 할 수는 있지만 much pens라고 할 수는 없거든요. 여기서 a, many, much 등과 같은 것들을 '한정사'라고 하며, 이 한정사의 개념과 명사에 관한 더 자세한 내용은 UNIT 02에서 다루도록 하겠습니다. ▶▶▶ 50쪽

2 명사의 대타, 대명사!

대명사란 '명사(구)를 대신하는 말'입니다.

어제 한 소개팅에 관해 친구와 얘기할 때, 상대방을 '친구가 소개해 준 사람'이라고 대화 내내 똑같이 지칭하는 것은 매우 비효율적입니다. 그래서 '그 사람, 그, 그녀' 등 짧은 단어로 대신하게 되는데, 영어에서도 이러한 역할을 하는 것이 바로 대명사입니다. 여러분이 잘 알고 있는 I, you, she, it, they 등이 대표적인 대명사입니다.

영어에서는 한 번 언급된 명사를 다시 말할 때 대명사를 쓴다는 원칙이 비교적 잘 지켜지고, 그 쓰임도 다양합니다. 이러한 대명사의 특징은 UNIT 03에서 더 자세히 살펴보도록 해요. ▶▶▶ 62쪽

3 문장의 기둥, 동사!

동사는 사람, 사물의 동작이나 상태를 나타내는 말입니다. 문장에서 주어와 함께 중요한 역할을 하죠. 아래 문장에서는 join(joined), wear(wears)가 바로 동사로 주어의 동작을 설명하고 있습니다.

> Ms. Thompson **joined** our team last year.
> 톰슨 씨는 작년에 우리 팀에 **합류했다**.
>
> The lab worker **wears** protective gloves. 실험실 직원은 보호 장갑을 **낀다**.

그런데 동사는 단순히 의미 전달만 하는 것은 아닙니다. 우리말에서 '만났다-만난다-만날 것이다' 등 어미를 바꿔 동작이나 상태의 '때'를 표현하는 것처럼, 영어의 동사도 형태를 변화시켜 '때'를 표현할 수 있습니다. 위에서 joined와 wears가 모두 그러한 예이고, 이를 '시제'라고 합니다. 이 밖에도 주어가 동작을 하는 것인지(능동) 당하는 것인지(수동)와 문장에 담긴 화자의 태도(직설과 가정) 역시 동사의 형태 변화를 통해 전달될 수 있습니다.

또한, 동사를 변화시켜 다른 품사처럼 쓰는 경우도 있습니다. 많이 들어 보셨을 부정사, 동명사, 분사가 바로 그러한 예에 해당되죠.

4 명사에 날개를 달아주는 형용사!

형용사란 사람이나 사물의 성질이나 상태를 설명하는 말입니다. 앞서 사람이나 사물의 이름을 '명사'라고 한 것 기억나시죠? 따라서 형용사는 명사와 매우 밀접한 관계가 있답니다. 소개팅에서 만난 사람을 그냥 '그 사람'이라고 하는 것보다 형용사를 사용하여 '멋진 사람', '그 사람 재미있어'라고 하면, 훨씬 구체적으로 상대를 설명할 수 있겠죠?

형용사는 아래 문장처럼 명사를 직접 수식할 수도 있고, 서술하여 나타낼 수도 있는데, UNIT 07에서 좀 더 확실히 알아보도록 합시다. 》》》120쪽

- **명사를 직접 수식**

  I met a **nice** guy yesterday. 나는 어제 **멋진** 사람을 만났다.

- **명사를 서술하여 나타냄**

  The product is **defective**. 그 제품은 **결함이 있다**.

5 내가 빠지면 섭하지~ 부사!

부사는 동사, 형용사, 다른 부사, 혹은 문장 전체의 의미를 좀 더 자세하고 명확하게 나타내기 위해서 덧붙이는 말입니다. 형용사가 명사를 수식하는 역할을 한다면, 부사는 동사, 형용사, 다른 부사, 혹은 문장 전체를 수식할 수 있다는 거죠. 소개팅에서 만난 사람에 대해 얘기할 때, '괜찮은 사람'과 '정말 괜찮은 사람'은 어감이 다릅니다. 괜찮은 정도가 어떤지 강조해 주는 '정말'이 바로 부사에 해당하는 것이죠. 부사는 아래처럼 쓰임이 다양하니 UNIT 07에서 형용사와 함께 더 자세히 알아보도록 해요. 》》 124쪽

- **동사 수식**
  Maria **really** likes her neighborhood. 마리아는 그녀의 이웃을 **정말** 사랑한다.

- **형용사 수식**
  She is **very** kind. 그녀는 **매우** 친절하다.

- **다른 부사 수식**
  He can speak English **quite** well. 그는 영어를 **꽤** 잘한다.

- **문장 전체 수식**
  Fortunately, he is an expert. **운 좋게도**, 그는 전문가이다.

6 명사를 달고 다니는 전치사!

전치사는 '명사나 대명사 앞(前)에 위치(置)하는 말(詞)'로서 시간, 장소, 수단, 원인 등의 의미를 나타내는 역할을 합니다. 전치사라는 말에서 알 수 있듯이, 전치사는 꼭 명사나 대명사, 동명사 앞에 쓰여요.

- **시간**
  The film starts **at** 6 P.M. 그 영화는 오후 6시에 시작한다.

- **장소**
  There are a lot of people **in** the theater. 극장에 사람들이 많다.

위 문장에서 in the theater와 같이 〈전치사+명사〉로 이루어진 형태를 '전치사구'라고 합니다. 이 전치사구는 앞서 배운 형용사나 부사처럼 다른 말들을 수식하는 역할을 한다고 보면 됩니다. 다양한 전치사의 형태와 의미는 UNIT 08에서 공부하도록 해요. 》》 136쪽

7 이어줘라, 접속사!

말과 말을 접속하는, 즉 연결해 주는 말을 접속사라고 합니다. 이러한 접속사에는 and, but, or, so, because 등이 있는데, 아래와 같이 단어와 단어뿐만 아니라, 두 단어 이상의 구나 절을 연결하기도 합니다.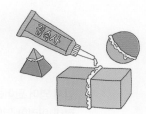

- **〈단어＋단어〉**

  Cash **or** card? 현금으로 하시겠습니까, **아니면** 카드로 하시겠습니까?

- **〈구＋구〉**

  Is it for here **or** to go? 여기서 드시겠습니까, **아니면** 가져가시겠습니까?

- **〈절＋절〉**

  Here is the receipt, **and** your coffee will be ready soon.
  영수증은 여기 있고 커피는 곧 준비됩니다.

접속사 역시 다양한 종류의 형태와 의미를 기억하는 것이 중요합니다. UNIT 12, 13에서 더 자세한 설명이 이어집니다.

>> 196쪽, 210쪽

8 오, 예! 감탄사!

감탄사란 말 그대로 '기쁨, 슬픔, 놀람, 아픔'과 같은 감정을 느낀 순간 내뱉는 말입니다. 우리말의 '어머!', '아야!', '헉!', '와~' 등을 생각해 보면 쉽게 와 닿을 거예요. 영어의 감탄사로는 Wow 우와~, Oh 외, Ouch 아얘, Oops 아이구~ 등이 있습니다. 품사의 하나이긴 하지만, 딱히 문법적인 설명이 필요치 않으므로 그냥 '아! 감탄사구나!' 정도로 생각하고 넘어가시면 됩니다.

각각 단어의 품사에 대해 알았다면, 그 단어가 모여 만드는 구와 절에 대해 알아야 문장의 구조를 알 수 있어요.

앞서 영어 단어는 그 쓰임에 따라 8가지 품사로 나눌 수 있다는 것에 대해 배웠습니다. 그런데 이러한 단어들은 두 개 이상 어울려 하나의 품사 역할을 하기도 합니다. 예를 들어, 'new computer(새 컴퓨터)'에서는 'new(새)'란 단어 하나가 컴퓨터를 수식하는 반면, 'the computer on the desk(책상 위에 있는 컴퓨터)'라고 할 때는 'on the desk(책상 위에 있는)'라는 세 단어가 컴퓨터를 꾸며 주고 있죠. 이처럼 두 단어 이상이 모여 특정한 의미를 갖고 하나의 품사처럼 쓰일 때 이를 '구'라고 합니다.

The new computer **on the desk** is mine.　**책상 위에 있는** 새 컴퓨터는 내 것이다.

▶ on the desk → computer를 수식하는 '형용사'처럼 쓰인 구!

그런데 두 단어 이상이 〈주어+동사〉를 포함한 채로 문장의 일부가 되는 경우가 있습니다. 이와 같은 것을 '절'이라고 부르는데, 아래 문장을 보면 굵게 표시된 부분이 '형용사'처럼 쓰였음을 알 수 있습니다.

This is my new computer **that I bought online**.
이것이 **내가 온라인에서 산** 나의 새 컴퓨터이다.

▶ that I bought online → computer를 수식하는 '형용사'처럼 쓰인 절!

그럼 구와 절에는 어떤 종류가 있는지 다음 페이지에서 좀 더 자세히 알아보도록 합시다.

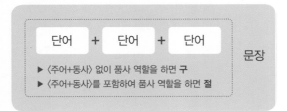

|단어|+|단어|+|단어|

문장

▶ 〈주어+동사〉 없이 품사 역할을 하면 **구**
▶ 〈주어+동사〉를 포함하여 품사 역할을 하면 **절**

1   구

〈주어+동사〉 없이 두 단어 이상이 모여서 여러 품사로 쓰이는 것을 '구'라고 합니다. 구는 문장 안에서의 역할에 따라 다음과 같이 명사구, 형용사구, 부사구로 나눌 수 있습니다. 용어에 너무 신경 쓰지 말고 진한 색으로 표시된 의미 단위를 '구'라고 한다는 것만 확실히 알고 넘어가시면 됩니다.

- **명사구**

  I want **to buy a gift for him**. 나는 그에게 줄 선물을 사기를 원한다.
  Choosing a gift for him is difficult. 그에게 줄 선물을 고르는 것은 어렵다.

- **형용사구**

  I will buy some chocolate **to give him**. 나는 그에게 줄 초콜릿을 살 것이다.
  The chocolate **at that store** looks fine. 저 상점의 초콜릿이 괜찮아 보인다.

- **부사구**

  To make him happy, I bought chocolate.
  그를 행복하게 해 주려고, 초콜릿을 샀다.
  I gave him chocolate **on Valentine's Day**.
  밸런타인 데이에 나는 그에게 초콜릿을 줬다.

2   절

'구'와 달리 '절'은 〈주어+동사〉를 포함한 채로 하나의 품사 역할을 하는데요, 그러다 보니 길이가 길어지는 경우가 많습니다. 그러나 절이 아무리 길어도 하나의 품사 역할을 하고 있다는 점을 기억하고, 한 덩어리처럼 의미 단위로 읽어내는 연습을 하는 것이 중요해요. 절도 구와 마찬가지로 명사절, 형용사절, 부사절로 나눌 수 있습니다.

- **명사절**

  I think **that she is interested in me**.
  나는 그녀가 나에게 관심이 있다고 생각한다.

- **형용사절**

  She is the first woman **that gave me chocolate**.
  그녀는 나에게 초콜릿을 준 첫 번째 여자이다.

- **부사절**

  I'll give her a gift in return **because she gave me chocolate**.
  그녀가 내게 초콜릿을 줬기 때문에 그녀에게 답례로 선물을 줄 것이다.

앞에서 8품사와 구, 절에 대해 알아보았습니다. 그런데 이러한 요소를 죽 나열한다고 해서 문장이 되는 것은 아닙니다. '단어, 구, 절'의 배열에 일정한 순서가 있고 그 순서를 '어순'이라고 합니다.

아래 문장들은 영어의 일반적인 문장 종류 다섯 가지를 대표하는 것들입니다. 하나씩 살펴보면서 어떤 '공통점'과 '차이점'이 있는지 알아봅시다.

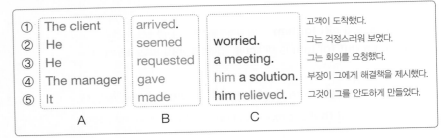

	A	B	C	
①	The client	arrived.		고객이 도착했다.
②	He	seemed	worried.	그는 걱정스러워 보였다.
③	He	requested	a meeting.	그는 회의를 요청했다.
④	The manager	gave	him a solution.	부장이 그에게 해결책을 제시했다.
⑤	It	made	him relieved.	그것이 그를 안도하게 만들었다.

위 문장들은 형태가 조금씩 다르지만 크게 문장의 주체가 되는 부분(A)과 이를 서술하는 부분(B+C)으로 나눌 수 있습니다. 즉 '주어(●)'와 이를 서술하는 '동사(●)'가 각 문장에 하나씩 있다는 공통점이 있죠. 그런데 위 문장들을 서로 다른 종류의 문장으로 만드는 것은 무엇일까요? 바로 동사 뒤에 따라오는 요소들(C)입니다.

위 문장들을 보면,
동사 뒤에 아무 것도 없는 것(①)과 특정한 요소가 있는 것(②③④⑤)이 있고, 특정한 요소가 하나만 있는 것(②③)과 두 개가 있는 것(④⑤)이 있으며, 하나의 요소도 주어를 설명하는 보어(●)와 행위의 대상이 되는 목적어(●)로 나뉘고, 두 개의 요소 역시 간접 목적어(●)가 추가되거나, 목적어를 설명하는 보어(●)가 추가된 것으로 다시 구분된다는 것을 알 수 있습니다.
이처럼 문장의 여러 구성 요소들이 특정한 방식으로 결합하여 서로 다른 종류의 문장을 만들며, 이러한 결합은 상당히 규칙적입니다. 즉, 위와 같이 다섯 가지 방식으로 문장을 만들 수 있고, 우리는 이를 5문형이라고 하는 거죠.
짐작하셨겠지만, 이 5문형에서 가장 중요한 것이 바로 '동사'입니다. 어떤 동사를 쓰느냐에 따라 뒤에 올 수 있는 요소들이 결정되기 때문입니다. 정리하자면, 영어의 문장은 기본적으로 〈주어+동사〉의 순서이며 동사의 성격에 따라 일반적으로 5문형이라는 다섯 가지 종류로 만들어집니다.

그럼 이 5문형에 대해 하나씩 살펴보도록 합시다.

1 1문형은 〈주어+동사〉

주어(●) 와 동사(●), 그리고 수식어(구)로만 이루어진 문장을 1문형이라고 합니다. 이는 동사가 보어나 목적어 없이도 주어의 동작, 상태를 서술하기에 충분하다는 말인데요. 물론, 부사와 같은 수식어(구)를 사용하여 문장의 의미를 좀 더 풍부하게 할 수도 있습니다. 이렇게 보어나 목적어 없이 홀로 문장을 만들 수 있는 동사를 '완전자동사'라고 합니다.

He smokes. 그는 담배를 피운다.
He smokes heavily. 그는 담배를 많이 피운다.

그런데 아래 go(went)나 begin(begins)과 같은 동사는 뒤에 upstairs(위층으로), at nine thirty(9시 30분에)와 같은 수식어(구)가 없으면 그 의미가 완전히 전달되지 않습니다. go(가다), begin(시작하다) 등은 그 자체로는 의미 전달이 불완전하기 때문이죠. 이럴 때에는 동사의 의미를 보조하는 수식어(구)가 꼭 필요합니다. 이처럼 수식어(구)가 꼭 필요한 경우도 있다는 점을 기억하시고, 이 수식어(구)들을 뒤에서 배울 보어나 목적어와 혼동하지 않도록 하세요.

She went upstairs. 그녀는 위층으로 갔다.
The team meeting begins at nine thirty. 팀 회의는 9시 30분에 시작한다.

2 2문형은 〈주어+동사+주격 보어〉

2문형은 주어(●) 와 동사(●) 외에 주격 보어(●)가 꼭 필요합니다. 여기서 주격 보어란 주어의 성질, 상태, 신분 등을 나타내어, 주어에 대한 정보를 보충해 주는 것을 말합니다. 주격 보어는 명사, 대명사, 형용사 등이 쓰일 수 있고, 이러한 주격 보어를 필요로 하는 동사를 '불완전자동사'라고 합니다. 1문형의 완전자동사에 비해 '보어'라는 요소가 필요하기 때문에 불완전자동사라고 하며, 대표적인 것으로 be동사가 있습니다.

He is a CEO. 그는 대표이사다. (그 = 대표이사)
He is busy. 그는 바쁘다. (그의 상태 = 바쁜)

위에서 주격 보어로 명사(CEO)가 쓰였는지, 형용사(busy)가 쓰였는지에 따라 해석에 차이가 있다는 점을 기억해두세요. 주격 보어가 명사이면 '주어=주격 보어', 주격 보어가 형용사이면 '주어의 상태/성질=주격 보어'가 된답니다. be동사 외에 2문형에서 쓰이는 불완전자동사들은 look[seem] ~처럼 보이다, become ~이 되다, remain ~인 상태로 남다 등과 같이 제한적이니까, 꼼꼼하게 살펴보시기 바랍니다. ≫≫ 38쪽

She became a top model. 그녀는 최고의 모델이 되었다. (그녀 = 최고의 모델)
You look happy today. 너 오늘 행복해 보인다. (너의 상태 = 행복한)

3 3문형은 〈주어＋동사＋목적어〉

3문형은 주어(●)와 동사(●) 뒤에 목적어(●)가 옵니다. 여기서 '목적어'란 동사의 동작이 행해지는 대상을 의미하고, 명사(구, 절), 대명사, to부정사, 동명사 등이 목적어로 쓰일 수 있습니다. 대부분의 동사는 목적어를 필요로 하기 때문에 3문형은 영어에서 가장 흔하게 접할 수 있는 문형이라 할 수 있습니다. 이처럼 목적어가 필수인 3문형에 쓰이는 동사들은 '완전 타동사'라고 합니다.

She drinks **five cups of coffee a day.** 그녀는 하루에 커피 다섯 잔을 마신다.
I forgot **to lock the door.** 나는 문을 잠그는 것을 잊었다.
We think **that he is right.** 우리는 그가 옳다고 생각한다.

그런데 아래 put off ～을 연기하다, look for ～을 찾다의 경우처럼 두 개 이상의 단어가 하나의 동사처럼 쓰이기도 합니다. 이러한 동사를 구동사라고 하는데, 뒤에 명사, 대명사와 같은 목적어가 올 경우 3문형의 타동사처럼 보면 됩니다.

We put off **the meeting.** 우리는 회의를 연기했다.
We're looking for **a solution.** 우리는 해결책을 찾고 있다.

4 4문형은 〈주어＋동사＋간접 목적어＋직접 목적어〉

3문형에 '간접 목적어'가 추가된 것을 4문형이라고 합니다. 앞서 3문형의 '완전타동사'가 목적어를 필요로 한다고 했는데, 이때 목적어는 주어의 행위가 직접적으로 영향을 미치는 대상으로 '～을[를]'로 해석됩니다. 그런데 간접 목적어는 행위의 방향을 나타내어 '～에게'로 해석된다는 점이 다릅니다. 즉, 주어(●)와 동사(●) 뒤에 '～에게'에 해당하는 간접 목적어(●)와 '～(을)를'에 해당하는 직접 목적어(●), 이렇게 두 개의 목적어가 오는 문장을 4문형이라고 합니다. 이때 간접 목적어와 직접 목적어의 순서를 혼동하는 경우가 있는데, 다음의 대표적인 예문을 기억해두면 도움이 됩니다.

He gave me **a lot of advice.** 그는 나에게 많은 충고를 해 주었다.
He gave **a lot of advice** me. (X)

이렇게 두 개의 목적어를 취하는 4문형 동사들은 대개 '~에게 …을 주다'란 뜻을 갖습니다. 이러한 동사들을 '수여동사'라고 부르는데, 뜻에 '주다'가 들어가는 동사들인 'give 주다, tell 말해 주다, show 보여 주다, send 보내 주다, teach 가르쳐 주다, buy 사 주다' 등이 이에 포함됩니다.

≫ 36쪽

She showed me **the painting**.   그녀는 나에게 그림을 보여 줬다.
He taught her **how to fix the printer**.   그는 그녀에게 프린터 고치는 법을 알려 줬다.
He bought his coworker **a nice lunch**.   그는 그의 동료에게 근사한 점심을 사 줬다.

5

5문형은 〈주어+동사+목적어+목적격 보어〉

5문형은 3문형에 '목적격 보어(●)'가 추가된 문장입니다. 2문형의 주격 보어가 주어를 보충 설명해 주는 것처럼 5문형의 목적격 보어는 목적어를 보충 설명해 줍니다. 이처럼 목적어와 목적격 보어를 필요로 하는 동사를 '불완전타동사'라고도 합니다. 목적어와 목적격 보어의 관계를 중심으로 아래 예문을 살펴봅시다.

≫ 38쪽

She found the room empty.
그녀는 방이 비어 있음을 알았다. (방의 상태 = 비어 있는)

They elected her mayor.
그들은 그녀를 시장으로 선출했다. (그녀 = 시장)

We call him Jack.
우리는 그를 잭이라고 부른다. (그 = 잭)

4 문단의 구성 요소

여러 문장이 모여 만드는 문단은 하나의 주제에 따라 전개된 문장의 흐름입니다.
PART 6와 PART 7은 이 흐름을 확실히 파악해야 잘 풀 수 있어요.

앞에서 단어와 문장에 대해 살펴봤는데요. '단어'란 의미를 나타내는 가장 최소 단위이고, 그 단어가 모여 하나의 문장을 만들게 된다고 했죠. 그럼, 문단(paragraph)이란 무엇일까요? 문단이란 하나의 주제에 대해 여러 개의 관련된 문장들이 일목요연하게 전개된 것을 의미합니다. 문장은 하나의 단편적인 사실이나 주장에 불과하지만, 문단에는 그 사실이나 주장을 뒷받침할 세부 사항들이 이어져 설득력을 가지게 되는 거죠.

그럼, 문단은 어떤 순서로 구성될까요? 중고등학생 때 많이 들어봤던 두괄식, 중괄식, 미괄식, 양괄식 구성 기억나죠? 우리말에서는 요점을 가장 마지막에 이야기하는 미괄식을 선호하는 편인데요. 영어는 이와 정반대입니다. 오히려, 하고자 하는 말을 앞에서 먼저 이야기해야 좋은 글이라고 할 수 있습니다. 따라서, 주장이나 사실을 담은 주제 문장이 제일 먼저 나오는 편입니다. 그다음에는 이를 부가적으로 설명해 주는 세부 정보들이 뒤따라오는데, 이는 주제 문장에 대한 구체적인 예이거나 정의, 혹은 부연 설명에 해당합니다. 마지막으로 결론에서 앞에서 말한 내용을 다시 한번 요약해 주면서 끝나게 됩니다. 이런 문단들이 모여 하나의 지문을 이루게 되는데요. 지문이란 문단과 문단이 하나의 주제 속에서 일관성 있게 연결된 것을 말합니다.

그런데 토익 같은 비즈니스 서식에도 '주제 문장'이 있냐며 의문을 가지실 분들이 있을 텐데요. 공지나 이메일의 경우 용건과 목적을 앞에서 분명히 밝히고 중간에서 구체적인 내용을 알려 주죠. 그리고 마지막으로 인사말로 마무리하고요. 따라서 세 단락 구성의 흐름은 같다고 보시면 됩니다.

WARM-UP에서 이렇게 어려운 이야기를 하는 이유는 PART 6&7의 가장 큰 특징이 바로 '문단의 흐름(문맥) 파악하기'이기 때문입니다.

PART 6의 '빈칸에 알맞은 문장을 고르는 유형'이나, PART 7의 '문장의 적절한 위치를 찾는 유형'은 지문 흐름을 파악해야 풀 수 있습니다. 그럼, 지금부터 지문의 흐름을 파악하는 중요한 근거가 되는 요소들을 차례대로 살펴보도록 할게요.

1 연결사의 법칙

(a) Originally, the year-end event was scheduled for December 21.
(b) The CEO thought this date might interfere with holiday plans.
(c) It has been moved to December 8.

세 문장의 연결이 어떤가요? 혹시 이해하기 어렵지는 않던가요? 그럼 아래 문장을 다시 읽어 보세요.

(a) Originally, the year-end event was scheduled for December 21.
(b) **However**, the CEO thought this date might interfere with holiday plans.
(c) **Therefore**, it has been moved to December 8.

자, 연결사가 추가되니 이해하기가 훨씬 편해졌죠?
(a) 문장은 애초의 계획, (b) 문장은 계획에 대한 부정적인 의견, (c) 문장은 계획의 변경 결과에 대해 이야기하고 있으므로 (a)와 (b) 사이에는 역접의 접속사인 However, (c)에는 결과를 나타내는 Therefore가 들어간 것이죠. 이렇게 연결사는 문장 사이의 논리적 흐름을 파악하게 해 주는 일등공신입니다. PART 6의 '빈칸에 알맞은 문장을 고르는 유형'과 PART 7의 '문장의 적절한 위치를 찾는 유형'의 경우 연결사가 단서가 되는 경우가 많으니 아래 연결사들을 꼭 기억해두세요.

- **역접 · 대조를 나타내는 연결사**

  but, however, yet, nevertheless, nonetheless, while, on the contrary, whereas, conversely, in contrast, on the other hand

- **원인을 나타내는 연결사**

  because, because of, due to, for this reason, owing to, thanks to

- **결과를 나타내는 연결사**

  therefore, so, thus, hence, consequently, as a result, in conclusion

- **첨가를 나타내는 연결사**

  in addition, additionally, besides, furthermore, moreover, what's more, also

- **예시를 나타내는 연결사**

  for example, for instance, for one thing, as an illustration

2 대명사의 법칙

지문의 논리적 흐름을 파악하게 도와주는 또 다른 수단은 '대명사'입니다. 기본적으로 한 문장은 '기존 정보'에서 '새로운 정보' 순으로 확장되는데요. 독자에게 이미 공유한 기존 정보를 문장의 앞에 제시하고, 이후에 새로운 정보를 제시해야 글을 읽으면서 이해하기 쉽기 때문입니다. 이때 유용하게 쓰이는 품사가 '대명사'예요. 하나의 주제에 대해 새로운 정보를 추가하며 이야기해야 하는데, 매번 같은 명사를 써주면 글도 길어지고 지루해지므로 대명사를 써 주는 것이죠.

따라서 긴 지문에는 반복을 피하기 위해 대명사가 자주 등장하므로, 글의 흐름을 파악하고 있지 않으면 대명사가 지칭하는 명사를 앞 문장에서 찾기 힘들기 때문에 해석에 애를 먹기 쉽습니다. 따라서 대명사가 가리키는 대상이 무엇인지 짚고 넘어가는 것은 지문을 제대로 이해하기 위해 반드시 필요한 작업입니다.

PART 6의 '알맞은 문장 고르는 유형'과 PART 7의 '문장의 적절한 위치를 찾는 유형'을 해결할 때, 이어지는 문장에 앞의 대상을 받는 대명사가 포함되어 있고, 이와 관련된 '새로운 정보'가 있다면 논리적 연결이 가장 자연스러운 것으로 판단할 수 있습니다. 특히, 대명사 this, that은 앞에 제시된 대상뿐만 아니라 문장 전체를 대신 받기도 하니 이 부분도 기억해 두세요.

(a) I hope that you find the training to be highly useful.
(b) **It** is expected <u>to take almost three hours</u>.
   　기존 정보　　　　　　　　신규 정보
   　(= training)

(a) Please view the attached list of required reading materials.
(b) **These** should be <u>read carefully prior to attending the training</u>.
   　기존 정보　　　　　　　　　　신규 정보
   　(= reading materials)

(a) Recently, we had a 'Black Friday Event' to get rid of stock.
(b) **This** resulted in <u>an huge increase in our sales</u>.
   　기존 정보　　　　　　　신규 정보
   　(= 앞 문장 전체)

3 패러프레이징의 법칙

앞에서 같은 명사의 반복을 피하기 위해 '대명사'를 쓴다고 했는데, 명사뿐 아니라 다른 품사의 경우에도 같은 단어의 반복을 싫어하기 때문에, 원래 의미는 유지하면서 다른 표현으로 바꾸어 쓰는 경우가 많습니다. 이를 패러프레이징 또는 바꿔 말하기라고 합니다. 하나의 주제에 대해 이야기하는 단락에서 같은 대상이 반복될 수 있으므로, 같은 단어를 쓰지 않고 다른 표현을 써 주는 것이죠. 토익 세계에 입문하면 귀에 딱지가 앉도록 반복해서 듣게 될 것이 바로 이 패러프레이징입니다.

패러프레이징의 가장 흔한 형태는 같은 의미의 동의어를 활용하는 것입니다. 좀 더 확장된 형태는 paper(종이) → office supplies(사무용품), dental insurance(치아 보험) → benefits package(복리후생 제도) 등의 상위어로 바꾸거나 문장 구조를 바꾸는 방법이 있습니다.

중요한 것은, 하나의 단락은 하나의 주제를 향해 결집해 있어야 하고, 각 문장의 내용은 '기존 정보 → 새로운 정보', '일반적 정보 → 세부적 정보'로 확장된다는 사실입니다. 지문의 정보는 확장되면서 유사한 의미의 다른 표현으로 패러프레이징된다는 사실을 기억하세요.

(a) [일반적 정보] I have just read your letter which you expressed **dissatisfaction** with our product in.
(b) [세부적 정보] According to your **complaint**, the blender stopped working after only a few uses.

(a) [일반적 정보] K Corp. released figures that showed a significant **boost** in profits.
(b) [세부적 정보] The CEO explained that the **increase** is the result of our user-friendly products.

4 지문 양식의 법칙

마지막은 앞의 세 가지 법칙과 비교해 가장 간단한 내용인데요. 토익 지문은 대부분 '목적과 용건-구체적인 내용-인사말'의 3단 구성을 따르고 있고, 앞부분의 용건과 마지막 인사말에서 자주 쓰이는 표현이 몇 가지로 정해져 있어요. 따라서 이 구조와 표현만 알면 지문 파악도 쉬워지고 PART 6의 '알맞은 문장 고르기 유형'과 PART 7의 '문장의 적절한 위치를 찾는 유형'도 거뜬히 해결되니 꼼꼼히 챙겨두세요.

PART

5 & 6

Reading Comprehension

"PART 5&6는 이렇게 풉니다"

STEP 1 선택지를 먼저 본다!

선택지를 보면 문제 유형이 보입니다. 선택지가 동일 어휘의 서로 다른 품사로 되어 있으면 구조·문법 유형이고, 동일 품사의 서로 다른 어휘들로 구성되어 있으면 어휘 유형의 문제예요. **(8-9쪽 참고)**

STEP 2 구조·문법 유형이라면, 빈칸 주변을 확인하자!

이들 유형은 대개 빈칸 주변의 어휘 형태만 보고도 쉽게 답을 고를 수 있어요. 주변 구조를 통해 빈칸에 적절한 품사 또는 문법 형태를 고르세요.

STEP 3 어휘 유형은 collocation과 문맥으로 풀자!

이 유형은 해석을 통해 문맥상 적절한 어휘를 정답으로 골라야 해요. 따라서 어휘를 학습할 때 함께 자주 등장하는 어휘들(collocation)도 같이 학습해야 합니다. PART 6의 경우, 지문의 흐름도 중요한 단서가 되므로 빈칸 주변 문장을 주의 깊게 살펴보세요.

PART 5&6 문장 구조편

UNIT 01

문장의 기본 구조
+제조 어휘(1)

우리는 언제나 함께야

주어

동사

영어의 일반적인 문장에는 주어와 동사가 하나씩 있습니다.
주어는 문장의 주체이고, 동사는 주어의 동작이나 상태를 설명하는 말이어서
둘이 짝을 이루어 〈주어+동사〉의 구조로 쓰입니다. 동사에 따라 뒤에 보어,
목적어를 필요로 하는 경우도 있고, 수식어구가 나올 수도 있어요.

---

1 주어와 동사 자리

2 목적어 자리

3 보어 자리

+ 제조 어휘(1)

1 주어와 동사 자리

The factory produces
a variety of goods.

주어 자리
- 주어 자리: 문장의 시작, 동사 앞
- 올 수 있는 형태: 명사(구, 절), 대명사

동사 자리
- 동사 자리: 주어 뒤
- 올 수 있는 형태: 《(조동사)+동사원형》, 《동사원형+-(e)s》 등
- 올 수 없는 형태: to부정사, 동명사, 분사 등

A 주어 자리

- 주어는 문장에서 어떤 동작이나 상태의 주체가 되는 말로, 우리말의 '~은[는]', '~이[가]'에 해당되는 말입니다.
- 주어 자리: 문장은 주로 주어로 시작하지만, 주어 앞뒤로 수식어(구)가 올 수 있어요.
  주어 뒤에는 동사가 따라오므로, 동사 앞도 주로 주어 자리입니다.
- 일반적으로 주어 자리에는 명사(구, 절), 대명사처럼 명사 역할을 하는 말이 옵니다.

명사	**The factory** <u>produces</u> a variety of goods. **그 공장은** 다양한 제품을 생산한다.
대명사	**It** <u>produces</u> a variety of goods. **그곳은** 다양한 제품을 생산한다.
명사구	**To control inventory** <u>is</u> his responsibility. **재고를 관리하는 것은** 그의 일이다. (to부정사구) **Meeting the deadline** <u>seems</u> impossible. **마감일을 맞추는 것은** 불가능해 보인다. (동명사구)
명사절	**That the plant moved to a new city** <u>is</u> true. (접속사절) **그 공장이 새로운 도시로 이전했다는 것은** 사실이다.

> **주의** '~이[가] 있다'라는 뜻으로 쓰이는 《There be[remain/exist] ~》의 경우, 주어는 동사 뒤에 위치한 명사입니다.
> <u>There is</u> **a work schedule** online. 온라인에 **작업 일정이** 있다. (주어 = a work schedule)

B 동사 자리

- 동사는 주어의 동작·상태를 설명하는 말입니다.
- 동사 자리: 주로 주어 뒤에 동사가 옵니다.
- 동사 자리에는 《(조동사)+동사원형》, 《동사원형+-(e)s》 등 다양한 형태가 올 수 있습니다.
  단, 준동사인 to부정사, 동명사, 분사(-ing, p.p.)는 동사가 아니라서 동사 자리에 올 수 없습니다.

  We **should speak** with our supervisor this week. 우리는 이번 주에 상사와 **이야기해야 한다.**
  ~~to speak, speaking, spoken~~

- 주어 뒤에 긴 수식어(구/절)가 붙어 있으면, 수식어를 건너뛰고 그 뒤에서 동사를 찾아요.

  수식어구 The partnership <u>between the companies</u> **increased** profits.
  그 회사들 간의 협력이 수익을 **증가시킨다.**

  수식어절 The parts <u>that he ordered yesterday</u> **will arrive** soon.
  그가 어제 주문한 부품들이 곧 **도착할 것이다.**

> **주의** '~해라, ~하세요'라고 상대에게 명령 또는 지시하는 명령문은 주어 you가 생략되어 문장이 동사로 시작합니다. 이때
> 동사는 -(e)s나 -(e)d가 붙지 않은 '동사원형'을 쓴다는 점에 주의하세요.
> (Please) **Explain** the standard procedure. 표준 절차를 **설명해 주세요.** (동사원형 explain 사용)

다음 괄호 안에서 알맞은 것을 고르세요.

|핵심 POINT 슬쩍 보기|

1 (Visitors / Visited) must wear a guest badge throughout the facility tour.

1 주어 자리에는 명사가 와요.

2 The human resources (department / depart) of the company handles employee contract renewals.

2 주어 앞뒤로 수식어(구)가 올 수 있어요.

3 The committee members (to agree / agree) on the terms of the contract.

3 주어 뒤는 동사 자리이며 준동 사는 동사 자리에 쓸 수 없어 요.

4 Advertisements for the vitamin (explain / explaining) its health benefits.

4 〈주어+수식어구〉 뒤에서 동사 를 찾아야 해요.

다음 빈칸에 알맞은 것을 고르세요.

5 The ------- for city mayor will be held on November 5.
빈출

(A) elects   (B) elective
(C) elections   (D) elected

7 There are many ------- to choose from for the new Web site.

(A) designs   (B) designed
(C) designable   (D) to design

6 For further information on the work schedule, please ------- to your managers.

(A) spoke   (B) speaking
(C) speak   (D) speaks

8 The supermarket chain ------- thirty stores across the country.
빈출

(A) operating   (B) operates
(C) operation   (D) operators

2 목적어 자리

She gave **me**
the instructions.

목적어 자리
- 목적어 자리: 동사 뒤
- 올 수 있는 형태: 명사(구, 절), 대명사

동사에 따른 목적어 자리
- 〈주어+3문형 동사+목적어〉
- 〈주어+4문형 동사+간접 목적어+직접 목적어〉

A 목적어 자리

- 목적어는 동사의 행위가 가해지는 대상으로, 우리말의 '～을(를)'에 해당되는 말입니다.
- 목적어 자리: 목적어는 주로 동사 뒤에 위치해요.
- 주어와 마찬가지로 목적어 자리에는 명사(구, 절), 대명사가 올 수 있어요.

명사	The host <u>sent</u> **invitations** to all of the sponsoring companies. 주최자는 모든 후원사에 **초대장을** 보냈다.
대명사	The safety inspector <u>found</u> **it**. 안전 감독관이 **그것을** 발견했다.
명사구	The charity <u>plans</u> **to hold a fundraising event** on April 5. (to부정사구) 그 자선단체는 4월 5일에 **모금 행사를** 개최할 예정이다. He <u>finished</u> **loading the boxes** onto the truck. (동명사구) 그는 트럭에 **상자들을 싣는 것을** 마쳤다.
명사절	The event organizer <u>announced</u> **that the tickets were sold out**. (접속사절) 행사 주최자는 **표가 매진되었다고** 알렸다.

B 동사에 따른 목적어 자리

ⓐ **3문형 동사들은 뒤에 한 개의 목적어를 취합니다.**

- 〈주어+동사+목적어〉의 순서로 쓰입니다.

명사   They <u>built</u> **factories** in suburban areas. 그들은 교외 지역에 **공장들을** 세웠다.

명사구   She <u>forgot</u> **to attach the label**. 그녀는 **이름표 부착하는 것을** 잊었다. (to부정사구)

ⓑ **4문형 동사들은 의미상 뒤에 두 개의 목적어를 취합니다.**

- 〈주어+동사+간접 목적어+직접 목적어〉의 순서로 쓰입니다.
- 간접 목적어(사람)는 '～에게', 직접 목적어(사물)는 '～을[를]'로 해석됩니다.

She <u>gave</u> **me the instructions**. 그녀는 **나에게 사용설명서를** 주었다.
        간접 목적어 ⟵┘   └⟶ 직접 목적어

- 두 개의 목적어를 취하는 4문형 동사들

give 주다	offer 제공해 주다	tell 말해 주다	show 보여 주다
send 보내 주다	grant 승인해 주다	bring 가져다주다	buy 사 주다

Ms. Jones <u>told</u> **me her idea**. 존스 씨는 **나에게 그녀의 생각을** 말해 줬다.
The foreman <u>showed</u> **the new employee the facility**. 현장 감독이 **신입사원에게 시설을** 보여 줬다.

핵심 POINT 확인하기

다음 괄호 안에서 알맞은 것을 고르세요.

1 The new software can improve (efficiency / efficient) by forty percent.

2 Many employees submitted (complain / complaints) about the long working hours.

3 Each guest must show the security guard (an invitation / with an invitations) at the entrance.

4 Ms. Stevens gives (inspect / inspectors) some useful advice for their tasks.

|핵심 POINT 슬쩍 보기|

1 목적어 자리에는 명사 형태가 와요.

2 3문형 동사 뒤에는 목적어가 필요해요.

3 동사 show는 4문형 동사로 뒤에 간접 목적어와 직접 목적어를 취할 수 있어요.

4 give는 4문형 동사로, 간접 목적어와 직접 목적어 자리에 모두 명사가 와요.

실전 감각 키우기

다음 빈칸에 알맞은 것을 고르세요.

5 Montgomery Bank completed ------- of a new building for its headquarters.

   (A) constructive   (B) construction
   (C) to construct   (D) constructed

6 빈출 Fairfax Communications offers ------- discounts on data roaming charges.

   (A) clients   (B) resources
   (C) services   (D) technologies

7 빈출 The manager sent the intern ------- on daily routines in the office.

   (A) directed   (B) direct
   (C) directs   (D) directions

8 Mr. Werner will provide ------- based on his findings during the inspection.

   (A) recommended   (B) recommendations
   (C) recommend   (D) recommends

3 보어 자리

supervisor

He is **a supervisor**.

보어 자리
- 보어 자리: 동사 뒤 또는 목적어 뒤
- 올 수 있는 형태: 명사, 형용사

주격 보어와 목적격 보어
- 〈주어+2문형 동사+주격 보어〉
- 〈주어+5문형 동사+목적어+목적격 보어〉

A 보어 자리

- 보어는 주어나 목적어의 성질, 상태, 신분 등을 보충 설명해 주는 말이에요.
- 보어 자리: 주어를 꾸미는 주격 보어는 동사 뒤에, 목적어를 꾸미는 목적격 보어는 목적어 뒤에 옵니다.
- 보어 자리에는 주로 명사나 형용사가 옵니다. 부사는 올 수 없어요.

명사	He is **a supervisor**. 그는 **감독관이다**. (그의 신분 = 감독관)
형용사	They found the supervisor **strict**. ~~strictly(부사)~~ 그들은 그 감독관이 **엄격하다고** 생각한다. (감독관의 성격 = 엄격한)

B 주격 보어: 〈주어+2문형 동사+주격 보어〉

- 주격 보어는 주어의 성질, 상태, 신분 등을 보충 설명해 주는 말이에요.
- 주격 보어를 취하는 대표적인 동사로는 be동사가 있습니다.

  명사　The information is **the instructions** for using the device.
  그 정보는 그 장비를 사용하기 위한 **사용설명서이다**. (그 정보 = 사용설명서)

  형용사　The information seems **important** to them.　그 정보는 그들에게 **중요해** 보인다. (그 정보 = 중요함)

- 주격 보어를 필요로 하는 2문형 동사들

look ~처럼 보이다	feel ~ 같다	become ~이 되다
sound ~처럼 들리다	seem ~인 것 같다	turn ~한 상태가 되다
remain 계속 ~인 상태이다	keep ~인 상태를 유지하다	fall ~한 상태가 되다

The production levels remained **stable**.　생산 수준이 계속해서 **안정적이었다**.

C 목적격 보어: 〈주어+5문형 동사+목적어+목적격 보어〉

- 목적격 보어는 목적어의 성질, 상태, 신분 등을 보충 설명해 주는 말이에요.

  명사　People elected her **union leader**.　사람들은 그녀를 **노조 위원장으로** 선출했다. (그녀 = 노조 위원장)
  형용사　Most employees found the manual **helpful**.
  　대부분의 직원이 지침서가 **도움이 된다고** 생각한다. (지침서 = 도움이 되는)

- 목적격 보어를 필요로 하는 5문형 동사들

elect ~를 …로 선출하다	name[appoint] ~를 …로 임명하다	consider ~가 …라고 여기다
find ~를 …라고 생각하다	make ~를 …하게 만들다	call ~를 …라고 부르다

Our team considers the project **valuable**.　우리 팀은 그 프로젝트가 **가치 있다고** 여긴다.

핵심 POINT 확인하기

다음 괄호 안에서 알맞은 것을 고르세요.

|핵심 POINT 슬쩍 보기|

1 Mr. Irving's qualifications are (impressive / impressively), so he is likely to get hired.

1 보어 자리에는 명사나 형용사가 쓰여요.

2 Ms. Patterson was the (won / winner) of the last architecture competition.

2 be동사는 보어를 필요로 하는 동사예요.

3 The building manager finds the security cameras (necessary / necessarily).

3 동사 find가 '~를 …라고 생각하다'라는 의미로 쓰이면, 뒤에는 〈목적어＋목적격 보어〉가 와요.

4 The company should appoint Mr. Smith (manage / manager) of its technology department.

4 동사 appoint는 목적어와 목적격 보어를 취하는 5문형 동사예요.

실전 감각 키우기

다음 빈칸에 알맞은 것을 고르세요.

5 빈출 The benefits package was -------, but the salary was too low.

(A) attractively   (B) attract
(C) attractive   (D) attraction

6 The library's online resources make information ------- to all users for free.

(A) access   (B) accesses
(C) accessible   (D) accessibly

7 Mr. Stern became an ------- at the firm right after his graduation.

(A) accounted   (B) accountant
(C) accountable   (D) accounting

8 The city government has named Ken Hurst ------- of the environmental project.

(A) supervisor   (B) supervised
(C) supervise   (D) supervising

앞에서 학습한 핵심 POINT를 떠올리며 빈칸을 완성해 보세요.

<table>
<tr><td>핵심
POINT
1</td><td>

주어와 동사 자리

주어 자리
- 주어 자리: 문장의 시작, ❶_____ 앞
- 올 수 있는 형태: 명사(구, 절), 대명사

동사 자리
- 동사 자리: ❷_____ 뒤
- 올 수 있는 형태: 〈(조동사)+❸_____〉, 〈동사원형+-(e)s〉 등
- 올 수 없는 형태: to부정사, 동명사, 분사 등

</td></tr>
</table>

<table>
<tr><td>핵심
POINT
2</td><td>

목적어 자리

목적어 자리
- 목적어 자리: ❹_____ 뒤
- 올 수 있는 형태: 명사(구, 절), ❺_____

동사에 따른 목적어 자리
- 〈주어+3문형 동사+목적어〉
- 〈주어+4문형 동사+❻_____ 목적어+❼_____ 목적어〉

</td></tr>
</table>

<table>
<tr><td>핵심
POINT
3</td><td>

보어 자리

보어 자리
- 보어 자리: 동사 뒤 또는 목적어 뒤
- 올 수 있는 형태: ❽_____, 형용사

주격 보어와 목적격 보어
- 〈주어+2문형 동사+❾_____〉
- 〈주어+5문형 동사+목적어+❿_____〉

</td></tr>
</table>

|빈칸 정답 살짝 보기|

❶ 동사 ❷ 주어 ❸ 동사원형 ❹ 동사 ❺ 대명사 ❻ 간접 ❼ 직접 ❽ 명사 ❾ 주격 보어 ❿ 목적격 보어

실전 감각 키우기

다음 빈칸에 알맞은 것을 고르세요.

1 ------- to *Economy Today* will expire without any formal notice after one year.

(A) Subscribe
(B) Subscribed
(C) Subscriptions
(D) Subscribes

2 Weather forecasts ------- the strong hurricane last week.

(A) prediction
(B) predicted
(C) predictable
(D) predictability

3 Our professionals will send you ------- about the renovation work as soon as possible.

(A) information
(B) informing
(C) inform
(D) informed

4 Relocating the headquarters to AG Tower did not look ------- because of the expensive rent.

(A) profitable
(B) profits
(C) profited
(D) profitability

[5-6] Questions 5-6 refer to the following e-mail.

Dear employees,

New equipment will be purchased soon to make our production process more efficient. At first, you will operate the machines only under close supervision. You will follow ------- by a certified technician. Once you are considered ready to work on your own, the
5.
technician will sign a document stating you have been trained. Please ------- the
6.
document attached to this e-mail to familiarize yourself with the machines in advance.

Thank you for your work.

5 (A) instruct
(B) instructs
(C) instructed
(D) instructions

6 (A) consultation
(B) consult
(C) consulting
(D) to consult

공장에서 제품을 생산하고 관리하는 상황에 관한 어휘들입니다.

equipment	명 장비, 기기	manufacturing **equipment** 제조 장비 *빈출 숙어인 be equipped with(~을 갖추고 있다)도 함께 알아두세요.
facility	명 시설 파 facilitate 용이하게 하다	modern **facilities** 현대적인 시설들
routine	형 정기적인, 일상적인 파 routinely 정기적으로, 일상적으로	a **routine** inspection 정기 점검
operate	동 작동시키다 파 operation 작동, 운영	**operate** the machinery 기계를 작동시키다
access	명 접근(권) 동 접근하다 파 accessible 접근 가능한	easy **access** to a site 현장에 용이한 접근
supervision	명 감독 파 supervise 감독하다 supervisor 감독관	under *one's* **supervision** ~의 감독하에
manufacture	동 제조하다 파 manufacturer 제조업체	**manufacture** the products 상품을 제조하다
capacity	명 생산[수용]량, 생산 능력	at full **capacity** 최대 생산[수용]량으로
procedure	명 절차 파 proceed 나아가다, 진행하다 파 process 과정, 절차; 가공하다	follow the **procedure** 절차를 따르다
inspector	명 검사관 파 inspect 검사[조사]하다	a safety **inspector** 안전 검사관
shift	명 교대 근무(조)	day[night] **shift** 주간[야간] 근무(조)
substitute	명 대신할 사람 동 대신하다 유 replace 대신하다	a **substitute** for *sb* ~를 대신할 사람
product	명 제품 유 goods 상품, 제품 merchandise 상품, 제품	a finished **product** 완제품
component	명 부품 유 part 부품	an electronic **component** 전자 부품
innovative	형 혁신적인 파 innovate 혁신하다	**innovative** technology 혁신적인 기술
efficient	형 효율적인 파 efficiency 효율성 efficiently 효율적으로	an **efficient** process 효율적인 과정
instructions	명 (제품 사용에 관한) 설명서 파 instruct 설명[지시]하다	detailed **instructions** 자세한 설명서
provide	동 제공[공급]하다 파 provider (서비스의) 공급업체	**provide** employees with handouts 직원들에게 유인물을 제공하다

파 파생어 유 유의어 반 반의어 관 관련 어휘

어휘 확인하기

다음 괄호 안에서 알맞은 것을 고르세요.

1 The production manager (provided / operated) each worker with safety goggles.

2 Not all employees have (procedure / access) to the factory floor.

3 A&N Co. (manufactures / substitutes) the components in these electronic devices.

4 Sandra's method seems (efficient / accessible) for handling multiple tasks at once.

실전 감각 키우기

다음 빈칸에 알맞은 것을 고르세요.

5 The manager inspected the ------- in the factory and ordered some new parts.

(A) procedure
(B) innovation
(C) construction
(D) equipment

6 Under the ------- of Francis Reed, the Oakdale plant processes about five hundred items per day.

(A) supervision
(B) indication
(C) completion
(D) generation

7 These modern machines increase the manufacturing ------- dramatically.

(A) component
(B) instrument
(C) capacity
(D) agreement

8 The diagnosis was first made during the patient's ------- checkup last October.

(A) routine
(B) accessible
(C) innovative
(D) efficient

주어진 문제를 제한시간에 맞추어 풀어 보세요.

Part 5 Choose the one word or phrase that best completes the sentence.

1. The new tracking system ------- the warehouse to ship goods more efficiently.

(A) will allow
(B) to allow
(C) allowance
(D) allowing

2. In the staff handbook, ------- for full-time employees are described in detail.

(A) regulated
(B) regulations
(C) regular
(D) regularly

3. The ------- laptop from Vida Co. received favorable reviews for its lightweight design.

(A) frequent
(B) innovative
(C) estimated
(D) reluctant

4. There remains a strong ------- for the two banks to merge in the future.

(A) possibilities
(B) possibly
(C) possibility
(D) possible

5. Some of the vehicle's ------- should be replaced because they are worn.

(A) capacities
(B) specifications
(C) procedures
(D) components

6. Office supply purchases over $100 require ------- from the finance department.

(A) approved
(B) approval
(C) approving
(D) approve

7. The walking paths became ------- after the maintenance work in the park.

(A) visible
(B) visibility
(C) vision
(D) visibly

8. Experienced technicians ------- the laboratory equipment carefully before an experiment begins.

(A) perform
(B) function
(C) instruct
(D) inspect

Part 6 Questions 9-12 refer to the following article.

GRENSTON, 11 June—CEO Ashton Murphy of Halta, Inc., has announced that the company will relocate its production plant to a cheaper area. Halta, Inc., manufactures electronics that it distributes across the Grenston region. "In order to keep its prices -------, Halta, Inc., needs to cut unnecessary expenses," Mr. Murphy stated. "One way
9.
to do that is to save on rent." Thus, while the stores will remain in the same locations, the production ------- will be moved to Hallsville. This city is popular among
10.
manufacturers because it offers industrial buildings ------- on rental prices. ------- .
11.   12.

9. (A) compete
    (B) competitors
    (C) competitive
    (D) competes

10. (A) facility
    (B) risk
    (C) capacity
    (D) safety

11. (A) reduces
    (B) reductions
    (C) reduce
    (D) reduced

12. (A) Visitors are attracted to the historical sites.
    (B) For special deals on phones, visit www.halta.com.
    (C) However, setting up a factory in Hallsville is very expensive.
    (D) In fact, several other electronics manufacturers are already based there.

PART 5&6 명사편

UNIT 02

명사
+제조 어휘(2)

명사란 사물이나 사람의 이름을 나타내는 말입니다.
명사는 크게 셀 수 있는 명사와 셀 수 없는 명사로 나눌 수 있습니다.
이 명사들이 각각 어떤 특징을 가지는지 알아볼까요?

1 명사의 역할과 종류
2 명사 자리와 한정사
3 헷갈리는 명사

+ 제조 어휘(2)

1 명사의 역할과 종류

The inspector
visits the restaurant.

명사
• 형태: -tion, -sion, -ness, -ance, -ment, -ship, -ty 등
• 역할: 문장의 주어, 목적어, 보어

명사의 종류
• 셀 수 있는 명사: 단수는 앞에 a(n)와, 복수는 뒤에 -(e)s가 함께 쓰임
• 셀 수 없는 명사: a(n), -(e)s는 함께 쓸 수 없고 the는 쓸 수 있음

A 명사

ⓐ **명사의 형태**: 다양한 형태로 쓰이지만, 단어의 끝부분을 보면 명사인지 알 수 있어요.

• 자주 쓰이는 명사형 어미: -tion, -sion, -ness, -ance, -ment, -ship, -ty 등
compens**ation** 보상   attend**ance** 참석   accomplish**ment** 성취   stabili**ty** 안정성

ⓑ **명사의 역할**: 명사는 주어, 목적어, 보어의 역할을 하므로, 각 성분의 자리에 들어갈 수 있습니다.

주어	**The inspector** visits the restaurant every four months. 그 **조사관**은 네 달에 한 번 그 식당을 방문한다.
목적어	The customer provided **the receipt** for the shirt. (동사의 목적어) 그 고객은 셔츠를 구매한 **영수증을** 제출했다. The bus will stop near **the library** at 4 P.M. (전치사의 목적어) 그 버스는 오후 4시에 **도서관** 근처에 정차할 것이다.
보어	Dorothy Helen became **the mayor** of Primville on June 14. (주격 보어) 도로시 헬렌 씨는 6월 14일에 프라임빌의 **시장이** 되었다. The boards appointed him **chairperson** of the committee. (목적격 보어) 이사회는 그를 위원회의 **회장으로** 임명했다.

B 명사의 종류

ⓐ **셀 수 있는 명사(가산명사)**

• 개수를 셀 수 있는 명사는 '가산명사'라고도 해요. 대부분의 명사가 가산명사입니다.
• 셀 수 있는 명사는 단수의 경우 앞에 관사 a(n)를, 복수의 경우 뒤에 -(e)s를 붙입니다.

The electronics company designed **a product**. 그 전자 회사는 **제품 하나를** 기획했다.

• 단수 명사 앞에는 a(n)가 아니더라도 꼭 한정사가 있어야 하고, 복수 명사는 한정사 없이도 쓸 수 있어요.

ⓑ **셀 수 없는 명사(불가산명사)**

• 개수를 셀 수 없는 명사는 '불가산명사'라고도 불러요.
• 셀 수 없으므로 a(n)도, -(e)s도 붙일 수 없지만, 관사 the는 붙일 수 있어요.

They are checking **the equipment**. 그들은 **장비를** 점검하고 있다.
~~an equipment, equipments~~

• 불가산명사는 셀 수 없는 것이 원칙이나, several pieces of 같은 단위 표현으로 수량을 나타낼 수 있습니다.

They are checking **several pieces of** equipment. 그들은 **여러 대의 장비를** 점검하고 있다.

빈출 불가산명사 equipment 장비, furniture 가구, consent 동의, access 접근(법), machinery 기계(류)

핵심 POINT 확인하기

다음 괄호 안에서 알맞은 것을 고르세요.

|핵심 POINT 슬쩍 보기||

1 (Employs / Employees) must file vacation request at least one week in advance.

1 주어 자리에는 명사가 쓰여요.

2 The board members named Ms. Kendal (manage / manager) of the store.

2 보어 자리에는 명사가 쓰여요.

3 As a safety precaution, the supervisor inspects (a / the) machinery once a month.

3 a(n)는 불가산명사와 함께 쓰일 수 없어요.

4 A lot of (luggage / luggages) looks similar, so please check the ID tag.

4 luggage는 불가산명사라 -(e)s를 붙여 쓸 수 없어요.

실전 감각 키우기

다음 빈칸에 알맞은 것을 고르세요.

5 Bornthon Industries will finish the ------- of its facility next month.

(A) renovation   (B) renovate
(C) renovative   (D) renovated

6 Sound Entertainment will succeed if it can expand consumer ------- to its services.

(A) access   (B) accessed
(C) accesses   (D) accessible

7 Relocating to Summit Building is a good ------- to building an extension on our current building.

(A) alternating   (B) alternated
(C) alternative   (D) alternates

8 The doctor cannot share a patient's medical history without -------.

(A) to consent   (B) consent
(C) consented   (D) consents

명사 자리와 한정사

his equipment

명사 자리
- 한정사 뒤: 〈한정사+(부사)+(형용사)+명사〉
- 형용사 뒤: 〈관사+형용사+명사〉, 〈소유격+형용사+명사〉

한정사와 명사의 형태
- 〈a(n)+단수 가산명사〉 a product ~~a products~~ ~~an information~~
- 〈the+모든 명사〉 the product the products the information

A 명사 자리

ⓐ 한정사 뒤

- 한정사는 명사의 의미를 명확히 해 주기 위해 〈한정사+(부사)+(형용사)+명사〉의 구조로 쓰입니다.
- 관사: '불특정한 하나'를 의미하는 부정관사 a(n)와 특정한 대상임을 나타내는 정관사 the가 있어요.

  부정관사 a(n) <u>a</u> **chair** 의자 하나   <u>a</u> comfortable **chair** 편안한 의자 하나

  정관사 the <u>the</u> **product** 그 제품   <u>the</u> new **product** 그 신제품

- 소유격 대명사: '누구의', '무엇의' 것인지 알려 주는 소유격 대명사 뒤는 명사 자리예요.

  <u>your</u> **supervisor** 당신의 상사   <u>his</u> **equipment** 그의 장비

- 수량 형용사: 수나 양을 표현해 주는 수량 형용사 뒤에는 명사가 와요.

  <u>every</u> **employee** 모든 직원   <u>many</u> **employees** 많은 수의 직원들   <u>much</u> **information** 많은 정보

- 지시대명사: '이', '저'의 의미로 쓰이는 지시대명사 뒤에 명사가 올 수 있어요.
  셀 수 있는 명사의 단수형 앞에는 this[that]이, 복수형 앞에는 these[those]가 쓰여요.

  <u>this[that]</u> **package** 이[저] 소포   <u>these[those]</u> **packages** 이[저] 소포들

ⓑ 형용사 뒤

- 〈관사+형용사+명사〉, 〈소유격+형용사+명사〉의 구조로 자주 쓰입니다.

  The <u>regular</u> **rate** for memberships will increase next month.
  회원권의 일반 **요금이** 다음 달부터 인상됩니다.

B 한정사와 명사의 형태

- 특정 한정사는 함께 쓸 수 있는 명사의 종류가 정해져 있어요.

구분		가산명사		불가산명사
		단수형	복수형	
관사	a(n)	a product	~~a products~~	~~an information~~
	the	the product	the products	the information
수량 형용사	each 각각의 every 모든 another 또 다른, 또 하나의	each product	~~each products~~	~~each information~~
	some 일부의 most 대부분의 all 모든	~~some product~~	some products	some information
	many 많은 a few 적은 few 거의 없는	~~many product~~	many products	~~many information~~
	much 많은 a little 적은 little 거의 없는	~~much product~~	~~much products~~	much information

핵심 POINT 확인하기

다음 괄호 안에서 알맞은 것을 고르세요.

1 Mr. Parker met with an (inspector / inspect) from the electrical safety department.

2 Mr. Andrews received many (estimate / estimates) from different construction companies.

3 Meeting participants use the main (enter / entrance) to the conference hall.

4 The railway company's seven-day train pass is an excellent (choice / choices) for tourists.

|핵심 POINT 슬쩍 보기|

1 한정사인 관사 a(n) 뒤에는 명사가 와요.

2 수량 형용사 many 뒤에는 가산 복수 명사를 써요.

3 관사와 형용사 다음에는 명사가 와야 해요.

4 a(n) 뒤에는 가산명사의 단수형이 나와요.

실전 감각 키우기

다음 빈칸에 알맞은 것을 고르세요.

5 Thanks to a new ------- of materials, the restaurant reduced its expenses.

(A) supplying   (B) supplied
(C) supplier   (D) suppliers

6 ------- files are vital and need to be sent to the accountant right away.

(A) Much   (B) A little
(C) That   (D) These

7 The shareholders talked about all the ------- on the meeting agenda.

빈출

(A) items   (B) itemized
(C) item   (D) itemize

8 Marketing head George Lee announced his ------- during the staff meeting.

(A) resigned   (B) resignation
(C) resigns   (D) to resign

3 헷갈리는 명사

applicant vs. application

핵심 POINT

사람 명사 vs. 추상 명사
- 사람 명사는 대개 가산명사로, -er[-or]이나 -ant로 끝남
- 추상 명사는 대개 불가산명사로, -ment, -ance, -tion으로 끝남

복합 명사
- 두 개 이상의 명사가 합쳐져 하나의 단어처럼 쓰이는 것
- 복수형을 나타내는 -e(s)는 마지막 단어에 붙임

A 사람 명사 vs. 추상 명사

- 같은 동사에서 파생되었지만 '사람을 나타내는 명사[사람 명사]'와 '추상적인 개념을 나타내는 명사[추상 명사]'는 서로 의미가 다릅니다.

사람 명사	동사	추상 명사
employer 고용주 employee 직원	employ 고용하다	employment 고용, 취업
applicant 지원자	apply 지원하다	application 지원(서)
investor 투자자	invest 투자하다	investment 투자
assistant 비서, 조수	assist 돕다, 보조하다	assistance 도움, 지원
supervisor 감독관, 상사	supervise 감독하다	supervision 감독
instructor 강사	instruct 지도하다	instruction 지도, 교육
consultant 상담가	consult 상담하다	consultation 상담

- 사람 명사의 경우, 대개 단어 끝이 -er[-or]이나 -ant로 끝나며, 셀 수 있는 가산명사입니다.
- 추상 명사는, 대개 단어 끝이 -ment, -ance, -tion으로 끝나고, 셀 수 없는 불가산명사입니다.

This **employer** gives generous benefits. 이 **고용주는** 넉넉한 수당을 준다.
It is easy to find full-time **employment** in the city. 그 도시에서 **정규직을** 찾는 것은 쉽다.

B 복합 명사

- 복합 명사는 두 개 이상의 명사가 합쳐져 하나의 단어처럼 쓰이는 것을 말해요.
- 복합 명사를 이루는 명사들은 다른 표현으로 대체할 수 없기 때문에, 한 단어처럼 외워야 합니다.

빈출 복합명사	job opening 채용 공고 (일자리) 공석 sales representative 영업 사원 training session 교육[연수] (기간) benefits package 복리후생 제도	awards ceremony 시상식 business proposal 사업 제안서 manufacturing process 제조 과정 employee productivity 직원 생산성

This **benefits package** is satisfactory. 이 **복리후생 제도는** 만족스럽다.

- 복합 명사는 복수형을 나타내는 -(e)s가 마지막 단어에 붙습니다.
  Many **job openings** will appear next month at Senset Inc.
  다음 달, 센셋 주식회사에 **일자리 공석이** 많이 있을 것이다.

핵심 POINT 확인하기

다음 괄호 안에서 알맞은 것을 고르세요.

1 The (investor / investment) in new equipment was highly profitable for the company.

2 The (supervisor / supervision) monitors the store's sales activity carefully.

3 My previous employer offered its entire staff a standard (beneficial / benefits) package.

4 Box Cutters plans to assess its (manufacturing / manufacturer) process next spring.

|핵심 POINT 슬쩍 보기|

1 사람 명사와 추상 명사는 해석으로 구분해요.

2 단어가 '-or'로 끝나면 사람 명사예요.

3 benefits package는 '복리 후생 제도'란 뜻의 복합 명사예요.

4 복합 명사를 이루는 명사들은 다른 표현으로 대체될 수 없어요.

실전 감각 키우기

다음 빈칸에 알맞은 것을 고르세요.

5 ------- will teach six different marketing courses at Bellmore Education in September.

(A) Instructions   (B) Instructors
(C) Instructive   (D) Instructed

6 Mr. Granger currently serves as a sales ------- for Tennessee Footwear.

(A) individual   (B) presenter
(C) record   (D) representative

7 To learn about possible retirement plans, visit Star Financial for a free one-hour -------.

(A) consults   (B) consulted
(C) consultant   (D) consultation

8 This year's annual awards ------- will be hosted at the prestigious High-Rise Hotel.

(A) ceremony   (B) title
(C) group   (D) winner

앞에서 학습한 핵심 POINT를 떠올리며 빈칸을 완성해 보세요.

핵심 POINT 1

명사의 역할과 종류

명사
- 형태: -tion, -sion, -ness, -ance, -ment, -ship, -ty 등
- 역할: 문장의 ❶_____, 목적어, ❷_____

명사의 종류
- 셀 수 있는 명사: ❸_____는 앞에 a(n)와, ❹_____는 뒤에 -(e)s가 함께 쓰임
- 셀 수 없는 명사: a(n), -(e)s는 함께 쓸 수 없고 the는 쓸 수 있음

핵심 POINT 2

명사 자리와 한정사

명사 자리
- ❺_____ 뒤: 〈한정사+(부사)+(형용사)+명사〉
- ❻_____ 뒤: 〈관사+형용사+명사〉, 〈소유격+형용사+명사〉

한정사와 명사의 형태
- 〈a[n]+단수 가산명사〉 a product a products an information
- 〈the+모든 명사〉 the product the products the information

핵심 POINT 3

헷갈리는 명사

사람 명사 vs. 추상 명사
- 사람 명사는 대개 ❼_____ 명사로, -er[-or]이나 -ant로 끝남
- 추상 명사는 대개 ❽_____ 명사로, -ment, -ance, -tion으로 끝남

❾_____ 명사
- 두 개 이상의 명사가 합쳐져 하나의 단어처럼 쓰이는 것
- 복수형을 나타내는 -e(s)는 ❿_____ 단어에 붙임

|빈칸 정답 살짝 보기|
❶ 주어 ❷ 보어 ❸ 단수 (명사) ❹ 복수 (명사) ❺ 한정사 ❻ 형용사 ❼ 가산 ❽ 불가산 ❾ 복합 ❿ 마지막[제일 끝]

실전 감각 키우기

다음 빈칸에 알맞은 것을 고르세요.

1 For the rest of the week, Ocean Surf has ------- on all of its swimwear.

(A) discounts
(B) discounted
(C) discountable
(D) discount

2 The main selling point of Marusuki Pedals bicycles is their ------- for everyday use.

(A) reliable
(B) relying
(C) relied
(D) reliability

3 Ms. Lawrence received a written ------- from her previous manager.

(A) refers
(B) referring
(C) referral
(D) referred

4 HanMed Pharmaceuticals posts the latest job ------ on its company Web site.

(A) chances
(B) abilities
(C) qualities
(D) openings

[5-6] Questions 5-6 refer to the following letter.

March 2

Rebecca Pauly

Human Resources

Dear Ms. Pauly,

I am highly interested in working for Orno, Inc., as a sales representative. Please find enclosed my résumé and a cover letter describing my -------. According to the job
5.
postings, ------- must submit the names of at least two references. I've included these in
6.
the cover letter. I look forward to hearing from you.

Sincerely,

Joshua Spence

5 (A) qualify
(B) qualifications
(C) qualified
(D) qualifying

6 (A) apply
(B) applications
(C) applicants
(D) applying

제품이 출시되어 보관·배송을 거쳐 소비자가 주문·구매하기까지의 과정에 관한 어휘들입니다.

release	몡 图 출시(하다)	**release** new products	신제품을 출시하다
launch	몡 图 출시(하다), 시작(하다)	**launch** a line of products 제품 라인을 출시하다 **launch** a program 프로그램을 시작하다	
feature	몡 특징 图 보여 주다, 특집으로 다루다	distinguishing **features** 두드러진 특징들	
superior	혱 뛰어난 밴 inferior 열등한	**superior** quality 뛰어난 품질 *superior[inferior] to는 '~보다 뛰어난[열등한]'이란 뜻이에요.	
sufficient	혱 충분한 틘 sufficiently 충분하게 윾 adequate 충분한, 적절한	**sufficient** space 충분한 공간 **sufficient** resources 충분한 자원	
strategy	몡 전략 퍄 strategic 전략적인 strategically 전략적으로	an aggressive marketing **strategy** 적극적인 마케팅 전략	
storage	몡 저장 퍄 store 저장하다	**storage** capacity 저장 용량	
inventory	몡 재고(품) 윾 stock 재고(품)	**inventory** control 재고 관리	
load	몡 짐, 화물 图 싣다, 태우다 밴 unload (짐을) 내리다	**load** boxes onto a truck 트럭에 상자를 싣다	
ship	图 배송하다 퍄 shipment 배송(품)	**ship** directly 직접 배송하다	
distribution	몡 유통 퍄 distribute 유통시키다, 배분하다	a **distribution** channel 유통 경로	
order	몡 图 주문(하다)	place[receive] an **order** 주문을 하다[받다]	
supplier	몡 공급업체 퍄 supply 공급(하다) 윾 provider 제공업체	a major **supplier** 주요 공급업체	
purchase	몡 图 구매(하다) 퐌 exchange 교환(하다) refund 환불(하다)	proof of **purchase** 구매의 증거	
transaction	몡 거래	a financial **transaction** 금융 거래	
pending	혱 미결의, 보류 중인, 임박한	a **pending** order 미결 주문	
complimentary	혱 무료의, 칭찬하는 윾 free 무료의	a **complimentary** breakfast 무료 조식 **complimentary** parking 무료 주차	
competitive	혱 경쟁력 있는 퐌 reasonable (가격이) 비싸지 않은 affordable (가격이) 알맞은	a **competitive** price 경쟁력 있는 가격	

퍄 파생어 윾 유의어 밴 반의어 퐌 관련 어휘

어휘 확인하기

다음 괄호 안에서 알맞은 것을 고르세요.

1 You can check the status of all (superior / pending) orders online.

2 Proya Corp. will (launch / attract) a brand-new line of cosmetics next month.

3 Hundreds of customers (released / purchased) the latest camera model this morning.

4 The warehouse does not have (complimentary / sufficient) space to store all of the items.

실전 감각 키우기

다음 빈칸에 알맞은 것을 고르세요.

5 Mr. Bowman introduced the laptop computer's -------, including its built-in Web cam.

(A) strategies
(B) deals
(C) features
(D) manuals

6 Some of the furniture was damaged when it was ------- onto the moving van.

(A) released
(B) recalled
(C) loaded
(D) ordered

7 Our exercise machines can be ------- directly to any location within the Bridgetown city limits.

(A) shipped
(B) launched
(C) rewarded
(D) compared

8 Hersey Company attracts customers by offering ------- rates.

(A) protective
(B) entire
(C) urgent
(D) competitive

주어진 문제를 제한시간에 맞추어 풀어 보세요.

Part 5 Choose the one word or phrase that best completes the sentence.

1. Consumers find Transcend's new ------- the best model on the market.

   (A) monitor
   (B) monitored
   (C) monitoring
   (D) will monitor

2. The article in *Tech World* analyzes the ------- of smartphone technology.

   (A) developed
   (B) develops
   (C) development
   (D) developmental

3. Mr. Logan became an established ------- more than twenty years ago.

   (A) architecture
   (B) architect
   (C) architecturally
   (D) architects

4. If you pay for your order after 6 P.M. on Friday, the ------- may not be processed until Monday morning.

   (A) distribution
   (B) observation
   (C) transaction
   (D) registration

5. Mr. Benn is preparing for the ------- of the twentieth anniversary of UCK Bank.

   (A) celebrate
   (B) celebrates
   (C) celebrating
   (D) celebration

6. In this workshop, participants will learn to create a business -------.

   (A) propose
   (B) proposal
   (C) proposed
   (D) proposals

7. Government ------- on the importation of goods will apply to all trading companies.

   (A) restricted
   (B) restrict
   (C) restrictions
   (D) restrictive

8. The entire staff must attend a training ------- about customer service twice a year.

   (A) skill
   (B) session
   (C) duration
   (D) point

Part 6 Questions 9-12 refer to the following e-mail.

From: Joanne Finnegan <jfinnegan@reiner.com>
To: Gary Murphy <gmurphy@reiner.com>
Subject: New Warehouse
Date: November 17

Dear Mr. Murphy,

We have had some issues recently with certain materials selling out quickly as we didn't

have sufficient space to store appropriate amounts. We need to maintain our high

standards and stay ahead of our -------. This is why Reiner Co. has decided to purchase
　　　　　　　　　　　　　　　　　9.

an additional warehouse. The timely ------- of materials to our clients is essential. A new
　　　　　　　　　　　　　　　　10.

storage facility would allow us to keep a larger ------- and thus provide better service.
　　　　　　　　　　　　　　　　　11.

We would like you to be in charge of selecting the location. Please start to research

possibilities. -------- . Thank you for your attention in this matter.
　　　　　　　12.

Sincerely,
Joanne Finnegan
Assistant Director, Reiner Co.

9. (A) competitive
    (B) compete
    (C) competitors
    (D) competed

10. (A) shipped
    (B) to ship
    (C) shipment
    (D) ship

11. (A) inventory
    (B) feature
    (C) location
    (D) merchandise

12. (A) You can expect to receive your order
        within a week.
    (B) If you have any questions, please
        contact me directly.
    (C) Our materials are all checked before
        being sent out.
    (D) However, we cannot approve your
        request.

PART 5&6 명사편

UNIT 03

대명사
+제조 어휘(3)

지난 주말에 제임스와 제임스의 친구들은 제임스의 집에서 제임스의 게임기를 가지고 제임스가 가장 좋아하는 게임을 하며 시간을 보냈다.

제임스?
제임스?

대명사는 명사를 대신하는 말입니다. 영어에서는 같은 명사를 반복해서 쓰지 않고, 대명사를 써요. 대명사는 가리키는 대상이 사람 또는 사물인지, 남성 또는 여성인지, 하나 또는 여럿인지에 따라 형태가 달라져요.

1 인칭대명사(주격·목적격·소유격 대명사)

핵심 POINT

인칭대명사
- 사람이나 사물을 가리키는 말
- 인칭, 성, 수, 격에 따라 형태가 다름

주격·목적격·소유격 대명사
- 주격은 동사 앞 주어 역할, 목적격은 동사와 전치사 뒤 목적어 역할
  소유격은 명사 앞에서 '~의'라는 의미의 한정사 역할

A 인칭대명사의 형태

- 인칭대명사는 'I(나), she(그녀), it(그것)'처럼 사람이나 사물을 가리키는 말입니다.
- 영어에서는 인칭, 성, 수, 격에 따라 인칭대명사의 형태가 달라집니다.

인칭/수		격	주격 ~은(는), ~이(가)	목적격 ~을(를), ~에게	소유격 ~의	소유대명사 ~의 것	재귀대명사 ~ 자신
1인칭	단수	나	I	me	my	mine	myself
	복수	우리	we	us	our	ours	ourselves
2인칭	단수	당신	you	you	your	yours	yourself
	복수	당신들	you	you	your	yours	yourselves
3인칭	단수	그	he	him	his	his	himself
		그녀	she	her	her	hers	herself
		그것	it	it	its	–	itself
	복수	그들, 그것들	they	them	their	theirs	themselves

참고 **인칭**은 나(1인칭), 당신(2인칭), 그·그녀(3인칭)처럼 말하는 사람·듣는 사람·제3자를 구분하는 것입니다. **성**은 남성·여성을, **수**는 단수·복수를 구분합니다. 또한, **격**은 문장에서 어떤 역할로 쓰이는지를 나타내요.

B 주격·목적격·소유격 대명사

- 인칭대명사는 문장에서 어떤 역할을 하느냐에 따라 주격, 목적격, 소유격으로 나누어집니다.
- 주격은 문장에서 주어로, 목적격은 동사나 전치사의 목적어로, 소유격은 명사 앞에서 한정사로 쓰여요.

주격	<u>Ms. Davidson</u> is not satisfied with the purchase. **She** wants a refund. 주어 데이비슨 씨는 구매한 물건이 마음에 들지 않는다. **그녀는** 환불을 원한다. (She = Ms. Davidson)
목적격	Mr. Bowey finished <u>the sales report</u>. He will send **it** to the supervisor. 동사의 목적어 보위 씨는 매출 보고서를 완료했다. 그는 **그것을** 상사에게 보낼 것이다. (it = the sales report)
소유격	<u>Ms. Park</u> wrote **her** address on the outside of the box. 명사를 꾸미는 한정사 박 씨는 **그녀의** 주소를 상자 겉면에 적었다. (her = Ms. Park's)

핵심 POINT 확인하기

다음 괄호 안에서 알맞은 것을 고르세요.

1 Ms. Jones left (their / her) laptop in the conference room.

2 (You / Your) can log on to the company's Web site to view the latest products.

3 The security officer gave (my / me) a visitor's badge at the entrance.

4 (Our / We) plan to relocate the company's factory abroad does not seem feasible.

|핵심 POINT 슬쩍 보기|

1 대명사가 가리키는 명사를 앞에서 찾아야 해요.

2 동사 앞 주어 자리에는 주격 인칭대명사가 와요.

3 동사 뒤 목적어 자리에는 목적격 인칭대명사를 써요.

4 명사 앞에서 '누구의' 것인지를 나타낼 때에는 소유격 인칭대명사를 써요.

실전 감각 키우기

다음 빈칸에 알맞은 것을 고르세요.

5 Mr. Kline is a noted engineer, so the electronics company hired ------- without hesitation.

(A) he
(B) him
(C) his
(D) himself

6 At Garmont Industries, ------- offer a customer service hotline twenty-four hours a day.

(A) me
(B) your
(C) we
(D) our

7 The position's benefits as well as ------- duties will be explained in the contract.

(A) they
(B) their
(C) it
(D) its

8 If you need supplies for next month, please order ------- by Friday.

(A) them
(B) it
(C) there
(D) she

2 인칭대명사(소유대명사·재귀대명사)

핵심 POINT

She is using **mine**.

소유대명사
- 〈소유격+명사〉의 역할을 하며, '~의 것'이라는 의미
- 명사 역할을 하므로 주어, 목적어, 보어로 쓰임

재귀대명사
- 재귀 용법: 주어와 목적어가 같은 대상을 가리킬 때, 목적어로 쓰임
- 강조 용법: 강조하고자 하는 말 바로 뒤 또는 문장 끝에 위치

A 소유대명사

- 소유대명사는 〈소유격+명사〉의 역할을 해서 붙여진 이름으로, '~의 것'이란 뜻이에요.
- 소유격 인칭대명사와 달리, 소유대명사는 그 자체로 명사 역할을 하기 때문에 문장에서 주어, 목적어, 보어로 사용될 수 있고, 뒤에 명사를 쓸 수 없어요.

주어	Although our <u>fabric</u> is made from recycled materials, **theirs**[their fabric] is cheaper. 우리 원단은 재활용 소재로 만들어지는데도, **그들의 것이** 더 저렴하다.
목적어	Ms. Thompson lost her <u>phone</u>, so she is using **mine**[my phone]. 탐슨 씨는 그녀의 전화기를 잃어버려서, **내 것을** 사용하고 있다.
보어	<u>The suitcase</u> behind the desk is **ours**[our suitcase]. 책상 뒤의 여행 가방이 **우리 것**이다.

B 재귀대명사

- 재귀대명사는 myself(나 자신), themselves(그들 자신)와 같이 '~ 자신'을 의미하는 말입니다.
- 인칭대명사의 소유격이나 목적격에 단수는 -self를, 복수는 -selves를 붙인 형태예요.
- 참고로 재귀대명사는 주어 자리에 쓸 수 없어요.

ⓐ 주어와 목적어가 같을 때(재귀 용법)

- 문장의 주어와 목적어가 같을 때 목적어 자리에 재귀대명사를 씁니다.
- 이때, 재귀대명사는 생략할 수 없습니다.

  <u>He</u> looked at **himself** in the mirror. 그는 거울에 비친 **자기 자신을** 보았다.
  <u>The technicians</u> introduced **themselves** to the managers. 기술자들은 부장들에게 **자신들을** 소개했다.

ⓑ 의미를 강조할 때(강조 용법)

- 주어, 목적어, 보어의 행위나 상태를 강조하기 위해, 강조하고자 하는 말 바로 뒤 또는 문장 마지막에 씁니다.
- 강조하기 위해 쓴 것이므로 생략해도 문장이 성립합니다.

  <u>She</u> (**herself**) streamlined the packaging process. 그녀가 **직접** 포장 과정을 간소화했다.
  = <u>She</u> streamlined the packaging process (**herself**).

ⓒ 관용 표현

by *oneself* 혼자서	for *oneself* 직접, 스스로	of *itself* 저절로

Her partner was busy, so <u>she</u> went to the conference **by herself**.
파트너가 바빠서 그녀는 **혼자** 학회에 갔다.

핵심 POINT 확인하기

다음 괄호 안에서 알맞은 것을 고르세요.

1 Mr. Chan mentioned that the blue folders on the desk were (his / him).

2 Dane Phillips introduced (hers / herself) to the investors at the conference.

3 The marketing department conducts product research (itself / its).

4 This quarter, we set a higher sales goal for (us / ourselves).

|핵심 POINT 슬쩍 보기|

1 소유대명사는 〈소유격+명사〉 역할을 해요.

2 주어와 목적어가 같으면, 목적 어 자리에는 재귀대명사를 써 요.

3 재귀대명사를 생략해도 문장이 성립한다면 의미를 강조하기 위해 쓰인 거예요.

4 for *oneself*는 '직접, 스스로' 라는 뜻이에요.

실전 감각 키우기

다음 빈칸에 알맞은 것을 고르세요.

5 빈출 While most of the reports contained only text, ------- included several graphs and photos.

(A) mine (B) myself
(C) me (D) my

6 The lab technician wears gloves to protect ------- from harmful chemicals.

(A) yourselves (B) himself
(C) myself (D) themselves

7 빈출 During Mr. Taylor's absence, Ms. Allen plans to organize the monthly meeting -------.

(A) she (B) hers
(C) her (D) herself

8 Mr. Franklin started his business by -------, and he became successful without any help.

(A) himself (B) his
(C) he (D) him

3 지시대명사

핵심 POINT

this와 that
- this/these는 '이것/이것들', that/those는 '저것/저것들'을 의미
- this/that은 단수 취급, these/those는 복수 취급

that/those만 쓸 수 있는 경우
- 같은 문장 내의 명사를 가리킬 때 that/those만 쓸 수 있음
- those who는 '~하는 사람들'이라는 뜻의 관용 표현

This is the new invoice.

A this와 that

- 지시대명사는 사람·사물을 가리키거나 이전에 언급된 내용을 가리킬 때 쓰입니다.
- 거리, 시간상 가까운 단수 명사를 가리킬 때 this(이것)를 쓰고, 먼 것을 가리킬 때 that(저것)을 씁니다. 복수형은 각각 these(이것들)와 those(저것들)이고 복수 취급해요.

사람·사물	**This[That]** is the new invoice. 이것[저것]은 새로운 운송장이다. **These[Those]** are our partners. 이들[저들]은 우리의 협력자들이다.
이전의 내용	The fragile item was wrapped carefully, and **this[that]** protected it. 그 깨지기 쉬운 물품은 조심스럽게 포장되었고, **이것[그것]**은 그것을 보호해 주었다.

참고 앞 단원에서 배운 것처럼 this와 that은 명사 앞에 위치하여 '이, 저'라는 의미를 더해주는 한정사로 쓰일 수 있어요. this[that] 뒤에는 단수 명사, these[those] 뒤에는 복수 명사가 옵니다.

> **This[That]** receipt is from last month. 이[저] 영수증은 지난달 것이다.
> **These[Those]** labels are ours. 이[저] 라벨들은 우리의 것이다.

B that/those만 쓸 수 있는 경우

ⓐ 같은 문장 안에 있는 명사를 가리킬 때
- 같은 문장 안에서 앞에 나온 명사를 가리킬 때는 지시대명사 that 또는 those를 씁니다.
- 가리키는 명사가 단수일 때는 that, 복수일 때는 those를 써요.

> This month's <u>production</u> surpassed **that** of last month. 이번 달의 생산량은 지난달의 **것을** 넘어섰다.
>   = the production

> Our <u>warranties</u> are better than **those** of our competitors. 우리의 품질 보증은 경쟁사의 **것들보다** 낫다.
>   = the warranties

참고 this와 these는 이런 쓰임이 없다는 것도 기억해두세요.

ⓑ those who: ~하는 사람들
- those는 일반적인 사람들(= people)을 가리키는 대명사로도 쓰입니다.
- those who(~하는 사람들)는 관용적으로 많이 쓰이니 통째로 기억해야 해요.

> **Those who** load the truck must be careful. 트럭에 짐을 싣는 **사람들은** 조심해야 한다.

- those 뒤의 〈who+be동사〉가 생략되어, those 뒤에 분사(-ing, p.p.)나 전치사구만 따라오는 경우도 있어요.

> We closely monitored **those** (**who were**) <u>unpacking</u> the crates.
> 우리는 상자를 푸는 **사람들을** 면밀히 관찰했다.

핵심 POINT 확인하기

다음 괄호 안에서 알맞은 것을 고르세요.

1 (This / These) is the best way to get to the harbor.

2 These (products / product) are available for purchase online only.

3 The staff size of Weston Bank is larger than (this / that) of its main competitor.

4 The workshop is helpful for (these / those) who don't know how to navigate the database.

|핵심 POINT 슬쩍 보기|

1 가리키는 대상이 단수이면 this, 복수이면 these를 써요.

2 한정사 these 뒤에는 복수 명사가 와요.

3 같은 문장 안에서 앞에 나온 명사는 that이나 those로 대신해요.

4 those who는 '~하는 사람들'이란 뜻의 관용적 표현이에요.

실전 감각 키우기

다음 빈칸에 알맞은 것을 고르세요.

5 빈출 The factory produces tons of waste each month, and ------- is a major cause of pollution.

(A) this
(B) ours
(C) these
(D) their

6 This year's sales report was more detailed than ------- of last year.

(A) they
(B) these
(C) them
(D) that

7 Please present ------- coupon to receive a 20 percent discount on our landscaping services.

(A) which
(B) this
(C) these
(D) whose

8 Only ------- holding a parking permit can park their cars in this section.

(A) that
(B) those
(C) them
(D) their

4 부정대명사

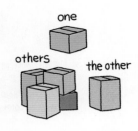

핵심 POINT

부정대명사의 의미와 쓰임
- 정해지지 않은 사람·사물을 가리킴
- some, any, most, all, both, each 등

one, another, other
- 한 개는 one, 다른 하나는 another, 나머지 중 일부는 others
- 나머지 한 개는 the other, 나머지 전부는 the others

A 부정대명사의 의미와 쓰임

- 부정대명사는 정해지지 않은 사람·사물을 가리킬 때 씁니다.
- 〈부정대명사+of the+명사〉의 형태로 '여러 개 중 일부'를 나타낼 때, 함께 쓰는 명사의 종류에 제약이 있어요.

some 일부	any 누구든/무엇이든	most 대부분	all 모두	+ of the + 모든 명사
many 많은	a few/few 적은/거의 없는	both 둘 다	each 각각	+ of the + 복수 가산명사
much 많은	a little/little 적은/거의 없는			+ of the + 불가산명사

Some of the staff has access to the staff lounge. 직원 중 **일부가** 직원 휴게실을 이용할 수 있다.

참고 some은 주로 긍정문에, any는 주로 부정문과 의문문에 쓰여요.

- every 모든, some 일부, any 누구든, 조금도, no ~ 아닌에 -one, -body, -thing이 붙어서 불특정한 사람·사물을 가리키는 부정대명사로 쓰여요.

Everyone made an effort to minimize costs. **모두가** 비용을 최소화하려는 노력을 했다.

- -one, -body, -thing 형태의 부정대명사는 뒤에 있는 형용사의 수식을 받아요.

Do you need **anything** new for the presentation? 발표를 위해 **무언가** 새로운 것이 필요한가요?

B one, another, other

- one, another, other은 여러 대상 중에 하나 또는 일부를 가리킬 때 쓰는 부정대명사입니다.

두 개 또는 세 개일 때	〈두 개〉 ☺ one (정해지지 않은) 하나	☺ the other 나머지 하나	〈세 개〉 ☺ one 하나	☺ another 다른 하나	☺ the other 나머지 하나
네 개 이상일 때	☺ ☺ ☺ ☺ ⋯ one 하나 another 다른 하나		☺ ☺ ☺ ☺ ⋯ one 하나 others (나머지 중) 일부		☺ ☺ ☺ ☺ one 하나 the others 나머지 전부

Both items aren't ready yet. We'll send **one** now and then **the other** later.
두 제품 모두 아직 준비되어 있지 않다. 우리는 **하나를** 지금 보내고 난 다음 **나머지 하나를** 나중에 보낼 것이다.

One product trial has been completed, and **others** are still being done.
하나의 제품 시험이 완료되었고, **(나머지 중) 일부는** 여전히 진행 중이다.

- each other(둘일 때)와 one another(둘 또는 다수일 때)는 '서로 (서로)'라는 의미의 관용 표현입니다.

The director and her assistant talk to **each other** daily. 그 이사와 그녀의 비서는 매일 **서로** 대화한다.

68 UNIT 03 대명사

UNIT 03

핵심 POINT 확인하기

다음 괄호 안에서 알맞은 것을 고르세요.

1 They will analyze (little / each) of the applications for this vacancy.

2 There was (nothing / any) negative about Ms. Dawson's job interview with Ferho Corporation.

3 One new product was released this year, and (much / others) are being developed.

4 Staff members should give (one another / the other) advice to improve their work.

|핵심 POINT 슬쩍 보기|

1 little은 불가산명사와, each 는 복수 가산명사와 어울려 쓰여요.

2 -thing, -one, -body 형태의 부정대명사는 뒤에 있는 형용사의 수식을 받아요.

3 여러 대상 중 일부를 나타낼 때 others는 '(나머지 중) 일부'를 나타내요.

4 one another은 '서로 (서로)' 라는 의미의 관용 표현이에요.

실전 감각 키우기

다음 빈칸에 알맞은 것을 고르세요.

5 ------- who uses a spare laptop registers at the IT department.

(A) Any   (B) Some
(C) Anyone   (D) That

6 If you encounter a problem within the thirty-day trial period, we will exchange your Home Gym 2000 for -------.

(A) other   (B) another
(C) them   (D) others

7 From scriptwriting to directing, the award-winning filmmaker managed ------- in the movie.

(A) other   (B) anybody
(C) whatever   (D) everything

8 Mr. Adams and Ms. Hill always get the best results when they collaborate with -------.

(A) another   (B) each other
(C) some   (D) the same

앞에서 학습한 핵심 POINT를 떠올리며 빈칸을 완성해 보세요.

핵심 POINT 1

인칭대명사(주격·목적격·소유격 대명사)

인칭대명사
- 사람이나 사물을 가리키는 말
- 인칭, 성, 수, ❶_____에 따라 형태가 다름

주격·목적격·소유격 대명사
- ❷_____은 동사 앞 주어 역할, 목적격은 동사와 전치사 뒤 목적어 역할
- ❸_____은 명사 앞에서 '~의'라는 의미의 한정사 역할

핵심 POINT 2

인칭대명사(소유대명사·재귀대명사)

소유대명사
- 〈❹_____+명사〉의 역할을 하며, '~의 것'이라는 의미
- 명사 역할을 하므로 주어, 목적어, 보어로 쓰임

재귀대명사
- 재귀 용법: 주어와 ❺_____가 같은 대상을 가리킬 때, 목적어로 쓰임
- 강조 용법: 강조하고자 하는 말 바로 뒤 또는 문장 끝에 위치

핵심 POINT 3

지시대명사

this와 that
- this/these는 '이것/이것들', that/those는 '저것/저것들'을 의미
- this/that은 ❻_____ 취급, these/those는 복수 취급

that/those만 쓸 수 있는 경우
- 같은 문장 내의 명사를 가리킬 때 that/those만 쓸 수 있음
- ❼_____는 '~하는 사람들'이라는 뜻의 관용 표현

핵심 POINT 4

부정대명사

부정대명사의 의미와 쓰임
- ❽_____ 사람·사물을 가리킴
- some 일부, any 누구든/무엇이든, most 대부분, all 모두, both 둘 다, each 각각 등

one, another, other
- 한 개는 one, 다른 하나는 ❾_____, 나머지 중 '일부'는 others
- 나머지 한 개는 the other, 나머지 '전부'는 ❿_____

| 빈칸 정답 살짝 보기 |

❶ 격 ❷ 주격 ❸ 소유격 ❹ 소유격 ❺ 목적어 ❻ 단수 ❼ those who ❽ 정해지지 않은(불특정한) ❾ another ❿ the others

실전 감각 키우기

다음 빈칸에 알맞은 것을 고르세요.

1 The charity workers met the mayor and thanked ------- for the donation.

(A) him
(B) them
(C) himself
(D) his

2 A welcome guide is provided so that guests can familiarize ------- with the hotel's amenities.

(A) himself
(B) itself
(C) yourself
(D) themselves

3 ------- who wish to attend the seminar should get in touch with Brenda from HR.

(A) These
(B) Whichever
(C) Those
(D) Them

4 The hardware store prefers ------- good at inventory management for the position.

(A) each other
(B) someone
(C) one another
(D) everyone

[5-6] Questions 5-6 refer to the following advertisement.

New Night Hikes up Emery Mountain!

Watch the sunrise from the top of Emery Mountain! ------- is an experience you will
　　　　　　　　　　　　　　　　　　　　　　　　　　　5.
never forget. Tours depart from the information center every day at 4:30 A.M. A guide will

walk you up the mountain for an hour-long hike. You will then enjoy a breakfast while

watching the sunrise. Note that the hike takes place at night, with no lighting. You may

bring ------- own flashlight or borrow one of ours for $5.
　　　　6.

5 (A) This
(B) These
(C) Them
(D) Those

6 (A) you
(B) your
(C) yours
(D) yourself

제품의 준비, 포장, 취급에 관한 어휘들입니다.

introduce	동 내놓다, 도입하다 파 introduction 도입	**introduce** a new product	신제품을 내놓다
measure	명 조치[정책], 척도[기준] 동 측정하다, 재다	implement a **measure**	조치를 시행하다
improve	동 개선하다 파 improvement 개선, 향상 improved 개선된, 향상된	**improve** a product	상품을 개선하다
install	동 설치하다 파 installation 설치	**install** a machine	기계를 설치하다
function	명 동 기능(하다) 파 malfunction 오작동(하다)	**function** properly	제대로 기능하다
standard	명 기준 형 일반적인 파 standardize 표준화하다	high[low] **standards**	높은[낮은] 기준
material	명 재료, 소재	raw **materials**	원자재
package	명 소포, 포장(물) 동 포장하다 유 wrap 포장하다	a **package** of goods	상품 한 상자
fragile	형 깨지기 쉬운 유 delicate 깨지기 쉬운, 연약한 반 durable 내구성 있는	**fragile** items	깨지기 쉬운 물품들
finalize	동 마무리하다, 완결하다 유 finish 끝내다, 마치다	**finalize** an operation	운영을 마무리하다
defective	형 결함이 있는 파 defect 결함, 장애 유 faulty 결함이 있는	a **defective** product	결함 있는 제품
transport	명 동 운송(하다) 파 transportation 운송	**transport** merchandise	제품을 운송하다
technician	명 기술자 파 technique 기술 technical 기술적인	a computer **technician**	컴퓨터 기술자
closely	부 면밀히 파 close 가까운; 가까이 유 thoroughly 철저히	**closely** monitor	면밀히 감시하다
compatible	형 (컴퓨터 등이) 호환되는	**compatible** with a device	기기와 호환되는
examine	동 검토하다 파 examination 검토, 조사	**examine** some results	결과를 검토하다
carefully	부 조심스럽게 파 careful 조심스러운	handle an item **carefully**	물품을 조심스럽게 다루다
effective	형 효과적인 파 effectively 효과적으로 반 ineffective 효과가 없는	**effective** measures	효과적인 방법들

파 파생어 유 유의어 반 반의어 관 관련 어휘

다음 괄호 안에서 알맞은 것을 고르세요.

1 Management will implement new (materials / measures) for safety tests.

2 The project leader must (transport / finalize) the proposal by tomorrow.

3 We offer full refunds for all (effective / defective) items without exception.

4 The UH charger is (compatible / delicate) with all standard devices.

다음 빈칸에 알맞은 것을 고르세요.

5 빈출 The technician ------- the air-conditioning units in the office last week.

(A) posted
(B) conducted
(C) installed
(D) introduced

6 The factory machinery is inspected once a month to ensure it ------- properly.

(A) changes
(B) functions
(C) simplifies
(D) transports

7 To avoid shipping damage, ------- items should be carefully packaged in bubble wrap.

(A) beneficial
(B) fragile
(C) supportive
(D) cautious

8 빈출 The new program is very ------- against computer viruses.

(A) total
(B) defective
(C) complete
(D) effective

주어진 문제를 제한시간에 맞추어 풀어 보세요.

Part 5 Choose the one word or phrase that best completes the sentence.

1. The final report cannot be written until ------- finish collecting the surveys.

   (A) us
   (B) our
   (C) we
   (D) ourselves

2. Products manufactured by Prosyris Enterprises are ------- monitored at every stage of the production process.

   (A) nearly
   (B) closely
   (C) approximately
   (D) technically

3. Ms. Mala has the same suitcase as the Harpers, and she accidentally took -------.

   (A) they
   (B) them
   (C) theirs
   (D) themselves

4. James repainted the interior walls ------- in order to save money.

   (A) his
   (B) he
   (C) him
   (D) himself

5. Ms. Bates must revise the poster design immediately, as her manager needs ------- tomorrow morning.

   (A) it
   (B) her
   (C) they
   (D) them

6. According to the airline's policy, ------- who possess first-class tickets may board the plane first.

   (A) this
   (B) those
   (C) both
   (D) these

7. ------- negotiates long-term contracts on behalf of the company better than Ms. Donovan.

   (A) Any
   (B) That
   (C) Nothing
   (D) Nobody

8. Acorn Supermarket has been praised for the high ------- of customer service in all its branches.

   (A) documents
   (B) guides
   (C) standards
   (D) precautions

어휘/해설 보기

UNIT 03

Part 6 Questions 9-12 refer to the following e-mail.

From: Claire Pascale
To: Penny Tran
Subject: Order #205354
Date: December 13

Dear Ms. Tran,

Thank you for your order of the RX250 oven. The oven will be delivered on Friday,
December 15, between 3 and 5 P.M. ------- installation will take approximately 45
                                       9.
minutes. A ------- will be there to oversee the process and ensure that the device works
            10.
properly.

Included in the delivery will be an instructions manual. Unfortunately, we recently noticed
errors in the book. ------- of the instructions were not updated accurately with our
                      11.
newest model. ------- . We will send you an updated version as soon as it is available.
                12.
In the meantime, if you have any questions, you may call our help line at 555-2966.

Sincerely,
Claire Pascale
Customer Service Representative, Yelex Co.

9. (A) It
    (B) Its
    (C) Their
    (D) His

10. (A) performer
    (B) quality
    (C) technician
    (D) function

11. (A) Both
    (B) Much
    (C) Any
    (D) Some

12. (A) As a result, you may be confused by
        parts of the manual.
    (B) We apologize for the delay in
        delivery and will refund the fee.
    (C) Please review the document in order
        to correct the mistakes.
    (D) We recommend ordering the most
        recent oven instead.

PART 5&6 동사편

UNIT 04

수일치
+회사 어휘(1)

문장에 없어서는 안 되는 주어와 동사는 아무렇게나 짝지어지는 게 아니에요.
단수 주어에는 단수 동사가 따라오고, 복수 주어에는 복수 동사가 따라오지요.
이것을 주어와 동사의 수일치라고 합니다.

---

1 주어와 동사의 수일치 ①
2 주어와 동사의 수일치 ②
3 수량 표현과 수일치

+ 회사 어휘(1)

1 주어와 동사의 수일치 ①

핵심 POINT

수일치
- 주어와 동사의 수를 일치시키는 것
- 단수 주어+단수 동사 / 복수 주어+복수 동사

단수 동사와 복수 동사의 형태
- 단수 동사는 〈동사원형+-e(s)〉, 복수 동사는 〈동사원형〉
- be동사는 과거 시제도 수일치가 적용됨

He + is/was/has/does
~~are/were/have/do~~

A 수일치

- 영어에서는 주어가 단수이면 동사도 단수 동사를, 주어가 복수이면 동사도 복수 동사를 씁니다. 이처럼 하나의 절 안에서 주어와 동사의 '수'를 서로 일치시키는 것을 수일치라고 합니다.

단수 주어+단수 동사	**He hires** the interns. 그는 인턴들을 **채용한다**.
복수 주어+복수 동사	**They accept** the proposal. 그들은 제안을 **받아들인다**.

B 단수 동사와 복수 동사의 형태

ⓐ 일반동사

- 단수 동사는 대개 동사원형에 -(e)s를 붙인 형태이고, 복수 동사는 동사의 기본형인 동사원형을 씁니다.

단수 동사	〈동사원형+-(e)s〉	**She attends** the job fair every year. 그녀는 매년 그 취업 박람회에 **참석한다**.
복수 동사	〈동사원형〉	**They attend** the job fair every year. 그들은 매년 그 취업 박람회에 **참석한다**.

참고 일반동사의 수일치는 현재 시제에만 적용되고, 과거나 미래 시제에는 적용되지 않아요.
She[They] attended the job fair last year. 그녀는[그들은] 작년에 그 취업 박람회에 **참석했다**.

ⓑ be동사 / do동사 / have동사

- be동사, do동사, have동사의 복수 동사 형태는 일반동사와 다릅니다.
- 특히, be동사는 현재 시제뿐만 아니라, 과거 시제에도 단수형과 복수형이 있다는 것에 주의하세요.

구분	be동사		do동사	have동사
	현재 시제	과거 시제		
단수 동사	(am), is	was	does	has
복수 동사	are	were	do	have

be동사   He **is[was]** reviewing the résumé. 그는 이력서를 검토하고 **있다[있었다]**.
They **are[were]** reviewing the résumé. 그들은 이력서를 검토하고 **있다[있었다]**.

do동사   He **does** not interview the job candidates. 그는 입사 지원자들을 **면접하지 않는다**.
They **do** not interview the job candidates. 그들은 입사지원자들을 **면접하지 않는다**.

have동사   She **has** participated in the event in the past. 그녀는 이전에 그 행사에 **참여한 적이 있다**.
They **have** participated in the event in the past. 그들은 이전에 그 행사에 **참여한 적이 있다**.

핵심 POINT 확인하기

다음 괄호 안에서 알맞은 것을 고르세요.

|핵심 POINT 슬쩍 보기|

1 Bryn Corp. employees (receive / receives) attractive bonuses every year in December.

1 주어가 복수이면, 동사는 〈동사원형〉을 써요.

2 Mr. Jackson (attend / attends) the board meeting every three months.

2 주어가 단수이면, 동사는 〈동사원형+-(e)s〉를 써요.

3 The (courier / couriers) has delivered the package to the reception desk.

3 has는 단수 동사예요.

4 The branch manager and her assistant (was / were) traveling to Tokyo.

4 일반동사와 달리 be동사는 과거 시제에도 복수형이 따로 있어요.

실전 감각 키우기

다음 빈칸에 알맞은 것을 고르세요.

5 Leading ------- agree that it is possible to develop an environmentally friendly fuel.

(A) chemist   (B) chemists
(C) chemical   (D) chemically

6 The highway expansion ------- the traffic problems in the area significantly.

(A) reducing   (B) reduced
(C) have reduced   (D) reduce

7 The ------- has greatly improved since the crisis ten years ago.

(A) economies   (B) economically
(C) economy   (D) economizes

8 Some retailers ------- for new suppliers following the closure of McKinley Wholesale.

(A) looks   (B) to look
(C) are looking   (D) looking

2 주어와 동사의 수일치 ②

핵심 POINT

주어의 단수/복수 구분
- 단수 주어: 단수 가산명사/단수 대명사/불가산명사/
  to부정사(구)·동명사(구)/명사절 등
- 복수 주어: 복수 가산명사/복수 대명사/A and B 등

주어를 찾기 어려운 경우의 수일치
- 주어 뒤의 수식어는 주어와 동사의 수일치에 영향을 주지 않음
- 〈There+be동사+주어〉에서, be동사는 그 뒤의 주어에 수일치
- 〈선행사(명사)+관계대명사+동사〉에서, 동사는 선행사에 수일치

A 주어의 단수/복수 구분

- 동사의 수를 결정하는 기준은 주어이므로, 주어가 단수인지 복수인지 잘 판단하여 동사의 수를 맞춥니다.

단수 주어	단수 가산명사 / 단수 대명사 / 불가산명사 / to부정사(구)·동명사(구) / 명사절 등
복수 주어	복수 가산명사 / 복수 대명사 / A and B 등

단수 주어 **Keeping the clients' addresses up-to-date is** important. (동명사구)
고객의 주소를 최신 정보로 유지하는 것은 중요하다.

복수 주어 **They enjoy** the magazine's fashion section. (복수 대명사)
그들은 그 잡지의 패션 코너를 **좋아한다.**

B 주어를 찾기 어려운 경우의 수일치

ⓐ 〈주어+수식어+동사〉의 수일치
- 수식어가 사이에 있어서 주어와 동사 거리가 멀어지면 수일치를 판단하기 어려워집니다.
- 수일치에 영향을 주지 않는 수식어를 찾아 제외하고, 그 다음 동사를 찾아 주어에 수일치 시키세요.
- 수식어로 쓰이는 것에는 부사, 전치사구, to부정사구, 분사구, 관계사절 등이 있어요.

부사 **The managers** frequently **monitor** our progress. 부장들이 종종 우리 진행 사항을 **점검한다.**
전치사구 **The benefits** at this corporation **are** generous. 이 회사의 **혜택들은** 후하다.
관계사절 **The briefcase** that I lost **has been found.** 내가 잃어버린 서류 가방이 **발견되었다.**

ⓑ 〈There+be동사〉의 수일치
- '~이[가] 있다'라는 뜻인 〈There+be동사〉 문장의 주어는 There이 아닌, be동사 뒤의 명사입니다.
  그러므로 〈There+is[was]+단수 명사〉 또는 〈There+are[were]+복수 명사〉 형태로 써야 해요.
  There **is a mistake** in one of the articles. 기사들 중 하나에 **오류가** 있다.

ⓒ 주격 관계대명사절의 동사는 선행사와 수일치
- 관계대명사절은 관계대명사 who, which, that 등으로 시작하는 절로, 앞에 있는 명사를 수식하는데, 수식을 받는 이 명사를 '선행사'라고 해요.
- 주격 관계대명사절의 경우, 관계대명사 뒤로 주어 없이 동사가 바로 이어지는데, 이 동사는 관계대명사절이 꾸미는 선행사에 수일치 시켜야 합니다.
  Employees who **don't** get promoted are disappointed. 승진하지 못한 **직원들은** 실망하고 있다.

UNIT 04

핵심 POINT 확인하기

다음 괄호 안에서 알맞은 것을 고르세요.

|핵심 POINT 슬쩍 보기|

1 Selecting high-quality ingredients (is / are) the first step in making Cobly peanut butter.

1 동명사 주어는 단수 취급해요.

2 The hotel's prices always (rises / rise) during the peak season.

2 주어와 동사 사이의 부사는 수 일치에 영향을 주지 않아요.

3 The catalogs sent out last month (lists / list) the store's brands.

3 주어 뒤의 과거분사(sent)를 동사와 혼동하지 않도록 하세요.

4 The manager who is on duty (handles / handle) all customer complaints.

4 주어 뒤의 관계사절을 괄호로 묶어 보세요.

실전 감각 키우기

다음 빈칸에 알맞은 것을 고르세요.

5 빈출 The manufacturer of children's toys ------- many strict policies to comply with the state's regulations.

(A) implementing   (B) implement
(C) implements   (D) to implement

6 There is increasing ------- for direct flights from Asia to Europe.

(A) demand   (B) demands
(C) demanding   (D) demanded

7 The company continuously ------- employees throughout their careers with monthly workshops.

(A) training   (B) trains
(C) have trained   (D) train

8 빈출 The people who ------- the subway system are mostly mechanical engineers.

(A) operates   (B) has operated
(C) operating   (D) operate

3 수량 표현과 수일치

수량 형용사와 수일치
- each/every+단수 명사+단수 동사
- many/several+복수 명사+복수 동사

주의해야 할 수량 표현의 수일치
- 〈부정대명사+of the+명사〉는 of 뒤의 명사에 동사의 수를 일치
  단, each of/one of+복수 명사+단수 동사
- a number of+복수 명사+복수 동사

A 수량 형용사와 수일치

● 수량 형용사는 뒤에 올 수 있는 명사의 종류에 제약이 있어서 동사도 그에 따라 수일치 시켜야 해요.

		+ 단수 가산명사 + 단수 동사
each 각각의	every 모든	+ 단수 가산명사 + 단수 동사
many (수가) 많은 a few (수가) 조금 있는	several 몇몇의 few (수가) 거의 없는	+ 복수 가산명사 + 복수 동사
much (양이) 많은	a little (양이) 조금 있는　little (양이) 거의 없는	+ 불가산명사　+ 단수 동사
some 약간의	most 대부분의　　all 모든	+ 복수 가산명사 + 복수 동사 + 불가산명사　+ 단수 동사

Many reports seem favorable.　많은 보고서가 호의적으로 보인다.
Much experience is needed for this position.　많은 경험이 이 직책에 필요하다.

B 주의해야 할 수량 표현의 수일치

ⓐ 부정대명사 수량 표현

- 부정대명사 뒤에 〈of the+명사〉가 붙어 전체의 일부분을 나타낼 때는 of 뒤의 명사에 동사의 수를 일치 시켜요.
- each와 one은 of 뒤에 복수 명사가 와도 단수 취급하여 단수 동사를 쓴다는 점에 유의하세요.

		+of the	+ 단수 가산명사/불가산명사 + 단수 동사 + 복수 가산명사　　　　　 + 복수 동사
most 대부분　all 전체　part 일부분　some 몇몇		+of the	
each 각각　one 하나		+of the	+ 복수 가산명사　　　　　+ 단수 동사

Most of the performance requires special lighting.　그 공연의 대부분은 특수 조명을 필요로 한다.

ⓑ 명사 수량 표현

- 〈a(n)+명사+of〉는 형용사처럼 쓰이는 수량 표현으로, 앞에 관사 a(n)가 있다고 해서 뒤에 무조건 단수 명사를 쓰는 것은 아닙니다.

a number of 다수의, 많은	a variety of 다양한	+ 복수 가산명사 + 복수 동사
a great deal of 상당량의	a large amount of 상당량의	+ 불가산명사 + 단수 동사

A number of people at the firm **are retiring** early.　그 회사의 많은 사람들이 일찍 퇴직하고 있다.

참고　the number of는 '~의 수'라는 뜻으로 뒤에 복수 명사, 단수 동사가 와요.
　　　The number of products rises every year.　제품의 수가 매년 늘어난다.

핵심 POINT 확인하기

다음 괄호 안에서 알맞은 것을 고르세요.

|핵심 POINT 슬쩍 보기|

1 Many (customers / customer) have indicated a preference for organic food in the survey.

1 many 뒤에는 복수 가산명사를 써요.

2 Most of the employees at the tire factory (was / were) exhausted from the extra work.

2 동사는 most of 뒤에 나온 명사에 수일치 시켜 줘요.

3 Each of the (dish / dishes) on the menu is suitable for vegetarians.

3 each of 뒤에는 복수 명사가 와요.

4 A number of shareholders (agree / agrees) with the acquisition.

4 a number of 다음에는 복수 명사와 복수 동사가 와요.

실전 감각 키우기

다음 빈칸에 알맞은 것을 고르세요.

5 Some of the candidates ------- going around the country to campaign for the elections.

(A) are　　　　(B) being
(C) is　　　　(D) was

6 A few board members ------- the overseas expansion as a risky business move.

(A) sees　　　　(B) be seen
(C) see　　　　(D) to see

7 ------- of the guest speakers at the robotics conference was Dr. Darren Williams.

(A) One　　　　(B) Most
(C) Some　　　　(D) Others

8 All ------- come with a five-year warranty and free repair service.

(A) product　　　　(B) products
(C) produce　　　　(D) producing

앞에서 학습한 핵심 POINT를 떠올리며 빈칸을 완성해 보세요.

핵심 POINT 1

주어와 동사의 수일치 ①

수일치
- 주어와 동사의 수를 일치시키는 것
- 단수 주어+❶_____ 동사 / 복수 주어+❷_____ 동사

단수 동사와 복수 동사의 형태
- 단수 동사는 〈동사원형+-(e)s〉, 복수 동사는 〈동사원형〉
- ❸_____는 과거 시제도 수일치가 적용됨

핵심 POINT 2

주어와 동사의 수일치 ②

주어의 단수/복수 구분
- 단수 주어: 단수 가산명사 / 단수 대명사 / ❹_____ / to부정사(구)·동명사(구) / 명사절 등
- 복수 주어: 복수 가산명사 / 복수 대명사 / ❺_____ 등

주어를 찾기 어려운 경우의 수일치
- 주어 뒤의 ❻_____는 주어와 동사의 수일치에 영향을 주지 않음
- 〈There+be동사+주어〉에서, be동사는 그 뒤의 주어에 수일치
- 〈선행사(명사)+관계대명사+동사〉에서, 동사는 선행사에 수일치

핵심 POINT 3

수량 표현과 수일치

수량 형용사와 수일치
- each/every+❼_____ 명사+단수 동사
- many/several+복수 명사+복수 동사

주의해야 할 수량 표현의 수일치
- 〈부정대명사+of the+명사〉는 of 뒤의 명사에 동사의 수를 일치
  단, each of/one of+복수 명사+❽_____ 동사
- a number of+❾_____ 명사+❿_____ 동사

| 빈칸 정답 살짝 보기 |

❶ 단수 ❷ 복수 ❸ be동사 ❹ 불가산명사 ❺ A and B ❻ 수식어 ❼ 단수 ❽ 단수 ❾ 복수 ❿ 복수

실전 감각 키우기

다음 빈칸에 알맞은 것을 고르세요.

1 Timely completion of the projects ------- on meeting all the deadlines.

(A) depends
(B) depend
(C) to depend
(D) depending

2 The managers who ------- in the service department will update the product return policy.

(A) work
(B) works
(C) working
(D) has worked

3 Some ------- from the business trip were not reimbursed by the company.

(A) expense
(B) expenses
(C) expend
(D) expensive

4 Guests should contact the front desk immediately if they ------- any changes in their reservation.

(A) requires
(B) to require
(C) requiring
(D) require

[5-6] Questions 5-6 refer to the following article.

MERIEN, August 2—Praxa, the popular online clothing retailer, has announced that it will open an actual store in Merien's city center. Owners Jake Finder and Molly Black -------
                                                                                             5.
to start construction next month. "We have earned a reputation as a reliable retailer," Mr.
Finder said. Indeed, ------- comment on Praxa's Web site gives the store an excellent
                       6.
review, and there is no doubt that this new project will be highly successful.

5 (A) intends
(B) intend
(C) to intend
(D) intending

6 (A) every
(B) many
(C) all
(D) several

회사 입사 지원 및 직원 채용, 복지 제도에 관한 어휘들입니다.

apply	동 지원하다 파 application 지원(서) applicant 지원자	**apply** for a job 일자리에 지원하다
submit	동 제출하다 유 hand in 제출하다	**submit** a résumé 이력서를 제출하다
experienced	형 숙련된 반 inexperienced 미숙한	**experienced** workers 숙련된 직원들
expertise	명 전문 지식 파 expert 전문가	technical **expertise** 기술적인 전문 지식
qualification 《pl.》	명 자격 (요건) 파 qualified 자격이 있는 유 requirements 자격 요건	have the **qualifications** 자격을 갖추다
recommend	동 추천하다 파 recommendation 추천	be highly **recommended** 강력 추천되다 a letter of **recommendation** 추천서
recruit	동 채용[모집]하다 유 hire 채용하다	**recruit** an employee 직원을 채용하다
capable	형 ~을 할 수 있는, 유능한 파 capability 능력, 역량 capacity (수용) 능력, 용량	be **capable** of designing 디자인하는 것을 할 수 있다
temporary	형 임시적인 파 temporarily 임시적으로, 임시로 반 permanent 영구적인	a **temporary** position 임시직 ↔ a permanent position 정규직
candidate	명 지원자, 후보자	successful **candidates** 합격한 지원자들
eligible	형 자격이 있는	**eligible** for a position 그 자리에 자격이 있는 *eligible for 또는 eligible to do의 형태로 '~할 자격이 있는'을 나타내요.
accept	동 받다, 받아들이다 파 acceptable 받아들일 수 있는	**accept** a proposal 제안을 받아들이다
benefit 《pl.》	명 (회사 등의 복지) 혜택, 수당	a **benefits** package 복리후생 제도 *셀 수 없는 명사 benefit으로 쓰일 때는 '이익, 이득'이란 뜻이에요.
earnings	명 (개인·회사의) 소득	annual **earnings** 연간 소득
previous	형 이전의, 예전의 파 previously 이전에	**previous** work experience 이전 업무 경험
flexible	형 유연성 있는	**flexible** working hours 유연 근무 시간제
enroll	동 등록하다 파 enrollment 등록	**enroll** in a training session 교육 과정에 등록하다 *enroll은 뒤에 전치사 in과 함께 enroll in(~에 등록하다)으로 써요.
retire	동 퇴직하다 파 retirement 퇴직, 은퇴	**retire** from a company 회사에서 퇴직하다

파 파생어 유 유의어 반 반의어 관 관련 어휘 《pl.》 주로 복수형

어휘 확인하기

다음 괄호 안에서 알맞은 것을 고르세요.

1 Mr. Berenson's former supervisor (recommended / retired) him for the marketing specialist position.

2 The (benefit / applicant) did not submit a cover letter with his résumé.

3 Donna Meyer (accepted / recruited) the award for Employee of the Year from the CEO at the ceremony.

4 The sales representative has (previous / capable) work experience as a branch manager.

실전 감각 키우기

다음 빈칸에 알맞은 것을 고르세요.

5 Workers who want to relocate to the Midwood branch should ------- a request to Mr. Watt.

(A) advise
(B) submit
(C) engage
(D) receive

6 Even though Ms. Anderson does not have the ------- for the role, she was given a chance to have an interview.

(A) positions
(B) careers
(C) qualifications
(D) rewards

7 Individuals with degrees in any science field are ------- to apply for the head researcher position.

(A) controlled
(B) flexible
(C) possible
(D) eligible

8 All employees must ------- in the course at least two weeks in advance.

(A) apply
(B) enroll
(C) hire
(D) afford

주어진 문제를 제한시간에 맞추어 풀어 보세요.

Part 5 Choose the one word or phrase that best completes the sentence.

1. Snadge Ltd.'s latest digital camera ------- very clear images even in low-light conditions.

   (A) products
   (B) produce
   (C) product
   (D) produces

2. Salary ------- are based on the employee's work history and performance.

   (A) increasingly
   (B) increasing
   (C) increases
   (D) increase

3. Mr. Wilkie lacks technical ------- in his field so he decided to attend the skills workshop.

   (A) impression
   (B) lecture
   (C) indication
   (D) expertise

4. ------- of the envelops for the confidential documents was properly sealed and kept in the safe.

   (A) Other
   (B) Each
   (C) Some
   (D) Most

5. All of the families affected by the earthquake ------- financial assistance from the government.

   (A) receives
   (B) receive
   (C) receiving
   (D) to receive

6. There are ------- local sales representatives at the fifteenth Narktowne Trade Fair.

   (A) many
   (B) much
   (C) others
   (D) plenty

7. The PR firm's ------- to expand into Asia includes hiring a local workforce.

   (A) plan
   (B) be planned
   (C) to plan
   (D) plans

8. Hafner Manufacturing requests that its more ------- workers assist new recruits whenever necessary.

   (A) eligible
   (B) previous
   (C) temporary
   (D) experienced

UNIT 04

Part 6 Questions 9-12 refer to the following advertisement.

Looking for Web Site Designer

Pilia Furniture is the area's leading furniture-building company, and a number of local

businesses ------- Pilia for their interior. Its furniture ------- famous around the region.
              9.   **10.**

Now is your chance to join this growing company. Pilia Furniture is looking for a Web

designer to manage the store's Web site. This is a permanent position with benefits.

The working hours are ------- and may be different from week to week. The successful
                             11.

candidate must have a bachelor's degree in graphic design or a related field. ------- .
                                                       12.

To apply, please submit a résumé, cover letter, and portfolio with at least three design

samples to piliahr@piliafurniture.com.

---

9. (A) uses
(B) use
(C) using
(D) to use

10. (A) to become
(B) have become
(C) has become
(D) becoming

11. (A) flexible
(B) essential
(C) qualified
(D) capable

12. (A) We are pleased to offer you the position.
(B) The program will prepare you for the job market.
(C) However, equivalent work experience will also be accepted.
(D) Therefore, we cannot process your application.

PART 5&6 동사편

UNIT 05

시제
+회사 어휘(2)

시제는 동사의 동작이 과거, 현재, 미래 중 어느 시점에 일어났는지 나타냅니다.
영어에서는 동사의 형태 변화를 통해 여러 가지 시제를 표현합니다.
시제에 따라 동사의 형태가 어떻게 달라지는지 확인해 보세요.

1 단순 시제
2 완료 시제
3 진행 시제

+ 회사 어휘(2)

핵심
POINT

He oversees
this department.

단순 시제
- 현재: 일반적인 사실이나 현재의 동작·상태, 반복되는 일, 습관 등
  단수 주어 〈동사원형+-e(s)〉, 복수 주어 〈동사원형〉
- 과거: 과거의 동작·상태, 특정 과거 시점의 일
  〈동사원형+-e(d)〉
- 미래: 앞으로 일어날 일, 미래에 대한 추측, 계획, 의지 등
  〈will+동사원형〉, 〈be going to+동사원형〉

A 현재

● 일반적인 사실, 현재의 동작이나 상태, 반복되는 일이나 습관, 일정 등을 표현할 때 써요.
〈동사원형〉 형태로 나타내며, 주어가 3인칭 단수일 때에는 〈동사원형+-(e)s〉를 씁니다.

일반적인 사실	Cooperation **is** important in the workplace. 직장에서 협력은 중요하다.
현재의 동작·상태	He **oversees** this department. 그가 이 부서를 감독한다.
반복되는 일·습관	We **participate** in the conference <u>every year</u>. 우리는 그 학회에 매년 참가한다.

중요 현재 시제와 함께 자주 쓰이는 표현들

always 항상	usually 대개, 보통	currently 현재	every[each] 매 ~
often 자주	regularly 정기적으로	generally 일반적으로	routinely 일상적으로

B 과거

● 과거의 동작이나 상태, 특정 과거 시점의 일을 말할 때, 〈동사원형+-(e)d〉 형태로 나타내요.

| 과거의 동작·상태 | He **entered** the meeting room. 그는 회의실로 들어갔다. |
| 특정한 과거 시점 | He <u>recently</u> **met** a new client. 그는 <u>최근에</u> 새로운 고객을 만났다. |

중요 과거 시제와 함께 자주 쓰이는 표현들

ago ~ 전에	before ~ 전에	yesterday 어제	last 지난 ~
recently 최근에	once 한때	previously 이전에	

● 〈동사원형+-(e)d〉 외에, 불규칙적으로 형태가 변화하는 동사들은 따로 기억해야 합니다.

불규칙 동사의 과거형	see 보다 → saw	give 주다 → gave	tell 말하다 → told	know 알다 → knew
	go 가다 → went	take 가지다 → took	eat 먹다 → ate	meet 만나다 → met

C 미래

● 미래에 대한 추측, 계획, 의지 등을 말할 때, 〈will[be going to]+동사원형〉 형태로 나타냅니다.

| 미래의 추측 | Mr. Han **will implement** new regulations. 한 씨는 신규 규제를 시행할 것이다. |
| 미래의 계획·의지 | They **are going to defend** their position. 그들은 그들의 입장을 고수할 것이다. |

중요 미래 시제와 함께 자주 쓰이는 표현들

next 다음 ~	shortly 곧	soon 곧, 조만간	tomorrow 내일

핵심 POINT 확인하기

다음 괄호 안에서 알맞은 것을 고르세요.

1 Dr. Jones currently (conducts / conducted) research at Gosho Pharmaceutical Company.

2 Ms. Anderson recently (returned / will return) from a business trip to Brazil.

3 A few international flights now (leave / will leave) the airport every day.

4 Several of the company's programmers (went / are going) to attend an IT workshop tomorrow.

| 핵심 POINT 슬쩍 보기 |

1 currently는 현재 시제와 함께 자주 쓰이는 표현이에요.

2 recently는 과거 시제와 함께 자주 쓰이는 표현이에요.

3 〈every+시간〉은 '매 ~(마다)'라는 뜻으로 어떤 일이 규칙적으로 반복됨을 나타내며 현재 시제와 자주 함께 쓰여요.

4 미래의 일은 동사원형 앞에 will이나 be going to를 써서 나타낼 수 있어요.

실전 감각 키우기

다음 빈칸에 알맞은 것을 고르세요.

5 To prevent accidents, the factory ------- a new set of safety procedures last month.

(A) suggests   (B) suggestion
(C) suggested   (D) suggesting

6 Next fall, the Metro Art Museum ------- local and national artists.

(A) will exhibit   (B) exhibit
(C) exhibiting   (D) exhibited

7 빈출 Usually, every editor of *Weekly Issue* ------- busy on Fridays.

(A) is   (B) been
(C) will be   (D) being

8 The general manager ------- China two weeks ago for the regular factory inspection.

(A) will visit   (B) visits
(C) visited   (D) visit

2 완료 시제

핵심 POINT

He has never met her before.

완료 시제

- 현재완료: 과거에 발생한 일이 현재까지 영향을 미칠 때
  〈have[has]+*p.p.*〉
- 과거완료: 대과거의 일이 과거까지 영향을 주거나, 대과거를 나타낼 때
  〈had+*p.p.*〉
- 미래완료: 미래 특정 시점까지 완료될 일을 나타낼 때
  〈will have+*p.p.*〉

A 현재완료

- 과거에 발생한 일이 현재까지 영향을 미칠 때, 〈have[has]+*p.p.*〉 형태로 나타냅니다.
- 현재완료는 대개 계속, 경험, 완료 등의 의미를 나타냅니다.

계속	She **has been** at the reception <u>for two hours</u>. 그녀는 환영회에 <u>두 시간 동안</u> **참석하고 있다.** **중요** 자주 함께 쓰이는 표현: for[over/in] ~ 동안 since ~ 이래로 over the last[past] 지난 ~ 동안
경험	He **has** <u>never</u> **met** her <u>before</u>. 그는 <u>전에</u> 그녀를 **만난 적이** <u>결코</u> 없다. **중요** 자주 함께 쓰이는 표현: never 결코 ~이 아닌 ever ~ 한 적 before 이전에
완료	The sales director **has** <u>just</u> **finished** his speech. 영업 부장이 <u>방금</u> 연설을 **끝냈다.** **중요** 자주 함께 쓰이는 표현: already 벌써, 이미 just 방금 yet 아직

참고 **현재완료 vs. 과거:** 현재완료는 현재에 영향을 주는 과거의 일을 나타내지만, 과거 시제는 과거의 일만 나타내요.
특히, 과거 시점을 명확하게 가리키는 말이 있다면 과거 시제를 써야 합니다.

현재완료	과거
The air conditioner **has broken down**. 에어컨이 (지금) **고장 나 있다.** → 과거에 고장이 났고, 현재에도 고장 난 상태.	The air conditioner **broke down** <u>yesterday</u>. 에어컨은 <u>어제</u> **고장이 났다.** → 과거에 고장이 났고, 현재는 그 상태를 알 수 없음.

B 과거완료·미래완료

ⓐ 과거완료

- 더 이전의 과거(대과거)에 발생한 일이 과거 어느 시점까지 영향을 미칠 때, 〈had+*p.p.*〉의 형태로 나타냅니다.

  She **had** never **contributed** her ideas <u>before</u> she <u>proposed</u> this measure.
  그녀는 이 방법을 제안하기 <u>전까지는</u> 자기 의견을 **말한 적이** 전혀 **없었다.** (경험)

- 과거완료는 과거보다 더 이전의 과거(대과거)에 발생한 일을 나타낼 때도 사용합니다.

  Mr. Shelby <u>repeated</u> the suggestion that he **had made** earlier.
  　　　　　　과거　　　　　　　　　　　　　　　대과거
  셸비 씨는 그가 이전에 **했던** 제안을 반복해서 말했다.

ⓑ 미래완료

- 어떤 사건·동작이 특정 미래 시점에 완료될 것임을 나타낼 때, 〈will have+*p.p.*〉 형태로 나타내요.

  She **will have conducted** fifty performance reviews <u>by May</u>.
  그녀는 <u>5월까지</u> 50개의 업무 평가를 **할 것이다.**

  중요 자주 함께 쓰이는 표현: by ~까지   by the time ~할 때까지   by the end of ~ 말까지

UNIT 05

핵심 POINT 확인하기

다음 괄호 안에서 알맞은 것을 고르세요.

|핵심 POINT 슬쩍 보기|

1 The Barnes family (operates / has operated) Barnes Manufacturing Company for seventy years.

1 과거부터 현재까지 계속되는 일에는 현재완료를 써요.

2 Yesterday, Avant Office Supplies (obtained / has obtained) the government's approval to open a new branch.

2 명백히 과거 시점을 가리키는 말이 있으면 과거 시제를 써야 해요.

3 Ms. Hanson (finishes / had finished) filling out the application before the doctor was ready.

3 과거보다 더 이전의 과거를 나타낼 때에는 과거완료 〈had+*p.p.*〉를 써요.

4 By three o'clock tomorrow, the manager (paid / will have paid) the building's utility bill.

4 미래의 특정 시점까지 완료될 일에는 미래완료 〈will have+*p.p.*〉를 써요.

실전 감각 키우기

다음 빈칸에 알맞은 것을 고르세요.

5 Due to limited funding, the traffic lights on Preston Street have not ------- been upgraded.

(A) early
(B) yet
(C) enough
(D) ever

6 Rounders, Inc., a furniture retailer, ------- about the prices before it placed an order.

(A) inquires
(B) had inquired
(C) will have inquired
(D) would be inquiring

7 Since he was hired ten years ago, Mr. Horton ------- to new departments several times.

(A) has transferred
(B) is transferring
(C) transfers
(D) transfer

8 Stan Doering ------- his first major film production by the end of next year.

빈출

(A) completed
(B) completes
(C) had completed
(D) will have completed

정답 및 해설 40쪽　**95**

3 진행 시제

핵심 POINT

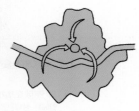

The team members **are gathering** now.

진행 시제
- 현재진행: 현재 진행 중인 일, 또는 가까운 미래의 일
  〈am[is/are]+*doing*〉
- 과거진행: 과거에 진행 중이던 동작·사건 〈was[were]+*doing*〉
- 미래진행: 미래에 진행 중일 동작·사건 〈will be+*doing*〉
- 완료진행: 완료 시제에서 동작이 진행 중임을 강조

A 현재진행·과거진행·미래진행

ⓐ 현재진행

- 현재 진행 중인 일을 나타낼 때, 〈am[is/are]+*doing*〉 형태로 나타냅니다.

The hiring committee **is** currently **reviewing** the applications. 채용 위원회가 현재 지원서를 검토 중이다.
The team members **are gathering** now. 팀원들이 지금 모이는 중이다.

중요 현재진행 시제와 자주 함께 쓰이는 표현들

now[at moment] 지금	currently[presently] 현재

참고 will이나 be going to를 쓰지 않고, 현재진행형으로 가까운 미래의 일을 나타낼 수도 있어요.
이때 soon 곧, tomorrow 내일, next week 다음 주 등 가까운 미래를 나타내는 말이 함께 쓰이기도 해요.
They **are leaving** next week. 그들은 다음 주에 떠날 것이다.

ⓑ 과거진행

- 과거에 진행 중이던 동작이나 사건을 나타낼 때, 〈was[were]+*doing*〉 형태로 나타냅니다.

She **was walking** to the reception center when I saw her.
내가 그녀를 보았을 때 그녀는 안내소로 걸어가고 있었다.

ⓒ 미래진행

- 미래에 진행 중일 동작이나 사건을 나타낼 때, 〈will be+*doing*〉 형태로 나타냅니다.

Developers **will be analyzing** the consumer feedback tomorrow morning.
개발자들은 내일 아침에 소비자 피드백을 분석하고 있을 것이다.

B 완료진행

- 완료 시제에서 사건이나 동작이 진행되고 있는 상태임을 강조할 때, 완료진행 시제를 써요.

현재완료진행 〈have[has] been+*doing*〉	She **has been planning** the merger for months. 그녀는 몇 달째 합병을 계획하는 중이다.
과거완료진행 〈had been+*doing*〉	The stock **had been dropping** for weeks when the CEO resigned. 그 CEO가 사임했을 때 주가는 몇 주간 떨어지는 중이었다.
미래완료진행 〈will have been+*doing*〉	The business **will have been operating** for forty years next quarter. 다음 분기가 되면 그 기업은 40년간 운영되어온 것이 된다.

핵심 POINT 확인하기

다음 괄호 안에서 알맞은 것을 고르세요.

1 Ms. Harper (met / is meeting) with the clothing distributor now.

2 The two departments (are merging / were merging) sometime next month.

3 The marketing team (has sent / will be sending) out questionnaires soon.

4 Pike Sports Store (has been offering / will be offering) special deals on tents for the past week.

|핵심 POINT 슬쩍 보기|

1 지금(now) 일어나고 있는 일에는 현재진행 시제를 쓸 수 있어요.

2 현재진행이 가까운 미래의 일을 나타내기도 해요.

3 미래에 진행 중일 일은 〈will be+doing〉을 써서 나타내요.

4 〈has been+doing〉은 현재완료에서 동작의 '진행'을 강조한 현재완료진행 형태예요.

실전 감각 키우기

다음 빈칸에 알맞은 것을 고르세요.

5 Presently, the director of Sodes Co. ------- the issue of the company's factory emissions.

(A) addressed
(B) is addressing
(C) has addressed
(D) was addressing

6 The lawyer ------- trouble establishing contract terms during the previous meeting.

(A) was having
(B) has
(C) will have had
(D) will have

7 A real estate agent ------- to appraise the building next week.

(A) came
(B) is coming
(C) coming
(D) had come

8 R&H Motors ------- its company foundation anniversary next Friday.

(A) celebrated
(B) had been celebrating
(C) has celebrated
(D) will be celebrating

앞에서 학습한 핵심 POINT를 떠올리며 빈칸을 완성해 보세요.

핵심 POINT 1

단순 시제

- 현재 시제: 일반적인 사실이나 현재의 동작·상태, **❶**_____되는 일, 습관 등

    ❷_____ 주어 〈동사원형+-e(s)〉, 복수 주어 〈동사원형〉

- 과거 시제: 과거의 동작·상태, 특정 과거 시점의 일

    〈동사원형+**❸**_____〉

- 미래 시제: 앞으로 일어날 일, 미래에 대한 추측, 계획, 의지 등

    〈will+동사원형〉, 〈be **❹**_____ to+동사원형〉

핵심 POINT 2

완료 시제

- 현재완료 시제: 과거에 발생한 일이 **❺**_____까지 영향을 미칠 때

    〈**❻**_____+p.p.〉

- 과거완료 시제: 대과거의 일이 과거까지 영향을 주거나, 대과거를 나타낼 때

    〈**❼**_____+p.p.〉

- 미래완료 시제: 미래 특정 시점까지 완료될 일을 나타낼 때

    〈will have+p.p.〉

핵심 POINT 3

진행 시제

- 현재진행 시제: 현재 진행 중인 일, 또는 가까운 **❽**_____의 일

    〈am[is/are]+doing〉

- 과거진행 시제: 과거에 진행 중이던 동작·사건

    〈**❾**_____+doing〉

- 미래진행 시제: 미래에 진행 중일 동작·사건

    〈will **❿**_____+doing〉

- 완료진행 시제: 완료 시제에서 동작이 진행 중임을 강조

|빈칸 정답 살짝 보기|

❶ 반복　❷ 단수　❸ -(e)d　❹ going　❺ 현재(지금)　❻ have[has]　❼ had　❽ 미래　❾ was[were]　❿ be

실전 감각 키우기

다음 빈칸에 알맞은 것을 고르세요.

1 Ms. Stanley ------- her new position as head of finances last Monday.

(A) is starting
(B) to start
(C) will start
(D) started

2 Over the past year, residents of Linsville -------- more than $10,000 to local charities.

(A) is donating
(B) have donated
(C) donate
(D) will donate

3 The hotel manager routinely ------- employee evaluations to all the workers.

(A) has given
(B) giving
(C) to give
(D) gives

4 Currently, the restaurant ------ with its sanitary problem in preparation for an inspection.

(A) dealt
(B) will deal
(C) is dealing
(D) to deal

[5-6] Questions 5-6 refer to the following memo.

To: Nautus Clinic Employees
From: Claudine Morask
Subject: Lobby Renovations
Date: January 18

We have decided to add new light fixtures to the waiting room. Workers ------- around
5.
10 A.M. Friday. Expect some noise and other disturbances. The work should be complete
by 1 P.M. The front desk staff has been notified of the plans ------- and has tried to
6.
schedule as few appointments as possible during those times, but we might still get
some walk-ins. Thank you for your cooperation.

5 (A) have arrived
(B) to arrive
(C) will be arriving
(D) arrived

6 (A) already
(B) soon
(C) anytime
(D) next

회사에서 수행하는 다양한 업무 및 그에 따른 성과에 관한 어휘들입니다.

conduct	명 동 수행(하다) 유 carry out 수행하다	**conduct** a survey 설문 조사를 하다
proceed	동 진행하다	**proceed** with a plan 계획을 진행하다 *proceed는 자동사라 목적어를 취하려면 with와 같은 전치사가 필요해요.
offer	명 동 제의[제안](하다) 유 propose 제안하다	**offer** a discount 할인을 제공하다
ensure	동 반드시 ~하게 하다, 보장하다	**ensure** the safety 안전을 보장하다
urgent	형 긴급한 파 urgency 긴급함, urgently 긴급히	an **urgent** matter 긴급한 문제
priority	명 우선 순위 파 prior 이전의	a top **priority** 최우선 순위
negotiate	동 협상하다 파 negotiation 협상 유 mediate 중재하다, 조정하다	**negotiate** with a union 노조와 협상하다
acquisition	명 (기업) 인수, 습득 파 acquire 인수[취득]하다	the **acquisition** of companies 회사의 인수
contract	명 계약(서) 동 계약하다 유 agreement 계약, 협정	sign a **contract** 계약서에 서명하다 renew a **contract** 계약을 갱신하다
determine	동 결정하다 파 determination 결정	**determine** prices 가격을 결정하다
implement	동 시행하다	**implement** a measure 조치를 취하다 *의미상 implement 뒤에는 주로 plan(계획), policy(방침), decision(결정) 등의 어휘가 와요.
collaborate	동 협력하다, 함께 일하다 파 collaboration 협업, 공동 작업	**collaborate** on a project 프로젝트에 있어 협력하다
perform	동 성과를 내다, 수행하다, 공연하다 파 performance 성과, 수행, 공연	**perform** strongly 좋은 성과를 내다
result	명 결과, 결실 동 발생하다	the **results** of a survey 그 설문의 결과 *result가 동사로 쓰일 때는 result from의 형태로 목적어를 취해요.
commitment	명 약속, 헌신 파 commit 약속하다, 헌신하다	fulfill a **commitment** 약속을 지키다
outstanding	형 놀라운, 뛰어난, 미지급의 유 excellent 훌륭한, 탁월한	**outstanding** success 놀라운 성공 an **outstanding** payment 미지급 결제
achieve	동 성취[달성]하다 파 achievement 성취[달성] 유 accomplish 성취하다	**achieve** a goal 목표를 달성하다
obtain	동 얻다, 획득하다	**obtain** accurate results 정확한 결과를 얻다

파 파생어 유 유의어 반 반의어 관 관련 어휘

어휘 확인하기

다음 괄호 안에서 알맞은 것을 고르세요.

1 The company (proceeds / offers) free workshops to all of its employees.

2 Careful market research (ensures / achieves) that the company stays up-to-date on current trends.

3 The survey (commitments / results) indicate a clear improvement in customer satisfaction.

4 The restaurant (collaborated / obtained) a permit to expand its dining area.

실전 감각 키우기

다음 빈칸에 알맞은 것을 고르세요.

5 Mr. Greggs plans to ------- a meeting with Japanese clients using videoconferencing equipment.

(A) respond
(B) conduct
(C) proceed
(D) accompany

6 The personnel manager will soon ------- new contracts with exceptional employees.

(A) present
(B) cooperate
(C) negotiate
(D) achieve

7 To increase productivity, Sulley Textiles Company has ------- an employee incentive plan.

(A) implemented
(B) protected
(C) collected
(D) separated

8 Jasper Cocker will receive an award for his ------- performance this year.

(A) increased
(B) outstanding
(C) urgent
(D) determined

주어진 문제를 제한시간에 맞추어 풀어 보세요.

Part 5 Choose the one word or phrase that best completes the sentence.

1. With great excitement, Mr. Thompson
------- yesterday that the company's
stocks are at an all-time high.

(A) announce
(B) announces
(C) announcing
(D) announced

2. Hanto Electronics plans to -------
Dobby Digital Company because of its
successful range of digital cameras.

(A) arrive
(B) perform
(C) acquire
(D) generate

3. Since its launch last year, the van
------- to the top of the domestic
market.

(A) will rise
(B) will be rising
(C) rises
(D) has risen

4. According to an article in *Business
Monthly*, MGV Inc. ------- with Paula
Corp. next year.

(A) merging
(B) will be merging
(C) has merged
(D) to merge

5. Risk management specialists -------
the best strategy for investment to
avoid losses.

(A) purchase
(B) move
(C) determine
(D) confess

6. Government agencies ------- check the
quality of the city's drinking water.

(A) regularly
(B) yet
(C) recently
(D) formerly

7. Before he asked to speak to the
manager, the client -------- a refund
from the cashier.

(A) requests
(B) will request
(C) had requested
(D) is requesting

8. By the time his next novel is released,
Juan Fuentes ------- five children's
books.

(A) published
(B) has published
(C) will have published
(D) is publishing

Part 6 Questions 9-12 refer to the following letter.

Dan Morrow
133 Strathern Road
Dundee, DD4 7PW, UK

Mr. Morrow,

------- . Please ignore my previous request to see samples of your work. I didn't realize
    9.
you ------- your portfolio already. I reviewed your pictures, and *Living Well* magazine
     10.
would be delighted to employ you as a contributing photographer. We are currently

writing a ------- for you. You'll receive it later this week. Please sign and return it to us.
        11.

After you are officially hired, your first task will be to visit the Montrose Flower Show,

which starts on April 22. Gail Halliwell ------- on this year's entries in the competition.
                                          12.
We would like you to go with her to take pictures of the winning flowers.

We look forward to working with you.

Sincerely,

Kathy Burke, *Living Well* magazine

9. (A) I would like to apologize for the
   damage to your photos.
   (B) Your annual subscription to *Living
   Well* has been renewed.
   (C) Thank you for taking the time to
   review my résumé.
   (D) I'm afraid a mistake I made may
   have caused some confusion.

10. (A) had sent
    (B) send
    (C) were sending
    (D) will send

11. (A) negotiation
    (B) contract
    (C) dialogue
    (D) meeting

12. (A) was reporting
    (B) reported
    (C) will be reporting
    (D) has been reporting

PART 5&6 동사편

UNIT 06

태

+회사 어휘(3)

태는 주어와 동사 사이의 관계를 나타내는 동사의 형태입니다.
주어가 동사의 동작을 행하는 주체이면 능동태로,
주어가 동사의 동작을 당하는 대상이면 수동태로 그 관계를 보여줍니다.

1 수동태의 개념과 형태
2 4문형·5문형 동사의 수동태
3 주의해야 할 수동태

+ 회사 어휘(3)

1 수동태의 개념과 형태

핵심 POINT

It **was painted** by da Vinci.

능동태와 수동태
- 주어가 동작을 직접 하면 능동태, 주어가 동작을 당하면 수동태
- 능동태는 '~하다'로, 수동태는 '~해지다, ~되다, ~받다'로 해석

수동태의 형태
- 기본 형태는 〈be동사+*p.p.*〉이고 뒤에 목적어를 쓰지 않음
- 동사의 행위자는 〈by+목적격〉으로 나타내나, 생략 가능함

A 능동태와 수동태

- 주어가 동사의 동작을 직접 하는 주체이면 능동태로 표현하며, '~하다'로 해석해요.
- 주어가 동사의 동작을 당하는 대상이면 수동태로 나타내며, '~해지다, ~되다, ~받다'로 해석해요.

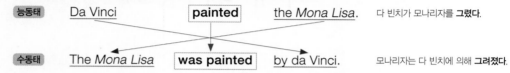

| **능동태** | Da Vinci | painted | the *Mona Lisa*. | 다 빈치가 모나리자를 **그렸다**. |

| **수동태** | The *Mona Lisa* | was painted | by da Vinci. | 모나리자는 다 빈치에 의해 **그려졌다**. |

B 수동태의 형태

- 수동태 동사의 기본 형태는 〈be동사+*p.p.*〉입니다.
- 일반적으로 수동태 문장은 동사 뒤에 목적어가 따라오지 않아요.
- 수동태에서는 〈by+목적격〉의 형태로 동사의 행위자를 나타냅니다.

The proposal **was accepted** by the manager. 그 제안은 **부장에 의해 받아들여졌다**.

그런데, 이 행위자가 불분명하거나 언급할 필요가 없을 때는 by와 함께 생략 가능합니다.

- 시제에 따라 형태가 조금씩 달라지지만 기본 형태인 〈be동사+*p.p.*〉는 변하지 않아요.

ⓐ 단순 시제: be+*p.p.*

현재	The newsletter **is published** every week. 그 소식지는 매주 **발행된다**.
과거	The newsletter **was published** yesterday. 그 소식지는 어제 **발행됐다**.
미래	The newsletter **will be published** tomorrow. 그 소식지는 내일 **발행될 것이다**.

ⓑ 진행 시제: be being+*p.p.*

현재진행	The team **is being trained** now. 그 팀은 지금 **교육받는 중이다**.
과거진행	The team **was being trained** last night. 그 팀은 어젯밤에 **교육받는 중이었다**.
미래진행	The team **will be being trained** at 8 P.M. 그 팀은 오후 8시에 **교육받는 중일 것이다**.

ⓒ 완료 시제: have been+*p.p.*

현재완료	My colleague **has been promoted** recently. 내 동료는 최근에 **승진했다**.
과거완료	My colleague **had been promoted** last year. 내 동료는 작년에 **승진했다**.
미래완료	My colleague **will have been promoted** by next week. 내 동료는 다음 주까지는 **승진할 것이다**.

핵심 POINT 확인하기

다음 괄호 안에서 알맞은 것을 고르세요.

1 The traffic law was (passing / passed) by members of Congress without much trouble.

2 The constructions at Bello Beach Resort will (complete / be completed) next week.

3 The plane tickets for Ms. Taylor's business trip are provided (by / for) the company.

4 A new convention hall has (built / been built) in the center of Springfield.

|핵심 POINT 슬쩍 보기|

1 주어가 동사의 동작을 당하는 대상이면 수동태를 써요.

2 수동태 동사 뒤에는 대개 목적어가 따라오지 않아요.

3 수동태에서 행위자는 by를 써서 표현해요.

4 완료 시제에서 수동태의 형태는 〈have been+*p.p.*〉예요.

실전 감각 키우기

다음 빈칸에 알맞은 것을 고르세요.

5 In accordance with the company policy, refunds are ------- for all defective products.

(A) guarantee
(B) guaranteed
(C) having guaranteed
(D) guaranteeing

6 The raw materials were ------- by quality experts before the production stage.

(A) test
(B) testing
(C) tested
(D) tests

7 Please try to avoid using the front doors while the sidewalk -------.

(A) is renovating
(B) renovates
(C) is being renovated
(D) has renovated

8 Because the merger -------, the labor union wants to discuss contracts.

(A) approve
(B) has approved
(C) will approve
(D) has been approved

2 4문형·5문형 동사의 수동태

4문형 동사의 수동태
- 〈주어+동사+간접 목적어+직접 목적어〉
→ 〈간접 목적어+be *p.p.*+직접 목적어+(by+행위자)〉 또는
  〈직접 목적어+be *p.p.*+to/for+간접 목적어+(by+행위자)〉

5문형 동사의 수동태
- 〈주어+동사+목적어+목적격 보어〉
→ 〈목적어+be *p.p.*+목적격 보어+(by+행위자)〉

They **were given** a special bonus.

A 4문형 동사의 수동태

- 앞서 배운 수동태 문장은 목적어를 하나만 가지는 3문형 동사로 만든 문장들입니다.
- 이와 달리, 4문형 동사는 두 개의 목적어를 가지는데, 이를 각각 주어로 하여 수동태 문장을 만들 수 있어요.

능동태	The company ⌈gave⌉ all employees a special bonus. 그 회사는 전 직원들에게 특별 수당을 **줬다.**
	간접 목적어 직접 목적어
수동태	〈간접 목적어+be *p.p.*+직접 목적어+(by+행위자)〉 All employees ⌈were given⌉ a special bonus by the company. 전 직원들은 회사로부터 특별 수당을 **받았다.** **주의** 간접 목적어가 주어로 쓰일 때, 남은 직접 목적어가 수동태 동사 뒤에 남는데, 이것을 보고 능동태 문장으로 생각하지 않아야 해요. 〈직접 목적어+be *p.p.*+to[for]+간접 목적어+(by+행위자)〉 A special bonus ⌈was given⌉ to all employees by the company. 특별 수당이 회사에 의해 전 직원들에게 **주어졌다.**

- 주요 4문형 동사: give, offer, ask, send, buy, tell, grant 등

B 5문형 동사의 수동태

- 5문형 동사는 목적어와 목적격 보어를 가지는데, 수동태 문장에서는 목적격 보어가 남아 동사 뒤에 옵니다.
  주의 목적어가 주어로 쓰이고 남은 목적격 보어가 수동태 동사 뒤에 따라오는데, 이것을 보고 능동태 문장으로 생각하지 않아야 해요.
- 주요 5문형 동사: call, name, appoint, consider, find, keep 등

능동태 Children ⌈call⌉ the mayor Uncle John. 아이들은 시장을 존 아저씨라고 **부른다.**
목적어 목적격 보어

수동태 〈목적어+be *p.p.*+명사(목적격 보어)+(by+행위자)〉
The mayor ⌈is called⌉ Uncle John by children. 시장은 아이들에 의해 존 아저씨라고 **불린다.**

능동태 Customers ⌈consider⌉ the company reliable. 고객들은 그 회사를 믿을 만하다고 **여긴다.**
목적어 목적격 보어

수동태 〈목적어+be *p.p.*+형용사(목적격 보어)+(by+행위자)〉
The company ⌈is considered⌉ reliable by customers.
그 회사는 고객들에 의해 믿음직스럽다고 **여겨진다.**

핵심 POINT 확인하기

다음 괄호 안에서 알맞은 것을 고르세요.

|핵심 POINT 슬쩍 보기|

1 For the interviews, applicants were (asked / asking) ten questions each.

1 4문형 동사의 수동태의 경우, 동사 뒤에 목적어가 하나 남아 있어요.

2 The annual fiscal reports have (sent / been sent) to the board of directors.

2 직접 목적어를 주어로 하는 수동태에서는, 간접 목적어 앞에 전치사 to[for]를 붙여요.

3 Harvey Electric (considers / is considered) the best manufacturer in the country.

3 5문형 동사인 consider가 수동태로 쓰이면 동사 뒤에 목적격 보어인 명사나 형용사가 와요.

4 According to the newsletter, Ms. Johns will (name / be named) branch manager by the CEO.

4 name은 '~를 …로 임명하다' 라는 뜻의 5문형 동사예요.

실전 감각 키우기

다음 빈칸에 알맞은 것을 고르세요.

5 Special awards are ------- to members of the board who have served the company for more than ten years.

(A) give   (B) gave
(C) given   (D) giving

6 Jaxen Supermart ------- customers a 10 percent discount for every purchase over $100.

(A) is offered   (B) offers
(C) will be offered (D) offering

7 Tixian Telecomms ------- bankrupt by its risky investment in a start-up smartphone manufacturer.

(A) left   (B) will leave
(C) was left   (D) leaves

8 Ms. Wade ------- chief finance officer of Manthu Fragrances last month.

(A) appoints   (B) appointing
(C) was appointed (D) appointed

3 주의해야 할 수동태

He will **be satisfied with** this report.

핵심 POINT

다양한 전치사와 함께 쓰이는 수동태
- be interested/engaged/involved/included+in
- be equipped/satisfied/pleased/frustrated+with
- be dedicated/related/sent+to
- be used+for

to부정사가 뒤따르는 수동태
- be advised/allowed/expected/intended+to *do*

A 다양한 전치사와 함께 쓰이는 수동태

- 보통 수동태는 by로 동작의 행위자를 나타내는데, 좀 더 다양한 의미를 나타내기 위해 다른 전치사와 함께 쓰이기도 합니다.

ⓐ in

be interested in ~에 흥미가 있다	be engaged in ~에 관심이 있다, ~에 종사하다
be involved in ~에 관련되다, ~에 참여하다	be included in ~에 포함되다

They **are involved in** administrative duties. 그들은 행정 업무에 **관련되어 있다.**

ⓑ with

be equipped with ~을 갖추다	be satisfied with ~에 만족하다
be pleased with ~에 기뻐하다	be frustrated with ~에 좌절하다[짜증 나다]

My manager will **be satisfied with** this report. 부장님은 이 보고서에 **만족할 것이다.**

ⓒ to/for

be dedicated to ~에 전념하다	be related to ~에 관련되다
be sent to ~에게 보내지다	be used for ~에 사용되다

The document **will be sent to** the supervisor. 그 문서는 감독관에게 **보내질 것이다.**

ⓓ 그 외의 전치사

be amazed[surprised] at[by] ~에 놀라다	be concerned about ~에 대해 걱정하다
be composed of ~로 구성되다	be overwhelmed by ~에 압도되다

The task force **is composed of** community leaders and policy analysts.
특별팀은 지역 사회 지도자들과 정책 분석가들로 **구성되어 있다.**

B to부정사가 뒤따르는 수동태

- 목적격 보어로 to부정사를 쓰는 동사 중, 수동태 형태가 하나의 표현처럼 쓰이는 경우도 있어요.

be advised to *do* ~하라고 조언받다	be allowed to *do* ~하도록 허용되다
be expected to *do* ~할 것으로 기대되다, ~할 예정이다	be intended to *do* ~하기로 의도되다

Interns **are allowed to apply** for the job vacancy. 인턴들은 공석에 지원하도록 **허용된다.**

핵심 POINT 확인하기

다음 괄호 안에서 알맞은 것을 고르세요.

1 The CEO is (concerned / concerning) about the drop in sales revenue this past quarter.

2 Users of the Web site were (frustrating / frustrated) with the complicated registration procedure.

3 The marketers are overwhelmed (in / by) the massive amount of paperwork.

4 Visitors to the park are advised (to watch /watching) their belongings at all times.

|핵심 POINT 슬쩍 보기|

1 be concerned about은 '~에 대해 걱정하다'라는 뜻입니다.

2 be frustrated with는 '~에 짜증 나다'라는 의미를 나타내요.

3 be overwhelmed by는 '~에 압도되다'라는 의미입니다.

4 동사 advise는 수동태로 쓰일 때 to부정사가 뒤따르기도 해요.

실전 감각 키우기

다음 빈칸에 알맞은 것을 고르세요.

5 Candidates who are -------- in this position should fill out an application form.

(A) interesting   (B) interest
(C) interests   (D) interested

6 If the high-speed rail is built, it will be used ------- transporting commuters.

(A) to   (B) for
(C) on   (D) over

7 All of the tourists ------- with the explanations the tour guide provided.

(A) satisfied   (B) are satisfying
(C) are satisfied   (D) will satisfy

8 The construction of the new highway is expected ------- until the end of June.

(A) to last   (B) lasted
(C) will last   (D) lasting

앞에서 학습한 핵심 POINT를 떠올리며 빈칸을 완성해 보세요.

핵심 POINT 1

수동태의 개념과 형태

능동태와 수동태
- 주어가 동작을 직접 하면 ❶_____, 주어가 동작을 당하면 ❷_____
- 능동태는 '~하다'로, 수동태는 '~해지다, ~되다, ~받다'로 해석

수동태의 형태
- 기본 형태는 〈be동사+❸_____〉이고 뒤에 목적어를 쓰지 않음
- 동사의 행위자는 주로 〈by+❹_____〉으로 나타내나, 생략 가능함

핵심 POINT 2

4문형·5문형 동사의 수동태

4문형 동사의 수동태
- 〈주어+동사+간접 목적어+직접 목적어〉
  → 〈간접 목적어+be *p.p.*+직접 목적어+(by+행위자)〉 또는
   〈직접 목적어+be *p.p.*+❺_____+간접 목적어+(by+행위자)〉

5문형 동사의 수동태
- 〈주어+동사+목적어+목적격 보어〉
  → 〈목적어+be *p.p.*+❻_____+(by+행위자)〉

핵심 POINT 3

주의해야 할 수동태

다양한 전치사와 함께 쓰이는 수동태
- be ❼_____ in ~에 흥미가 있다   be engaged in ~에 관심이 있다   be involved in ~에 관련되다
- be equipped with ~을 갖추다   be ❽_____ with ~에 만족하다   be pleased with ~에 기뻐하다
- be dedicated to ~에 전념하다   be related to ~에 관련되다   be sent to ~에게 보내지다
- be used ❾_____ ~에 사용되다

to부정사가 뒤따르는 수동태
- be ❿_____ to *do* ~하라고 조언받다   be allowed to *do* ~할 것을 허가받다
  be expected to *do* ~할 것으로 기대되다   be intended to *do* ~하기로 의도되다

|빈칸 정답 살짝 보기|

❶ 능동태 ❷ 수동태 ❸ *p.p.* ❹ 목적격 ❺ to/for ❻ 목적격 보어 ❼ interested ❽ satisfied ❾ for ❿ advised

실전 감각 키우기

다음 빈칸에 알맞은 것을 고르세요.

1 The prestigious journalism award ------- to Mr. Angus following his recent article on environmental policy.

(A) give
(B) was given
(C) will give
(D) has given

2 Elaine Sturrock has recently ------- to head of personnel at Bacary Pharmaceuticals, Inc.

(A) promoting
(B) promoted
(C) been promoted
(D) to promote

3 All board members ------- in drafting the offer for the acquisition of Gerlife Insurance.

(A) will be involved
(B) have involved
(C) are involving
(D) will be involving

4 The employees in the sales department always ------- their duties properly.

(A) perform
(B) to perform
(C) are performed
(D) performance

[5-6] Questions 5-6 refer to the following notice.

To: Accounting Department
Subject: Software Upgrade

As we discussed in the meeting, all computers in the department are going to be equipped ------- state-of-the-art software. The new software will simplify how financial
5.
claims are processed and billing statements are submitted.

With our current software, bills for various categories ------- separate. As a result, the
6.
billing process is too complex. I think you will all save a lot of time with the new software.

5 (A) with
(B) in
(C) for
(D) to

6 (A) keep
(B) kept
(C) keeping
(D) are kept

회사 내 조직 및 인사, 직원 관리에 관한 어휘들입니다.

headquarters	명 본사 관 subsidiary 자회사 branch 지점, 지사	the UN **headquarters** UN 본사 *headquarters는 항상 복수형으로 써요.
board	명 이사회, 위원회 유 council/committee 위원회	a **board** of directors 이사회
administrative	형 관리[행정]의 파 administer 관리[행정]하다 administration 관리[행정]	**administrative** staff 관리 직원
representative	명 대표, 대리인 형 대표하는 파 represent 대표하다	send a **representative** 대리인을 보내다
spokesperson	명 대변인	a **spokesperson** for a company 회사 대변인
reorganization	명 (조직) 개편	the **reorganization** of a company 회사의 조직 개편 *reorganization은 organization(조직) 앞에 '다시'를 의미하는 re-가 붙은 형태예요.
promotion	명 승진, (제품 관련) 홍보, 판촉 파 promote 승진시키다	get a **promotion** 승진하다
allocate	동 할당하다 파 allocation 할당(량)	**allocate** work to the staff 직원들에게 일을 할당하다
transfer	동 전근 가다, 이동하다 유 relocate 전근 가다	**transfer** to another office 다른 사무실로 전근 가다
contribution	명 공헌, 기여 파 contribute 공헌하다	a valuable **contribution** 소중한 공헌
dedicate	동 헌신하다 파 dedication 헌신	**dedicate** one's life to a job 삶을 일에 헌신하다
colleague	명 동료 유 coworker 동료	a former **colleague** 이전의 동료
manage	동 운영하다, 경영하다 파 management 관리, 경영	**manage** day-to-day operations 일상적인 업무를 관리하다
encourage	동 격려[고무]하다 반 discourage 막다, 좌절시키다	**encourage** employees[workers] 직원들을 격려하다
oversee	동 감독하다	**oversee** a project 업무를 감독하다 *oversee – oversaw – overseen의 동사 변화도 기억해두세요.
regulation	명 규정, 규제 파 regulate 규제[단속]하다	comply with **regulations** 규정을 따르다
official	형 공식적인 명 관리, 공무원 파 officially 공식적으로	an **official** training program 공식 교육 프로그램
assess	동 평가하다, 가늠하다 파 assessment 평가	**assess** some work 업무를 평가하다 *assess는 형태가 비슷한 access(접근하다)와 혼동하기 쉬워요.

파 파생어 유 유의어 반 반의어 관 관련 어휘

어휘 확인하기

다음 괄호 안에서 알맞은 것을 고르세요.

1 A (representative / contribution) of Hyan Corp. confirmed the firm's plans to relocate.

2 Henry Pilner and Daisy Smith are (boards / colleagues) at a publishing company.

3 All office workers are (allocated / encouraged) to attend a workshop.

4 Each leader (oversees / transfers) a team of eight to ten members.

실전 감각 키우기

다음 빈칸에 알맞은 것을 고르세요.

5 On January 1, Rob's Burgers will hold a training program at its -------.

(A) headquarters
(B) residences
(C) procedures
(D) promotions

6 The ------- for Garrido Electronics announced that the company will hire a new director of sales.

(A) outcome
(B) spokesperson
(C) patron
(D) reputation

7 Ms. Dawson will be ------- to the factory in Chengdu next year to oversee its expansion.

(A) placing
(B) assessing
(C) calculating
(D) transferring

8 All employees must comply with the restaurant's new health and safety -------.

(A) admissions
(B) contributions
(C) regulations
(D) observations

주어진 문제를 제한시간에 맞추어 풀어 보세요.

Part 5 Choose the one word or phrase that best completes the sentence.

1. Clients ------- by customer service representatives about pending concerns within one day.

   (A) have contacted
   (B) will be contacted
   (C) will contact
   (D) are contacting

2. Sherman and Lopez's law team is ------- to providing exceptional legal advice.

   (A) satisfied
   (B) distributed
   (C) supportable
   (D) dedicated

3. In light of the national recall, customers ------- any Gilmore product without proof of purchase.

   (A) to be returned
   (B) may return
   (C) returning
   (D) should be returned

4. After the old coffee machine broke down, a new coffee maker ------- for the employees on the second floor.

   (A) orders
   (B) were ordered
   (C) was ordered
   (D) order

5. Business First ------- the best nonprofit group for assisting entrepreneurs.

   (A) considered
   (B) is considered
   (C) consider
   (D) to consider

6. Since last year, most of the negotiations with our partners ------- by Bogart International.

   (A) will be conducted
   (B) have conducted
   (C) have been conducted
   (D) was conducting

7. The marketing team is ------- with the feedback customers have given.

   (A) pleased
   (B) pleasing
   (C) pleasure
   (D) pleasant

8. The winner of the presidential election ------- promptly at six o'clock tomorrow night.

   (A) is announcing
   (B) has been announced
   (C) will announce
   (D) will be announced

Part 6 Questions 9-12 refer to the following memo.

From: George Jameson, General Manager
To: All New Staff
Subject: Re: Training Sessions

We ------- a new skills-improvement program. On Friday morning, a senior sales
    9.
representative will lead a mandatory training session.

This session will include information on the structure of our organization. You'll also learn
about the best techniques for managing your time. The class will take at least three
hours. ------- . Once you pass it, you ------- an official document for completing the
    10.   **11.**
program. We believe that this training will help us ------- your needs and skills and that it
         12.
will be highly beneficial to the company.

Thank you.

9. (A) are started
(B) are starting
(C) will be started
(D) were starting

10. (A) I hope you have enjoyed this
workshop.
(B) Please let us know whether you can
participate.
(C) Some customers have complained
that this is too long.
(D) The final thirty minutes will consist
of a short written test.

11. (A) are giving
(B) will give
(C) will be given
(D) have given

12. (A) allocate
(B) assess
(C) command
(D) contribute

PART 5&6 수식어편

UNIT 07

형용사·부사
+업무 어휘(1)

형용사와 부사 모두 다른 말을 꾸며 주는 수식어입니다.
형용사는 명사만을 꾸며 주는 반면에 부사는 동사, 형용사, 다른 부사
그리고 문장 전체를 모두 꾸며 줄 수 있어요.

1 형용사의 개념과 쓰임

2 주의해야 할 형용사

3 부사의 개념과 쓰임

4 주의해야 할 부사

+ 업무 어휘(1)

1 형용사의 개념과 쓰임

The product is **defective**.

형용사의 개념과 형태
- 명사의 상태, 성질 등을 나타냄
- 형태: -able[ible], -ful, -less, -ive, -ous, -en, -al, -ary 등

형용사의 쓰임과 자리
- 명사 수식: 수식하는 명사 앞, -thing, -body 뒤
  한정사와 쓰이면 〈한정사+형용사+명사〉 순서
- 보어 역할: 주격 보어일 때는 동사 뒤, 목적격 보어일 때는 목적어 뒤

A 형용사의 개념과 형태

- 형용사는 명사를 수식하여 그 명사의 상태나 성질 등을 나타내는 역할을 합니다.

  Expensive <u>goods</u> should be handled with care. **값비싼** 제품은 조심해서 다뤄야 한다.

- 형용사의 형태: 다양한 형태로 쓰이지만, 명사처럼 끝부분의 형태를 보면 알 수 있어요.

  자주 쓰이는 형용사 어미: -able[-ible], -ful, -less, -ive, -ous, -en, -al, -ary 등

comfort**able** 편안한	care**ful** 조심스러운	meaning**less** 의미 없는	attract**ive** 매력적인
danger**ous** 위험한	wood**en** 목재의	natur**al** 자연의	imagin**ary** 상상의

B 형용사의 쓰임과 자리

ⓐ 명사 수식: 명사 앞에서 명사를 수식하여 의미를 더해주는 역할을 합니다.

- 이때 형용사가 주로 명사를 앞에서 수식하지만, -thing, -body로 끝나는 명사는 뒤에서 수식합니다.

  I need a **durable** <u>product</u>. **내구성이 있는** 제품이 필요하다.

  I need <u>something</u> **durable**. **내구성 있는** 것이 필요하다.

- 관사나 소유격 같은 한정사와 함께 쓰일 경우, 〈한정사+형용사+명사〉의 순서로 씁니다.

  A **recent** <u>study</u> showed promising results for cancer treatments.
  최근의 연구가 암 치료에 대한 유망한 결과를 보여주었다.

ⓑ 보어 역할: 주어나 목적어로 쓰인 명사의 성질이나 상태를 나타내는 보어의 역할도 해요.

- 이때 형용사의 자리는 주격 보어일 때는 동사 뒤, 목적격 보어일 때는 목적어 뒤입니다.

주격 보어	The product is **defective**. 이 제품은 **결함이** 있다. 주어 　　　　 주격 보어
목적격 보어	He found the product **worthless**. 그는 그 제품이 **가치 없다고** 생각했다. 　　　　 목적어 　　 목적격 보어

참고 보어 자리에는 형용사뿐만 아니라 명사도 쓰일 수 있는데, 보어가 주어·목적어와 동격이면 명사를, 주어·목적어의 성질이나 상태를 나타내면 형용사를 고르면 됩니다.

명사　The company appointed <u>Mr. Kim</u> **manager**. 회사는 **김 씨를 관리자로** 임명했다. (김 씨 = 관리자)

형용사　The manager made <u>the process</u> **simple**. 부장은 **절차를 단순하게** 만들었다.

핵심 POINT 확인하기

다음 괄호 안에서 알맞은 것을 고르세요.

| 핵심 POINT 슬쩍 보기 |

1 (Comfort / Comfortable) chairs help employees maintain proper posture at their desks.

1 명사를 수식하는 것은 형용사예요.

2 The new theater will be (function / functional) by October 5.

2 주어의 성질을 나타내는 보어 역할을 하는 것은 형용사예요.

3 Ms. Garcia didn't do anything (special / specially) during her time off.

3 -thing으로 끝나는 명사의 경우, 형용사가 명사를 뒤에서 수식해요.

4 The recent drop in the stock market made investors (cautious / cautiously).

4 목적격 보어 자리에는 명사나 형용사가 쓰여요.

실전 감각 키우기

다음 빈칸에 알맞은 것을 고르세요.

5 The client was impressed with Mr. Miller's ------- ideas for the television commercial.

(A) creatively   (B) creative
(C) creativeness   (D) create

7 During winter, transport authorities consider the slippery roads very -------.

(A) dangers   (B) dangerous
(C) danger   (D) dangerously

6 With its aggressive marketing tactics, Zalbrec is quite ------- in selling its newest laptop.

(A) succeed   (B) success
(C) successful   (D) succeeded

8 The educational programs at the community center have had a beneficial ------- on residents.

(A) impact   (B) impacted
(C) impacting   (D) to impact

2 주의해야 할 형용사

핵심 POINT

economical (O)
economic (X)

같은 단어에서 파생된 두 가지 형용사
· considerable/considerate, economic/economical 등

분사형 형용사
· leading, existing, lasting, detailed, limited 등

〈be동사＋형용사＋전치사〉 어구
· be available for, be aware of, be familiar with, be useful to, be responsible for 등

A 같은 단어에서 파생된 두 가지 형용사

· 같은 단어에서 파생되었지만 서로 다른 어미가 붙어 다른 의미를 가지는 형용사들이 있습니다.

considerable 상당한	confident 확신하는	sensible 합리적인, 분별 있는
considerate 사려 깊은	confidential 기밀의	sensitive 민감한
comparable 비슷한	respectable 존경할 만한	economic 경제의
comparative 비교의	respective 각각의	economical 알뜰한, 경제적인

Our prices are **comparable** to theirs. 우리 가격들은 그들의 것과 **비슷하다**.
The **comparative** method we used was helpful. 우리가 사용한 **비교** 방식은 유용했다.

B 분사형 형용사

· 현재분사(doing) 또는 과거분사(p.p.) 형태인 형용사는 동사와 헷갈리지 않도록 주의해야 합니다.

현재분사형(doing)		과거분사형(p.p.)	
leading 선도하는	lasting 지속되는	detailed 자세한	qualified 자격(증)이 있는
existing 기존의	missing 분실된, 누락된	limited 제한된	complicated 복잡한

Proteus Corp. is the **leading** supplier of raw materials in the region.
프로테스 사는 지역 내 **선도적인** 원자재 공급사이다.

The room reserved for the meeting has **limited** seating.
회의를 위해 예약된 그 공간은 좌석이 **제한되어 있다**.

C 〈be동사＋형용사＋전치사〉 어구

· 어떤 형용사들은 특정 전치사와 어울려 〈be동사＋형용사＋전치사〉 형태로 하나의 표현처럼 쓰여요.

be available for ~이 이용 가능하다	be aware of ~을 알다
be capable of ~을 할 수 있다	be compliant with ~에 부합하다
be confident in ~에 자신이 있다	be exempt from ~에서 면제되다
be familiar with ~에 익숙하다[잘 알다]	be useful to ~에 유용하다
be responsible for ~에 책임이 있다	be similar to ~와 유사하다

The factory's working conditions **are compliant with** the safety standards.
그 공장의 근무 환경은 안전 기준에 **부합한다**.

The results of the consumer survey **were useful to** the marketers.
소비자 조사의 결과는 마케팅 담당자들에게 **유용했다**.

핵심 POINT 확인하기

다음 괄호 안에서 알맞은 것을 고르세요.

1 It is not easy to sustain (economic / economical) growth over a long period.

2 The management team took (sensible / sensitive) measures to protect the fragile goods.

3 The manager noticed something (miss / missing) from Ms. Austin's sales report.

4 The brochure about cultural heritage sites is (using / useful) to tourists.

|핵심 POINT 슬쩍 보기|

1 economic은 '경제의', economical은 '알뜰한, 경제적인'이라는 뜻을 나타내요.

2 sensible은 '합리적인', sensitive는 '민감한'이라는 뜻을 나타내요.

3 missing은 현재분사 형태로 쓰이는 형용사예요.

4 be useful to는 '~에 유용하다'라는 의미의 어구예요.

UNIT 07

실전 감각 키우기

다음 빈칸에 알맞은 것을 고르세요.

5 Numerous companies spend money on protecting their ------- trade strategies from competitors.

(A) confidence   (B) confidential
(C) confident   (D) confidentially

6 Lyon Shipping is not ------- for delivery delays due to poor weather conditions.

(A) responsibility   (B) responsible
(C) responding   (D) responsibly

7 The manager prepared a ------- product description of the newly released vehicles.

(A) detailing   (B) details
(C) detailed   (D) detail

8 The conference hall is ------- of accommodating over one thousand people.

(A) capability   (B) capably
(C) capabilities   (D) capable

부사의 개념과 쓰임

부사의 개념과 형태
- 부사는 동사, 형용사, 부사, 문장 전체를 수식함
- 형태: 일반적으로 〈형용사+-ly〉의 형태

부사의 쓰임과 자리
- 동사 수식: 일반동사의 앞/뒤, 조동사·be동사·have동사 뒤 등
- 형용사, 부사, 문장 전체 수식: 대개 꾸미는 말 앞, 문장의 앞/뒤

He sent it **immediately**.

A 부사의 개념과 형태

- 부사는 동사, 형용사, 다른 부사, 문장 전체를 꾸며 방법이나 정도 등을 부가 설명합니다.
  만약 문장에서 빈칸을 생략해도 문장이 완전하다면, 그 빈칸은 부사(구) 자리입니다.
- 부사는 일반적으로 〈형용사+-ly〉의 형태이지만, 그렇지 않은 경우도 있으니 주의하세요.

형용사+-ly	**quickly** 빨리	**simply** 간단히	**fully** 충분히, 완전히	**angrily** 화내며, 성내며
형용사와 같은 형태	**fast** 빠른; 빨리	**early** 이른; 일찍	**late** 늦은; 늦게	**high** 높은; 높게
이외의 형태	**very** 매우	**too** 너무	**well** 잘	**soon** 곧

B 부사의 쓰임과 자리

ⓐ **동사 수식**: 부사는 동사를 수식해서 의미를 더욱 구체적으로 만들어 줍니다.

- 이때 부사의 자리는 일반동사의 앞/뒤, 조동사·be동사·have동사의 뒤, 문장의 앞/뒤입니다.

부사+동사	They **finally** <u>decided</u> to investigate the problem.

그들은 **결국** 그 문제를 조사하기로 <u>했다</u>.

동사+(목적어)+부사	He <u>sent</u> the statistics **immediately**. 그는 **즉시** 그 통계 자료를 <u>보냈다</u>.
조동사+부사+본동사	We <u>will</u> **completely** <u>finish</u> the analysis. 우리는 분석을 **완전히** 끝낼 것이다.
be동사+부사+-ing[p.p.]	The gym <u>is</u> **temporarily** <u>allowing</u> members to bring guests.
have동사+부사+p.p.	The company <u>has</u> **continually** <u>expanded</u> its global operations.

그 체육관은 **한시적으로** 회원들이 손님을 데려오는 것을 허락하고 있다.

그 회사는 **계속해서** 해외 사업을 확장해오고 있다.

ⓑ **형용사·부사·문장 전체 수식**: 부사는 동사 외에도 형용사·부사·문장 전체를 수식합니다.

- 부사는 대개 수식하는 말 앞에 오지만, 부사의 위치는 비교적 자유로워 문장의 맨 앞이나 맨 뒤에 오기도
  합니다.

부사+형용사	It was an **absolutely** <u>successful</u> project. 그것은 **틀림없이** <u>성공적인</u> 프로젝트였다.
부사+수량 표현	The training sessions last for **approximately** <u>two</u> hours.
부사+부사	The lawyer knows the judge **very** <u>well</u>. 그 변호사는 그 판사를 **아주** 잘 안다.
부사+문장	**Actually**, <u>he quit his job</u>. **사실**, <u>그는 일을 그만두었다</u>.

연수 과정들이 **약** <u>두</u> 시간 동안 지속된다.

핵심 POINT 확인하기

다음 괄호 안에서 알맞은 것을 고르세요.

|핵심 POINT 슬쩍 보기|

1 The Victoria Hotel was too (expenses / expensive) for our travel budget.

1 too는 부사이므로, 형용사를 수식할 수 있어요.

2 Several teams in the existing factory will relocate to the new facility (permanent / permanently).

2 괄호 없이도 문장이 완전할 때, 그 자리에는 부사가 와요.

3 The new staff members are (strong / strongly) encouraged to participate in the workshop.

3 수동태를 이루는 be동사와 과거분사 사이에 올 수 있는 것은 부사뿐이에요.

4 Redwood Furnishings' operations are envisioned to grow (steadily / steady) for five years.

4 동사를 수식할 수 있는 것은 부사예요.

실전 감각 키우기

다음 빈칸에 알맞은 것을 고르세요.

5 Ms. Thomas ------- reviews each article in the newspaper every morning.

(A) personal (B) personally
(C) personable (D) personalize

6 Most visitors to the Vinita Gallery are ------- interested in the sculpture collection.

(A) particularly (B) particularity
(C) particular (D) particulars

7 Delma Shipping has ------- awarded college scholarships to numerous deserving students.

(A) generously (B) most generous
(C) generous (D) generosity

8 The company is becoming ------- reliant on a few key markets in Asia and Europe.

(A) increased (B) increase
(C) increasing (D) increasingly

4 주의해야 할 부사

late (O)　lately (X)

형용사와 의미가 달라지는 부사
- late/lately, short/shortly, near/nearly, high/highly 등

부정의 의미가 담긴 부사
- 문장 내에서 not 또는 다른 부정어와 함께 쓰일 수 없음
- never, barely, hardly/scarcely/rarely/seldom 등

빈출 부사
- already, yet, soon, still

A 형용사와 의미가 달라지는 부사

● 대개 형용사에 -ly를 붙이면 의미가 비슷한 부사가 되지만, 형용사에 -ly를 붙여 완전히 다른 뜻의 부사가 되는 경우도 있어요.

late 늦은; 늦게	short 짧은; 짧게	near 가까운; 가까이	high 높은; 높게
lately 최근에	shortly 곧, 이내	nearly 거의	highly 아주, 매우, 대단히
hard 열심히 하는; 열심히	clear 깨끗한, 분명한	most 대부분의; 가장	close 가까운; 가깝게
hardly 거의 ~않는	clearly 또렷하게	mostly 주로, 일반적으로	closely 면밀히, 밀접하게

The corporation has not developed any new products **lately**.
그 기업은 **최근에** 어떠한 신제품도 개발하지 않았다.

Our welfare costs have **nearly** doubled over the last five years.
우리의 복지 비용은 지난 5년 동안 **거의** 두 배가 되었다.

B 부정의 의미가 담긴 부사

● 부정의 의미를 가진 접두사 un-이나 dis-가 없는데도, 부정의 의미를 나타내는 부사들이 있어요. 이러한 부사들은 그 자체로 not의 의미를 포함하고 있기 때문에, 문장 안에서 not과 같은 부정어들과 함께 쓰일 수 없습니다.

never 결코[전혀] ~ 않는	barely 간신히 ~하는
hardly[scarcely/rarely/seldom] 거의 ~않는, 좀처럼 ~않는	

Thames Organic **hardly** uses artificial ingredients in its snacks.
~~does not hardly use~~　테임즈 오가닉 사는 과자에 인공 재료를 **거의** 쓰지 **않는다**.

C 그 외 빈출 부사

already 이미, 벌써	완료 시제와 주로 쓰임	yet 아직, 이미	부정문(아직), 의문문(이미)에 주로 쓰임
soon 곧, 금방	미래 시제와 주로 쓰임	still 여전히, 지금껏	긍정문·부정문·의문문에 모두 쓰임

Several local corporations have **already** entered into international markets.
몇몇 현지 기업들은 **이미** 국제 시장에 진출했다.

The engineer has **still** needs to modify the design of the device.
그 기술자는 **여전히** 그 장치의 디자인을 수정해야 한다.

핵심 POINT 확인하기

다음 괄호 안에서 알맞은 것을 고르세요.

1 Investors (close / closely) monitor the stock market for any changes in stock prices.

2 The agenda for Grande Bank's next board meeting will be announced (short / shortly).

3 Audience members in the back row could (hard / hardly) hear the speaker.

4 The departure of the flight to Atlanta has (already / mostly) been delayed by the severe weather.

|핵심 POINT 슬쩍 보기|

1 close는 '가까운; 가깝게', closely는 '면밀히, 밀접하게' 라는 뜻이에요.

2 shortly는 '곧'이라는 뜻이에요.

3 hardly는 '거의 ~ 않는'이라는 부정의 의미를 갖고 있어요.

4 already는 '이미, 벌써'라는 뜻으로 완료 시제와 같이 자주 쓰이는 부사예요.

실전 감각 키우기

다음 빈칸에 알맞은 것을 고르세요.

5 빈출 The weekend's free concert was attended by ------- five thousand people.

(A) near   (B) nearer
(C) nearest   (D) nearly

6 The writers of controversial articles ------- reveal the sources of their information.

(A) less   (B) very
(C) not   (D) seldom

7 빈출 The research and development team will ------- finish the automobile's engine design.

(A) still   (B) yet
(C) already   (D) soon

8 Due to the road widening project, most of the employees arrived very ------- for work.

(A) late   (B) lately
(C) latest   (D) later

UNIT 07

앞에서 학습한 핵심 POINT를 떠올리며 빈칸을 완성해 보세요.

핵심 POINT 1-2

형용사의 개념과 형용사의 쓰임

형용사의 개념과 형태
- ❶_____의 상태, 성질 등을 나타냄
- 형태: -able[ible], -ful, -less, -ive, -ous, -en, -al, -ary 등

형용사 쓰임과 자리
- 명사 수식: 수식하는 명사 ❷_____, -thing, -body 뒤
  한정사와 쓰이면 〈한정사＋형용사＋명사〉 순서
- 보어 역할: 주격 보어일 때는 동사 뒤, ❸_____일 때는 목적어 뒤

주의해야 할 형용사
- considerable 상당한/considerate 사려 깊은, economic 경제의/economical 알뜰한, 경제적인 등
- leading 선도하는, ❹_____ 기존의, lasting 지속되는, detailed 자세한, limited 제한된 등
- be ❺_____ for ~이 이용 가능하다, be aware of ~을 알다, be familiar with ~에 익숙하다 등

핵심 POINT 3-4

부사의 개념과 부사의 쓰임

부사의 개념과 형태
- 부사는 동사, 형용사, 부사, 문장 전체를 수식함
- 형태: 일반적으로 〈형용사＋❻_____〉의 형태

부사의 쓰임과 자리
- 동사 수식: 일반동사의 앞/뒤, 조동사·be동사·have동사 뒤 등
- 형용사, 부사, 문장 전체 수식: 대개 꾸미는 말 ❼_____, 문장의 앞/뒤

주의해야 할 부사
- late 늦은: 늦게/ ❽_____ 최근에, short 짧은: 짧게/shortly 곧, 이내 등
- ❾_____ 결코[전혀] ~ 않는, barely 간신히 ~하는, hardly/scarcely/rarely/seldom 거의 ~않는 등
- ❿_____ 이미, 벌써, yet 아직, 이미, soon 곧, 금방, still 여전히, 지금껏 등

|빈칸 정답 살짝 보기|⋯⋯⋯

❶ 명사 ❷ 앞 ❸ 목적격 보어 ❹ existing ❺ available ❻ -ly ❼ 앞 ❽ lately ❾ never ❿ already

실전 감각 키우기

다음 빈칸에 알맞은 것을 고르세요.

1 The staff at *In Our World Magazine* is dedicated to publishing ------- articles.

(A) informative
(B) informs
(C) to inform
(D) has informed

2 Those who plan to attend seminars abroad need to get permission from their ------- supervisors.

(A) respectably
(B) respect
(C) respecting
(D) respective

3 Film critics have ------- recommended the World War II movie *Pacific Soldiers*.

(A) highly
(B) highest
(C) high
(D) higher

4 The building for the headquarters of V&V Inc. is ------- new.

(A) completed
(B) complete
(C) completely
(D) completing

[5-6] Questions 5-6 refer to the following letter.

Thank you for choosing Bassell Tours. We've been operating exciting bus tours across the country for ------- thirty years, so we know how to make your trip perfect. We know
5.
you will enjoy your upcoming tour of Riverwell National Park. Enclosed you will find your ticket and information about your tour. As there is ------- space for luggage, please
6.
follow the enclosed guidelines carefully so that everyone can place their belongings.

5 (A) approximate
(B) approximated
(C) approximation
(D) approximately

6 (A) limit
(B) limits
(C) to limit
(D) limited

제품 개발 및 시장 조사, 고객 관찰에 관한 어휘들입니다.

develop	동 개발하다 파 development 개발, 발전 developmental 개발의	**develop** a new model 신형을 개발하다
analyze	동 분석하다 파 analysis 분석, analyst 분석가	**analyze** data 자료를 분석하다
modify	동 수정하다 파 modification 수정, 변경	**modify** a design 디자인을 수정하다
alternative	명 대안 형 대체 가능한 파 alternate 번갈아 나오는	find an **alternative** 대안을 찾다
demonstrate	동 시연하다, 설명하다 파 demonstration 시연, 설명, 시위	**demonstrate** a new product 신제품을 시연하다
deadline	명 마감일 유 due date 예정일, 마감일	meet[miss] a **deadline** 마감일을 맞추다[놓치다]
expand	동 확장[확대]하다 파 expansion 확장, 확대	**expand** a market 시장을 확장하다
additional	형 추가의 파 add 더하다, addition 추가(된 것)	ten **additional** workers 10명의 추가 작업자 *명사형 addition은 '~에 더하여'라는 뜻의 구전치사 in addition to 형태로도 쓰여요.
fluctuation	명 변동 파 fluctuate 변동을 거듭하다	a price **fluctuation** 가격 변동
flexibility	명 유연성 파 flexible 유연성 있는	**flexibility** in a schedule 일정의 유연성
available	형 이용 가능한, 구매 가능한 파 availability 구매 가능성	**available** tickets 구매 가능한 입장권
research	명 동 조사(하다) 파 researcher 조사원, 연구원	conduct market **research** 시장 조사를 하다 extensive **research** 광범위한 조사
communication	명 의사소통 파 communicate 의사소통하다	**communication** with customers 고객들과의 의사소통
investigate	동 조사하다 파 investigation 조사	**investigate** product sales 상품 판매를 조사하다
prefer	동 더 좋아하다, 선호하다 파 preferred 선호하는	**prefer** an applicant 지원자를 선호하다
indicate	동 나타내다, 보여주다 파 indication 징후, 표시, 조짐	**indicate** a positive response 긍정적인 답변을 보여주다
expectation	명 기대, 예상 파 expect 기대[예상]하다	meet[exceed] *someone's* **expectations** 기대를 충족시키다[넘어서다]
respond	동 대응하다, 응답하다 파 response 대응, 응답 respondent 응답자	**respond** to the fashion trend 패션 트렌드에 대응하다

파 파생어 유 유의어 반 반의어 관 관련 어휘

어휘 확인하기

다음 괄호 안에서 알맞은 것을 고르세요.

1 The article explains some of the latest (developments / analysts) in technology.

2 Finding an (alternative / preferred) supplier will reduce the restaurant's costs.

3 A sales representative (modified / demonstrated) the product's various functions to customers.

4 A number of people (researched / responded) to the customer satisfaction survey.

실전 감각 키우기

다음 빈칸에 알맞은 것을 고르세요.

5 Product developers set the ------- of April 22 for unveiling a prototype.

(A) advice
(B) income
(C) deadline
(D) possibility

6 Fillmore Couture hopes to ------- its customer base by creating a range of men's clothing.

(A) refer
(B) require
(C) expand
(D) arrive

7 Once our new laptop computer has been developed, it will be ------- in all major electronics stores.

(A) responsible
(B) available
(C) desirable
(D) flexible

8 The market research team is ------- possible reasons why the product does not appeal to customers.

(A) investigating
(B) contacting
(C) preferring
(D) removing

주어진 문제를 제한시간에 맞추어 풀어 보세요.

Part 5 Choose the one word or phrase that best completes the sentence.

1. The steps for replacing the air purifier's filter are explained quite ------- in the user manual.

   (A) clearing
   (B) clearable
   (C) clearly
   (D) clearest

2. Mr. Peterson has ------- the consumer survey data and is satisfied with the results.

   (A) analyzed
   (B) regarded
   (C) required
   (D) vacated

3. Immigrants are eligible for citizenship after they have lived in the country ------- for four years.

   (A) continue
   (B) continued
   (C) continuous
   (D) continuously

4. Conference fees are fully ------- to participants who cancel their registration by May 30.

   (A) refunding
   (B) refund
   (C) refunds
   (D) refundable

5. Security cameras were ------- placed in the building's main hallways.

   (A) strategy
   (B) strategic
   (C) strategize
   (D) strategically

6. Management wants to find a ------- solution to the fast employee turnover at the company.

   (A) lastly
   (B) lasting
   (C) lasts
   (D) lasted

7. Family members of the play's performers are ------- from admission fees on opening night.

   (A) exempt
   (B) distinct
   (C) ready
   (D) delayed

8. The sales figures for this month are ------- similar to expectations.

   (A) remarks
   (B) remarkably
   (C) remarked
   (D) remark

Part 6 Questions 9-12 refer to the following article.

Male Skincare Products Gaining Popularity

In a recent study, close to 75 percent of males in the nation responded that they --‐‐‐‐‐
9.
use some kind of skin-treatment product. --‐‐‐‐‐ . The full findings will be published in
10.
the magazine's next issue.

After examining the data, many cosmetics companies now plan to carry out their own

--‐‐‐‐‐ studies. They want to determine the needs and --‐‐‐‐‐ of men who purchase and
11.   12.
use skincare products.

Industry leader NTS Cosmetics says it could expand its skincare lines for men by up to

20 percent this year. Other companies are likely to do the same if the decision proves

profitable.

UNIT 07

9. (A) regular
(B) regularly
(C) regulation
(D) regulating

11. (A) investigate
(B) investigative
(C) investigated
(D) to investigate

10. (A) If you wish to participate, please
respond to the survey.
(B) The most popular product is a
moisturizing lotion.
(C) This study was conducted by *Lyke
Monthly*.
(D) Nevertheless, several problems were
discovered.

12. (A) expectations
(B) invitations
(C) variations
(D) relations

PART 5&6 수식어편

UNIT 08

전치사

+업무 어휘(2)

전치사 +명사 대명사 동명사

전치사는 '앞에 위치하는 말'이라는 뜻으로,
주로 명사나 대명사, 동명사 앞에 쓰여 다양한 의미를 나타내요.
특히, 〈전치사+명사〉의 형태로 다른 말을 꾸며 주기도 합니다.

1 전치사의 개념과 쓰임

2 시점·기간을 나타내는 전치사

3 장소·방향을 나타내는 전치사

4 그 외 주요 전치사

5 특별한 형태의 전치사와 관용 표현

+ 업무 어휘(2)

1 전치사의 개념과 쓰임

핵심
POINT

전치사의 개념
- 명사 앞에 쓰여 시간, 장소, 이유 등 다양한 의미를 나타냄
- 전치사의 목적어 자리에는 명사(구, 절), 목적격 대명사, 동명사 등이 옴

전치사구의 쓰임
- 〈전치사+명사(구, 절)〉의 전치사구는 형용사 또는 부사의 역할을 함
- 형용사로 쓰이면 명사를 수식하거나 보어의 역할을, 부사로 쓰이면 동사, 형용사, 부사 또는 문장 전체를 수식함

A 전치사의 개념

- 전치사는 명사 앞에 쓰여 **on** Monday 월요일에, **at** the office 사무실에서, **with** anger 화가 나서처럼 시간, 장소, 이유 등의 다양한 의미를 나타냅니다.

| 장소 | **in** the room 방 안에 | 방향 | **to** the building 건물로 |
| 위치 | **by** the museum 박물관 옆에 | 이유 | **for** the traffic jam 교통 체증 때문에 |

- 전치사 뒤에 나오는 명사를 '전치사의 목적어'라고 해요.
  전치사의 목적어 자리에는 명사(구, 절), 대명사(목적격), 동명사 등이 쓰여요.

명사	The reporter is interviewing the author **of** <u>the book</u>. 기자는 <u>그 책의</u> 저자와 인터뷰하고 있다.
목적격 대명사	Mr. Jacob contacted Ms. Cobbs to collaborate **with** <u>her</u> on a project. 제이콥 씨는 콥스 씨에게 연락해서 <u>그녀와</u> 프로젝트를 같이 하자고 했다.
동명사	Ms. Hayes was tasked **with** <u>planning</u> the retirement party. 헤이스 씨는 퇴직 파티를 <u>계획하는 일을</u> 맡았다.

B 전치사구의 쓰임

- 〈전치사+명사(구, 절)〉 형태의 전치사구는 문장 내에서 형용사 또는 부사의 역할을 합니다.

ⓐ 형용사 역할

- 전치사구가 형용사처럼 쓰인 경우, 명사를 수식하거나 주격 보어, 목적격 보어의 역할을 합니다.

| 명사 수식 | Here are the <u>workbooks</u> **for the training session**. 연수를 위한 <u>교재들이</u> 여기 있다. |
| 주격 보어 | <u>This notice</u> is **about how companies can book the venue**.
<u>이 공지는</u> 회사들이 장소를 예약할 수 있는 방법에 관한 것이다. |

ⓑ 부사 역할

- 전치사구가 부사로 쓰인 경우 동사, 형용사, 부사 또는 문장 전체를 수식합니다.

동사 수식	Mr. Miller has to <u>arrive</u> at the airport **by 5 P.M.** 밀러 씨는 **오후 다섯 시까지** 공항에 도착해야 한다.
형용사 수식	The business courses were <u>popular</u> **for two years**. 그 경영 과정은 **2년 동안** 인기 있었다.
문장 수식	**In my opinion**, <u>we should ask for approval</u>. **내 생각에**, <u>우리는 승인을 요청해야 한다.</u>

핵심 POINT 확인하기

다음 괄호 안에서 알맞은 것을 고르세요.

|핵심 POINT 슬쩍 보기|

1 The staff members of ABK Appliances respond to (complain / complaints) from customers promptly.

1 전치사 뒤에는 명사가 와요.

2 Feel free to leave your luggage with (we / us) during the tour.

2 전치사의 목적어로 대명사가 올 경우, 목적격을 써야 해요.

3 A large room (some / for) hosting parties is located at the back of the restaurant.

3 전치사는 뒤에 나온 동명사와 함께 형용사 역할도 해요.

4 The office building will be sold (after / later) the holiday season.

4 전치사는 뒤에 나온 명사와 함께 부사 역할을 할 수 있어요.

UNIT 08

실전 감각 키우기

다음 빈칸에 알맞은 것을 고르세요.

5 빈출 Several methods of ------- can be used when making purchases at the festival's booths.

(A) pays   (B) payment
(C) payable   (D) pay

7 The company's profits have increased dramatically ------- the last few years.

(A) more   (B) over
(C) about   (D) further

6 The west parking lot will be closed ------- Friday due to maintenance work.

(A) already   (B) those
(C) some   (D) until

8 빈출 The building contractor is still far from ------- the lobby renovation.

(A) completed   (B) will complete
(C) completing   (D) to complete

2 시점·기간을 나타내는 전치사

in 2030, in July

핵심 POINT

시점·기간을 나타내는 전치사
- in+연도, 계절, 월, morning, evening 등
- on+날짜, 요일
- at+시각, noon, night 등
- from은 시작 시점만, since는 현재까지 계속됨을 표현
- by는 동작의 완료를, until은 동작의 계속을 표현
- for+구체적인 기간 / during+행사, 사건

A 시점을 나타내는 전치사

in, on, at ~에	• **in**+(긴 시간: 연도, 계절, 월, morning, afternoon, evening) **in** 2030 2030년에 **in** spring 봄에 **in** March 3월에 **in** the morning 아침에 • **on**+(특정 시간: 날짜, 요일) **on** March 28 3월 28일에 **on** Monday 월요일에 • **at**+(짧은 시간: 시각, noon, night, midnight) **at** seven o'clock 7시에 **at** noon 정오에
from, since ~부터	• **from**: 시작하는 시점만 나타내므로 현재의 상황은 알 수 없어요. She began working at the agency **from** last week. 그녀는 지난 주**부터** 그 대리점에서 일했다. (현재는 알 수 없다.) • **since**: 현재까지 계속됨을 나타내므로 현재의 상황도 알 수 있어요. She has been working at the agency **since** last week. 그녀는 지난 주**부터** 그 대리점에서 일해 오고 있다. (지금도 일을 하고 있다.)
by, until[till] ~까지	• **by**: 동작의 '완료'에 초점을 둬요. He will complete the inquiry **by** Thursday. 그는 질문서를 목요일**까지** 완성할 것이다. • **until[till]**: 동작이 '계속되는 상태'를 강조해요. Our registration booth is open **until** six o'clock. 우리 등록 부스는 6시**까지** 연다.
in ~ 후에 **within** ~ 이내에	We will submit the first draft **in** two days. 우리는 이틀 **후에** 초안을 제출할 것이다. The agenda will be ready **within** two days. 안건은 이틀 **이내에** 준비될 것이다.
before ~전에 **after** ~후에	The concert director gave a lecture **before** the performance. 콘서트 감독은 공연에 **앞서** 강연을 했다. They will serve dinner **after** the awards ceremony. 그들은 시상식 **후에** 저녁 식사를 내올 것이다.

B 기간을 나타내는 전치사

for, during ~ 동안	• **for**+구체적인 기간 **for** ten years 10년 **동안** **for** the last three months 지난 석 달 **동안** • **during**+행사·사건을 나타내는 명사 **during** the convention 총회 **동안** **during** the awards ceremony 시상식 **동안**
over ~ 동안 **throughout** **[through]** ~ 동안 죽, 내내	**Over** the last several years, conference attendance has doubled. 지난 몇 년 **동안**, 학회 참석 인원이 두 배로 늘었다. I go on many business trips **throughout[through]** the year. 나는 일 년 **내내** 많은 출장을 간다.

핵심 POINT 확인하기

다음 괄호 안에서 알맞은 것을 고르세요.

|핵심 POINT 슬쩍 보기|

1 Mr. Andrews went to London (in / on) December for a business trip.

1 비교적 긴 시간 앞에는 전치사 in을 써요.

2 The engineer is going to stay in the city (for / during) three days to inspect the factory.

2 숫자로 된 구체적인 기간과 함께 쓰일 수 있는 것은 for예요.

3 Ms. Morgan must submit the leave form to her supervisor (by / until) tomorrow morning.

3 by는 '동작의 완료'에, until은 '계속되는 상태'에 쓰여요.

4 Sitio Resort offers free scuba diving lessons to its guests (on / throughout) the summer.

4 throughout에는 '~동안 죽, 내내'라는 의미가 있어요.

실전 감각 키우기

다음 빈칸에 알맞은 것을 고르세요.

5 The interest rate on home mortgages has remained steady ------- the past year.

(A) over (B) to
(C) out (D) from

7 Each application for renewing a driver's license is processed ------- two weeks.

(A) around (B) within
(C) through (D) behind

6 The store employees discussed window display ideas for the products ------- the meeting.

(A) about (B) into
(C) during (D) along

8 Visitors are required to pass through metal detectors ------- entering Panthec Towers.

(A) before (B) across
(C) around (D) until

UNIT 08

정답 및 해설 68쪽　**139**

3 장소·방향을 나타내는 전치사

장소·방향을 나타내는 전치사
- at+지점
- in+넓은 장소
- over와 under는 표면과 접촉한 경우, 떨어진 경우 모두 사용 가능
- above와 below는 표면과 물체 사이에 공간이 있는 경우 사용
- between+두 개의 장소/대상 · among+불특정 다수의 장소/대상
- from은 위치, 출신, 출처, 시각 등 여러 가지 의미를 나타냄

A 장소·공간을 나타내는 전치사

at, in ~에(서)	· **at**+지점 · **in**+넓은 장소 **at** the entrance 입구에 **in** the lobby 로비에
on ~의 위에[표면에] **in[inside]** (내부) ~ 안에	**on** the desk 책상 위에 **in** the box 상자 안에
in front of ~ 앞에 ↔ **behind** ~ 뒤에 **next to[by, beside]** ~ 옆에	**in front of** the building 건물 앞에 ↔ **behind** the counter 카운터 뒤에 **next to** the elevator 엘리베이터 옆에
over ~ (바로) 위에 걸쳐서 ↔ **under** ~ (바로) 아래 **above** ~보다 위쪽에 ↔ **below** ~보다 아래쪽에	· **over**와 **under**는 물체가 표면과 접촉한 경우, 떨어진 경우 모두 사용 가능해요. **over** the fence 담장 위에 걸쳐서 ↔ **under** the chair 의자 아래 · **above**와 **below**는 주로 표면과 물체 사이에 공간이 있는 경우에 사용해요. **above** the shelf 선반 위쪽에 ↔ **below** the window 창문 아래쪽에
between, among ~ 사이에, ~ 중에	· **between**+두 개의 대상 · **among**+불특정 다수의 대상 **between** John and Mary 존과 메리 사이에 **among** staff members 직원들 중에
near ~ 근처에 **around** ~의 주변에[주위에] **throughout[across]** ~의 도처에[전역에]	**near** the station 역 근처에 **around** the neighborhood 동네 주변에 **throughout** the world 세계 도처에
against ~에 기대어	**against** the wall 벽에 기대어

B 이동 방향을 나타내는 전치사

toward[for] ~을 향해 **from** ~에서(부터)	**toward** the sea 바다를 향해 **from** Pittsburgh 피츠버그에서 참고 from은 이외에도 '(출처·기원) 출신의[~에서 나온]', '(시작 시각)부터', '(판단의 근거로 보아' 등 여러 가지 의미를 가진 전치사로 시험에 자주 출제됩니다.
into ~ 안으로 ↔ **out of** ~ 밖으로	**into** the auditorium 강당 안으로 ↔ **out of** the office 사무실 밖으로
through ~을 통과하여 **along** ~을 따라	**through** a tunnel 터널을 통과하여 **along** the river 강을 따라

핵심 POINT 확인하기

다음 괄호 안에서 알맞은 것을 고르세요.

|핵심 POINT 슬쩍 보기|

1 Ms. Bingley arrives (on / at) the office before 9:00 A.M. every day.

1 특정한 지점은 at을 써서 나타내요.

2 Diners who order the lunch set can choose (between / among) soup and salad.

2 둘 사이에는 between, 불특정 다수 사이에는 among을 써요.

3 Security placed a surveillance camera (under / above) the entrance of every office.

3 under는 '~ (바로) 아래', above는 '~보다 위쪽에'를 나타냅니다.

4 Shoppers in the supermarket rushed (toward / throughout) the exit when the fire alarm went off.

4 toward는 '~을 향해', throughout은 '~의 도처에' 라는 뜻으로 쓰여요.

실전 감각 키우기

다음 빈칸에 알맞은 것을 고르세요.

5 The name and address of the recipient should be clearly written ------- the outside of the package.

(A) with   (B) to
(C) on   (D) for

7 빈출 Sheila Colton ------- Dhalster Network was a speaker at the mass media summit.

(A) about   (B) by
(C) to   (D) from

6 빈출 Medical history files for all the patients should be kept ------- this cabinet.

(A) into   (B) through
(C) in   (D) at

8 Ancient Egyptian artifacts are on display ------- the museum.

(A) against   (B) throughout
(C) onto   (D) toward

4 그 외 주요 전치사

그 외 주요 전치사
- 수단·목적: by, with, for
- 원인·이유: for, from, at
- 관련 주제: about, of, on
- 기타: despite[in spite of], except (for), as

A 수단·목적을 나타내는 전치사

by ~에 의해, ~함으로써	The decision was made **by** the assistant. 그 결정은 비서에 의해 이뤄졌다. He consented **by** nodding his head. 그는 고개를 끄덕임으로써 동의했다. 참고 특히, 동명사와 함께 by+*doing*(~함으로써)의 형태로 시험에 자주 등장합니다.
with ~로	They increased the profit margin **with** a new product. 그들은 신제품으로 이익률을 높였다. 중요 '(도구, 수단)으로'라는 의미 외에 '~와 함께'라는 뜻으로도 사용됩니다. 반대말은 '~ 없이'라는 뜻의 without으로 'without electricity 전기 없이'처럼 쓰이니 함께 알아두세요.
for ~을 위해	They did their best **for** the informative presentation. 그들은 유익한 발표를 위해 최선을 다했다.

B 원인·이유를 나타내는 전치사

for ~ 때문에, ~로 인해	We had to cancel the event **for** lack of interest. 우리는 관심 부족으로 인해 행사를 취소해야 했다.
from ~로 인해	He was tired **from** working all day. 그는 종일 일한 것으로 인해 피곤했다.
at ~에	She was surprised **at** the outdated materials. 그녀는 시대에 뒤떨어진 자료에 놀랐다.

C 기타 전치사

about, of, on ~에 대해	How do you feel **about** people's reaction? 사람들의 반응에 대해 어떻게 생각하십니까? He told me the news **of** the accident. 그는 사고에 대한 소식을 나에게 말했다. The resolution **on** membership was approved. 회원권에 대한 해결책이 승인되었다.
despite, in spite of ~에도 불구하고	**Despite** the inconvenient location, the store was full of people. 불편한 위치에도 불구하고 그 가게는 사람들로 가득 차 있었다.
except (for) ~을 제외하고	Everyone **except (for)** salespeople should attend the meeting. 영업자들을 제외하고 전원이 그 회의에 참석해야 한다.
as ~로서	He made an important suggestion **as** manager. 그는 부장으로서 중요한 제안을 했다.

핵심 POINT 확인하기

다음 괄호 안에서 알맞은 것을 고르세요.

1 Many travelers were attracted (by / of) the airline's generous rewards program.

2 Applicants (except / without) at least three years of experience will not be considered.

3 The seminar (on / by) good leadership will be held this Thursday.

4 (Despite / Throughout) the bad weather, management did not cancel the anniversary party.

|핵심 POINT 슬쩍 보기|

1 수단을 나타낼 때에는 전치사 by를 쓸 수 있어요.

2 without은 '~ 없이'라는 뜻이에요.

3 on은 '~에 대해'라는 의미로 쓰여요.

4 '~에도 불구하고'라는 양보의 의미를 나타낼 때에는 전치사 despite을 써요.

실전 감각 키우기

다음 빈칸에 알맞은 것을 고르세요.

5 All waterproof clothes ------- ski jackets are eligible for a substantial discount this week.

(A) between (B) along
(C) before   (D) except

6 The plant manager requested additional machines ------- sealing product packages.

(A) for   (B) within
(C) through (D) into

7 빈출 The Tourism Department collaborated ------- the Environment Bureau to promote the Maishee Caves.

(A) out (B) up
(C) with (D) at

8 The manager of the Laurel building told Mr. Patterson ------- the repaving of the parking lot.

(A) about (B) between
(C) only (D) as

5 특별한 형태의 전치사와 관용 표현

두 단어 이상의 구전치사
* because of, in addition to, prior to, regardless of 등

-ing로 끝나는 전치사
* regarding, following, concerning, considering 등

전치사 관용 표현
* 〈동사+전치사〉 apply to, enroll in, participate in 등
* 〈명사+전치사〉 access to, increase in, reason for 등

prior to departure

A 두 단어 이상의 구전치사

* 두 단어 이상이 모여 만들어진 전치사로, 자주 출제되는 아래 구전치사들을 잘 기억해두세요.

because of[due to] ~ 때문에	in addition to(= besides) ~ 외에
prior to(= before) ~ 전에	regardless of ~에 상관없이
instead of ~ 대신에	according to ~에 따라(서)
in spite of(= despite) ~에도 불구하고	as to[as for] ~에 관해
in case of[in the event of] ~의 경우에	on behalf of ~을 대신[대표]해서

I missed the meeting **due to** a prior commitment. 나는 선약 **때문에** 그 회의를 놓쳤다.

Please arrive at the airport at least two hours **prior to** departure.
공항에 최소 출발 2시간 **전에** 도착해 주세요.

B -ing로 끝나는 전치사

* 동사원형에 -ing를 붙인 형태라, 문장의 동사나 동명사로 착각하기 쉬운 전치사들입니다.
* 뒤에 전치사의 목적어로 명사(구, 절)를 취하지만, 형태가 같은 동명사만은 목적어로 쓸 수 없습니다.

regarding ~에 관해	following ~ 후에	concerning ~에 관해
considering ~을 고려하면	excluding ~을 제외하고	including ~을 포함해서

They have some concerns **regarding** the topic of the address.
그들은 연설의 주제**에 관해** 몇 가지 사항을 우려하고 있다.

Mr. Reid received the e-mail **concerning** the new working hours.
레이드 씨는 새로운 업무 시간**에 대한** 이메일을 받았다.

C 전치사 관용 표현

apply to ~에 적용되다, ~에 지원하다	enroll in ~에 등록하다	participate in ~에 참석하다
specialize in ~을 전문으로 하다	contribute to ~에 공헌하다	work with ~와 함께 일하다
access to ~로의 접근	increase[decrease] in ~의 증가[감소]	reason for ~에 대한 이유

Many people **participated in** the discussion following the presentation.
많은 사람들이 그 발표 후에 이어진 논의에 **참석했다.**

This change resulted in a huge **increase in** sales. 이 변화가 매출에 큰 **증가를** 일으켰다.

핵심 POINT 확인하기

다음 괄호 안에서 알맞은 것을 고르세요.

1 Budrow Books published more of the author's novels (because of / instead of) high demand.

2 Mr. Young wants to purchase the antique desk (on behalf of / regardless of) the price.

3 You'll probably arrive at the station late, (considering / considered) the heavy traffic.

4 (Following / Follow) an interview with supervisors, the most qualified applicant will be hired.

|핵심 POINT 슬쩍 보기|

1 because of는 이유를 나타 내는 구전치사예요.

2 regardless of는 '~에 상관 없이'라는 뜻을 나타내요.

3 considering은 '~을 고려하 면'이라는 의미의 전치사예요.

4 following은 전치사로 '~ 후 에'라는 뜻이에요.

UNIT 08

실전 감각 키우기

다음 빈칸에 알맞은 것을 고르세요.

5 ------- distributing paper copies of the monthly newsletter, the company will post it online.

(A) Due to　　　(B) Beyond
(C) Instead of　　(D) Among

6 Please speak to Dr. Walsh about any concerns ------- the medical treatment.

(A) regards　　　(B) regarding
(C) regarded　　 (D) regard

7 ------- a survey, 16 percent of office workers ride bikes to work.

(A) In addition to　(B) Instead of
(C) In front of　　 (D) According to

8 YanTech creates software programs, ------- quality-assurance applications, for manufacturing companies.

(A) below　　　(B) including
(C) between　　(D) regarding

정답 및 해설 71쪽　**145**

핵심 POINT 다시 보기

앞에서 학습한 핵심 POINT를 떠올리며 빈칸을 완성해 보세요.

핵심 POINT 1

전치사의 개념과 쓰임

전치사의 개념
- ❶ _____ 앞에 쓰여 시간, 장소, 이유 등 다양한 의미를 나타냄
- 전치사의 ❷ _____ 자리에는 명사(구, 절), 목적격 대명사, 동명사 등이 옴

전치사구의 쓰임
- 〈전치사+명사(구, 절)〉의 전치사구는 형용사 또는 부사의 역할을 함
- 형용사로 쓰이면 ❸ _____ 를 수식하거나 보어의 역할을 함
- ❹ _____ 로 쓰이면 동사, 형용사, 부사 또는 문장 전체를 수식함

핵심 POINT 2-5

여러 가지 전치사

시점·기간을 나타내는 전치사
- (시간)에: ❺ _____ +연도, 계절, 월 등   on+날짜, 요일   at+시각, noon, night 등
- (언제)부터: from은 시작 시점만   since는 현재까지 계속됨을 표현
- (언제)까지: ❻ _____ 는 동작의 완료를   until은 동작의 계속을 표현
- ~ 동안: for+구체적인 기간   ❼ _____ +행사, 사건

장소·방향을 나타내는 전치사
- (장소)에: ❽ _____ +지점   in+넓은 장소
- (장소/대상) 사이에: ❾ _____ +두 개의 장소/대상   among+불특정 다수의 장소/대상

그 외 주요 전치사
- 수단·목적: by ~에 의해, with ~로, for ~을 위해
- 관련 주제: about, of, on ~에 대해
- 원인·이유: for ~해서, from ~로 인해, at ~에
- 기타: despite[in spite of] ~에도 불구하고, except (for) ~을 제외하고, as ~로서

특별한 형태의 전치사와 관용 표현
- because of ~때문에, in ❿ _____ to ~ 외에, prior to ~ 전에 , regardless of ~에 상관없이
- ⓫ _____ ~에 관해, following ~ 후에, concerning ~에 관해, considering ~을 고려하면
- 〈동사+전치사〉 apply to ~에 적용하다, enroll ⓬ _____ ~에 등록하다, participate in ~에 참가하다
- 〈명사+전치사〉 access ⓭ _____ ~로의 접근, increase in ~의 증가, reason for ~에 대한 이유

|빈칸 정답 살짝 보기|··
❶ 명사 ❷ 목적어 ❸ 명사 ❹ 부사 ❺ in ❻ by ❼ during ❽ at ❾ between ❿ addition ⓫ regarding ⓬ in ⓭ to

실전 감각 키우기

다음 빈칸에 알맞은 것을 고르세요.

1 Visit the nearest bank in person to get more information ------- small business loans.

(A) out
(B) around
(C) to
(D) about

2 The new books' titles must be entered into the database ------- the product bar codes.

(A) by
(B) onto
(C) at
(D) with

3 A significant amount of air pollution comes ------- private cars.

(A) after
(B) for
(C) down
(D) from

4 The board met several times ------- approving the company's new logo design.

(A) beyond
(B) among
(C) before
(D) within

[5-6] Questions 5-6 refer to the following article.

New Exhibition at the Toscano Gallery

April 28—The Toscano Gallery has announced plans to host an exhibition of paintings by Luisella DeRose that will start ------- May 2. Ms. DeRose is among the nation's top
5.
artists, and she has won numerous awards for her work.

The exhibition will feature watercolor paintings of the Italian countryside. Museum visitors can take advantage of the informative signs located throughout the exhibition.
------- explanations about the background of each painting, these feature original poems
6.
written by the artist.

5 (A) for
(B) until
(C) on
(D) to

6 (A) In addition to
(B) Because of
(C) Despite
(D) Regardless of

제품 판촉 및 고객 서비스, 보상 등 고객 관련 업무에 관한 어휘들입니다.

discount	명 동 할인(하다)	give[offer] a **discount** 할인해 주다 *전치사 on과 함께 discount an(~에 대한 할인) 형태로 자주 쓰여요.
reduction	명 할인, 감소 파 reduce 줄이다, (가격을) 낮추다	a price **reduction** 가격 할인
installment	명 할부, 분납 파 install 설치하다 installation (기계 등의) 설치	pay in **installments** 할부로 지불하다
display	명 동 진열(하다), 전시(하다) 유 exhibit (작품 등을) 전시하다	a window **display** 창가 진열
reasonable	형 알맞은, 비싸지 않은, 타당한 유 budget 저렴한, 실속 있는	at a **reasonable** price 알맞은 가격에
frequently	부 자주, 빈번히 파 frequent 잦은, 빈번한	**frequently** asked questions 자주 묻는 질문
complaint	명 불만 사항 파 complain 불평[항의]하다	deal with customer **complaints** 고객 불만을 처리하다 file a **complaint** 불만을 제기하다
inquiry	명 문의 파 inquire 문의하다	respond to an **inquiry** 문의에 답하다 *형태가 비슷한 require(요구하다), acquire(얻다)도 함께 알아두세요.
satisfaction	명 만족(도) 파 satisfy 만족시키다	customer **satisfaction** 고객 만족(도)
refund	명 환불(금)	a full **refund** 전액 환불
warranty	명 품질 보증서	under **warranty** 보증 기간 내인
expire	동 만료되다 파 expiration 만료	**expire** in July 7월에 만료되다 *명사형이 쓰인 표현 expiration date(유효기간)도 알아두세요.
policy	명 정책, 방침	make adjustments to **policies** 정책을 수정하다 *'보험 계약 (증서)'라는 의미도 있어서, renew the policy(보험을 갱신하다) 와 같이 쓰여요.
replacement	명 교체, 후임자 파 replace 교체하다	the **replacement** of some parts 부품 교체
guarantee	명 동 보장(하다)	**guarantee** the quality 품질을 보장하다 *〈guarantee[ensure]+that절〉은 '~임을 보장하다'라는 뜻이에요.
review	명 비평, 후기 동 검토하다, 비평하다	a customer's product **review** 고객 상품 후기 consult an online **review** 온라인 후기를 참고하다
detailed	형 상세한, 자세한 파 detail 세부 사항, 상세 항목	**detailed** instructions 상세 사용 설명서 a **detailed** product description 상세 상품 설명
permanent	형 영구적인, 상설의 유 lasting 지속적인	on **permanent** display 상시 전시

파 파생어 유 유의어 반 반의어 관 관련 어휘

어휘 확인하기

다음 괄호 안에서 알맞은 것을 고르세요.

1 Price (installments / reductions) have helped attract more people to the store.

2 Several editors (reviewed / satisfied) the advertisement before its publication.

3 The manual provides (permanent / detailed) instructions for the book shelf's construction.

4 The store manager immediately offered a (policy / refund) for the broken item.

실전 감각 키우기

다음 빈칸에 알맞은 것을 고르세요.

5 The restaurant in Guzman Hotel offers a variety of dishes at ------ prices.

(A) reasonable
(B) cautious
(C) temporary
(D) durable

6 Ms. Jordan is in charge of dealing with customer -------- about product defects.

(A) purchases
(B) complaints
(C) satisfaction
(D) requirements

7 The warranty on your Zolo X50 stereo system ------- two years from the date of purchase.

(A) recalls
(B) requires
(C) confirms
(D) expires

8 We can ------- one-hour processing of your photographs if you pay ten cents per picture.

(A) notice
(B) afford
(C) guarantee
(D) display

정답 및 해설 74쪽 **149**

주어진 문제를 제한시간에 맞추어 풀어 보세요.

Part 5 Choose the one word or phrase that best completes the sentence.

1. Hawthorne Hotels provides upscale accommodations at fifty locations ------- North America.

   (A) behind
   (B) among
   (C) over
   (D) across

2. ------- the special guest, Ms. Jacobs will give the opening remarks for Perchatown's founding celebration.

   (A) As
   (B) Except
   (C) Off
   (D) Along

3. Our technical support team responds to all ------- within thirty minutes.

   (A) refunds
   (B) inquiries
   (C) discounts
   (D) positions

4. The winding mountain roads are cleared regularly ------- the winter to ensure greater safety for motorists.

   (A) throughout
   (B) without
   (C) among
   (D) down

5. Using the telecommunication technology, employees can complete their assignments without ------- home.

   (A) leaves
   (B) leaving
   (C) leave
   (D) left

6. The production of the company brochures is handled ------- the creative department.

   (A) about
   (B) by
   (C) of
   (D) during

7. The labor minister will answer questions ------- the proposed minimum wage increase.

   (A) excluding
   (B) since
   (C) further
   (D) concerning

8. The air-conditioning unit in the conference room needs to be ------- because it makes too much noise.

   (A) replaced
   (B) requested
   (C) worked
   (D) coordinated

Part 6 Questions 9-12 refer to the following e-mail.

From: Swann Auto Shop <jsnow@swann.com>
To: Mary Robinson <mrobinson@mymail.com>
Date: November 2
Subject: Re: Damage to your car

Dear Ms. Robinson,

I'm sorry about the damage caused to your vehicle by our staff. ------- our policy, you
9.
are entitled to a refund for the recent work on your car. ------- .
10.

As a token of goodwill, we would also like to offer you a fifty percent -------. It will be
11.
applied to your next visit for maintenance work conducted by our company.

We would like to remind you that we really do value you as a customer. -------, we
12.
guarantee our prices will always be lower than those of our competitors.

Regards,

James Snow, Swann Auto Shop

---

9. (A) On behalf of
(B) Compared to
(C) According to
(D) Instead of

10. (A) We offer a wide range of services.
(B) Please return to our shop to claim it.
(C) Your car requires a new coat of paint.
(D) We recommend changing your engine's oil.

11. (A) profit
(B) satisfaction
(C) discount
(D) warranty

12. (A) Furthermore
(B) Nevertheless
(C) Otherwise
(D) By contrast

UNIT 08

PART 5&6 준동사편

UNIT 09

부정사
+업무 어휘(3)

동사인듯, 동사 아닌 동사 같은 너~

준동사

우리말에서 동사인 '달리다'를 '달리기'로 바꾸어 명사로 쓰거나, '달리는'으로 바꾸어 형용사로 쓸 수 있습니다. 영어에서도 동사의 형태를 바꾸어 다른 품사로 쓰이는 말이 있는데, 이를 준동사라고 해요. 준동사에는 to부정사(to+동사원형), 동명사(동사원형+-ing), 분사(동사원형+-ing, *p.p.*) 등이 있어요.

1 to부정사의 개념과 형태

They decided
to publish the article.

to부정사
- 〈to+동사원형〉 형태로 문장에서 명사, 형용사, 부사 역할
- 뒤에 목적어나 보어가 올 수 있고 수식어구도 올 수 있음

to부정사의 형태
- 기본형: 〈to+동사원형〉
- 부정형: 〈not to+동사원형〉
- 수동형: 〈to+be *p.p.*〉
- 완료형: 〈to+have *p.p.*〉

A 준동사의 개념

- 준동사는 동사에서 비롯되었으나 문장에서 명사, 형용사, 부사 등 다른 품사로 쓰이는 말입니다. 앞으로 배울 to부정사, 동명사, 분사가 여기에 포함됩니다.

동사	He **arranges** the meetings. 그는 그 회의를 준비한다.
to부정사	**To arrange** the meetings, I contacted him. 회의를 준비하기 위해, 나는 그에게 연락했다.
동명사	**Arranging** the meetings was difficult for me. 회의를 준비하는 것은 나에게 어려웠다.
분사	I will attend the meetings **arranged** by the marketing team. 나는 마케팅 팀에 의해서 **준비된** 회의에 참석할 것이다.

B to부정사의 개념과 형태

ⓐ to부정사의 개념

- to부정사는 동사를 명사, 형용사, 부사처럼 쓰기 위해 〈to+동사원형〉의 형태로 바꾼 것입니다.
- to부정사는 동사에서 비롯되었지만, 준동사라서 동사 자리에는 올 수 없습니다. 하지만, 동사의 성질을 갖고 있어서 뒤에 목적어나 보어, 수식어구(부사(구), 전치사구)가 올 수 있어요.

to부정사+목적어	They decided **to publish** the article. 그들은 그 기사를 내기로 결정했다.
to부정사+수식어(구)	The monthly budget started **to decrease** steadily. 월간 예산이 서서히 줄기 시작했다.

ⓑ to부정사의 형태

기본형 〈to+동사원형〉	**To raise** prices regularly is a common practice among local restaurants 정기적으로 가격을 올리는 것은 지역 식당들 사이에서 흔한 관례이다.
부정형 〈not to+동사원형〉	The intern has decided **not to apply** for a full-time position. 그 인턴은 정규직에 지원하지 않기로 결정했다.
수동형 〈to+be *p.p.*〉	• to부정사와 주어의 관계가 수동일 때 사용해요. Ms. Jones hadn't expected **to be nominated** for the award. 존스 씨는 그 상에 후보로 지명될 것이라고 기대하지 않았다. → 존스 씨는 후보를 지명한 것이 아니라, 후보로 지명된 대상(수동)
완료형 〈to+have *p.p.*〉	• 문장의 동사보다 이전 시점에 일어난 일을 나타내요. The passengers are upset **to have waited** so long. 승객들은 너무 오래 기다린 것에 화가 났다. → 화가 난 것은 현재, 기다린 것은 과거(대과거)

핵심 POINT 확인하기

다음 괄호 안에서 알맞은 것을 고르세요.

|핵심 POINT 슬쩍 보기|

1 (Place / To place) an order after 6 P.M., please visit our Web site at www.cosetimarket.com.

1 동사처럼 생겼으나, 문장을 수식하는 부사 역할을 하는 것은 준동사 to부정사예요.

2 We want (to advertise / advertisement) our products in a popular weekly magazine.

2 to부정사는 동사의 성질도 갖고 있어서, 뒤에 목적어가 올 수 있어요.

3 Mr. Walton is ready (applied / to apply) for the researcher position at JAX Pharmaceuticals.

3 to부정사는 부사처럼 쓰여서 앞에 나온 형용사를 수식할 수도 있어요.

4 The architect has promised not (exceed / to exceed) the construction budget.

4 to부정사의 부정형은 앞에 not을 붙여서 만들어요.

UNIT 09

실전 감각 키우기

다음 빈칸에 알맞은 것을 고르세요.

5 The number of online banking customers is likely to increase ------- over the next five years.

(A) steady
(B) steadily
(C) steadied
(D) steadiness

6 Isis Biomedical claims ------- an effective cure for a major disease.

(A) to discover
(B) discover
(C) discovered
(D) to have discovered

7 빈출 Mr. Geller has contacted the personnel manager to obtain ------- for the order of office supplies.

(A) approve
(B) approved
(C) approves
(D) approval

8 Poor ticket sales caused the concert ------- for a later date.

(A) is rescheduling
(B) to be rescheduled
(C) will be rescheduled
(D) to reschedule

2 to부정사의 쓰임

핵심 POINT

I want **to help** a charity.

to부정사의 역할
- 명사 역할: '~하는 것', '~하기' 주어, 목적어, 보어 역할
- 형용사 역할: '~할', '~하는' 명사를 뒤에서 수식
- 부사 역할: '~하기 위해', '~하게 되어' 동사, 형용사, 문장 수식

가주어와 의미상의 주어
- to부정사 주어를 뒤로 보내고 대신 가주어 it을 씀
- 의미상의 주어: ⟨for+명사[목적격 대명사]⟩ 형태

A to부정사의 역할

ⓐ 명사 역할
- to부정사는 문장에서 명사로 쓰여 주어, 목적어, 보어 자리에 쓰일 수 있어요.

주어	**To succeed in politics** is not easy. 정치계에서 성공하는 것은 쉽지 않다.

> **참고** to부정사 주어는 단수 취급하므로 단수 동사를 사용해요.

목적어	I want **to help a charity**. 나는 자선단체를 돕기를 원한다.
주격 보어	My job is **to install security cameras**. 내 일은 보안카메라를 설치하는 것이다.
목적격 보어	I encouraged him **to change the book's cover**. 나는 그에게 책 표지를 바꿀 것을 권했다.

ⓑ 형용사 역할
- 명사 뒤에서 앞의 명사를 수식하며, '~할', '~하는'으로 해석됩니다.

명사 수식	He found a charity **to help**. 그는 도울 자선단체를 찾았다.

ⓒ 부사 역할
- 부사처럼 동사, 형용사, 문장 전체를 수식할 수 있으며, 주로 '목적(~하기 위해)'의 의미를 나타냅니다.
- 형용사를 수식할 때는 '감정의 원인(~하게 되어)'이나 '판단의 근거(~하다니)'를 나타내는 경우가 많아요.

동사 수식(목적)	Please complete this form **to register**. 등록하시려면 이 양식을 작성해 주세요.
형용사 수식(원인)	She was glad **to help the charity**. 그녀는 그 자선단체를 돕게 되어 기뻤다.
문장 수식(목적)	**To help the charity**, she made a donation. 그 자선단체를 돕기 위해, 그녀는 기부를 했다.

- to부정사가 부사 역할을 할 때, 아래 구문의 형태로도 쓰입니다.

in order to *do*(= so as to *do*) ~하기 위해서	too + 형용사[부사] + to *do* 너무 ~해서 …할 수 없다

I studied hard **in order to[so as to]** pass the exam. 나는 그 시험을 통과하기 위해서 열심히 공부했다.

B 가주어와 의미상의 주어
- to부정사가 주어로 쓰여 길어진 경우, 이것을 문장 맨 뒤로 보내고 그 자리에 가주어 it을 쓸 수 있습니다.

To check the weather forecast is important. 일기예보를 확인하는 것은 중요하다.

= It is important **to check the weather forecast**.

> **참고** 가주어 it을 쓴 문장에서 to부정사가 나타내는 행위의 주체(의미상의 주어)를 밝혀야 하는 경우에는 ⟨for+명사[목적격 대명사]⟩의 형태로 to부정사 앞에 써서 나타냅니다.
> It is difficult for journalists **to uncover the truth**. 기자들이 진실을 폭로하기는 어렵다.

핵심 POINT 확인하기

다음 괄호 안에서 알맞은 것을 고르세요.

|핵심 POINT 슬쩍 보기|

1 The goal is (to resolve / resolved) the problems in our production line.

1 to부정사는 명사 역할을 할 수 있기 때문에, 주격 보어로 쓰일 수 있어요.

2 Mr. Smith made the decision (to suspend / suspends) the renovation work due to budget issues.

2 형용사 역할의 to부정사는 명사를 뒤에서 수식할 수 있어요.

3 The marketing department must work late in order to (meet / meeting) the deadline.

3 in order to *do*는 '~하기 위해서'라는 뜻의 to부정사 구문이에요.

4 It is important for job applicants (to include / including) all their qualifications on their résumés.

4 주어가 it으로 시작하면 진주어는 뒤에 나오는 to부정사가 아닌지 확인해요.

UNIT 09

실전 감각 키우기

다음 빈칸에 알맞은 것을 고르세요.

5 The CEO of the investment firm plans ------- stock in at least three corporations.

(A) purchased (B) purchases
(C) are purchasing (D) to purchase

6 Ms. Samson received an invitation ------- the twelfth Annual Green Planet Convention next month.

(A) is attending (B) attends
(C) to attend (D) attend

7 It is essential for sales representatives ------- the daily figures to the head office.

(A) send (B) is sending
(C) will send (D) to send

8 ------- cooperation, the operations manager has placed employees in diverse project teams.

(A) Encouragement (B) To encourage
(C) To be encouraged (D) Encouraged

to부정사와 함께 쓰이는 표현

to부정사와 어울려 쓰이는 동사
- 〈동사+to부정사〉 plan, wish, hope, want, ask, decide, expect
- 〈동사+목적어+to부정사〉 tell, advise, allow, encourage

to부정사와 어울려 쓰이는 형용사·명사
- 〈형용사+to부정사〉 be able to *do*, be likely to *do*
- 〈명사+to부정사〉 ability to *do*, chance to *do*, plan to *do*

I want / hope / wish **to *do***

A to부정사와 어울려 쓰이는 동사

ⓐ 〈동사+to부정사〉: to부정사를 목적어로 쓰는 동사들

- to부정사는 '미래'의 의미를 내포해서 주로 희망, 계획, 결정을 의미하는 동사와 함께 쓰입니다.

plan 계획하다	wish[hope] 바라다[희망하다]	want 원하다	
ask 요청하다	decide 결정하다	expect 기대하다	+to *do*
agree 동의하다	choose 선택하다	offer 제안하다	

The company <u>decided</u> **to give** all the employees an annual bonus.
회사에서 전 직원에게 연간 보너스를 **주기로** 결정했다.

(참고) want, ask, expect, choose 등은 〈동사+목적어+to *do*〉 형태로도 쓰여요.

ⓑ 〈동사+목적어+to부정사〉: to부정사를 목적격 보어로 쓰는 동사들

tell 말하다	advise 충고하다	allow 허용하다	
encourage 장려[격려]하다	persuade 설득하다	remind 상기시키다	+목적어+to *do*

The city <u>encourages</u> <u>residents</u> **to attend the music festival**.
　　　　　　　　　목적어　　　　　　목적격 보어　　　　시는 거주민들에게 **음악 축제에 참여할 것을** 장려한다.

(참고) 위의 동사들이 수동태로 쓰이면, 〈be+*p.p.*+to *do*〉의 형태가 됩니다.
Mr. Ken <u>was advised</u> **to reduce** his business expenses. 켄 씨는 출장 경비를 **줄이도록** 조언받았다.

B to부정사와 어울려 쓰이는 형용사·명사

ⓐ 〈형용사+to부정사〉

be able to *do* ~할 수 있다	be likely to *do* ~할 것 같다	be willing to *do* 기꺼이 ~하다
be unable to *do* ~할 수 없다	be pleased to *do* ~하게 되어 기쁘다	be eligible to *do* ~할 자격이 있다
be eager to *do* 몹시 ~하고 싶다	be ready to *do* ~할 준비가 되다	be reluctant to *do* ~하기를 꺼리다

All employees **are eligible to apply** for a promotion after one year.
모든 직원은 1년 후에 승진에 **지원할 자격이 있다**.

ⓑ 〈명사+to부정사〉

ability to *do* ~할 능력	chance[opportunity] to *do* ~할 기회	plan to *do* ~할 계획
attempt to *do* ~하려는 시도	effort to *do* ~하려는 노력	way to *do* ~하는 방법

Mr. Masterson had **the opportunity to practice** his Spanish during his business trip.
매스터슨 씨는 출장 중에 스페인어를 **연습할 기회가** 있었다.

핵심 POINT 확인하기

다음 괄호 안에서 알맞은 것을 고르세요.

|핵심 POINT 슬쩍 보기|

1 The Caring Hands Organization hopes (raise / to raise) over $10,000 from the benefit event.

1 hope는 목적어로 to부정사를 취하는 동사예요.

2 Mr. Garland reminded me (to create / creating) a banner for the new sports shoes.

2 remind는 목적격 보어로 to 부정사를 취하는 동사예요.

3 The contractor was able (to submit / submitted) the design for the renovation on time.

3 형용사 able은 to부정사의 수식을 받아 be able to do의 형태로 자주 쓰여요.

4 The shareholders approved the proposal (to transform / transform) the building into a hotel.

4 명사 proposal은 to부정사의 수식을 받아 자주 쓰여요.

실전 감각 키우기

다음 빈칸에 알맞은 것을 고르세요.

5 The TMC foundation chose ------- Professor Yates for his dedication to helping others.

(A) to honor (B) will honor
(C) to be honored (D) would honor

6 Ms. Wilson asked her assistant ------- for the job fair.

(A) prepare (B) to prepare
(C) prepares (D) preparation

7 The global economic slowdown is expected ------- challenges for major businesses.

(A) presents (B) to present
(C) presenting (D) presentation

8 The internship at M&K Accounting is a good opportunity ------- useful information about the industry.

(A) learn (B) learning
(C) has learned (D) to learn

앞에서 학습한 핵심 POINT를 떠올리며 빈칸을 완성해 보세요.

핵심 POINT 1

to부정사의 개념과 형태

to부정사
- 〈to+동사원형〉 형태로 문장에서 ❶_____, 형용사, 부사 역할
- 뒤에 ❷_____나 보어가 올 수 있고, 수식어구도 올 수 있음

to부정사의 형태
- 기본형: 〈to+동사원형〉
- 수동형: 〈to+❸_____ p.p.〉
- 부정형: 〈not to+동사원형〉
- 완료형: 〈to+have p.p.〉

핵심 POINT 2

to부정사의 쓰임

to부정사의 역할
- 명사 역할: '~하는 것', '~하기' 주어, 목적어, 보어 역할
- ❹_____ 역할: '~할', '~하는' 명사를 뒤에서 수식
- 부사 역할: '~하기 위해', '~하게 되어' 동사, 형용사, 문장 수식

가주어와 의미상의 주어
- to부정사 주어를 뒤로 보내고 대신 가주어 ❺_____을 씀
- 의미상의 주어: 〈❻_____+명사[목적격 대명사]〉형태

핵심 POINT 3

to부정사와 함께 쓰이는 표현

to부정사와 어울려 쓰이는 동사
- 〈동사+to부정사〉 ❼_____ 계획하다, wish 바라다, hope 희망하다, want 원하다, ask 요청하다
- 〈동사+목적어+to부정사〉 tell 말하다, advise 충고하다, ❽_____ 허용하다, encourage 장려하다

to부정사와 어울려 쓰이는 형용사·명사
- 〈형용사+to부정사〉 be ❾_____ to do ~할 수 있다, be likely to do ~할 것 같다
- 〈명사+to부정사〉 ability to do ~할 능력, ❿_____ to do ~할 기회, plan to do ~할 계획

|빈칸 정답 살짝 보기|

❶ 명사 ❷ 목적어 ❸ be ❹ 형용사 ❺ it ❻ for ❼ plan ❽ allow ❾ able ❿ chance[opportunity]

실전 감각 키우기

다음 빈칸에 알맞은 것을 고르세요.

1 Bob Hilditch has the ability ------- his core tasks more efficiently than the other customer service representatives.

(A) perform
(B) performing
(C) be performed
(D) to perform

2 It is standard procedure ------- defective appliances back to manufacturers.

(A) to send
(B) sent
(C) sends
(D) will send

3 Management policies are likely ------- from one business unit to another.

(A) differing
(B) difference
(C) to differ
(D) differ

4 Supervisors do not allow their employees ------- confidential materials from the premises.

(A) remove
(B) to remove
(C) removing
(D) removed

[5-6] Questions 5-6 refer to the following e-mail.

Dear Ms. Chandler,

As you may remember, we met at the recent fundraising gala at Caird Hall. You were understaffed, and it was my pleasure ------- you with the setting up of the food tables.
5.

Afterwards, I mentioned that I needed to find a caterer for an upcoming event, and you said you could handle the job.

Could you let me know what your rates are? We need to serve approximately fifty people. I would be happy ------- a phone meeting to discuss the options further.
6.

5 (A) assists
(B) assisted
(C) to be assisted
(D) to have assisted

6 (A) arranged
(B) to arrange
(C) would arrange
(D) to be arranged

직장에서의 회의 및 각종 행사, 문서 작업과 관련된 어휘들입니다.

attend	⑧ 참석하다 ㉿ attendance 참석(률), 참석자	**attend** a conference 회의에 참석하다
agenda	⑲ 의제, 안건	an item on the **agenda** 의제의 항목
consent	⑲ ⑧ 동의(하다) ㉫ refusal 거절	written **consent** 서면 동의 give **consent** 동의하다
settle	⑧ 해결하다 ㊌ resolve 해결하다	**settle** a problem 문제를 해결하다
presentation	⑲ 발표 ㉪ speech 연설, 담화	give a **presentation** 발표를 하다
postpone	⑧ 연기하다, 미루다	an event is **postponed** 행사가 연기되다
ceremony	⑲ 의식, 행사	an awards **ceremony** 시상식 an opening **ceremony** 개막식
venue	⑲ 장소	the **venue** for an event 행사를 위한 장소 *venue는 회의 등의 개최 '장소'를, site는 건축, 공사 등의 '현장'을 나타내요.
limited	⑱ 제한된, 한정된 ㉿ limit 제한(하다) limitation 한계, 취약점	**limited** time 제한된 시간 **limited** to ~까지 제한된, ~에게 제한된
address	⑧ (문제 등을) 다루다, 연설하다 ⑲ 연설, 주소	**address** an issue 문제를 다루다 **address** an audience 청중에게 연설하다
instructor	⑲ 강사 ㉿ instruct 가르치다	a qualified **instructor** 자격 있는 강사
complete	⑧ 완료하다 ⑱ 완벽한, 완전한	**complete** a course 과정을 완료하다 **complete** control 완전한 통제
documentation	⑲ (공식적인) 문서, 서류, 문서화 ㉿ document 서류; 기록하다	additional **documentation** 추가 서류
draft	⑲ 초안 ㉪ manuscript (책 등의) 원고	write a first **draft** 초안을 작성하다
outline	⑧ 요약하다 ⑲ 개요, 윤곽 ㊌ summarize 요약하다	**outline** a proposal 제안서를 요약하다
implement	⑧ 실행[이행]하다 ㉿ implementation 실행, 이행	**implement** a procedure 절차를 실행하다
restricted	⑱ 제한된 ㉿ restrict 제한하다 restriction 제한, 규제	**restricted** access 제한된 접근
approval	⑲ 승인, 결재 ㉿ approve 승인하다, 찬성하다	receive final **approval** 최종 승인을 받다

㉿ 파생어 ㊌ 유의어 ㉫ 반의어 ㉪ 관련 어휘

어휘 확인하기

다음 괄호 안에서 알맞은 것을 고르세요.

1 The host of the contest has decided to (implement / limit) the number of entries.

2 The meeting was (addressed / postponed) until further notice.

3 More than twenty people (attended / settled) the seminar.

4 The reception hall has (restrictions / ceremonies) on event type, number of people, and other elements.

실전 감각 키우기

다음 빈칸에 알맞은 것을 고르세요.

5 Ms. Spencer will go over each item on the ------- in detail.

(A) agenda
(B) process
(C) function
(D) presentation

6 Organizers are still trying to reserve a suitable ------- for the Annual Broadcasting Awards Dinner.

(A) candidate
(B) venue
(C) promotion
(D) benefit

7 Front desk receptionists must ------- the hotel's training program before they work alone.

(A) cooperate
(B) consent
(C) participate
(D) complete

8 Do not make any travel plans until you receive ------- from your supervisor.

(A) materials
(B) admission
(C) approval
(D) comments

주어진 문제를 제한시간에 맞추어 풀어 보세요.

Part 5 Choose the one word or phrase that best completes the sentence.

1. The employees started a carpool program as an attempt ------- to work in a more environmentally friendly way.

   (A) commute
   (B) commutes
   (C) commuted
   (D) to commute

2. The branch manager must give ------- prior to any personnel changes, including department transfers.

   (A) consent
   (B) evidence
   (C) attention
   (D) influence

3. Mr. Sawyer is ------- busy to answer the phone at the moment.

   (A) now
   (B) too
   (C) very
   (D) not

4. It is necessary ------- this form for advanced classes registration.

   (A) signature
   (B) to be signed
   (C) signing
   (D) to sign

5. In an effort ------- the hiring process, the HR department will set up a new job application Web site.

   (A) simplify
   (B) to simplify
   (C) simplifies
   (D) simplification

6. The information pamphlet ------- the steps for applying for a loan at Havana Bank.

   (A) approves
   (B) produces
   (C) outlines
   (D) allows

7. ------- image quality, Altrox redesigned its smartphone's high-resolution camera.

   (A) Enhances
   (B) To enhance
   (C) To be enhanced
   (D) Enhanced

8. Museum visitors were eager ------- some Egyptian artifacts in the main exhibition hall.

   (A) to have examined
   (B) examine
   (C) examined
   (D) to examine

Part 6 Questions 9-12 refer to the following e-mail.

To: Ericka J. Flores <florese@wayneinc.com>, Rita Sheppard <sheppardr@wayneinc.com>
From: Dennis Bickley <bickleyd@wayneinc.com>
Date: June 8
Subject: Conference room booking

Ms. Flores and Ms. Sheppard,

Due to a system error, the conference room has been double-booked for June 16.

Unfortunately, both of you need to meet with clients at the same time. It is important to

------- this problem as soon as possible.
  9.

Here's what I propose. ------- . Then, the other person can select a new date. To -------
      10.   11.
the new time slot, that person should also cancel the current one in the system.

I'm sorry for any inconvenience this may cause, and I hope that one of you will be able

------- her schedule.
  12.

Sincerely,

Dennis Bickley, Administration Department

9. (A) attend
(B) maintain
(C) settle
(D) predict

10. (A) I'll fix the problem with the site soon.
(B) The room can be shared because of its spaciousness.
(C) The room's available times are posted online.
(D) Please decide who will take the original date between you.

11. (A) reserving
(B) reserve
(C) have reserved
(D) reservation

12. (A) to change
(B) changing
(C) changed
(D) change

UNIT 09

PART 5&6 준동사편

UNIT 10

동명사
+사회 어휘(1)

우리말에서 동사인 '보다'를 '보기'로 바꾸어 명사로 쓸 수 있습니다.
영어에서는 바로 이 '～하기'에 해당하는 것이 '-ing'인데요.
동사원형에 -ing를 붙여서 명사처럼 사용할 수 있어요.

---

1 동명사의 개념과 형태
2 동명사와 함께 쓰이는 표현
3 동명사 vs. 명사 vs. to부정사

+ 사회 어휘(1)

1 동명사의 개념과 형태

His duty is
collecting information.

동명사
- 형태: 〈동사원형+-ing〉
- 문장에서 명사처럼 주어, 목적어, 보어 역할

동명사의 형태
- 기본형: 〈동사원형+-ing〉
- 부정형: 〈not+동사원형+-ing〉
- 수동형: 〈being *p.p.*〉
- 완료형: 〈having *p.p.*〉

A 동명사의 개념

- 동명사는 준동사로, 동사가 〈동사원형+-ing〉의 형태로 쓰이는 것을 말합니다.

동사 ~하다	He **collects** information. 그는 정보를 **수집한다**.
동명사 ~하는 것, ~하기	His duty is **collecting** information. 그의 임무는 정보를 **수집하는 것**이다.

- 동명사는 명사처럼 문장에서 주어, 목적어, 보어 역할을 합니다.
- 동사의 성질을 갖고 있어서 뒤에 목적어, 보어, 수식어구가 올 수 있어요.

주어		**Discussing** politics is my favorite activity. 정치에 대해 **토론하는 것**은 내가 가장 좋아하는 활동이다. (참고) 동명사 주어는 단수 취급하므로, 단수 동사를 써야 해요.
목적어	동사의 목적어	I enjoy **discussing** politics. 나는 정치에 대해 **토론하는 것**을 즐긴다.
	전치사의 목적어	We can learn about the issues by **discussing** politics. 우리는 정치에 대해 **토론함으로써** 그 쟁점들에 대해 알 수 있다.
보어		My main interest is **discussing** politics. 나의 주된 관심사는 정치에 대해 **토론하는 것**이다.

- 동명사의 행위 주체를 밝혀줘야 할 때, 〈소유격[목적격]+동명사〉 형태로 나타냅니다.

  We appreciate your[you] **helping** us. 귀하께서 저희를 **도와주신 것**에 대해 감사드립니다.

B 동명사의 형태

기본형 〈동사원형+-ing〉	**Satisfying** its clients is the company's main objective. 고객들을 **만족시키는 것**은 그 회사의 주된 목표이다.
부정형 〈not+동사원형+-ing〉	The board considered **not changing** company policies. 이사회는 회사 방침을 **변경하지 않는 것**을 고려했다.
수동형 〈being *p.p.*〉	• 동명사와 주어의 관계가 수동일 때 사용돼요. He is proud of **being promoted** to the new position. 그는 새로운 직위로 **승진된 것**을 자랑스러워한다. → 그가 승진시킨 것이 아니라, 승진된 대상(수동)
완료형 〈having *p.p.*〉	• 문장의 동사보다 이전 시점에 일어난 일을 나타내요. Helen was satisfied with **having increased** the profits. 헬렌 씨는 수익이 **높아졌던 것**에 대해 만족했다. → 만족한 것은 과거, 수익이 높아진 것은 그 이전의 과거(대과거)

핵심 POINT 확인하기

다음 괄호 안에서 알맞은 것을 고르세요.

|핵심 POINT 슬쩍 보기|

1 (Maintained / Maintaining) the trust of its clients is important to Fidelis Industries.

1 동사는 〈동사원형+-ing〉 형태로 명사처럼 쓰일 수 있어요.

2 The intern denied (working / worked) for the company's competitor in the past.

2 동명사는 명사처럼 목적어로 쓰여요.

3 Conducting customer surveys (allow / allows) companies to obtain valuable feedback.

3 동명사 주어는 단수 취급해요.

4 Despite Ms. Howson's lack of experience, Mr. Gibbs approves of (she / her) leading the project team.

4 동명사의 행위 주체는 소유격 또는 목적격으로 나타내요.

UNIT 10

실전 감각 키우기

다음 빈칸에 알맞은 것을 고르세요.

5 Ms. Lang's main responsibility is ------- the promotion of the company's latest products.

  (A) handling   (B) handle
  (C) handlers   (D) handled

7 Mr. Walters plans on ------- the firm's 빈출 sales goals for the coming year at the shareholders meeting.

  (A) outline   (B) outliner
  (C) outlining   (D) being outlined

6 Ms. Wilkie was congratulated for ---------- the first interview.

  (A) passes   (B) will pass
  (C) passed   (D) having passed

8 In addition to ------- his own catering firm, Mr. Borrell also gives lectures at Grimley College.

  (A) manage   (B) manageable
  (C) manages   (D) managing

2 동명사와 함께 쓰이는 표현

핵심 POINT

He avoided
paying the customs duty.

동명사와 어울려 쓰이는 동사
- 〈동사+동명사〉: consider, avoid, finish, quit, stop, give up

동명사 관용 표현
- 〈to+*doing*〉: be committed to *doing*, contribute to *doing*, looking forward to *doing*, be related to *doing*
- 기타: feel like *doing*, it is no use *doing*, be worth *doing*, be busy *doing*

A 동명사와 어울려 쓰이는 동사

- 〈동사+동명사〉의 구조로 동명사를 목적어로 취하는 동사들이 있습니다.
- 동명사는 '과거'의 의미가 강해서, 중지, 지연, 제안 등을 의미하는 동사의 목적어로 주로 쓰여요.

consider 고려하다	avoid 피하다	finish 끝내다	
quit[stop] 그만두다	give up 포기하다	postpone[delay] 미루다	+*doing*
suggest 제안하다	recommend 권하다	deny 부인하다	

I <u>suggested</u> **buying** a new car. 나는 새 차를 **사는 것을** <u>제안했다</u>.
He <u>avoided</u> **paying** the customs duty. 그는 관세를 **내는 것을** <u>피했다</u>.

B 〈전치사 to+*doing*〉

- 전치사 to 다음에 동명사가 와야 하는 표현이에요. to부정사의 to와 헷갈리지 않도록 주의하세요.

be committed to *doing* ~하는 것에 전념하다	contribute to *doing* ~하는 것에 기여하다
look forward to *doing* ~하는 것을 고대하다	be related to *doing* ~하는 것에 관련되다
be used to *doing* ~하는 것에 익숙하다	lead to *doing* ~하는 것을 초래하다
object to doing[be opposed to *doing*] ~하는 것에 반대하다	

I <u>look forward to</u> **sharing** my opinions. 나는 내 의견을 **공유하기를** <u>기대한다</u>.
~~share~~

We <u>are used to</u> **making** the arrangements ourselves. 우리는 직접 준비를 **하는 것에** <u>익숙하다</u>.
~~make~~

C 기타 동명사 관용 표현

- 동명사와 함께 관용적으로 쓰이는 표현이에요. 통째로 외우면 답을 고르는 시간을 줄일 수 있어요.

feel like *doing* ~하고 싶어 하다	it is no use *doing* ~해 봐야 소용없다
be worth *doing* ~할 가치가 있다	be busy *doing* ~하느라 바쁘다
spend time[money] *doing* ~하는 데 시간[돈]을 쓰다	cannot help *doing* ~하지 않을 수 없다
have trouble[difficulty] (in) *doing* ~하는 데 어려움을 겪다	upon[on] *doing* ~하자마자

The customs officer <u>spent time</u> **interviewing** travelers. 세관원은 여행객들을 **인터뷰하는 데** <u>시간을 보냈다</u>.
The diplomats <u>were busy</u> **negotiating** trade policies. 외교관들은 무역 정책을 **협상하느라** 바빴다.

핵심 POINT 확인하기

다음 괄호 안에서 알맞은 것을 고르세요.

|핵심 POINT 슬쩍 보기|

1 Mr. Quinn recommends (purchasing / purchase) recycled products to help protect the environment.

1 recommend는 동명사를 목적어로 취하는 동사예요.

2 To prevent accidents, avoid (operating / operate) the machine near water or wet surfaces.

2 avoid는 동명사를 목적어로 취하는 동사예요.

3 Ms. Traynor is used to (dealt / dealing) with customer complaints over the phone.

3 be used to *doing*은 '~하는 것에 익숙하다'라는 뜻이에요.

4 Ms. Bora was busy (analyze / analyzing) the survey results all week.

4 be busy *doing*은 '~하느라 바쁘다'라는 뜻을 갖고 있어요.

UNIT 10

실전 감각 키우기

다음 빈칸에 알맞은 것을 고르세요.

5 The board delayed ------- the advertising firm's headquarters to New York.

(A) relocate   (B) has relocated
(C) relocating   (D) is relocating

7 Breetowne's government officials are committed to ------- the people to their fullest capacity.

(A) served   (B) serving
(C) services (D) serves

6 The construction team finished ------- a new subway exit on Forester Road.

(A) building   (B) will build
(C) build   (D) builds

8 Mr. Park had some difficulty ------- to his new job, as he had never worked in the field.

(A) adjusting   (B) adjustment
(C) adjust   (D) adjusted

동명사 vs. 명사 vs. to부정사

동명사 vs. 명사
- 동명사만 뒤에 목적어를 취할 수 있음
- 명사만 앞에 한정사와 형용사가 올 수 있음

동명사 vs. to부정사
- 동명사만 전치사의 목적어 자리에 가능, to부정사는 불가
- prefer, begin, start, continue+동명사[to부정사](같은 의미)
- remember, forget+동명사(과거 의미)/to부정사(미래 의미)

A 동명사 vs. 명사

- 동명사와 명사의 가장 큰 차이점은 동명사에 '동사적 성질'이 남아 있다는 점입니다.
  그래서 동명사는 뒤에 목적어를 취할 수 있어요.

  동명사 **Attending** <u>the meeting</u> is required for all volunteers.
  목적어
  그 회의에 참석하는 것은 모든 자원봉사자들에게 필수이다.

- 반대로, 명사 앞에는 한정사 또는 형용사가 올 수 있지만, 동명사는 이들과 함께 쓰일 수 없습니다.

  명사 He checked his passport before the **departure**. 그는 **출발** 전에 자기 여권을 확인했다.
  한정사 ~~departing~~

B 동명사 vs. to부정사

ⓐ **전치사의 목적어 자리에는 동명사만 쓰입니다.**

- 명사 역할을 하는 동명사는 전치사의 목적어로 쓰일 수 있어요.
  to부정사도 명사 역할을 할 수 있지만, 전치사의 목적어가 될 수는 없어요.

  동명사 Ms. Jones was worried <u>about</u> **imposing** strict regulations.
  전치사 ~~to impose~~
  존스 씨는 엄격한 규정을 도입하는 것에 대해 걱정했다.

ⓑ **동사의 목적어 자리에는 동명사와 to부정사가 둘 다 쓰일 수 있는 경우도 있어요.**

- 의미의 구분 없이 동명사와 to부정사 모두 목적어로 쓰는 동사가 있어요.

prefer 선호하다　begin[start] 시작하다　continue 계속하다　intend 의도하다	+동명사[to부정사]

I <u>prefer</u> **following**[**to follow**] the agenda closely. 나는 의제를 충실히 **따르는 것을** <u>선호한다</u>.

- 그러나 remember, forget 등의 동사는 목적어가 동명사일 때와 to부정사일 때 의미가 달라져요.
  동명사는 '과거'의 의미, to부정사는 '미래'의 의미라는 것을 기억하면 구분하기 쉬워요.

remember[forget] *doing* ~했던 것을 기억하다[잊다]	remember[forget] to *do* ~할 것을 기억하다[잊다]

동명사 We <u>remembered</u> **hearing** his inspiring speech.
우리는 그의 인상적인 강연을 **들었던 것을** <u>기억했다</u>.

to부정사 We <u>remembered</u> **to wear** our name tags. 우리는 이름표를 **착용할 것을** <u>기억했다</u>.

다음 괄호 안에서 알맞은 것을 고르세요.

|핵심 POINT 슬쩍 보기|

1 Management should consider (replacing / replacement) the company's old computers with new ones.

1 명사 역할을 하면서, 뒤에 목적어가 있으면 동명사 자리예요.

2 Every day, the investor reads articles about new (development / developing) in modern technology.

2 형용사의 수식을 받을 수 있는 건 동명사가 아니라 명사예요.

3 Diona Textiles, Inc., is accused of (hiring / to hire) unqualified workers to save on labor costs.

3 전치사 뒤에는 to부정사가 올 수 없어요.

4 Airline employees must not forget (to check / checking) the validity of each passenger's passport.

4 forget to do는 '~할 것을 잊다'로, forget doing은 '~했던 것을 잊다'로 해석돼요.

UNIT 10

다음 빈칸에 알맞은 것을 고르세요.

5 The county government depends on donations from local businesses for ------- historical buildings.

(A) maintaining
(B) maintain
(C) maintains
(D) maintenance

6 Starting in May, the program updates will begin ------- the newest version of the software.

(A) supportive
(B) supporting
(C) supported
(D) support

7 Applicants should submit three letters of ------- with their application forms.

(A) to recommend
(B) recommended
(C) recommendation
(D) recommending

8 A front desk employee's duties include ------- guest room reservation in the hotel's database.

(A) confirmation
(B) confirms
(C) confirming
(D) confirmed

앞에서 학습한 핵심 POINT를 떠올리며 빈칸을 완성해 보세요.

핵심 POINT 1

동명사의 개념과 형태

동명사
- 형태: 〈동사원형+-ing〉
- 문장에서 ❶ _____ 처럼 주어, 목적어, 보어 역할

동명사의 형태
- 기본형 〈동사원형+-ing〉
- 수동형 〈❷ _____ *p.p.*〉
- 부정형 〈not+동사원형+-ing〉
- 완료형 〈having *p.p.*〉

핵심 POINT 2

동명사와 함께 쓰이는 표현

동명사와 어울려 쓰이는 동사
- 〈동사+동명사〉: ❸ _____ 고려하다   avoid 피하다   finish 끝내다
  ❹ _____ 그만두다   stop 멈추다   give up 포기하다

동명사 관용 표현
- 〈to+동명사〉: be ❺ _____ to *doing* ~하는 것에 전념하다 contribute to *doing* ~하는 것에 기여하다
  looking forward to *doing* ~하는 것을 고대하다 be related to *doing* ~하는 것에 관련되다
- 기타: feel like *doing* ~하고 싶어 하다   it is no use *doing* ~해봐야 소용없다
  be ❻ _____ *doing* ~할 가치가 있다   be busy *doing* ~하느라 바쁘다

핵심 POINT 3

동명사 vs. 명사 vs. to부정사

동명사 vs. 명사
- ❼ _____ 만 뒤에 목적어를 취할 수 있음
- ❽ _____ 만 앞에 한정사와 형용사가 올 수 있음

동명사 vs. to부정사
- ❾ _____ 만 전치사의 목적어 자리에 가능, ❿ _____ 는 불가
- prefer 선호하다, begin 시작하다, start 시작하다, continue 계속하다+동명사[to부정사](같은 의미)
- remember 기억하다 forget 잊다+동명사(과거 의미)/to부정사(미래 의미)

|빈칸 정답 살짝 보기|

❶ 명사 ❷ being ❸ consider ❹ quit ❺ committed ❻ worth ❼ 동명사 ❽ 명사 ❾ 동명사 ❿ to부정사

실전 감각 키우기

다음 빈칸에 알맞은 것을 고르세요.

1 ------- deleted files is sometimes possible if you contact the IT department.

(A) Recover
(B) Recovery
(C) Recovered
(D) Recovering

2 The directors postponed ------- an additional member to their board.

(A) to appoint
(B) appointing
(C) appointed
(D) appoint

3 Ms. Peters will receive the ------- for her magazine article next Monday.

(A) paying
(B) pays
(C) payment
(D) paid

4 Employees expressed interest in ------- a foreign language in preparation for business trips overseas.

(A) learning
(B) learn
(C) to learn
(D) be learned

[5-6] Questions 5-6 refer to the following e-mail.

Dear Mr. Hayes,

I appreciate your -------- our organically-grown fruit and vegetables.
5.

My business partner informed me that you would like to meet with us at 9 A.M. on

Tuesday because you are interested in stocking our produce in your supermarket. We

look forward to ------- you on Tuesday. Let's use this time for discussing ways that our
6.

businesses can help each other.

5 (A) ordered
(B) having ordered
(C) order
(D) orders

6 (A) see
(B) being seen
(C) seeing
(D) saw

언론, 출판 및 시사 문제, 사회 현상에 관한 어휘들입니다.

publish	⑧ 출판[발행]하다, 게재하다 ㈜ publication 출판(물)	**publish** a journal 잡지를 출판하다
issue	⑲ (잡지·신문 등의) 호, 쟁점 ⑧ 발행[발급]하다	the May **issue** of *Newstime* 〈뉴스타임〉 지의 5월호
confidential	⑱ 기밀의	**confidential** documents 기밀 문서 *confident(자신감 있는, 확신하는)와 의미를 혼동하지 않도록 유의하세요.
periodical	⑲ 정기 간행물 ㈜ period 주기, 기간 　periodically 정기적으로	a management **periodical** 경영 관련 정기 간행물
subscriber	⑲ (정기) 구독자 ㈜ subscribe 구독하다 　subscription (정기) 구독(료)	be cancelled by a **subscriber** 구독자에 의해 취소되다
forecast	⑲ ⑧ 예보[예측](하다) ㈜ predict 예측하다 　foresee 예견하다, 내다보다	the weather **forecast** 일기 예보
extensive	⑱ 광범위한 ㈜ comprehensive 포괄적인	**extensive** damage 광범위한 피해
session	⑲ (특정 활동을 위한) 기간, 회의	an emergency **session** 긴급 회의
adequate	⑱ 적절한, 충분한 ㈜ inadequate 부적절한, 불충분한	an **adequate** measure 적절한 조치
initiative	⑲ 방안, 구상	environmental improvement **initiative** 환경 개선 방안
indicator	⑲ 지표 ㈜ indicate 나타내다, 보여주다	a social **indicator** 사회적인 지표
conservation	⑲ 보호 ㈜ conserve 보호하다	wildlife **conservation** 야생 동식물 보호
security	⑲ 보안, 경비 ㈜ secure 보호하다; 안전한	a **security** camera 보안 카메라
recognition	⑲ 인정 ㈜ recognize 인정하다, 깨닫다	international **recognition** 국제적인 인정
figure	⑲ 수치, 숫자 ㈜ statistics 통계	population **figures** 인구 수치
steady	⑱ 지속적인, 안정적인 ㈜ continuous 지속적인, 계속되는	a **steady** decline 지속적인 감소
annual	⑱ 연간의, 매년의 ㈜ annually 매년 　biannual 연 2회의	an **annual** budget 연간 예산
suggestion	⑲ 제안, 건의, 의견 ㈜ suggest 제안하다, 제의하다	**suggestion** for[on] a problem 문제에 대한 제안

㈜ 파생어 ㈜ 유의어 ㈜ 반의어 ㈜ 관련 어휘

어휘 확인하기

다음 괄호 안에서 알맞은 것을 고르세요.

1 The next (forecast / issue) of *Mirror Magazine* will feature an interview with a famous chef.

2 The subscription will expire after a (period / figure) of twelve months.

3 Without (adequate / published) funding, the project will have to be abandoned.

4 Mr. Newman makes a (steady / confidential) income by writing articles for newspapers.

실전 감각 키우기

다음 빈칸에 알맞은 것을 고르세요.

5 Professor Johnson will soon ------- his research paper in a popular medical journal.

(A) admit
(B) generate
(C) publish
(D) broadcast

6 CCTV cameras have been set up for ------- reasons in the neighborhood.

(A) security
(B) efficiency
(C) recognition
(D) diversity

7 Loretta Laing gained international ------- for reducing poverty in the region.

(A) indicator
(B) standard
(C) recognition
(D) council

8 ABB Network received an award for its ------- coverage of the presidential election.

(A) tentative
(B) extensive
(C) potential
(D) illegal

UNIT 10

주어진 문제를 제한시간에 맞추어 풀어 보세요.

Part 5 Choose the one word or phrase that best completes the sentence.

1. As a travel agent, Thomas Wilkinson's job involves ------- itineraries to check for scheduling problems.

   (A) to reviewing
   (B) reviewing
   (C) reviewed
   (D) review

2. Only upper management employees have access to -------- documents related to criminal backgrounds.

   (A) cautious
   (B) surrounding
   (C) confidential
   (D) limiting

3. ------- to articles from past issues are handled by the science journal's chief editor, Mr. Kang.

   (A) Corrections
   (B) Correct
   (C) Correcting
   (D) Corrected

4. Whizz Electronic Goods will continue ------- its e-reader despite the item's increasingly poor sales.

   (A) is stocking
   (B) stock
   (C) has stocked
   (D) stocking

5. Mr. Rooney was given the responsibility of ------- an ideal venue for the company banquet.

   (A) find
   (B) to find
   (C) finding
   (D) found

6. According to several studies, high levels of unemployment are clear ------- of economic decline.

   (A) indicators
   (B) operators
   (C) contractors
   (D) instructors

7. Before the end of the year, the supervisors must spend time ------- each worker's contribution to the company.

   (A) evaluate
   (B) evaluating
   (C) evaluated
   (D) being evaluated

8. Due to ------- negative feedback about the product, Mr. Lee wants to change its design.

   (A) having received
   (B) received
   (C) be receiving
   (D) has received

Part 6 Questions 9-12 refer to the following e-mail.

From: Frank Milano
To: Karl Lovett
Subject: Hospital Renovations
Date: July 2

Dear Mr. Lovett,

As you requested, I have attached the estimated cost for our upcoming project. The ------- includes the total price of the materials and the wages of all workers. This will
9.
cost a lot but it is ------- investing that amount for our hospital.
10.

Along with the installation of new facilities, our contractor suggested ------- our existing
11.
machinery. Some machinery will be serviced by engineers next week.

These changes will increase the number of patients we can serve. The work is expected to take six months to fully complete.

------- .
12.

Frank Milano

General Operations Manager, Chapman Hospital

9. (A) connection
   (B) problem
   (C) figure
   (D) procedure

10. (A) worth
    (B) forward
    (C) use
    (D) spent

11. (A) upgrading
    (B) will upgrade
    (C) to be upgraded
    (D) are being upgraded

12. (A) Feel free to send copies to my office for review.
    (B) I look forward to hearing from you about our service.
    (C) Your help in recruiting volunteers was essential.
    (D) Please let me know if you have any questions about the cost.

PART 5&6 수식어편

UNIT 11

분사

+사회 어휘(2)

우리말에서 '말하다'라는 동사를 '말하는'으로 바꾸어 형용사처럼 쓸 수 있습니다.

영어에서도 동사의 형태를 바꾸어 형용사처럼 쓸 수 있는데, 이것을 분사라고 합니다.

분사는 명사를 수식하거나 보어로 쓰이는 형용사 역할을 해요.

분사의 개념과 쓰임

분사의 개념과 형태

- 현재분사 〈동사원형+-ing〉: 능동, 진행의 의미
- 과거분사 〈동사원형+-(e)d/불규칙변화〉: 수동, 완료의 의미

분사의 쓰임과 위치

- 형용사 역할: 명사 수식, 주격·목적격 보어
- 명사를 수식할 때, 수식하는 명사의 앞이나 뒤에 위치
- 주격 보어일 때는 동사 뒤, 목적격 보어일 때는 목적어 뒤에 위치

A 분사의 개념과 형태

- 분사는 동사원형에 -ing나 -ed를 붙여 동사를 형용사처럼 쓸 수 있게 만든 것입니다.
- 동사에서 만들어져서 동사의 성질을 지니고 있으므로 뒤에 목적어, 보어, 수식어구가 올 수 있습니다.

현재분사 〈동사원형+-ing〉	과거분사 〈동사원형+-(e)d/불규칙변화〉
능동(~ 하는), 진행(~하고 있는)	수동(~해진, ~당한), 완료(~된)
the expert **providing** the estimate 견적서를 **제공하는** 전문가	the estimate **provided** by the expert 전문가에 의해 **제공된** 견적서
developing countries (지금) 개발 중인 국가들	**developed** countries (이미) 개발된 국가들

B 분사의 쓰임과 위치

- 분사는 형용사처럼 명사를 수식하거나, 주격 보어·목적격 보어로 쓰입니다.
- 명사를 수식할 때는 명사의 앞이나 뒤에, 주격 보어로 쓰일 때는 동사 뒤에, 목적격 보어로 쓰일 때는 목적어 뒤에 옵니다.

명사 앞에서 수식	the **confusing** process 혼란을 일으키는 절차
명사 뒤에서 수식	the agency **regulating** the industry 그 산업을 **규제하는** 기관
주격 보어	The investors felt **confused**. 투자자들은 **혼란스럽다고** 느꼈다.
목적격 보어	The government had the industry **regulated**. 정부는 그 산업이 **규제받도록** 했다.

- 현재분사나 과거분사 중 하나의 형태가 굳어져 형용사처럼 쓰이는 관용 표현도 있어요.

an **experienced** applicant 경력있는 지원자	a **surrounding** area 인근 지역
existing equipment 기존의 장비	**preferred** means 선호되는 수단
an **attached** file 첨부 파일	a **limited** budget 한정된 예산
a **complicated** process 복잡한 절차	an **appointed** member 임명된 회원
a **traveling** time 이동 시간	a **scheduled** time 예정된 시각
a **rewarding** career 보람 있는 직업	a **lasting** impression 지속적인 인상
remaining work 남은 일	a **challenging** problem 어려운 문제

핵심 POINT 확인하기

다음 괄호 안에서 알맞은 것을 고르세요.

1 Clients can choose their (preferred / prefer) means of communication between telephone and e-mail.

2 Mr. Davids will attend an international economics conference (begin / beginning) next Monday.

3 Selling the product will become (challenged / challenging) when the advertising campaign ends.

4 Mr. Pirelli had his consumer study (publishes / published) last week.

|핵심 POINT 슬쩍 보기|

1 분사는 형용사 역할을 하기 때문에 명사를 수식할 수 있어요.

2 분사는 명사를 뒤에서도 수식할 수 있어요.

3 분사는 형용사 역할을 하기 때문에 주격 보어로도 쓰여요.

4 목적격 보어 자리에도 분사가 올 수 있어요.

실전 감각 키우기

다음 빈칸에 알맞은 것을 고르세요.

5 After correcting some errors, Bennet Advertising Inc. sent the ------- proposal to all of its clients.

(A) revise (B) revises
(C) revising (D) revised

6 Management is considering holding 빈출 training sessions ------- on customer service skills.

(A) focus (B) focusing
(C) have focused (D) will focus

7 The city's traffic laws have become ------- over the past few years.

(A) is complicated (B) complicated
(C) complicates (D) to complicate

8 Alfresco Craftwork, a furniture maker ------- in outdoor furnishings, will open another branch.

(A) specializing (B) specializes
(C) will specialize (D) is specializing

UNIT 11

2 현재분사 vs. 과거분사

현재분사와 과거분사의 구분
- 현재분사: 명사와 분사의 관계가 능동인 경우
- 과거분사: 명사와 분사의 관계가 수동인 경우
- 목적어가 있으면 현재분사, 없으면 과거분사

감정과 관련된 동사의 현재분사와 과거분사
- 수식 받는 명사가 감정을 유발하는 주체이면 현재분사, 감정을 느끼는 대상이면 과거분사를 씀
- 사물은 주로 현재분사와, 사람은 주로 과거분사와 쓰임

A 현재분사와 과거분사의 구분

ⓐ 현재분사: 명사와 분사의 관계가 능동인 경우
- 수식 받는 명사가 분사가 나타내는 행위를 직접 행하는 주체이면 '능동' 관계이므로 현재분사를 씁니다.

명사 수식 They are searching for a **motivating** incentive.
그들은 **동기를 부여하는** 장려책을 찾고 있다. → incentive는 '동기를 부여하는' 주체

주격 보어 The outcome of the negotiations was **surprising**.
그 협상의 결과는 **놀라웠다**. → outcome은 '놀랍게 하는' 주체

ⓑ 과거분사: 명사와 분사의 관계가 수동인 경우
- 수식 받는 명사가 분사가 나타내는 행위를 당하는 대상이면 '수동' 관계이므로 과거분사를 씁니다.

명사 수식 The article **completed** by Ms. Ross has many errors.
로스 씨에 의해 **완성된** 기사에 오류가 많다. → article은 '완성된' 대상

목적격 보어 The artist left the painting **unfinished** in his studio.
그 예술가는 작품을 **미완성된 상태로** 그의 작업실에 두었다. → painting은 '미완성된' 대상

ⓒ 목적어 유무 여부에 따른 구별
- 명사를 뒤에서 수식할 때 현재분사 뒤에는 목적어가 올 수 있지만 과거분사 뒤에는 올 수 없어요.

현재분사	The man **signing** the contract is my boss. 계약서에 **서명하는** 사람은 내 상사이다. 목적어
과거분사	The deal **made** yesterday is for selling the property. 수식어 어제 **맺은** 계약은 부동산 매각에 관한 것이다.

B 감정과 관련된 동사의 현재분사와 과거분사
- 감정을 나타내는 동사들은 분사 형태 자체가 형용사로 굳어져 쓰이는 경우가 많습니다.
- 수식 받는 명사가 감정을 유발하는 주체이면 현재분사, 감정을 느끼는 대상이면 과거분사를 써요.

interesting — interested	fascinating — fascinated	surprising — surprised
흥미로운 흥미를 느낀	흥미진진한 흥미를 느낀	놀라운 놀란
satisfying — satisfied	concerning — concerned	disappointing — disappointed
만족할 만한 만족스러운	걱정스러운 걱정하는	실망스러운 실망한

The audience found the presentation **interesting**. 청중들은 발표가 **흥미롭다고** 생각했다.
The presenter kept the audience **interested**. 발표자는 청중들이 계속 **흥미를 느끼도록** 했다.

핵심 POINT 확인하기

다음 괄호 안에서 알맞은 것을 고르세요.

|핵심 POINT 슬쩍 보기|

1 The new advertising campaign is a (contributing / contributed) factor to Hinxon's recent success.

1 분사와 수식 받는 명사가 능동 관계에 있으면 현재분사를 써요.

2 The figures released by the firm were lower than the (anticipating / anticipated) annual earnings.

2 분사와 수식 받는 명사가 수동 관계에 있으면 과거분사를 써요.

3 The foreman noticed him (operating / operated) the factory machinery in the wrong way.

3 명사를 뒤에서 수식할 때, 현재 분사 뒤에만 목적어가 올 수 있어요.

4 The publisher is (surprising / surprised) by the increasing number of *Planters Magazine* subscribers.

4 놀라움을 주는 주체이면 surprising, 놀라움을 느끼는 대상이면 surprised를 써요.

UNIT 11

실전 감각 키우기

다음 빈칸에 알맞은 것을 고르세요.

5 Chairman Park will review the ------- budget for the petroleum firm's expansion program.

(A) propose   (B) proposing
(C) proposes   (D) proposed

7 Dominic Weston won the Independent Cinema Award for his ------- documentary.

(A) fascinating   (B) fascinated
(C) fascinate   (D) fascination

6 The Odeon Theater is pleased to announce a new film festival ------- the work of local filmmakers.

(A) feature   (B) features
(C) featuring   (D) featured

8 The staff of the production department is ------- with the new equipment.

(A) satisfied   (B) satisfy
(C) to satisfy   (D) satisfying

3 분사구문

분사구문의 개념
- 〈접속사+주어+동사〉 → 〈(접속사)+분사〉
- 문장에서 시간, 이유 등을 나타내는 부사 역할을 함

분사구문의 형태
- 주절의 주어와 분사가 능동 관계면 현재분사, 수동 관계면 과거분사
- 분사구문이 주절의 시제보다 앞서면 〈having (been)+*p.p.*〉

A 분사구문의 개념

- 분사구문이란 〈접속사+주어+동사〉 형태의 부사절을 분사 형태의 부사구로 간결하게 만든 것입니다.
- 분사구문은 시간, 이유 등 다양한 의미의 부사 역할을 합니다.

① When ② I ③ unpacked the goods, I broke a plate. ↓ **(When) Unpacking** the goods, I broke a plate. 제품을 **꺼낼 때**, 나는 접시 하나를 깨뜨렸다.	① 부사절의 접속사를 생략합니다. ② 부사절과 주절의 주어가 같으므로 부사절의 주어를 생략합니다. ③ 능동태 동사 unpacked를 〈동사원형+-ing〉 형태의 현재분사로 만듭니다.

- 수동태 동사는 〈being *p.p.*〉 형태가 되는데 being은 생략하고 *p.p.*만 남아요.
- 주로 접속사를 생략하지만, when ~할 때, as ~ 대로, after ~ 후에 등의 접속사가 올 경우, 정확한 의미 전달을 위해 남겨두기도 해요.

  When opening the business, he recruited investors. **사업을 시작할 때**, 그는 투자자들을 모집했다.

B 분사구문의 형태

능동형 〈동사원형+-ing〉	• 분사구문의 분사와 주절의 주어 사이의 관계가 능동이면 현재분사를 씁니다. **Briefing** them, he pointed to the board. = As he briefed them, … 그들에게 **요약 설명을 하면서**, 그는 칠판을 가리켰다. (요약 설명을 한 사람 = 그)
수동형 〈*p.p.*〉	• 분사구문의 분사와 주절의 주어 사이의 관계가 수동이면 과거분사를 씁니다. **Briefed** at the meeting, they knew the procedure. = Because they were briefed at the meeting, … 회의에서 **요약 설명을 들었기 때문에**, 그들은 절차에 대해 알았다. (요약 설명을 들은 사람 = 그들)
완료형 〈Having+*p.p.*〉	• 주절의 시제보다 분사구문의 내용이 먼저 일어난 경우, 완료형을 씁니다. 〈having+*p.p.*〉는 '~하고 난 후'로 해석합니다. **Having watched** the news, I knew about the problem. = Since I had watched the news, … 뉴스를 **보고 난 후라서**, 나는 그 문제에 대해 알고 있었다. (뉴스를 본 것이 문제에 대해 안 것보다 먼저)
완료수동형 〈Having been+*p.p.*〉	• 〈having been+*p.p.*〉는 '~된 후'로 해석합니다. **Having been briefed** at the meeting, they knew the procedure. = Because they have been briefed at the meeting, … 회의에서 **요약 설명을 들은 후라서**, 그들은 절차에 대해 알았다.

핵심 POINT 확인하기

다음 괄호 안에서 알맞은 것을 고르세요.

|핵심 POINT 슬쩍 보기|

1 (Creation / Creating) several new dishes, Chef Gordon hopes to improve the restaurant's menu.

1 〈접속사+주어+동사〉의 부사절 대신, 간단히 분사구문을 쓸 수 있어요.

2 While (discussing / discussed) the library renovation, Mr. Norris suggested that the budget is too low.

2 분사구문에서 분사와 주절의 주어가 능동의 관계이면 현재분사를 써요.

3 (Repairing / Repaired) only last week, the photocopier should be working perfectly.

3 분사구문에서 수동의 관계는 과거분사로 나타내요.

4 (Provided / Having provided) good service to our company for five years, Ettrick Office Supplies will remain as our main supplier.

4 분사구문의 내용이 주절의 내용보다 앞서 일어난 경우에는 완료형인 〈having+p.p.〉를 써요.

UNIT 11

실전 감각 키우기

다음 빈칸에 알맞은 것을 고르세요.

5 ------- more than one thousand salespeople nationwide, Altus Telecom is the largest firm in its field.

(A) Employ (B) Employing
(C) Employed (D) Employment

6 ------- to work over the weekend, the project team was able to finish the proposal before the deadline.

(A) Instruct (B) Instructs
(C) Instructing (D) Instructed

7 ------- inspecting the contents prior to shipping, our staff always checks for damaged items.

(A) Because (B) Despite
(C) When (D) Yet

8 ---------- the new member to the council, the chairperson began discussing the first item on the agenda.

(A) Introduced (B) Will introduce
(C) Has introduced (D) Having introduced

앞에서 학습한 핵심 POINT를 떠올리며 빈칸을 완성해 보세요.

핵심 POINT 1

분사의 개념과 쓰임

분사의 개념과 형태

- 현재분사 〈동사원형+-ing〉: ❶_____, 진행의 의미
- 과거분사 〈동사원형+-(e)d/불규칙변화〉: ❷_____, 완료의 의미

분사의 쓰임과 위치

- ❸_____ 역할: 명사 수식, 주격·목적격 보어
- 명사를 수식할 때, 수식하는 명사의 앞이나 뒤에 위치
- 주격 보어일 때는 ❹_____ 뒤, 목적격 보어일 때는 목적어 뒤에 위치

핵심 POINT 2

현재분사 vs. 과거분사

현재분사와 과거분사의 구분

- ❺_____분사: 명사와 분사의 관계가 능동인 경우
- ❻_____분사: 명사와 분사의 관계가 수동인 경우
- 목적어가 있으면 현재분사, 없으면 과거분사

감정과 관련된 동사의 현재분사와 과거분사

- 수식 받는 명사가 감정을 유발하는 주체이면 ❼_____분사,
  감정을 느끼는 대상이면 ❽_____분사를 씀
- 사물은 주로 현재분사와, 사람은 주로 과거분사와 쓰임

핵심 POINT 3

분사구문

분사구문의 형태와 개념

- 〈접속사+주어+동사〉 → 〈(접속사)+❾_____〉
- 문장에서 시간, 이유 등을 나타내는 ❿_____ 역할을 함

분사구문의 형태

- 주절의 주어와 분사가 능동 관계면 현재분사, 수동 관계면 과거분사
- 분사구문이 주절의 시제보다 앞서면 〈⓫_____ (been)+*p.p.*〉

|빈칸 정답 살짝 보기|

❶ 능동 ❷ 수동 ❸ 형용사 ❹ 동사 ❺ 현재 ❻ 과거 ❼ 현재 ❽ 과거 ❾ 분사 ❿ 부사 ⓫ having

실전 감각 키우기

다음 빈칸에 알맞은 것을 고르세요.

1 The new audio equipment was severely ------- during the delivery.

(A) damage
(B) damaging
(C) damages
(D) damaged

2 Before ------- a physical therapy session, a patient must first be examined by a doctor.

(A) will schedule
(B) scheduling
(C) scheduled
(D) is scheduling

3 The marketing team's survey received an ------- number of responses from potential customers.

(A) overwhelming
(B) overwhelmed
(C) overwhelms
(D) overwhelm

4 Once -------, your order of mechanical components will be delivered to your premises.

(A) confirm
(B) confirmed
(C) confirming
(D) to confirm

[5-6] Questions 5-6 refer to the following article.

Hillman Apartments Makes Changes after Fire

Due to last week's fire at Hillman Apartments, the building owners have decided to implement stricter safety measures. As indicated in the safety officer's report, the owners must conduct regular fire drills and improve the signs ------- people to exits.
5.

Tenants are ------- as they are still unsure which route to take in case of a fire. These
6.
new measures should help them feel safer.

5 (A) director
(B) directed
(C) directing
(D) direct

6 (A) concerning
(B) concern
(C) concerns
(D) concerned

UNIT 11

사회를 구성하는 크고 작은 공동체 및 정부, 조직, 그리고 정치와 관련된 어휘들입니다.

conference	명 총회, 학회 관 seminar 세미나	attend a **conference** 총회에 참석하다 hold a **conference** 학회를 열다
conflict	명 갈등, 충돌 동 상충하다 관 argument 논쟁	handle **conflicts** 갈등을 조정하다 **conflicting** opinions 상충되는 의견
concern	명 동 우려(하다), 걱정(하다)	a specific **concern** 구체적인 우려 be **concerned** about a slowdown 침체에 대해 걱정하다
conventional	형 관습적인, 관례적인 파 convention 관습, 관례, 대회, 총회	a **conventional** manner 관습적인 방식
reputation	명 명성, 평판 관 renowned 잘 알려진	gain a **reputation** 명성을 얻다
voluntary	형 자발적인 파 volunteer 자원봉사자; 자원하다	a **voluntary** donation 자발적인 기부
government	명 정부 파 govern 통치하다	a **government** policy 정부 방침 **government** officials 공무원
comply with	동 따르다, 응하다 파 compliance 준수, 따름	**comply with** new standards 새로운 기준을 따르다
declare	동 선언하다 파 declaration 선언, 단언	**declare** a state of emergency 비상 사태를 선언하다
constitute	동 구성하다 파 constitution 구조, 헌법	**constitute** a committee 위원회를 구성하다
institution	명 기관, 협회 파 institute 기관[협회]; 도입하다	a national **institution** 국가 기관
charge	동 요금을 청구하다 명 요금, 사용료, 책임, 담당	in **charge** of an organization 기관을 담당하고 있는
election	명 선거 파 elect 선출하다 유 vote 투표(하다)	a presidential **election** 대통령 선거
enforce	동 (법률 등을) 시행하다, 집행하다 파 enforcement 시행, 집행	**enforce** a rule 규정을 시행하다
support	명 동 지지(하다) 반 oppose 반대하다	**support** a policy 그 정책을 지지하다
authority	명 권위, 권한 파 authorize 재가[인가]하다	a governor's **authority** 주지사의 권한 *health authorities(보건 당국)처럼 '당국, 기관'의 뜻으로 쓰일 때는 복수형을 써요.
reform	명 동 개선(하다) 유 improve 개선하다 　 restore 회복시키다, 복구하다	**reform** a system 제도를 개선하다
delegate	명 대표자 동 위임하다 파 delegation (조직 등의) 대표단	meet a **delegate** 대표를 만나다

파 파생어　유 유의어　반 반의어　관 관련 어휘

어휘 확인하기

다음 괄호 안에서 알맞은 것을 고르세요.

1 The Reika Organization holds more fundraising events than (compliant / conventional) charities.

2 The road development project was paid for by (delegate / government) funds.

3 Workers must (comply / constitute) with the safety regulations of the factory floor.

4 The lawyer's client was not (charged / enforced) for the first consultation.

실전 감각 키우기

다음 빈칸에 알맞은 것을 고르세요.

5 The local government has ------- a state of emergency in the town due to the flooding.

(A) declared
(B) reformed
(C) enlarged
(D) prohibited

6 The mayor of Garrity has gained a ------- for listening closely to the concerns of citizens.

(A) destination
(B) renewal
(C) reputation
(D) transfer

7 The city council tried to resolve a ------- between local homeowners and Wickham Construction.

(A) combination
(B) prevention
(C) following
(D) conflict

8 Castleford locals largely ------- the plan to transform the parking lot into a park.

(A) suppose
(B) propose
(C) support
(D) reform

UNIT 11

주어진 문제를 제한시간에 맞추어 풀어 보세요.

Part 5 Choose the one word or phrase that best completes the sentence.

1. The ------- warranty card must be completed and registered within thirty days of purchase.

   (A) enclosing
   (B) to enclose
   (C) be enclosed
   (D) enclosed

2. The governor expressed his ------- about the high level of pollution in the area.

   (A) stability
   (B) intrigue
   (C) concern
   (D) need

3. Unfortunately, the exercise machine was shipped without some vital parts, -------- it useless.

   (A) made
   (B) making
   (C) will make
   (D) has made

4. Ms. Arnett was ------- by the lack of features on the digital camera, considering the price that she paid.

   (A) disappointed
   (B) disappointedly
   (C) disappointing
   (D) disappoint

5. By following the guidelines ------ in the user manual, you can prolong the life of the product.

   (A) outlining
   (B) outlined
   (C) outline
   (D) outlines

6. In order to provide the local community with a greater sense of identity, the Winterborne Historical Society was ------- in 1946.

   (A) constituted
   (B) limited
   (C) explored
   (D) diminished

7. Staff members are reminded to turn off the air conditioning when ------- the meeting room.

   (A) exit
   (B) exited
   (C) exits
   (D) exiting

8. Due to an increase in thefts, tourists are ------- to watch their belongings at all times.

   (A) advising
   (B) advised
   (C) advisor
   (D) advise

Part 6 Questions 9-12 refer to the following article.

Harington Set to Begin Local Clean-up

10 May—Harington Council has announced the launch of a new environmental project, Clean Up Harington. This project aims to improve the facilities of the town for all residents. It will be carried out by community members through ------- work.
 9.

Workers will first turn their attention to Blighty Park, where they will focus on trash removal from the pond and ------- area. This park used to be a beautiful, clean area
 10.
------- by many Harington residents. ------- .
 11.   12.

In a recent interview, the mayor told of his delight at receiving local support for the project. He said, "We consider providing the town with these services extremely important."

---

9. (A) consistent
    (B) conventional
    (C) previous
    (D) voluntary

10. (A) surround
    (B) surrounding
    (C) surrounded
    (D) have surrounded

11. (A) enjoy
    (B) enjoying
    (C) enjoyed
    (D) to enjoy

12. (A) Safety is a top priority for the city's parks.
    (B) The department is considering planting flowers.
    (C) However, it has become dirty due to the lack of regular maintenance.
    (D) Alternatively, there are indoor spaces for various activities.

PART 5&6 연결어·구문편

UNIT 12

접속사와 명사절 접속사
+사회 어휘(3)

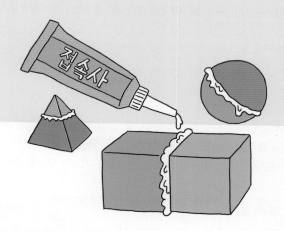

접속사는 단어와 단어, 구와 구, 절과 절을 이어 주는 역할을 하는
접착제 같은 말입니다. 접속사를 알면 긴 문장의 구조도 쉽게 파악할 수 있어요.
명사절은 문장 안에서 명사의 역할을 하는 절을 말합니다.

---

1 접속사의 개념과 종류

2 등위접속사

3 종속접속사 – 명사절접속사

+ 사회 어휘(3)

1 접속사의 개념과 종류

Blair and I
were surprised.

접속사의 개념
- 접속사: 단어와 단어, 구와 구, 절과 절을 연결

접속사의 종류
- 등위접속사: 문법적으로 서로 같은 성격의 단어, 구, 절을 대등하게
  연결하는 접속사
- 종속접속사: 명사절, 부사절, 형용사절을 이끌어 주절과 연결하는
  접속사

A 접속사의 개념

- 문장 내에서 단어와 단어, 구와 구, 절과 절을 연결하는 역할을 하는 것을 접속사라고 합니다.

[단어+단어]	Blair **and** I were surprised at the number of participants. 블레어와 나는 참석자 수에 놀랐다.
[구+구]	The museum director **or** a volunteer guide will show you the exhibition. 미술관 담당자나 자원봉사 가이드가 그 전시회를 보여 줄 것이다.
[절+절]	**Before** the reception started, we set up the stage. 연회가 시작되기 **전에**, 우리는 무대를 설치했다.

B 접속사의 종류

- 등위접속사는 문법적으로 서로 같은 성격의 단어, 구, 절을 대등하게 연결합니다.
- 종속접속사는 주절과 종속절(명사절, 부사절, 형용사절)을 연결합니다.
  종속접속사에는 명사절을 이끄는 명사절 접속사, 부사절을 이끄는 부사절 접속사, 형용사절을 이끄는 관계
  사가 있습니다.

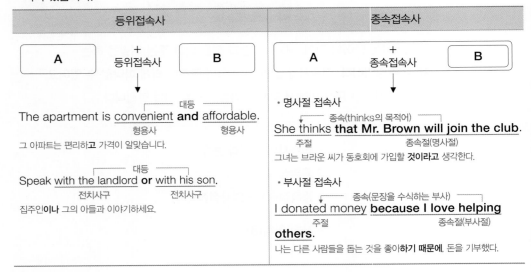

핵심 POINT 확인하기

다음 괄호 안에서 알맞은 것을 고르세요.

|핵심 POINT 슬쩍 보기|

1 Vero Insurance promotes its products through e-mails (of / and) calls.

1 단어와 단어를 연결할 때에는 접속사가 필요해요.

2 He suggested meeting at the concert venue (its / or) at the nearest station.

2 접속사는 구와 구를 연결할 수 도 있어요.

3 We wanted to attend the lecture, (but / to) the tickets were sold out.

3 절과 절을 연결하는 것은 접속 사예요.

4 New supervisors think (that / but) managing people in organizations is a challenging task.

4 등위접속사 but은 대등한 절 만 연결할 수 있어요.

실전 감각 키우기

다음 빈칸에 알맞은 것을 고르세요.

5 Ms. Smith applied for a home loan, ------- her application was approved by the bank.

(A) during   (B) through
(C) and   (D) over

6 Please sign up online ------- go to the HR department to register for the training.

(A) ever   (B) though
(C) at   (D) or

7 Market research shows ------- young consumers are spending more on travel these days.

(A) this   (B) that
(C) for   (D) and

8 Ms. Wu didn't want to take the medication ------- she was concerned about its side effects.

(A) just   (B) following
(C) from   (D) because

UNIT 12

2 등위접속사

핵심 POINT

등위접속사의 개념과 종류
- 문법적으로 대등한 두 요소를 연결
- so와 for는 결과 절만 연결

상관접속사: 짝을 이루는 등위접속사
- both A and B: 복수 취급
- either A or B, neither A nor B, not only A but also B: B에 수일치

A 등위접속사의 개념과 종류

- 등위접속사는 문법적으로 대등한 성격의 두 요소를 연결합니다.

첨가: and 그리고	선택: or 또는, 그렇지 않으면	대조: but 그러나, 하지만
이유: for 왜냐하면	결과: so 그래서	대조: yet 그렇지만, 그런데도

- 대등한 두 요소가 등위접속사로 나란히 연결된 것을 '병렬 구조'라고 합니다.

The new banquet hall is <u>spacious</u> **yet** <u>expensive</u>. 새로운 연회장은 넓지**만** 비싸다.
형용사 단어 · 형용사 단어

He is interested in <u>establishing a charity</u> **or** <u>donating money</u>.
동명사구 · 동명사구

그는 자선단체를 설립하**거나** 돈을 기부하는 데 관심이 있다.

- 다른 등위접속사와 달리 so와 for는 절과 절만을 연결할 수 있습니다.

<u>The residents were pleased</u>, **for** <u>the city held outdoor events in the summer</u>.
절 · 절

주민들은 만족스러워 했는데, 시에서 여름에 야외 행사를 개최했기 **때문이다.**

B 상관접속사: 짝을 이루는 등위접속사

- 상관접속사는 등위접속사의 일종으로, 두 단어 이상이 짝을 이루는 형태의 접속사예요.
- 상관접속사로 연결된 두 요소도 '병렬 구조'가 되어야 합니다.

both A and B A와 B 둘 다	either A or B A나 B 둘 중 하나
not A but B A가 아니라 B	neither A nor B A도 B도 둘 다 아닌
not only A but (also) B[B as well as A] A뿐만 아니라 B도	

They should examine **both** <u>the exterior</u> **and** <u>the interior</u>. 그들은 외부**와** 내부 **둘 다** 점검해야 한다.
Some participants **neither** <u>completed the form</u> **nor** <u>submitted it to the staff</u>.
일부 참가자들은 양식을 작성**하지도**, 그것을 직원에게 제출**하지도 않았다.**

- 상관접속사로 연결된 말이 주어로 쓰일 때, (both) A and B를 제외하고는 모두 B에 동사를 수일치 시켜요.

(both) A and B	복수 취급	**Both** <u>the ceiling</u> **and** <u>the wall</u> <u>need</u> to be repainted. 천장**과** 벽 **모두** 페인트칠을 다시 해야 한다.
either A or B neither A nor B not only A but (also) B = B as well as A	B에 수일치	**Neither** <u>the managers</u> **nor** <u>the CEO</u> <u>favors</u> the idea. 관리자들**과** 대표이사 **둘 다** 그 생각을 선호하지 **않는다.**

핵심 POINT 확인하기

다음 괄호 안에서 알맞은 것을 고르세요.

1 The town's household trash is collected and (recycling / recycled) properly.

2 Mr. Lee's flight arrived late, (but / so) he missed the ceremony.

3 Quality inspections must be conducted (either / both) closely and consistently.

4 Either the security guards or the manager (lock / locks) the main entrance so that no one enters after 6 P.M.

|핵심 POINT 슬쩍 보기|

1 등위접속사 and로 연결되는 두 성분은 문법적으로 대등해야 해요.

2 so는 결과를 나타내는 접속사로, 절과 절을 연결해요.

3 상관접속사 either는 or와, both는 and와 짝을 이뤄요.

4 either A or B가 주어로 쓰이면, 수일치는 B에 해 줘요.

실전 감각 키우기

다음 빈칸에 알맞은 것을 고르세요.

5 In most stores in Lilletowne Outlet, customers can pay in cash ------- with credit cards.

(A) or (B) up
(C) nor (D) if

6 The reading club usually meets in ------- the employee lounge or the cafeteria.

(A) still (B) either
(C) both (D) neither

7 Mr. Nelson's position involves ------- news articles and generating original content for the magazine.

(A) revising (B) revised
(C) revise (D) to revise

8 Neither audio recording equipment nor video cameras ------- in the theater.

(A) allowing (B) is allowed
(C) are allowed (D) to allow

UNIT 12

3 종속접속사 – 명사절 접속사

핵심 POINT

Whether the price will increase is unknown.

명사절과 명사절 접속사
- 명사절: 명사처럼 주어, 목적어, 보어 역할을 하는 절
- 명사절 접속사: 명사절을 이끄는 접속사(that, whether, if 등)

명사절 접속사의 쓰임
- that: 주어, 동사의 목적어, 보어 역할의 명사절을 이끎
- whether: 주어, 목적어, 보어 역할의 명사절을 이끎
- if: 동사의 목적어, 보어 역할의 명사절만 이끎

A 명사절과 명사절 접속사

- 명사절은 명사처럼 주어, 목적어, 보어 역할을 하는 절입니다.
  이런 명사절을 이끄는 접속사를 '명사절 접속사'라고 하며, that, whether, if 등이 대표적입니다.

  I can't believe **that** he got injured. 나는 **그가 부상당했다는 것을** 믿을 수 없다. (목적어 역할)
  ────────명사절────────

B 명사절 접속사의 쓰임

ⓐ that: ~라는 것

주어	**That** the store needs more employees is certain. 매장에 직원이 더 필요하다는 것은 확실하다. = It is certain **that** the store needs more employees. (참고) 주어가 긴 경우 가주어 it을 사용하여 긴 주어를 뒤로 보내요.
목적어	He knows **(that)** he should pay the bill. 그는 **청구액을 지불해야 한다는 것을** 알고 있다. (참고) that절이 목적어일 때 접속사 that은 생략 가능합니다.
보어	Her hope is **that** she can move in next week. 그녀의 희망은 **그녀가 다음 주에 이사 가는 것이다.**

(참고) 주절에 아래와 같은 〈요청·제안·주장·권유〉를 나타내는 동사가 쓰이면 목적어로 쓰인 that절 안의 동사는 주절의 시제와 상관없이 〈(should) + 동사원형〉을 씁니다.

insist 주장하다	request 요청하다	demand 요구하다	suggest 제안하다	recommend 추천하다

The legal consultant <u>suggested</u> **that** some terms in the agreement <u>(should) be</u> changed.
법률 컨설턴트가 계약서 상의 몇 가지 조항이 변경되어야 한다고 말했다.

ⓑ whether, if: ~인지 아닌지

주어	**Whether** the price will increase is unknown. 가격이 오를지 안 오를지는 알려져 있지 않다. (참고) 주어로 쓰일 때는 if가 아닌 whether만을 쓰는 것이 원칙입니다.
목적어	She will decide **whether[if]** the treatment is necessary. 그녀는 **치료가 필요한지 여부를** 결정할 것이다. The shop's owner is still talking about **whether** the operating hours are too short or <u>not</u>. 매장 주인은 **영업 시간이 너무 짧은지 아닌지에** 관해 여전히 얘기하는 중이다. (참고) 전치사의 목적어일 때 역시 whether만 쓸 수 있습니다.
보어	My concern is **whether** the expenses will increase. 내 관심사는 **비용이 오를지 아닐지**이다.

(참고) if와 달리, whether는 뒤에 절이 아닌 to부정사구가 와서 〈whether+to do〉의 형태로도 쓰입니다.

He hasn't decided **whether** to take out a lease. 그는 **임대계약을 맺을지 말지를** 결정하지 않았다.

200 UNIT 12 접속사와 명사절 접속사

핵심 POINT 확인하기

다음 괄호 안에서 알맞은 것을 고르세요.

1 The delivery company assured (and / that) the equipment would arrive at the client's office tomorrow.

2 The belief of the chairman of the board is (that / if) more foreign investment is needed.

3 Mr. Tao wonders (that / if) buying a house is better than renting one.

4 Wayne cannot decide (whether / if) to enroll in online courses or study at a local institute.

|핵심 POINT 슬쩍 보기|

1 동사 assured의 목적어가 필요하므로 명사절 접속사가 와야 해요.

2 명사절 접속사 중에서 '~라는 것'이란 의미를 나타내는 것은 that이에요.

3 if와 whether는 '~인지 아닌지'라는 불확실한 상황을 나타내요.

4 whether의 경우, 〈whether to do〉의 형태로도 쓸 수 있어요.

실전 감각 키우기

다음 빈칸에 알맞은 것을 고르세요.

5 The secretary will ask ------- the director can join the video conference tomorrow afternoon.

(A) if
(B) despite
(C) to
(D) however

6 Members of the homeowners association will discuss ------- to plant some trees around the parking lot.

(A) about
(B) whether
(C) after
(D) that

7 It is imperative ------- workers wear protective gear at all times on the project site.

(A) whether
(B) beyond
(C) that
(D) each

8 A poll conducted by the newspaper indicates ------- most voters are in favor of the proposal.

(A) like
(B) that
(C) but
(D) them

앞에서 학습한 핵심 POINT를 떠올리며 빈칸을 완성해 보세요.

핵심 POINT 1 — 접속사의 개념과 종류

접속사의 개념
- 접속사: 단어와 단어, 구와 구, 절과 절을 **❶**_____

접속사의 종류
- **❷**_____ : 문법적으로 서로 같은 성격의 단어, 구, 절을 대등하게 연결하는 접속사
- **❸**_____ : 명사절, 부사절, 형용사절을 이끌어 주절과 연결하는 접속사

핵심 POINT 2 — 등위접속사

등위접속사의 개념과 종류
- 문법적으로 **❹**_____한 두 요소를 연결
- so 그래서와 for 왜냐하면는 절과 절만 연결

상관접속사: 짝을 이루는 접속사
- both A and B A와 B 둘 다: **❺**_____ 취급
- **❻**_____ A or B A나 B 둘 중 하나, **❼**_____ A nor B A도 B도 둘 다 아닌, not only A but also B A뿐만 아니라 B도: B에 수일치

핵심 POINT 3 — 종속접속사 – 명사절 접속사

명사절과 명사절 접속사
- 명사절: 명사처럼 주어, 목적어, 보어 역할을 하는 절
- 명사절 접속사: **❽**_____을 이끄는 접속사(that, whether, if 등)

명사절 접속사의 쓰임
- that ~라는 것: 주어, 동사의 목적어, **❾**_____ 역할의 명사절을 이끎
- whether ~인지 아닌지: 주어, 목적어, 보어 역할의 명사절을 이끎
- if ~인지 아닌지: **❿**_____의 목적어, 보어 역할의 명사절만 이끎

실전 감각 키우기

다음 빈칸에 알맞은 것을 고르세요.

1 Rice ------- corn are the two main agricultural products exported by ACM Corporation.

(A) other
(B) and
(C) either
(D) likewise

2 Doeville Repairs will temporarily shut down, ------- the business is relocating to the commercial district.

(A) or
(B) through
(C) behind
(D) for

3 Doctors recommend ------- walking and biking as ways to have a healthier lifestyle.

(A) neither
(B) alike
(C) both
(D) none

4 Clients must specify ------- they will pay for the magazine subscription annually or quarterly.

(A) whether
(B) but also
(C) both
(D) neither

[5-6] Questions 5-6 refer to the following e-mail.

Dear Ms. Hernandez,

As you know, there has been a series of avoidable accidents at our company recently.

To address this issue, not only the president but also the directors ------- to form a
5.
workplace health and safety committee.

We believe ------- a group of members should meet regularly to assess current
6.
conditions and give recommendations for improving the working environment.

Please let me know how we can start organizing this.

5 (A) agrees
(B) to agree
(C) agreeable
(D) have agreed

6 (A) if
(B) so
(C) that
(D) what

무역, 경기 및 경제에 관한 어휘들입니다.

decrease	명 동 감소(하다)	a **decrease** in exports 수출의 감소 *increase(증가)와 마찬가지로 뒤에 전치사 in과 자주 쓰여요.
compete	동 경쟁하다 파 competition 경쟁 competitive 경쟁적인, 경쟁력 있는	**compete** in the market 시장에서 경쟁하다
cooperation	명 협력, 협조 파 cooperate 협력하다	international **cooperation** 국제 협력 *접두사 co-에는 '함께, 공동'이라는 의미가 있어요.
investment	명 투자 파 invest 투자하다 investor 투자자	foreign **investment** 해외 투자 make **investments** 투자하다
customized	형 맞춤형의, 맞춤제작한 파 customize 맞춤제작하다	a **customized** car 맞춤형 자동차
remarkable	형 두드러진 파 remark 언급(하다)	**remarkable** success 두드러진 성공
factor	명 요인, 요소	a key **factor** in a decision 결정상의 주요 요인
strategic	형 전략적인 파 strategy 전략	**strategic** investment 전략적인 투자
immediate	형 즉각의, 즉시의, 당면한 파 immediately 즉각적으로	**immediate** measures 즉각적인 조치
consumption	명 소비(량) 파 consume 소비하다 consumer 소비자	encourage **consumption** 소비를 장려하다
enhance	동 향상시키다 파 enhancement 향상, 개선	**enhance** the quality of life 삶의 질을 향상시키다
stable	형 안정된 유 secure 안전한, 확실한	a **stable** economic situation 안정된 경제 상황
property	명 부동산, 재산, 소유물 유 real estate 부동산 (중개업)	the **property** market 부동산 시장 personal **property** 개인 소유물
corporation	명 (대)기업	a private **corporation** 사기업 *기업명 뒤의 Corp.는 corporation 또는 corporal의 줄임말이에요.
excessive	형 과도한 파 exceed 초과하다, 넘어서다 excess 초과(량), 과도	**excessive** regulations 과도한 규제
significant	형 중요한, 상당한 파 significance 중요성	**significant** results 중요한 결과
consistent	형 변함 없는, 일관된 파 consistently 일관되게, 한결같이 유 constant 끊임없는, 계속되는	**consistent** growth 변함 없는 성장
estimate	동 추정하다 명 추정(치), 견적	**estimate** economic value 경제적 가치를 추정하다 a rough **estimate** 대략의 견적

파 파생어 유 유의어 반 반의어 관 관련 어휘

어휘 확인하기

다음 괄호 안에서 알맞은 것을 고르세요.

1 Several companies worked in (property / cooperation) to organize this technology convention.

2 Many (factors / customizations) contributed to triggering the current economic crisis.

3 Mago Corp.'s market shares (immediately / competitively) plunged following the CEO's announcement.

4 To limit (excessive / remarkable) spending, the city council has decided to review the budget.

실전 감각 키우기

다음 빈칸에 알맞은 것을 고르세요.

5 Mr. Tetley's initial ------- entitles him to a thirty percent share of the company.

(A) delivery
(B) investment
(C) delay
(D) consumption

6 Even though much of Europe has suffered a recession, the economic situation is ------- in Belgium.

(A) coupled
(B) mutual
(C) excessive
(D) stable

7 Following the merger with the Chinese firm, we experienced ------- growth in Asian markets.

(A) complete
(B) significant
(C) correct
(D) approximate

8 Due to the ------- decline in exports, the government has encouraged citizens to buy domestic goods.

(A) strategic
(B) enhanced
(C) consistent
(D) competitive

주어진 문제를 제한시간에 맞추어 풀어 보세요.

Part 5 Choose the one word or phrase that best completes the sentence.

1. We couldn't have been successful without the team's strong support and full -------.

   (A) cooperator
   (B) cooperation
   (C) cooperated
   (D) cooperate

2. The HR department's problem is ------- the employees and management refuse to compromise on the additional benefits.

   (A) while
   (B) this
   (C) that
   (D) since

3. To meet the particular requirement of each client, every product of Wein & Gaber is individually -------.

   (A) customized
   (B) resolved
   (C) preferred
   (D) invested

4. The patient had health insurance, ------- the policy did not cover medical treatment while out of the country.

   (A) or
   (B) but
   (C) if
   (D) then

5. Ticket holders of the postponed concert will be refunded or ------- with vouchers.

   (A) providing
   (B) provided
   (C) provide
   (D) provides

6. The magazine gives useful tips for ------- saving money and staying organized.

   (A) many
   (B) neither
   (C) few
   (D) both

7. The CEO congratulated the entire staff on the ------- sales figures this month.

   (A) remarkable
   (B) forceful
   (C) sensible
   (D) deliverable

8. In the event of the manager's absence, the receptionist usually asks ------- the caller would like to leave a message or try again later.

   (A) for
   (B) either
   (C) despite
   (D) whether

Part 6 Questions 9-12 refer to the following article.

SpeedyTrak Partners with Competitor

Two rivals in the rail industry announced ------- they are planning to form one company.
9.
After having competed with each other for many years, the two largest rail firms in the

country, Speedy Trak and FastLink, have decided to merge and operate under the name

FastTrak.

Industry experts expect that, in doing so, they will be able to produce trains equipped

with the most modern technology. Speedy Trak and FastLink have both expressed their

goal as not only improving speed and comfort, ------- developing more eco-friendly
10.
trains.

A spokesperson for FastTrak stated that they hope to ------- the experience of rail travel
11.
through the purchase of more modern vehicles and the renovation of train stations.

------- .
12.

---

9. (A) that
    (B) moreover
    (C) as for
    (D) despite

11. (A) enhance
    (B) describe
    (C) illustrate
    (D) accelerate

10. (A) only if
    (B) but also
    (C) along with
    (D) and then

12. (A) This is great news for travelers tired
        of outdated amenities.
    (B) Mergers are common in the energy
        production industry.
    (C) The competition was at its maximum
        a few years ago.
    (D) Research indicates that consumers
        are looking for cheaper tickets.

UNIT 12

PART 5&6 연결어·구문편

UNIT 13

부사절 접속사

+생활 어휘(1)

부사절

부사절 접속사

주절

부사절은 문장 안에서 부사 역할을 하는 절을 말합니다.
주어와 동사로 구성된 절 앞에 부사절 접속사가 붙어서
주절을 꾸며주는 역할을 합니다.

1 시간·이유의 부사절 접속사
2 조건·양보의 부사절 접속사
3 접속사 vs. 전치사 vs. 접속부사

+ 생활 어휘(1)

1 시간·이유의 부사절 접속사

핵심 POINT

부사절과 부사절 접속사
- 부사절: 부사처럼 주절을 수식하는 절로, 주절의 앞뒤에 위치
- 부사절 접속사: 시간, 이유, 조건, 양보 등 다양한 의미의 부사절을 이끄는 종속접속사

시간·이유를 나타내는 부사절 접속사
- 시간: when, as, while, before, after
- 이유: because, as, since, now that, in that

A 부사절과 부사절 접속사

- 부사절은 부사처럼 주절을 수식하는 절로, 주절의 앞뒤에 모두 위치할 수 있어요.
- 이런 부사절을 이끄는 접속사는 종속접속사의 하나로, '부사절 접속사'라고 합니다. 시간, 이유, 조건, 양보 등 다양한 의미를 나타내어 쓰여요.

접속사 when

Most of the tenants moved out. The monthly rent doubled.
<u>절</u>　　　　　　　　　　　　　　　　　　　　　<u>절</u>

Most of the tenants moved out **when** the monthly rent doubled.
　　　　　　　　　　　　　　　　　주절을 수식하는 부사절

= **When** the monthly rent doubled, most of the tenants moved out.
월세가 두 배가 되었을 때, 대부분의 세입자들이 이사를 나갔다.

B 시간을 나타내는 부사절 접속사

when ~할 때, ~하면	as ~할 때	while ~하는 동안에
before ~하기 전에	after ~한 후에	until ~할 때까지
once ~하자마자, ~할 때	since ~한 이래로	as soon as ~하자마자

주의 before, after, until, since는 접속사와 같은 의미의 전치사로도 쓰여요.

- 특히, when은 '어떤 한 시점'을 나타내고, while은 '기간'을 나타냅니다.
  - **시점** The coverage will start **when** the payment is received. **납입금이 접수되면** 보장이 시작될 것이다.
  - **기간** **While** I tried on clothes, my friend waited. **내가 옷을 입어 보는 동안에**, 내 친구는 기다렸다.
  - **참고** while은 '~ 반면에'라는 대조의 의미로도 쓰이며, 이때는 whereas와 같은 뜻이에요.

- 시간의 부사절에서 미래의 일을 나타낼 때 미래 시제 대신에 현재 시제를 쓴다는 것에 주의하세요.
  The meeting will begin **as soon as** the investor **arrives**. **투자자가 도착하자마자** 회의가 시작될 것이다.
  ~~will arrive~~

C 이유를 나타내는 부사절 접속사

because, as, since, now that, in that ~이기 때문에, ~이므로

참고 as와 since는 시간을 나타내는 접속사로도 쓰이므로, 각각의 의미를 구분해서 알아두세요.

Since the item was faulty, I asked for a refund. **제품이 불량이었기 때문에**, 나는 환불을 요청했다.

As the rate was favorable, I exchanged some currency. **환율이 좋았기 때문에**, 나는 몇몇 통화를 환전했다.

핵심 POINT 확인하기

다음 괄호 안에서 알맞은 것을 고르세요.

1 Please turn off the lights in the conference room (when / because) you leave.

2 The corrected invitations will be distributed (after / before) they are reprinted.

3 Mr. Whelan didn't get the job (while / since) he didn't have the proper qualifications.

4 Traffic is flowing smoothly (as soon as / now that) the new bridge has been opened.

|핵심 POINT 슬쩍 보기||

1 when은 '~할 때', because는 '~이기 때문에'라는 뜻의 접속사예요.

2 이후 시점을 나타낼 때에는 after, 이전을 나타낼 때에는 before를 써요.

3 since는 시간뿐만 아니라 이유를 나타내는 접속사로도 쓰여요.

4 as soon as는 '~하자마자', now that은 '~이므로'란 뜻이에요.

실전 감각 키우기

다음 빈칸에 알맞은 것을 고르세요.

5 Pharmaceutical companies cannot sell medicine or supplements ------- the products pass an inspection.

(A) by   (B) even
(C) during   (D) until

6 빈출 Employees must get approval from a supervisor at least one week ------- they plan to use vacation time.

(A) from   (B) before
(C) later   (D) about

7 빈출 The town council rejected the proposal for a community park ------- the project was expensive.

(A) so   (B) because
(C) then   (D) however

8 Mr. Hall no longer handles questions from the press ------- he transferred to another department last month.

(A) as   (B) when
(C) yet   (D) before

UNIT 13

2 조건·양보의 부사절 접속사

핵심 POINT

I'll bring some flowers **if** the hospital allows it.

조건을 나타내는 부사절 접속사
- 조건: if, unless, once, in case, as long as
- 시간과 조건의 부사절에서는 현재 시제로 미래를 나타냄

양보·대조를 나타내는 부사절 접속사
- 양보: (even) though, although, even if
- 대조: while, whereas

A 조건을 나타내는 접속사

- 조건을 나타내는 부사절 접속사는 주절의 전제 조건이 되는 절을 이끌 때 사용됩니다.
- 두 단어 이상이거나, 분사 형태의 접속사도 있으니 유의하세요.

if ~라면	unless[if ~ not] ~가 아니라면	once 일단 ~하면
in case (that) ~한 경우에 (대비하여)	as long as ~하는 한	provided[providing] (that) ~한다면

- if, unless 모두 조건의 부사절을 이끌지만, unless는 'if ~ not'이므로 부정의 의미입니다.
  I'll bring her some flowers **if** the hospital allows it. _{병원이 허락한다면} 나는 그녀에게 꽃을 가져갈 것이다.
  Unless the item is on sale, we cannot afford it. _{제품이 할인 중이 아니라면} 우린 그것을 살 여유가 없다.

- 시간의 부사절과 마찬가지로, 조건의 부사절에서는 미래의 일을 나타낼 때 현재 시제를 씁니다.
  If we **win** this bid, Mr. Watson will give us all bonuses.
  ~~will win~~ 이 입찰을 따내면, 왓슨 씨가 우리 모두에게 보너스를 줄 것이다.

B 양보·대조를 나타내는 접속사

- 어떤 원인에 대해 예상치 못한 결과나 반대되는 내용을 나타낼 때 씁니다.

양보	(even) though, although, even if (비록) ~이지만, ~에도 불구하고
대조	while, whereas ~인 반면

양보 **Though** he visited numerous stores, he didn't buy anything.
그는 여러 매장을 방문했지만, 아무것도 사지 않았다.

대조 **While** some reports are too complicated, his report was simple and clear.
몇몇 보고서는 너무 복잡했지만, 그의 보고서는 단순하고 명료했다.

C 기타 접속사

목적	so that, in order that ~하기 위해서, ~이 되도록
결과	so+형용사[부사]+that, such+a(n)+(형용사)+명사+that 매우 ~해서 …하다

목적 Please fill out this form **so that** we can know your medical history.
당신의 병력을 알 수 있도록 이 양식을 작성해 주세요.

결과 The piece of jewelry was **so** beautiful **that** we decided to buy it.
그 보석은 매우 아름다워서 우리는 그것을 사기로 결정했다.

결과 The hospital had **such** a crowded waiting room **that** some people had to stand.
그 병원은 대기실이 매우 혼잡해서 몇몇 사람들은 서 있어야 했다.

핵심 POINT 확인하기

다음 괄호 안에서 알맞은 것을 고르세요.

|핵심 POINT 슬쩍 보기|

1 Customers can return a defective product (if / unless) they have a receipt.

> **1** if는 '~라면', unless는 '~가 아니라면'이란 뜻의 부사절 접속사예요.

2 The team members have their supervisor's personal phone number (in case / so that) they encounter a problem on a weekend.

> **2** in case는 '~한 경우에'라는 조건을, so that은 '~하기 위해서'라는 목적을 나타내요.

3 The film failed at the box office (as long as / even though) it was a high-budget movie.

> **3** as long as는 '~하는 한', even though는 '(비록) ~이지만'으로 해석돼요.

4 The vase is (so / such) fragile that it must be shipped in special packaging.

> **4** so 다음에는 형용사[부사]가 오는 반면, such 다음에는 명사(구)가 와요.

실전 감각 키우기

다음 빈칸에 알맞은 것을 고르세요.

5 빈출 The project cannot progress any further ------- the board approves the proposed budget increase.

(A) otherwise (B) unless
(C) if (D) because

6 빈출 The video presentation was brief, ------- it explained the marketing plan in detail.

(A) although (B) also
(C) in case (D) so that

7 The company's finances are managed by the accounting department ------- salaries are handled by Mr. Hardy.

(A) despite (B) unless
(C) through (D) while

8 The writing in the article must be clear ------- all readers can understand the complex issue.

(A) while (B) as though
(C) so that (D) neither

UNIT 13

3 접속사 vs. 전치사 vs. 접속부사

접속사 vs. 전치사
- 접속사 자리: ⟨**접속사**+주어+동사⟩
- 전치사 자리: ⟨**전치사**+명사(구, 절)⟩

접속사 vs. 접속부사
- 접속사: 두 개의 절을 의미와 구조면에서 하나의 문장으로 연결
- 접속부사: 의미 연결만 가능, 문장에서 콤마(,)와 함께 나옴

Despite its popularity,
the store closed.

A 접속사 vs. 전치사

- 토익에서는 의미가 비슷한 접속사와 전치사 중에서 정답을 골라야 하는 문제가 자주 출제됩니다.

종류	⟨접속사+주어+동사⟩	의미	⟨전치사+명사(구/절)⟩
시간	while	~하는 동안	during
	as soon as	~하자마자	upon[on] *doing*
	before	~ 전에	before, prior to
	after	~ 후에	after, following
	by the time	~(할 때)까지	by
이유	because, as, since, now that	~ 때문에	because of, due to, owing to
조건	in case (that), in the event (that) unless, if ~ not	~인 경우에 ~가 아니라면	in case of, in the event of without
양보	(even) though, although, even if	(비록) ~이지만	despite, in spite of, notwithstanding

- 접속사 뒤에는 ⟨주어+동사⟩가 포함된 절이, 전치사 다음에는 명사(구, 절)가 와야 합니다.

  접속사   A nurse entered **while** <u>the patient</u> <u>was having</u> a consultation with the doctor.
                                     접속사   주어   동사
  환자가 의사에게 상담을 받고 있는 **동안에** 간호사가 들어왔다.

  전치사   **Despite** <u>its popularity</u>, the store closed.   매장의 인기에도 **불구하고**, 그곳은 폐업했다.
                전치사   명사구

B 접속사 vs. 접속부사

- 접속부사는 의미상 접속사와 헷갈리기 쉽지만, **부사라서 두 개의 절을 하나의 문장으로 연결하지는 못합니다.**

첨가	moreover, in addition, besides 게다가 furthermore 더욱이, in fact 사실은	대조	however 그러나, otherwise 반면에 nevertheless 그럼에도 불구하고
결과	therefore 따라서, as a result 그 결과	예시	for example, for instance 예를 들어

- 접속부사는 두 문장의 의미만 연결하고 문장에서는 콤마(,)와 함께 나옵니다.

  접속사   **Because** the homeowner had insurance, the damage was repaired at no cost.
  집주인이 보험에 들었기 **때문에**, 피해는 비용 없이 복구되었다.

  접속부사   The homeowner had insurance. **Therefore**, the damage was repaired at no cost.
  집주인은 보험이 있었다. **따라서**, 피해는 비용 없이 복구되었다.

핵심 POINT 확인하기

다음 괄호 안에서 알맞은 것을 고르세요.

1 The historical artwork was not properly preserved (since / because of) the museum's lack of equipment.

2 This year's music festival had a low turnout (despite / although) it had a lot of publicity.

3 The post office was already closed (by / by the time) Ms. Simpson arrived.

4 Silverware at Bon Appétit is extremely expensive; (nevertheless / although), many customers still visit the shop.

|핵심 POINT 슬쩍 보기|

1 접속사 다음에는 〈주어＋동사〉 가, 전치사 다음에는 명사(구, 절)가 나와요.

2 despite는 전치사, although 는 접속사예요.

3 〈전치사＋명사〉, 〈접속사＋주 어＋동사〉를 기억해두세요.

4 두 개의 절을 한 문장으로 연결 할 때에는 접속사를, 의미만 연 결할 때에는 접속부사를 써요.

실전 감각 키우기

다음 빈칸에 알맞은 것을 고르세요.

5 ------- the air conditioner is in operation, please keep the door closed securely.

(A) While (B) Throughout
(C) Within (D) During

6 The picnic has been postponed until next week ------- a forecast of heavy rain.

(A) because (B) although
(C) instead of (D) due to

7 Kellenvue Repair contacts clients ------- their watches are ready for pickup.

(A) as soon as (B) until
(C) upon (D) ahead of

8 Mr. Gorash landed more than an hour late in Philadelphia and ------- he missed his connection.

(A) because (B) therefore
(C) whereas (D) however

UNIT **13**

앞에서 학습한 핵심 POINT를 떠올리며 빈칸을 완성해 보세요.

핵심 POINT 1

시간·이유의 부사절 접속사

부사절과 부사절 접속사

- 부사절: 부사처럼 주절을 수식하는 절로, 주절의 **❶**_____에 위치
- 부사절 접속사: 시간, 이유, 조건, 양보 등 다양한 의미의 부사절을 이끄는 종속접속사

시간·이유를 나타내는 부사절 접속사

- 시간: **❷**_____ ~할 때, ~하면, as ~할 때, **❸**_____ ~하는 동안에, before ~전에, after ~후에
- 이유: because, as, since, now that, in that ~이기 때문에, ~이므로

핵심 POINT 2

조건·양보의 부사절 접속사

조건을 나타내는 부사절 접속사

- 조건: **❹**_____ ~라면, **❺**_____ ~가 아니라면, once 일단 ~하면
- 시간과 조건의 부사절에서는 **❻**_____ 시제로 미래를 나타냄

양보·대조를 나타내는 부사절 접속사

- 양보: (even) though, **❼**_____, even if (비록) ~이지만, ~에도 불구하고
- 대조: **❽**_____, whereas ~인 반면

핵심 POINT 3

접속사 vs. 전치사 vs. 접속부사

접속사 vs. 전치사

- **❾**_____ 자리: 〈**❾**_____+주어+동사〉
- **❿**_____ 자리: 〈**❿**_____+명사(구, 절)〉

접속사 vs. 접속부사

- 접속사: 두 개의 절을 의미와 구조면에서 하나의 문장으로 연결
- 접속부사: 의미 연결만 가능, 문장에서 콤마(,)와 함께 나옴

|빈칸 정답 살짝 보기|..

❶ 앞뒤 ❷ when ❸ while ❹ if ❺ unless ❻ 현재 ❼ although ❽ while ❾ 접속사 ❿ 전치사

실전 감각 키우기

다음 빈칸에 알맞은 것을 고르세요.

1 Your travel expenses will not be reimbursed ------- official receipts are submitted.

(A) providing
(B) that
(C) unless
(D) as long as

2 Customers can track the shipment of their purchases online ------- the goods are in transit.

(A) during
(B) while
(C) in case
(D) without

3 Keyace Motors only sells pre-owned cars ------- other dealerships carry new and used vehicles.

(A) whereas
(B) in case
(C) as soon as
(D) unlike

4 More moviegoers went to see *Crovella* ------- the film received an award.

(A) following
(B) next to
(C) after
(D) regarding

[5-6] Questions 5-6 refer to the following e-mail.

Dear Mr. Bowers,

I am writing ------- the elevator in the west wing is out of order. Despite numerous
   5.
requests to the maintenance team, this problem has not been resolved.

I realize that there is another elevator available on the east side of the building. -------,
                                                                                      6.
we need the west wing elevator fully functioning.

As the owner of the building, you are responsible for all repairs. I ask that you take care

of this matter as soon as possible.

5 (A) because
(B) even if
(C) however
(D) not only

6 (A) While
(B) Whereas
(C) For example
(D) Nevertheless

지역 사회·단체 및 지역 행사, 주거 생활에 관한 어휘들입니다.

resident	📖 거주자, 주민 📰 residential 주택의, 주거용의	a **resident** of the town 도시 거주자
community	📖 지역 사회, 지역 주민	belong to a **community** 지역 사회에 속하다
conveniently	📖 편리하게 📰 convenient 편리한 convenience 편리, 편의 시설	**conveniently** located 편리하게 위치한
intend	📖 ~할 생각[계획]이다, 의도하다 📰 intention 의도, 의향, 계획	**intend** to attend a forum 포럼에 참석할 생각이다 be **intended** for the residents 주민을 대상으로 하다
establish	📖 설립하다	**establish** an organization 단체를 설립하다
reliable	📖 믿을 만한 📰 rely (on) (~에) 의지하다 📖 dependable 믿을 만한	a **reliable** source 믿을 만한 출처
participate	📖 참석하다 📰 participation 참석 participant 참석자	**participate** in a seminar 세미나에 참석하다
charity	📖 자선 (단체) 📰 charitable 자선의 📎 donation 기부	a local **charity** 지역 자선 단체
exhibition	📖 전시회 📰 exhibit 전시하다	open an **exhibition** 전시회를 열다
celebrate	📖 축하하다 📰 celebration 축하[기념] (행사)	**celebrate** a victory 승리를 축하하다 *celebrity(유명인사)와 혼동하지 않도록 주의하세요.
reception	📖 축하연, 환영회	hold a **reception** 환영회를 열다 *호텔 등의 로비에 위치한 '안내 데스크, 접수대'를 의미하기도 해요.
entitled	📖 권리가 있는	be **entitled** to a free medical checkup 무료 의료 검진을 받을 권리가 있다
notify	📖 알리다, 통보하다 📰 notification 통지, 공고, 통보	**notify** residents of changes 주민들에게 변경사항에 대해 알리다
separate	📖 분리된, 따로 떨어진 📰 separation 분리 separately 따로따로, 별도로	**separate** rooms 분리된 방들
appliance	📖 (가정용) 기기, 전기제품 📖 device 장치, 기구	a kitchen **appliance** 주방 기구
outdoor	📖 야외의 📰 indoor 실내의	an **outdoor** swimming pool 야외 수영장
disposal	📖 처리, 처분 📰 dispose (of) (~을) 처리하다	sewage **disposal** systems 하수 처리 시스템
rental	📖 임대[대여]료 📖 임대[대여]의 📰 rent 세내다, 빌리다	**rental** car fleets 렌터카 보유 차량 a **rental** car 대여 자동차

📰 파생어 📖 유의어 📰 반의어 📎 관련 어휘

어휘 확인하기

다음 괄호 안에서 알맞은 것을 고르세요.

1 Tenants must (intend / notify) the landlord before doing any repairs in a housing unit.

2 (Participation / Disposal) in this year's arts festival was much higher than anticipated.

3 The museum is featuring a special (exhibition / individual) on ancient art.

4 The city held a (celebration / rental) to mark the one hundredth anniversary of its founding.

실전 감각 키우기

다음 빈칸에 알맞은 것을 고르세요.

5 As a long-time ------- of Watson City, Edwin Anderson was familiar with its historical sites.

(A) resident
(B) gathering
(C) foundation
(D) community

6 Stratford Towers is ------- located within walking distance of a shopping center and Regina Beach.

(A) previously
(B) commonly
(C) increasingly
(D) conveniently

7 The corporation plans to host a small ------- to honor Mr. Kohl's thirty years of service.

(A) reception
(B) completion
(C) establishment
(D) accomplishment

8 The ------- scheduled to be delivered on Saturday requires installation by a skilled technician.

(A) invoice
(B) appliance
(C) address
(D) directory

주어진 문제를 제한시간에 맞추어 풀어 보세요.

Part 5 Choose the one word or phrase that best completes the sentence.

1. ------ Jaspoint Restaurant first started, it had a lot of positive reviews online.

   (A) For
   (B) When
   (C) Through
   (D) Until

2. The Winter Hills Hotline provides citizens with ------- information about the city's attractions.

   (A) residential
   (B) portable
   (C) approximate
   (D) reliable

3. The effects of the new strategy can be determined ------- the figures have been analyzed.

   (A) once
   (B) almost
   (C) so that
   (D) away

4. ------- the other manufacturing companies experienced a slowdown last year, Milltown Industries profits increased.

   (A) Except for
   (B) Besides
   (C) Only if
   (D) While

5. ------- the director approves the proposal from the security department, employees will be issued electronic key cards.

   (A) Provide
   (B) Provides
   (C) Provided
   (D) Provision

6. The video game system includes only one wireless controller, but extra controllers can be purchased -------.

   (A) suddenly
   (B) loosely
   (C) separately
   (D) accidentally

7. Golden Ferry still allows motorcycles on its vessels ------- larger vehicles are temporarily banned on board.

   (A) owing to
   (B) even though
   (C) whether
   (D) despite

8. All merchandise can be returned within thirty days of purchase ------- it was a custom order.

   (A) in case
   (B) during
   (C) instead
   (D) unless

Part 6 Questions 9-12 refer to the following advertisement.

Let Sherman Realty Help You

Since it was ------- nearly ten years ago, Sherman Realty has become a trusted source
        9.
for high-quality real estate in Maryville.

------- our real estate brokers are selected to work for us, we provide them with an
  10.
intensive in-house training program. ------- . So we're confident you'll be fully satisfied
                                         11.
with your experience working with us.

-------, we do a high volume of business and have more listings than any other realtor in
  12.
the region. That means you'll have more properties to view and to choose from. From
residential homes to commercial buildings, Sherman Realty is your number one
resource.

---

9. (A) settled
    (B) established
    (C) arranged
    (D) produced

10. (A) After
    (B) During
    (C) Rather
    (D) So that

11. (A) The training sessions are usually
        held in the mornings.
    (B) We recommend registering for the
        program as early as possible.
    (C) This equips staff with a high degree
        of professionalism.
    (D) If you have experience, feel free to
        apply to work with us.

12. (A) Furthermore
    (B) Otherwise
    (C) Supposing
    (D) Because

UNIT 13

PART 5&6 연결어·구문편

UNIT 14

관계사
+생활 어휘(2)

Will is an executive **who** often travels abroad.

관계사는 앞 문장에 나온 대상을 뒤 문장에서 반복할 경우, 다른 말로 가리키면서
두 문장을 연결하는 기능까지 함께 합니다. 반복되는 대상이 사람·사물과 같은 명사이면,
관계대명사가, 반복되는 대상이 시간·이유와 같은 부사이면 관계부사가 쓰입니다.

---

1 관계대명사의 개념과 쓰임

2 주격·목적격·소유격 관계대명사

3 관계대명사 that과 what

4 관계부사와 복합관계사

+ 생활 어휘(2)

1 관계대명사의 개념과 쓰임

a flight attendant **who**
works for the Airline

관계대명사의 개념과 선행사
- 〈접속사+대명사〉로 두 문장을 연결하면서, 뒤 문장의 명사를 대신함
- 선행사: 관계대명사절의 수식을 받는 명사(구)
- 관계대명사절은 〈관계대명사+불완전한 절〉, '~(하)는'으로 해석

선행사에 따른 관계대명사의 종류
- 선행사가 사람: who, that
- 선행사가 사물/동물: which, that

A 관계대명사의 개념: 〈접속사＋대명사〉
- 관계대명사는 접속사와 대명사의 역할을 동시에 하는 연결어입니다.
- 어떤 명사(구)가 뒤의 문장에서 반복될 때, 두 문장을 연결하면서 반복되는 명사 대신 사용합니다.

I know **a flight attendant**, and she works for the Airline.　나는 **한 승무원**을 알고 있는데,
　　　　　　절　　　　　　　　　　　　　　절　　　　　**그녀는** 그 항공사에서 일한다.

I know **a flight attendant** who works for the Airline.　나는 그 항공사에서 일하는 **한 승무원**을 안다.

B 관계대명사와 선행사
- 선행사는 관계대명사 앞에서 관계대명사절의 수식을 받는 명사(구)를 뜻합니다.

There are three **agents who** check boarding passes.　탑승권을 확인하는 **담당자가** 세 명 있다.
　　　　　　선행사 ◀──────────────── 관계대명사절

> 참고　또한, 선행사가 관계대명사 바로 앞에 오지 않고, 그 사이에 수식어(구)가 들어가는 경우도 있습니다.
> 그러므로 관계대명사 바로 앞에 있는 명사(구)가 항상 선행사인 것은 아니라는 점을 기억하세요.
> There were **some passengers** *on this flight* **who[that]** checked excess baggage.
> 　　　　　　선행사 ◀─┴─────── 수식어　　　　　 이 비행편에는 초과되는 짐을 부친 **승객들이 몇몇** 있었다.

- 관계대명사절에서는 반복되는 명사(구) 대신 관계대명사를 쓰기 때문에, 관계대명사절은 〈관계대명사+불완전한 절〉의 형태입니다.
- 관계대명사절은 선행사를 뒤에서만 수식할 수 있으며, 명사를 수식하는 형용사 역할을 하기 때문에 일반적으로 '~(하)는'으로 해석합니다.

C 선행사에 따른 관계대명사의 종류
- 관계대명사는 선행사가 사람/사물인지에 따라 구분합니다.
  또, 관계대명사절 안에서의 역할에 따라 주격, 목적격, 소유격으로 구분해요.
- that은 소유격을 제외하고 선행사의 종류와 관계 없이 사용할 수 있어요.

선행사	사람	사물/동물	사람/사물
주격 관계대명사	who	which	that
목적격 관계대명사	who(m)	which	that
소유격 관계대명사	whose	of which, whose	-

> **사람**　Kevin is a truck driver **who[that]** has a valid license.　케빈 씨는 유효 면허증을 가진 **트럭 운전사**이다.
> **사물/동물**　You have to take the documents **which[that]** are on the cabinet.
> 　　　　　캐비닛 위에 있는 **문서를** 가지고 가야 합니다.

핵심 POINT 확인하기

다음 괄호 안에서 알맞은 것을 고르세요.

1 Mr. Hunt hired a lawyer (he / who) is an expert in corporate law.

2 Conchi Incorporated should develop a recycling program, (and / which) would reduce its industrial waste.

3 Ms. Hall explained the benefits of the merger to shareholders, (who / and) they discussed the matter.

4 The newspaper listed the (residents / residences) who participated in the local clean-up drive.

|핵심 POINT 슬쩍 보기|

1 접속사와 대명사 역할을 동시에 할 수 있는 것은 관계대명사예요.

2 관계대명사는 '접속사'와 '대명사'의 기능이 모두 필요할 때에만 쓸 수 있어요.

3 완전한 두 절은 접속사로 연결해요.

4 관계대명사 who가 이끄는 절을 통해 선행사가 무엇일지를 파악하세요.

실전 감각 키우기

다음 빈칸에 알맞은 것을 고르세요.

5 Ms. Wanda recently met the artist ------- painted the portrait of a famous musician.

(A) who
(B) so
(C) they
(D) few

6 In *Crusaders*, Ben Porter played the lead role, ------- required him to learn another language.

(A) who
(B) which
(C) whom
(D) whose

7 The company has a new attendance policy, and ------- will be implemented next month.

(A) who
(B) these
(C) this
(D) which

8 The long-running musical features ------- who have delighted audiences across the globe.

(A) performance
(B) perform
(C) performers
(D) performing

UNIT 14

2 주격·목적격·소유격 관계대명사

the route **which**
takes the least time

주격 관계대명사
- 주격 관계대명사: 관계대명사 뒤에 주어 없이 동사가 이어짐
- 관계대명사절의 동사는 관계대명사 앞의 선행사에 수일치

목적격 관계대명사·소유격 관계대명사
- 목적격 관계대명사: 관계대명사 뒤에 주어와 동사만 이어짐
  목적격 관계대명사는 생략 가능, 전치사가 앞에 있으면 생략 불가
- 소유격 관계대명사: 선행사와 관계대명사 뒤의 명사가 소유 관계

A 주격 관계대명사

- 관계대명사가 관계대명사절 안에서 주어 역할을 하면 주격 관계대명사입니다.
- 대개 관계대명사 뒤에 주어 없이 바로 동사가 이어지면 주격 관계대명사로 볼 수 있어요.
- 선행사가 사람이면 who나 that, 사물이면 which나 that을 사용해요.

  사람 선행사 Will is an executive **who[that]** often travels abroad.
  윌 씨는 자주 해외 출장을 가는 경영자이다.

  사물 선행사 I will follow the route **which[that]** takes the least time.
  나는 시간이 가장 적게 걸리는 노선을 따를 것이다.

- 주격 관계대명사절의 동사는, 관계대명사 앞의 선행사에 수일치를 해줍니다.
  The cooks **who** work at this restaurant are very talented. 이 식당에서 일하는 요리사들은 매우 재능 있다.
  복수 명사   복수 동사

B 목적격 관계대명사

- 관계대명사가 관계대명사절 안에서 목적어 역할을 하면 목적격 관계대명사입니다.
- 관계대명사 뒤에 주어와 타동사가 있는데, 목적어가 없으면 목적격 관계대명사라고 할 수 있어요.
- 선행사가 사람이면 who(m)나 that, 사물이면 which나 that을 씁니다.

  사람 선행사 I know the representative **who(m)[that]** the company sent.
  나는 그 회사에서 보낸 직원을 알고 있다.

  사물 선행사 The storm caused a delay **which[that]** we can't handle.
  폭풍은 우리가 해결할 수 없는 지연을 야기했다.

  참고 목적격 관계대명사는 생략할 수 있으나, 바로 앞에 전치사가 함께 있는 경우는 불가능해요.
  A colleague (**whom**) I was acquainted with accompanied me on the trip.
  A colleague with **whom** I was acquainted accompanied me on the trip.
  아는 동료가 여행에 나를 동반했다.

C 소유격 관계대명사

- 관계대명사절 내에서 선행사가 관계대명사 뒤의 명사를 소유하는 관계이면 소유격 관계대명사입니다.
- 선행사와 관계대명사 뒤의 명사가 '~의 …'로 해석되면 소유격 관계대명사로 볼 수 있어요.
- 선행사의 종류에 관계없이 주로 whose를 씁니다.
  This is the motorist **whose** vehicle was damaged. 이 사람이 손상된 차량의 운전자이다.(운전자의 차량)

  참고 목적격과 소유격 관계대명사 뒤에는 둘 다 〈주어+동사〉가 와서 혼동됩니다.
  관계대명사절에 주어와 목적어가 다 있으면 소유격 관계대명사가 와야 해요.
  There are travelers **whose** passports have many stamps. 여권에 스탬프가 많은 여행객들이 있다.

핵심 POINT 확인하기

다음 괄호 안에서 알맞은 것을 고르세요.

|핵심 POINT 슬쩍 보기|

1 All employees who (wish / wishes) to retire early must submit a formal letter to their managers.

1 주격 관계대명사 뒤의 동사는 선행사에 수일치 시켜요.

2 Borsa and Associates is a law firm (whose / who) lawyers specialize in corporate conflicts.

2 선행사가 관계대명사 뒤의 명사를 소유하는 관계이면 소유격 관계대명사를 써요.

3 The Sandyport beach resort has airport shuttles (whose / which) guests can ride for free.

3 관계대명사절에 목적어 자리가 비어 있다면 목적격 관계대명사를 골라야 해요.

4 I have not met the assistant (whom / whose) the general manager hired last week.

4 목적격과 소유격 관계대명사를 구분할 때에는 관계대명사절의 목적어를 확인하세요.

실전 감각 키우기

다음 빈칸에 알맞은 것을 고르세요.

5 빈출 Anyone ------- collects vintage cars must attend the tenth Mewshire Classica Auto Show.

(A) whom　　　　(B) whose
(C) who　　　　　(D) which

6 Mr. Daniels paid $50 extra for the overdue SUV ------- he rented from Union Cars.

(A) through　　　(B) which
(C) thus　　　　　(D) who

7 빈출 A singer ------- most recent album sold more than one million copies will give a live concert in Pembroke Park tomorrow.

(A) that　　　　　(B) which
(C) their　　　　　(D) whose

8 The main tunnel that ------- the national zoo and the art museum will be out of service this weekend.

(A) connection　　(B) connects
(C) connect　　　　(D) connecting

UNIT 14

3 관계대명사 that과 what

I bought
what they wanted.

관계대명사 that
- 관계대명사 who(m)나 which를 대신할 수 있음
- 관계대명사 that+불완전한 절 / 명사절 접속사 that+완전한 절

선행사를 포함한 관계대명사 what
- 선행사를 이미 포함한 관계대명사로, 앞에 선행사가 없음
- what이 이끄는 절은 명사절로, 문장에서 주어, 목적어, 보어 역할
- 관계대명사 what+불완전한 절

A 관계대명사 that

- 관계대명사 that은 who(m)와 which를 대신하여 선행사의 종류와 격에 상관없이 쓰일 수 있어요.
  단, 전치사 뒤의 목적격 관계대명사 whom이나 which를 대신해서는 쓰일 수 없습니다.
- 또한 관계대명사 that은 소유격으로는 쓰이지 않아요.

The designer tried the software **that[which]** Ms. Pearson recommended.
디자이너는 피어슨 씨가 추천한 소프트웨어를 한번 써 봤다.

The museum curator talked to a professor **whose[that]** specialty is modern history.
그 박물관 큐레이터는 전공이 현대사인 교수와 이야기했다.

참고 관계대명사 that은 명사절을 이끄는 접속사 that과 구분해야 합니다.
관계대명사 that은 주어나 목적어 역할을 하므로 뒤에 불완전한 절이 오지만,
명사절 접속사 that은 절과 절을 연결하는 역할을 하므로 뒤에 완전한 절이 옵니다.

관계대명사 that	The appointment **that** I arranged is urgent. 내가 잡은 약속은 시급하다. (불완전한 절)
명사절 접속사 that	**That** I arranged the appointment is a fact. 내가 약속을 잡은 것은 사실이다. (완전한 절)

B 선행사를 포함한 관계대명사 what

- 관계대명사 what(= the thing which)은 선행사를 포함한 관계대명사로, 앞에 선행사가 오지 않아요.
- 관계대명사 what이 이끄는 절은 명사절로, 문장에서 주어, 목적어, 보어로 쓰이며 '~하는 것'으로 해석돼요.

주어 **What** the highway needs is a carpool lane. 그 고속도로에 필요한 것은 카풀 노선이다.

목적어 We will determine **what** the highway needs. 우리는 그 고속도로에 필요한 것을 결정할 것이다.

보어 This express check-in option is **what** the airline's customers asked for.
이 빠른 수속 옵션은 항공사 고객들이 요구했던 것이다.

참고 관계대명사 that과 what 뒤에는 모두 불완전한 문장이 와서 헷갈려요.
이때는 선행사의 유무를 확인하세요.
관계대명사 that 앞에는 선행사가 있고, 관계대명사 what 앞에는 선행사가 없어요.

관계대명사 that	I bought the car **that** my family wanted. 나는 우리 가족이 원했던 차를 샀다. (선행사 있음)
관계대명사 what	I bought **what** my family wanted. 나는 우리 가족이 원했던 것을 샀다. (선행사 없음)

핵심 POINT 확인하기

다음 괄호 안에서 알맞은 것을 고르세요.

|핵심 POINT 슬쩍 보기|

1 The Louvre is the museum in (which / that) Leonardo da Vinci's *Mona Lisa* is displayed.

1 관계대명사 that은 전치사 뒤에서는 쓰이지 않아요.

2 A research study indicates (that / whom) Questo Bank offers the country's most convenient online banking service.

2 명사절 접속사 that 뒤에는 완전한 절이 와요.

3 (Which / What) the brochure mainly describes is a practical way to reduce household waste.

3 문장에서 주어로 쓰이는 명사절을 이끌 수 있는 것은 관계대명사 what이에요.

4 The supervisor explained (that / what) employees should do in case of emergency.

4 관계대명사 what 앞에는 선행사가 올 수 없어요.

실전 감각 키우기

다음 빈칸에 알맞은 것을 고르세요.

5 The server ------- takes your order will make recommendations for a variety of menu selections.

(A) neither   (B) that
(C) each   (D) what

6 ------- we allocated for the retirement dinner was not enough to cover the unexpected expenses.

(A) Those   (B) What
(C) Therefore   (D) Which

7 The quality control staff selected ------- needed to be sent back to the manufacturer.

(A) what   (B) this
(C) that   (D) who

8 The latest research suggests ------- vitamin supplements from EZ-Med prevent colds.

(A) to   (B) what
(C) you   (D) that

UNIT 14

4 관계부사와 복합관계사

핵심
POINT

the place **where**
you board the plane

관계부사
- 〈접속사+부사〉의 역할을 하며, 뒤에 완전한 절이 옴
- 선행사가 장소이면 where, 시간이면 when,
  이유이면 why, 방법이면 how를 씀

복합관계사
- 〈관계사+-ever〉의 형태
- 복합관계대명사는 명사절·부사절을, 복합관계부사는 부사절을 이끎

A 관계부사

- 관계대명사가 〈접속사+대명사〉의 역할을 하듯이, 관계부사는 〈접속사+부사〉의 역할을 합니다.
- 관계부사는 선행사의 종류에 따라 구분될 뿐, 격의 구분은 없어요.

장소: where	시간: when	이유: why	방법: how
the place **where**	the time **when**	the reason **why**	**how**[the way]

This is <u>the place</u> **where** you board the plane.　여기가 고객님이 비행기에 탑승하는 곳입니다.

We look forward to <u>the time</u> **when** we take our summer vacation.
우리는 여름 휴가를 떠날 때를 기대하고 있다.

We don't know <u>the reason</u> **why** the traffic congestion is getting worse.
저희는 교통 정체가 더 심각해지는 이유를 모릅니다.

- 다른 관계부사와 달리, how는 선행사 the way와 나란히 쓰이지 않고 둘 중 하나만 씁니다.

  This is **how** they use the bus.　이것이 그들이 버스를 이용하는 방법이다.
  = This is **the way** they use the bus.

  참고 뒤에 불완전한 절이 오는 관계대명사와 달리, 관계부사는 뒤에 완전한 절이 옵니다.
  This is the parking lot **which** <u>they left their vehicle in.</u>　이곳은 그들이 차량을 주차한 주차장이다. (관계대명사)
  This is the parking lot **where** <u>they left their vehicle.</u>　이곳은 그들이 차량을 주차한 주차장이다. (관계부사)

B 복합관계사

- 복합관계사는 〈관계사+-ever〉 형태로, 복합관계대명사와 복합관계부사가 있어요.
- 복합관계대명사는 명사절·부사절을 이끌 수 있어요. 선행사를 포함하고 있어서 앞에 선행사가 올 수 없습니다.
- 복합관계부사는 부사절만을 이끕니다.

복합관계대명사	명사절	복합관계부사	부사절
who(m)ever	~하는 사람은 누구나	whenever	언제든지 (= no matter when)
whatever	~하는 것은 무엇이나	wherever	어디든지 (= no matter where)
whichever	~하는 것은 어느 것이나	however	아무리 ~ 한다 해도 (= no matter how)

Whoever <u>enters the venue</u> must be on the guest list.
그 장소에 들어가는 사람은 **누구나** 손님 명단에 올라 있어야 한다. (명사절−주어 역할)

Whenever <u>someone logs in</u>, the application sends a notification.
누군가 로그인할 때는 **언제나** 그 애플리케이션은 알림을 보낸다. (부사절)

핵심 POINT 확인하기

다음 괄호 안에서 알맞은 것을 고르세요.

|핵심 POINT 슬쩍 보기|

1 Police officers examined the intersection (which / where) the accident occurred.

1 관계부사 뒤에는 완전한 절이 와요.

2 The publisher didn't explain the reason (why / how) the manuscript was rejected.

2 the reason why는 '~하는 이유'라는 뜻이에요.

3 Employees can sign up for a workshop in (whatever / whose) they prefer.

3 목적어 역할을 하는 명사절을 이끌 수 있는 것은 복합관계대명사예요.

4 Customers may call the Halk Electronics technical support hotline (whenever / which) they need help with products.

4 whenever는 '언제든지'라는 뜻으로 부사절을 이끌어요.

실전 감각 키우기

다음 빈칸에 알맞은 것을 고르세요.

5 From 8 A.M. to 11 A.M., parking is prohibited on the street ------- the parade is scheduled to take place.

(A) until   (B) where
(C) beside   (D) near

6 Members of our rewards club can receive substantial discounts on the day ------- the store celebrates its anniversary.

(A) whose   (B) when
(C) which   (D) what

7 빈출 Please send this letter to ------- is in charge of handling mutual funds and investment at your company.

(A) whatever   (B) wherever
(C) whoever   (D) whichever

8 ------- limited the given time was, the marketing team still produced a great advertising campaign.

(A) Whenever   (B) Why
(C) Which   (D) However

UNIT 14

앞에서 학습한 핵심 POINT를 떠올리며 빈칸을 완성해 보세요.

핵심 POINT 1-2

관계대명사

관계대명사의 개념과 쓰임
- 〈①_____+대명사〉의 역할로 두 문장을 연결하면서, 뒤 문장의 명사를 대신함
- ②_____ : 관계대명사의 수식을 받는 명사(구)

선행사에 따른 관계대명사의 종류
- 선행사가 사람: who, that
- 선행사가 사물/동물: which, that

격에 따른 관계대명사의 종류
- 주격 관계대명사: 관계대명사 뒤에 주어 없이 동사가 이어짐
  관계대명사절의 동사는 관계대명사 앞의 ③_____에 수일치
- 목적격 관계대명사: 관계대명사 뒤에 주어와 동사만 이어짐
  생략 가능하나, 전치사가 앞에 있으면 생략 불가
- 소유격 관계대명사: 선행사와 관계대명사 뒤의 명사가 소유 관계

핵심 POINT 3

관계대명사 that과 what

관계대명사 that
- 관계대명사 who(m)나 ④_____를 대신할 수 있음
- ⑤_____ that+불완전한 절
- 명사절 접속사 that+완전한 절

선행사를 포함한 관계대명사 what
- 선행사를 이미 포함한 관계대명사로, 앞에 선행사가 없음
- what이 이끄는 절은 ⑥_____로, 문장에서 주어, 목적어, 보어 역할
- 관계대명사 what+불완전한 절

핵심 POINT 4

관계부사와 복합관계사

관계부사
- 〈접속사+⑦_____〉의 역할을 하며, 뒤에 완전한 절이 옴
- 선행사가 장소이면 ⑧_____, 시간이면 when, 이유이면 ⑨_____, 방법이면 how를 씀

복합관계사
- 〈관계사+⑩_____〉의 형태
- 복합관계대명사는 명사절·부사절을, 복합관계부사는 부사절을 이끎

|빈칸 정답 살짝 보기|

❶ 접속사　❷ 선행사　❸ 선행사　❹ which　❺ 관계대명사　❻ 명사절　❼ 부사　❽ where　❾ why　❿ -ever

실전 감각 키우기

다음 빈칸에 알맞은 것을 고르세요.

1 Candidates ------- meet the minimum requirements will be contacted for an interview and examination.

(A) who
(B) they
(C) which
(D) when

2 ------- attracts consumers to H-TEC Electronics is its affordable prices.

(A) That
(B) Both
(C) What
(D) Each

3 Telcom Inc. promoted Ms. Dumas, ------- excellent market analysis helped to foresee several trend changes.

(A) who
(B) whom
(C) which
(D) whose

4 Customer service representatives are trained to deal with -------- customers report about products and services.

(A) whoever
(B) whatever
(C) whomever
(D) whichever

[5-6] Questions 5-6 refer to the following memo.

The editorial meeting for next month's issue of the magazine has been moved. It was originally scheduled to take place in the conference room ------- last month's meeting
5.
was held. However, the ceiling has started leaking.

While repairs are being made, the room will be off limits. Therefore, please come to my office instead. As usual, we will try to choose a theme ------- readers will find interesting.
6.
Please think of some unique and exciting topics in advance.

5 (A) which
(B) where
(C) when
(D) whose

6 (A) of which
(B) such as
(C) what
(D) that

UNIT 14

생활 어휘(2)

쇼핑·요금 및 주택·보험, 병원에 관한 어휘들입니다.

retail	명 소매 반 wholesale 도매	a **retail** outlet 소매점
delivery	명 배달, 배송 파 deliver 배달하다, 배송하다	an on-time **delivery** 정시 배송 a **delivery** date for a purchase 구매 물품의 배송일
bill	명 요금 청구서 유 invoice (공급 물품에 대한) 청구서	a telephone **bill** 전화 요금 청구서
exchange	명 동 교환[환전](하다) 관 currency 통화, 화폐	**exchange** an item for another model 상품을 다른 모델로 교환하다
afford	동 (~을 살·할) 여유가 있다 파 affordable 살 만한 가격의	**afford** (to buy) a car 차를 살 여유가 있다
payment	명 지불(금), 결제(금)	the date of a **payment** 지불 날짜 **payment** in advance 선불
deposit	명 보증금	pay a **deposit** 보증금을 지불하다
lease	명 임대차 계약 동 임대[임차]하다 유 rent 임대[임차]하다	renew a **lease** 임대 계약을 갱신하다
expense	명 비용 파 expenditure 지출	a repair **expense** 수리 비용 *복수형인 expenses는 출장, 접대 등의 업무상 '경비'를 나타내요.
policy	명 (보험) 증서	issue an insurance **policy** 보험 증서를 발행하다 *기관이나 단체의 '정책, 방침'이란 뜻도 있어요.
claim	명 동 (보험료 등을) 청구(하다)	file a **claim** 청구하다
coverage	명 보장 파 cover (보험으로) 보장하다	insurance **coverage** 보험 보장 범위
pharmacy	명 약국 파 pharmaceutical 약학의, 제약의 관 prescription 처방(전)	a hospital **pharmacy** 병원 약국
treatment	명 치료(법) 유 cure 치료(법), remedy 치료(약) medication 약물 (치료)	emergency **treatment** 응급 치료
consultation	명 상담, 진찰 파 consult 상담하다	a **consultation** with a doctor 의사와의 상담
information	명 정보, 자료 파 inform 알리다, 통지하다 informed 정보력이 있는	detailed **information** about an insurance policy 건강 보험에 대한 상세 정보
cancel	동 취소하다, 중지하다 파 cancellation 취소, 중지	**cancel** an appointment 예약을 취소하다
injury	명 부상 파 injure 부상을 입다	a serious **injury** 심각한 부상 *동사에 -y가 붙어서 명사가 되는 경우에요. ex. recover 회복하다 → recovery 회복

파 파생어 유 유의어 반 반의어 관 관련 어휘

어휘 확인하기

다음 괄호 안에서 알맞은 것을 고르세요.

1 The customer asked to (lease / exchange) the shirt for a bigger size.

2 Ms. Edmonds went to the (pharmacy / treatment) to pick up a prescription.

3 Pia Insurance provides more (injury / coverage) than its competitors at a lower price.

4 Mr. Flinch filed a (claim / refund) with his insurance company for the roof repairs.

실전 감각 키우기

다음 빈칸에 알맞은 것을 고르세요.

5 If the clerk doesn't accept the discount coupon, Ms. Morgan cannot ------- the watch.

(A) rearrange
(B) verify
(C) afford
(D) exchange

6 The ------- of repairing the wall will be fully covered by the moving company.

(A) premiums
(B) wage
(C) advantage
(D) expense

7 Ms. Teller read the insurance ------- carefully before signing it.

(A) policy
(B) payment
(C) method
(D) lease

8 Patients can make decisions about their treatment after the initial -------.

(A) consultation
(B) activity
(C) machine
(D) information

UNIT 14

주어진 문제를 제한시간에 맞추어 풀어 보세요.

Part 5 Choose the one word or phrase that best completes the sentence.

1. Celebrax is a company ------- supplies a wide range of party products for all types of events.

(A) who
(B) whoever
(C) that
(D) whichever

2. Ms. Everton spent months trying to find an effective ------- for her medical condition.

(A) involvement
(B) treatment
(C) injury
(D) origin

3. Junior executives who ------- to attend seminars abroad must get clearance from their supervisors two weeks in advance.

(A) need
(B) is needing
(C) needs
(D) to need

4. Seaside Restaurant, ------- chef underwent intensive training in Italy, received positive reviews from food critics.

(A) which
(B) who
(C) whatever
(D) whose

5. The caterer sends updates to his regular customers ------- he adjusts the prices of the packages.

(A) whenever
(B) however
(C) moreover
(D) whoever

6. The shipment requested by local customers was ------- to the Marks & Vaughn warehouses in Slough yesterday.

(A) connected
(B) delivered
(C) observed
(D) afforded

7. Its poor business model is ------- caused the software developer to go bankrupt.

(A) whose
(B) who
(C) what
(D) which

8. The admission ticket shows the time ------- the performance begins.

(A) which
(B) how
(C) when
(D) their

Part 6 Questions 9-12 refer to the following advertisement.

Stylish Living at City Suites

Be a part of the energy and excitement of downtown! City Suites is a luxury apartment complex ------- is located in the heart of Toronto. Units of various sizes are available
_{9.}
now, and tenants have the option of signing a one- or two-year -------.
_{10.}

City Suites is the ideal home for anyone who ------- to enjoy urban life. In addition, it has
_{11.}
easy access to shopping and dining.

Stop by our rental office on the first floor of City Suites, at 142 Avenue Road, for a tour.
------- . So please have your financial documents ready. This will allow us to accept your
_{12.}
initial payment quickly and get you into your new home as soon as possible.

We look forward to seeing you!

---

9. (A) which
   (B) where
   (C) what
   (D) whenever

10. (A) license
    (B) budget
    (C) subscription
    (D) lease

11. (A) wanting
    (B) to want
    (C) wants
    (D) want

12. (A) You can visit www.city-suites.com to view photos.
    (B) We are even able to provide a contract on the same day.
    (C) There is a free parking area for guests in the underground.
    (D) Many of our tenants have lived here for a long time.

PART 5&6 연결어·구문편

UNIT 15

특수 구문

+생활 어휘(3)

만약에 …

여기에서는 특수 구문인 비교 구문과 가정법 구문을 배우게 되는데요.
비교 구문은 둘 이상의 것을 비교할 때, 가정법 구문은 실제로 일어나지 않았거나
일어날 가능성이 거의 없는 일을 가정할 때 쓰는 구문입니다.

1 원급·비교급·최상급과 원급 비교

2 비교급·최상급 비교

3 가정법의 종류와 쓰임

4 가정법 및 기타 구문의 도치

+ 생활 어휘(3)

1 원급·비교급·최상급과 원급 비교

핵심 POINT

원급·비교급·최상급의 형태와 의미
- 원급: 형용사/부사의 원래 형태. '~한[하게]'의 의미
- 비교급: 〈원급+-er〉 또는 〈more+원급〉, '더 ~한[하게]'의 의미
- 최상급: 〈원급+-est〉 또는 〈most+원급〉, '가장 ~한[하게]'의 의미

원급 비교
- 〈as+원급+as〉: …만큼 ~한[하게]
- 〈as+원급+as possible〉: 가능한 ~한[하게]

A 원급·비교급·최상급의 형태와 의미

- 원급은 형용사와 부사의 원래 형태를 말하며, '~한[하게]'라는 의미입니다.
- 이 원급의 형태를 변형해서 비교급과 최상급을 만들 수 있어요.

비교급	최상급
형태: 〈원급+-er〉 또는 〈more+원급〉 의미: 더 ~한[하게]	형태: 〈원급+-est〉 또는 〈most+원급〉 의미: 가장 ~한[하게]

- 대개 형용사/부사가 1음절이면 뒤에 -er[-est]를, 2음절 이상이면 앞에 more[most]를 붙입니다.
  그러나 모든 단어에 적용되는 것은 아니므로, 불규칙 변화하는 형용사/부사는 따로 기억해두어야 해요.

형용사/부사의 형태	원급	비교급	최상급
1음절 단어	young 어린	young**er** 더 어린	young**est** 가장 어린
2음절 이상의 단어	quickly 빨리	**more** quickly 더 빨리	**most** quickly 가장 빨리
불규칙 변화	good[well] 좋은[잘] bad[ill] 나쁜[아픈] many, much 많은 little 적은	better 더 나은[더 잘] worse 더 나쁜[더 아픈] more 더 많은 less 더 적은	best 최상의[가장 잘] worst 최악의[가장 아픈] most 가장 많은 least 가장 적은

B 원급 비교

- 원급 비교는 두 대상의 상태가 동등함을 나타내며, 기본 형태는 〈as+원급+as〉 입니다.
- as ~ as 사이에 〈형용사+명사〉도 들어갈 수 있어요.
  특히 〈as+many+복수 명사+as〉 또는 〈as+much+불가산 명사+as〉 형태로 자주 쓰입니다.

as+원급+as …만큼 ~한[하게]	The outlet store is **as big as** the department store. 그 아웃렛은 백화점**만큼 크다.** (형용사) We will send the replacement **as quickly as possible**. **가능한 한 빨리** 교체품을 보내드리겠습니다. (부사) **참고** 〈as+원급+as possible〉은 '가능한 한 ~한[하게]'라는 의미예요.
as+형용사+명사+as …만큼 ~한 '명사'	We didn't have **as many complaints as** last month. 우리는 지난달**만큼 많은 불만**을 받지 않았다. (many+복수 명사) This event received **as much attention as** the others. 이번 행사는 다른 행사**만큼 많은 관심**을 받았다. (much+불가산 명사)

핵심 POINT 확인하기

다음 괄호 안에서 알맞은 것을 고르세요.

1 Big Travels is growing (rapidly / more rapidly) than any of its competitors.

2 A recent study said Praville had the (stronger / strongest) economy in the region last year.

3 The design team's newest member is as (competent / more competent) as some of the older members.

4 Interns work as (many / much) hours as full-time staff members.

|핵심 POINT 슬쩍 보기|

1 다른 대상보다 '더 ~한[하게]' 라는 의미를 나타낼 때에는 비교급을 써요.

2 여러 대상 중에서 '가장 ~한 [하게]'이라는 의미를 나타낼 때에는 최상급을 써요.

3 원급 비교에서 as와 as 사이에는 형용사나 부사의 원급이 쓰여요.

4 as ~ as 사이에는 〈many+ 복수 명사〉 또는 〈much+불가산 명사〉가 들어가기도 해요.

실전 감각 키우기

다음 빈칸에 알맞은 것을 고르세요.

5 The convention will be attended by some of the ------- politicians in the country.

(A) most prominent (B) prominence
(C) more prominently (D) prominently

6 Pillhurst Express is as ------- to client requests as larger courier companies.

(A) most responsive (B) responsive
(C) responsiveness (D) responsively

7 The results of medical checkups are sent to patients ------- as possible.

(A) as soon (B) so that
(C) much to (D) as of

8 Journalists from the *Montgomery Gazette* gathered ------- information about the scandal as the police department did.

(A) more than (B) as much
(C) so many (D) the most

UNIT 15

2 비교급·최상급 비교

비교급 비교
- 〈비교급+than〉: …보다 더 ~한[하게]
- 〈less+원급+than〉: …보다 덜 ~한[하게]
- 비교급 강조 부사: much, even, still, far, a lot 훨씬

최상급 비교
- 〈the+최상급+of[in] …〉: … 중에서 가장 ~한[하게]
- 〈the+서수+최상급〉: …번째로 ~한[하게]
- 〈one of the+최상급+복수 명사〉: 가장 ~한 '명사'들 중 하나

A 비교급 비교와 구문

- 두 대상을 비교하여 '…보다 더 ~한[하게]'의 의미를 나타내며, 기본 형태는 〈비교급+than〉입니다.
- 전치사 than 뒤에는 비교 대상이 등장하며, 그 대상을 문맥상 알 수 있는 경우는 than과 함께 생략 가능합니다.

비교급+than …보다 더 ~한[하게]	The current unemployment rate is **higher than** it was last year. 현재 실업률은 작년**보다 높다.** They've decided to offer discounts **more often** (**than** before). 그들은 (예전**보다**) 더 **자주** 할인을 해 주기로 결정했다.
less+원급+than …보다 덜 ~한[하게]	The new printer is **less noisy than** the old one. 새 프린터는 오래된 것**보다 덜 시끄럽다.**

- 부사 much, even, still, far, a lot 등은 비교급 앞에 쓰여 '훨씬'의 의미로 비교급을 강조해요.

The outlet store is **much bigger** than the department store.   아웃렛은 백화점보다 **훨씬 더 크다.**

The responses were **far more positive** than in the last survey.
응답은 지난 번 설문에 비해 **훨씬** 더 긍정적이었다.

참고 비교급과 함께 '더 이상 …아닌'이라는 의미의 부사 no longer도 자주 출제되니 기억해두세요.
The training video is **no longer** available online.   이 교육 영상은 **더 이상** 인터넷에서 이용할 수 없습니다.

B 최상급 비교

- 셋 이상의 대상을 비교하여 '가장 ~한[하게]'라는 의미를 나타내며, 기본 형태는 〈the+최상급〉입니다.
- 비교 범위를 나타내기 위해 최상급 뒤에 〈of+복수 명사〉 혹은 〈in+장소〉를 쓰기도 해요.

(the+) 최상급+of[in] … 중에서 가장 ~한[하게]	The store is **the newest building in** this area. 그 가게는 이 지역에서 **가장 새 건물이다.** Among the team members, John works **most quickly.** 존은 팀원들 중에서 **가장 빨리** 일한다. 참고 형용사와 달리, 부사의 최상급 앞에는 보통 정관사 the를 쓰지 않아요.
the+서수+최상급 …번째로 ~한[하게]	They conducted **the third largest** recall in history. 그들은 사상 **세 번째로 규모가 큰** 제품 회수를 시행했다.
one of the+최상급+복수 명사 가장 ~한 '명사'들 중 하나	This model is **one of the fastest cars** on the market. 이 모델은 시중에서 **가장 빠른 차들 중에 하나입니다.**

핵심 POINT 확인하기

다음 괄호 안에서 알맞은 것을 고르세요.

1 No one on the team works (hard / harder) than Mr. Murphy.

2 This experiment requires laboratory scales that are much (sensitive / more sensitive).

3 Mr. Tratoni is the (greater / greatest) designer in the country.

4 Aloya Station is the third (busier / busiest) station in the city at the moment.

|핵심 POINT 슬쩍 보기|

1 비교 대상을 나타내는 전치사 than은 비교급과 함께 쓰여요.

2 much, even, far 등은 비교급 앞에 쓰여 비교급을 강조하는 부사들이에요.

3 최상급 비교는 〈the+최상급+in[of]〉 형태로 나타내요.

4 〈the+서수+최상급〉은 '…번째로 ~한[하게]'라는 뜻이에요.

실전 감각 키우기

다음 빈칸에 알맞은 것을 고르세요.

5 Some staff members from satellite offices are ------- familiar with the company's policies than others.

(A) less   (B) quite
(C) so   (D) fewer

6 Outsourcing the billing procedures is considerably cheaper ------- performing the work in-house.

(A) within   (B) between
(C) than   (D) to

7 These days, government inspectors examine factory machinery even ------- than before.

(A) more careful   (B) most careful
(C) most carefully   (D) more carefully

8 Ravenbam Tower is the ------- of all structures in Attium City.

(A) higher   (B) high
(C) highest   (D) highly

UNIT 15

3 가정법의 종류와 쓰임

핵심 POINT

가정법 과거
- 현재 사실에 대한 가정(~하다면 …할 텐데)
- 〈If+주어+과거 동사, 주어+would[could/might]+동사원형〉

가정법 과거완료
- 과거 사실에 대한 가정(~했다면 …했을 텐데)
- 〈If+주어+had *p.p.*, 주어+would[could/might]+have *p.p.*〉

A 가정법 과거

- 현재의 사실을 반대로 가정하거나, 일어나지 않은 일, 일어날 가능성이 희박한 일을 나타내요.

형태	〈If+주어+**과거 동사**, 주어+**would[could/might]+동사원형**〉
의미	(현재) ~하다면 …할 텐데

If she **knew** the neighborhood, she **would recommend** a place to visit.
그녀가 동네를 **알고 있다면**, 방문할 만한 곳을 **추천해 줄 텐데**.
→ 그녀가 동네에 대해 모른다는 현재의 사실에 대한 반대 상황을 가정

- 가정법 if절의 동사가 be동사일 때, 주어의 단·복수에 상관없이 주로 were를 씁니다.

If he **were** at home, I **could contact** him. 그가 집에 **있다면**, 그에게 **연락할 수 있을 텐데**.

B 가정법 과거완료

- 가정법 과거와 비슷하지만, 현재가 아닌 과거의 사실을 반대로 가정할 때 가정법 과거완료를 씁니다.

형태	〈If+주어+**had *p.p.***, 주어+**would[could/might]+have *p.p.***〉
의미	(과거에) ~했다면 …했을 텐데

If he **had known** earlier, he **would have made** a reservation.
그가 더 일찍 **알았더라면**, 예약을 **했을 텐데**.
→ 그가 늦게 알아서 예약하지 못했던 과거의 사실에 대한 반대 상황을 가정

C 가정법 미래

- 일어날 가능성이 낮은 미래의 일을 가정할 때 주로 사용합니다.

형태	〈If+주어+**should+동사원형**, 주어+**would(will)[could(can)/might(may)]+동사원형**〉
의미	(미래에) ~한다면 …할 텐데

If Jill **should attend** the performance, she **would[will] invite** us.
만일 질이 공연에 **참가한다면**, 우리를 **초대할 텐데**.

참고 〈If+주어+should+동사원형, 명령문(동사원형)〉 형태로 말하는 사람의 정중한 태도를 나타낼 수 있습니다.
If you **should make** a purchase, **get** a receipt. 혹시 구매를 **하시면**, 영수증을 **받으세요**.
If you **should go** hiking, **bring** some water with you. 만일 하이킹을 **가면**, 물을 약간 **가지고 가세요**.

핵심 POINT 확인하기

다음 괄호 안에서 알맞은 것을 고르세요.

1 If the company went bankrupt, shareholders would (lose / have lost) large amounts of money.

2 If a suitable location (was found / were found), Estus Enterprises would seriously consider relocating its headquarters.

3 If the supervisor had known about the problem, he could (have done / done) something to solve it.

4 If you should (have seen / see) an error message on the printer, check for a paper jam.

|핵심 POINT 슬쩍 보기|

1 가정법 과거에서는 주절의 동사로 〈would[could/might]+동사원형〉을 써요.

2 가정법 과거의 if절에서 be동사는 수일치와 상관없이 주로 were를 써요.

3 가정법 과거완료에서 주절의 동사로 〈would[could/should]+have p.p.〉를 써요.

4 주절이 명령문이면 가정법 미래를 써요.

실전 감각 키우기

다음 빈칸에 알맞은 것을 고르세요.

5 빈출 If the manager ------- them enough time, the staff could have prepared a presentation for the potential investors.

(A) had given   (B) gives
(C) will give   (D) gave

6 If the machine ------- capable of producing more units per hour, we might install it in our factory.

(A) be   (B) were
(C) is   (D) been

7 빈출 If Ms. Etherington had not made the payment on June 30, ownership of the vehicle ------- to the original seller.

(A) will revert   (B) being reverted
(C) has reverted (D) would have reverted

8 If you ------- to end your magazine subscription early, send an e-mail to our customer service department.

(A) had wished   (B) have wished
(C) should wish   (D) wished

UNIT 15

핵심
POINT

가정법 If의 생략과 도치
- if절의 동사가 were[had/should]일 때, if 생략 후 주어, 동사 도치
- 〈Should+주어+동사〉 구조의 가정법 미래 문장에 유의

기타 구문의 도치
- 부정어 강조: 〈부정어 Not[Never/Seldom]+동사+주어〉
- 보어 강조: 〈Enclosed[Attached/Among]+동사+주어〉

A 가정법 If의 생략과 도치

- 도치란 문장에서 주어와 동사의 순서가 바뀌어 〈동사+주어〉형태로 쓰이는 것을 말해요.
- 가정법 if절의 동사가 were[had/should]일 때 if를 생략하고 주어와 동사를 도치시켜요.
  특히, should로 시작하는 도치된 형태의 가정법 미래 문장이 자주 등장하니 잘 기억해두세요.

가정법 과거	**If**+주어+**were** ~,	→	**Were**+주어 ~,
가정법 과거완료	**If**+주어+**had** *p.p.* ~,	→	**Had**+주어+*p.p.* ~,
가정법 미래	**If**+주어+**should**+동사원형 ~, 생략　　　　도치	→	**Should**+주어+동사원형 ~,

가정법 과거　**If** the hotel **were** close to the museum, I would reserve it.
→ **Were** the hotel close to the museum, I would reserve it.
그 호텔이 미술관에 **가깝다면**, 그곳을 예약할 텐데.

가정법 과거완료　**If** he **had** cleaned the garage, I could have parked my car.
→ **Had** he **cleaned** the garage, I could have parked my car.
그가 차고를 **청소했다면**, 내 차를 주차할 수 있었을 텐데.

가정법 미래　**If** you **should become** ill at night, go to the all-night pharmacy.
→ **Should** you **become** ill at night, go to the all-night pharmacy.
혹시 밤에 **아프면**, 밤새 여는 약국으로 가세요.

B 기타 구문의 도치

ⓐ 부정어 강조

- 문장의 부정어를 강조하려고 문장 맨 앞으로 옮기고 주어와 동사를 도치시킬 수 있습니다.
  I **have never seen** such a beautiful painting.
  → **Never have** I **seen** such a beautiful painting.　나는 이렇게 아름다운 그림을 **본 적이 없다.**

ⓑ 보어 강조

- 보어를 강조하기 위해 문장 앞으로 옮기고 주어와 동사를 도치시킨 형태로, enclosed, attached, among 등은 하나의 표현처럼 뒤에 주어, 동사가 도치된 형태로 자주 등장하므로 기억해두세요.
  A check is **enclosed** in the amount of $200.
  → **Enclosed** is a check in the amount of $200.　200달러 상당의 수표가 동봉되었습니다.

핵심 POINT 확인하기

다음 괄호 안에서 알맞은 것을 고르세요.

|핵심 POINT 슬쩍 보기|

1 (Were / If) the invitations sent out earlier, the event would be filled to capacity.

1 가정법 과거에서 if가 생략되면, 동사가 주어 앞으로 도치돼요.

2 (Should / Although) you have any inquiries about our products, please call BirzaTech at 800-1256.

2 if가 생략되어서 조동사가 주어 앞으로 도치된 형태예요.

3 (Has / Had) Ms. Olsen studied harder, she might have passed the computer proficiency test.

3 가정법 과거완료에서 if가 생략되면, 〈Had+주어+p.p.〉가 돼요.

4 Never (will anyone / anyone will) be able to come into the office under our surveillance system.

4 부정어 never가 앞으로 오면 주어와 동사가 도치돼요.

실전 감각 키우기

다음 빈칸에 알맞은 것을 고르세요.

5 ------- Brionext Graphics invested in online game development, it could have significantly grown its business.

(A) Have   (B) Never
(C) Had   (D) Should

6 ------- is the invoice for the completed Olevao Clubhouse landscaping project.

(A) To attach   (B) Attach
(C) Attached   (D) Attaches

7 ------- any machinery malfunction, please report the incident to the plant manager immediately.

빈출

(A) Should   (B) Even so
(C) As well as   (D) Somewhere

8 ------- does Veestan Hardware miss its monthly sales target of $5,000.

(A) Still   (B) While
(C) Until   (D) Seldom

UNIT 15

앞에서 학습한 핵심 POINT를 떠올리며 빈칸을 완성해 보세요.

핵심 POINT 1-2

원급·비교급·최상급 비교

원급·비교급·최상급

- **①** _____: 형용사/부사의 원래 형태 ~한[하게]
- 비교급: 〈원급+-er〉 또는 〈**②** _____+원급〉 더 ~한[하게]
- 최상급: 〈원급+**③** _____〉 또는 〈most+원급〉 가장 ~한[하게]

비교 구문

- 원급 비교: 〈as+원급+as〉 …만큼 ~한[하게], 〈as+원급+as **④** _____〉 가능한 ~한[하게]
- 비교급 비교: 〈비교급+than〉 …보다 더 ~한[하게], 〈**⑤** _____+원급+than〉 …보다 덜 ~한[하게]
  - 비교급 강조 부사: much, even, still, far, a lot 훨씬
- 최상급 비교: 〈the+최상급+of[in] …〉 …에서 가장 ~한[하게], 〈the+서수+최상급〉 …번째로 ~한[하게]
  - 〈one of the+최상급+복수 명사〉 가장 ~한 '명사'들 중 하나

핵심 POINT 3-4

가정법의 종류와 쓰임

가정법 과거

- **⑥** _____ 사실에 대한 가정 ~하다면 …할 텐데
- 〈If+주어+과거 동사, 주어+would[could/might]+**⑦** _____〉

가정법 과거완료

- 과거 사실에 대한 가정 ~했다면 …했을 텐데
- 〈If+주어+**⑧** _____, 주어+would[could/might]+have p.p.〉

가정법 및 기타 구문의 도치

- 가정법: If절 동사가 were[had/should]일 때, if 생략 후 주어, 동사 도치
  - 〈**⑨** _____+주어+동사〉 구조의 가정법 미래 문장에 유의
- 기타 구문: 부정어 강조 〈부정어 **⑩** _____[Never/Seldom]+동사+주어〉
  - 보어 강조 〈Enclosed[Attached/Among]+동사+주어〉

|빈칸 정답 살짝 보기|

① 원급 **②** more **③** -est **④** possible **⑤** less **⑥** 현재 **⑦** 동사원형 **⑧** had p.p. **⑨** Should **⑩** Not

다음 빈칸에 알맞은 것을 고르세요.

1 The northern part of Berpo City is ----- populated than the southern area.

(A) more densely
(B) most densely
(C) more dense
(D) most dense

2 Ms. Davenport is considered the ------- senior executive of Yanpro Insurance, Inc.

(A) eloquence
(B) more eloquent
(C) eloquently
(D) most eloquent

3 If Emanti Ventures had provided better benefits, many former employees ------- with the company.

(A) were staying
(B) had stayed
(C) be staying
(D) would have stayed

4 ------- the store clerk been able to assist the shopper, the customer's feedback would have been more positive.

(A) Had
(B) Whenever
(C) Although
(D) If fact

[5-6] Questions 5-6 refer to the following memo.

To: All employees

From: Karen Spencer, Office Manager

Starting May 1, we will use a software program to track employees' days off. This program will allow us to process vacation requests twice ------- as we did with the paper
5.
system.

Instead of gathering signatures from multiple supervisors, employees will file requests centrally on the company's Web site.

Should you encounter any problems with the software, ------- Klaus Meldon in the IT
6.
department.

5 (A) fastest
(B) as fast
(C) faster
(D) as faster

6 (A) contacts
(B) contacted
(C) contact
(D) to contact

UNIT 15

휴양 및 휴식, 레저와 관련된 어휘들입니다.

departure	몡 출발(편) 파 depart (from) (~에서) 출발하다 반 arrival 도착	a **departure** gate 탑승구
delay	몡 통 지연(시키다) 파 delayed 지연된 유 postpone[put off] 연기하다	a flight **delay** 비행편 지연 without **delay** 지체 없이, 즉시
domestic	혱 국내의 파 domestically 국내적으로	a **domestic** flight 국내선 비행기 ↔ an international flight 국제선 비행기
valid	혱 유효한 반 invalid 효력 없는, expired 만료된	possess a **valid** passport 유효한 여권을 소지하다
belongings	몡 소지품, 짐 유 possessions 소지품, 소유물	personal **belongings** 개인 소지품
view	몡 경관, 견해 통 보다, 생각하다	in the **view** of the publisher 출판사의 견해로는
transportation	몡 교통, 운송 파 transport 운송(하다)	use public **transportation** 대중 교통 수단을 이용하다
vehicle	몡 차량	a parked **vehicle** 주차된 차량
license	몡 면허증, 자격증 유 certificate 증명서 permit 허가(증); 허가하다	a driver's **license** 운전 면허증 a **license** holder 면허증 소지자
congestion	몡 정체, 혼잡 파 congest 정체시키다 congested 정체된, 혼잡한	traffic **congestion** 교통 정체
park	통 주차하다	**park** in a garage 차고 안에 주차하다
upcoming	혱 곧 있을	an **upcoming** business trip 곧 있을 출장 *형용사이지만 명사를 앞에서 수식하는 기능만 있고, 보어로는 쓰이지 않아요.
itinerary	몡 (여행) 일정표 유 schedule 일정	a detailed **itinerary** 상세한 일정표
expand	통 확대되다, 늘리다 파 expansion 확대, 확장	**expand** a distribution area 유통 구역을 확대하다 **expand** a factory 공장을 확장하다
extend	통 연장하다, 늘리다 파 extensive 광범위한, 포괄적인 extended 장기간에 걸친, 늘어난	**extend** the stay for a week 체류 기간을 일주일 연장하다 *extend는 expand와 달리 범위뿐 아니라 시간을 늘린다는 뜻으로도 써요.
confirm	통 확인하다 파 confirmation 확인	**confirm** some dates 날짜를 확인하다
arrange	통 정하다 파 arrangement 준비, 마련	**arrange** an appointment 약속을 정하다
accommodate	통 수용하다 파 accommodations 숙박시설	**accommodate** a guest 투숙객을 수용하다

파 파생어 유 유의어 반 반의어 관 관련 어휘

어휘 확인하기

다음 괄호 안에서 알맞은 것을 고르세요.

1 Rooms with (views / vehicles) on the sea are more expensive.

2 Orsus Co. is preparing for an overseas (expansion / itinerary) of its business.

3 All of our travel agents have (extensive / upcoming) experience customizing vacation packages.

4 The hotel's event hall can (expand / accommodate) up to seventy-five people.

실전 감각 키우기

다음 빈칸에 알맞은 것을 고르세요.

5 Meadow Railways cannot process ticket changes within one hour of the scheduled -------.

(A) baggage
(B) direction
(C) departure
(D) location

6 Please follow the boarding procedures to ensure the flight can depart without -------.

(A) destination
(B) favor
(C) belongings
(D) delay

7 Additional lanes will be built in order to avoid ------- during rush hour.

(A) congestion
(B) transportation
(C) climates
(D) pavement

8 Send an e-mail to the public relations department to ------- a private tour of the facility.

(A) intend
(B) arrive
(C) arrange
(D) communicate

UNIT 15

주어진 문제를 제한시간에 맞추어 풀어 보세요.

Part 5 Choose the one word or phrase that best completes the sentence.

1. If his video conference with investors finished earlier, the CEO ------- to the product launch.

   (A) go
   (B) would go
   (C) will go
   (D) gone

2. The regional manager will explain the details of the ------- relocation to Fraize Lake.

   (A) numerous
   (B) adjacent
   (C) upcoming
   (D) frequent

3. If the promotional displays ------- in a more visible spot, a greater number of customers would have purchased the products.

   (A) placed
   (B) had been placed
   (C) has placed
   (D) are placed

4. Experts say that employees who receive ------- feedback perform better than others.

   (A) more precise
   (B) precisely
   (C) most precise
   (D) as precise

5. Please ------- your appointment with Mr. Walsh by calling his assistant no later than June 12.

   (A) confirm
   (B) remind
   (C) agree
   (D) comply

6. Ms. Scott's speech at the technology conference was ------- longer than the keynote address.

   (A) too
   (B) so
   (C) even
   (D) more

7. Mr. Burnage may contact some successful local business owners ------- extra funding be required to start his new restaurant.

   (A) when
   (B) should
   (C) in fact
   (D) through

8. Freetelecomm's revenue has increased continuously over the year, but Internet bundles sales grew ------- last June.

   (A) most quickly
   (B) quickness
   (C) more quickly
   (D) quick

Part 6 Questions 9-12 refer to the following letter.

Irene Reynolds

318 Saint Francis Way

Brookfield, WI 53005

Dear Ms. Reynolds,

Thank you for your interest in our European Summer Tour, one of our -------- tour

  9.

packages so far. The trip is fully booked at this time, but I have added you to the waiting

list. If a spot ------- up, I will let you know right away.

  10.

In the event of a last-minute cancellation, I'd like you to be fully prepared. All tour

participants must possess a ------- passport with at least one blank page remaining.

  11.

The trip package includes all hotel stays, travel costs, and admission fees to sites for the

duration of the tour. However, please keep in mind that you will be responsible for

transportation to the starting point, which is in Paris.

------- .

  12.

Tamara Indell

Customer Service Agent, Go Abroad Tours

---

9.   (A) popular
     (B) more popular
     (C) popularity
     (D) most popular

10. (A) should open
     (B) had opened
     (C) opened
     (D) to open

11. (A) domestic
     (B) valid
     (C) distinctive
     (D) relevant

12. (A) The hotels we have reserved have
         excellent service.
     (B) Paris is well-known for its many
         tourist attractions.
     (C) We hope you will be able to travel
         with us soon.
     (D) Please send in your application in a
         timely manner.

PART

7

Reading Comprehension

"PART 7은 이렇게 풉니다"

STEP 1 · 문제와 선택지를 먼저 읽자!

PART 7 지문은 길이가 길어서 독해 시간을 줄이려면 문제에서 묻고 있는 내용을 중심으로 핵심만 빠르게 파악하는 것이 중요합니다. 문제와 선택지를 먼저 읽고, 핵심어에 동그라미를 쳐 보세요.

STEP 2 · 지문 앞부분에서 핵심 내용을 파악하자!

토익에서는 지문의 핵심 내용이 제목이나 첫 번째 문단에 집약되어 있는 경우가 많아요. 이 부분들을 먼저 꼼꼼히 확인하고 뒤에 이어질 내용을 예측하면서 읽으세요.

STEP 3 · 문제에서 묻는 내용을 지문에서 찾아 보자!

PART 7 문제의 단서는 지문 안에 명확히 담겨 있어요. 이때, 지문의 표현이 문제나 선택지에서는 다른 표현으로 바뀌어 표현(패러프레이징)된다는 점을 기억해두세요.

PART 7 문제 유형편

UNIT 16

문제 유형

+패러프레이징(1)

화장실에 가고 싶을 때는
어떻게 하나요?

일반적 내용을 묻는 유형

- PART 7의 가장 기본적인 문제 유형으로, 지문별로 한 문제씩 출제돼요.
- 이 유형의 문제는 주로 글의 〈목적, 주제, 대상〉을 물어봅니다.
  예를 들어, 이메일/편지에서는 글을 쓴 목적을, 공지/메모에서는 글의 주제나 대상을, 광고에서는 광고하는 상품에 대해 묻습니다.
- 또한, 이 유형은 글의 전반적인 내용과 관련 있기 때문에 순서상 주로 첫 번째 문제로 나옵니다.

목적	**What** is the **purpose** of the letter? 이 편지의 **목적은?** **Why** was the letter written? 이 편지가 쓰여진 **이유는?**
주제	**What** is the article **mainly discussing**? 이 기사의 **주제는?** **What** is the memo **mainly about**? 이 메모는 주로 무엇에 관한 것인가?
사람·사물	**For whom** is the announcement **intended**? 이 공고가 의도하고 있는 **대상은?** **What** is being advertised? 광고되고 있는 것은 **무엇인가?**

핵심 POINT

하나! 앞부분에 주목
지문 앞부분의 주제나 제목을 확인하고, 주제문(topic sentence)을 먼저 확인하세요.

둘! 전체 훑어 읽기
파악한 주제를 중심으로 전체 내용을 훑어 읽어(skimming) 가면서 정답을 찾으세요.

To: Joel Swanson <j_swanson@acefoods.com>
From: ABC Supplies <service@abcsupplies.com>
Date: January 18
단서1 Subject: Your order

단서1 Order number 2894-4029 for Joel Swanson will not arrive on January 19. Unfortunately, **단서2** our delivery trucks are behind schedule due to heavy snow. Your merchandise is now scheduled to arrive on January 22. **단서2** We're pleased to offer you a coupon for 10 percent off your next order as an apology for the inconvenience.

Sincerely,

The ABC Supplies Team

>>> **단서1 지문 앞부분에서 주제 파악**
제목(Subject:) 부분을 보니 주문에 관한 이메일이네요. 이제 지문 앞부분의 주제문을 살펴보세요. 주문품이 예정된 날짜에 도착하지 않을 것이라는 내용을 통해 배송이 지연되었음을 알 수 있어요.

단서2 전반적인 내용 파악
'배송 지연'에 관한 정보를 중심으로 글을 훑어 읽으세요. 늦어진 이유가 폭설 때문이며, 이에 대한 보상으로 할인 쿠폰을 제공할 것이라고 하네요.

Q. What is the purpose of the e-mail?

(A) To advertise a sale
(B) To request a payment
(C) To report a delivery delay
(D) To place an order

>>> 글의 목적을 묻는 문제
앞부분에서 주문품이 예정일에 도착하지 못함을 알려준 후, 뒤이어 그 이유와 보상에 대해 설명하고 있으므로 정답은 (C)입니다.

한 단락 지문 연습하기

다음 지문을 읽고 질문에 답하세요.

On behalf of Worldwind Travel, I'd like to inform you that you are eligible for 25 percent off any travel package booked between February 1 and March 31. This includes cruises, guided tours, and luxury vacations. This discount is available to preferred members only.

1 Why was this letter written?

(A) To introduce a special offer
(B) To correct an error in a bill
(C) To send a travel itinerary
(D) To recommend a travel destination

실전 감각 키우기

Questions 2-3 refer to the following announcement.

Announcement

The lease on our office here in the Utica Building will expire soon, so we are moving to a new place. A real estate agent has finally found a space that is suitable for our needs. The office is newly built, and it can accommodate all of our staff. Employees will be responsible for packing their personal belongings. If you need any materials such as boxes or tape, please talk to your supervisor. I'm sure everyone will enjoy the spacious new office.

Regards,

Donna Harris

2 What is the purpose of the announcement?

(A) To show appreciation to staff
(B) To describe job responsibilities
(C) To explain a new policy
(D) To announce a location change

3 For whom is the announcement intended?

(A) Project supervisors
(B) Job applicants
(C) Staff members
(D) Apartment tenants

세부 내용을 묻는 유형

- 세부 내용을 묻는 문제는 PART 7에서 40~50% 이상을 차지하는 가장 중요한 문제 유형입니다.
- 이 유형은 구체적인 내용을 묻기 때문에, 〈누가(Who), 어디서(Where), 어떻게(How), 언제(When), 무엇을(What), 왜(Why)〉의 의문사를 활용한 다양한 질문이 등장해요.
- 주로 일반적 내용을 묻는 유형의 문제 다음에 배치되며, 매 지문 당 최소 한 문제 이상 출제돼요.

사람	**Who** is in charge of the marketing strategies? 마케팅 전략을 담당하는 **사람은?**
장소	**Where** will they hold the meeting? 그들이 회의를 할 **장소는?**
방법	**How** does Mr. Smith place an order? 스미스 씨가 주문을 하는 **방법은?**
시간	**When** did the new item arrive? 신상품이 도착한 **때는?**
대상	**What** is included in the letter? 편지에 첨부된 **것은?**
이유	**Why** does Ms. Walling propose the idea? 월링 씨가 아이디어를 제안한 **이유는?**

핵심 POINT

하나! 질문의 키워드 파악
지문보다 질문을 먼저 읽고 질문의 키워드를 파악하세요. 이 키워드를 잘 기억한 후 지문 읽기를 시작해야 합니다.

둘! 키워드 찾아 읽기(scanning)
지문을 읽으면서 질문에서 묻지 않는 내용들은 빠르게 지나가고 키워드가 나오는 부분을 집중적으로 읽어서 정답을 찾으세요.

Dear Ms. Zimmerman,

Jeanette Robinson is highly recommended for the position of manager of the human resources department. She has given a strong performance during her five years at Fritz Financial. 단서2 Management is especially impressed with her ability to keep her work organized despite working on multiple projects at the same time.

Regards,

Paul Dreher

>>> 단서1 **질문 먼저 읽고 키워드 파악**
질문에서 '경영진이 로빈슨 씨에게 감명을 받은 이유'를 묻고 있으니까 키워드는 management(경영진)와 impressed(감명을 받은)예요.

단서2 **지문에서 해당 키워드 찾기**
질문의 키워드가 지문의 네 번째 줄에 등장해요. 이 부분을 보면 경영진은 '그녀가 일을 체계화하는 능력'에 감명 받았음을 알 수 있어요.

Q. 단서1 Why is management impressed with Ms. Robinson?

(A) She worked as a project leader.
(B) She can finish the work quickly.
(C) She developed a good financial plan.
(D) She has excellent organizational skills.

>>> **이유를 묻는 문제**
질문의 키워드가 등장하는 지문 부분에서 로빈슨 씨가 '일을 체계화하는 능력이 있다'고 했으므로 정답은 (D)예요.

다음 지문을 읽고 질문에 답하세요.

We have recently signed a contract with Prime Co. to advertise the Carter-360 washing machine. We're confident that the campaign designed by Prime Co. will be a success, as the company specializes in promoting products that are new to the market.

1 What is Prime Co.'s specialty?

(A) Repairing washing machines
(B) Manufacturing electronics
(C) Advertising new products
(D) Transporting merchandise

Questions 2-3 refer to the following letter.

Etta Stuart
Knight Apartments, #302
1791 Columbia Road
Philadelphia, PA 19108

Dear Ms. Stuart,

The maintenance team has reviewed your request for renovation work on September 19. The apartment owner approved it on September 23. A crew is going to start the renovation at 10 A.M. on Saturday, September 27, and it will be completed in around four hours. A crew member will pick up the key from the rental office, so you don't have to be home at that time. Someone from the rental office will stop by the following day to make sure you are satisfied with the finished result.

Sincerely,

The Knight Apartments Staff

2 When will the renovation be finished?

(A) On September 19
(B) On September 23
(C) On September 27
(D) On September 28

3 Where will a crew member get the key?

(A) From Ms. Stuart
(B) From the rental office
(C) From the crew supervisor
(D) From the maintenance office

UNIT 16

NOT이 포함된 유형

- PART 7 문제 중 '언급되지 않은 내용은?', '사실이 아닌 것은?'과 같이, 선택지 중에서 한 개의 틀린 정보가 어느 것인지 묻는 문제를 이 유형으로 분류할 수 있어요.
- 이 유형은 전체 문제 중 15% 정도의 비율로 출제되며, 사실상 세부 내용을 묻는 유형과 같아요.
- 그러나 지문 곳곳을 확인하여 맞는 내용의 선택지를 제외하고, 틀리거나 없는 내용의 선택지 하나만 골라야 하기 때문에 난이도가 높은 편입니다.

What is **NOT** mentioned as a requirement of the job? 일자리의 자격 요건으로 언급되지 **않은** 것은?
What is **NOT** going to happen at the annual event? 연례 행사에서 일어나지 **않을** 일은?
What is **NOT** included in the message? 메시지에 포함되지 **않은** 것은?
What is **NOT** true about room service? 룸서비스에 관해 사실이 **아닌** 것은?

핵심 POINT

하나! 선택지의 키워드 찾기
먼저 질문과 선택지를 읽은 후, 각 선택지에서 핵심 키워드를 찾아 표시하세요.

둘! 대조 소거법 이용
지문을 읽어가며 해당 키워드가 등장할 때마다 선택지와 대조하세요. 맞는 것들을 모두 소거하면, 틀리거나 언급되지 않은 내용의 선택지 하나가 정답으로 남게 돼요.

Managers should prepare the factory for the inspection tomorrow. 단서 2B Please check the machinery, 단서 2C give safety goggles and gloves to your employees, 단서 2D and throw away all boxes and containers that we are not using. Let's work together to improve our score compared to last year.

>>> 단서 1 **선택지의 키워드 파악**
질문을 먼저 읽고 선택지마다 키워드에 동그라미 하세요. '관리자의 업무'에 대해 물었으니 (A)는 Posting, (B)는 equipment, (C)는 protective gear, (D)는 Throwing away가 키워드가 될 수 있겠네요.

단서 2 **선택지에서 지문 내용 대조 소거**
지문에서 선택지에 등장한 키워드가 나오는지 살펴 보세요. 단서 2B 에서 기계 확인, 단서 2C 에서 안전 장비 제공, 단서 2D 에서 필요 없는 물품 버리기와 같은 키워드 내용을 대조해 소거하니 (A)만 남네요.

Q. 단서 1 What is NOT mentioned as a task that managers >>> should do?

(A) Posting a safety notice
(B) Checking some equipment
(C) Giving workers protective gear
(D) Throwing away unnecessary items

언급되지 않은 내용을 찾는 문제
단서 2B ~ 단서 2D 의 내용들이 각각 선택지에 패러프레이징되어 나오므로, 언급되지 않은 (A)가 정답이에요.

다음 지문을 읽고 질문에 답하세요.

Ms. Hutchinson would be an excellent candidate for the hotel manager position. She has nearly ten years of experience in the tourism industry, and she planned training programs at her former job. In addition, she is proficient in three languages, which would be useful for communicating with international travelers.

1 What is NOT indicated as one of Ms. Hutchinson's qualifications?

(A) The ability to plan training
(B) Proficiency in multiple languages
(C) Work history in the tourism industry
(D) Experience in international business

Questions 2-3 refer to the following notice.

At the Lakeville Community Center meeting on April 2, upcoming activities for local residents were announced. Participants can take classes in watercolor painting, yoga, choir singing, and more.

Sign up for any activity by clicking on the "Registration" button on our homepage. Community members of all ages are invited to participate. The deadline for registration for the summer session is May 15. Remember, because of generous financial support from the community, all classes are offered free of charge.

2 What is NOT an activity residents can do at the center?

(A) Take swimming classes
(B) Practice yoga
(C) Learn to paint
(D) Participate in a choir

3 What is NOT true about the registration?

(A) It can be done online.
(B) It is open only to adults.
(C) It ends on May 15.
(D) It is offered at no cost.

UNIT 16

4

추론 유형

- PART 7 문제 중 약 10% 정도 출제되는 추론 유형은 '추론할 수 있는 것은?', '암시하는 것은?', '아마 ~일 것 같은 것은?'과 같이 '추론, 추측, 예상'을 통해 답을 찾는 유형이에요.
- 이 유형의 질문에는 imply, infer, expect, suggest와 같은 동사나 probably, most likely 같은 부사 표현이 등장해요.
- 정답의 단서가 직접적으로 제시되지 않고, 단서 문장의 함축적 의미를 유추해야 답을 찾을 수 있습니다.

> What does the memo **imply** about Mr. Smith? 메모에서 스미스 씨에 대해 **암시하는** 것은?
> What can be **inferred** about AVT Air? AVT 항공에 대해 **추론할** 수 있는 것은?
> What is **probably** true about the meeting? 회의에 대해 **아마** 사실인 것은?
> What does Ms. Clifton **most likely** think about the project?
> 클리프턴 씨가 프로젝트에 대해 생각할 **것 같은 것은?**

핵심 POINT

하나! 지문에서 단서 파악

추론 문제라 해도 내용을 상상해서는 안 되고 반드시 지문에서 정답의 단서를 찾아야 해요. 추론 문제 여도 단서는 꼭 등장하니까요.

둘! 함축적 의미 파악

단서 문장에서 간접적으로 전달하고 있는 정보를 파악하여 정답을 고르세요.

Please join us for personnel manager Valerie Wiley's retirement dinner on August 13. All employees are invited, and it will be a great opportunity for everyone to meet Travis Harding. 단서1 단서2 Mr. Harding will be in charge of all personnel and administrative employees after the departments are combined next month.

>> 단서1 **지문에서 정답 단서 파악**
질문의 동사 imply를 보니 추론 유형이네요. '회사에 대해 암시된 내용'을 지문에서 빠르게 찾아 보니, 맨 마지막 문장에서 '부서가 다음 달에 통합이 된다'고 했어요.

단서2 **단서 문장의 함축적 의미 파악**
단서 문장에서 부서가 통합된다는 말은 조직의 구성이 바뀐다는 의미니까 '부서가 재구성된다'는 내용을 추론할 수 있어요.

Q. 단서1 What is implied about the company?

(A) It is moving to a new location.
(B) It currently has a job opening.
(C) It has recently hired Valerie Wiley.
(D) It plans to restructure its departments.

>> 추론 문제
단서2 에서 두 부서의 통합을 간접적으로 알리고 있으므로, 부서의 재구성(restructure its departments)이란 표현이 있는 (D)가 정답이에요.

한 단락 지문 연습하기

다음 지문을 읽고 질문에 답하세요.

Movie fans are highly anticipating the release of *Space Dust II*. Its fantastic special effects are certain to make it even more popular than the original, which was a box-office hit. This action film from director Ryan Ressler is the second in a series of three.

1 What can be inferred about *Space Dust II*?

(A) It stars a popular actor.
(B) It was recently released.
(C) It will get many viewers.
(D) Its director won an award.

실전 감각 키우기

Questions 2-3 refer to the following announcement.

Over the past few months, our company has experienced a decrease in sales. Since other companies have cut their prices significantly, it has been difficult for us to maintain our previous sales volume. While our sales representatives are doing their best, we need to develop a new strategy. Therefore, we will be adding more staff to the marketing team and investing more in this side of the business. We want to show customers that our high-quality goods are well worth the price.

---

2 What is implied about the decrease in sales?

(A) It was predicted by the sales representatives.
(B) It was due to inexperienced employees.
(C) It was influenced by other companies.
(D) It was stopped by reducing prices.

3 What is probably true about the company's plan?

(A) It will be tested with some customers.
(B) It will focus on marketing the products.
(C) It will be based on a previous strategy.
(D) It will involve hiring more sales employees.

UNIT 16

5

동의어 찾기 유형

- 동의어를 찾는 문제 유형은 '지문의 특정 어휘와 가장 가까운 뜻으로 쓰인 단어'를 찾는 문제예요.
- 문제는 〈The word "~" in paragraph ~, line ~, is closest meaning to〉의 형태로 제시되며, 단일 지문 유형과 다중 지문 유형에서 각각 한 개씩, 보통 두 문제 정도가 출제돼요.
- 해당 단어의 대표 뜻만을 떠올려 답을 고르면 안 되고, 반드시 지문의 문맥에서 쓰인 의미를 파악해서 답을 골라야 해요.

> The word "overlooked" in paragraph 1, line 3, is closest in meaning to
> 첫째 단락 세 번째 줄의 단어 "overlooked"와 의미상 가장 가까운 단어는?
> In the e-mail, the word "retain" in paragraph 2, line 2, is closest in meaning to
> 이메일에서, 둘째 단락 두 번째 줄의 단어 "retain"과 의미상 가장 가까운 단어는?

핵심 POINT

하나! 단어의 위치 파악
질문을 먼저 읽으면서 해당 단어가 몇 번째 문단의 몇 번째 줄에 등장하는지 빠르게 파악하고 읽기 전에 밑줄을 그어 놓으세요.

둘! 문맥으로 의미 파악
단어가 포함된 문장을 정확하게 해석하면서 문맥상 단어의 뜻을 파악하세요. 뜻이 애매하다면 선택지에 주어진 단어들을 하나씩 넣으면서 문맥과 어울리는지 비교해 보세요.

단서2 The Norcross Museum is proud to present the early 단서1 pieces of painter Marco Pirozzi. Visitors are asked to follow all museum guidelines. Do not bring food or beverages into the gallery. You may take pictures of the paintings, but please remember that flash photography is not allowed.

>>> 단서1 질문의 단어 위치 파악
질문을 보고 지문의 첫째 단락 두 번째 줄에 있는 단어 pieces를 찾아서 밑줄을 그어 놓으세요. 밑줄을 그어 놓으면 지문을 읽어 내려갈 때 해당 단어의 의미에 집중할 수 있어요.

>>> 단서2 어휘의 문맥적 의미 파악
해당 단어가 들어간 문장을 읽어 보니, 박물관이 화가인 마르코 피로치 씨의 '초기 pieces를 보여주게 되어' 자랑스럽다고 했네요. 문맥상 pieces는 '작품'이라는 의미로 쓰였음을 알 수 있어요.

Q. 단서1 The word "pieces" in paragraph 1, line 2, is closest in meaning to

(A) belongings
(B) duties
(C) artworks
(D) careers

>>> 동의어 찾기 문제
(A)부터 (D)까지의 어휘를 지문에 넣어보면서 가장 유사한 어휘를 찾아보세요. (C) artworks(예술품)란 단어가 해당 단어 pieces(작품들)와 가장 근접하네요. (A)는 소지품, (B)는 의무, (D)는 직업이란 의미로 문맥에 어울리지 않아요. 정답은 (C).

다음 지문을 읽고 질문에 답하세요.

Enroll in BizCo's business seminars and see excellent results! Our specially designed courses will give you an edge in the market. You will learn how to manage others effectively and address customer needs. This will help you increase production and experience company growth.

1 In the advertisement, the word "edge" in paragraph 1, line 3, is closest in meaning to

(A) advantage
(B) side
(C) profit
(D) change

실전 감각 키우기

Questions 2-3 refer to the following article.

Tower Communications and Telelinx, Inc., have announced plans for joint operations. Beginning March 1, the two companies will merge in order to use each other's strengths to serve customers better. The companies will be able to reach more customers in Glenwood and the surrounding areas. According to William Howell, the CEO of Telelinx, plans are set for an expansion of the telecommunications network. "With the population increase in Glenwood, it is necessary to install more telephone lines," Howell said.

2 The word "reach" in paragraph 1, line 3, is closest in meaning to

(A) arrive
(B) stretch
(C) aim
(D) serve

3 The word "set" in paragraph 1, line 5, is closest in meaning to

(A) ready
(B) useful
(C) agreed
(D) unusual

UNIT 16

6

화자의 의도를 묻는 유형

- 화자의 의도를 묻는 유형의 문제는 대화체 지문인 '문자 메시지 지문'과 '온라인 채팅 지문'에서 출제되며, 매회 평균 2문제씩 나와요.
- 특정 시각에 화자가 언급한 표현에 대해 그것의 숨은 의도나 의미를 물어봅니다.
- 항상 동일한 형태로 출제되며, 메시지를 보낸 시각을 명시해 주고 화자의 표현을 따옴표(" ")로 나타냅니다.
- 이 유형은 어휘나 문장 구조가 상대적으로 쉬운 대화체 지문에서 출제되므로 내용 파악은 쉬우나, 해당 표현의 앞뒤 문맥을 제대로 파악하지 못하면 틀릴 수 있으니 주의해야 해요.

> At 10:11 A.M., what does Mr. Lee mean when he writes, "It's no problem?"
> 오전 10시 11분에, 이 씨가 "문제 없어요"라고 한 것에서 그가 의도한 것은?

핵심 POINT

하나! 대화 주제와 화자 간의 관계 파악!
지문을 읽어 내려가면서 '대화의 주제'와 '화자 간의 관계'를 잘 파악하세요. 내용의 흐름을 정확히 이해해야 그 맥락 안에서 화자가 한 말의 의미를 파악할 수 있기 때문이에요.

둘! 문맥 추론을 통한 핵심 단서 파악
해당 표현의 앞뒤 문장에는 정답을 찾을 수 있는 핵심 단서가 숨어 있어요. 문맥을 통해 이 단서를 찾아내야 정확한 답을 골라낼 수 있어요.

GEORGIA HUGHES   6:41 P.M.
Have you left for the banquet hall yet?

ANTHONY PEREIRA   6:42 P.M.
No. Why?

GEORGIA HUGHES   6:44 P.M.
I'm here setting up, but I left the storage device on my desk.

GEORGIA HUGHES   6:45 P.M.
단서1 Can you grab it and bring it with you?

ANTHONY PEREIRA   6:49 P.M.
You bet. 단서2 I'll be there in twenty minutes.

단서1 주제와 화자 간의 관계 파악
한 화자가 특정 물건을 책상에 놓고 온 상황으로, 다른 화자에게 그것을 가져다 달라고 하는 내용의 대화예요. 대화의 주제는 '놓고 온 물건'에 대한 것이고 두 사람 간의 관계는 직장 동료 정도로 파악이 가능해요.

단서2 문맥 속 핵심 단서 파악
해당 표현 앞에서 휴즈 씨가 요청을 하고 있는 상황이고, 해당 표현 뒤의 문장을 보면 I'll be there ~라는 표현이 나와요. 즉, 상대가 요구하는 것을 가져가겠다는 의미의 결정적 단서예요. 그렇다면 질문의 You bet.은 상대의 요청에 대한 '수락'임을 알 수 있어요. You bet이 Of course와 같은 의미라는 것을 알면 더 쉽게 답을 고를 수 있어요.

Q. At 6:49 P.M., what does Mr. Pereira mean when he writes, "You bet"?

(A) He will buy a storage device.
(B) He will leave as soon as possible.
(C) He will take a forgotten item with him.
(D) He will meet Ms. Hughes outside a venue.

의도 문제
저장장치를 가져다 달라는 요청에 그렇게 해 주기로 했다는 내용의 (C)가 정답이에요. 지문의 bring, it(a storage device)가 각각 take, a forgotten item으로 바꾸어 표현되었어요.

한 단락 지문 연습하기

다음 지문을 읽고 질문에 답하세요.

TERRANCE KOLB	3:26 P.M.

I'm at the eye doctor's. Apparently I need to have surgery.

MICAELA PAYNE	3:28 P.M.

Oh, really? When?

TERRANCE KOLB	3:29 P.M.

Tomorrow morning. I won't be able to attend the meeting at 11 A.M. tomorrow. Can you do that for me?

MICAELA PAYNE	3:32 P.M.

Definitely. Where is the information I need for the meeting?

TERRANCE KOLB	3:35 P.M.

There is a file on my desk. Thanks.

1 At 3:32 P.M., what does Ms. Payne mean when she writes, "Definitely"?

(A) She will give a speech for Mr. Kolb.

(B) She is agreeing to distribute some files.

(C) She is allowing Mr. Kolb to take time off.

(D) She will be present at a meeting.

실전 감각 키우기

Questions 2-3 refer to the following online chat discussion.

Heather Nelsen [2:25 P.M.]	Good morning. Does anyone have the revised program for the conference?
Carlos Palmer [2:26 P.M.]	The head of HR was supposed to send it to the department managers, but I didn't get any e-mail yet.
Carlos Palmer [2:27 P.M.]	He should send it soon. The conference is in less than three weeks, and I'm not sure when my team is scheduled to give the marketing presentation.
Katrina Burnings [2:28 P.M.]	You can find the schedule on the company's Web site. HR decided to post it there so that everyone could easily see it.
Heather Nelsen [2:29 P.M.]	Oh, I didn't think to check the Web site. I see it now. Thanks.

2 Which department does Mr. Palmer most likely work for?

(A) Web design

(B) Customer service

(C) Human Resources

(D) Marketing

3 At 2:29 P.M., what does Ms. Nelsen mean when she says, "I see it now"?

(A) She has updated the Web site.

(B) She has found a schedule online.

(C) She has just received an e-mail.

(D) She has met with a coworker.

- 주어진 문장의 지문 내 가장 적절한 위치를 묻는 유형으로 매 시험마다 2문제가 출제됩니다.
- 주어진 문장은 보통 '첨가, 부연, 예시, 인과, 대조, 양보' 등의 내용을 담고 있어요.
- 주어진 문장은 따옴표(" ")로 표기되며, [1], [2], [3], [4]의 선택지는 각각 지문 내에 위치합니다.
- 문장 삽입 위치인 선택지가 지문 전체에 걸쳐서 분포하므로, 세부 정보에 집중하기보다는 전반적인 글의 흐름을 이해하고 접근해야 해요.

> In which of the positions marked [1], [2], [3], and [4] does the following sentence best belong? [1], [2], [3], [4]번으로 표시된 위치들 중 다음 문장이 들어가기에 가장 적절한 곳은?
>
> "However, this was admitted at a press conference yesterday."
> "그러나, 이것은 어제 기자 회견에서 사실로 인정됐습니다."

핵심 POINT

하나! 주어진 문장 먼저 분석
지문을 읽기 전에 주어진 문장의 내용을 완전히 숙지하고 있어야, 지문과 주어진 문장을 여러 번 읽지 않고 시간을 절약할 수 있어요.

둘! 대명사와 연결사로 문장 연결성 파악
지시대명사(this, that 등), 인칭대명사(he, it, they 등), 접속부사(therefore, also, however 등), 접속사(although, because 등) 등을 통해 앞뒤 문장과의 연결성을 확인하세요.

Hello all,

—[1]—. Motivational speaker Glenn Castor will be delivering several talks in the city next month. —[2]—. I attended his presentation in New York last year, and I highly recommend that you go and hear him speak. —[3]—. 단서2 I advise you to book in advance because tickets are selling out quickly. —[4]—. So act fast if you want to go.

Best regards,

Bailey Ruffolo

>>> **단서1 주어진 문장 분석**
주어진 문장은 '그것들의 절반이 이미 팔렸음이 분명하다'라는 내용이에요. 해당 문장의 내용을 먼저 숙지하는 것은 시간 절약의 핵심이에요.

단서2 문장 연결성 파악
주어진 문장 안의 대명사인 them을 단서로, 지문에서 '팔릴 수 있는' 대상을 찾아야 해요. 지문 속의 단서2 에 있는 복수 명사 tickets가 them이 가리킬 수 있는 유일한 표현임을 알 수 있어요.

Q. In which of the positions marked [1], [2], [3], and [4] does the following sentence best belong?

" 단서1 Apparently, half of 단서2 them have been sold already."

(A) [1]
(B) [2]
(C) [3]
(D) [4]

>>> **문장 위치 찾기 문제**
복수 명사인 tickets가 언급된 뒤에 그것을 가리키는 대명사 them이 나오는 것이 자연스러우므로 주어진 문장은 [4]번에 위치해야 해요. 정답은 (D).

다음 지문을 읽고 질문에 답하세요.

Join the Costello, Inc., Team!

—[1]—. Costello, Inc. is seeking a public relations manager. —[2]—. Your primary role will be to supervise a team of marketing and media specialists. We are looking for someone who is capable of working with diverse personalities and thrives under pressure. —[3]—. If you think you match this description, then we want to hear from you! Applications must be submitted by February 23. —[4]—.

1 In which of the positions marked [1], [2], [3], and [4] does the following sentence best belong?

"Willingness to travel is also necessary."

(A) [1]
(B) [2]
(C) [3]
(D) [4]

Questions 2-3 refer to the following notice.

Attention Staff

—[1]—. With the temperature getting colder, many people are using personal heaters at their desks. —[2]—. Recently, it has been noted that several staff members consistently forget to turn their heaters off before going home. It is a fire hazard to leave unattended heaters running throughout the night. —[3]—. Therefore, we would like all staff members to be more careful when they leave. —[4]—. We can address this issue by working together.

Thank you,

Management

2 What is the problem with personal heaters?

(A) They are difficult to move around.
(B) They increase the utility costs.
(C) They could cause a fire.
(D) They raise the temperature too much.

3 In which of the positions marked [1], [2], [3], and [4] does the following sentence best belong?

"If someone near you has accidentally left their heater running, please shut it down."

(A) [1] (B) [2] (C) [3] (D) [4]

PART 7의 경우, 지문에 나온 단서 표현을 정답에서 똑같이 제시하지 않고, 다르지만 비슷한 표현을 통해 나타내요. 이를 '바꿔 말하기(패러프레이징)'라고 하며, PART 7에서 정답을 쉽게 찾기 위해서는 이 패러프레이징에 익숙해져야 해요.

check the **equipment** of a factory 공장의 장비를 검사하다	inspect the **machinery** of a factory 공장의 기계를 검사하다
replace some automobile **parts** 몇몇 자동차 부품들을 교체하다	replace some automobile **components** 몇몇 자동차 부품들을 교체하다
go over a product manual 제품 안내서를 검토하다	**review** a product manual 제품 안내서를 검토하다
contain **breakable** items 깨지기 쉬운 제품들을 포함하다	contain **fragile** articles 부서지기 쉬운 물건들을 포함하다
be **provisionally shut down** 잠정적으로 휴업하다	be **temporarily closed** 임시로 문을 닫다
furnished with up-to-date items 현대식 물품들을 갖춘	**equipped with state-of-the-art** items 최신식 물품들을 갖춘
be **tailored to** the customers' needs 고객의 요구에 맞춰지다	be **customized for** customers' needs 고객의 요구에 맞춤제작되다
visit a production plant 생산 공장을 방문하다	**stop by a manufacturing facility** 제조 시설에 들르다
become more efficient 더 효율적으로 되다	**increase productivity** 생산성을 높이다
must **wear a hard hat at all times** 항상 안전모를 써야 한다	must **always wear safety gear** 항상 안전 장비를 착용해야 한다

패러프레이징 연습하기

[1~4] 다음 빈칸에 알맞은 것을 고르세요.

1 inspect the machinery
→ check the -------

(A) equipment
(B) merchandise

2 visit the production plant
→ stop by the manufacturing -------

(A) facility
(B) headquarters

3 go over an instruction manual
→ ------- an instruction booklet

(A) produce
(B) review

4 become more efficient
→ increase -------

(A) productivity
(B) demand

패러프레이징 도전하기

[5~7] 다음 문장과 같은 의미의 문장을 고르세요.

5 These items are breakable and must be handled with care.

(A) These items are broken and need to be changed soon.

(B) You must be careful when handling these fragile items.

6 The facilities are temporarily closed because of renovations.

(A) State-of-the-art equipment was installed at the warehouse.

(B) Due to construction, the place is provisionally shut down.

7 Some of the machine's components need to be replaced.

(A) The device has parts that should be changed.

(B) The factory must produce new computer products.

[8~9] 다음 지문을 읽고 문제의 답을 고르세요.

On July 7, we will start to manufacture a new product. We already produce many tools and machines to be used in hospitals and by doctors. However, there is a lot of demand for clothing that is specially designed for nurses. Thus, this new line of clothing will be tailored to the needs of medical workers and feature pants, scrubs, masks, and hats. More information will be sent out soon.

8 What is being announced?

(A) The company will produce some new merchandise.

(B) Some tools will be redesigned by medical workers.

9 What will be special about the line of clothing?

(A) It will be customized for medical workers.

(B) It will be produced using new technology.

UNIT 16

주어진 문제를 제한시간에 맞추어 풀어 보세요.

Questions 1-2 refer to the following letter.

Cloud Nine Airlines
1264 Hyde Park Road, Los Angeles, CA 90017
Phone: 310-341-3870

January 14

Jason Welkins
519 Nields Street
El Monte, CA 91731

Dear Mr. Welkins,

Your application to become a member of the Cloud Nine Airlines frequent flyer program has been approved. When you book a flight with us or any of our partners, you will now earn points. These points can be used for discounts on seat upgrades, airport purchases, and airfare. Enclosed with this letter is your membership card. The next time you fly with us, please show it to the airport staff when you check in. This will ensure that your account receives the appropriate number of points. If you have any questions, visit our Web site at www.cloudnineairlines.com/frequentflyers.

We look forward to your next flight with us.

Sincerely,

Peggy Marcos
Cloud Nine Airlines, Frequent Flyer Program Manager

1. For whom is the letter intended?

   (A) A flight attendant
   (B) A travel agent
   (C) A new member
   (D) An airline manager

2. How can Mr. Welkins make sure he gets points on his account?

   (A) By presenting his card to a staff member
   (B) By purchasing some goods at the airport
   (C) By upgrading his seat at the check-in desk
   (D) By logging into the Cloud Nine Airlines Web site

Questions 3-5 refer to the following Web page.

https://www.cometcourse.com/reviews/

| Home | Classes | Teachers | Fees | **Reviews** |

Great class!

Review by Aurora Harrison

I highly recommend attending a Comet program. I took the public speaking course over the summer. I had heard good things about it, but it was even better than I had expected. The instructor gave practical advice and provided many opportunities for hands-on practice. The class size was small, so the professor could give feedback to each of us individually.

Before the class, every time I presented my company's products to potential clients, I would have difficulty explaining things, and the clients would seem bored. Thanks to this class, my speech is now organized and clear. I can tell that, as a result, my audience is interested. In fact, my sales have gone up by several percentage points since I completed the course. I have no doubt that this is due to my improved public-speaking skills. The only criticism I have about the class is that it is quite expensive. Despite this, I would advise anyone trying to improve their skills to join a Comet program.

3. In paragraph 1, line 3, the word "practical" is closest in meaning to

(A) cheap
(B) comfortable
(C) useful
(D) complex

4. What is probably true about Ms. Harrison?

(A) She regularly gives presentations for her work.
(B) She teaches public speaking.
(C) She is the best salesperson at her company.
(D) She recently started a new job.

5. What does Ms. Harrison criticize about the Comet program?

(A) Its price
(B) Its topic
(C) Its class size
(D) Its instructor

UNIT 16

Questions 6-7 refer to the following text message.

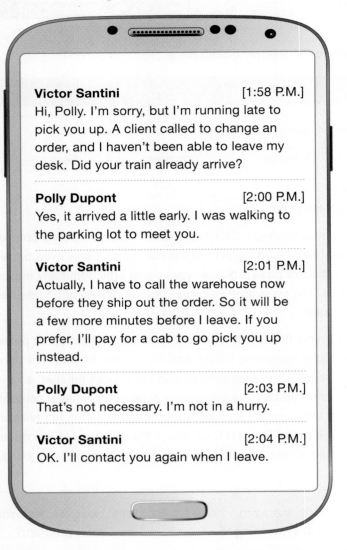

Victor Santini [1:58 P.M.]
Hi, Polly. I'm sorry, but I'm running late to pick you up. A client called to change an order, and I haven't been able to leave my desk. Did your train already arrive?

Polly Dupont [2:00 P.M.]
Yes, it arrived a little early. I was walking to the parking lot to meet you.

Victor Santini [2:01 P.M.]
Actually, I have to call the warehouse now before they ship out the order. So it will be a few more minutes before I leave. If you prefer, I'll pay for a cab to go pick you up instead.

Polly Dupont [2:03 P.M.]
That's not necessary. I'm not in a hurry.

Victor Santini [2:04 P.M.]
OK. I'll contact you again when I leave.

6. Where did Mr. Santini and Ms. Dupont plan to meet?

(A) At an office
(B) In a train station
(C) At a warehouse
(D) In a parking lot

7. At 2:03 P.M., what does Ms. Dupont most likely mean when she writes, "That's not necessary"?

(A) She will take a taxi to the office.
(B) She can call the warehouse herself.
(C) She will wait for Mr. Santini.
(D) She does not need to pay for the shipment.

A New Turn for Portsmouth

PORTSMOUTH (18 November)—A recent report on Portsmouth's economic status shows that the city's retailers and restaurants have had a high increase in business over the past year. —[1]— . While the city has seen steady growth for about a decade, the last few months mark a sharp rise. —[2]— .

Economists believe that this sudden growth is due to the opening of a new manufacturing plant right outside the city. —[3]— . As a result, unemployment in the area is at an all-time low, and the average income of local residents has increased. "With job security and higher incomes, consumers are more willing to spend money," explains Maria Denton, who helped write the report.

—[4]— . Moreover, experts agree that the growth will continue well into the upcoming year. Real estate companies have noticed the trend and the resulting population increase. They have already started building new apartments with up-to-date appliances, and property prices in Portsmouth are increasing. It is thus safe to assume that the city will keep developing.

---

8. What is the purpose of the article?

(A) To encourage consumers to spend money
(B) To discuss an economic trend
(C) To announce new job openings
(D) To recommend some business strategies

9. What is NOT indicated about Portsmouth?

(A) Business had been increasing continuously for ten years.
(B) Residents of the city are earning higher salaries.
(C) Apartments with state-of-the-art appliances are being built.
(D) Real estates in Portsmouth have become more affordable.

10. Who most likely is Ms. Denton?

(A) A real estate owner
(B) A factory worker
(C) An economist
(D) A job seeker

11. In which of the following positions marked [1], [2], [3], and [4] does the following sentence best belong?

"This new facility has created more than a thousand new jobs."

(A) [1]
(B) [2]
(C) [3]
(D) [4]

UNIT 16

PART 7 지문 유형편

UNIT 17

빈출 일반 지문
+패러프레이징(2)

- 이메일과 편지는 PART 7 지문 중 40% 이상 출제되는 비중 있는 지문 유형이에요.
- 이 지문들의 주요 특징은 지문의 상·하단에 수신과 발신 정보가 등장한다는 점입니다.
  즉, (이메일) 주소와 수신자명 (To:), 발신자명(From:), 날짜(Date:), 제목(Subject:)이 구체적으로 제시돼요.
- 이러한 형식적 측면의 정보를 먼저 정확히 파악하면 지문 이해와 문제 풀이가 훨씬 수월해져요.

핵심 POINT

〈대표적인 지문 흐름〉

1 글을 쓰는 목적	I'm writing this e-mail[letter] to *do* ~ 저는 ~하기 위해 이 이메일[편지]를 씁니다 The purpose of this e-mail[letter] is to *do* ~ 이 이메일[편지]의 목적은 ~하는 것입니다

▼

2 세부 내용과 핵심 요청 사항	I would appreciate it if ~	만약 ~해 주시면 감사하겠습니다
	Please let me know ~	~을 저에게 알려 주십시오
	Could you do me a favor?	제 부탁 좀 들어 주시겠습니까?

▼

3 추가 내용 및 첨부, 끝인사	I have included ~	~을 동봉합니다
	Enclosed[Attached] is ~	동봉된[첨부된] 것은 ~입니다

대표 상황별 빈출 어휘

여행 예약 확인	reservation 예약 book 예약하다 destination 목적지 confirmation 확인 accommodation 숙박 시설 itinerary 여행 일정(표)
티켓 구매 문의	inquire 문의하다 purchase 구매(하다) performance 공연 exhibition 전시회 sold out (표가) 매진된 in advance 미리
제품 불만 제기	exchange 교환(하다) refund 환불(하다) policy 방침, 정책 invoice 송장 complimentary 무료의 receipt 영수증

실전 지문에 적용하기

To: Bernie Collins <bcollins@collinssupplies.com>
From: Margaret Ling <mling@webmail.com>
Date: October 18
Subject: Recent order

Dear Mr. Collins,

1 글의 목적 **I'm writing to report a problem with a recent delivery.** I purchased a photocopier from your store, and it was delivered yesterday. The machine is in perfect working order, and I am pleased with it.

2 세부 내용과 요청 사항 However, I also ordered a box of extra ink cartridges for the machine, and that was not included with the delivery. I checked the invoice later and saw that I was charged for the cartridges. **Please let me know by e-mail what the problem is and when I can expect the delivery.**

3 추가 내용 및 첨부 We are going to need the cartridges very soon, so I hope to receive them as quickly as possible. **I have attached a copy of my invoice for your reference.**

Sincerely,

Margaret Ling
Appleton Office

>>> **1 글의 목적**

"저는 최근 배송에 대한 문제를 알리기 위해 이 메일을 쓰고 있습니다."

이메일의 목적은 대개 지문 도입부에 제시되며, I'm writing to *do*와 같은 표현을 쓸 수 있어요. 여기에서는 최근 배송에 문제가 있음을 밝히고 있네요.

|출제되는 문제 유형|
Q. What is the main purpose of the e-mail? 이메일의 주된 목적은?
A. To report a problem with an order 주문의 문제를 알리기 위해서

2 세부 내용과 요청 사항

"무엇이 문제인지 그리고 언제 배송을 받을 수 있을지를 이메일로 알려 주세요."

목적을 밝힌 다음, 문제의 세부 내용과 요청 사항이 이어집니다. 여기서는 Please let me know라는 표현을 썼네요. 이 밖에도 I would appreciate it if ~(만약 ~해주시면 감사하겠습니다) 등의 표현도 쓸 수 있어요.

|출제되는 문제 유형|
Q. What does Ms. Ling ask Mr. Collins to do? 링 씨가 콜린 씨에게 해달라고 요청한 것은?
A. Inform her of an estimated delivery date 그녀에게 예상 도착 날짜 알려주기

3 추가 내용 및 첨부

"참고하실 수 있도록 송장 한 부를 첨부합니다."

이메일의 후반부에는 물품이 빨리 오면 좋겠다고 희망하는 내용과 함께 송장을 첨부한다고 했네요. attach(첨부하다)나 include(동봉하다) 등의 동사를 기억해두세요.

|출제되는 문제 유형|
Q. What has Ms. Ling included with the letter? 링 씨가 편지에 동봉한 것은?
A. A transaction document 거래 서류

UNIT 17

Questions 1-2 refer to the following letter.

Angela Manzo
445 Maven Avenue
Boston, MA 02210

Dear Ms. Manzo,

I am sending you this letter to officially offer you the job of regional branch manager. I was very impressed with your qualifications and experience. The job will start on May 3. Please let me know as soon as possible if you would like to accept our offer. You can call me at (508) 555-0283 anytime between 9 A.M. and 5 P.M. Enclosed are a copy of the contract and a copy of our employee handbook. These outline the terms and conditions of the position.

I look forward to meeting you again soon.

Gary Carter
Director of Personnel, LTV Electronics

1. Why did Mr. Carter write the letter?

(A) To schedule a job interview
(B) To offer a position to Ms. Manzo
(C) To request an employee handbook
(D) To apply for a job at LTV Electronics

2. What does Mr. Carter ask Ms. Manzo to do?

(A) Inform him of her decision
(B) Come in for a meeting
(C) Revise a handbook
(D) Send some contact information

Questions 3-5 refer to the following e-mail.

To:	Rover Rentals <reservations@roverrentals.com>
From:	Ronald Lloyd <ronald@buzzmail.com>
Subject:	Rental request
Date:	June 9

Dear Sir or Madam,

A colleague of mine visited Auckland recently and recommended your agency to me. I'm writing to inquire if you have a minivan available that seats six people. My family and I will be arriving in Auckland on July 2 for our summer vacation. We will be staying in the city for six days and will need the vehicle during that time. If a minivan is unavailable, I will need a list of the other options you have. In addition, I'll also need to know how much you charge per day and if you offer any weekly rental packages.

You can respond to this e-mail or call me at (082) 555-8823. My current insurance plan has coverage for vehicle rentals, so I have included a copy of my policy in an attachment for reference. Thanks for your time, and I hope to hear from you soon.

Regards,

Ronald Lloyd

3. What is the purpose of the e-mail?

(A) To inquire about renting a vehicle
(B) To make reservations for a hotel
(C) To request changes to a trip itinerary
(D) To ask about city attractions

4. What does Mr. Lloyd mention about his trip?

(A) It will last for more than a week.
(B) It will include stops in numerous cities.
(C) It will be with members of his family.
(D) It will be paid for by his company.

5. What is included with the e-mail?

(A) A rental application form
(B) A hotel information brochure
(C) A copy of an insurance policy
(D) A receipt for an upcoming trip

UNIT 17

2 기사/정보문 Article/Information

- 여러 사실 정보가 나열되는 기사와 정보문은 객관적 어조로 쓰이고 어려운 어휘도 많이 사용되어 PART 7에서 가장 어려운 유형의 지문입니다.
  그러나, 매 시험에 최소 두세 지문씩 출제되므로 반드시 공부해야 합니다.
- 주로 도입부에서 주제와 출처를 먼저 밝히고, 본론에서 주제와 관련된 세부 정보를 다룬 후에 마지막에 미래 계획이나 추가 조사 방법 등을 언급합니다.
- 이렇게 형식을 갖춘 지문은 지문의 흐름만 잘 파악해도, 문제에서 묻는 내용을 빨리 찾을 수 있습니다.

핵심 POINT

〈대표적인 지문 흐름〉

1 주제와 출처	In a press release[statement] ~ At a press conference ~ According to A ~	언론 발표[성명서]에서 ~ 기자 회견에서 ~ A에 따르면 ~

▼

2 주제 관련 세부 정보	A took place[will take place] ~ A was held[will be held] ~ A lasted for[will last for] ~ A가 ~ 동안 지속되었다[지속될 것이다]	A가 일어났다[일어날 것이다] A가 개최되었다[개최될 것이다]

▼

3 미래 계획, 추가 정보	A also plans to *do* ~ A는 또한 ~할 계획이다 Additional information can be found ~ 추가 정보는 ~에서 찾을 수 있다 For further details on A, you can *do* ~ A에 관한 추가 정보를 보시려면, ~하시면 됩니다

대표 상황별 빈출 어휘

장소 이전 안내	relocate 이전[이동]하다 move 이사하다 district 지구, 지역 lease 임대(하다) headquarters 본사 branch 지사, 지점 rent 임대료
공사 안내	expansion 확장, 확대 estimate 견적 construction 건설, 공사 location 장소
연구 결과 소개	findings 연구 결과 compare 비교하다 respondent 응답자 result 결과 survey 설문 조사 analyze 분석하다 gather 모으다

실전 지문에 적용하기

Ingram Properties' Building Project

1 주제와 출처 On July 8, international property developer Ingram Properties will begin construction of a shopping mall in Calgary. **In a recent press release, the company said the facility will contain units for 200 retailers, parking facilities, and 20 restaurants.**

2 세부 정보 **Work will last for three years at a cost of $380 million.** Ingram will provide nearly 60 percent of the funding, while the city will provide the rest as an investment. The company chose to build the mall to offer residents a convenient shopping venue.

3 미래 계획 **Ingram Properties also plans to add an upscale hotel to the mall in the future.** However, that project would not begin for at least four years.

>>> **1 주제와 출처**

"최근의 언론 발표에서, 회사는 이 시설이 200개의 소매업체, 주차 시설, 20개의 식당을 포함할 것이라고 말했다."

In a recent press release라는 표현은 정보의 출처를 알려 줘요. 이후에 글의 주제가 나오죠. 여기서는 한 부동산 회사가 매장, 주차장, 식당을 포함한 대규모 시설을 짓는다는 걸 알 수 있어요.

| 출제되는 문제 유형 |

Q. What does the company plan to do? 회사가 하려고 계획하는 것은?
A. Construct a retail facility 소매 시설 짓기

2 세부 정보

"작업은 3억 8천만 달러의 비용으로 3년 동안 지속될 것이다."

본론에서는 주제와 관련된 세부 정보가 나열됩니다. 여기에서는 건축 기간과 비용 등을 설명하고 있어요.

| 출제되는 문제 유형 |

Q. How long will the construction project last? 건설 프로젝트가 지속될 기간은?
A. For three years 3년간

3 미래 계획

"인그램 프로퍼티즈 사는 또한 향후 그 쇼핑몰에 고급 호텔도 추가할 계획이다."

기사의 마지막 부분에서는 주로 plan, further details, additional information 등의 표현과 함께 미래의 계획이나 추가 정보에 대해 설명해요. 여기서는 plan to do를 이용해 회사가 시설에 고급 호텔을 추가할 계획임을 밝히고 있어요.

| 출제되는 문제 유형 |

Q. What will Ingram Properties most likely do in the future?
인그램 프로퍼티즈 사가 향후에 할 것 같은 일은?
A. Build a luxury hotel 고급 호텔 짓기

UNIT 17

Questions 1-2 refer to the following article.

LEVITTOWN, December 5—Tourism in Levittown and its suburbs has decreased this past year. In response to this, Mayor Rodham announced at a recent press conference that he would launch a campaign aimed at emphasizing Levittown's artistic attractions. As part of the campaign, he plans to talk to several contractors about building a new convention hall. He hopes this will encourage performers and artists from various fields to organize more events in Levittown rather than go to the neighboring city of Sillaville, and thus attract audience members from around the country. "Levittown is a city full of diversity," Mayor Rodham explained. "We want people to come see the wonderful art that can be produced by this diversity." For further details on the plan, you can visit Levittown's Web site at www.levittownnews.net.

1. Why is Mayor Rodham launching a campaign?

(A) To encourage citizens to vote
(B) To attract more visitors to the city
(C) To raise funds for a construction project
(D) To advertise artists and musicians

2. What can readers find at the Levittown Web site?

(A) More information about a project
(B) A performance schedule
(C) Contract terms and conditions
(D) A map to a new convention hall

Questions 3-5 refer to the following article.

Study Results Show Surprising Findings

At a press conference on Monday morning, professors from Billington University announced the findings of a study comparing the health of residents in large cities and rural areas. The research project started a decade ago, with scientists gathering information from 500 urban residents and 500 participants who live in rural areas. Both groups filled out health information surveys four times a year for the past ten years. The results were obtained from the data gathered through the surveys.

Many experts were surprised that the health of country residents was poorer than that of city residents. Nearly 70 percent of city residents reported good health, with the figure only at 62 percent for country participants. Experts say there are several reasons for this, including the lack of healthcare facilities and educational programs in rural areas. The study also showed that those living in cities had healthier diets.

However, country residents did show fewer signs of stress. Of the city participants, 43 percent said they had stressful lives, while the rate was only 22 percent for country residents.

3. What was the study conducted by Billington University mainly about?

(A) Improved healthcare facilities
(B) Rising rates of urban populations
(C) The health of two groups of residents
(D) Increasing levels of medical problems

4. What is indicated about the results of the study?

(A) They are not completely accurate.
(B) They are based on several surveys.
(C) They were not surprising to experts.
(D) They will be updated at a later time.

5. What does the article mention about people living in cities?

(A) They have poorer medical care facilities.
(B) They are dissatisfied with educational programs.
(C) They eat healthier food than country residents.
(D) They have less stressful lives.

UNIT 17

3 제품/서비스 광고 Product/Service Advertisement

- 제품/서비스 광고 유형은 매회 두 지문에서 네 지문까지 출제되는 중요한 지문 유형 중 하나예요.
- 이 유형의 지문은 제품과 서비스의 특장점을 부각시켜 고객의 구매 욕구를 자극하는 것이 목적이에요.
- 따라서 광고의 시작 부분에서는 광고하고자 하는 것이 무엇인지 명확하게 밝히고, 본론에서는 제품/서비스의 가장 매력적인 장점들이 묘사돼요. 마지막 부분에서는 구매 방법이나 이용이 가능한 장소를 알려 주는 것으로 마무리됩니다.

핵심 POINT

〈대표적인 지문 흐름〉

1 광고 제품 [서비스]	**Are you looking for ~?** ~을 찾고 계신가요? **Then look no further than ~** 그렇다면 ~말고는 더 볼 필요가 없습니다 **Are you tired of ~?** ~에 싫증나셨나요?

▼

2 제품[서비스]의 특장점	**We are (well) known for ~** 저희는 ~로 (잘) 알려져 있습니다 **Our product comes equipped with ~** 저희 제품은 ~이 갖춰져 나옵니다 **We provide quality products[services]** 저희는 질 좋은 제품[서비스]를 제공합니다

▼

3 제품[서비스] 구매 방법, 장소	**So why not purchase[book/visit] ~?** 그러니 구매[예약/방문]하시는 게 어떨까요? **You can find our product ~** 저희 제품은 ~에서 찾으실 수 있습니다 **To purchase our products, ~** 저희 제품을 구매하시려면, ~

대표 상황별 빈출 어휘

식당 광고	ingredient 재료 affordable (가격이) 알맞은, 저렴한 advantage 장점
재고품 할인 판매	warehouse 창고 merchandise 상품 bargain 특가 clearance sale 재고 정리 판매 special offer 특별가 할인
호텔 서비스 광고	accommodation 숙박 complimentary 무료의 belongings 소지품 courtesy 정중함 reservation 예약 stay 머무름, 체류

실전 지문에 적용하기

Pangea! Always a smooth flight!

1 광고 제품[서비스] **Are you looking for an airline with fewer flight delays and cancellations?** With Pangea International Airlines, you can stop worrying about those problems and enjoy your trip. **2 특장점** **We are known for having the lowest rates of delays and cancellations of all airlines,** and we will take you safely to one of more than 100 destinations worldwide. We've been the winner of the Customer Service Award from the Global Airline Organization for the past two years.

3 구매 방법, 장소 **So why not book your next flight by visiting our Web site at www.pangeaintairlines.com and experience our excellent service for yourself?**

We hope to see you aboard one of our flights soon!

>>> **1 광고 제품[서비스]**

"항공편 연착과 취소가 더 적은 항공사를 찾고 계십니까?"

광고하고자 하는 제품이나 서비스는 글의 제목과 도입부에서 제시되는데, 특히 Are you looking for ~? 뒤에 자주 등장합니다. 여기에서는 항공사를 광고하고 있네요.

|출제되는 문제 유형|

Q. What is being advertised?
광고되고 있는 것은?

A. A global airline 국제 항공사

2 특장점

"저희는 모든 항공사 중 가장 낮은 연착률과 취소율로 알려져 있으며."

광고는 본론 부분에서 제품[서비스]의 특장점을 부각시켜요. We are known for라는 어구 뒤에 해당 항공사의 특장점으로 가장 낮은 연착률과 취소율을 들고 있어요.

|출제되는 문제 유형|

Q. What is indicated about Pangea International Airlines?
팡지아 인터내셔널 항공사에 대해 시사된 것은?

A. It has few delays. 거의 지연이 없다.

3 구매 방법, 장소

"그러니 저희 웹사이트인 www.pangeaintairlines.com으로 방문하셔서 여러분의 다음 항공편을 예약하시고, 저희의 훌륭한 서비스를 직접 경험해 보시는 게 어떨까요?"

So why not ~?이라는 권유 표현은 구매 방법이나 구매 장소를 알려 주는 신호가 될 수 있어요. 여기에서는 항공사 사이트에서 항공편을 예약할 수 있다고 알려 주고 있네요.

|출제되는 문제 유형|

Q. How can tickets be purchased?
티켓을 구매할 수 있는 방법은?

A. By going to a Web site 웹사이트에 가서

UNIT 17

Questions 1-2 refer to the following advertisement.

EASY-BACK 2300!

Do you need a comfortable office chair that supports your back? Then look no further than the all-new Easy-Back 2300! This chair was created by a team of designers and medical experts who developed a structure that supports the back. Unlike others, our chairs come equipped with a spinal support system which is ideal for office workers or those spending long periods sitting down.

Each chair is crafted from stainless steel and genuine leather. We also provide a money-back guarantee for one year. You can find our chairs at Business-Co office supply stores nationwide, or at many office furniture retailers. For a list of outlets, visit our Web site at www.easybackchairs.com.

1. What is a characteristic of the Easy-Back 2300?

(A) It has adjustable parts.
(B) It includes a lifetime guarantee.
(C) It is less expensive than similar items.
(D) It comes with a unique support system.

2. How can the Easy-Back 2300 be purchased?

(A) By visiting a Web site
(B) By filling out a form
(C) By going to a retail store
(D) By placing a phone call

Questions 3-5 refer to the following advertisement.

Maharani's Kitchen Introduces
HOME DELIVERY SERVICE!

Are you tired of eating the same thing for dinner every day? Then add some spice to your life and order a home delivery meal from Maharani's Kitchen, located at 629 Bohemia Boulevard. We provide quality foods, using only the freshest ingredients, at prices that anyone can afford. To promote this brand-new service, the following meals are offered at only $28:

- *Beef curry meal: includes curry, rice, flat bread, and salad*
- *Tandoori chicken meal: includes chicken, rice, and salad*
- *Vegetable curry meal: includes curry, rice, and salad*

Take advantage of this special offer this week only from June 6 to 12. To place an order, simply call us at (604) 555-7676. This service is only available to residents of this city. Delivery time usually takes between 30 and 40 minutes. Orders will not be taken within 1 hour of our closing time of 10 P.M.

To learn about our other menu options and special offers, or to inquire about delivery services, visit the restaurant's Web site at www.maharaniskitchen.com.

3. What is being advertised?

(A) Added menu items
(B) A new service
(C) Extended business hours
(D) A banquet event

4. What is mentioned about Maharani's Kitchen?

(A) It has affordable prices.
(B) It only uses local ingredients.
(C) It accepts orders any time of day.
(D) It opened for business a week ago.

5. What is NOT available on the Web site?

(A) Details on delivery services
(B) A list of other food offerings
(C) Information on special promotions
(D) An online order form

UNIT 17

4 구인 광고 Job Advertisement

- 회사나 기관에서 사람을 채용하려는 목적의 글인 구인 광고는 토익에서 단골로 출제되는 유형입니다.
- 먼저 어떤 자리가 공석(opening)으로 나왔는지를 밝힌 후, 이에 대한 자격 요건(qualifications)및 직무 (duties)를 설명해요.
- 또한 회사에서 제공하는 복지 혜택(benefits package), 보험의 보장 범위(insurance coverage), 임금 (salary) 등에 대한 안내가 추가로 등장하기도 합니다.
- 마지막으로 이력서(résumé), 자기 소개서(cover letter), 추천서(a letter of recommendation) 등의 제출 서류와 지원 방법을 알려 줍니다.

핵심 POINT

〈대표적인 지문 흐름〉

1 광고되고 있는 일자리[직위]	(Our company) is looking for ~ (저희 회사는) ~를 찾고 있습니다 We currently have a vacant position in ~ 저희는 현재 ~에 공석이 있습니다 We have a job opening for ~ 저희는 ~에 대한 공석이 있습니다

▼

2 자격 요건 및 직무 내용, 복지 혜택	(degree[experience]) is required ~ (학위[경력])이 필요합니다 Successful candidates must have ~ 합격자들은 반드시 ~가 있어야 합니다 The selected applicant will ~ 선택된 지원자는 ~을 하게 됩니다

▼

3 지원 방법	To apply for the job[position], ~ 일자리[직위]에 지원하려면, ~하세요 Send a résumé, cover letter, and a letter of reference 이력서, 자기 소개서, 그리고 추천서를 보내 주세요 Fill out an application form 지원서를 작성해 주세요

대표 상황별 빈출 어휘

회사 교대 근무조 채용	vacancy 공석 shift 교대 근무조 applicant 지원자 temporary 임시직의 competitive salary 경쟁력 있는 급여
환경 단체 직원 채용	requirement 요구 조건 fundraising (자금) 모금 application 지원서 monitor 감독하다 environmental 환경의, 환경적인 regulate 규제하다
호텔 직원 채용	candidate 후보자 proficient in ~에 능숙한 deal with 처리하다 booking 예약 a letter of reference[recommendation] 추천서

실전 지문에 적용하기

POSITION NOW AVAILABLE:
Edward Regency Hotel

1 일자리[직위] 명시 **The Edward Regency Hotel is currently looking for two new members for its housekeeping staff.** The selected applicants will start the job on May 20. **2 자격 요건, 직무, 복지 혜택** **A minimum of two years of housekeeping experience is required,** but training will be provided. Knowledge of cleaning equipment is also an asset. Candidates should be willing to work some weekend shifts. We offer good salaries with a generous benefits package. Employees are provided two weeks of annual vacation and receive insurance coverage.

3 지원 방법 **To apply for a position, drop off a copy of your résumé at the hotel's administrative office,** located at 443 Ninth Avenue. Only selected candidates will be contacted for interviews, which will take place on May 16.

---

1 일자리[직위] 명시

"에드워드 리젠시 호텔에서 현재 새로운 청소 직원 두 명을 구하고 있습니다."

구인 광고는 글의 시작 부분에 정확히 어떤 사람이 필요한지에 대해 밝혀요. 특히 (Our company) is (currently) looking for라는 표현 뒤에 관련 내용이 나오게 되니 이 부분을 잘 살펴보세요. 지문에서는 '청소 직원'을 뽑고 있네요.

|출제되는 문제 유형|

Q. What type of job is being advertised?
광고되고 있는 직업의 종류는?

A. Cleaner 청소부

2 자격 요건, 직무, 복지 혜택

"최소 2년의 호텔 청소 경력이 요구되지만,"

자격 요건과 업무 내용, 복지 혜택과 관련된 문제를 풀 때는 본론 부분에 집중하세요. 특히, 자격 요건은 be required[needed]와 같은 표현을 써서 나타낼 수 있어요. 여기에서는 최소 2년의 경력을 요구하고 있습니다.

|출제되는 문제 유형|

Q. What is a requirement of the position? 일자리의 자격 요건은?

A. Previous work experience
이전 업무 경험

3 지원 방법

"일자리에 지원하시려면, 이력서를 9번가 443번지에 위치한 호텔의 행정실에 갖다 내세요."

To apply for라는 표현 뒤에 구체적인 지원 방법과 제출 서류가 나와요. 지문에서는 이력서를 직접 제출하라고 나와 있네요. 지원 방법으로 e-mail, letter, fax도 자주 나와요.

|출제되는 문제 유형|

Q. How can interested people apply for the job?
관심있는 사람들이 일자리에 지원할 방법은?

A. By submitting a résumé
이력서를 제출함으로써

Questions 1-2 refer to the following advertisement.

Appleton Bakery, located at 913 Vineyard Avenue, is a family-run business that has been in operation for forty years. We currently have a vacant position for a morning shift sales clerk. Some weekend shifts may also be required on occasion, but overtime pay will be provided. We offer competitive salaries and a standard benefits package. Applicants should have at least one year of experience in retail.

Please send a résumé, cover letter, and at least one reference to anitachoi@appletonbakery.com. Make sure to include your contact information so that we may call you for an interview. Only those who meet the requirements for the position will be contacted.

1. Who is the business looking to hire?

(A) A full-time baker
(B) A sales assistant
(C) A delivery person
(D) A kitchen cook

2. What should people interested in the position do?

(A) E-mail the bakery
(B) Fill out the provided forms
(C) Visit an establishment
(D) Call the business's owner

Questions 3-5 refer to the following advertisement.

Heathcliff Savings Bank
POSITION AVAILABLE

Heathcliff Savings Bank has a job opening for a full-time manager for a team of bank tellers and customer service associates. A university degree in management or a related field is required. Only those with at least five years of previous bank managerial experience will be considered. The successful candidate will report directly to the branch manager.

The selected applicant will be responsible for providing training, scheduling work shifts, handling payroll, dealing with vacation requests, and making sure the employees maintain high levels of service in the bank.

It is necessary for applicants to send a résumé, cover letter, and two references to: Adam Lewis, Branch Manager, Heathcliff Savings Bank, 3388 Sullivan Street, Edgewood, WI 53072. Telephone interviews will be conducted first, and then final candidates will be invited to visit our offices to meet with a panel of bank executives.

3. What position is Heathcliff Savings Bank looking to fill?

(A) Bank teller
(B) Branch manager
(C) Team leader
(D) Customer service employee

4. What is NOT mentioned as a responsibility of the selected applicant?

(A) Training employees
(B) Making schedules
(C) Handling vacation requests
(D) Dealing with customers

5. What is suggested about the hiring process?

(A) It takes at least a week.
(B) It involves more than one interview.
(C) It is conducted twice a year.
(D) It requires e-mailed documents.

'바꿔 말하기(패러프레이징)'는 간단하게 '단어'만 바꿀 수도 있지만 두 단어 이상의 '구' 단위나 '문장'을 전체적으로 바꿔서도 표현할 수 있어요. 다양한 바꿔 말하기 표현에 익숙해져야 PART 7에서 정답을 찾을 수 있으므로 꾸준히 패러프레이징 연습을 해야 합니다.

start a new **job** 새로운 일을 시작하다	start a new **position** 새로운 직위를 시작하다
a list of **candidates** 후보자 명단	a list of **applicants** 지원자 명단
reject an offer 제안을 거절하다	**turn down** an offer 제안을 거절하다
collaborate on a project 일에 협력하다[공동 작업하다]	**work together on** a project 일을 함께 하다
the **location of** a conference 회의의 장소	the **venue for** a conference 회의를 위한 장소
be eligible for a promotion 승진 자격이 있다	**be entitled to an advancement** 승진 자격이 있다
meet to **negotiate some terms** 조건을 협상하기 위해 만나다	meet to **discuss a contract** 계약을 논의하기 위해 만나다
receive **a revised work schedule** 수정된 작업 일정을 받다	receive **an updated shift timetable** 업데이트 된 교대근무 시간표를 받다
accommodate fifty people 50명을 수용하다	**have seating for** fifty people 50명을 위한 자리가 있다
show ID 신분증을 보여 주다	**present some identification** 신분증을 제시하다

패러프레이징 연습하기

[1~4] 다음 빈칸에 알맞은 것을 고르세요.

1 difficult to reject the offer
→ hard to ------- the proposal

(A) turn down
(B) discuss

2 frequently work together on advertisements
→ often -------- on commercials

(A) collaborate
(B) negotiate

3 the start day of a job
→ the first day in a -------

(A) membership
(B) position

4 show ID
→ ------- some identification

(A) display
(B) present

[5~7] 다음 지문과 같은 의미의 문장을 고르세요.

5 The company met with the supplier in order to discuss a contract.

(A) The company and the provider gathered to negotiate some terms.
(B) The supplier signed a contract that the company proposed.

6 The human resources manager has interviewed some candidates.

(A) People are interested in the interview for the human resources position.
(B) Some applicants were interviewed by the department manager.

7 The department head will attach a revised work schedule to the e-mail.

(A) The department head will send a new job advertisement by e-mail.
(B) An updated shift timetable will be attached to the e-mail by the team leader.

[8~9] 다음 지문을 읽고 문제의 답을 고르세요.

I am writing to let you know that I have reserved the Rosehill Convention Center for the Marketing Strategies Conference on June 1. It was the venue for the awards ceremony last year. The main room there can accommodate a hundred people. Tables and chairs are provided, and we will hire a catering service to have some refreshments during the event. You asked whether you would be able to show some slides for your presentation, and I did get confirmation that the room has a projector.

8 The word "venue" in paragraph 1, line 2, is closest in meaning to

(A) location
(B) reservation

9 What is NOT indicated about the main room?

(A) It provides free catering services.
(B) It has seating for a hundred people.

UNIT 17

PART 7 지문 유형편

UNIT 18

빈출 특수 지문

+패러프레이징(3)

1 공지/메모 Announcement/Memorandum

- 공지와 메모 모두 **특정 대상에게 중요한 내용을 집약적으로 전달하는 것**이 목적입니다.
- 두 지문 유형은 합쳐서 약 7% 비율로 출제되므로 흐름과 특징을 알아두어야 해요.
- 공지 유형은 내용이 바로 전개되는 반면, 메모 유형은 이메일처럼 상단에 수신(To:), 발신(From:), 제목 (Subject:), 날짜(Date:) 등이 먼저 등장한 후 내용이 이어집니다.
- 일반적으로 지문의 앞부분에서는 대상이나 주제가 명시되고, 중간에서는 핵심 세부 내용이, 마지막에는 요청, 제안, 문의 등과 관련된 내용이 나와요.
- 앞부분을 통해 대상과 주제를 정확히 파악해야 이후의 세부 내용에 대한 이해가 쉬워져요.

핵심 POINT

〈대표적인 지문 흐름〉

1 대상과 주제	This notice is for ~	이 공지는 ~를 위한 것입니다
	This is to notify A that ~	이것은 A에게 ~을 알리기 위한 것입니다
	I want to let you know ~	저는 당신에게 ~을 알려 드리고 싶습니다

▼

2 핵심 정보와 세부 사항	Please be reminded that ~	~라는 것을 기억하세요
	Please note that ~	~라는 것에 유의하세요
	The important thing is ~	중요한 것은 ~입니다

▼

3 요청, 제안, 문의	We request that ~	우리는 ~할 것을 요청합니다
	You are advised to *do* ~	~하실 것을 권합니다
	If you require further information ~	추가 정보가 필요하시면 ~

대표 상황별 빈출 어휘

예정된 연수	upcoming 다가오는 immediate supervisor 직속 상관 permission 허락[허가] training 연수, 교육 session (특정 활동을 위한) 시간
아파트 수리	repair 수리 entrance 현관 advance notice 사전 공지 closure 폐쇄
은행 계좌 개설	account 계좌 verify 확인[입증]하다 interest rate 이자율 balance 잔액
추가 근무 요청	volunteer 지원자 operation 운영 overtime 초과근무 cooperation 협력, 협동

실전 지문에 적용하기

NOTICE: Entrance Closure

1 공지 대상 **This notice is for all tenants in Westerly Towers.** **2 핵심 정보와 세부 사항** **Please be reminded that the building's main entrance on Carlin Avenue will be closed tomorrow, April 29.** The floors in the main lobby will undergo repairs, and the entrance will be closed for the convenience of the work crew.

3 요청 및 요구 사항 **We request that all tenants use the rear entrance of the building or the side doors on Leighton Avenue instead.** The main entrance will be available for use again from April 30. Please contact us if you have any questions. We apologize for the inconvenience and thank you for your cooperation in this matter.

Westerly Towers Building Administration

>>> **1 공지 대상**

"이 공지는 웨스터리 타워즈의 모든 세입자를 위한 것입니다."

공지 유형은 일반적으로 시작 부분에서 대상자를 명시합니다. 여기서는 This notice is for ~라는 표현 뒤에 온 tenants(세입자)가 공지의 대상자예요.

|출제되는 문제 유형|
Q. For whom is the notice intended?
공지가 의도하고 있는 대상은?
A. Building tenants 건물 세입자들

2 핵심 정보와 세부 사항

"칼린 로 쪽의 건물 중앙 출입구가 내일 4월 29일에 폐쇄될 예정이라는 것을 기억하세요."

Please be reminded that ~ 이후에 핵심 세부 내용이 제시됩니다. 내일부터 건물 출입구가 폐쇄된다는 것을 알리는 내용이에요.

|출제되는 문제 유형|
Q. What are tenants reminded about?
세입자들이 재안내를 받은 것은?
A. The closure of the main entrance
중앙 출입구의 폐쇄

3 요청 및 요구 사항

"대신 모든 세입자들이 건물의 후문이나 라이튼 로 쪽의 옆문을 이용하시기를 요청합니다."

요청은 보통 지문 마지막에 나와요. We request that이라는 표현 다음에 건물의 후문이나 옆문을 이용하라는 내용이 나오네요.

|출제되는 문제 유형|
Q. What does the building administration request that tenants do?
건물 관리측이 세입자들에게 하도록 요청하는 것은?
A. Use other entrances
다른 출입구 이용하기

UNIT 18

Questions 1-2 refer to the following memo.

MEMO

To: Front desk staff
From: Elena Klum, Hotel Manager
Subject: Holiday work schedule
Date: December 18

The holiday season is coming, so I want to let you know about some opportunities to earn some extra income. As this is a busy time of year at the hotel, we are looking for people to work additional shifts on December 24 and 25. Those of you who choose to work on those days will be eligible for overtime pay. Moreover, you will receive two additional vacation days to use in the future. Please send me an e-mail by Friday with your availability and preferred shifts. If you require further information, feel free to contact me anytime. Thank you for your cooperation.

1. What is the main purpose of the memo?

(A) To thank employees for their hard work
(B) To request payment for a hotel reservation
(C) To invite personnel to an end-of-year party
(D) To announce a chance to get additional pay

2. What do front desk employees need to do by Friday?

(A) Send a response by e-mail
(B) Update a reservations list
(C) Fill out a vacation request form
(D) Provide their contact details

Questions 3-5 refer to the following announcement.

IMPORTANT ANNOUNCEMENT: Dellacourt City Transit Authority

This is to notify all passengers of the Dellacourt City subway system that the regular hours of operation will be changed for the upcoming long weekend. Train service will be offered from 7 A.M. to 10 P.M. from Saturday, July 2 to Monday, July 4. In addition, trains will arrive at stations every fifteen minutes rather than every eight minutes. Subway service will return to the regular hours of operation on July 5. The airport line's schedule will remain the same during this time, departing every thirty minutes.

You are advised to check the holiday service schedules posted at ticketing counters in each station for further details. You may also log on to our Web site at www.dellacourttransit.com to view the modified timetables or call us at 555-0097. We thank you for your cooperation and understanding and hope you enjoy the holiday.

3. What is the announcement mainly about?

(A) Employee work timetables for a holiday
(B) Scheduling changes for a transit service
(C) New policies for requesting a transport pass
(D) Upcoming maintenance work on a subway system

4. What will take place on July 5?

(A) Regular hours of operation will resume.
(B) A subway system will shorten its hours.
(C) An airport train will stop its services.
(D) Departure schedules will be posted.

5. What are people asked to do?

(A) Purchase tickets in advance
(B) Make reservations online
(C) Check temporary schedules
(D) Apply for transit passes

2 대화체 지문 Text Message/Chat Discussion

- 대화체 지문은 문자 메시지 지문과 온라인 채팅 지문으로 총 2가지 유형이에요.
- 매회 각각 한 지문씩 출제되며, 화자의 의도를 묻는 유형의 문제가 항상 같이 출제됩니다.
- 보통 문자 메시지 지문은 두 명의 화자가, 온라인 채팅 지문은 세 명 이상의 화자가 등장해요.
- 업무나 자료 요청, 시간이나 일정 변경, 프로젝트 진행 상황 보고 등의 내용이 자주 나와요.
- 대화체 지문은 어휘나 문장 구조가 상대적으로 쉽지만, 문장이 짧고 설명이 적어서 지시어나 연결어 등을 잘 보지 않으면 내용의 흐름을 놓칠 수 있으므로 주의해야 해요.

핵심 POINT

〈대표적인 지문 흐름〉

1 용건	There's[There are] ~	(용건) ~이 있습니다
	It looks like ~	~인 것 같습니다
	That means ~	그것은 ~라는 의미입니다

▼

2 구체적인 질문 및 요청 사항	Do you think you could ~?	~을 해 주실 수 있습니까?
	Would you please ~?	~해 주시겠어요?
	I'd like you to ~	당신이 ~해 주셨으면 합니다

▼

3 마무리	I'm sorry about ~	~에 대해 죄송합니다
	I really appreciate ~	~에 정말 감사드립니다
	I'll go over ~	~를 검토해 보겠습니다

대표 상황별 빈출 어휘

교통 상황 관련	express train 급행 열차 traffic jam 교통 체증 ride 태워주기 delay 연착되다 public transportation 대중 교통 in time for ~에 맞춰서
업무 상황 관련	budget 예산 contractor 계약자 distributor 유통업체 expire 만료되다 call back 다시 전화하다 particular 특정한 specialize in ~을 전문으로 하다
주거 및 생활 관련	lease 임대[계약] real estate agency 부동산 cozy 편안한 comfortable 편안한 affordable 저렴한 convenient 편리한

실전 지문에 적용하기

LUIS ZIRINSKY   4:12 P.M.

1 용건 설명 There's a lot of traffic on the road, and I won't make it back to our office before the end of the day.

LUIS ZIRINSKY   4:13 P.M.

So I need you to do me a favor.

ELISE KELLER   4:14 P.M.

Sure, what is it?

LUIS ZIRINSKY   4:16 P.M.

I have an important package on my desk that needs to be mailed out today. 2 요청 사항 Would you please send it for me?

ELISE KELLER   4:22 P.M.

OK. I'll take it over to the post office now.

ELISE KELLER   4:24 P.M.

Do you want me to send it by regular mail?

LUIS ZIRINSKY   4:27 P.M.

3 마무리 Yes, that's fine. I really appreciate your help.

>>> 1 용건 설명

"도로에 정체가 상당해서 퇴근 시간 전에 사무실로 돌아가지 못할 것 같아요."

보통 문자 메시지에서는 인사말 없이 단도직입적으로 용건부터 이야기되기도 합니다. 첫 번째 메시지를 통해 지린스키 씨가 교통 체증으로 사무실에 늦게 들어가게 되었음을 알 수 있네요.

|출제되는 문제 유형|

Q. What is true about Mr. Zirinsky?
지린스키 씨에 대해 사실인 것은?

A. He cannot return to the office on time.
그는 제시간에 사무실로 복귀할 수 없다.

2 요청 사항

"저 대신 소포를 보내 줄래요?"

지문 중간 부분에는 메시지를 보낸 용건인 질문이나 요청 내용이 나와요. 이 지문에서는 지린스키 씨가 본인의 책상에 있는 중요한 소포를 대신 발송해 달라고 요청하고 있어요.

|출제되는 문제 유형|

Q. What is Ms. Keller asked to do?
켈러 씨가 요청받은 일은?

A. Mail a package 소포 보내기

3 마무리

"네, 그게 좋겠어요. 도와줘서 정말 고마워요."

마지막에는 대화를 마무리하는 표현들이 나오는데요. 이 부분에서는 앞의 요청사항에 대해 세부 항목을 확인하는 질문에 관한 대답과 감사 표현으로 대화를 마무리하고 있네요. 다양한 응답 표현을 알아두면 좋아요.

|출제되는 문제 유형|

Q. At 4:27 P.M., what does Mr. Zirinsky mean when he writes, "that's fine"?
오후 4시 27분에 지린스키 씨가 "그게 좋겠어요"라고 했을 때, 그가 의도한 것은?

A. He is confirming a preferred mailing option. 선호하는 배송 방법을 확인해 주고 있다.

UNIT 18

Questions 1-2 refer to the following text message chain.

BRENT DORRIAN	2:01 P.M.
Are you still at the stationery store?	
LARISSA PERKINS	2:02 P.M.
Yes, I'm here now.	
LARISSA PERKINS	2:03 P.M.
I'm waiting in line to order the invitations for our fundraiser.	
BRENT DORRIAN	2:14 P.M.
Great. I've decided to add a few more agencies to the guest list. Can you change the size of our order?	
LARISSA PERKINS	2:19 P.M.
How many more are you thinking?	
BRENT DORRIAN	2:21 P.M.
About twenty-five extra.	
LARISSA PERKINS	2:24 P.M.
Got it.	
LARISSA PERKINS	2:26 P.M.
Is there anything else you need?	
BRENT DORRIAN	2:31 P.M.
No. Thanks.	

1. Why did Mr. Dorrian contact Ms. Perkins?

(A) To remind her of a party's budget
(B) To ask to design event invitations
(C) To inform her of changes to an order
(D) To thank her for donating to a fundraiser

2. At 2:24 P.M., what does Ms. Perkins mean when she writes, "Got it"?

(A) She will stop by the stationery store again.
(B) She is confirming a project's budget.
(C) She received the guest list in advance.
(D) She will increase the number of invitations.

Questions 3-5 refer to the following online chat discussion.

Meredith Hawking [11:11 A.M.]
Hey, Vincent and Robert. I'm overseeing the theater project, and we're almost out of bricks. It looks like we didn't order enough for the east wall.

Vincent Purcell [11:12 A.M.]
I checked the order. It seems that we ordered more than enough bricks according to the measurements. Something is not right.

Robert Schmidt [11:13 A.M.]
Ah, I forgot to tell you about this. The supplier called us this morning and explained that they couldn't deliver all of the bricks at once. So there will be a second delivery. They said it would be made between 2 and 2:30. Is that a problem?

Meredith Hawking [11:14 A.M.]
Actually, I have to leave the site to meet another client at 2. So I won't be here when they make the delivery. Vincent, do you think you could stop by around that time?

Vincent Purcell [11:15 A.M.]
Sure, no problem. I can be there from 1:30 to 3. When the delivery people arrive with the second part of the order, I'll go over it to make sure everything is correct.

Robert Schmidt [11:17 A.M.]
Thanks, Vincent. That would be great.

---

3. Where most likely is Ms. Hawking?

(A) In an office building
(B) At a construction site
(C) In a performance hall
(D) At a supplier's headquarters

4. Why did a supplier make a phone call?

(A) To explain that an item is sold out
(B) To request that a fee be paid in full
(C) To warn that two deliveries would be made
(D) To confirm that an order amount was modified

5. At 11:15 A.M., what does Mr. Purcell mean when he writes, "I'll go over it"?

(A) He will review a delivery.
(B) He will meet a client.
(C) He will change an order.
(D) He will set up an appointment.

3 웹페이지 Web Page

- 웹페이지 유형은 인터넷 사용률이 높은 최신 경향을 반영해 출제되는 독특한 지문 유형이에요.
- 매 시험마다 2지문 이상씩 출제되고 있으며, PART 7의 7% 정도를 차지하는 중요한 유형 중 하나에요.
- 실제 웹페이지처럼 지문 상단에 사이트 주소, 제목, 탭 메뉴 등이 상세하게 나와요.
- '제품[서비스] 설명과 판매', '전시 목록 및 시간', '교통 일정 변경', '관광 안내' 등의 내용이 출제되었어요.
- 웹페이지 지문의 독특한 형식을 숙지하고, 대표적으로 출제되는 상황별 어휘를 학습하세요.

핵심 POINT

〈대표적인 지문 흐름〉

1 인사 및 소개	Welcome to ~	~에 오신 걸 환영합니다
	We are proud to *do* ~	저희는 ~하게 되어서 자랑스럽습니다
	We are the area's leading ~	저희는 지역의 선도적인 ~입니다

▼

2 웹페이지의 세부 정보	Search for ~ on this page	이 페이지에서 ~를 찾아보세요
	We offer the following ~	저희는 이하의 ~를 제공합니다
	Here you can find ~	여기서 ~을 찾으실 수 있습니다

▼

3 이용 방법 및 추가 정보 찾기	Please click here to *do* ~	~하시려면 여기를 클릭해주세요
	To find out more about ~, visit ~ page	~에 관해 더 찾으시려면, ~ 페이지를 방문하세요
	To browse ~, go to ~	~를 살펴보시려면, ~로 가세요

대표 상황별 빈출 어휘

제품[서비스] 안내	serve ~를 위해 일하다 inventory 재고(품) deal 거래 bargain 특가, 유리한 거래 special offer 특별 할인 quality 품질, 고급의
전시회 소개 및 내용	unique 독특한 contemporary 현대의, 동시대의 sculpture 조각품 feature 특징[특집]으로 하다 extraordinary 뛰어난, 비상한 original 독창적인
여행지나 경로 소개	entrance 입구 destination 목적지 sightseeing 관광, 유람 ranger 삼림 경비관 sign 표지(판) spectator 관중 trail 산길, 오솔길 terrain 지형

실전 지문에 적용하기

---

http://www.kalakafabrics.com/

| **HOME** | PRODUCTS | CART | CONTACT |

KALAKA FABRICS
Thank you for visiting Kalaka Inc.!

1 인사 및 소개 We are the area's leading apparel retailer. We've been around for more than ten years, and we can provide everything you need to stay warm in the winter and cool in the summer! We hold more items than any of our competitors, and now is a great time to shop! **2 웹페이지의 세부 정보** We offer the following deals every winter season:

30% off sweaters

20% off coats

10% off pants

There is no need to download any coupon. When you check out, simply enter SNOWFLAKE in the code box. Hurry up before items become sold out! **3 추가 정보** To browse our winter apparel, go to the "Products" page and enter a search term.

>>> **1 인사 및 소개**

"저희는 지역의 선도적인 의류 소매업체입니다."

We are the area's leading ~으로 시작하는 업체 소개의 전형적인 도입부입니다. 이 부분을 통해 해당 업체가 어떤 일을 하는지 알 수 있어요. 지문에서는 의류 소매업체라고 소개하고 있네요.

|출제되는 문제 유형|

Q. What type of business is Kalaka Inc.? 칼라카 주식회사의 사업 종류는?

A. A clothing store 의류 업체

2 웹페이지의 세부 정보

"저희는 겨울철마다 다음의 혜택을 제공합니다."

해당 웹페이지의 주요 정보가 구체적으로 드러나는 부분이에요. 특히 We offer라는 표현 뒤에는 '주로 제공하는 제품[서비스]'나 '특별 혜택 및 할인'의 세부 내용이 등장해요.

|출제되는 문제 유형|

Q. Why is Kalaka Inc. giving discounts? 칼라카 주식회사가 할인을 제공하는 이유는?

A. It is having a seasonal sale. 계절에 따른 할인 판매를 하기 때문이다.

3 추가 정보

"저희의 겨울 의상을 살펴보시려면, '제품' 페이지로 가셔서 검색어를 입력하세요."

주로 웹페이지 마지막 부분에서는 제품이나 서비스를 이용할 수 있는 방법이나 추가 정보를 찾는 방법이 나와요. To browse ~ 이후의 내용에 집중해 보세요.

|출제되는 문제 유형|

Q. What can users do on the "Products" page? 사용자들이 "제품" 페이지에서 할 수 있는 것은?

A. Look through some items 몇몇 제품 살펴보기

UNIT 18

Questions 1-2 refer to the following Web page.

http://www.pietragallery.com/Exhibitions

| ABOUT | **EXHIBITIONS** | MEMBERSHIP | CONTACT |

PIETRA GALLERY EXHIBITIONS

We are proud to announce that our April exhibition theme is the sea. Here you can find the dates for each week-long exhibition. As usual, we will host our monthly guest speaker lecture at the gallery on the first of the month from 6 to 8 P.M.

Dates	Artist	Exhibition Title
April 2 – 8	Paulina Smith	*Sailors of Tomorrow*
April 9 – 15	Ivan Lucas	*Underwater Worlds*
April 16 – 22	Noel Lee	*Deep Thoughts*
April 23 – 29	Mia Jackson	*Water Colors*

April 30, 7 P.M. to 9 P.M.: Closing event *
Join us for dinner at the Bruge Hotel. A five-course meal will be served for $45 per person.

*Due to limited space, advanced reservation is required, though payment can be made at the door. Please click **here** to reserve a seat.

1. How often does Pietra Gallery invite guest speakers?

(A) Every day
(B) Every week
(C) Once a month
(D) Once a year

2. How can visitors sign up for the closing event?

(A) By following a link
(B) By going to the gallery
(C) By displaying their artwork
(D) By paying a fee

Questions 3-5 refer to the following Web page.

| **HOME** | HOURS | WILDLIFE | HIKING TRAILS | LIVE CHAT |

http://www.mountmarjoriepark.com/trails/

Welcome to Mount Marjorie Park's Web site! Mount Marjorie is a mountain with wonderful views. It features many trails of different difficulties. Visit the "**Hiking Trails**" page to find a list of trails and explanations of their difficulty levels. Be sure to consult the "**Hours**" page before coming. You may not enter the park after the main center closes at 6 P.M.

In addition, Mount Marjorie Park is the home of diverse wildlife. Descriptions for all of the animals are on the "**Wildlife**" page. Search for the creatures you want to see on this page by entering a keyword in the search box. The page will suggest the paths where you are most likely to see the animal.

Note that Mount Marjorie Park is a protected area, and visitors are asked to respect the environment at all times. If you wish to donate money to our efforts to protect the local wildlife, please call 555-8282.

Finally, to find out more about the park, try a live chat with one of our park rangers. Simply click on "**Live Chat**" to write directly to staff members.

3. What is NOT mentioned about Mount Marjorie?

(A) It features beautiful scenery.
(B) It has many animals living in it.
(C) It is the highest mountain in the area.
(D) It has various paths with different difficulties.

4. Why should visitors visit the "Wildlife" page?

(A) To report endangered species
(B) To register for a tour
(C) To make a donation
(D) To look up an animal

5. How can visitors learn more about Mount Marjorie Park?

(A) By calling a number
(B) By chatting online
(C) By going to another Web site
(D) By visiting the center after 6 P.M.

4 양식 Form

- 양식 지문은 다양한 형태로 등장한다는 점이 가장 큰 특징이에요.
  예를 들어, 등록 양식에는 개인 정보 칸이 등장하고, 고객 설문 조사 양식에서는 공란에 제품의 장단점이나 선호도를 적게 되어 있어요.
  또한, 주문 관련 영수증이나 송장/명세서 등에서는 구매 제품명, 금액, 할인 등의 내용이 표로 나와요.
- 양식의 공통적인 전개 방식은 시작 부분에 대상과 목적을 밝힌다는 거예요.
  그리고 나서 본론 부분에서는 구체적인 정보들이 나오고, 마지막에는 문제나 질문에 대한 해결 방법들이 제시돼요.

〈대표적인 지문 흐름〉

1 양식의 대상과 목적	This form[receipt] is for ~ 이 양식[영수증]은 ~을 위한 것입니다 This is to confirm ~ 이것은 ~을 확인하기 위한 것입니다 The following is information on ~ 다음은 ~에 대한 정보입니다

▼

2 구체적인 정보	The following information includes ~ 다음 정보는 ~을 포함합니다 Please check the following information 다음의 정보를 확인해 주세요 This information will help us to *do* ~ 이 정보는 우리가 ~하도록 도와줄 겁니다

▼

3 문제 및 질문 해결 방법	If you find an error, please ~ 오류를 발견하시면, ~해 주세요 If you have a question regarding ~ 관련 질문이 있으시면, ~하세요 To report an error, please ~ 오류를 보고하려면, ~해 주세요

대표 상황별 빈출 어휘

외국어 수업 등록서	sign up for ~을 등록하다 course (수업) 과목 instruct 가르치다, 교육하다 fee 수업료
수프 요리법 (recipe)	tender 부드러운 pour 붓다, 따르다 dissolve 녹이다 stir 젓다
레스토랑 만족도 평가	cleanliness 청결 appetizer 전채 요리 chef's special 오늘의 특선 요리 atmosphere 분위기 ingredient 재료

실전 지문에 적용하기

Augustus Fitness Center

1 대상, 목적 This form is for current members of Augustus Fitness Center who wish to renew or extend their membership.

2 구체적인 정보 The following information includes necessary details to be filled in. Please hand in the form to a staff member at the front desk after completing it.

NAME	Albert Brookside
ADDRESS	2119 Rosemont Crescent, Portland OR
PHONE	(503) 555-3847
PAYMENT METHOD	Credit card
EXTENSION OR RENEWAL REQUESTED	Annual membership renewal

3 문의 해결 방법 If you have a question regarding our fees, packages, or services, please speak to a membership coordinator. Those renewing or extending their membership will receive a ten percent discount.

Thank you for your business.

>>> 1 대상, 목적

"이 양식은 회원권을 갱신하거나 연장하기를 원하는 아우구스투스 피트니스 센터의 기존 회원들을 위한 것입니다."

양식에서는 시작 부분에 대상과 목적을 반드시 명시해요. 이 글은 회원권 갱신이나 연장을 하려는 회원을 위한 양식이네요.

|출제되는 문제 유형|

Q. What is the purpose of the form?
양식의 목적은?

A. To renew a sports facility membership
스포츠 시설 회원권을 갱신하기 위하여

2 구체적인 정보

"다음은 기입하실 필수 세부 사항을 포함하고 있습니다."

양식 지문의 특성에 따라, 세부 정보는 다양한 형태로 제시됩니다. 이 지문에서는 표를 이용해 등록에 필요한 개인정보 사항(name, address, phone 등)을 한눈에 살펴볼 수 있게 했어요.

|출제되는 문제 유형|

Q. What information did Mr. Brookside NOT provide?
브룩사이드 씨가 제공하지 않은 정보는?

A. An e-mail address 이메일 주소

3 문의 해결 방법

"요금, 패키지, 또는 서비스에 관해 문의 사항이 있으면, 회원권 조정 담당자에게 말씀해 주세요."

If you have a question regarding 뒤에 문의 해결 방법을 제시하면서 글이 마무리돼요. 문의는 회원권 조정 담당자에게 하라고 하네요.

|출제되는 문제 유형|

Q. What should members do if they have a question?
회원들이 질문이 있으면 해야 할 일은?

A. Talk to a coordinator
담당자에게 이야기하기

UNIT 18

Questions 1-2 refer to the following form.

Gryllis Stationery
2715 Granville Lane
Weehawken, NJ 07872
www.gryllisstationery.com

Invoice: 130259
Date placed: October 13

Ship to: Pedros Solex
1391 Shearwood Forest Drive
Keene, NJ 07463

This is to confirm that we have received your online order. Your order number is 130259. Please submit a payment for the amount stated by transfer or credit card payment. We will then ship your order. If we do not receive the due amount by October 20, the order will be canceled automatically. If you have a question regarding this order, please contact our customer service at 555-2957.

Item	Quantity	Unit Price	Total
Large Whiteboard	3	$80.00	$240.00
Scissors	5	$12.00	$60.00
Plastic Container	15	$10.00	$150.00
Subtotal			$450.00
Shipping			$30.00
AMOUNT DUE			$480.00

Once you receive your order, feel free to leave a comment in the review section of our Web site, www.gryllisstationery.com.

Thank you for shopping at Gryllis Stationery.

1. What can be inferred about Mr. Solex?

(A) He recently placed an order on a Web site.
(B) He has paid $450 using a credit card.
(C) He is a regular customer of Gryllis Stationery.
(D) He requested that an order be canceled.

2. What will happen if payment is not submitted by October 20?

(A) A fee will be applied.
(B) A reminder will be sent.
(C) The order will be canceled.
(D) The delivery will be delayed.

Questions 3-5 refer to the following form.

SJJ Supermarket   SURVEY FORM

Thank you for agreeing to participate in our survey. The following information will help us to improve our services and bring you better products. Please provide the following information and drop off the completed form at SJJ Supermarket.

FULL NAME	Cathy Tan
E-MAIL*	ctan@goal.com

How often do you shop for groceries? <u>About twice a week</u>
How often do you shop at SJJ Supermarket? <u>Maybe four to five times a month</u>
What products do you purchase every week? <u>Milk, bread, fruit, and vegetables</u>
What suggestions do you have for SJJ Supermarket?
<u>I would like to see a better produce section. I usually buy my fruits and vegetables from other markets, as the section is better.</u>

*Please provide your e-mail address if you would like to receive information on upcoming promotions or sales.

Our employees are always here to assist you at the service counter. Please hand in this form to one of them when it is completed.

---

3. Why is SJJ Supermarket conducting a survey?

(A) To help provide better items
(B) To decide how to promote its products
(C) To find out how to compete with other stores
(D) To determine where new branches should be opened

4. What is NOT indicated about Ms. Tan?

(A) She wants to receive information on sales.
(B) She only buys groceries once every week.
(C) She purchases vegetables at another store.
(D) She shops at SJJ Supermarket several times a month.

5. What is suggested about SJJ Supermarket?

(A) It is considering an expansion of its operations.
(B) It has numerous outlets across the country.
(C) It provides a customer service counter in the store.
(D) It sends out flyers with information on special promotions.

PART 7에서 자주 사용되는 바꿔 말하기(패러프레이징) 방법은 지문 속에 등장한 표현을 문제와 선택지에서 다른 표현으로 바꾸어 나타내는 것입니다. 따라서 바꿔 말하기에 익숙해지면 독해 문제를 풀 때 정답을 쉽게 고를 수 있고, 문제 푸는 속도도 빨라집니다.

book a hotel room 호텔 객실을 예약하다	→ **reserve** a hotel room 호텔 객실을 예약하다
be a **regular** customer 단골 고객이 되다	→ be a **loyal** customer 단골 고객이 되다
subscribe to a membership program 회원 프로그램에 가입하다	→ **become a member** of a program 프로그램의 회원이 되다
have **the authority** to *do* ~할 권한을 가지다	→ have **permission** to *do* ~할 허가를 얻다
go through **difficult economic times** 힘든 경제 시기를 겪다	→ go through **an economic crisis** 경제 위기를 겪다
plan to **take some time off** 휴가 가는 것을 계획하다	→ plan to **take a vacation** 휴가 가는 것을 계획하다
pick a coworker **up** from the airport 공항에서부터 동료를 차에 태워 주다	→ **give** a coworker **a ride** from the airport 공항에서부터 동료를 차에 태워 주다
sell some goods **to a foreign country** 외국에 제품을 팔다	→ **export** some goods **overseas** 해외로 제품을 수출하다
the unemployment rate has gone down 실업률이 감소하다	→ the number of unemployed people has **decreased** 실업자의 수가 감소하다
hold a press conference 기자 회견을 열다	→ announce to the public 공표하다

패러프레이징 연습하기

[1~4] 다음 빈칸에 알맞은 것을 고르세요.

1 reserve their tickets in advance
→ ------- their seats ahead of time

(A) book
(B) print

2 struggling in the difficult economic times
→ having difficulties in the -------

(A) economic crisis
(B) dangerous circumstances

3 loyal customers at this restaurant
→ ------- patrons of the establishment

(A) first-time
(B) regular

4 have the authority to supervise the workers
→ have ------- to oversee the employees

(A) permission
(B) abilities

[5~7] 다음 지문과 같은 의미의 문장을 고르세요.

5 We will hold a press conference soon about the merger.

(A) A decision will be made soon about the merger.
(B) The merger will soon be announced to the public.

6 The CEO told Ms. Hertz to pick him up from the airport.

(A) The CEO asked Ms. Hertz to give him a ride from the airport.
(B) The CEO asked Ms. Hertz to reserve a plane ticket from the airport.

7 Thanks to new building projects, the unemployment rate has gone down.

(A) Employers advertised fewer job openings despite the new projects.
(B) The number of unemployed people has decreased because of the construction.

[8~9] 다음 지문을 읽고 문제의 답을 고르세요.

Dear Ms. Manning,

Thank you for telling me about the Benson Arts Festival next month. Unfortunately, I am taking that week off from work and will be out of the country until the following weekend. I booked my flight a month ago and cannot change my dates. It's a shame because the festival looks like it will be a lot of fun. I'm glad it's an annual event so that I can go next year. I hope you enjoy it even though I can't go.

Sincerely,

Karen Carlson

---

8 Why is Ms. Carlson unable to attend the festival?

(A) She is taking a vacation at that time.
(B) She has a lot of work to do that week.

9 How often does the Benson Arts Festival take place?

(A) Quarterly
(B) Yearly

UNIT 18

PART 7 지문 유형편

UNIT 19

두 개의 지문

누가 이렇게 많이 쓴거야?
카드사에 이메일로 물어봐야 겠다.

카드 명세서 →

1 이메일/편지(E-mail/Letter) 이중 지문
2 공지(Announcement) 이중 지문
3 양식(Form) 이중 지문

이메일/편지(E-mail/Letter) 이중 지문

- 이메일/편지는 의사소통 수단이라는 특성 때문에 관련 정보를 묻고 답하는 PART 7의 연계 지문으로 자주 출제됩니다.
- 특히 〈문의에 대한 답변 이메일/편지〉, 〈공지에 대한 문의 및 조정 이메일/편지〉, 〈기사문에 대한 정정 요청 이메일/편지〉 등이 자주 출제됩니다.

핵심 POINT

〈대표적인 지문 흐름〉

첫 번째 지문: e-mail	두 번째 지문: e-mail
관심 표명과 문의 사항 "임대용 사무실에 관심이 있습니다." "입주일 정보가 다릅니다."	**문의 사항 해결과 관심에 대한 응대** "입주일은 4월 28일입니다." "화요일 3시에 둘러볼 수 있습니다."

〈그 밖에 등장할 수 있는 유형과 상황들〉
- **이메일+이메일:** 배송 지연 문의+도착 날짜와 보상에 대한 설명
- **공지+이메일:** 팀 회의 및 연수 일정 공지+개인 사정으로 인한 일정 조정 요청
- **기사+이메일/편지:** 박물관 건설에 대한 정부 지원 보도+잘못된 보도에 대한 내용 정정 요청

지문 읽기 전략

step1 이메일의 수신자와 발신자의 관계를 파악하자!
주고 받는 사람들 간의 관계를 파악하는 게 이메일과 편지 지문 읽기의 기본이에요. 지문 위 아래에 명시되는 수신자와 발신자를 먼저 살피세요. ○, △와 같은 도형을 이용해 수신자와 발신자를 구별해두면 내용 이해에 혼동을 줄일 수 있습니다.

step2 첫 번째 이메일/편지의 주제와 목적을 분명히 파악하자!
이메일/편지 지문에는 분명한 목적이 있는데, 주로 내용 문의나 요청 사항 등입니다. 지문을 읽으면서 이와 관련된 내용이 나오면 밑줄을 그어 표시해두세요.

step3 두 번째 이메일/편지의 핵심은 연계 내용임을 기억하자!
두 번째 이메일/편지는 첫 번째 이메일/편지에 대한 응답이므로, 앞서 나온 문의나 요청에 따른 내용 확인과 해결 방법 등이 반드시 제시될 것입니다. 따라서 연계된 내용 파악에 중점을 두세요.

실전 지문에 적용하기

step1 To: Metro Realty <info@metro-realty.net>
From: Diane Coleman <d.coleman@inbox4u.com>

To whom it may concern:

step2 I am interested in the office space for rent on the fourth floor of the Frederickson Building. The location is convenient because it's within walking distance of the subway.

Q However, there are two different pieces of information detailing the moving-in dates for this space. The local newspaper said it is available from April 5 while your Web site says the moving-in date is April 28.

step2 Please let me know which is correct. Also, I would like to schedule a time to view the office space. You can reply to this message or call my office at 555-2040 anytime before 6 P.M. today.

Regards,

Diane Coleman

---

step1 To: Diane Coleman <d.coleman@inbox4u.com>
From: Metro Realty <info@metro-realty.net>

Dear Ms. Coleman,

Thank you for pointing out the error. We hadn't noticed that two different dates had been listed. step3 Q The correct moving-in date is April 28. I hope that will work out for your business.

I've attached a brochure to this e-mail that has lots of pictures of the office. As you can see, it is quite spacious. step3 I can give you a tour on Tuesday afternoon at 3 P.M. If you're busy then, just let me know, and I'll try to rearrange my schedule.

Sincerely,

Fred Logan
Real Estate Agent, Metro Realty

>>> step1 수신자/발신자 관계 파악

지문 1 수신: 메트로 부동산
발신: 다이앤 콜맨
지문 2 수신: 다이앤 콜맨
발신: 메트로 부동산

부동산 중개인과 고객 간에 주고 받은 이메일임을 확인할 수 있어요.

step2 주제와 목적 파악

"프레드릭슨 빌딩의 4층 임대용 사무실에 관심이 있습니다."
"어느 쪽이 올바른지 알려 주세요. 또한 사무실을 구경할 시간을 정하고 싶습니다."

임대용 사무실에 대한 관심을 시작으로 입주 가능한 날짜에 대한 문의와 임대 공간을 둘러보고 싶다는 내용이 나와요.

step3 두 지문의 연계성 파악

"올바른 입주일은 4월 28일입니다."
"화요일 오후 3시에 둘러보실 수 있게 해드릴 수 있습니다."

첫 지문의 문의 사항에 대한 해결로 올바른 입주 날짜를 제시하였고, 관심에 대한 응대로 임대 공간 방문 일정을 제안하고 있어요.

➕ 연계 유형 문제

Q. Where can an error be found?

   (A) In a previous e-mail
   (B) In a newspaper listing
   (C) On a Web site
   (D) In a company brochure

Q. 오류가 발견될 수 있는 곳은?
〈지문1〉에서 발신자가 문의한 두 가지 정보 중 틀린 것 하나를 〈지문2〉에서 가려내는 문제입니다. 입주일이 4월 28일이 맞다고 했으므로, 오류가 있는 쪽은 4월 5일이라고 한 신문이 되므로 정답은 (B).

UNIT 19

Questions 1-5 refer to the following e-mails.

To: Kevin Reilly <reillyk@inboxnow.net>
From: Rahul Kilam <rkilam@acrosstn.com>
Date: October 29
Subject: Open position

Dear Mr. Reilly,

Thank you for your interest in working for *Across the Nation*. Please note that our current full-time science writer is leaving on November 10. Therefore, her replacement should start three days before that. That way, she can train the new reporter.

This position has many benefits. The salary is higher than average for our industry. You will also get to choose when you work, as long as it adds up to forty hours per week. That means you are in charge of your own schedule. Finally, we offer a bonus every December, which is based on your job performance.

Having looked at your submitted résumé, I would like to invite you for an interview at our headquarters at 10 A.M. on November 1. Please let me know if this is suitable for you. Also, could you please send a sample article so I can review your writing style before the interview?

Thanks,

Rahul Kilam
HR manager, *Across the Nation*

To: Rahul Kilam <rkilam@acrosstn.com>
From: Kevin Reilly <reillyk@inboxnow.net>
Date: October 29
Subject: RE: Open position

Dear Mr. Kilam,

Thank you for considering me for an interview. The file you requested is attached to this e-mail. I think I would make a great addition to your team because I have a lot of experience as a science writer. As you saw on my résumé, I spent three years writing for the science and technology section of *Janesburg News*. It is no problem to meet on November 1 at 10 A.M. In fact, my apartment is only a five-minute walk from your headquarters in the

Madison Building. I look forward to meeting you and explaining my experience in greater detail.

Sincerely,

Kevin Reilly

1. When does the new position start?

(A) November 1
(B) November 7
(C) November 10
(D) November 11

2. What is NOT mentioned as a benefit of the position?

(A) Many vacation days
(B) Flexible working hours
(C) A year-end bonus
(D) A generous salary

3. What is attached to Mr. Reilly's e-mail?

(A) A work schedule
(B) An updated résumé
(C) A recommendation letter
(D) A writing sample

4. How long has Mr. Reilly worked as a science writer?

(A) Two years
(B) Three years
(C) Five years
(D) Eight years

5. What can be inferred about Mr. Reilly?

(A) He has met Mr. Kilam before.
(B) He prefers to arrive before 10 A.M.
(C) He lives near the Madison Building.
(D) He studied science in college.

2

공지(Announcement) 이중 지문

- 공지 지문은 다수의 사람들에게 일방적으로 정보를 알리는 목적을 가지고 있으므로, 공지를 본 사람들로 부터 문의나 요청이 뒤따르는 형태의 연계 지문이 빈번하게 출제됩니다.
- 공지와 자주 연계되는 지문으로는, 〈유지보수 관련 공지에 대해 문의하는 이메일/편지〉, 〈행사나 대회 공 지에 대한 확인 요청 이메일/편지〉 등이 있어요.

핵심 POINT

〈대표적인 지문 흐름〉

첫 번째 지문: announcement	두 번째 지문: e-mail
공지 대상 명시, 핵심 정보 전달 "고객 서비스 부서를 4개 부문으로 나눌 것입니다."	**핵심 정보 관련 요청 또는 문의** "골드 패키지로 바꾸는 게 나을 것 같습니다."

〈그 밖에 등장할 수 있는 유형과 상황들〉

- **공지+이메일:** 건물 유지보수에 관한 공지+관련 내용 문의 및 확인
- **공지+편지:** 자선 행사에 대한 공지+참가 신청/봉사 활동 독려
- **공지+공지:** 직원들에게 조사 준비를 지시하는 공지+기관 및 정부의 조사 계획 공지 첨부

지문 읽기 전략

step1 첫 번째 공지의 대상자를 먼저 확인하자!
공지 대상자에 따라 공지의 대략적인 내용을 미리 파악해 볼 수 있습니다. 따라서 공지의 맨 윗부분에서 수신자를 의미하는 To:(~에게)라는 표현에 밑줄을 그어 놓으세요.

step2 첫 번째 공지의 핵심 내용이 무엇인지를 파악하자!
중요 내용은 보통 본론 부분에 등장하므로, 이 부분부터 집중력을 최대한 발휘해야 해요. 명확 한 내용 전달은 공지의 특징이므로 간결하고 핵심적인 문체로 서술된다는 점도 기억하세요.

step3 두 번째 지문에 등장한 요청이나 문의의 연계성을 파악하자!
두 번째 지문에서는 첫 번째 지문의 정보에 관련된 요청이나 문의 내용을 담은 글이 이어집니 다. 연계되는 부분에서 주로 문제가 출제되니 이 부분들을 확실히 표시해두세요.

실전 지문에 적용하기

step1 To: Tri-State Cellular Customers
From: Tri-State Cellular Customer Service
        Department
Date: September 30

step1 To offer more efficient service, Tri-State Cellular is separating its customer service department into four sections. Please contact the manager who is in charge of the section you need. You will receive a response within one working day.

step2
Contract Details – Ann Dunigan <a.dunigan@tristate.com>: For renewing or ending your contract with Tri-State Cellular

Payments and Invoices – Greg Foster <g.foster@tristate.com>: For questions about current or past payments and invoices

Ⓠ Service Packages – Edward Fields <e.fields@tristate.com>: For upgrading or changing your cell phone service package

Warranty Inquiries – Susan Dean <s.dean@tristate.com>: For obtaining warranty information about your cell phone

---

step3 Ⓠ To: Edward Fields <e.fields@tristate.com>
From: David McNeil <davidmc@inbox99.com>
Date: October 3
Subject: Inquiry

Hello,

I currently have a two-year contract with Tri-State Cellular. It is the Silver Package, which has 450 minutes per month. I got a new job, so now I use my phone a lot more than I used to. The past two months, I exceeded my monthly limit. step3 Ⓠ Therefore, I think it would be better to change to the Gold Package because it has unlimited minutes. Please e-mail me a copy of the forms I need in order to make this change. I'd like to do it as soon as possible.

Thank you,

David McNeil

≫ step1 공지 대상자 확인

"수신: 트리-스테이트 휴대폰 고객들"
"더 효율적인 서비스를 제공하기 위해"

공지의 첫 번째 줄에서 휴대전화 업체가 고객들을 대상으로 하는 공지라는 걸 알 수 있어요. 더 나은 서비스를 제공하기 위한 새로운 정책을 안내하고 있어요.

step2 공지의 핵심 정보 파악

"계약 세부사항, 지불 및 명세서, 서비스 패키지, 보증서 문의"
"서비스 패키지 – 에드워드 필즈"
공지의 핵심 정보로 서비스와 관련해서 총 네 가지 부서의 업무와 담당자 정보가 나오네요.

step3 요청/문의 내용 파악

"수신: 에드워드 필즈"
"그래서 제 생각에 골드 패키지로 바꾸는 게 나을 것 같습니다."

두 번째 이메일의 수신자인 에드워드 필즈 씨는 첫 번째 지문을 보면 서비스 패키지(Service Packages) 담당자임을 알 수 있어요. 고객인 데이비드 씨가 골드 패키지로 바꾸고 싶다는 의사를 밝히고 있습니다.

✚ 연계 유형 문제

Q. Which section did Mr. McNeil contact?

(A) Contract Details
(B) Payments and Invoices
(C) Service Packages
(D) Warranty Inquiries

Q. 맥닐 씨가 연락한 부서는?
〈지문 2〉에서 맥닐 씨가 연락한 사람의 이름을 보고, 〈지문 1〉에서 그 사람이 어떤 부서의 담당자인지 찾아야 하는 문제예요. 〈지문 2〉에서 에드워드 필즈 씨가 이메일 수신인이므로, 〈지문 1〉에서 등장한 네 개의 부서 중 맥닐 씨가 연락한 부서는 (C)임을 알 수 있어요.

Questions 1-5 refer to the following announcement and e-mail.

Announcement from the Rose Foundation

The Rose Foundation provides a variety of services to the underprivileged in our community. Please contact one of the following departments to get involved:

Financial Services
Make a donation by check or bank transfer.
Contact Fang Shih at fshih@rosefd.org.

Outreach Department
Plan your own event to raise funds for the Rose Foundation.
Contact Anna Soranen at asoranen@rosefd.org.

Volunteer Department
We offer a free dinner every Sunday. Prepare food and serve the dinner.
Contact Jean Williams at jwilliams@rosefd.org.

Professional Services
Provide health services to those in need at our on-site clinic. Medical professionals only.
Contact Raymond Carter at rcarter@rosefd.org.

To: Anna Soranen <asoranen@rosefd.org>
From: Lauren Shafer <l_shafer@inboxtime.net>
Date: February 19
Subject: The Rose Foundation

Dear Ms. Soranen,

I am interested in assisting the Rose Foundation by hosting an event. The work your organization does for the community is necessary, and I know that many people have been helped by your services. As a local business owner, I would love the opportunity to support such important work. I run a small coffee shop downtown, and I know a lot of customers who would be interested in attending an event for the Rose Foundation. My shop is located right next to the Horner Gallery, which is where I'd like to hold the event. The gallery's owner has generously offered to provide the space for free.

My plan is to hold a formal party with drinks and appetizers. I've never planned an event like this before, so your advice would be quite useful to me. It would be easiest to meet in person. You could tell me about some of the previous fundraising events that others have held. Could you visit the proposed venue sometime next week? Then we could discuss the plan.

Thank you,
Lauren Shafer

어휘/해설 보기

1. What is the purpose of the announcement?

(A) To ask people to attend an annual event
(B) To promote an organization's opening
(C) To recruit people to help an organization
(D) To explain changes in a service

2. What is indicated about the Rose Foundation?

(A) It accepts donations by credit card.
(B) It receives funding from the government.
(C) It provides a free meal once a week.
(D) It is working with a nearby clinic.

3. Which department did Ms. Shafer contact?

(A) Financial Services
(B) Outreach Department
(C) Volunteer Department
(D) Professional Services

4. In the e-mail, the word "run" in paragraph 1, line 4, is closest in meaning to

(A) operate
(B) continue
(C) race
(D) compete

5. Where would Ms. Shafer like to meet?

(A) At a gallery
(B) At a charity
(C) At a coffee shop
(D) At a restaurant

3 양식(Form) 이중 지문

- 양식 지문은 송장, 일정표, 고객 설문지 등 일상생활에서 접할 수 있는 서식들로, 그 내용이 실용적이고 형태가 다양하다는 특징을 가집니다.
  따라서 연계 지문들도 양식의 종류에 따라 다양한 내용과 형태로 등장해요.
- 주로 〈제품[서비스] 송장이나 확인서에 대한 오류 문의 이메일〉, 〈제품 카탈로그를 보고 문의나 주문을 하는 이메일〉 등이 양식 지문과 연계되어 나옵니다.

핵심 POINT

〈대표적인 지문 흐름〉

첫 번째 지문: form	두 번째 지문: e-mail
영수증 세부 내역 "환불 영수증" "결제 금액: 200달러/환불 금액: 100달러"	▶ **문제 제기와 해결 요청** "잘못된 환불 금액을 확인했습니다" "전액이 환불되어야 합니다."

〈그 밖에 등장할 수 있는 유형과 상황들〉
- **양식+이메일**: 제품[서비스] 송장이나 확인서+오류 확인 요청 메일
- **양식+이메일[편지]**: 제품[서비스] 리스트+문의나 주문 메일
- **메모+양식**: 작업 시간 변경 알림+작업 일정표

지문 읽기 전략

step1 **주어진 양식 유형을 먼저 파악하자!**
양식은 지시문에 그 종류가 명시되므로, 먼저 유형부터 파악하세요. 만약 직접적으로 명시되어 있지 않은 경우에는 지문의 전반적인 정보를 보고 양식의 유형을 추론해야 해요.

⌄

step2 **양식의 세부 사항을 살펴보자!**
송장, 영수증, 확인서, 작업 일정표, 고객 평가서 등의 양식은 그 세부 내역이 소항목으로 파악하기 쉽게 정리되어 있는 편이에요. 따라서 열거된 항목들을 중심으로 세부 사항을 빠르게 파악하세요.

⌄

step3 **연계 지문의 문제 제기 및 해결 요청 내용을 확인하자!**
두 번째 지문에서는 보통 첫 번째 지문의 세부 내역 중 하나에 문제가 있어서 해결해 달라는 식으로 내용이 전개돼요. 이 부분을 제대로 파악해야 정답을 고를 수 있어요.

실전 지문에 적용하기

---

step1 Salinas Hotel

step1 Refund Receipt

Customer: Orika Mori
Customer reservation number: CP396
Venue: Grand Ballroom
Reservation date: March 27
step2 **Q** Payment received: $200
       Refund amount: $100

According to the hotel refund policy, the above amount will be refunded to the credit card that was used for the original reservation. If you do not receive the refund within 60 days, contact our booking department at reservations@salinashotel.com.

To: Salinas Hotel <reservations@salinashotel.com>
From: Orika Mori <orikamori@edgeacct.com>
Date: April 20
Subject: Refund

To whom it may concern:

I recently canceled an event at Salinas Hotel. When I looked at my credit card statement, step3 I saw that the wrong refund amount had been sent. At first, I thought that it was my mistake. However, after checking the contract, I discovered that the problem must be with your hotel. Because I gave more than two weeks' notice for the cancellation, step3 **Q** my full payment should have been returned. Please e-mail me back to let me know how soon you can resolve this issue.

Thank you,

Orika Mori

>>> step1 양식 유형 확인

"살리나스 호텔"
"환불 영수증"

양식 제목을 포함한 앞부분을 통해서 호텔에서 고객에게 보내는 환불 영수증임을 알 수 있어요.

step2 양식 세부 사항 확인

"결제 금액: 200달러"
"환불 금액: 100달러"

양식의 유형을 확인했으면, 빠르게 그 세부 내용을 확인해야 해요. 원래 호텔에 지불했던 금액은 200달러이고 환불 받은 금액은 100달러입니다.

step3 요청 내용 파악

"잘못된 환불 금액이 보내진 것을 알게 되었습니다."
"전체 금액이 환불되어야 합니다."

이메일에서 발신자가 잘못된 환불 금액이 들어왔다고 이야기하네요. 이 문제의 해결 방법으로 '전액 환불'을 요청하고 있는 상황임을 알 수 있습니다.

+ 연계 유형 문제

Q. What is suggested about Ms. Mori?

(A) She attended an event on March 27.
(B) She expected to receive $200.
(C) She paid for a reservation in cash.
(D) She needs a new copy of a contract.

Q. 모리 씨에 대해 암시된 것은?

〈지문 2〉에서 모리 씨는 전액 환불을 요청했고 〈지문 1〉에서 모리 씨가 원래 지불한 금액이 200달러임을 알 수 있어요. 따라서 모리 씨가 200달러를 받을 것이라고 예상했던 것이므로 정답은 (B).

UNIT 19

Questions 1-5 refer to the following form and letter.

Itinerary from Jetset Travel

Passenger: Sylvia Jenkins
Confirmation code: 9304-3950
Booking date: April 8
Total charge: USD 856.00

April 29	
Depart Manila, Philippines 8:10 A.M. Ninoy Aquino International Airport (MNL) **Arrive** Hong Kong, Hong Kong 10:20 A.M. Hong Kong Airport (HKG)	Rica Airlines Flight RZ993 Class: First Seat number: B2 Flight duration: 2hrs 10min Meal: Breakfast

May 5	
Depart Hong Kong, Hong Kong 7:25 P.M. Hong Kong Airport (HKG) **Arrive** Manila, Philippines 9:40 P.M. Ninoy Aquino International Airport (MNL)	Rica Airlines Flight RZ120 Class: First Seat number: C1 Flight duration: 2hrs 15min Meal: Dinner

Baggage allowance: Two pieces of free checked luggage for first-class passengers. One piece of free checked luggage for economy passengers. Extra luggage will be charged at a rate of $30 per bag.

A fee of $20 will be charged for any changes to the above itinerary. Please note that this is a non-refundable ticket, so cancellations cannot be made without penalty.

Thank you for choosing Jetset Travel. To book another trip with us, call 1-800-555-4097.

Jetset Travel
1332 Coral Way Avenue
Manila Bay, Manila, Philippines

To whom it may concern:

I received the itinerary for my upcoming trip. However, since I have to visit a manufacturing plant during my business trip, I'd like to make one change. On April 29, I need to take the Rica Airlines 6:30 A.M. flight to Hong Kong instead of the one I booked. I hope you are able to accommodate this request. The return flight doesn't need any changes at all.

Additionally, the total cost of the trip was much higher than I expected. I didn't realize that the figure you told me over the phone did not include taxes. In the future, please let me know exactly how much will be charged to my credit card before it is processed.

The day before my return flight, I'll have quite a bit of free time in the afternoon. Can you recommend some famous places to visit? I'd love to see what the city has to offer. Any information you could share would be greatly appreciated. Please send my updated itinerary to my e-mail address at s_jenkins@athacorp.com.

Thank you,

Sylvia Jenkins

1. What is indicated about the trip?

(A) It was booked through a Web site.
(B) A meal will be served on both flights.
(C) The return flight will arrive at noon.
(D) It can be changed at no extra charge.

2. How much will Ms. Jenkins be charged if she checks two bags?

(A) $0.00
(B) $20.00
(C) $30.00
(D) $60.00

3. What is the purpose of Ms. Jenkins' letter?

(A) To cancel an upcoming trip
(B) To make an itinerary change
(C) To complain about an error
(D) To request payment information

4. In the letter, the word "figure" in paragraph 2, line 2, is closest in meaning to

(A) plan
(B) shape
(C) proposal
(D) amount

5. What will Ms. Jenkins most likely do on May 4?

(A) Go sightseeing in the city
(B) Visit a manufacturing plant
(C) Have a meeting with investors
(D) Return to her departure city

PART 7 지문 유형편

UNIT 20

세 개의 지문

1 광고(Advertisement) 삼중 지문

- 광고는 제품 및 서비스 광고, 구인 광고 등 종류가 다양해서 시험에 자주 출제되는 지문이에요.
- 단일 지문으로 출제될 뿐만 아니라 광고를 보고 문의를 하거나 구매를 하는 등의 여러 가지 상황이 이어질 수 있어 연계 지문에서도 출제 빈도가 높은 편입니다.
- 세 개의 지문이라고 해서 지문의 길이에 겁먹지 말고 우선 각 지문의 제목과 첫 문단을 통해 대략의 상황 및 흐름을 파악하는 것이 중요합니다.

핵심 POINT

〈대표적인 지문 흐름〉

첫 번째 지문: advertisement	두 번째 지문: notice	세 번째 지문: form
제품[서비스] 소개와 특장점	제품[서비스] 관련 공지사항	영수증
"공사 뒤 식당 재개업" "멋진 음식, 우수한 바텐더"	"손님들의 좌석 배치 시 주의사항"	"날짜: 6월 21일" "합계: 1057.69달러"

〈그 밖에 등장할 수 있는 유형과 상황들〉

- 광고+이메일+이메일: 인력 충원 광고+자격 요건 관련 문의+인사 담당자 답변
- 광고+양식+이메일: 신규 상품 및 서비스 광고+구매 영수증[송장]+주문 관련 이메일
- 광고+양식+이메일/편지: 봉사활동 참여를 독려하는 광고+지원 신청서 양식+지원 이메일/편지

지문 읽기 전략

step1 각 지문의 제목과 첫 줄을 통해 연관성을 파악하라!
세 개 지문의 제목과 첫 줄을 읽고 각각의 지문이 어떤 상황으로 연결되는지를 파악하세요.

step2 앞 두 지문의 구체적인 정보에 집중하라!
광고 다음에 나오는 공지사항에서는 주로 앞의 광고에서 언급된 제품 및 서비스의 이용 조건이나 제품의 반품/교환/취소 정책 등이 주로 언급돼요. 광고와 공지 관련 세부 내용을 묻는 유형의 문제가 자주 등장하므로, 질문을 먼저 읽고 해당 세부 정보를 지문에서 빠르게 찾으세요.

step3 세 번째 지문에서 무조건 연계 문제의 힌트를 찾자!
영수증에서는 상품 및 서비스의 세부 항목, 구매 관련 할인 혜택 및 배송 조건에 대한 정보가 등장하는데, 이들 정보가 대부분 위의 두 지문과 연계되어 있으므로 꼼꼼히 읽어야 해요.

실전 지문에 적용하기

---

step1 **Falleni's Restaurant Now Open!**

step1 Falleni's Restaurant is proud to announce that after months of construction, we are officially opening for business. In addition to amazing food, we have a contest-winning bartender on staff. step2 Our grand opening will take place on Friday, June 19. step3 **Q** **And all groups with more than twenty diners will save ten percent on their bills as a special promotion that month.**

---

step1 **How to Seat Tonight's Guests**

step2 Tonight's dinner service includes several bookings for large parties. All of these groups cannot be in the same section because there would be too many patrons for one server. Please distribute big groups evenly throughout the restaurant. Each server should have not only the same number of tables, but approximately the same number of customers as well.

---

step1 **Falleni's Restaurant**

Date: 21/06   Time: 8:57 P.M.
step3 **Q** Guests: 25   Table #: 2

Food Total	1147.43
step3 **Q** Discount	114.74
Subtotal	1032.69
Tip	25.00
TOTAL	1057.69

SIGN X *Trisha Nakao*

+ 연계 유형 문제

Q. Why did Ms. Nakao receive a discount?

(A) She ate in the restaurant on opening night.
(B) She came as part of a large group.
(C) She presented a coupon to the hostess.
(D) She shared a table with other groups.

>> step1 **각 지문의 연관성 파악**

"팔레니 레스토랑이 이제 문을 엽니다!"
"오늘 저녁 손님들의 좌석 배치 방법"
"팔레니 레스토랑"

각 지문의 제목과 첫 줄을 통해서 레스토랑의 재개업을 알리는 광고와 손님들의 좌석 배치 방법에 관한 공지, 그리고 식사 영수증이 이어지고 있음을 파악합니다.

step2 **세부 공지사항 주목**

"6월 19일에 개점 예정"
"6월 중 방문하는 20인 이상 단체에게 10% 할인 제공"
"대규모의 단체 예약이 예정되어 있음"

세부 정보 중 날짜, 할인 등의 특이사항은 문제화되는 경우가 많으니 주의해서 보세요.

step3 **앞 지문과 연계 정보 파악**

"인원: 25명"
"할인: 114.74달러"

식사 영수증은 보통 날짜, 테이블 번호, 메뉴, 식사 가격, 서비스 요금 등의 항목으로 구성돼요. 여기서는 고객이 6월 21일에 25명의 단체의 일원으로 레스토랑에서 식사를 했고, 할인 혜택을 받았음을 알 수 있어요.

Q. 나카오 씨가 할인을 받은 이유는?

〈지문 3〉의 25명의 단체 손님이라는 단서와, 〈지문 1〉의 20명 이상이라는 할인 조건을 연계하여 푸는 문제. 〈지문 3〉을 보면 나카오 씨의 단체는 25명이며 할인을 받았고, 〈지문 1〉에서 20명 이상일 경우 10%를 할인해 준다고 했으므로 정답은 (B)입니다.

UNIT 20

Questions 1-5 refer to the following advertisement, notice, and receipt.

Convenient Cars is here for you!

Convenient Cars vehicles can be booked in advance or reserved at the last minute, depending on availability. Prices are based on vehicle category: compact, full size, and luxury. For an additional charge, larger vehicles are also available to move furniture.

To rent a car, drivers must be 21 years of age or older. Renters 21 through 24 years of age are considered "young drivers". They can only rent compact through full-size cars and will be subject to a $20.00/day young-driver fee.

Convenient Cars sends staff members to pick up and drop off customers at their homes before and after rental car use. Also included in the rental fees is twenty-four hour roadside assistance in the case of an emergency.

RETURN POLICY

Please follow these return instructions after our business hours. Simply park the car, lock its doors, and place the car keys inside the slot of this sealed drop box. Before you return a vehicle, please verify that you have filled up the fuel tank.

Convenient Cars Business Hours:

Monday	7:30 A.M.–6:00 P.M.
Tuesday	7:30 A.M.–6:00 P.M.
Wednesday	7:30 A.M.–6:00 P.M.
Thursday	7:30 A.M.–6:00 P.M.
Friday	7:30 A.M.–6:00 P.M.
Saturday	9:00 A.M.–12:00 P.M.
Sunday	CLOSED

Convenient Cars Rental Receipt

RESERVATION SUMMARY	TOTAL COST SUMMARY	
Pickup Location	For a(n) COMPACT rental	
219 Eagle St., Pinckneyville, IL 62274 Tel.: (618)-894-9820	1 Day @ $33.14 USD	$33.14 USD
Dates & Times	GPS Rental Fee	$23.62 USD
	Daily Insurance Fee	$60.48 USD
Pickup: Friday @ 5:00 P.M. Rental Period: 24-hours	Driver Fee	$20.00 USD
	Sales Tax	$23.74 USD
Renter's Information	-----------------------------	
Mr. Byron Hetzel Tel.: (618)-357-0004	Total Charges	$160.98 USD

1. What is NOT a service provided by Convenient Cars?

(A) Customer pickup
(B) Large vehicles rental
(C) Roadside assistance
(D) Free GPS service

2. In the notice, the word "sealed" in paragraph 1, line 2, is closest in meaning to

(A) stamped
(B) authorized
(C) secured
(D) marked

3. What is indicated about service on weekends?

(A) Special rates are available.
(B) Office hours are shortened.
(C) Fewer vehicles are available.
(D) The pickup area is reduced.

4. Why was Mr. Hetzel charged a $20 fee?

(A) He kept a vehicle longer than specified.
(B) He requested additional driver's insurance.
(C) He is under the age of twenty-five.
(D) He did not refill the fuel tank.

5. What can be inferred about Mr. Hetzel's rental car?

(A) It was returned after hours.
(B) It was reserved at the last minute.
(C) It was rented from an airport.
(D) It was the only vehicle available.

2 기사(Article) 삼중 지문

- 언제, 어디서, 누가, 무엇을, 어떻게, 왜 등과 같은 육하원칙의 정보를 다루는 기사 지문은 내용이 길고 구체적이기 때문에, 한 개의 지문으로만 나와도 어렵게 느껴질 수 있습니다. 하지만 세 개의 지문에서는 기사도 더 짧고 나머지 연계 지문도 상대적으로 쉬우니 겁먹을 필요는 없어요.
- 대표적인 출제 유형으로는 〈출시 제품에 대한 기사와 제품 구매 광고 및 주문 이메일〉, 〈승진 기사와 축하 이메일 및 답장〉 등이 있어요.

핵심 POINT

〈대표적인 지문 흐름〉

첫 번째 지문: article		두 번째 지문: e-mail		세 번째 지문: form
주제 제시, 구체적인 정보 나열 "제품 회수 결정" "전액 환불 예정"	▶	문의 및 요청 사항 "제품을 떨어뜨려 고장" "환불 가능 여부 문의"	▶	자격요건, 참고양식 "회수 제품에 대한 보상 정책"

〈그 밖에 등장할 수 있는 유형과 상황들〉
- **기사+공지+이메일**: 최근 출시된 제품에 대한 기사+제품 구매에 대한 사내 공지+제품 주문 이메일
- **공지+기사+이메일**: 마케팅 전략 강화 사내 공지+경기불황 첨부 기사+전략 회의 요청 이메일
- **기사+이메일+이메일**: 승진 관련 인사이동 기사+승진을 축하하는 이메일+축하 이메일에 대한 답장

지문 읽기 전략

step1 **기사가 어려우면 두 번째 지문부터 파악하라!**
기사 연계 삼중 지문의 경우 주로 기사를 보고 이에 문의나 항의를 하고, 또 이에 답변하는 내용으로 이어집니다. 기사 지문이 어렵게 느껴지면 두 번째 지문부터 먼저 읽어 대략의 상황을 파악하세요.

≫

step2 **기사의 주제 및 세부 내용을 제대로 파악하자!**
육하원칙을 중심으로 기사의 세부 내용을 파악합니다. 그러면 뒤의 두 지문의 상황적 배경을 이해하는 데 도움이 됩니다.

≫

step3 **세 번째 지문에서는 앞의 두 지문과의 연계 내용을 찾자!**
세 번째 지문에서는 기사와 관련하여 단순 문의에 대해 답변을 해 주거나 내용 정정 등의 요청에 대해 해결을 해 주는 흐름으로 전개됩니다. 따라서 앞 지문과 유기적으로 관련된 부분을 찾아서 표시해두도록 합니다.

실전 지문에 적용하기

step2 **Mahier Inc. Recalls Ceiling Fans**
By Anne Collier

Last week, Mahier Inc. recalled forty-three ceiling fan models because of malfunctioning motors. This is the second time in three months that Mahier has recalled a potentially dangerous product. According to a Mahier spokesperson, step2 customers should return fan model J45 to stores for a full refund.

To: Customer Service <cs@mahier.com>
From: Mariah Reyes <mreyes@usernet.mail>
Date: May 14
Subject: Recall procedures

Hello,

I purchased the J45 ceiling fan a week ago. When taking it out of the box, step1 🄳 I accidentally dropped and broke it. Since the product is being recalled anyway, am I entitled to a refund?

Kind thanks,

Mariah Reyes

---

step3 Mahier Coverage Policy for Recalled Products

Condition of recalled item	Refund (%)
Broken during delivery (courier responsible for compensation)	0%
step3 🄳 Broken by customer	50%
Broken due to improper installation	75%
Unopened or intact	100%

✚ 연계 유형 문제

Q. How much of a refund will Ms. Reyes receive?

(A) 0%
(B) 50%
(C) 75%
(D) 100%

>>> step1 이메일의 목적 파악

"제품을 바닥에 떨어뜨려 고장이 났습니다. 저도 환불 자격이 되나요?"

두 번째 지문을 먼저 보면, 환불 자격에 관한 단순 문의 이메일입니다. 이메일 뒤에 문의에 대한 답변이 될 만한 내용이 등장할 것임을 예측해 볼 수 있겠네요.

step2 기사의 세부 내용 파악

"마이어 주식회사, 천장 선풍기를 회수하다"
"고객들은 전액 환불을 받으려 J45 모델을 매장에 반납해야 한다."

기사 제목에서 '마이어 주식회사가 제품을 회수한다'는 주제가 등장하네요. 또한 기사 후반부에서 구체적으로 'J45 모델'이라고 언급합니다. 이를 바탕으로 두 번째 지문이 쓰인 배경을 더잘 이해할 수 있습니다.

step3 위 지문과의 연계성 파악

"회수 제품에 대한 마이어 사의 환불 정책"
"고객에 의한 파손: 50% 보상"

회수 제품 환불 정책에 대한 양식입니다. 회수된 제품의 상태에 따른 환불 조건 내용을 보고, 두 번째 지문과 연계성을 가진다는 것을 알 수 있습니다.

Q. 레이예스 씨가 받게 될 환불 비율은?

질문의 Ms. Reyes라는 이름을 보자마자 지문에서 해당 이름을 빠르게 찾아야 합니다. 〈지문 2〉에서 이메일의 발신자가 레이예스 씨이고 회수되어야 할 제품이 그녀에 의해 망가졌음을 알 수 있는데, 〈지문 3〉에서 고객에 의해 파손된 제품에는 50%를 환불해 준다고 했으므로 정답은 (B)입니다.

Questions 1-5 refer to the following article, e-mail, and agenda.

Miami City Convention Center Finally Open

October 1—After nearly nine months of building, the City Convention Center has officially opened in downtown Miami. Construction plans for the convention center included a 47,000 square-foot ballroom; 88,300 square-foot public lobby, concourse, and registration area; and 151,100 square feet of exhibition space that can accommodate over 800 exhibit booths.

As a promotional incentive for organizations to start using the new space, rental fees will be lowered by 15% for any conferences before the end of the year.

To: Adele Dresner <adele@employmentsolutions.com>

From: Bernard Pender <bernard@employmentsolutions.com>

Date: November 14

Subject: Management Seminar

Attachment: Seminar Agenda

Dear Adele,

Everything has been finalized for your seminar tomorrow. I've confirmed the arrangements with the convention center, and there are fifty participants in total. However, there's been a change. We won't have the discussion after all. We concluded that it would overlap too much with the previous period, and it makes the day too long. So we'll just end the event after the Q&A session. Then, you will need to make an announcement informing participants of the new schedule.

Thanks,
Bernard Pender

Management Seminar Agenda

Miami City Convention Center, Miami, November 15
Conducted by Adele Dresner, Leadership Consultant, Employment Solutions

MORNING AGENDA	AFTERNOON AGENDA
10:30 SESSION 1–EFFECTIVE BUDGETING TECHNIQUES **11:30** Coffee break **11:45** SESSION 2–KEEPING YOUR STAFF MOTIVATED **12:45** Lunch	**14:00** SESSION 3–WRITING REFERENCE LETTERS FOR FORMER EMPLOYEES **15:00** SESSION 4–BEST INTERVIEW QUESTIONS TO ASK CANDIDATES **16:00** Question & answer period **16:30** Discussion **17:00** End of Event

1. In the article, the word "accommodate" in paragraph 1, line 9, is closest in meaning to

(A) submit
(B) arrange
(C) contain
(D) approve

2. What is probably true about Employment Solutions?

(A) It received a discount on a room reservation.
(B) It has a partnership with the Miami Convention Center.
(C) It limits seminar participation to only fifty attendees.
(D) It visits local businesses to provide leadership seminars.

3. What will Ms. Dresner make an announcement about?

(A) The order of two sessions will be switched.
(B) The program has been modified.
(C) One of the seminars has been canceled.
(D) The question & answer session will be extended.

4. What time will the seminar conclude?

(A) At 16:00
(B) At 16:30
(C) At 17:00
(D) At 17:30

5. What will participants hear following the first refreshment break?

(A) Tips for managing a budget
(B) Information about writing a reference letter
(C) Advice on asking good interview questions
(D) A talk about employee motivation strategies

- 인터넷과 모바일 환경이 발달하면서, 시험에서 웹페이지 지문의 출제 비율도 높아지고 있습니다.
- 웹이라는 점만 다를 뿐 제품 및 서비스를 광고하거나 고객 대상으로 중요 공지사항을 알리는 등, 내용 면에서는 광고나 공지와 크게 다르지 않습니다.
- 또한, 실제 웹페이지처럼 가격표, 영수증, 일정표 등의 형태로 등장할 수도 있어요.
- 웹페이지 지문의 본래 목적은 어떤 내용을 알리는 데 있으므로 이를 중심으로 내용을 파악하면 어렵지 않습니다.

핵심 POINT

〈대표적인 지문 흐름〉

첫 번째 지문: Web page	두 번째 지문: form	세 번째 지문: letter
목적 및 지시사항	설문 문항과 세부내용	결과 전달, 요청 및 문의
"고객 설문 참여 요청" "경품 증정 예정"	"설문 작성자: 크리스틴" "설문 문항과 답변"	"당첨자로 선정됨" "경품 배송 일정 안내"

〈그 밖에 등장할 수 있는 유형과 상황들〉
- 웹사이트+이메일+양식: 호텔 가격 정보 화면+예약 확인 이메일+서비스에 대한 고객 평가 양식
- 웹사이트+이메일+이메일: 제품 홍보 화면+주문 문의 이메일+문의에 대한 답변 이메일

지문 읽기 전략

step1 지문의 주제와 목적을 제대로 파악하자!
개별 지문의 분량이 단일 지문이나 이중 지문에 비해 상대적으로 짧아서 도입부만 보아도 중심 내용을 쉽게 알 수 있어요. 세 지문의 도입부를 빠르게 훑어보며 각 지문의 목적을 파악하세요.

step2 지문에 등장한 세부 사항들에 주목하자!
웹페이지는 정보를 알리는 목적을 가지고 있으므로 세부 사항들이 많이 등장합니다. 그러므로 양식의 설문 항목과 같은 세부 사항들을 꼼꼼히 검토해두도록 합니다.

step3 결과 전달, 요청 및 문의 내용을 파악하자!
세 번째 지문에는 주로 앞의 두 지문을 바탕으로 하여 결론이 되는 내용이 오게 되는데, 주로 결과 전달, 요청, 문의와 관련된 내용이 등장한다는 사실을 알아두세요.

실전 지문에 적용하기

www.arcoil.com/customersurvey

step1 **Tell us what you think!**

Throughout January, customers who purchase gasoline from one of our stations will be asked to fill out a feedback survey. As a thank-you, step2 two-dozen participants will be randomly selected from the responses. **Q You could win a premium gas card, which will provide free gasoline for seven days.** Those who aren't selected will also receive a car-wash coupon for $5 off. Don't miss out on this fantastic chance.

---

step1 **Arc Oil Customer Survey**

step2 **Name:** Christine Stout
address: 72 Spinnaker Lane, Chicago

1. **How much do you spend on gasoline each month?**
   $100–$200
2. **Why do you choose our gas station?**
   It offers low prices, and it's close to work.

---

step3 **Q Christine Stout**
72 Spinnaker Lane, Chicago, IL 60654

Dear Ms. Stout:

step1 **Q Congratulations!** step3 **Your name was randomly selected as one of our 24 prize winners.** You should receive your thank-you gift through the mail within 4 to 6 weeks.

Thank you once again for your participation,

Arc Oil

✚ 연계 유형 문제

Q. What will be mailed to Ms. Stout?

(A) A gift card for complimentary gasoline
(B) A detailed customer survey form
(C) A coupon for free oil changes
(D) A discount voucher for a vehicle cleaning

》》 step1 **지문의 주제 및 목적 파악**

"여러분의 생각을 말해 주세요."
"아크 주유소 고객 설문"
"축하드립니다!"

각 지문의 도입부를 훑어봄으로써, 고객들에게 설문을 독려하는 광고, 광고를 보고 참여한 고객의 설문지, 그리고 설문 후 경품에 당첨되었다는 결과를 전달하는 편지임을 알 수 있습니다.

step2 **세부 정보 확인**

"24명의 무작위 당첨자에게 일주일 무료 주유 카드 지급"
"설문 작성자: 크리스틴 스타우트"

앞의 두 지문에 등장하는 세부적인 정보들에 집중합니다. 24명의 설문 작성자가 무작위로 당첨될 것이라 했고, 스타우트 씨가 설문에 참여했으므로 당첨될 가능성이 있겠네요.

step3 **지문 연계성 파악**

"수신인: 크리스틴 스타우트"
"24명의 당첨자 중 한 명으로 뽑히셨습니다."

세 번째 지문은 스타우트 씨에게 쓰여진 편지로, 수신인인 스타우트 씨가 경품에 당첨되었으므로 첫 번째 지문에서 언급된 '일주일 무료 주유권'을 받게 될 것임을 알 수 있어요.

Q. 스타우트 씨에게 우편으로 발송될 것은?
〈지문 1〉과 〈지문 3〉을 연계해야 풀 수 있는 문제. 그녀가 설문에 참여해서 경품에 당첨되었고, 〈지문 1〉에서 당첨 상품이 '무료 주유 카드'임을 알 수 있으므로 정답은 (A)입니다.

Questions 1-5 refer to the following Web page, form and letter.

 www.platinumbank.com/onlineapplicationresults

Congratulations, Ms. Coleton!

Your online application for a Platinum Bank Air Miles credit card has been approved. If you are already an air miles collector, you will receive an initial 25,000 air miles credited to your account immediately.

In 3 to 5 weeks, you will receive your new credit card at the address you submitted on the previous screen. Once it has arrived, you can activate it by calling 1-866-254-6486. After selecting a personalized code for your new card, you can use it right away.

Platinum Bank Air Miles Credit Card Statement

Account Holder: Ruth Coleton
Account Number: 263-8934-985
Air Miles Number: 754-567-923
Statement Period: Dec. 1 to Dec. 31

Current Purchases: $815.00
Previous Balance: $400.00
Total Amount Due: $1,215.00

TRANSACTION DATE	PURCHASE	AMOUNT
December 06	Bambino Airport Café	$15.00
December 13	Express Fuel Gas Station	$50.00
December 16	Deckard Bookstore	$150.00
December 22	Golden's Grocery & Market	$600.00
	Total	$815.00

Minimum payment due: $40.00   **Payment due date:** January 7

For inquiries about this statement or your account, contact 1-866-254-5475, or write to Platinum Bank, Credit Card Services, 480 Hawthorne Avenue, Benton Harbor, Michigan 49022.

Platinum Bank
480 Hawthorne Avenue
Benton Harbor, Michigan 49022
January 2

To whom it may concern,

I recently received my credit card statement in the mail, and I wanted to inform you of an error.

My statement says that I have a balance carried over from my previous statement. However, I paid this amount in full on December 2 and the payment has been received. I verified that the money was taken out of my bank account, so please update your records accordingly.

Sincerely,

Ruth Coleton

1. How did Ms. Coleton obtain a new credit card?

(A) By applying on a Web site
(B) By filling out a form at an airport
(C) By speaking with a bank teller
(D) By reporting a stolen card

2. What is implied about Ms. Coleton?

(A) She earned additional air miles.
(B) She activated her card at the bank.
(C) She requested a credit limit increase.
(D) She lives in Benton Harbor.

3. Where did Ms. Coleton NOT make a purchase?

(A) At a coffee shop
(B) At a grocery store
(C) At a fuel station
(D) At a pharmacy

4. Why did Ms. Coleton send the letter?

(A) To mail a payment by check
(B) To correct a mistake on a bill
(C) To close a credit card account
(D) To request a lower interest rate

5. According to Ms. Coleton, how much did she pay in December?

(A) $400
(B) $600
(C) $815
(D) $1,215

ACTUAL TEST

Reading Comprehension

실전
모의
고사

In the Reading test, you will read a variety of texts and answer several different types of reading comprehension questions. The entire Reading test will last 75 minutes. There are three parts, and directions are given for each part. You are encouraged to answer as many questions as possible within the time allowed.

You must mark your answers on the separate answer sheet. Do not write your answers in the test book.

PART 5

Directions: A word or phrase is missing in each of the sentences below. Four answer choices are given below each sentence. Select the best answer to complete the sentence. Then mark the letter (A), (B), (C), or (D) on your answer sheet.

101. The straps on this bag are ------- to each person simply by pulling on them.

(A) adjustable
(B) adjustment
(C) adjusting
(D) adjust

102. Come to Melinka's special summer sale and check out our many great ------- on shoes and accessories.

(A) dealer
(B) dealing
(C) deal
(D) deals

103. Members must present both a membership card ------- photo ID to receive the discount.

(A) but
(B) through
(C) and
(D) or

104. Audience members are asked to find their seats ------- ten minutes before the start of the show.

(A) at least
(B) so that
(C) but also
(D) no less

105. By investing in stocks and bonds, Zoe Harvey hopes ------- money in the long run.

(A) earning
(B) to earn
(C) having earned
(D) to be earned

106. The presenter's ------- usually help the audience understand the graph on the screen.

(A) clarification
(B) clarify
(C) clarified
(D) clarifications

107. All trains to Stephenville depart from track 2 unless ------- noted on the display screen.

(A) otherwise
(B) once
(C) forward
(D) each

108. By switching suppliers for the raw materials, Corofa Corp. was able to cut production ------- by a significant amount.

(A) costs
(B) currency
(C) origin
(D) results

109. On the cruise, tourists have to pay for drinks, but they can order ------- they want from the menu.

(A) another
(B) them
(C) whatever
(D) some

110. The Reina Maritime Museum ------- all visitors to check their bags at the entrance.

(A) covers
(B) opens
(C) requires
(D) decides

111. Cell phones must be turned off ------- the concert out of respect for the performers.

(A) upon
(B) during
(C) while
(D) when

112. By the time Mr. Cramer arrived at the conference hall, the first presentation had ------- started.

(A) already
(B) yet
(C) before
(D) as soon as

113. The runner managed to maintain a ------- speed throughout the course and win the race.

(A) best
(B) faulty
(C) final
(D) steady

114. Yorta Automobiles sold over one million vehicles this year, ------- all other years by several hundred thousands.

(A) surpassing
(B) surpass
(C) surpasses
(D) surpassed

115. This neighborhood houses a diverse population and has the highest ------- of immigrants in the city.

(A) difference
(B) conference
(C) variation
(D) concentration

116. This year's year-end office party will have ------- attendants than last year's because of the venue's location.

(A) some
(B) fewer
(C) higher
(D) as well

117. People with disabilities and the elderly may use the elevators at the end of the hall -------- walk up the stairs.

(A) instead
(B) rather than
(C) for instance
(D) except for

118. All of the interns performed ------- in their temporary assignments, and most were offered permanent positions.

(A) admire
(B) admired
(C) admirable
(D) admirably

119. Only managers who are ------- to make changes to the payroll can log into this computer.

(A) automated
(B) authorized
(C) avoided
(D) postponed

120. The documentary was not as ------- to the younger generation as the book it was based on.

(A) attractive
(B) attract
(C) attracts
(D) attractively

GO ON TO THE NEXT PAGE

121. It is Alison Horton who ------- greets clients at the airport when they come to visit the headquarters.

(A) momentarily
(B) customarily
(C) progressively
(D) seemingly

122. Henny Co. offered all of its employees ------- for having them work on a holiday.

(A) compensate
(B) compensating
(C) compensation
(D) compensates

123. The new coffee shop is offering a free cookie to the first fifty customers each day to ------- customers.

(A) charge
(B) reject
(C) inform
(D) attract

124. ------- you wish to return this product for any reason, please refer to the customer service desk.

(A) Should
(B) Whereas
(C) Anywhere
(D) Resulting in

125. Jonathan Perkin's retirement party will be held in March, and further details about the event will be given as ------- approaches.

(A) he
(B) they
(C) it
(D) his

126. ------- he was first hired five years ago as an IT consultant, Thomas Finslor has been promoted twice.

(A) Since
(B) Yet
(C) However
(D) When

127. After her company opened several new branches overseas, Emily Elkins became interested in the ------- of working abroad.

(A) routine
(B) supply
(C) rejection
(D) prospect

128. The doctor provided the patient with information on topics ------- the illness, such as advice on lifestyle and eating habits.

(A) beyond
(B) against
(C) inside
(D) apart

129. *This Time*, a painting by Gertrude Mitchell, was ------- revealed at the Stelton Gallery before being moved to the Garata Museum.

(A) previously
(B) passively
(C) heavily
(D) essentially

130. Due to the difficult economic times, by this time next year, Stanic Electronics ------- the majority of its factories.

(A) will be closed
(B) has been closed
(C) will have closed
(D) has closed

PART 6

Directions: Read the texts that follow. A word, phrase, or sentence is missing in parts of the each text. Four answer choices for each question are given below the text. Select the best answer to complete the text. Then mark the letter (A), (B), (C), or (D) on your answer sheet.

Questions 131-134 refer to the following article.

PRIMAVILLE, August 13—Primaville is quickly becoming the tourism capital of the area.

-------, the number of tourists to Primaville has more than doubled this year compared to
   131.

last. ------- . The event, which features various arts and crafts made of local -------, was
    132.   **133.**

launched two years ago and has been a huge success. Citizens of Primaville ------- this
                                                              134.

sudden spark in tourism as a great opportunity to increase business and make the city

more dynamic.

131. (A) However
    (B) At first
    (C) In fact
    (D) Even so

132. (A) With many famous historic sites, Primaville is a fascinating place to visit.
    (B) Information on tourist attractions is displayed throughout the city.
    (C) This rise in touristic appeal is largely due to the Primaville Arts Festival.
    (D) We would like to invite you to an event on August 20.

133. (A) materials
    (B) artists
    (C) benefits
    (D) residents

134. (A) are seen
    (B) see
    (C) sees
    (D) seeing

GO ON TO THE NEXT PAGE

Questions 135-138 refer to the following instruction.

Thank you for purchasing the Scorpio X printer. ------- . Regularly remove dust and
                                                    135.

paper particles using compressed air and wipe down the paper-handling mechanism

with a damp cloth. In case of a paper jam, open the drawer and ensure that the paper

path is ------- from any obstructions. If you notice changes in colors or if some elements
       136.

are not ------- aligned in your printouts, you may have to perform a head cleaning or
       137.

print head alignment. ------- for these functions in the system preferences of the
              138.

accompanying software's main menu.

---

135. (A) All of our devices are on sale for up to 60 percent off.
    (B) Please follow these directions for maintaining your printer.
    (C) We apologize for the issues with your equipment.
    (D) However, your payment has not been processed properly.

136. (A) free
    (B) absent
    (C) evident
    (D) trivial

137. (A) corrected
    (B) correcting
    (C) correctly
    (D) correct

138. (A) Look
    (B) Change
    (C) Accept
    (D) Call

Questions 139-142 refer to the following article.

Two months ago, Veria Tech gathered data ------- hundreds of survey respondents about
139.
what functions they'd like to see in the next smartphone. Now, with only a few weeks left

before the new Veria XD 5 smartphone hits the market, the company has ------- an
140.
aggressive marketing campaign specifically targeting the needs expressed by these

survey respondents. By highlighting the exact features people expressed the most

interest in, Veria Tech has managed to build up excitement surrounding the new

smartphone. ------- . Critics have high expectations for the Veria XD 5's interface, which
141.
was completely redesigned for the ------- user experience.
142.

139. (A) from
(B) above
(C) in
(D) since

140. (A) launched
(B) advertised
(C) failed
(D) misplaced

141. (A) This was in part due to the negative
feedback from the survey.
(B) Indeed, it has exceeded all previous
models in number of preorders.
(C) Unfortunately, this particular model
is sold out at the moment.
(D) It is therefore imperative that more
research be done in marketing.

142. (A) optimize
(B) optimization
(C) optimizes
(D) optimal

GO ON TO THE NEXT PAGE

Questions 143-146 refer to the following information.

Visitors to the Taurus Gym may use the changing rooms located in the east wing of the building. Please do not leave ------- lying around in the changing rooms. ------- . These
                              143.   **144.**
are secured by a code of your choosing and are large enough to hold all of your articles.

------- requires a deposit of $1.00, which is returned to the user. If you forget your
145.

passcode, please report to the main desk, which is open from 8 A.M. to 9 P.M. daily. Note

that it will take ------- thirty minutes to resolve the issue.
                     146.

143. (A) machinery
(B) clothing
(C) facilities
(D) locations

144. (A) Instead, please place your items in one of the lockers.
(B) Once you're done changing, you may use equipment.
(C) For directions, please check the floor plan on the wall.
(D) We apologize for this temporary inconvenience.

145. (A) Every
(B) Another
(C) Each
(D) Either

146. (A) approximate
(B) approximated
(C) approximation
(D) approximately

PART 7

Directions: In this part, you will read a selection of texts, such as magazine and newspaper articles, e-mails, and instant messages. Each text or set of texts is followed by several questions. Select the best answer for each question and mark the letter (A), (B), (C), or (D) on your answer sheet.

Questions 147-148 refer to the following Web page.

The first trailer for director Tyler Morton's newest movie, *Comets*, was just released. As the last chapter of the *Meteor Shower* trilogy, *Comets* is the most anticipated science-fiction movie of the year. It will be in theaters on July 1.

To view the trailer, click here: www.cometsmovie.com/trailer1

Share the trailer on any of your social media pages to be automatically entered to win two seats at the premiere! Contest winners will get to meet director Tyler Morton and lead actor Jed Barrings for a question-and-answer session! Winners will be contacted by e-mail on May 13.

147. What will happen on July 1?

(A) A participant will be chosen.
(B) A director will be interviewed.
(C) A movie will be released.
(D) A trailer will be shown.

148. How can people participate in the contest?

(A) By purchasing movie tickets
(B) By sharing a video
(C) By sending an e-mail
(D) By filling out a form

GO ON TO THE NEXT PAGE

Questions 149-150 refer to the following e-mail.

To: Employees <customerservicestaff@jplusluggage.com>
From: Gerard Keaton <gkeaton@jplusluggage.com>
Subject: Web Site Change
Date: February 1

As you know, our Web site was recently updated, and you'll notice that customers now go through a different procedure to leave comments about our products and services. These comments are now all made public, and customers must provide proof of purchase to contribute. If you notice a negative comment from a customer, please respond to the review by starting with a polite sentence using the person's name and acknowledging the issue. Then, please offer a solution or explanation. See the example below.

> Meredith McGuire, we are very sorry to hear that the suitcase you received was not of the quality you expected. Please note that our products come with a warranty, and we'd be happy to replace your suitcase. You can fill out a request at this link: www.jplusluggage.com/exchangeform/.

If you have any questions, feel free to contact me.

Gerard Keaton
Customer Service Manager

149. What did the company recently change?

(A) Its return policy
(B) Its feedback process
(C) Its product prices
(D) Its Web site address

150. Who is Ms. McGuire?

(A) An airline agent
(B) A customer service representative
(C) A department manager
(D) A product reviewer

Questions 151-153 refer to the following e-mail.

From: GJ Bank <customerservice@gjbank.com>
To: Mary Princeton <m_princeton@theonemail.com>
Subject: Your GJ Bank Card
Date: January 3

Dear Ms. Princeton,

We've noticed that some irregular transactions were recently made with your GJ Bank card. To protect you from fraud, we have frozen your account. — [1] — . To remove the freeze, you must call us at 5332-5726 or visit any GJ Bank branch. — [2] — . You will be asked to prove your identity and to verify some transactions. — [3] — .

We'd like to remind you that lost cards and unrequested transactions should be reported as soon as they are noticed in order to avoid funds being stolen. — [4] — . We also recommend changing your password often to ensure that your account is protected.

Sincerely,

GJ Bank Customer Service

151. Why was the e-mail sent to Ms. Princeton?

(A) To notify her of unusual activities
(B) To request payment for a recent order
(C) To inform her of a new banking policy
(D) To thank her for being a loyal customer

152. What is Ms. Princeton advised to do?

(A) Open a new account
(B) Modify security codes
(C) Request transaction receipts
(D) Always carry an ID card

153. In which of the positions marked [1], [2], [3], and [4] does the following sentence best belong?

"Thus, no transaction can be done using your bank card."

(A) [1]
(B) [2]
(C) [3]
(D) [4]

GO ON TO THE NEXT PAGE

Questions 154-155 refer to the following online chat discussion.

Richard Webster [12:03 P.M.]	Hey, Helen and Tarah. I saw a listing for an office on Chestnut Street online.
Tarah Layman [12:05 P.M.]	I think I know which place you're talking about. It looks perfect for our new law offices. It has everything we are looking for.
Richard Webster [12:05 P.M.]	Yes, so I contacted the landlord, and he said he's available now until two. Do you want to check it out?
Helen Nord [12:06 P.M.]	We were just about to go to lunch. Is it possible to visit it tomorrow instead?
Richard Webster [12:07 P.M.]	Well, it probably is, but it is really nice, and apparently, he's getting a lot of interest. So I think it's better for us to go see it as soon as possible.
Tarah Layman [12:08 P.M.]	OK. I guess we can just eat lunch later. You're not at the office, right? Shall we meet at the subway station on Chestnut Street?
Richard Webster [12:09 P.M.]	I can pick you up. I'm only a couple of minutes from the office. I'm leaving now.

154. What is most likely true about the writers?

(A) They are planning to move to another place.
(B) They currently work on Chestnut Street.
(C) They are the owners of several properties.
(D) They have been trying to contact their landlord.

155. At 12:09 P.M., what does Mr. Webster mean when he writes, "I'm leaving now"?

(A) He is already on the subway.
(B) He has just finished eating lunch.
(C) He is taking the rest of the day off.
(D) He will meet his coworkers soon.

MEMO

To: Customer Service Staff
From: Bianca Dargan
Date: March 2
Subject: Name Badges

A few months ago, we distributed name badges to all of our staff. We'd like to emphasize once again that it is imperative that all customer service personnel have their names clearly visible. The badge must be worn on the left side of your shirt, right below the shoulder. We have noticed several customer service representatives not wearing a name badge or wearing it in the wrong place. Studies show that customers tend to respond in a much friendlier way and have a more positive view of an interaction when they know the customer service representative's name. We must therefore insist that you make every effort to follow this policy. If you have misplaced your badge or if it is damaged, please immediately request a new one from human resources.

156. What is the purpose of the memo?
(A) To remind employees of a rule
(B) To inform staff of a recent study's results
(C) To announce the hiring of new members
(D) To report an increase in negative feedback

157. What should employees do if they have a problem with their badge?
(A) Tell customers their names
(B) Contact a department
(C) Check a policy manual
(D) Speak with their supervisors

GO ON TO THE NEXT PAGE

●●●   ↗

From: Pasha Beauty <customerservice@pashabeauty.com>
To: Mia Robert <miarobert@cleanmail.com>
Subject: Order 36694
Date: May 4

Dear customer,

Thank you for shopping at Pasha Beauty, your one-stop online store for all cosmetics and beauty products! We are writing to inform you that your order has shipped. Your order number is 36694 and you may track the package by following this link: www.denverspeeddelivery.com/ordertracking/125a55.
Below is a summary of your order:

1 Tinty Hand Cream 225mL	$15.50
1 Tinty Hand Cream 50mL	$5.00
1 Laloo Eye Shadow Kit	$17.75
TOTAL	**$38.25**

For returns, exchanges, or any other issues, you may respond to this e-mail or call 494-8813 to speak to a customer service representative.

We hope you enjoy your Pasha Beauty items and shop with us again soon. After you receive your merchandise, please review our products! We and other customers would love to hear what you think.

Sincerely,
Pasha Beauty Customer Service

---

158. What is the purpose of the e-mail?

(A) To confirm shipment of a package
(B) To thank a shopper for a review
(C) To provide an update on item availability
(D) To inform a customer of a declined payment.

159. What is implied about the Tinty hand cream?

(A) It was on sale at the time of the order.
(B) It comes in more than one size.
(C) It is currently out of stock.
(D) It was shipped separately.

160. What is Ms. Robert asked to do?

(A) Contact customer service
(B) Refer a friend
(C) Return one of the items
(D) Provide some feedback

Tessa Museum is extending its hours starting in September. Come check out our newest artifacts and exhibitions!

Museum Hours
Tuesday to Thursday: 9 A.M. to 6 P.M.
Friday to Saturday: 10 A.M. to 8 P.M.
Sunday: 8 A.M. to 7 P.M.

Special Exhibit: *Metal in Art*
October 3 to October 31
The Tessa Museum of Art has a special exhibit on metal and its artistic value. The exhibit gives a history of metal and its use throughout history with chronologies, artifacts from a variety of countries and time periods, photographs of famous items, and videos showing art being made. It explains the role that metal has played in shaping our society and the way it has been used in art to convey a wide range of messages. The exhibit will also feature many modern metal art pieces, contributions from Gabriel Harrah's private collection.

In addition, the museum's curator, Dr. Dmitri Raja, will give a lecture on October 20 at 5:00 P.M. Dr. Raja will talk about *Black Crystals*, artist Valery Borjes's most recent piece, which is featured in the exhibit. While the exhibit is free, the lecture costs $20.00 to attend. Reserve your seat by calling 555-3270.

161. What is indicated about the Tessa Museum of Art?

(A) It closes later on weekends.
(B) It first opened on October 3.
(C) It focuses on modern art.
(D) It charges an extra fee for exhibits.

162. What is NOT mentioned as featured in the *Metal in Art* exhibit?

(A) Examples of artwork
(B) Historical timelines
(C) Pictures of artists
(D) Educational films

163. Who is Mr. Harrah?

(A) A museum curator
(B) A world historian
(C) An art collector
(D) A metal artist

164. What will the lecture on October 20 be about?

(A) Metal's history
(B) An artist's life
(C) Artistic methods
(D) A work of art

GO ON TO THE NEXT PAGE

Questions 165-168 refer to the following text-message chain.

Wilfried Parkson 11:33 A.M.	Hello. I'm with FFD Co. I was given this contact number for the retirement lunch. I'm in charge of setting up the buffet and setting the tables.
Jessica Fern 11:35 A.M.	Hi. Yes, I'm the event organizer for today. Is there something I can help you with?
Wilfried Parkson 11:36 A.M.	I've just arrived at the venue, the Natalia room at Tran Ly Hotel. I've noticed that the room has only thirty chairs. I was told you have a party of thirty-five. I want to make sure you are aware of that.
Jessica Fern 11:38 A.M.	Oh, I didn't know. That is strange. The hotel had told us the room could accommodate thirty-five people. Anyway, is it possible for you to provide some?
Wilfried Parkson 11:39 A.M.	Well, that shouldn't be a problem. I have to make a couple more trips back to the headquarters anyway. But chair rental is not free.
Jessica Fern 11:40 A.M.	Yes, I assumed so. That's fine. Just add it to the bill. We still have some room in the budget.
Wilfried Parkson 11:41 A.M.	OK. I'll go get those for you now. Everything should be ready by 1 P.M.

165. Who most likely is Mr. Parkson?

(A) A caterer
(B) A hotel manager
(C) An event organizer
(D) A furniture store owner

166. What is mentioned about the Natalia room?

(A) It is already set up for a party.
(B) It does not have enough seating.
(C) It was double-booked.
(D) It does not have audiovisual equipment.

167. What is indicated about Mr. Parkson?

(A) He will be retiring soon.
(B) He has made a reservation.
(C) He needs to go back to his company.
(D) He is on a business trip.

168. At 11:40 A.M., what does Ms. Fern mean when she writes, "I assumed so"?

(A) She guessed that a service was not free.
(B) She is aware of Mr. Parkson's tight budget.
(C) She had to return to the headquarters.
(D) She has already made a payment.

Questions 169-171 refer to the following e-mail.

From: Constance Milavich <constance@payapa.com>
To: Patrick Sienna <psienna@pjubusinessschool.edu>
Subject: International Business Lecture Series
Date: September 14

Dear Mr. Sienna,

I wish to register for one of the Communication Abroad seminars from the international business lecture series that your company is offering on September 22 at 5:00 P.M. I am a doctoral student writing a thesis on the subject of international relations, so I believe I am entitled to a discount, as all events organized by PJU Business School are supposed to be discounted for doctoral students. Please remember to take this into account when you send me the bill for my attendance.

Also, the flyer I saw mentioned that the lecture would be held on PJU Campus, but that university has two campus locations, so I was wondering whether it will be on the North Campus or South Campus.

Thank you for your help.

Sincerely,

Constance Milavich

169. What is the purpose of the e-mail?

(A) To reserve a seat for a lecture
(B) To suggest a topic for a class
(C) To inform of a venue change
(D) To request a partial refund

170. What does Ms. Milavich ask Mr. Sienna to do?

(A) Transfer some funds
(B) Hire a student worker
(C) Review her thesis
(D) Apply a discount

171. What does Ms. Milavich suggest about the flyer?

(A) It did not mention the lecture times.
(B) It featured inaccurate information.
(C) It did not include directions.
(D) It was designed for her thesis.

GO ON TO THE NEXT PAGE

HICKSVILLE, February 16—Penny Stationery will be moving its store from the outskirts of the city to the center of Hicksville, in the heart of the commercial zone.

Since its opening three years ago, the stationery store has grown its business into a very healthy one, with profits increasing almost every month. —[1]— This is all despite its relatively remote location, a good twenty-minute drive from the city. The store has managed to make a name for itself simply by word of mouth. "Now that we've saved up enough money," says store owner Melanie Walker, "we can finally afford to move downtown, close to where our customers are."

There is no doubt that relocating to the center of town will bring more foot traffic to the store. —[2]— First, rent is much higher in the city, and profits need to be higher to offset the additional expense. —[3]— One other concern is that Penny Stationery will no longer be in the large wooden cottage that it became renowned for. —[4]— Indeed, when asked what they liked most about the store, customer Elizabeth Arroya said, "They have nice products. But the biggest attraction is the atmosphere. I love the space, the wooden walls, and the rustic décor. I don't know any other store like that."

Penny Stationery is not likely to have the same look in its new home, as the downtown facilities will be modern and much smaller.

172. What is the purpose of the article?

(A) To review a new retailer
(B) To announce a relocation
(C) To explain a rise in rent prices
(D) To attract tourists to a city

173. How did Penny Stationery become famous?

(A) By its store being in a high traffic area
(B) By its owner creating some commercials
(C) By people talking to one another about it
(D) By a newspaper publishing an article on it

174. What does Ms. Arroya say she likes most about Penny Stationery?

(A) Its products are unique.
(B) Its interior design is appealing.
(C) Its facilities are modern.
(D) Its prices are reasonable.

175. In which of the positions marked [1], [2], [3], and [4] does the following sentence best belong?

"Yet the move presents a few risks for the retailer."

(A) [1]
(B) [2]
(C) [3]
(D) [4]

GO ON TO THE NEXT PAGE

From: Burt Lincoln <b.lincoln@beautynow.com>
To: Colin Kinsley <c.kinsley@beautynow.com>
Subject: Image Editing Workshop
Date: August 21
Attachment: Workshop Flyer

Dear Mr. Kinsley,

I was wondering how much we are authorized to spend on workshops and how we can get funds for them. As you know, we have a few new workers on our team who started just a couple of weeks ago. While all of them are highly qualified, I think it would be beneficial for them to attend some workshops to ensure they feel confident in their new jobs.

I've attached a flyer about an upcoming workshop for image editing. It seems to be highly relevant to our work, especially since we plan to start working on the advertisements for the new lipstick line soon. The individual cost is $120 per person, but we should be able to get a discount if all six of the new employees attend. There is limited seating, so I think we should reserve now and simply cancel later if the budget isn't sufficient.

I look forward to hearing from you about this matter.

Sincerely,

Burt Lincoln
Marketing Department Manager

IMAGE EDITING WORKSHOP

Location: Piora Center, Room 120
Date: September 2
Time: 2 P.M. to 5 P.M.
Registration: August 20 to August 30
Instructor: Laura Goryl

This image editing workshop is for people with beginner to intermediate skills. You will learn to modify an image to achieve various goals. Participants will be provided with four images of completely different genres and walked through the step-by-step processes to edit each in order to make it more appealing, eye-catching, and convincing. With a primary emphasis on marketing, this workshop is ideal for those in the advertisement business as it teaches both technical and theoretical knowledge.

The class is limited to twenty-five participants. Seats are available on a first come, first serve basis. All reservations are final and may not be refunded in case of cancelation. Cost is $120 per person. Group rates are available starting at five attendees. Please contact 222-5934 for more information about this.

176. What is the purpose of the e-mail?

(A) To suggest changing a job requirement

(B) To promote an upcoming product line

(C) To request budget information

(D) To provide feedback about a workshop

177. According to the e-mail, what will the marketing department do soon?

(A) Hire more qualified workers

(B) Run a workshop series

(C) Increase its advertising budget

(D) Launch a marketing campaign

178. In the flyer, the word "primary" in paragraph 1, line 5, is closest in meaning to

(A) initial

(B) temporary

(C) main

(D) simple

179. What has Mr. Lincoln misunderstood about the workshop?

(A) Its group rates

(B) Its class size limit

(C) Its cancelation policy

(D) Its registration process

180. What is suggested about Ms. Goryl in the flyer?

(A) She has only basic image editing skills.

(B) She will help students edit some pictures.

(C) She requested a minimum of twenty-five students.

(D) She works for an advertising firm.

GO ON TO THE NEXT PAGE

Reah Ring Park and Its Controversies

By Vincent Benjamin

Trinity, April 22—Reah Ring Park, a park that circles around Reah Lake, is finally open to the public. The park covers a one-kilometer-wide ring around the body of water and includes a bike path, a walkway, and several rest areas.

Construction had been delayed several times due to unexpected issues, mostly related to the quality of the soil, which makes it difficult to build a solid foundation. The park's opening had also been delayed after a bridge over a small stream was deemed unsafe in a safety inspection and had to be rebuilt. The city's decision to reject proposed plans to include a playground for children sparked further controversy. "After careful analysis of the environment, we have concluded that building a playground would be too costly due to environmental factors," explained Mayor Peter Garrett. Nevertheless, city council member Veronica McDonnell, who first suggested building a playground, continued to search for a contractor. And she may have found one in Loyden Co.'s Linda Joyce. At a recent town hall meeting, Ms. McDonnell claimed that, "Ms. Joyce has inspected the area, and she believes that she could design something that would be feasible on a small budget."

Despite these drawbacks, the project was finally completed and the park opened its doors on April 20, welcoming hundreds of visitors on its first day. So far, the park has gotten great reviews from visitors who all seem pleased with the results.

Letter to the Editor

Trinity News Daily
77 Park Avenue
Trinity, PA 19636

Dear *Trinity News Daily*,

I was one of the first visitors to Reah Ring Park on Monday, and I was quite surprised by the article that you published about it. I think you've included some misleading information about how the park was received. There are several negative comments on the forums that complain about the lack of parking, and most importantly, the lack of facilities for children. The project proposed by city council member Veronica McDonnell was rejected for no good reason. It is well-known that there are funds left over from the construction that would be sufficient to go ahead with the project. I recommend you interview the contractor that Ms. Donnell mentioned to the mayor at the last town hall meeting. I believe we would gain more insightful information from hearing a different point of view.

Sincerely,

Jarrod Kline

181. What is the purpose of the article?

(A) To explain a delay in construction

(B) To detail some safety precautions

(C) To announce a park's opening

(D) To encourage donations for a project

182. What is suggested about Reah Ring Park?

(A) It is built on unstable ground.

(B) It was entirely funded by donations.

(C) It is mainly targeted at young children.

(D) It is closed indefinitely due to safety issues.

183. What does Mr. Kline say is inaccurate in the article?

(A) The information concerning security

(B) The names of the people involved

(C) The listing of available facilities

(D) The description of the public response

184. What opinion does Mr. Kline express?

(A) That the playground should have been approved

(B) That safety procedures have not been followed

(C) That more town hall meetings should be held

(D) That a budget should be increased

185. Who does Mr. Kline suggest the *Trinity News Daily* interview?

(A) Mr. Benjamin

(B) Mr. Garrett

(C) Ms. McDonnell

(D) Ms. Joyce

GO ON TO THE NEXT PAGE

Questions 186-190 refer to the following Web page, e-mail and schedule.

---

https://greenfieldscommunity.com/events ⚙ •••

| HOME | ABOUT | **EVENTS** | NEWS | CONTACT |

Greenfields Technology Convention

Attention job seekers!

Learn about the various careers that exist in technology and land a job in a field you love! At the Greenfields Technology Convention (GTC), you will have the chance to meet real professionals, including employers, who will be collecting résumés and giving out business cards. This is a networking opportunity you can't afford to miss. In addition, a series of presentations by experts in tech will provide insight into the requirements and expectations of several growing technological areas. See the program below.

Cybersecurity	Saturday, June 8, 10:30 A.M. to 12:00 P.M.
Big Data	Saturday, June 8, 2:00 P.M. to 4:00 P.M.
Graphic Design	Sunday, June 9, 11:00 A.M. to 12:15 P.M.
Robotics	Sunday, June 9, 1:00 P.M to 2:15 P.M.

••• </>

To: Joe Glax <joeglax@byaincorporated.com>
From: Linda Planter <lindaplanter@byaincorporated.com>
Subject: Chris's Promotion Party
Date: May 30

Hi Joe,

I got the message about Chris's promotion party on Saturday. I know you need an exact head count by tomorrow, so I want to tell you about my situation. Unfortunately, I will be at the Greenfields Technology Convention on that day. I can't miss it since I'm giving a presentation. I reserved a return ticket for Sunday morning already. However, I can easily cancel it and make a new reservation. Then, I could leave on the first train after my presentation Saturday and be at Cander Station around 2:30. I can take a taxi from the station and be at the party venue around 3 P.M., which means I'd still miss lunch. Is it okay for me to arrive late at the party?

Let me know what you think.

Cheers,
Linda Planter

Weekend Train Schedule
Greenfields-Cander Route

Train Number	Departure Station	Destination	Departure Time	Arrival Time
884	Greenfields	Cander	10:30 A.M.	12:30 P.M.
624	Greenfields	Cander	12:30 P.M.	2:30 P.M.
197	Cander	Greenfields	10:30 A.M.	12:30 P.M.
499	Cander	Greenfields	2:40 P.M.	4:40 P.M.

186. On the first Web page, the word "land" in paragraph 1, line 1, is closest in meaning to

(A) arrive
(B) reject
(C) offer
(D) acquire

187. What is NOT something participants can do at the Greenfield Technology Convention?

(A) Meet business contacts
(B) Try new technological equipment
(C) Interact with professionals
(D) Attend lectures by experts

188. Which train did Ms. Planter reserve a ticket for originally?

(A) Train 884
(B) Train 624
(C) Train 197
(D) Train 499

189. Who most likely is Mr. Glax?

(A) A software developer
(B) A train station worker
(C) An event organizer
(D) An employee benefits advisor

190. In what field does Ms. Planter most likely work?

(A) Cybersecurity
(B) Big data
(C) Graphic design
(D) Robotics

GO ON TO THE NEXT PAGE

Questions 191-195 refer to the following advertisement, e-mail and invoice.

Wishing Well Resort Diving Week Event

It's time for this year's Diving Week! Relax at Wishing Well Resort while staying active and learning new skills. For one week, June 2 to June 8, we are partnering with Aronnax Diving to offer you great deals on unforgettable undersea adventures. Join us on any or all of the following:

Monday: reef dive 1
Tuesday: reef dive 2
Wednesday: night dive
Thursday: wreck dive

Guests staying at the Wishing Well Resort for one or more nights that week will receive a 10 percent discount on all of these dives. During Diving Week, all guests get to use the Wishing Well pool for free. In addition, to help you have enough energy for your adventures, the breakfast buffet is complimentary for the whole week!
For specific rates and reservations, call 555-2957.

From: Aronnax Diving <frank.elser@aronnaxdiving.com>
To: Wishing Well Resort <pdenzel@wishingwellresorts.com>
Subject: Invoice
Date: June 15
Attachment: Invoice

Dear Ms. Denzel,

Attached is the invoice for the Diving Week of June 2 to June 8. It includes $415.00 for the person who decided to get certified. This rate was cleared by the resort staff manager on duty at the time.

I also wanted to point out that many people came to us asking to join the night dive, but we had already reached the limit of the number of people, so we had to turn a lot of people down. If you choose to have this promotion again next year, consider scheduling an additional night dive instead of the second reef one, which didn't have a lot of demand. I think we could easily fill up a second night excursion.

Thank you for your business,

Frank Elser
Diving Instructor, Aronnax Diving

Aronnax Diving Invoice

Bill to: Wishing Well Resort

	Price	Number of Participants	Number of Instructors
Reef Dive 1	$180.00	14	2
Reef Dive 2	$180.00	8	1
Night Dive	$200.00	15	3
Wreck Dive	$185.00	17	4
Certification	$415.00	1	2

191. According to the advertisement, what is NOT offered during Diving Week?

(A) Reduced prices on dives
(B) Free breakfast
(C) Complimentary nights
(D) Access to the pool

192. In the e-mail, the word "cleared" in paragraph 1, line 2, is closest in meaning to

(A) approved
(B) experienced
(C) refunded
(D) requested

193. What is suggested about the night dive?

(A) It could include only fifteen people.
(B) It was not as popular as the reef dives.
(C) It was available only to certified divers.
(D) It had to be canceled at the last minute.

194. What does Mr. Elser recommend?

(A) Offering certifications
(B) Increasing the limit per dive
(C) Reducing room prices
(D) Substituting an excursion

195. How many instructors went diving on Thursday?

(A) 1
(B) 2
(C) 3
(D) 4

GO ON TO THE NEXT PAGE

Job opening: Library Assistant

The Treasure Cove Library is looking to hire a library assistant to work at the front desk. Candidates must have prior experience working in a public library and have great people skills. The job entails greeting library patrons, renewing library accounts, checking items in and out, putting away books, and taking overdue fines among various other tasks. This is a part-time job with flexible hours, but the library assistant must work twenty hours a week and on at least one weekend day. To apply, please send a résumé and cover letter to Sophie Travia at stravia@tclibrary.org by September 10.

To: Sophie Travia <stravia@tclibrary.org>
From: Matthew Hunter <matthunter@forevermail.com>
Date: September 9
Subject: Application for Library Assistant
Attachment: résumé, cover letter

Dear Ms. Travia,

I wish to apply for the position of Library Assistant at Treasure Cove.

Although I have not worked in a library before, I have extensive experience in customer service. As such, I believe that I would excel at serving patrons and ensuring that all of their requests are fulfilled. Moreover, I am currently pursuing a master's degree in library science. I am already halfway through my degree, and as I keep progressing, I will continue to gain knowledge that will be useful on the job.

I've attached my résumé and a cover letter with further details about my experience and background.

Sincerely,
Matthew Hunter

To: Circulation Staff<circulation@tclibrary.org>
From: Sophie Travia <stravia@tclibrary.org>
Subject: Library Assistant Position
Date: September 11

Hi all,

We didn't get many candidates for the library assistant job. I recommend loosening our requirements so that we can find at least five interviewees. For example, Matthew Hunter does not have all of the qualifications that we listed. However, he might still be suitable for the job. He has never worked in a library, but his current situation suggests that he is familiar with the environment and that he would be able to adapt quickly.

On the other hand, Ms. McCawley has all of the necessary qualifications, but she is not able to work on Saturdays or Sundays. It would be difficult for us to rearrange the schedule to accommodate her. Thus, I think we might have to find someone else to interview instead of her.

I look forward to hearing your suggestions.

Regards,

Sophie Travia
Head of Library Circulation

---

196. According to the advertisement, what is a duty of the library assistant?

(A) Purchasing books
(B) Collecting money
(C) Repairing items
(D) Creating accounts

197. What does Mr. Hunter think his biggest strength is?

(A) His background in finance
(B) His in-depth knowledge
(C) His ability to work long hours
(D) His people skills

198. What is the purpose of the second e-mail?

(A) To recommend offering a job to a candidate
(B) To reject an incomplete application package
(C) To suggest making hiring criteria more flexible
(D) To explain the necessary qualifications for a position

199. What does Ms. Travia think makes Mr. Hunter suitable for the job?

(A) His relevant field of study
(B) His extensive work experience
(C) His ideal financial situation
(D) His outgoing personality

200. What is implied about Ms. McCawley?

(A) She is looking for a full-time job.
(B) She was already interviewed by Ms. Travia.
(C) She has worked in a public library before.
(D) She is applying for a master's degree in library science.

Stop! This is the end of the test. If you finish before time is called,
you may go back to Parts 5, 6, and 7 and check your work.

지은이

NE능률 영어교육연구소

NE능률 영어교육연구소는 혁신적이며 효율적인 영어교재를 개발하고
영어 학습의 질을 한 단계 높이고자 노력하는 NE능률의 연구 조직입니다.

이미영

[현] YBM어학원 (종로센터) 대표 토익 강사
[현] YBM CLASS 인강 RC 스타 강사
[전] YBM어학원 (신촌센터) RC 전 타임 마감 기록 대표 토익 강사
한국외국어대학교 TESOL 대학원 ELT 석사
한국외국어대학교 사범대학 졸업 (졸업 우수상 수상)

[저서] 넥서스 나혼자 끝내는 토익 PART7, 넥서스 토익 파트별 실전 문제 PART7, 토마토 BASIC RC 3rd edition, 토마토 TOEFL iBT READING, 토마토 토익 COMPACT실전리딩/리스닝/PART3&4, 토마토 토익 INTENSIVE 1st/2nd edition

토마토 BASIC RC 전면 개정판

펴 낸 이	주민홍
펴 낸 곳	서울특별시 마포구 월드컵북로 396(상암동) 누리꿈스퀘어 비즈니스타워 10층
	(주)NE능률 (우편번호 03925)
펴 낸 날	2018년 6월 15일 개정판 제1쇄
	2023년 10월 31일 제11쇄
전 화	02 2014 7114
팩 스	02 3142 0356
홈페이지	www.neungyule.com
등록번호	제 1-68호
정 가	16,000원
I S B N	979-11-253-2175-0

NE 능률

고객센터

교재 내용 문의: contact.nebooks.co.kr (별도의 가입 절차 없이 작성 가능)
제품 구매, 교환, 불량, 반품 문의: 02-2014-7114
☎ 전화 문의는 본사 업무 시간 중에만 가능합니다.

토마토 TOEIC 실전 1000제만의
따라 올 수 없는 혜택!

| 토마토 TOEIC 실전 1000제 RC | 토마토 TOEIC 실전 1000제 LC |

해설집
무료 제공

스크립트, 해설, 해석,
어휘 등 토마토 TOEIC 실전
1000제 교재 한 권이면
이 모든 것을 다 보실 수
있습니다.

테스트별 & 문항별 MP3
(온라인/모바일 제공)

실전 테스트 보듯 한 번에
들을 수도, 복습 시 문항별로
들을 수도 있는 MP3를
제공합니다. 다운로드는 물론
모바일로도 들을 수 있습니다.

복습어휘리스트
어휘 MP3 제공

문제에서 풀었던 단어들을
복습할 수 있도록 해당
단어들의 어휘리스트와 MP3를
제공합니다. 따로 단어장을
구매할 필요가 없습니다.

新 토익 추가 핵심 문항
2 SETS 제공

나만의 강약점 진단을 위
온라인 모의고사 2 SET
무료로 제공합니다.

토익이 쉬워지는

토마토
BASIC

정답 및 해설 ■

NE Books 공식 홈페이지
www.nebooks.co.kr

토익 입문서 베스트셀러

RC

NE 능률

토마토
BASIC
RC 정답 및 해설

UNIT 01 문장의 기본 구조

1 주어와 동사 자리

교재 35쪽

1 Visitors **2** department **3** agree **4** explain **5** (C) **6** (C) **7** (A) **8** (B)

---

1 (**Visitors** / Visited) must wear a guest badge / throughout the facility tour.

해석 | 방문객들은 시설 견학 내내 방문자 배지를 착용해야 한다.

어휘 | badge 배지, 명찰 facility 시설, 기관

해설 | must wear가 문장의 동사이므로 그 앞은 문장의 주어 자리이다. 주어 자리에는 명사가 와야 하므로, '방문객'이라는 의미의 Visitors가 정답.

---

2 The human resources (**department** / depart) of the company / handles employee contract renewals.

해석 | 그 회사의 인사부서에서 직원 계약 갱신을 처리한다.

어휘 | human resources 인사(부) department 부서, 부 renewal 갱신

해설 | handles가 문장의 동사이므로 그 앞부분은 주어이다. 괄호 앞 The human resources와 괄호 뒤 of the company는 수식어이므로 괄호가 문장의 주어이다. 따라서 주어가 될 수 있는 명사 department가 정답.

---

3 The committee members (to agree / **agree**) / on the terms of the contract.

해석 | 위원회 구성원들은 계약 조건에 동의한다.

어휘 | committee 위원회 agree 동의하다 terms 조건 contract 계약

해설 | 주어 The committee members의 동사가 없으므로 괄호는 동사가 들어갈 자리이다. 따라서 정답은 agree. to agree는 to부정사로, 문장에서 동사 외의 역할을 하므로 동사 자리에 올 수 없다.

---

4 Advertisements for the vitamin / (**explain** / explaining) its health benefits.

해석 | 그 비타민 광고들은 비타민의 건강상 이점을 설명한다.

어휘 | advertisement 광고 explain 설명하다 benefit 이점

해설 | 주어인 Advertisements가 for the vitamin의 수식을 받고 있다. 문장에 동사가 없으므로 〈주어+수식어구〉 뒤 괄호가 동사 자리이므로 explain이 정답.

---

5 The **elections** for city mayor / will be held / on November 5.
(A) elects (B) elective (C) **elections** (D) elected

해석 | 시장 선거는 11월 5일에 열릴 것이다.

어휘 | election 선거 mayor 시장 hold 열다, 개최하다

해설 | 빈칸은 for city mayor의 수식을 받는 주어 자리이므로, 명사인 (C)가 정답.

---

6 For further information on the work schedule, / please **speak** to your managers.
(A) spoke (B) speaking (C) **speak** (D) speaks

해석 | 업무 일정에 대한 더 많은 정보를 얻으려면, 본인의 매니저에게 문의하세요.

어휘 | further 추가의, 더 이상의

해설 | 빈칸 앞에 주어가 될 만한 명사가 없고 please가 있는 것으로 보아, 주어 없이 동사로 시작하는 명령문임을 알 수 있다. 명령문은 동사원형으로 시작하므로 정답은 (C).

---

7 There are many **designs** to choose from / for the new Web site.
(A) **designs** (B) designed (C) designable (D) to design

해석 | 새 웹사이트를 위해 고를 수 있는 디자인이 많이 있다.

해설 | 문장은 '~이[가] 있다'라는 뜻으로 쓰이는 〈There be[remain/exist] ~〉 구문으로, 빈칸은 주어 자리이다. 따라서 주어 자리에 올 수 있는 명사 (A)가 정답.

---

8 The supermarket chain **operates** thirty stores / across the country.
(A) operating (B) **operates** (C) operation (D) operators

해석 | 그 슈퍼마켓 체인점은 전국적으로 서른 곳의 매장을 운영한다.

어휘 | operate 운영하다 across ~의 전역에 걸쳐

해설 | 빈칸 앞의 The supermarket chain이 주어로, 빈칸은 동사 자리이다. 동명사인 (A)와 명사인 (C), (D)는 동사 자리에 올 수 없다. 따라서 정답은 (B).

2 목적어 자리

1 efficiency **2** complaints **3** an invitation **4** inspectors **5** (B) **6** (A) **7** (D) **8** (B)

---

1 The new software can improve (**efficiency** / efficient) / by forty percent.

해석 | 새로운 소프트웨어는 40%나 효율성을 향상시킬 수 있다.

어휘 | improve 향상시키다 efficiency 효율성

해설 | 괄호 앞에 문장의 동사인 can improve 가 있으므로 괄호는 동사의 목적어 자리. 따라서 명사인 efficiency가 정답이다. efficient는 '효율적인'이란 뜻의 형용사이므로, 목적어로 쓸 수 없다.

---

2 Many employees submitted (complain / **complaints**) / about the long working hours.

해석 | 많은 직원들이 긴 근무 시간에 대해 항의서를 제출했다.

어휘 | submit 제출하다 complaint 항의(서), 불만 working hours 근무 시간

해설 | 괄호는 동사 submitted의 목적어 자리 이므로, 명사가 들어가야 한다. '항의서'란 뜻의 명사 complaints가 정답. complain은 '불평 하다'라는 뜻의 동사이다.

---

3 Each guest must show the security guard (**an invitation** / with an invitation) / at the entrance.

해석 | 각각의 손님들은 입구에서 보안요원에게 초대장을 보여줘야 합니다.

어휘 | security guard 보안요원 invitation 초대장 entrance 입구

해설 | 동사 show는 〈show+간접 목적어+직 접 목적어〉의 형태로, '~에게 …을 보여 주다'라 는 의미를 나타낸다. 동사 바로 뒤에 security guard라는 간접 목적어가 나오므로, 괄호 안에 직접 목적어로 쓰이는 명사가 들어가야 알맞다. 따라서 an invitation이 정답. 〈전치사+명사〉 는 수식어로, 목적어가 될 수 없다.

---

4 Ms. Stevens gives (inspect / **inspectors**) some useful advice / for their tasks.

해석 | 스티븐슨 씨는 조사관들에게 그들의 업무에 관한 몇몇 유용한 조언을 해 준다.

어휘 | inspect 조사하다, 점검하다 advice 조언, 충고 task 업무, 과제

해설 | 동사 give는 간접 목적어와 직접 목적어 를 취하여 '~에게…을 주다'라는 의미로 쓰인다. 괄호 뒤에 직접 목적어 some useful advice 가 있으므로 괄호는 간접 목적어 자리이다. 따라 서 명사인 inspectors가 정답.

---

5 Montgomery Bank completed **construction** of a new building / for its headquarters.
(A) constructive (B) **construction** (C) to construct
(D) constructed

해석 | 몽고메리 은행은 본사로 쓰일 새 건물의 건설을 완료했다.

어휘 | complete 완료하다 construction 건설, 공사 headquarters 본사

해설 | 문장의 동사는 completed이므로 빈칸 은 목적어가 들어갈 자리이다. 따라서 목적어 역 할을 할 수 있는 명사인 (B)가 정답.

---

6 Fairfax Communications offers **clients** discounts / on data roaming charges.
(A) **clients** (B) resources (C) services (D) technologies

해석 | 페어팩스 커뮤니케이션즈 사는 고객들에게 데이터 로밍 요금에 대해 할인을 제공한 다.
(A) 고객 (B) 자원 (C) 서비스 (D) 기술

어휘 | discount 할인 data roaming charge 데이터 로밍 요금

해설 | 빈칸에는 동사 offer와 빈칸 뒤의 명사 discounts와 어울리는 것이 들어가야 한다. 빈 칸의 대상에게 할인을 제공한다는 의미가 되어야 하므로 할인을 받는 대상이 될 수 있는 clients 가 정답이다. 참고로, offer는 4문형 동사이기 때문에 뒤에 〈간접 목적어(사람)+직접 목적어(사 물)〉를 취한다.

---

7 The manager sent the intern **directions** / on daily routines / in the office.
(A) directed (B) direct (C) directs (D) **directions**

해석 | 관리자는 인턴 사원에게 사무실에서의 일상 업무에 대한 지시 사항을 보냈다.

어휘 | directions 지시 (사항)(㉆ instructions) daily 매일의 routine 일과, 일상

해설 | 동사 send는 '~에게 …을 보내다'는 의 미로, 간접 목적어와 직접 목적어를 취하는 동사 이다. 동사 sent 다음에 the intern이라는 간접 목적어가 나왔으므로, '무엇'을 보냈는지 나타내 는 직접 목적어가 빈칸에 와야 한다. 따라서 목적 어로 쓰일 수 있는 명사 (D)가 정답.

---

8 Mr. Werner will provide <u>recommendations</u> / based on his findings / during the inspection.
(A) recommended **(B) recommendations** (C) recommend (D) recommends

해석ㅣ 베르너 씨는 시찰하는 동안 그가 발견한 것들을 토대로 권고해 줄 것이다.

어휘ㅣ recommendation 권고, 추천 based on ~을 토대로, ~에 기초하여 finding ((pl.)) (조사 등의) 발견, 결과 inspection 시찰, 점검

해설ㅣ will provide가 동사이므로 빈칸은 목적어 자리임을 쉽게 알 수 있다. 따라서 정답은 명사인 (B). recommend는 '권고하다, 추천하다'라는 뜻의 동사이다.

---

3 보어 자리

1 impressive **2** winner **3** necessary **4** manager **5** (C) **6** (C) **7** (B) **8** (A)

---

1 Mr. Irving's qualifications are (**impressive** / impressively), / so he is likely to get hired.

해석ㅣ 어빙 씨의 자격 요건이 인상적이어서, 그는 채용될 것 같다.

어휘ㅣ qualification ((pl.)) 자격 (요건) impressive 인상적인 be likely to do ~할 것 같다 get hired 채용되다

해설ㅣ 괄호는 be동사 are의 보어가 들어갈 자리이다. 보어 자리에는 형용사나 명사가 올 수 있으나, 부사는 올 수 없으므로 형용사인 impressive가 정답.

---

2 Ms. Patterson was the (won / **winner**) / of the last architecture competition.

해석ㅣ 패터슨 씨는 지난 건축 대회의 우승자였다.

어휘ㅣ architecture 건축(학) competition 대회, 경쟁

해설ㅣ 괄호는 be동사 was의 보어가 들어갈 자리이다. 보어 자리에는 형용사 또는 명사가 쓰일 수 있으나, 동사는 올 수 없으므로 명사인 winner가 정답.

---

3 The building manager finds / the security cameras (**necessary** / necessarily).

해석ㅣ 건물 관리인은 보안 카메라가 필요하다고 생각한다.

어휘ㅣ security 보안, 경비 necessary 필요한

해설ㅣ 동사 find는 '~를 …라고 생각하다'라는 뜻으로 쓰일 때 〈주어+동사+목적어+목적격 보어〉의 구조를 취한다. the security cameras가 목적어이고, 괄호는 목적격 보어 자리이므로 형용사인 necessary가 들어가야 한다. 부사인 necessarily는 보어 자리에 올 수 없다.

---

4 The company should appoint Mr. Smith (manage / **manager**) / of its technology department.

해석ㅣ 회사는 스미스 씨를 기술 부서의 관리자로 임명해야 한다.

어휘ㅣ appoint 임명[지명]하다 technology 기술

해설ㅣ 동사 appoint는 '~를 …로 임명하다'라는 의미로 쓰일 때 목적어와 목적격 보어를 취한다. 동사 appoint 뒤에 목적어인 Mr. Smith가 왔으므로 빈칸에는 목적격 보어가 와야 한다. 따라서 정답은 보어로 쓸 수 있는 명사 manager.

---

5 The benefits package was **attractive**, / but the salary was too low.
(A) attractively (B) attract **(C) attractive** (D) attraction

해석ㅣ 복리후생 제도는 매력적이었으나, 급여가 너무 낮았다.

어휘ㅣ benefits package 복리후생 제도 salary 급여

해설ㅣ 빈칸은 동사 was의 보어가 들어갈 자리이므로 부사인 (A)와 동사인 (B)는 제외한다. 보어로 형용사와 명사 모두 가능하지만, 문맥상 주어인 복리후생 제도(benefits package)가 매력적이었다는 내용이 자연스러우므로 주어의 상태를 설명해 주는 형용사 (C)가 정답. (D)는 명사로 '매력, (관광) 명소'를 뜻하므로 문맥상 어색해서 오답이다.

6 The library's online resources make information **accessible** / to all users for free.
(A) access (B) accesses **(C) accessible** (D) accessibly
해석 | 도서관의 온라인 자료는 모든 사용자들이 무료로 정보를 이용할 수 있도록 해 준다.
어휘 | resource 자원, 자료 accessible 접근 가능한 for free 무료로

해설 | 동사 make가 '~를 …하게 만들다'라는 뜻으로 쓰일 때는 뒤에 〈목적어+목적격 보어〉의 구조를 취한다. information이 목적어이므로 빈칸에는 목적격 보어 자리에 들어갈 수 있는 명사 (A)와 형용사 (C)가 정답 후보. 문맥상 '정보를 이용 가능하도록 만들어 준다'는 내용이 자연스러우므로 형용사 (C)가 빈칸에 들어가야 알맞다.

7 Mr. Stern became an **accountant** / at the firm / right after his graduation.
(A) accounted **(B) accountant** (C) accountable
(D) accounting
해석 | 스턴 씨는 졸업 직후에 그 회사의 회계사가 되었다.
어휘 | accountant 회계사 firm 회사 right 즉시, 곧바로 graduation 졸업

해설 | 빈칸은 동사 became의 보어 자리이므로 명사 또는 형용사가 들어가야 한다. 문맥상 '스턴 씨가 회계사가 되었다'는 내용이 자연스러우므로 명사인 (B)가 정답. (C)는 '책임이 있는'이라는 뜻의 형용사이고, (D)는 '회계'라는 뜻의 명사이지만 문맥상 어울리지 않는다.

8 The city government has named Ken Hurst / **supervisor** of the environmental project.
(A) supervisor (B) supervised (C) supervise
(D) supervising
해석 | 시 정부는 켄 허스트 씨를 환경 프로젝트 책임자로 임명했다.
어휘 | supervisor 책임자 environmental 환경의

해설 | name이 동사로 쓰이면 '~를 …로 임명하다'라는 뜻이다. 이때 목적어로는 사람, 목적격 보어로는 직책이 주로 나온다. 빈칸 앞의 사람 이름 Ken Hurst가 목적어이므로 목적격 보어 자리인 빈칸에는 직책을 나타내는 supervisor(책임자)가 들어가야 알맞다.

REVIEW 핵심 POINT 다시 보기

교재 41쪽

1 (C) 2 (B) 3 (A) 4 (A) 5 (D) 6 (B)

1 **Subscriptions** to *Economy Today* / will expire / without any formal notice after one year.
(A) Subscribe (B) Subscribed **(C) Subscriptions**
(D) Subscribes
해석 | 〈이코노미 투데이〉 지에 대한 구독이 1년 후에 공식 통지 없이 만료될 것입니다.
어휘 | subscription 구독 expire 만료되다 formal 공식적인 notice 통지, 알림

해설 | will expire이 문장의 동사이고 to *Economy Today*는 수식어이므로 빈칸은 주어 자리이다. 따라서 빈칸에는 주어가 될 수 있는 명사 (C)가 정답. (A) Subscribe는 '구독하다'라는 의미의 동사이므로 오답.

2 Weather forecasts **predicted** the strong hurricane / last week.
(A) prediction **(B) predicted** (C) predictable
(D) predictability
해석 | 일기 예보에서 지난 주에 강력한 허리케인을 예측했다.
어휘 | weather forecast 일기 예보 predict 예측[예견]하다

해설 | 주어인 Weather forecasts의 동사가 없으므로 빈칸은 동사가 들어갈 자리이다. 따라서 정답은 (B). 명사인 (A), (D)와 형용사인 (C)는 동사 자리에 올 수 없으므로 오답이다.

3 Our professionals will send you **information** / about the renovation work / as soon as possible.
(A) information (B) informing (C) inform (D) informed
해석 | 저희의 전문가들이 여러분께 보수 작업에 대한 정보를 가능한 한 빨리 보내 드릴 것입니다.
어휘 | professional 전문가 renovation 보수, 개조 as soon as possible 가능한 한 빨리

해설 | 동사 send는 뒤에 you라는 간접 목적어가 나왔으므로, 빈칸에는 '무엇을' 보낼지를 나타내는 직접 목적어가 들어가야 한다. 따라서 목적어 역할을 하는 명사 (A)가 정답.

4 Relocating the headquarters to AG Tower / did not look **profitable** / because of the expensive rent.
(A) profitable (B) profits (C) profited (D) profitability

해석 | 본사를 AG 타워로 이전하는 것은 비싼 임대료 때문에 수익성이 있을 것 같아 보이지 않았다.

어휘 | relocate 이전[이동]하다 profitable 수익성이 있는 because of ~ 때문에 rent 임대료

해설 | look은 '~처럼 보이다'라는 의미로 주격 보어를 필요로 하는 2문형 동사이다. 따라서 빈칸에는 보어로 쓰일 수 있는 형용사나 명사가 들어가야 한다. 문맥상 본사를 AG 타워로 이전하는 것이 '수익성이 있어 보이지 않는다'는 내용이 자연스러우므로, 정답은 형용사 (A). 참고로 profit은 '이익, 이득(을 얻다)'라는 뜻의 명사나 동사로 쓰이고 profitability는 '수익성'이라는 뜻의 명사로 쓰인다.

5-6

Dear employees,

New equipment will be purchased soon to make our production process more efficient. At first, you will operate the machines only under close supervision. You will follow **instructions** by a certified technician. Once you are considered ready to work on your own, the technician will sign a document stating you have been trained. Please **consult** the document attached to this e-mail to familiarize yourself with the machines in advance.

Thank you for your work.

직원 여러분께

우리의 생산 과정을 더 효율적으로 하기 위해 곧 신규 장비를 구매할 것입니다. 처음에는, 여러분은 철저한 감독하에서만 장비를 조작하게 될 것입니다. 여러분은 자격을 갖춘 기술자의 **지시를** 따르게 될 것입니다. 여러분이 혼자서 일할 준비가 되었다고 판단되면, 기술자는 당신이 숙달되었음을 명시하는 문서에 서명할 것입니다. 미리 장비에 익숙해지려면 이 이메일에 첨부된 문서를 **참고하세요.**

노고에 감사드립니다.

어휘 | equipment 장비, 설비 process 과정, 절차 operate (기계를) 조작하다, 가동하다 supervision 감독, 관리 certified 자격증을 가진, 보증된 state 명시하다, 말하다 familiarize 익숙하게 하다 in advance 미리, 사전에

5 You will follow **instructions** / by a certified technician.
(A) instruct (B) instructs (C) instructed (D) instructions

해설 | 빈칸 앞에 문장의 동사 will follow가 있으므로 빈칸은 목적어 자리이다. 따라서 목적어 역할을 할 수 있는 명사 (D)가 정답.

---

6 Please **consult** the document attached to this e-mail / to familiarize yourself with the machines / in advance.
(A) consultation (B) consult (C) consulting (D) to consult

해설 | 주어 없이 문장이 시작하고 있으므로 명령문이다. 명령문은 주어 없이 동사원형으로 시작하거나 공손함을 나타내기 위해 동사 앞에 Please를 붙인다. 따라서 빈칸에는 동사원형인 (B)가 들어가는 것이 알맞다.

VOCABULARY 제조 어휘(1)

교재 43쪽

1 provided 2 access 3 manufactures 4 efficient 5 (D) 6 (A) 7 (C) 8 (A)

---

1 The production manager (**provided** / operated) each worker / with safety goggles.

해석 | 생산 관리자는 각 작업자에게 보안경을 제공했다.

어휘 | safety goggles 보안경

해설 | '각 작업자에게 보안경을 제공했다'는 내용이 가장 자연스러우므로 정답은 provided. provide A with B는 'A에게 B를 제공하다'의 의미이다.

---

2 Not all employees have (procedure / **access**) / to the factory floor.

해석 | 모든 직원이 작업 현장에 접근 권한을 가진 것은 아니다.

어휘 | factory floor 작업 현장

해설 | 괄호 뒤의 전치사 to와 어울려 '~에의 접근 권한'이라는 의미가 내용상 어울리므로 정답은 access.

3 A&N Co. (**manufactures** / substitutes) the components / in these electronic devices.

해석 | A&N 사는 이 전자 기기들에 들어가는 부품을 생산한다.

어휘 | component 부품, 요소 electronic device 전자 기기

해설 | 동사의 목적어가 the components이므로, 이와 자연스럽게 어울리는 동사는 '생산하다'라는 의미의 manufactures이다.

---

4 Sandra's method seems (**efficient** / accessible) / for handling multiple tasks at once.

해석 | 샌드라의 방식은 여러 가지 업무를 동시에 해내는 데 효과적인 것 같다.

어휘 | method 방식, 방법 multiple 다수의 at once 동시에, 한 번에

해설 | 괄호 앞 seems는 2문형 동사로, 괄호는 주어인 method의 특징을 서술하는 주격 보어 자리이다. '방법이 효과적이다'라는 내용이 자연스러우므로 정답은 efficient.

---

5 The manager inspected the **equipment** in the factory / and ordered some new parts.
(A) procedure (B) innovation (C) construction (D) equipment

해석 | 관리자는 공장의 장비를 점검하고 몇몇 새 부품을 주문했다.

(A) 절차, 순서 (B) 혁신 (C) 건설 (D) 장비

어휘 | inspect 점검하다 part 부품

해설 | 점검하고 부품을 주문할 수 있는 대상은 선택지에서 equipment(장비)뿐이므로 정답은 (D).

---

6 Under the **supervision** of Francis Reed, / the Oakdale plant processes / about five hundred items per day.
(A) supervision (B) indication (C) completion (D) generation

해석 | 프란시스 리드 씨의 감독하에 오크데일 공장은 하루에 약 500개의 제품을 가공한다.

(A) 감독 (B) 징후, 표시 (C) 완성 (D) 발생

어휘 | plant 공장 process 가공하다, 처리하다 item 제품

해설 | 공장이 '~의 감독하에' 가동되고 있다는 내용이 가장 자연스러우므로 정답은 (A)이다. under the supervision(감독하에)이라는 표현을 통째로 기억해두자.

---

7 These modern machines increase / the manufacturing **capacity** dramatically.
(A) component (B) instrument (C) capacity (D) agreement

해석 | 이 최신 기계들은 제조 능력을 급격하게 증가시킨다.

(A) 부품 (B) (과학) 기구 (C) 능력, 용량 (D) 합의

어휘 | modern 최신의, 현대적인 increase 증가시키다 manufacturing 제조 dramatically 급격하게

해설 | 빈칸은 동사 increase의 목적어 자리로, 동사와 자연스럽게 어울리는 명사를 골라야 한다. 선택지 중 정도나 수를 늘릴 수 있는 대상은 '능력, 용량'의 의미인 (C)뿐이다. 따라서 정답은 (C).

---

8 The diagnosis was first made / during the patient's **routine** checkup / last October.
(A) routine (B) accessible (C) innovative (D) efficient

해석 | 지난 10월 그 환자의 정기 검진에서 처음으로 그 진단이 내려졌다.

(A) 정기적인 (B) 접근 가능한 (C) 혁신적인 (D) 효율적인

어휘 | diagnosis (질병의) 진단 during ~ 동안에 checkup (건강) 검진

해설 | '진단이 환자의 정기 검진에서 내려졌다'는 내용이 가장 자연스러우므로 정답은 (A).

1 (A)　**2** (B)　**3** (B)　**4** (C)　**5** (D)　**6** (B)　**7** (A)　**8** (D)　**9** (C)　**10** (A)　**11** (B)　**12** (D)

---

1 The new tracking system <u>will allow</u> / the warehouse to ship goods more efficiently.
(A) will allow　(B) to allow　(C) allowance　(D) allowing

해석| 새로운 추적 시스템은 창고에서 더 효율적으로 상품을 배송하도록 해 줄 것이다.

어휘| tracking 추적　allow A to *do* A가 ~하는 것이 가능하게 하다　warehouse 창고　ship 배송하다　goods 상품, 제품　efficiently 효율적으로

해설| **동사 자리**
빈칸 앞 주어 The new tracking system의 동사가 없으므로 빈칸은 동사 자리이다. 선택지에서 동사 역할을 할 수 있는 것은 (A)뿐이다. 오답| to부정사 (B)와 동명사 (D)는 동사 자리에 올 수 없고, (C)는 명사이므로 오답.

---

2 In the staff handbook, / <u>regulations</u> for full-time employees / are described / in detail.
(A) regulated　(B) regulations　(C) regular　(D) regularly

해석| 직원 안내서에는 정직원을 위한 규정들이 자세하게 설명되어 있다.

어휘| regulation 규정　describe 설명하다, 묘사하다　in detail 상세하게

해설| **주어 자리**
적절한 품사를 묻는 문제의 경우 주어와 동사부터 파악하는 습관을 기르자. 문장의 동사가 are described이므로 빈칸부터 employees까지가 주어이면서 for full-time employees는 빈칸을 수식하는 수식어구이다. 따라서 빈칸은 주어 자리이므로 명사인 (B)가 정답이다.

---

3 The <u>innovative</u> laptop from Vida Co. / received favorable reviews / for its lightweight design.
(A) frequent　(B) innovative　(C) estimated　(D) reluctant

해석| 비다 사에서 나온 혁신적인 노트북 컴퓨터는 경량 디자인으로 호의적인 평가를 받았다.

(A) 빈번한 (B) 혁신적인 (C) 예측된 (D) 꺼리는

어휘| favorable 호의적인　review 평가　lightweight 경량의, 가벼운

해설| **형용사 어휘 innovative**
빈칸 뒤의 명사 laptop을 수식하기에 알맞은 형용사 어휘를 고르는 문제이다. 경량 디자인으로 호의적인 평가를 받은 노트북에 대한 수식어로 '혁신적인'이라고 하는 것이 의미상 가장 알맞으므로 (B)가 정답.

---

4 There remains a strong <u>possibility</u> / for the two banks / to merge / in the future.
(A) possibilities　(B) possibly　(C) possibility　(D) possible

해석| 향후 두 은행이 합병할 가능성이 크다.

어휘| possibility 가능성　merge 합병[병합]하다　in the future 장차, 미래에

해설| **주어 자리**
빈칸은 〈There be[remain/exist] ~〉 구문의 주어 자리. 따라서 주어 역할을 할 수 있는 명사 (A)와 (C)가 정답 후보. 빈칸 앞쪽에 단수를 나타내는 부정관사 a가 쓰였으므로, 단수 명사인 (C)가 정답.

---

5 Some of the vehicle's <u>components</u> / should be replaced / because they are worn.
(A) capacities　(B) specifications　(C) procedures
(D) components

해석| 차량 부품 중 일부가 닳았기 때문에 교체되어야 한다.

(A) 능력, 용량 (B) (제품) 사양, 명세 (C) 절차 (D) 부품

어휘| vehicle 차량　replace 교체하다　worn 닳은, 해진

해설| **명사 어휘 component**
빈칸에는 빈칸 앞 vehicle's와 어울려, 차량의 일부이면서 교체될 수 있는 대상을 나타내는 명사 어휘가 와야 한다. 또한 빈칸 어휘를 가리키는 대명사 they가 닳았다(worn)고 했으므로 적절한 것은 (D)이다.

---

6 Office supply purchases over $100 require <u>approval</u> / from the finance department.
(A) approved　(B) approval　(C) approving　(D) approve

해석| 100달러 이상의 사무용품 구매는 재무부서의 승인을 필요로 한다.

어휘| office supply 사무용품　purchase 구매　require 필요로 하다　approval 승인　finance department 재무부서

해설| **목적어 자리**
문장의 동사는 빈칸 앞 require이고 빈칸은 동사의 목적어 자리이다. 따라서 명사인 (B)가 정답. approval은 -al 형태의 명사라는 점에 유의하자.

---

7 The walking paths became **visible** / after the maintenance work in the park.
(A) visible　(B) visibility　(C) vision　(D) visibly
해석| 공원에서 정비 작업을 한 후에 보행로가 보이게 되었다.
어휘| walking path 보행로　visible (눈에) 보이는　maintenance 정비, 관리

해설| **보어 자리**
빈칸은 2문형 동사 become 뒤의 주격 보어 자리이다. 따라서 형용사 (A)와 명사 (B), (C)가 정답 후보. '보행로가 잘 보이게 되었다'라는 내용이 자연스러우므로 정답은 (A).
오답| (B)는 '시정, 가시성', (C)는 '시력, 시야'라는 뜻으로 '보행로가 시정/시력이 되는 것'은 내용상 자연스럽지 않아 오답.

8 Experienced technicians **inspect** the laboratory equipment carefully / before an experiment begins.
(A) perform　(B) function　(C) instruct　**(D) inspect**
해석| 실험이 시작되기 전에 경험 많은 기술자들이 실험실 장비를 세심하게 점검한다.
(A) 수행하다 (B) 기능하다, 작용하다 (C) 지시하다 (D) 점검하다
어휘| experienced 경험 많은　technician 기술자　laboratory 실험실　experiment 실험

해설| **동사 어휘 inspect**
빈칸 뒤의 the laboratory equipment(실험실 장비)를 목적어로 취해서 의미가 자연스러운 것은 '점검하다'라는 뜻의 (D)이다.
오답| perform은 목적어로 task(업무), experiment(실험) 등의 업무 관련 내용이 와야 하고, function은 '(기계가) 정상 작동하다'의 의미로 문맥상 어색하므로 오답이다.

9-12

GRENSTON, 11 June—CEO Ashton Murphy of Halta, Inc., has announced that the company will relocate its production plant to a cheaper area. Halta, Inc., manufactures electronics that it distributes across the Grenston region. "In order to keep its prices **competitive**, Halta, Inc., needs to cut unnecessary expenses," Mr. Murphy stated. "One way to do that is to save on rent." Thus, while the stores will remain in the same locations, the production **facility** will be moved to Hallsville. This city is popular among manufacturers because it offers industrial buildings **reductions** on rental prices. **In fact, several other electronics manufacturers are already based there.**

그렌스톤, 6월 11일—할타 주식회사의 CEO인 애쉬튼 머피 씨는 회사가 자사의 생산 공장을 더 저렴한 지역으로 이전할 것이라고 발표했다. 할타 주식회사는 그렌스톤 지역 전역에 유통되는 전자제품을 생산한다. "가격을 계속 **경쟁력 있게** 유지하려면, 할타 주식회사는 불필요한 비용을 줄여야 합니다."라고 머피 씨는 말했다. "그렇게 하는 한 가지 방법은 임대료를 아끼는 것입니다." 그래서 매장은 동일한 장소에 남겨지는 반면, 생산 **시설**은 홀스빌로 이전될 것이다. 이 도시는 산업용 건물에는 임대료 **할인**을 제공하고 있어서 제조사들 사이에 인기가 있다. **사실, 몇몇 다른 전자제품 제조사들은 이미 그곳을 기반으로 하고 있다.**

어휘| announce 발표하다, 알리다　production 생산　plant 공장　area 지역　distribute 유통시키다, 분배하다　unnecessary 불필요한　expense 비용, 경비　industrial 산업[공업]의　rental price 임대료

9 "In order to keep its prices **competitive**, / Halta, Inc., needs to cut unnecessary expenses," / Mr. Murphy stated.
(A) compete　(B) competitors　(C) competitive　(D) competes

해설| **보어 자리**
동사 keep은 '~을 …하게 유지하다'라는 의미로, 목적어와 목적격 보어를 취하는 5문형 동사이다. 빈칸은 동사 keep의 목적격 보어 자리로 명사인 (B), 형용사인 (C)가 정답 후보. '가격을 경쟁력 있게 유지한다'는 내용이 자연스러우므로 정답은 (C).

10 Thus, while the stores will remain in the same locations, / the production **facility** will be moved to Hallsville.
(A) **facility**　(B) risk　(C) capacity　(D) safety
(A) 시설 (B) 위험 (C) 용량 (D) 안전

해설| **명사 어휘 facility**
문단의 첫 문장에서 할타 주식회사가 생산 공장을 이전할 것이라고 했으므로, 같은 내용인 '생산 시설이 옮겨질 것이다'라는 내용이 자연스럽다. 정답은 '시설'이라는 뜻의 (A).

11 This city is popular among manufacturers / because it offers industrial buildings <u>reductions</u> / on rental prices.
(A) reduces　(B) reductions　(C) reduce　(D) reduced

해설 | **목적어 자리**

빈칸 앞쪽의 offers는 because가 이끄는 절의 동사이다. offer는 '~에게 …를 제공하다'라는 뜻의 4문형 동사로, 간접 목적어와 직접 목적어를 취한다. offers 뒤에 industrial buildings가 간접 목적어이고, 빈칸은 직접 목적어 자리이므로 빈칸에 들어갈 정답은 명사인 (B).

---

12 (A) Visitors are attracted to the historical sites.
(B) For special deals on phones, visit www.halta.com.
(C) However, setting up a factory in Hallsville is very expensive.
(D) In fact, several other electronics manufacturers are already based there.

(A) 방문객들은 유적지에 매력을 느낀다.
(B) 핸드폰 특가 상품을 보시려면, www.halta.com을 방문하세요.
(C) 그러나, 홀스빌에 공장을 세우는 것은 매우 비싸다.
(D) 사실, 몇몇 다른 전자제품 제조사들은 이미 그곳을 기반으로 하고 있다.

해설 | **알맞은 문장 고르기**

빈칸 앞에 생산 공장을 옮길 지역에서는 산업용 건물 임대료 할인을 제공해서 제조사들에게 인기가 많다는 내용이 나왔으므로, 빈칸에는 이미 그곳을 기반으로 하는 다른 제조사들이 있다는 내용이 들어가는 것이 자연스럽다. 따라서 정답은 (D).

오답 | (A)는 지문과 관련 없는 유적지에 대한 내용이므로 오답. (B)는 고객을 대상으로 하는 광고에 어울리는 내용이므로 오답이다. (C)는 지문에서 서술된 낮은 임대료와는 상반된 내용이므로 오답.

UNIT 02 명사

1 명사의 역할과 종류

1 Employees **2** manager **3** the **4** luggage **5** (A) **6** (A) **7** (C) **8** (B)

---

1 (Employs / **Employees**) must file vacation request / at least one week in advance.

해석 | 직원들은 최소한 일주일 전에 휴가 신청서를 제출해야 한다.

어휘 | file 제출하다 request 요청 at least 적어도

해설 | 괄호 뒤 must file이 문장의 동사이므로 괄호는 문장의 주어 자리이다. 따라서 주어 역할을 할 수 있는 명사 Employees가 정답.

---

2 The board members named Ms. Kendal (manage / **manager**) / of the store.

해석 | 이사들은 켄달 씨를 그 매장의 매니저로 임명했다.

어휘 | name ~를 …로 임명하다

해설 | 5문형 동사 named가 문장의 동사이고 그 뒤의 명사 Ms. Kendal이 목적어이다. 괄호는 목적어를 꾸며 주는 목적격 보어 자리이므로, 보어 역할을 할 수 있는 명사 manager가 정답.

---

3 As a safety precaution, / the supervisor inspects (a / **the**) machinery / once a month.

해석 | 안전 예방 조치의 일환으로, 감독관은 한 달에 한 번 기계를 점검한다.

어휘 | precaution 예방 조치 machinery 기계(류)

해설 | '기계(류)'를 뜻하는 machinery는 불가산 명사로 a(n)와 함께 쓰일 수 없다. 따라서 정답은 the. 관사 the는 가산명사의 단수형과 복수형, 불가산명사 앞에 모두 쓸 수 있다. 참고로 '(개별) 기계'를 의미하는 machine은 가산명사임을 기억해둘 것.

---

4 A lot of (**luggage** / luggages) looks similar, / so please check the ID tag.

해석 | 많은 짐이 비슷해 보이니 이름표를 확인하도록 하세요.

어휘 | similar 비슷한, 유사한 ID tag 이름표, 명찰

해설 | luggage가 불가산명사임을 알고 있어야 풀 수 있는 문제. 불가산명사는 복수형으로 쓸 수 없으므로 정답은 luggage이다. 참고로 '짐'을 의미하는 luggage, baggage는 불가산명사이나, 비슷한 의미의 suitcase는 가산명사로 쓰인다는 것도 알아두자.

---

5 Bornthon Industries will finish the **renovation** / of its facility next month.
(A) renovation (B) renovate (C) renovative (D) renovated

해석 | 본던 산업은 자사의 시설 개조를 다음 달에 끝마칠 것이다.

해설 | 빈칸은 동사 will finish의 목적어 자리이면서 빈칸 앞 관사 the의 수식을 받는 명사 자리이다. 따라서 정답은 명사인 (A). 동사인 (B), (D)와 형용사 (C)는 목적어 자리에 올 수 없으므로 오답이다.

---

6 Sound Entertainment will succeed / if it can expand consumer **access** / to its services.
(A) access (B) accessed (C) accesses (D) accessible

해석 | 사운드 엔터테인먼트 사는 서비스에 대한 소비자의 접근을 확대할 수 있다면 성공할 것이다.

어휘 | succeed 성공하다 expand 확대[확장]하다 access 접근(법)

해설 | 빈칸은 앞의 consumer와 어울려 동사 expand의 목적어가 되는 명사 자리이다. 선택지에서 목적어로 쓸 수 있는 명사는 (A)와 (C)인데, access는 셀 수 없는 명사이므로, 뒤에 -es가 붙을 수 없다. 따라서 정답은 (A). access to는 '~에 대한 접근'이라는 의미로 외워두자.

---

7 Relocating to Summit Building is a good **alternative** / to building an extension / on our current building.
(A) alternating (B) alternated (C) alternative (D) alternates

해석 | 서밋 빌딩으로 이전하는 것은 현재 우리 건물을 증축하는 것의 좋은 대안이다.

어휘 | alternative 대안, 선택 가능한 것 extension 증축, 확장 current 현재의

해설 | 빈칸 앞쪽의 문장의 동사 is로 보아 빈칸은 주어를 보충 설명하는 주격 보어 자리이다. 빈칸 앞쪽에 관사 a가 있으므로 빈칸은 명사 자리임을 알 수 있다. 따라서 정답은 (C). -ive는 형용사를 만드는 접미사로 주로 쓰이지만, alternative는 형용사와 명사로 모두 쓸 수 있다.

---

8 The doctors cannot share a patient's medical history / without <u>consent</u>.
(A) to consent **(B) consent** (C) consented (D) consents

해석 | 의사들은 동의 없이 환자의 병력을 공유할 수 없다.

어휘 | share 공유하다 medical history 병력 consent 동의

해설 | 빈칸은 전치사 without의 목적어 자리이므로 명사가 들어가야 한다. 선택지에서 명사는 (B)와 (D)인데 명사 consent는 셀 수 없는 명사이므로 뒤에 -(e)s를 붙일 수 없다. 따라서 정답은 (B).

---

2 명사 자리와 한정사

교재 51쪽

1 inspector **2** estimates **3** entrance **4** choice **5** (C) **6** (D) **7** (A) **8** (B)

---

1 Mr. Parker met with an (**inspector** / inspect) / from the electrical safety department.

해석 | 파커 씨는 전기 안전 부서에서 나온 조사관을 만났다.

어휘 | inspector 조사관 electrical 전기의, 전기를 이용하는 safety 안전

해설 | 괄호는 전치사 with의 목적어 자리로, 괄호 앞에 불특정한 '하나'를 의미하는 부정관사 an이 있는 것으로 보아 명사 inspector가 정답.

---

2 Mr. Andrews received many (estimate / **estimates**) / from different construction companies.

해석 | 앤드류 씨는 각각 다른 건설사로부터 많은 견적서를 받았다.

어휘 | receive 받다

해설 | estimate는 '견적(서)'이라는 뜻의 가산 명사로, 앞에 many라는 수량 형용사가 나왔으므로 복수형인 estimates가 정답이다.

---

3 Meeting participants use the main (enter / **entrance**) / to the conference hall.

해석 | 회의 참석자들은 회의장으로 들어가는 중앙 출입구를 사용한다.

어휘 | participant 참가자 main 주된, 가장 큰 conference hall 회의장

해설 | 괄호는 동사 use의 목적어 자리로 명사 자리이다. 괄호 앞에 정관사 the와 형용사 main이 있으므로 이들의 수식을 받는 명사 entrance가 정답. 〈관사＋형용사＋명사〉의 구조에서 명사 자리를 묻는 문제가 많으므로 이 구조를 꼭 기억해두자.

---

4 The railway company's seven-day train pass is an excellent (**choice** / choices) / for tourists.

해석 | 그 철도회사의 일주일짜리 패스는 여행객들에게 탁월한 선택이다.

해설 | 괄호 앞의 부정관사 an을 보자마자 가산 명사의 단수형을 떠올려야 한다. 정답은 choice. excellent는 choice를 꾸며주는 형용사로 관사와 명사 사이에 위치함을 기억하자.

---

5 Thanks to a new <u>supplier</u> of materials, / the restaurant reduced its expenses.
(A) supplying (B) supplied **(C) supplier** (D) suppliers

해석 | 새로운 재료 공급업체 덕분에 그 식당은 비용을 줄였다.

어휘 | supplier 공급업체 material 재료, 자재 reduce 줄이다

해설 | 빈칸은 전치사 to의 목적어 자리이므로 명사인 (C)와 (D)가 정답 후보. 빈칸에 들어갈 명사는 빈칸 앞 부정관사 a의 수식을 받을 수 있어야 하므로 단수형인 (C)가 정답.

---

6 <u>These</u> files are vital and need to be sent / to the accountant / right away.
(A) Much (B) A little (C) That **(D) These**

해석 | 이 파일들은 매우 중요한 것으로 지금 당장 회계사에게 보내야 한다.

어휘 | vital 매우 중요한 right away 지금 당장

해설 | 선택지를 보니 빈칸에 알맞은 한정사를 고르는 문제. 빈칸의 한정사는 바로 뒤의 복수 명사 files를 수식하므로 불가산명사를 수식하는 (A)와 (B)는 정답 후보에서 제외. 복수 명사와 어울려 쓰일 수 있는 (D)가 정답이다. (C)는 단수 명사와 어울려 쓰이므로 오답.

---

7 The shareholders talked about all the **items** / on the meeting agenda.
(A) items (B) itemized (C) item (D) itemize
해석 | 주주들은 회의 안건의 모든 항목들에 대해 이야기 했다.
어휘 | shareholder 주주 item 항목, 사항 agenda 안건, 의제

해설 | 빈칸은 전치사 about의 목적어 자리로 명사가 들어가야 한다. 따라서 명사인 (A)와 (C)가 정답 후보. 빈칸 앞 수량 형용사 all은 가산명사의 복수형과 함께 쓰이므로 정답은 복수형인 (A).

8 Marketing head George Lee announced his **resignation** / during the staff meeting.
(A) resigned (B) resignation (C) resigns (D) to resign
해석 | 마케팅 책임자 조지 리 씨는 직원 회의에서 그의 사임을 발표했다.
어휘 | head 책임자, 수장 resignation 사임, 사직

해설 | 빈칸은 동사 announced의 목적어이면서 소유격 대명사 his의 수식을 받으므로 명사 자리이다. 따라서 명사인 (B)가 정답.

---

3 헷갈리는 명사

교재 53쪽

1 investment **2** supervisor **3** benefits **4** manufacturing **5** (B) **6** (D) **7** (D) **8** (A)

---

1 The (investor / **investment**) in new equipment / was highly profitable / for the company.
해석 | 새 장비에 대한 투자는 회사에 매우 유익했다.
어휘 | investor 투자자

해설 | 문맥상 새 장비에 대해 할 수 있는 것은 '투자'가 되어야 자연스러우므로 investment가 정답이다. 참고로 investment는 '투자금'의 의미인 가산명사와 '투자'의 의미인 불가산명사로 모두 쓸 수 있다.

2 The (**supervisor** / supervision) monitors the store's sales activity / carefully.
해석 | 그 관리자는 매장의 판매 활동을 면밀하게 관찰한다.
어휘 | supervision 감독 monitor 관찰하다, 감시하다 sales 판매의

해설 | 문맥상 매장의 판매 활동을 관찰하는 주체는 사람이어야 하므로 supervisor가 정답이다. '감독하다'라는 뜻의 동사 supervise에 사람을 나타내는 어미 -or이 붙어 '관리자, 감독관'이라는 의미로 쓰인다.

3 My previous employer offered its entire staff a standard (beneficial / **benefits**) package.
해석 | 내 이전 고용주는 전 직원에게 통상적인 복리후생 제도를 제공했다.
어휘 | previous 이전의 employer 고용주 entire 전체의 standard 통상적인, 표준의; 기준, 수준

해설 | 고용주가 직원에게 제공하는 것이므로 '복리후생 제도, 복지 혜택'을 뜻하는 benefits package가 되어야 알맞다. 따라서 정답은 benefits. benefits package는 토익에 자주 출제되는 복합 명사이므로 반드시 기억해둘 것.

4 Box Cutters plans to assess / its (**manufacturing** / manufacturer) process / next spring.
해석 | 박스 커터스 사는 내년 봄에 자사의 제조 과정을 평가할 계획이다.

해설 | 괄호에는 뒤에 있는 process와 함께 '제조과정'이라는 의미의 복합 명사를 이루는 manufacturing이 들어가야 알맞다.

5 <u>Instructors</u> will teach six different marketing courses / at Bellmore Education / in September.
(A) Instructions **(B) Instructors** (C) Instructive (D) instructed
해석 | 강사들은 9월에 벨모어 에듀케이션 사에서 6개의 다른 마케팅 과정을 가르칠 것이다.
어휘 | course 과정, 강좌

해설 | 빈칸은 문장의 주어 자리이므로 명사인 (A)와 (B)가 정답 후보이다. 문맥상 '마케팅 과정을 가르치는' 주체는 강사이므로 정답은 (B). (A)는 '지도, 교육'이라는 의미의 추상 명사이므로 내용과 어울리지 않는다.

6 Mr. Granger currently serves as a sales **representative** / for Tennessee Footwear.
(A) individual (B) presenter (C) record **(D) representative**
해설| 그레인저 씨는 현재 테네시 풋웨어 사의 영업 사원으로 근무하고 있다.
(A) 개인 (B) 발표자 (C) 기록 (D) 대표자, 대리인
어휘| currently 현재, 지금 serve 근무하다, 일하다

해설| 빈칸은 전치사 as의 목적어 자리이므로 명사가 들어가야 한다. 빈칸 앞의 명사 sales와 함께 짝을 이루어 sales representative가 '영업 사원'이라는 뜻의 복합 명사로 쓰임을 알고 있다면 쉽게 정답이 (D)임을 찾을 수 있다.

7 To learn about possible retirement plans, / visit Star Financial / for a free one-hour **consultation**.
(A) consults (B) consulted (C) consultant **(D) consultation**
해설| 가능한 은퇴 대비책에 대해 알아보시려면, 스타 파이낸셜 사를 방문하셔서 1시간 무료 상담을 받으세요.
어휘| possible 가능한 retirement 은퇴

해설| 빈칸은 전치사 for의 목적어이면서 앞에 나온 a free one-hour의 수식을 받고 있는 명사 자리이므로 (C)와 (D)가 정답 후보. 문맥상 '1시간 무료 상담'이라는 뜻이 되어야 알맞으므로, (D)가 정답. (C) consultant는 '상담가'라는 의미의 사람 명사로 문맥상 적절하지 않다.

8 This year's annual awards **ceremony** / will be hosted / at the prestigious High-Rise Hotel.
(A) ceremony (B) title (C) group (D) winner
해설| 올해의 연례 시상식은 명성 있는 하이 라이즈 호텔에서 개최될 것이다.
(A) 의식, 행사 (B) 제목, 직함 (C) 집단 (D) 우승자, 수상자
어휘| annual 연례의 host 개최하다 prestigious 명성 있는, 명망 높은

해설| 문장의 동사가 will be hosted이므로 빈칸은 문장의 주어 자리이다. '개최되다'라는 동사에 어울리는 주어는 '시상식'이라는 뜻의 복합 명사 awards ceremony이다. 따라서 정답은 (A).

REVIEW 핵심 POINT 다시 보기

교재 55쪽

1 (A) **2** (D) **3** (C) **4** (D) **5** (B) **6** (C)

1 For the rest of the week, / Ocean Surf has **discounts** / on all of its swimwear.
(A) discounts (B) discounted (C) discountable (D) discount
해설| 이번 주의 남은 기간 동안, 오션 서프 사는 수영복 전 품목에 대해 할인을 해 준다.
어휘| rest 나머지 have a discount on ~에 대해 할인을 해 주다 swimwear 수영복

해설| 빈칸은 동사 has의 목적어 자리이므로 명사가 와야 한다. 따라서 정답 후보는 (A)와 (D). discount는 가산명사이므로 앞에 한정사가 없다면 반드시 복수형으로 써야 한다. 따라서 복수형인 (A)가 정답.

2 The main selling point of Marusuki Pedals bicycles / is their **reliability** / for everyday use.
(A) reliable (B) relying (C) relied **(D) reliability**
해설| 마루스키 페달스 자전거의 주요 판매 강점은 일상적으로 사용함에 있어서 자전거의 안정성이다.
어휘| selling point 판매 강점 reliability 안정성, 신뢰도

해설| 문장의 동사는 is이고 빈칸에는 주격 보어가 들어가야 하므로 보어로 쓸 수 있는 형용사나 명사가 정답으로 적절하다. 그런데 빈칸은 바로 앞 소유격 대명사 their의 수식을 받고 있으므로 빈칸에는 명사가 들어가야 한다. 정답은 (D).

3 Ms. Lawrence received a written **referral** / from her previous manager.
(A) refers (B) referring **(C) referral** (D) referred
해설| 로렌 씨는 그녀의 이전 매니저로부터 추천서를 받았다.
어휘| referral 추천, 소개

해설| 빈칸에는 빈칸 앞의 형용사 written의 수식을 받으며 동사 received의 목적어가 되는 명사가 필요하다. 따라서 정답은 명사인 (C).

4 HanMed Pharmaceuticals posts the latest job **openings** / on its company Web site.

(A) chances (B) abilities (C) qualities **(D) openings**

해석 | 한메드 제약회사는 최신 채용 공고를 회사 웹사이트에 게시한다.

(A) 기회 (B) 능력, 재능 (C) 품질 (D) 빈자리, 공석

어휘 | pharmaceuticals 제약회사 post 게시하다 latest 최신의

해설 | 빈칸은 동사 post(게시하다)의 목적어로 앞의 명사 job과 어울려 '채용 공고, (일자리) 공석'이라는 의미를 이루는 openings가 들어가는 것이 적절하다. 따라서 정답은 (D). job openings는 토익에 자주 출제되는 복합 명사이므로 기억해두자.

5-6

March 2

Rebecca Pauly

Human Resources

Dear Ms. Pauly,

I am highly interested in working for Orno, Inc., as a sales representative. Please find enclosed my résumé and a cover letter describing my **qualifications**. According to the job postings, **applicants** must submit the names of at least two references. I've included these in the cover letter. I look forward to hearing from you.

Sincerely,

Joshua Spence

3월 2일

레베카 파울리

인사팀

파울리 씨께

저는 오노 주식회사에서 영업 사원으로 일하는 것에 매우 흥미가 있습니다. 저의 **자격 요건을** 설명한 이력서와 자기 소개서를 동봉합니다. 구인 광고에 따르면, **지원자들은** 반드시 최소 두 명의 추천인 이름을 제출해야 하더군요. 자기 소개서에 그것들을 포함시켜 두었습니다. 귀하의 답변을 듣기를 고대하고 있겠습니다.

조슈아 스펜스 드림

어휘 | highly 매우, 대단히, 크게 enclosed 동봉된 résumé 이력서 cover letter 자기 소개서 reference 추천인

5 Please find enclosed my résumé and a cover letter / describing my **qualifications**.

(A) qualify **(B) qualifications** (C) qualified (D) qualifying

해설 | 빈칸은 describing의 목적어 자리이면서, 빈칸 앞의 소유격 대명사 my의 수식을 받는 명사 자리임을 알 수 있다. 따라서 정답은 명사인 (B).

6 According to the job postings, / **applicants** must submit the names / of at least two references.

(A) apply (B) applications **(C) applicants** (D) applying

해설 | 빈칸 뒤에 동사 must submit이 있으므로 빈칸은 문장의 주어 자리이다. 따라서 동사인 (A)는 정답 후보에서 제외. 문맥상 '추천인의 이름을 제출하는' 주체는 사람이 되는 것이 자연스러우므로 '지원자'라는 의미의 (C)가 정답. application은 '지원'이라는 의미의 추상 명사이다.

VOCABULARY 제조 어휘(2) 교재 57쪽

1 pending 2 launch 3 purchased 4 sufficient 5 (C) 6 (C) 7 (A) 8 (D)

1 You can check the status / of all (superior / **pending**) orders / online.

해석 | 모든 미결 주문의 상태를 온라인으로 확인하실 수 있습니다.

어휘 | status 상태, 상황

해설 | 괄호 뒤의 명사 orders를 수식하는 알맞은 형용사를 고르는 문제이다. orders와 어울려 '미결 주문'이라는 의미를 가지는 pending이 정답.

2 Proya Corp. will (**launch** / attract) a brand-new line of cosmetics / next month.

해석 | 프로야 사는 다음 달에 완전히 새로운 라인의 화장품을 출시할 것이다.

어휘 | attract 끌다, 매료시키다   brand-new 완전히 새 것의, 신상품의

해설 | 괄호에는 문장의 목적어인 a brand-new line of cosmetics(완전히 새로운 라인의 화장품)와 어울리는 동사가 들어가야 한다. 정답은 '출시하다'라는 의미의 launch.

---

3 Hundreds of customers (released / **purchased**) the latest camera model / this morning.

해석 | 오늘 아침에 수백 명의 고객이 최신 모델의 카메라를 구매했다.

해설 | 문장의 목적어인 the latest camera model(최신 모델의 카메라)과 호응할 수 있는 동사를 골라야 한다. 정답은 '구매하다'라는 의미의 purchased.

---

4 The warehouse does not have (complimentary / **sufficient**) space / to store all of the items.

해석 | 그 창고에는 모든 물품들을 보관할 만한 충분한 공간이 없다.

어휘 | space 공간, 자리   store 보관하다, 저장하다

해설 | 괄호 뒤 명사 space를 수식하는 알맞은 형용사를 고르는 문제. 창고에 '충분한 공간'이 없다는 내용이 자연스러우므로 '충분한'이라는 의미의 sufficient가 정답.

---

5 Mr. Bowman introduced the laptop computer's <u>features</u>, / including its built-in Web cam.
(A) strategies (B) deals **(C) features** (D) manuals

해석 | 바우만 씨는 내장형 웹캠을 포함한 노트북의 특징들을 소개했다.

(A) 전략 (B) 거래 (C) 특징 (D) 설명서

어휘 | introduce 소개하다   built-in 내장된, 붙박이의

해설 | 빈칸은 동사 introduced의 목적어로, '내장형 웹캠을 포함한 노트북의 특징을 소개했다'는 내용이 자연스러우므로 빈칸에는 '특징'이라는 의미의 (C)가 들어가야 한다.

---

6 Some of the furniture was damaged / when it was <u>loaded</u> onto the moving van.
(A) released (B) recalled **(C) loaded** (D) ordered

해석 | 가구 중 일부가 화물용 차량에 실릴 때 손상되었다.

(A) 출시하다 (B) 회수하다 (C) 싣다 (D) 주문하다

어휘 | furniture 가구   damaged 손상된   moving van 화물용 차량

해설 | 빈칸은 접속사 when이 이끄는 절의 동사 자리로, 절의 주어 it은 앞에 나온 '일부 가구'를 가리킨다. 가구가 화물용 차량에 '실릴' 때 손상되었다는 의미가 자연스러우므로 '싣다'라는 의미의 동사 (C)가 정답.

---

7 Our exercise machines can be <u>shipped</u> directly to any location / within the Bridgetown city limits.
(A) shipped (B) launched (C) rewarded (D) compared

해석 | 저희 운동기구는 브리지타운 시 안에 있는 어떤 지역에라도 직접 배송이 가능합니다.

(A) 배송하다 (B) 출시하다 (C) 보상하다 (D) 비교하다

어휘 | directly 직접, 바로   location 장소   limit 경계, 한도

해설 | 문맥상 특정 제품이 어떤 지역 내에서 '배송될 수 있다'는 내용이 자연스럽다. 따라서 정답은 (A).

---

8 Hersey Company attracts customers / by offering **competitive** rates.
(A) protective (B) entire (C) urgent **(D) competitive**

해석 | 허시 사는 경쟁력 있는 가격을 제시함으로써 고객들을 유치한다.

(A) 보호하는 (B) 전체의 (C) 긴급한 (D) 경쟁력 있는

어휘 | offer 제공하다   rate 가격, 요금

해설 | 빈칸 뒤의 명사 rates를 꾸며 주는 알맞은 형용사를 골라야 한다. 수단을 나타내는 전치사 by로 고객을 유치하는 방법을 나타내고 있으므로, '경쟁력 있는 가격'이라는 의미를 만드는 (D)가 정답. competitive rates는 '다른 회사의 가격과 비교해서 뒤지지 않는 가격'이라는 뜻으로 토익에 자주 출제된다.

1 (A) **2** (C) **3** (B) **4** (C) **5** (D) **6** (B) **7** (C) **8** (B) **9** (C) **10** (C) **11** (A) **12** (B)

---

1 Consumers find Transcend's new **monitor** / the best model / on the market.
(A) monitor (B) monitored (C) monitoring (D) will monitor

해석 | 소비자들은 트랜센드 사의 새 모니터를 시장에서 가장 좋은 모델이라고 생각한다.

해설 | 명사 자리

문장의 동사인 find는 '~을 …라고 생각하다'라는 의미일 때, 〈find+목적어+목적격 보어〉의 구조로 쓰이는 5문형 동사이다. 빈칸 뒤에 명사구 the best model이 목적격 보어이고, 빈칸이 동사의 목적어 자리이므로 명사인 (A)가 정답. monitor는 '감시하다'라는 뜻의 동사로도 쓰인다.

---

2 The article in *Tech World* / analyzes the **development** / of smartphone technology.
(A) developed (B) develops **(C) development**
(D) developmental

해석 | 〈테크 월드〉 지에 실린 그 기사는 스마트폰 기술의 발달을 분석한다.

어휘 | article 기사, 논문 analyze 분석하다 development 발달, 개발

해설 | 명사 자리

빈칸은 동사 analyzes의 목적어이고, 빈칸 앞 정관사 the의 수식을 받는 명사 자리이다. 따라서 정답은 명사인 (C).

---

3 Mr. Logan became an established **architect** / more than twenty years ago.
(A) architecture **(B) architect** (C) architecturally
(D) architects

해석 | 로건 씨는 20년도 더 전에 인정받는 건축가가 되었다.

어휘 | established 인정받는 architect 건축가

해설 | 명사 자리+수일치

문장의 동사가 became이므로 빈칸은 주격 보어 자리이다. 보기에서 주격 보어로 쓰일 수 있는 명사는 (A), (B), (D)인데, 문맥상 '인정받는 건축가가 되었다'는 것이 자연스러우므로 '건축가'라는 뜻의 (B)와 (D)가 정답 후보. 빈칸 앞에 부정관사 an이 있으므로 답은 단수 명사인 (B).

오답 | (A) architecture은 '건축술, 건축학'이라는 뜻으로 문맥상 어울리지 않는다.

---

4 If you pay for your order / after 6 p.m. on Friday, / the **transaction** may not be processed / until Monday morning.
(A) distribution (B) observation **(C) transaction**
(D) registration

해석 | 주문품에 대해 금요일 저녁 6시 이후에 결제하면, 그 거래는 월요일 아침까지 처리되지 않을 수도 있습니다.
(A) 유통 (B) 관찰 (C) 거래 (D) 등록

어휘 | pay for ~의 값을 지불하다 order 주문(품) until ~까지

해설 | 명사 어휘 transaction

선택지를 보니 문맥상 가장 적절한 명사를 고르는 문제이다. 동사 process와 어울려 특정 시각 이후에 결제하면 '거래가 처리되지 않을 수 있다'는 의미가 적절하므로 정답은 (C).

---

5 Mr. Benn is preparing for the **celebration** / of the twentieth anniversary / of UCK Bank.
(A) celebrate (B) celebrates (C) celebrating **(D) celebration**

해석 | 벤 씨는 UCK 은행의 20주년 기념 행사를 준비하고 있다.

어휘 | prepare 준비하다 anniversary 기념일

해설 | 명사 자리

빈칸은 전치사 for의 목적어 자리이고, 빈칸 앞 정관사 the의 수식을 받으므로 명사 자리임을 알 수 있다. 따라서 명사인 (D)가 정답이다.

6 In this workshop, / participants will learn to create a business <u>proposal</u>.
(A) propose **(B) proposal** (C) proposed (D) proposals
해석| 이번 워크숍에서 참가자들은 사업 제안서를 작성하는 법을 배우게 됩니다.
어휘| create 만들다 proposal 제안(서)

해설| **복합 명사 business proposal**
빈칸은 동사 create의 목적어 자리로, 빈칸 앞 명사 business와 어울려 '제안서'라는 의미로 쓰이는 복합명사 business proposal을 안다면 명사인 (B)와 (D)로 정답 후보를 줄일 수 있다. 빈칸 앞쪽의 부정관사 a는 셀 수 있는 명사의 단수형과 어울려 쓰이므로 정답은 단수인 (B).

---

7 Government <u>restrictions</u> on the importation of goods / will apply to all trading companies.
(A) restricted (B) restrict **(C) restrictions** (D) restrictive
해석| 제품 수입에 대한 정부 규제가 모든 무역 회사에 적용될 것이다.
어휘| importation 수입 apply to ~에 적용되다

해설| **명사 자리**
빈칸은 빈칸 앞 Government와 빈칸 뒤 on부터 goods까지의 수식을 받는 문장의 주어 자리이다. 따라서 주어 자리에 들어갈 수 있는 명사 (C)가 정답.

---

8 The entire staff must attend a training <u>session</u> / about customer service / twice a year.
(A) skill **(B) session** (C) duration (D) point
해석| 모든 직원들은 일 년에 두 번 고객 서비스에 대한 교육에 참석해야 한다.
(A) 기술 (B) 시간, 기간 (C) 지속, 기간 (D) 요점
어휘| attend 참석하다

해설| **복합 명사 training session**
빈칸 앞의 명사 training과 어울려 '교육[연수](기간)'의 의미의 복합 명사를 구성하는 (B)가 정답. session과 유사한 의미인 (C) duration도 있지만, 복합 명사의 단어는 다른 단어로 대체할 수 없음을 기억하자.

9-12

From: Joanne Finnegan <jfinnegan@reiner.com>
To: Gary Murphy <gmurphy@reiner.com>
Subject: New Warehouse
Date: November 17

Dear Mr. Murphy,

We have had some issues recently with certain materials selling out quickly as we didn't have sufficient space to store appropriate amounts. We need to maintain our high standards and stay ahead of our <u>competitors</u>. This is why Reiner Co. has decided to purchase an additional warehouse. The timely <u>shipment</u> of materials to our clients is essential. A new storage facility would allow us to keep a larger <u>inventory</u> and thus provide better service.

We would like you to be in charge of selecting the location. Please start to research possibilities. <u>If you have any questions, please contact me directly.</u> Thank you for your attention in this matter.

Sincerely,
Joanne Finnegan
Assistant Director, Reiner Co.

발신: 조앤 피네건 〈jfinnegan@reiner.com〉
수신: 게리 머피 〈gmurphy@reiner.com〉
제목: 새 창고
날짜: 11월 17일

머피 씨에게,

우리는 적절한 수량을 보관할 장소가 없어서 특정 자재들이 빠르게 매진되는 문제를 최근에 겪었습니다. 우리는 우리의 높은 기준을 유지해야 하며, 우리 **경쟁자들보다** 앞서 나가야 합니다. 이것이 레이너 사가 추가 창고를 구입하기로 결정한 이유입니다. 고객에게 적시에 자재를 **배송하는 것은** 중요합니다. 새로운 보관 시설은 우리가 더 많은 **재고를** 보유할 수 있게 하여 더 나은 서비스를 제공할 수 있게 해 줄 것입니다.

우리는 당신이 장소 선정을 맡아주기를 원합니다. 가능한 장소들을 찾기 시작해 주세요. **질문이 있으면, 저에게 직접 연락해 주세요.** 이 문제에 대한 당신의 관심에 감사드립니다.

레이너 사, 부책임자
조앤 피네건 드림

어휘| recently 최근에 sufficient 충분한 appropriate 적절한 amount 양, 총액 maintain 유지하다 ahead of ~보다 앞서서 additional 추가의 timely 시기 적절한, 때맞춘 essential 필수적인 thus 그러므로, 따라서 be in charge of ~을 담당하다 location 장소 attention 주의, 주목

9 We need to maintain our high standards / and stay ahead of our **competitors**.
(A) competitive   (B) compete   **(C) competitors**   (D) competed

빈칸은 전치사 of의 목적어 자리이고, 빈칸 앞의 소유격 대명사 our의 수식을 받으므로, 명사 자리이다. 따라서 정답은 명사인 (C).

---

10 The timely **shipment** of materials to our clients / is essential.
(A) shipped   (B) to ship   **(C) shipment**   (D) ship

해설 | **명사 자리+명사 어휘**
문장의 동사가 is이므로 The부터 clients가 주어이다. 빈칸 앞에 정관사 the와 형용사 timely가 있으므로 빈칸은 이들의 수식을 받으며 주어 역할을 하는 명사 자리이다. 정답은 명사인 (C).
오답 | (D)도 '배'라는 의미의 명사이지만, 문맥상 빈칸에 어울리지 않는다.

---

11 A new storage facility would allow us / to keep a larger **inventory** / and thus provide better service.
(A) inventory   (B) feature   (C) location   (D) merchandise
(A) 재고 (B) 특징 (C) 장소 (D) 물품, 상품

해설 | **명사 어휘 inventory**
'새 보관 시설은 우리가 더 많은 재고를 보유할 수 있게 한다'는 의미가 자연스러우므로 정답은 (A).
오답 | (D)의 merchandise도 '물품, 상품'이라는 의미로 가능해 보이나 불가산명사이므로 빈칸 앞의 부정관사 a와는 함께 쓰일 수 없어 오답이다.

---

12 (A) You can expect to receive your order within a week.
(B) If you have any questions, please contact me directly.
(C) Our materials are all checked before being sent out.
(D) However, we cannot approve your request.
(A) 일주일 내로 주문품을 받으실 수 있을 것입니다.
(B) 질문이 있으면, 저에게 직접 연락해 주세요.
(C) 우리 자재들은 보내지기 전에 모두 확인됩니다.
(D) 그러나, 귀하의 요청을 승인할 수 없습니다.

해설 | **알맞은 문장 고르기**
빈칸 바로 앞에서 머피 씨에게 새로운 창고를 위한 가능한 장소들을 조사해 달라고 부탁했고, 다음 문장에서 이메일을 마무리하는 인사를 전하고 있으므로 빈칸에는 질문이 있으면 연락해 달라는 내용의 (B)가 들어가는 것이 적절하다.
오답 | (A)는 고객에게 보내는 주문 확인 메일에 등장할 수 있는 내용이므로 오답. (C)는 고객에게 제품의 배송이나 품질에 대한 안내를 하는 내용이므로 오답. 빈칸 앞에서 요청을 받은 것은 이메일 수신자이므로 (D)의 내용은 어울리지 않으므로 오답이다.

UNIT 03 대명사

1 인칭대명사(주격·목적격·소유격 대명사)

1 her **2** You **3** me **4** Our **5** (B) **6** (C) **7** (D) **8** (A)

1 Ms. Jones left (their / **her**) laptop / in the conference room.
해석 | 존스 씨는 회의실에 그녀의 노트북을 두고 왔다.
어휘 | laptop 노트북 컴퓨터

해설 | 괄호 뒤에 있는 명사 laptop을 꾸미는 알맞은 소유격 인칭대명사를 고르는 문제. 여성인 3인칭 단수 명사인 Ms. Jones를 가리키는 소유격 인칭대명사는 her이다.

---

2 (**You** / Your) can log on to the company's Web site / to view the latest products.
해석 | 최신 상품들을 보시려면 회사 웹사이트에 접속하시면 됩니다.
어휘 | log on to ~에 접속하다 view 보다

해설 | 괄호는 동사 can log on 앞의 주어 자리이므로 주격 인칭대명사가 들어가야 한다. 따라서 정답은 You. 소유격 Your 뒤에는 반드시 명사가 와야 하므로 오답.

---

3 The security officer gave (my / **me**) a visitor's badge / at the entrance.
해석 | 경비원이 입구에서 나에게 방문객 명찰을 주었다.
어휘 | security officer 경비원

해설 | 괄호는 동사 gave의 목적어 자리이므로 목적격 인칭대명사가 들어가야 한다. 참고로, give는 대표적인 4문형 동사로 〈give+간접 목적어+직접 목적어〉의 구조로 쓰인다는 것도 알아두자. 정답은 me.

---

4 (**Our** / We) plan to relocate the company's factory abroad / does not seem feasible.
해석 | 회사 공장을 해외로 이전하려는 우리의 계획은 실현 가능해 보이지 않는다.
어휘 | abroad 해외로, 해외에 feasible 실현 가능한

해설 | 문장의 동사는 does not seem이므로 괄호 뒤의 plan은 동사가 아니라 명사이다. 명사 plan 앞에 쓸 수 있는 인칭대명사는 소유격뿐이므로 정답은 Our.

---

5 Mr. Kline is a noted engineer, / so the electronics company hired **him** / without hesitation.
(A) he **(B) him** (C) his (D) himself
해석 | 클라인 씨는 유명한 엔지니어여서, 그 전자 회사는 주저 없이 그를 채용했다.
어휘 | noted 유명한 hire 고용하다 without hesitation 주저 없이

해설 | 선택지를 보니 빈칸에 알맞은 인칭대명사를 고르는 문제. 빈칸은 동사 hired의 목적어 자리이다. 따라서 목적격 인칭대명사인 (B)가 정답.

---

6 At Garmont Industries, / **we** offer a customer service hotline / twenty-four hours a day.
(A) me (B) your **(C) we** (D) our
해석 | 저희 가먼트 산업에서는 하루 24시간 고객 서비스 상담 전화를 제공합니다.
어휘 | hotline (직통) 상담 전화

해설 | 빈칸 뒤에 동사 offer가 나온 것으로 보아, 빈칸은 주어 자리이다. 따라서 주격 인칭대명사인 (C)가 정답.

---

7 The position's benefits / as well as **its** duties / will be explained in the contract.
(A) they (B) their (C) it **(D) its**
해석 | 그 직책에 따른 업무뿐 아니라 복지도 계약서에서 설명될 것이다.
어휘 | position (일)자리, 직위 benefit 《pl.》 복지, 혜택 as well as ~뿐만 아니라 duty 업무, 의무

해설 | 선택지를 보니 빈칸에 알맞은 인칭대명사를 고르는 문제. 빈칸은 뒤의 명사 duties 앞에서 한정사로 쓰이는 소유격 인칭대명사 자리이므로 (B)와 (D)가 정답 후보. 내용상 the position's를 대신하는 단수형이 와야 하므로 정답은 (D).

8 If you need supplies for next month, / please order **them** by Friday.

(A) them   (B) it   (C) there   (D) she

해석 | 다음 달에 쓸 비품이 필요하시면, 금요일까지 주문하세요.

어휘 | supply 《pl.》 비품   order 주문하다

해설 | 빈칸은 동사 order의 목적어 자리이므로 목적격 인칭대명사인 (A)와 (B)가 정답 후보. 문맥상 주문할 수 있는 것은 '비품'이므로 빈칸에는 복수 명사인 supplies를 가리키는 말이 들어가야 하므로 정답은 복수인 (A). (C) there(거기에)는 부사이므로 목적어 자리에 올 수 없다.

2	**인칭대명사(소유대명사·재귀대명사)**	교재 65쪽

1 his   **2** herself   **3** itself   **4** ourselves   **5** (A)   **6** (B)   **7** (D)   **8** (A)

---

1 Mr. Chan mentioned / that the blue folders on the desk were (**his** / him).

해석 | 첸 씨는 책상 위의 파란 서류철이 그의 것이라고 말했다.

어휘 | mention 말하다, 언급하다   folder 서류철, 폴더

해설 | 동사 were의 보어 자리에 알맞은 인칭대명사를 고르는 문제. 주어 blue folders는 him(그)이 아니라 his(그의 것)이므로 정답은 소유대명사 his.

---

2 Dane Phillips introduced (hers / **herself**) / to the investors / at the conference.

해석 | 데인 필립스 씨는 회의에서 투자자들에게 자신을 소개했다.

해설 | 괄호는 동사 introduced의 목적어 자리인데, 문맥상 주어인 Dane Phillips를 가리킨다. 주어와 목적어가 같을 때 목적어 자리에는 재귀대명사를 쓰므로 herself가 정답.

---

3 The marketing department conducts product research / (**itself** / its).

해석 | 마케팅 부서가 직접 제품 연구를 수행했다.

어휘 | conduct 수행하다

해설 | 괄호 없이도 완전한 문장이므로, 괄호에는 의미를 강조하기 위해 쓰는 재귀대명사 itself가 들어가야 알맞다. 주어인 The marketing department를 강조해 '마케팅 부서가 직접 수행했다'는 의미로 재귀대명사가 쓰였다.

---

4 This quarter, / we set a higher sales goal / for (us / **ourselves**).

해석 | 이번 분기에, 우리는 우리 스스로 더 높은 매출 목표를 설정했다.

어휘 | quarter 분기, 사분기   set (목표 등을) 정하다

해설 | 전치사 for 뒤의 괄호에는 목적격 인칭대명사와 재귀대명사 모두 올 수 있으므로 문맥을 보고 정답을 판단해야 한다. 전치사 for와 어울려 '직접, 스스로'의 뜻이 되어야 자연스러우므로 정답은 ourselves.

---

5 While most of the reports contained only text, / **mine** included several graphs and photos.

(A) mine   (B) myself   (C) me   (D) my

해석 | 대부분의 보고서에는 글만 있었지만, 내 것은 그래프와 사진들을 여러 개 포함했다.

어휘 | contain 포함하다   include 포함하다   several 여럿의

해설 | 선택지를 보니 알맞은 인칭대명사를 고르는 문제이다. 빈칸은 동사 included 앞의 주어 자리. 대명사 중에서 단독으로 주어 자리에 올 수 있는 것은 주격 인칭대명사와 소유대명사이다. 따라서 소유대명사인 (A)가 정답. 문맥상 mine은 my report를 뜻한다.

---

6 The lab technician wears gloves / to protect **himself** from harmful chemicals.

(A) yourselves   **(B) himself**   (C) myself   (D) themselves

해석 | 실험실 기술자는 해로운 화학물질로부터 스스로를 보호하기 위해서 장갑을 착용한다.

어휘 | lab 실험실   harmful 해로운   chemical 《pl.》 화학물질

해설 | 선택지를 보니 알맞은 재귀대명사를 고르는 문제. 빈칸은 동사 protect의 목적어 자리인데 문맥상 주어인 The lab technician을 가리킨다. 주어가 3인칭 단수이므로 정답은 (B).

7 During Mr. Taylor's absence, / Ms. Allen plans to organize the monthly meeting / <u>herself</u>.
(A) she   (B) hers   (C) her   (D) herself
해석 | 테일러 씨의 부재 기간 동안, 앨런 씨가 직접 월례 회의를 준비할 계획이다.
어휘 | absence 부재   plan to *do* ~할 계획이다   organize 준비하다   monthly 월 1회의, 매달의

해설 | 빈칸 없이도 완전한 문장이므로, 빈칸에는 강조 용법으로 쓰이는 재귀대명사가 들어가야 알맞다. 따라서 (D)가 정답.

---

8 Mr. Franklin started his business / by <u>himself</u>, / and he became successful / without any help.
(A) himself   (B) his   (C) he   (D) him
해석 | 프랭클린 씨는 그의 사업을 혼자 시작했고, 그는 어떠한 도움도 없이 성공했다.
어휘 | successful 성공한, 성공적인   without ~ 없이

해설 | 빈칸 앞에 전치사 by가 있으므로 전치사의 목적어로 쓰일 수 있는 재귀대명사 (A)와 목적격 인칭대명사 (D)가 정답 후보. 문맥상 전치사 by와 어울려 '혼자서'라는 뜻을 이루는 재귀대명사가 들어가는 것이 알맞다. 따라서 정답은 (A).

---

3 지시대명사

1 This   **2** products   **3** that   **4** those   **5** (A)   **6** (D)   **7** (B)   **8** (B)

---

1 (**This** / These) is the best way / to get to the harbor.
해석 | 이것이 항구까지 가는 가장 좋은 방법이다.
어휘 | get to ~에 도착하다   harbor 항구

해설 | 괄호가 가리키는 대상이 the best way라는 단수 명사이므로, 단수형인 This를 써야 한다. 참고로 This가 단수이기 때문에 동사도 단수형인 is가 쓰였다.

---

2 These (**products** / product) are available / for purchase online only.
해석 | 이 제품들은 온라인 구매만 가능하다.
어휘 | available 구할[이용할] 수 있는

해설 | 괄호 앞에 '이'라는 뜻을 더해 주는 한정사 These가 있다. These는 복수 명사 앞에 쓰이므로 괄호 안에는 복수 명사가 들어가야 한다. 따라서 products가 정답.

---

3 The staff size of Weston Bank / is larger than (this / **that**) of its main competitor.
해석 | 웨스턴 은행의 직원 규모는 주요 경쟁사의 그것보다 더 크다.
어휘 | staff (전체) 직원   competitor 경쟁사

해설 | 괄호 안의 지시대명사는 앞서 나온 단수 명사 The staff size를 가리키는 것이므로 둘 다 정답이 될 수 있다고 생각할 수 있으나, 같은 문장 안에서 앞에 나온 명사를 가리킬 때는 that/those만을 쓴다. 따라서 정답은 that.

---

4 The workshop is helpful / for (these / **those**) who don't know / how to navigate the database.
해석 | 그 워크숍은 데이터베이스를 탐색하는 방법을 모르는 사람들에게 도움이 된다.
어휘 | helpful 도움이 되는   navigate 길을 찾다, 돌아다니다

해설 | 문맥상 '~하는 사람들'이라는 뜻을 나타내는 those who가 되어야 알맞다. 따라서 정답은 those. those who는 토익에 자주 나오는 관용 표현이므로 반드시 기억해두자.

---

5 The factory produces tons of waste each month, / and <u>this</u> is a major cause of pollution.
(A) **this**   (B) ours   (C) these   (D) their
해석 | 그 공장은 매달 몇 톤씩 폐기물을 만들어 내고, 이것이 주된 오염원이다.
어휘 | waste 폐기물, 쓰레기   major 주요한   cause 원인   pollution 오염

해설 | and가 이끄는 절의 동사 is 앞에 주어가 없으므로, 빈칸은 주어 자리이다. 주어로 쓸 수 있는 지시대명사 (A), (C)와 소유대명사 (B)가 정답 후보. 내용상 빈칸에는 앞서 언급된 내용 전체를 가리키는 대명사가 들어가야 하는데, 절은 단수 취급하므로 정답은 단수형 지시대명사 (A). (B)도 단수 명사 대신 쓸 수 있으나, 내용상 어색하므로 오답이다.

6 This year's sales report was more detailed / than **that** of last year.
(A) they   (B) these   (C) them   **(D) that**
해석| 올해의 판매 보고서는 작년 것보다 더 상세하다.
어휘| detailed 상세한

해설| 선택지를 보니 빈칸에 알맞은 대명사를 고르는 문제. 문맥상 앞서 나온 sales report를 대신하여 쓰이는 지시대명사인 (D)가 정답. 참고로, (B)도 지시대명사이지만 this/these는 앞서 나온 명사를 대신하여 쓸 수 없다.

7 Please present **this** coupon / to receive a 20 percent discount / on our landscaping services.
(A) which   **(B) this**   (C) these   (D) whose
해석| 저희 조경 서비스에 대해 20% 할인을 받으려면 이 쿠폰을 제시하세요.
어휘| discount 할인   landscaping 조경

해설| 빈칸 뒤에 명사 coupon이 있으므로 빈칸에는 명사의 의미를 한정해 주는 한정사가 들어가야 한다. 선택지에서 한정사로 쓰일 수 있는 것은 (B)와 (C)인데, 단수 명사 coupon 앞에 쓰여야 하므로 (B)가 정답.

8 Only **those** holding a parking permit / can park their cars in this section.
(A) that   **(B) those**   (C) them   (D) their
해석| 주차 허가증을 소지하고 있는 사람들만 이 구역에 자기 차를 주차할 수 있다.
어휘| parking permit 주차 허가증

해설| holding부터 permit까지가 빈칸을 수식하는 구조로, 빈칸은 주어 자리이다. 주어로 쓸 수 있는 지시대명사 (A)와 (B)가 정답 후보. '주차 허가증을 소지하고 있는 사람들'이라는 내용이 자연스럽다. 따라서 those who 형태로 '~하는 사람들'의 뜻으로 쓰이는 (B)가 정답. those 뒤의 who are가 생략되어 분사구 holding a parking permit이 바로 이어지는 구조이다.

4 부정대명사

교재 69쪽

1 each   **2** nothing   **3** others   **4** one another   **5** (C)   **6** (B)   **7** (D)   **8** (B)

1 They will analyze (little / **each**) of the applications / for this vacancy.
해석| 그들은 이 공석에 대한 각각의 지원서들을 검토할 것이다.
어휘| vacancy 공석, 결원

해설| 부정대명사는 〈부정대명사+of the+명사〉 구조로 여러 개 중 일부를 나타내기도 한다. 괄호 다음 of 뒤의 명사가 복수 가산명사 applications인 것으로 보아, each가 정답. 참고로 little은 불가산명사와 어울려 쓰인다.

2 There was (**nothing** / any) negative / about Ms. Dawson's job interview / with Ferho Corporation.
해석| 페로 사와 진행한 도슨 씨의 면접에서 부정적인 것은 아무것도 없었다.
어휘| negative 부정적인

해설| 문맥을 통해 적절한 부정대명사를 골라야 한다. 문맥상 '부정적인 것은 아무것도 없었다'는 내용이 자연스러우므로 nothing이 정답. 참고로 any는 형용사의 수식을 받을 수 없다.

3 One new product was released this year, / and (much / **others**) are being developed.
해석| 신제품 하나는 올해 출시되었고, 다른 것들은 지금 개발 중이다.
어휘| develop 개발하다

해설| 괄호는 and로 연결된 절의 주어 자리이다. 문맥상 앞서 말한 신제품 하나를 제외한 '나머지 다른 것들이 개발 중'이라는 내용이 자연스러우므로 정답은 others. much는 셀 수 없는 명사의 수량을 나타내어 쓰인다.

4 Staff members should give (**one another** / the other) advice / to improve their work.
해석| 직원들은 그들의 업무를 개선하기 위해 서로에게 조언을 해 주어야 한다.

해설| 문맥상 '서로에게 조언을 해 주다'라는 의미가 적절하므로 정답은 one another. the other은 여러 개 중에서 나머지 하나를 가리킬 때 사용되는 부정대명사이다.

5 <u>Anyone</u> / who uses a spare laptop / registers at the IT department.

(A) Any (B) Some **(C) Anyone** (D) That

해석 | 예비용 노트북을 사용하는 사람은 누구든 IT 부서에 등록한다.

어휘 | spare 예비의, 여분의 register 등록하다, 기재하다

해설 | 선택지를 보니 알맞은 대명사를 고르는 문제. 빈칸은 문장의 주어 자리로, '노트북을 사용하는 사람은 누구든지'의 의미가 자연스러우므로 정답은 사람을 가리키는 부정대명사 (C). 참고로 any가 긍정문에 쓰이면 '어떤 ~라도'라는 의미이다.

---

6 If you encounter a problem / within the thirty-day trial period, / we will exchange your Home Gym 2000 / for <u>another</u>.

(A) other **(B) another** (C) them (D) others

해석 | 30일의 시범 사용 기간 내에 문제가 있으면, 고객님의 홈짐 2000 제품을 다른 것으로 교환해 드리겠습니다.

어휘 | encounter (문제에) 부딪히다 trial period 시험 사용 기간 exchange A for B A를 B로 교환해 주다

해설 | 빈칸에 들어갈 알맞은 대명사를 고르는 문제. 빈칸에는 앞의 명사 Home Gym 2000을 가리키는 대명사가 필요하므로, 단수 명사 대신 쓸 수 있는 (B)가 정답. (A)는 '나머지 하나'의 의미로 쓰이려면 정관사 the와 함께 쓰이며, 내용상으로도 어울리지 않고, 복수형인 (C)와 (D)는 문장 앞쪽에 가리킬 만한 복수 명사가 없으므로 오답.

---

7 From scriptwriting to directing, / the award-winning filmmaker managed <u>everything</u> / in the movie.

(A) other (B) anybody (C) whatever **(D) everything**

해석 | 대본 집필부터 연출까지, 상을 받은 영화 제작자는 영화의 모든 것을 해냈다.

어휘 | directing 연출 filmmaker 영화 제작자

해설 | 빈칸은 동사 managed의 목적어 자리이므로 목적어로 쓸 수 있는 부정대명사 (A), (B), (D)가 정답 후보. 문맥상 '모든 것을 해냈다'는 내용이 자연스러우므로 (D)가 정답. (B) anybody는 사람을 나타내므로 어색하다.

---

8 Mr. Adams and Ms. Hill always get the best results / when they collaborate with <u>each other</u>.

(A) another **(B) each other** (C) some (D) the same

해석 | 아담스 씨와 힐 씨는 서로 협력하여 일할 때 항상 최상의 결과를 얻는다.

어휘 | result 결과 collaborate with ~와 협력하다

해설 | 문맥상 빈칸에는 두 사람이 '서로'라는 뜻을 갖는 말이 들어가야 자연스러우므로 정답은 (B). (A) another은 '다른 하나', (C) some은 '일부', (D) the same은 '똑같은 것'의 의미로 문맥상 어색하다.

핵심 POINT 다시 보기   교재 71쪽

1 (A) 2 (D) 3 (C) 4 (B) 5 (A) 6 (B)

---

1 The charity workers met the mayor / and thanked <u>him</u> for the donation.

(A) him (B) them (C) himself (D) his

해석 | 자선 단체의 직원들은 시장을 만났고 그에게 기부에 대해 감사를 전했다.

어휘 | charity 자선 단체 donation 기부, 기증

해설 | 빈칸은 동사 thanked의 목적어 자리로, 소유격 인칭대명사 (D)를 제외하고 모두 가능하므로 문맥을 통해 정답을 찾아야 한다. 문맥상 빈칸은 앞의 단수 명사 the mayor를 가리켜 '시장에게 감사했다'는 내용이 자연스러우므로 정답은 단수 명사를 대신할 수 있는 (A).

---

2 A welcome guide is provided / so that guests can familiarize <u>themselves</u> / with the hotel's amenities.

(A) himself (B) itself (C) yourself **(D) themselves**

해석 | 손님들이 호텔의 편의시설에 익숙해질 수 있도록 안내 책자가 제공됩니다.

어휘 | welcome guide 안내 책자 provide 제공하다 so that ~하도록 familiarize A with B A를 B에 익숙해지게 하다 amenity ((pl.)) 편의시설

해설 | 선택지를 보니 적절한 재귀대명사를 고르는 문제. 빈칸이 동사 familiarize의 목적어 자리인 것으로 보아 재귀용법으로 쓰였음을 알 수 있다. 따라서 주어인 guests에 맞게 3인칭 복수형인 (D)가 정답.

3 <u>Those</u> / who wish to attend the seminar / should get in touch with Brenda / from HR.
(A) These (B) Whichever **(C) Those** (D) Them
해석ㅣ 세미나에 참석하기를 원하는 사람들은 인사팀의 브렌다 씨에게 연락해야 한다.
어휘ㅣ get in touch with ~와 연락[접촉]하다

해설ㅣ 빈칸은 빈칸 뒤 who부터 seminar까지의 수식을 받는 주어 자리이다. 문맥상 '~하는 사람들'이라는 뜻을 나타내는 Those who ~ 구조가 되어야 알맞으므로 정답은 (C). 이 경우 Those 대신 (A) These는 쓸 수 없다.

---

4 The hardware store prefers **someone** good at inventory management / for the position.
(A) each other **(B) someone** (C) one another (D) everyone
해석ㅣ 철물점에서는 그 자리에 재고 관리를 잘하는 사람을 선호한다.
어휘ㅣ hardware store 철물점 prefer ~을 선호하다 inventory 재고 management 관리, 운영

해설ㅣ 빈칸에 들어갈 알맞은 부정대명사를 고르는 문제. 문맥상 '재고 관리를 잘하는 누군가를 선호한다'는 의미가 자연스러우므로 정답은 '누군가'를 뜻하는 (B). (A)와 (C)는 '서로 (서로)'라는 의미로 어울리지 않고, (D)는 내용상 특정 일자리에 '모두'를 선호할 수 없으므로 오답.

5-6

New Night Hikes up Emery Mountain!

Watch the sunrise from the top of Emery Mountain! **This** is an experience you will never forget. Tours depart from the information center every day at 4:30 a.m. A guide will walk you up the mountain for an hour-long hike. You will then enjoy a breakfast while watching the sunrise. Note that the hike takes place at night, with no lighting. You may bring **your** own flashlight or borrow one of ours for $5.

새로운 에머리 산 야간 산행!

에머리 산 꼭대기에서 일출을 보세요! **이것은** 당신이 절대 잊지 못할 경험입니다. 투어는 안내소에서 매일 오전 4시 30분에 출발합니다. 가이드가 한 시간의 산행 동안 당신과 산을 오를 것입니다. 그리고 나서 일출을 보며 아침 식사를 즐기시게 됩니다. 산행이 조명 없이 밤에 진행된다는 점을 유념하세요. **자기** 손전등을 가지고 오거나, 5달러에 저희 손전등 중 하나를 빌릴 수 있습니다.

어휘ㅣ sunrise 일출, 해돋이 depart 출발하다 walk ~을 (걸어서) 바래다주다 borrow 빌리다, 꾸다

5 <u>This</u> is an experience / you will never forget.
(A) This (B) These (C) Them (D) Those

해설ㅣ 선택지를 보니 알맞은 대명사를 고르는 문제. 빈칸에는 바로 앞 문장 전체를 가리키는 대명사가 들어가야 한다. 절은 단수 취급하므로 지시대명사 (A)가 정답.

---

6 You may bring **your** own flashlight / or borrow one of ours / for $5.
(A) you **(B) your** (C) yours (D) yourself

해설ㅣ 빈칸은 빈칸 뒤 명사 flashlight를 수식하는 한정사 자리로, 보기 중에 한정사로 쓸 수 있는 것은 소유격 인칭대명사인 (B)뿐이다. 따라서 정답은 (B).

VOCABULARY 제조 어휘(3) 교재 73쪽

1 measures 2 finalize 3 defective 4 compatible 5 (C) 6 (B) 7 (B) 8 (D)

---

1 Management will implement new (materials / **measures**) / for safety tests.
해석ㅣ 경영진은 안전 검사를 위한 새로운 조치를 시행할 것이다.
어휘ㅣ implement 시행하다

해설ㅣ 빈칸 앞쪽의 동사 implement와 어울려 '조치를 시행하다'라는 의미가 자연스러우므로 '조치[정책]'이라는 뜻의 measures가 정답.

2 The project leader must (transport / **finalize**) the proposal / by tomorrow.

해석 | 그 프로젝트 관리자는 내일까지 제안서를 마무리 지어야 한다.

해설 | 괄호 안에서 적절한 동사를 찾는 문제. 괄호 뒤의 목적어 proposal과 어울려 문맥상 '내일까지 제안서를 마무리 짓는다'는 내용이 적절하므로 답은 finalize.

---

3 We offer full refunds for all (effective / **defective**) items / without exception.

해석 | 저희는 결함이 있는 모든 물품들에 대해 예외 없이 전액 환불을 제공합니다.

어휘 | full refund 전액 환불　exception 예외, 이례

해설 | 괄호 뒤의 명사 items를 수식하는 형용사를 고르는 문제. 문맥상 전액 환불을 받을 수 있는 대상은 '결함이 있는 물품들'이라는 내용이 되어야 자연스러우므로 답은 defective.

---

4 The UH charger is (**compatible** / delicate) / with all standard devices.

해석 | 그 UH 충전기는 모든 표준 기기와 호환된다.

어휘 | charger 충전기　delicate 부서지기 쉬운

해설 | 괄호는 주어인 The UH charger를 보충 설명하는 주격 보어 자리. '충전기가 모든 표준 기기와 호환된다'는 내용이 자연스러우므로 compatible이 답이다.

---

5 The technician _installed_ the air-conditioning units / in the office last week.

(A) posted　(B) conducted　(**C**) **installed**　(D) introduced

해석 | 지난주에 그 기술자가 사무실에 에어컨을 설치했다.

(A) 게시하다 (B) 수행하다 (C) 설치하다 (D) 도입하다

해설 | 빈칸 앞뒤의 주어, 목적어와 어울려 '기술자가 에어컨을 설치했다'는 의미가 가장 자연스러우므로 정답은 (C).

---

6 The factory machinery is inspected once a month / to ensure it _functions_ properly.

(A) changes　(**B**) **functions**　(C) simplifies　(D) transports

해석 | 공장 기계는 제대로 작동하는지 확실히 하기 위해 한 달에 한 번씩 점검된다.

(A) 변하다 (B) (기계 등이) 기능하다 (C) 간소화하다 (D) 운반하다

어휘 | inspect 점검하다　ensure (that) ~을 확실히 하다　properly 제대로

해설 | 선택지를 보니 적절한 동사를 고르는 문제. 점검의 목적은 제대로 '작동하는지' 확실히 하기 위함이므로 정답은 (B).

---

7 To avoid shipping damage, / _fragile_ items should be carefully packaged / in bubble wrap.

(A) beneficial　(**B**) **fragile**　(C) supportive　(D) cautious

해석 | 배송 중 손상을 피하기 위해, 깨지기 쉬운 제품은 비닐 기포 포장지에 꼼꼼하게 포장해야 한다.

(A) 유익한 (B) 깨지기 쉬운 (C) 지원하는 (D) 조심하는

어휘 | avoid 피하다, 꺼리다　damage 손상, 피해

해설 | 포장지에 꼼꼼하게 포장해야 할 것은 '깨지기 쉬운' 물품이라는 내용이 가장 자연스러우므로 정답은 (B).

---

8 The new program is very _effective_ / against computer viruses.

(A) total　(B) defective　(C) complete　(**D**) **effective**

해석 | 그 새로운 프로그램은 컴퓨터 바이러스에 매우 효과적이다.

(A) 전체의 (B) 결함이 있는 (C) 완벽한 (D) 효과적인

어휘 | against (백신 등이) ~에 대해

해설 | 문맥상 '컴퓨터 바이러스에 대해 새로운 프로그램이 효과적이다'라는 내용이 되어야 자연스러우므로 정답은 (D).

1 (C) **2** (B) **3** (C) **4** (D) **5** (A) **6** (B) **7** (D) **8** (C) **9** (B) **10** (C) **11** (D) **12** (A)

---

1 The final report cannot be written / until **we** finish collecting the surveys.
(A) us (B) our (C) we (D) ourselves

해석 | 최종 보고서는 우리가 설문 조사지 수거를 마칠 때까지는 작성할 수 없다.

어휘 | collect 모으다, 수집하다 survey 설문 조사

해설 | **인칭대명사**
빈칸은 접속사 until이 이끄는 절의 주어 자리이므로 주격 인칭대명사인 (C)가 정답이다.

---

2 Products manufactured by Prosyris Enterprises / are **closely** monitored / at every stage of the production process.
(A) nearly (B) closely (C) approximately (D) technically

해석 | 프로시리스 엔터프라이즈 사에서 제조된 제품들은 생산 과정의 매 단계마다 면밀하게 점검된다.
(A) 거의 (B) 면밀하게 (C) 대략 (D) 기술적으로

어휘 | manufacture 제조하다 stage 단계

해설 | **부사 어휘 closely**
선택지를 보니 빈칸에 알맞은 부사를 고르는 문제. 빈칸 앞뒤의 be monitored와 연결되어 '면밀하게 점검된다'는 의미가 자연스러우므로 정답은 (B).

---

3 Ms. Mala has the same suitcase as the Harpers, / and she accidentally took **theirs**.
(A) they (B) them (C) theirs (D) themselves

해석 | 말라 씨는 하퍼 씨 가족의 것과 같은 여행 가방을 갖고 있었고, 그녀는 실수로 그들의 것을 가져갔다.

어휘 | suitcase 여행 가방 accidentally 우연히

해설 | 선택지를 보니 알맞은 인칭대명사를 고르는 문제. 빈칸은 빈칸 앞 동사 took의 목적어 자리로, 주격 인칭대명사인 (A)를 제외한 모든 선택지가 정답 후보. '하퍼 씨 가족의 것'을 가져갔다는 의미가 되어야 알맞으므로 소유대명사 (C)가 정답. (B)는 앞에 가리킬 만한 복수 명사가 없고, (D)는 주어와 목적어가 같지 않으므로 쓸 수 없다.

---

4 James repainted the interior walls **himself** / in order to save money.
(A) his (B) he (C) him (D) himself

해석 | 제임스는 돈을 아끼기 위해서 실내 벽을 직접 다시 칠했다.

어휘 | repaint 페인트칠을 다시 하다 interior 실내의; 실내 in order to do ~하기 위해

해설 | **재귀대명사**
빈칸 앞에 주어(James)와 동사(repainted), 목적어(the interior walls)가 모두 갖춰져 있는 완전한 문장이 있으므로 빈칸에는 생략 가능한 강조 용법으로 쓰인 재귀대명사가 들어가야 알맞다. 따라서 정답은 (D).

---

5 Ms. Bates must revise the poster design immediately, / as her manager needs **it** / tomorrow morning.
(A) it (B) her (C) they (D) them

해석 | 베이츠 씨는 포스터 디자인을 당장 수정해야 하는데, 그녀의 매니저가 내일 아침에 그것을 필요로 할 것이기 때문이다.

어휘 | revise 수정[변경]하다 immediately 즉시, 즉각

해설 | **인칭대명사**
빈칸은 동사 needs의 목적어 자리이므로 목적격 인칭대명사인 (A), (B), (D)가 정답 후보. 빈칸이 가리키는 명사가 3인칭 단수의 사물 명사인 poster design이므로 정답은 (A).

---

6 According to the airline's policy, / **those** who possess first-class tickets / may board the plane first.
(A) this (B) those (C) both (D) these

해석 | 항공사 규정에 따르면, 일등석 탑승권을 소지한 사람들은 먼저 비행기에 탑승할 수 있다.

어휘 | according to ~에 따르면 airline 항공사 policy 규정, 방침 possess 소지하다 board 탑승하다

해설 | **지시대명사**
선택지의 those와 빈칸 뒤의 who를 보면 관용 표현 those who를 묻는 문제가 아닌지 의심해 봐야 한다. 문맥상 '일등석 탑승권을 소지한 사람들'이라는 의미이므로 답은 (B).

7 **Nobody** negotiates long-term contracts / on behalf of the company / better than Ms. Donovan.
(A) Any (B) That (C) Nothing **(D) Nobody**
해석ㅣ 도너번 씨보다 회사를 대표하여 장기 계약을 더 잘 협상하는 사람은 없다.
어휘ㅣ negotiate 협상하다 long-term 장기적인 on behalf of ~을 대표[대신]하여

해설ㅣ **부정대명사**
빈칸은 동사 negotiates의 앞이므로 주어가 들어갈 자리이다. 선택지 모두 대명사로 주어 역할을 할 수 있어서 해석을 통해 가장 적절한 것을 골라야 한다. '도너번 씨보다 협상을 더 잘할 사람은 아무도 없다'라는 의미가 자연스러우므로 정답은 '아무도 ~ 않다'라는 부정의 의미를 가진 (D)이다.

8 Acorn Supermarket has been praised / for the high **standards** of customer service / in all its branches.
(A) documents (B) guides **(C) standards** (D) precautions
해석ㅣ 에이콘 슈퍼마켓은 모든 지점에서 높은 수준의 고객 서비스로 칭찬을 받아왔다.
(A) 문서 (B) 지침 (C) 수준, 기준 (D) 예방책
어휘ㅣ praise 칭찬하다 branch 지점

해설ㅣ **명사 어휘 standard**
칭찬을 받는 이유로 빈칸 앞의 형용사 high와 호응할 수 있는 명사 어휘를 골라야 한다. 따라서 정답은 (C). high standards는 '높은 수준'이라는 뜻으로 하나의 표현처럼 쓰이므로 기억해두자.

9-12

From: Claire Pascale
To: Penny Tran
Subject: Order #205354
Date: December 13

Dear Ms. Tran,

Thank you for your order of the RX250 oven. The oven will be delivered on Friday, December 15, between 3 and 5 p.m. **Its** installation will take approximately 45 minutes. A **technician** will be there to oversee the process and ensure that the device works properly.

Included in the delivery will be an instructions manual. Unfortunately, we recently noticed errors in the book. **Some** of the instructions were not updated accurately with our newest model. **As a result, you may be confused by parts of the manual.** We will send you an updated version as soon as it is available. In the meantime, if you have any questions, you may call our help line at 555-2966.

Sincerely,
Claire Pascale
Customer Service Representative, Yelex Co.

발신: 클레어 파스칼
수신: 페니 트렌
제목: 주문 번호 205354
날짜: 12월 13일

트렌 씨에게,

RX250 오븐을 구매해 주셔서 감사합니다. 오븐은 12월 15일 금요일 오후 3시에서 5시 사이에 배송될 것입니다. **그것의** 설치는 45분 정도 소요될 것입니다. **기술자가** 그 과정을 감독하고 오븐이 제대로 작동하는지 확인하기 위해 그 자리에 있을 것입니다.

배송품에는 사용 설명서가 포함됩니다. 유감스럽게도, 저희는 최근 책자에서 오류를 발견했습니다. 사용 설명서 중 **일부가** 저희의 최신 모델과 정확히 일치하도록 업데이트 되지 않았습니다. **결과적으로, 설명서의 일부분에 의해 혼란을 느끼실 수도 있습니다.** 업데이트된 버전이 사용 가능하게 되는 즉시 보내드리도록 하겠습니다. 그 사이에 문의가 있으시면, 저희의 문의 센터인 555-2966으로 전화 주세요.

옐렉스 사, 고객 서비스 상담원
클레어 파스칼 드림

어휘ㅣ installation 설치, 설비 approximately 약, 거의 oversee 감독하다 unfortunately 유감스럽게도 accurately 정확히, 정밀하게 in the meantime 그동안

9 **Its** installation will take / approximately 45 minutes.
(A) It **(B) Its** (C) Their (D) His

해설 | **인칭대명사**

빈칸은 빈칸 뒤 명사 installation을 꾸미는 한정사 자리. 명사 앞의 한정사 자리에 올 수 있는 것은 소유격 인칭대명사이므로 (B), (C), (D)가 정답 후보. 문맥상 '오븐의 설치'가 자연스러우므로 3인칭 단수인 사물 명사 oven을 가리킬 수 있는 (B)가 정답.
오답 | 문장의 시작이라고 해서 무조건 빈칸을 주어 자리로 보고 주격 인칭대명사인 (A)를 고르지 않도록 하자.

---

10 A **technician** will be there / to oversee the process / and ensure / that the device works properly.
(A) performer (B) quality **(C) technician** (D) function
(A) 연기자, 연주자 (B) 품질 (C) 기술자 (D) 기능

해설 | **명사 어휘 technician**

제품 설치의 과정과 제품 작동을 확인하는 것은 '기술자'가 하는 일이므로 (C)가 정답.

---

11 **Some** of the instructions were not updated accurately / with our newest model.
(A) Both (B) Much (C) Any **(D) Some**

해설 | **부정대명사**

빈칸은 문장의 주어 자리이다. 선택지 모두 대명사로 주어 역할을 할 수 있으므로 문맥상 가장 적절한 것을 골라야 한다. '사용 설명서 중 일부가 업데이트 되지 않았다'라는 의미가 자연스러우므로 정답은 '일부'를 뜻하는 (D).

---

12 **(A) As a result, you may be confused by parts of the manual.**
(B) We apologize for the delay in delivery and will refund the fee.
(C) Please review the document in order to correct the mistakes.
(D) We recommend ordering the most recent oven instead.
(A) 결과적으로, 설명서의 일부분에 의해 혼란을 느끼실 수도 있습니다.
(B) 배송 지연에 대해 사과드리며 비용을 환불해 드리겠습니다.
(C) 오류를 바로잡기 위해 그 서류를 검토해 주시기 바랍니다.
(D) 대신에 가장 최신 모델의 오븐을 주문하는 것을 권해 드립니다.

해설 | **알맞은 문장 고르기**

빈칸 앞에서 설명서의 일부에 오류가 있다고 했으므로, 빈칸에는 인과관계를 나타내는 접속부사 As a result로 연결되어 오류가 있는 설명서를 사용하면서 생길 수 있는 문제에 대해 경고하는 (A)가 들어가는 것이 적절하다.
오답 | (B) 지문은 배송 지연이 아니라, 설명서 오류에 대해 이야기하고 있으므로 오답. (C) 오류를 바로 잡는 것은 이메일 발신자의 일이므로 고객에게 보내는 이메일인 지문에 어울리지 않아 오답. (D)는 특정 모델의 오븐에 대한 문의 답변에 어울리는 문장이므로 오답이다.

1 주어와 동사의 수일치 ①

교재 79쪽

1 receive **2** attends **3** courier **4** were **5** (B) **6** (B) **7** (C) **8** (C)

---

1 Bryn Corp. employees (**receive** / receives) attractive bonuses / every year in December.

해석| 브린 사의 직원들은 매년 12월에 멋진 보너스를 받는다.

해설| 주어가 복수 명사 employees이므로 동사도 복수 동사 receive를 써야 한다.

---

2 Mr. Jackson (attend / **attends**) the board meeting / every three months.

해석| 잭슨 씨는 3개월마다 한 번씩 이사회 회의에 참석한다.

어휘| board 이사회, 위원회

해설| 주어 Mr. Jackson이 3인칭 단수이므로 동사도 끝에 -(e)s를 붙인 형태의 단수 동사 attends를 써야 한다.

---

3 The (**courier** / couriers) has delivered the package / to the reception desk.

해석| 택배 기사가 소포를 접수대로 배달했다.

어휘| courier 배달원, 택배 회사 deliver 배달하다 package 소포, 짐 reception desk 접수대

해설| 괄호 뒤에 단수 동사 has가 쓰였으므로 주어 자리인 괄호에는 단수 명사인 courier가 들어가는 것이 적절하다.

---

4 The branch manager and her assistant (was / **were**) traveling / to Tokyo.

해석| 지점 관리자와 그녀의 비서는 도쿄로 출장 중이었다.

어휘| assistant 비서, 보조 travel 출장 가다

해설| 주어인 The branch manager and her assistant는 두 명을 나타내므로 복수 주어이다. 따라서 이에 맞는 복수 동사 were를 골라야 한다. be동사는 과거 시제에서도 수일치가 적용됨을 기억하자.

---

5 Leading **chemists** agree / that it is possible to develop / an environmentally friendly fuel.
(A) chemist (B) **chemists** (C) chemical (D) chemically

해석| 뛰어난 화학자들은 친환경 연료를 개발하는 것이 가능하다는 데에 동의한다.

어휘| leading 뛰어난, 선두적인 chemist 화학자 chemical 화학 물질; 화학의 environmentally friendly 친환경의, 환경친화적인 fuel 연료

해설| 빈칸은 문장의 주어이면서 빈칸 앞 형용사 Leading의 수식을 받는 명사 자리. 따라서 주어 자리에 올 수 있는 명사인 (A), (B), (C)가 정답 후보. 빈칸 뒤 동사가 복수 동사인 agree이므로 정답은 복수 명사인 (B)이다. (C) chemical은 '화학 물질'이라는 뜻으로 문맥상 어울리지 않아 오답.

---

6 The highway expansion **reduced** the traffic problems / in the area / significantly.
(A) reducing (B) **reduced** (C) have reduced (D) reduce

해석| 고속도로 확장은 그 지역의 교통 문제를 현저히 줄여 주었다.

어휘| expansion 확장, 확대 significantly 크게, 상당히

해설| 빈칸 앞 주어 The highway expansion의 동사가 없으므로 빈칸은 동사 자리이다. 따라서 동사인 (B), (C), (D)가 정답 후보. 주어인 단수 명사 expansion과 함께 쓰일 수 있는 단수 동사가 없으므로 과거 시제 동사인 reduced가 정답. 일반동사의 수일치가 과거 시제에는 적용되지 않음을 기억해두자.

---

7 The **economy** has greatly improved / since the crisis / ten years ago.
(A) economies (B) economically (C) **economy** (D) economizes

해석| 10년 전 경제 위기 이후로 경기가 크게 좋아졌다.

어휘| greatly 대단히 crisis 위기

해설| 빈칸 뒤에 동사 has가 있으므로 빈칸은 문장의 주어 자리이다. 따라서 부사인 (B)와 동사인 (D)는 오답으로 제외. 빈칸 뒤에 단수 동사 has가 쓰였으므로 빈칸에는 단수 명사 (C)가 알맞다.

---

8 Some retailers **are looking** for new suppliers / following the closure of McKinley Wholesale.
(A) looks (B) to look **(C) are looking** (D) looking

해석 | 몇몇 소매업자들은 매킨리 도매점의 폐점 이후 새 공급업체를 찾는 중이다.

어휘 | retailer 소매업자 following ~ 후에 closure 폐점, 폐쇄 wholesale 도매(업)

해설 | 문장에 동사가 없으므로 빈칸은 동사 자리이다. 따라서 동사인 (A)와 (C)가 정답 후보. 빈칸 앞 주어 Some retailers가 복수 명사이므로, be동사의 복수형 are가 쓰인 (C)가 정답.

---

2 주어와 동사의 수일치 ②

교재 81쪽

1 is **2** rise **3** list **4** handles **5** (C) **6** (A) **7** (B) **8** (D)

---

1 Selecting high-quality ingredients (**is** / are) the first step / in making Cobly peanut butter.

해석 | 고품질의 재료를 엄선하는 것이 코블리 땅콩 버터를 만드는 첫 번째 단계입니다.

어휘 | select 선발[선택]하다 high-quality 고급의 ingredient 재료, 구성 요소

해설 | 괄호 안에 알맞은 동사를 고르는 문제. 주어가 동명사 Selecting이므로 단수 취급한다. 따라서 정답은 be동사의 단수형인 is.

---

2 The hotel's prices always (rises / **rise**) / during the peak season.

해석 | 성수기에는 호텔 가격이 항상 오른다.

어휘 | rise 오르다, 증가하다 peak season 성수기

해설 | 주어가 복수 명사인 prices이므로 복수 동사인 rise가 정답. 참고로 빈도부사인 always는 일반동사 앞이나 조동사와 be동사 뒤에 위치한다는 것도 기억해두자.

---

3 The catalogs sent out last month / (lists / **list**) the store's brands.

해석 | 지난달에 발송된 카탈로그는 매장의 브랜드들을 열거하고 있다.

어휘 | list 열거하다, 목록이 나와 있다; 목록

해설 | The catalogs가 주어이고 sent out last month는 주어를 수식하는 분사구이다. 따라서 괄호에는 주어인 복수 명사 catalogs에 맞는 복수 동사 list가 들어가야 한다. list가 동사로도 쓰인다는 것을 알아두자.

---

4 The manager / who is on duty / (**handles** / handle) all customer complaints.

해석 | 근무 중인 매니저가 모든 고객 불만 사항을 처리하고 있다.

어휘 | on duty 근무 중인

해설 | who부터 duty까지는 주어를 수식하는 관계사절이고 주어는 단수 명사 manager이므로 괄호 안의 동사는 단수 동사인 handles가 알맞다.

---

5 The manufacturer of children's toys / **implements** many strict policies / to comply with the state's regulations.
(A) implementing (B) implement **(C) implements**
(D) to implement

해석 | 그 어린이 장난감 제조사는 주 정부의 규정을 준수하기 위해 많은 엄격한 방침들을 시행한다.

어휘 | strict 엄격한 comply with 준수하다, 지키다 regulation 규정

해설 | 문장에 동사가 없으므로 빈칸은 동사 자리이다. 따라서 동사인 (B)와 (C)가 정답 후보. of children's toys는 수식어구이고 단수 명사 manufacturer가 주어이므로, 정답은 단수 동사 (C). 빈칸 바로 앞의 toys를 주어로 착각하여 복수 동사 (B)를 정답으로 고르지 않도록 주의해야 한다.

---

6 There is increasing **demand** / for direct flights from Asia to Europe.
(A) demand (B) demands (C) demanding (D) demanded

해석 | 아시아에서 유럽으로 가는 직항 항공편에 대해 증가하는 수요가 있다.

어휘 | demand 수요, 요구 direct 직행[직통]의

해설 | '~이[가] 있다'라는 의미의 〈There+be동사〉 구조에서는 주어가 There이 아니라 be동사 뒤에 나오는 명사임을 기억해야 한다. 단수 동사 is를 보면 주어가 단수 명사임을 알 수 있으므로 정답은 (A).

7 The company continuously **trains** employees / throughout their careers / with monthly workshops.
(A) training **(B) trains** (C) have trained (D) train

해설| 그 업체는 직원들이 근무하는 내내 월별 워크숍을 통해 직원들을 지속적으로 교육한다.

어휘| continuously 지속적으로, 끊임 없이 train 교육하다, 양성하다 throughout ~ 동안 내내

해설| 문장의 주어 The company의 동사가 없으므로 빈칸은 동사 자리이다. 따라서 동명사 (A)는 정답 후보에서 제외. 빈칸 앞의 부사는 수일치에 영향을 주지 않으므로 더 앞쪽에 있는 주어의 수를 확인해야 한다. 주어가 단수 명사 The company이므로 단수 동사인 (B)가 정답.

8 The people / who **operate** the subway system / are mostly mechanical engineers.
(A) operates (B) has operated (C) operating **(D) operate**

해설| 지하철 시스템을 가동하는 사람들은 주로 기계 기술자들이다.

어휘| mostly 주로 mechanical 기계로 작동되는, 기계와 관련된

해설| who부터 system까지는 선행사 people을 꾸며 주는 주격 관계대명사절로, 빈칸은 이 절의 동사 자리이다. 따라서 동사인 (A), (B), (D)가 정답 후보. 이 동사는 복수 명사인 선행사 people에 수일치 시켜야 하므로 정답은 복수 동사 (D).

---

3 **수량 표현과 수일치**   교재 83쪽

1 customers **2** were **3** dishes **4** agree **5** (A) **6** (C) **7** (A) **8** (B)

1 Many (**customers** / customer) have indicated a preference / for organic food in the survey.

해석| 많은 고객들이 설문 조사에서 유기농 식품에 대한 선호를 보여 주었다.

어휘| indicate 보여 주다, 나타내다 preference 선호, 애호 organic 유기농의

해설| 괄호는 바로 앞의 수량 형용사 Many의 수식을 받는 주어 자리이다. 따라서 괄호에는 복수 명사 customers가 와야 한다. many는 뒤에 복수 명사와 복수 동사를 취한다.

2 Most of the employees at the tire factory / (was / **were**) exhausted from the extra work.

해석| 타이어 공장에 있는 대부분의 근로자들은 추가 근무로 지쳐 있었다.

어휘| exhausted 지친 extra 추가의, 여분의

해설| most of는 '대부분의'란 뜻으로 of 뒤의 명사에 동사의 수를 일치시킨다. most of 뒤의 명사 employees가 복수이므로 정답은 복수 동사인 were. at the tire factory는 주어를 수식하는 수식어구이므로 factory를 주어로 착각하여 was를 고르지 않도록 주의할 것.

3 Each of the (dish / **dishes**) on the menu / is suitable for vegetarians.

해석| 메뉴에 있는 각각의 요리들은 채식주의자들에게 적합하다.

어휘| dish 요리, 접시 suitable 적당한, 알맞은 vegetarian 채식주의자

해설| each of는 '각각의'라는 뜻으로 뒤에 복수 명사와 단수 동사를 취한다. 따라서 정답은 복수 명사인 dishes.

4 A number of shareholders (**agree** / agrees) / with the acquisition.

해석| 많은 주주들이 그 인수에 동의한다.

어휘| acquisition 인수, 습득

해설| 맨 앞의 관사 A만 보고 단수 주어로 착각하지 않도록 주의할 것. A number of는 '다수의, 많은'이라는 뜻이므로 뒤에는 복수 명사가 오며, 복수 동사를 쓴다. 따라서 agree가 정답.

5 Some of the candidates **are** going around the country / to campaign for the elections.
(A) are (B) being (C) is (D) was

해석| 일부 출마자들은 선거를 위한 캠페인을 벌이기 위해 전국을 돌아다니고 있다.

어휘| candidate 출마자, 입후보자 campaign 캠페인[운동]을 벌이다

해설| 문장에 동사가 없으므로 빈칸은 동사 자리이다. 따라서 동명사 (B)는 정답 후보에서 제외. ⟨most/all/part/some+of⟩ 형태의 수량 표현들은 of 뒤에 나오는 명사에 동사의 수를 일치시킨다. Some of 뒤에 복수 명사 candidates가 나왔으므로 복수 동사 (A)가 정답.

6 A few board members <u>see</u> the overseas expansion / as a risky business move.

(A) sees (B) be seen **(C) see** (D) to see

해석 | 몇 명의 이사들은 해외 진출을 위험한 사업적 움직임이라고 생각한다.

어휘 | board member 이사 overseas 해외의, 외국의 risky 위험한

해설 | 빈칸은 문장의 동사 자리로, 동사인 (A), (B), (C)가 정답 후보. 빈칸 앞 주어인 board members가 '(수가) 조금 있는'의 뜻인 a few 의 수식을 받는 복수 명사이므로 복수 동사인 (C)가 정답이다.

---

7 <u>One</u> of the guest speakers / at the robotics conference / was Dr. Darren Williams.

(A) One (B) Most (C) Some (D) Others

해석 | 로봇 공학 학회의 초청 연사 중 한 명은 대런 윌리엄스 박사였다.

어휘 | robotics 로봇 공학

해설 | 선택지를 보니 빈칸에 알맞은 부정대명사를 고르는 문제. 부정대명사는 어울려 쓰이는 명사와 동사에 제약이 있어서 그것을 확인하여 정답을 찾는다. 문장의 동사가 단수인 was이므로 주어는 단수여야 한다. 선택지 중 단수를 의미하는 것은 One뿐이므로 정답은 (A). (B)나 (C)의 경우 단수 동사와 어울려 쓰이려면 of 뒤에 단수 명사가 와야 하는데 빈칸 뒤 명사가 guest speakers로 복수형이라 오답이다.

---

8 All <u>products</u> come with a five-year warranty / and free repair service.

(A) product **(B) products** (C) produce (D) producing

해석 | 모든 제품은 5년 품질 보증과 무료 수리 서비스가 딸려 나온다.

어휘 | come with ~이 딸려 나온다 warranty 보증(서) repair 수리, 보수 produce 농산물; 생산하다

해설 | 빈칸은 문장의 동사 come 앞의 주어 자리로, 주어 자리에 올 수 있는 명사 (A), (B), (C)가 정답 후보. 빈칸 앞 수량 형용사 all은 복수 명사와 어울려 쓰이고, 문장의 동사인 come도 복수 동사이므로 정답은 복수 명사인 (B).

REVIEW | 핵심 POINT 다시 보기

교재 85쪽

1 (A) 2 (A) 3 (B) 4 (D) 5 (B) 6 (A)

---

1 Timely completion of the projects / <u>depends</u> / on meeting all the deadlines.

(A) depends (B) depend (C) to depend (D) depending

해석 | 프로젝트를 제시간에 완료하는 것은 모든 마감 기한을 지키는 것에 달려있다.

어휘 | completion 완료, 완성 deadline 마감 기한, 마감 일자

해설 | 빈칸은 문장의 동사 자리이므로 동사인 (A)와 (B)가 정답 후보. of the projects는 주어를 수식하는 전치사구이고 단수 명사 completion이 주어이므로, 단수 동사인 (A)가 정답이다. 빈칸 바로 앞의 projects를 주어로 생각하고 복수 동사 (B)를 답으로 고르지 않도록 주의하자.

---

2 The managers / who <u>work</u> in the service department / will update the product return policy.

(A) work (B) works (C) working (D) has worked

해석 | 고객 서비스 부서에서 일하는 관리자들이 반품 정책을 업데이트할 것이다.

어휘 | service department 고객 서비스 부서 return policy 환불 정책

해설 | 문장의 동사는 will update이고 who 부터 department까지가 주어 The managers를 수식하는 관계대명사절이다. 따라서 빈칸은 관계대명사절의 동사 자리이므로, 동사인 (A), (B), (D)가 정답 후보. 이 중 선행사인 복수 명사 managers와 쓰일 수 있는 복수 동사 (A)가 정답.

---

3 Some <u>expenses</u> from the business trip / were not reimbursed / by the company.

(A) expense **(B) expenses** (C) expend (D) expensive

해석 | 출장에서 발생한 일부 비용은 회사가 변제해 주지 않았다.

어휘 | reimburse 변제하다, 상환하다

해설 | 문장의 동사는 were not reimbursed 이고, 빈칸은 빈칸 앞뒤의 Some과 from the business trip의 수식을 받는 주어 자리이다. 따라서 명사인 (A)와 (B)가 정답 후보. 수량 형용사 Some의 수식을 받고 문장의 동사 were도 복수 동사이므로 복수 명사인 (B)가 정답.

4 Guests should contact the front desk immediately / if they **require** any changes / in their reservation.
(A) requires (B) to require (C) requiring **(D) require**

해석| 투숙객들은 만약 예약에 어떠한 변경이라도 필요한 경우, 즉시 프런트 데스크로 연락해야 한다.

어휘| contact 연락하다 reservation 예약

해설| 빈칸은 접속사 if가 이끄는 절의 동사 자리이다. 수일치는 절 안의 주어와 동사에도 적용된다. 따라서 절의 주어인 복수 명사 they와 함께 쓸 수 있는 복수 동사 (D)가 정답.

5-6

MERIEN, August 2—Praxa, the popular online clothing retailer, has announced that it will open an actual store in Merien's city center. Owners Jake Finder and Molly Black **intend** to start construction next month. "We have earned a reputation as a reliable retailer," Mr. Finder said. Indeed, **every** comment on Praxa's Web site gives the store an excellent review, and there is no doubt that this new project will be highly successful.

메리엔, 8월 2일—인기 있는 온라인 의류 소매업체 프렉사 사가 메리엔의 도심에 업체의 실제 매장을 열 것이라고 발표했다. 기업주인 제이크 파인더 씨와 몰리 블랙 씨는 다음 달 공사를 시작할 **생각이다**. "저희는 신뢰할 만한 소매업체라는 평판을 얻었습니다."라고 파인더 씨가 말했다. 실제로, 프렉사 사 웹사이트의 **모든** 댓글이 업체에 대해 호평을 하고 있고, 이 새로운 프로젝트는 매우 성공적일 것임에 의심의 여지가 없다.

어휘| owner 주인, 소유자 earn a reputation 평판을 얻다 comment 댓글, 논평, 언급 doubt 의심, 의구심

5 Owners Jake Finder and Molly Black **intend** to start construction / next month.
(A) intends **(B) intend** (C) to intend (D) intending

해설| 주어가 Owners로 복수 명사이므로 복수 동사인 (B)가 정답. 빈칸 바로 앞의 Molly Black만 보고 단수 주어로 생각하여 단수 동사인 (A)를 고르지 않도록 한다.

---

6 Indeed, / **every** comment on Praxa's Web site / gives the store an excellent review, / and there is no doubt / that this new project will be highly successful.
(A) every (B) many (C) all (D) several

해설| 선택지를 보니 알맞은 수량 형용사를 고르는 문제. 빈칸 뒤에 단수 명사 comment가 왔고, 문장의 동사 gives도 단수 동사이다. 따라서 뒤에 단수 명사와 단수 동사를 취하는 수량 형용사 every가 정답. 나머지 선택지는 모두 뒤에 단수 명사를 취할 수 없으므로 오답.

VOCABULARY 회사 어휘(1)

교재 87쪽

1 recommended 2 applicant 3 accepted 4 previous 5 (B) 6 (C) 7 (D) 8 (B)

1 Mr. Berenson's former supervisor (**recommended** / retired) him / for the marketing specialist position.

해석| 베런슨 씨의 이전 상사가 그를 마케팅 전문가 자리에 추천했다.

어휘| former 이전의 supervisor 상사 specialist 전문가

해설| 괄호 뒤에 동사의 목적어로 쓰인 인칭대명사 him이 있다. retire은 '퇴직하다'라는 의미로 쓰일 때 뒤에 목적어를 갖지 않는 자동사이다. 따라서 '~을 추천하다'라는 의미의 타동사 recommended가 정답.

---

2 The (benefit / **applicant**) did not submit a cover letter / with his résumé.

해석| 그 지원자는 자기 소개서를 이력서와 함께 제출하지 않았다.

해설| 문맥상 '이력서를 제출하는' 주체는 사람이 되어야 자연스러우므로 '지원자'라는 의미의 applicant가 정답. applicant는 동사 apply(지원하다)의 파생어로 사람을 나타내는 어미 -ant가 붙은 사람 명사이다.

3 Donna Meyer (**accepted** / recruited) the award for Employee of the Year / from the CEO at the ceremony.

해석| 도나 메이어 씨는 시상식에서 CEO로부터 올해의 직원상을 받았다.

어휘| award 상 ceremony 식, 의식

해설| 괄호 뒤의 목적어인 the award of Employee of the Year와 문맥상 어울리는 동사를 찾아야 한다. 주어인 특정 인물이 올해의 직원상을 '받는다'는 의미가 자연스러우므로 정답은 accepted.

---

4 The sales representative has (**previous** / capable) work experience / as a branch manager.

해석| 그 영업 사원은 지점장으로 일했던 이전 업무 경험이 있다.

어휘| branch manager 지점장, 지사장

해설| 괄호 뒤의 명사 work experience와 잘 어울리는 형용사를 고르는 문제. 문맥상 '이전의 업무 경험이 있다'고 하는 것이 자연스러우므로 정답은 previous이다.

---

5 Workers / who want to relocate to the Midwood branch / should <u>submit</u> a request to Mr. Watt.
(A) advise **(B) submit** (C) engage (D) receive

해석| 미드우드 지점으로 전근하고 싶은 직원들은 와트 씨에게 신청서를 제출해야 한다.

(A) 조언하다 (B) 제출하다 (C) 고용하다 (D) 받다

어휘| relocate to ~로 전근하다 request 신청(서)

해설| 문장의 주어가 Workers이므로 주어와 어울리는 동사를 찾아야 한다. '전근을 원하는 직원들이 신청서를 제출한다'는 내용이 자연스러우므로 정답은 (B).

---

6 Even though Ms. Anderson does not have the <u>qualifications</u> for the role, / she was given a chance / to have an interview.
(A) positions (B) careers **(C) qualifications** (D) rewards

해석| 앤더슨 씨는 그 역할에 대한 자격을 갖추지 않았지만, 면접을 볼 기회가 주어졌다.

(A) 직위, 자리 (B) 경력 (C) 자격 (요건) (D) 보상

어휘| role 역할 have an interview 면접을 보다

해설| '가지다'라는 뜻의 동사 have의 목적어로 어울리는 명사를 고르는 문제. 문맥상 '자격을 갖추다'라는 의미가 되어야 하므로 (C)가 알맞다. 비슷한 의미의 meet the requirements(자격 요건을 충족시키다) 라는 표현도 함께 알아두자.

---

7 Individuals with degrees in any science field / are <u>eligible</u> to apply for the head researcher position.
(A) controlled (B) flexible (C) possible **(D) eligible**

해석| 어느 과학 분야에서라도 학위가 있는 사람들은 선임 연구원직에 지원할 자격이 있다.

(A) 통제된 (B) 유연성 있는 (C) 가능한 (D) 자격이 있는

어휘| individual 개인 degree 학위 head researcher 선임 연구원

해설| 빈칸은 주어 Individuals의 상태를 보충 설명하는 보어 자리로, '특정 분야의 학위를 소지한 개인은 선임 연구원직에 지원할 수 있는 자격이 있다'는 내용이 자연스럽다. 따라서, to부정사를 수식어로 취해 eligible to do(~할 자격이 있는)로 쓰이는 (D)가 정답.

---

8 All employees must <u>enroll</u> in the course / at least two weeks in advance.
(A) apply **(B) enroll** (C) hire (D) afford

해석| 모든 직원은 적어도 2주 전에 강좌에 등록해야 한다.

(A) 신청하다, 적용하다 (B) 등록하다 (C) 채용하다 (D) 제공하다

해설| 빈칸에 알맞은 동사 어휘를 고르는 문제로, 빈칸 뒤에 in이 나오는 것에 주의한다. enroll은 '~에 등록하다'라는 뜻으로 뒤에 in을 수반하여 목적어를 취한다. 따라서 (B)가 정답. (A) apply도 유사한 의미이나, '~에 지원하다'의 의미로 쓰일 때 전치사 for나 to와 함께 쓰이므로 오답.

실전 문제에 적용하기

1 (D)　**2** (C)　**3** (D)　**4** (B)　**5** (B)　**6** (A)　**7** (A)　**8** (D)　**9** (B)　**10** (C)　**11** (A)　**12** (C)

---

1 Snadge Ltd.'s latest digital camera **produces** very clear images / even in low-light conditions.
(A) products　(B) produce　(C) product　**(D) produces**

해석 | 스내지 사의 최신 디지털 카메라는 빛이 적은 환경에서도 아주 선명한 이미지를 만들어 낸다.

어휘 | clear 또렷한, 알아보기 쉬운　conditions 환경, 상태

해설 | 동사 자리＋수일치

빈칸 앞 camera가 문장의 주어이고 빈칸은 동사 자리로 동사인 (B)와 (D)가 정답 후보. 주어가 단수 명사이므로 빈칸에 들어갈 정답은 단수 동사인 (D).

오답 | (A), (C)는 명사이므로 동사 자리에 들어갈 수 없다.

---

2 Salary **increases** are based / on the employee's work history and performance.
(A) increasingly　(B) increasing　**(C) increases**　(D) increase

해석 | 급여 인상은 직원의 업무 이력과 성과에 기반한다.

어휘 | salary 급여　be based on ～에 기반하다　history 이력

해설 | 명사 자리＋수일치

빈칸 뒤에 동사 are가 있으므로 빈칸에는 Salary와 구를 이루어 주어로 쓸 수 있는 명사가 들어가야 한다. 따라서 명사인 (C)와 (D)가 정답 후보. are가 복수 동사이므로 정답으로 어울리는 것은 복수 명사 (C)이다.

---

3 Mr. Wilkie lacks technical **expertise** / in his field / so he decided to attend the skills workshop.
(A) impression　(B) lecture　(C) indication　**(D) expertise**

해석 | 윌키 씨는 자기 분야에 대한 기술적인 전문 지식이 부족해서 기술 워크숍에 참석하기로 결정했다.
(A) 인상 (B) 강연 (C) 표시 (D) 전문 지식

어휘 | lack ～이 부족하다　technical 기술적인　field 분야

해설 | 명사 어휘 expertise

결과를 나타내는 접속사 so로 두 절이 연결되어 있으므로 기술 워크숍에 참석하기로 한 원인이 so 앞에 나와야 한다. '기술적인 전문 지식이 부족하다'는 내용이 자연스러우므로 '전문 지식'의 의미인 (D)가 알맞다. expertise(전문 지식)와 함께 '전문가'라는 뜻의 expert도 알아두자.

---

4 **Each** of the envelops for the confidential documents / was properly sealed / and kept in the safe.
(A) Other　**(B) Each**　(C) Some　(D) Most

해석 | 기밀 문서가 담긴 각각의 봉투들은 제대로 밀봉되어서 금고에 보관되었다.

어휘 | envelop 봉투　confidential 기밀의　document 문서, 서류　seal 밀봉하다, 밀폐하다　safe 금고

해설 | 부정대명사＋수일치

빈칸은 〈부정대명사＋of the＋명사〉 구조의 부정대명사 자리이다. of 뒤의 명사가 복수형 envelops이고 문장의 동사가 단수 동사 was인 것으로 보아 빈칸에 올 수 있는 부정대명사는 '각각'을 의미하여 단수 취급하는 each이므로 정답은 (B).

오답 | (C)와 (D)는 〈부정대명사＋of the＋명사〉 구조로 쓰일 때, of 뒤에 복수 명사를 쓰면 복수 동사가 뒤따라야 하므로 오답이다.

---

5 All of the families affected by the earthquake / **receive** financial assistance / from the government.
(A) receives　**(B) receive**　(C) receiving　(D) to receive

해석 | 지진으로 인해 영향을 받은 모든 가정은 정부에서 금전적 도움을 받는다.

어휘 | affect 영향을 미치다　earthquake 지진　assistance 도움, 원조　government 정부

해설 | 동사 자리＋수일치

문장에 동사가 없으므로 빈칸은 동사 자리이다. 따라서 동사인 (A)와 (B)가 정답 후보. 빈칸 앞 주어를 살펴보면 〈all＋of the＋명사〉 구조로, of 뒤에 오는 명사에 동사 수를 맞춰야 한다. of 뒤에는 복수 명사 families가 쓰였으므로 복수 동사인 (B)가 정답. affected부터 earthquake까지는 주어인 families를 수식하는 분사구로, affected를 동사로 착각하지 않도록 주의하자.

---

6 There are **many** local sales representatives / at the fifteenth Narktowne Trade Fair.

(A) many　(B) much　(C) others　(D) plenty

해석 | 제15회 나크타운 무역 박람회에는 많은 지역 영업 사원들이 있다.

(A) (수가) 많은 (B) (양이) 많은 (C) 다른 것들 (D) 많은 양

어휘 | local 지역의, 현지의　representative 대표　trade fair 무역[산업] 박람회

해설 | **수량 형용사**

빈칸은 빈칸 뒤의 명사를 수식하는 형용사 자리이므로 수량 형용사인 (A)와 (B)가 정답 후보. 빈칸 뒤에 복수 명사 representatives가 왔으므로 빈칸에는 '(수가) 많은'이라는 뜻으로, 가산 명사의 복수형과 함께 쓰이는 many가 들어가는 것이 적절하다.

오답 | (B) much는 셀 수 없는 명사 앞에 쓰여 '(양이) 많은'이라는 의미를 나타내므로 적절하지 않다.

---

7 The PR firm's **plan** to expand into Asia / includes hiring a local workforce.

(A) plan　(B) be planned　(C) to plan　(D) plans

해석 | PR 사의 아시아로의 확장 계획은 현지 노동인력을 고용하는 것을 포함한다.

어휘 | workforce 노동인구, 노동력

해설 | **명사 자리+수일치**

문장의 동사는 includes이고, 빈칸 뒤 to부터 Asia까지는 주어를 꾸미는 수식어구이다. 따라서 빈칸은 주어 자리이므로, 주어로 쓸 수 있는 명사인 (A), (D)와 to부정사 (C)가 정답 후보. 문장에 단수 동사 includes가 쓰였으므로, 복수 명사인 (D)는 정답 후보에서 제외. to부정사는 한정사(소유격)의 수식을 받을 수 없으므로 (C)도 제외되고, 단수 명사인 (A)가 정답이다.

---

8 Hafner Manufacturing requests / that its more **experienced** workers assist new recruits / whenever necessary.

(A) eligible　(B) previous　(C) temporary　(D) experienced

해석 | 하프너 제조사는 필요시에는 언제든지 더 숙련된 직원들이 신입 사원들을 도와주라고 요구한다.

(A) ~을 할 수 있는 (B) 이전의 (C) 임시적인 (D) 숙련된

어휘 | request 요청하다　assist 돕다　new recruit 신입 사원　whenever ~할 때 언제든지

해설 | **형용사 어휘 experienced**

동사 requests의 목적어로 that절이 쓰였다. that절 이하의 내용으로는 '숙련된' 직원들이 신입 사원들에게 도움을 줘야 한다는 것이 적절하다. 따라서 정답은 (D).

9-12

Looking for Web Site Designer

Pilia Furniture is the area's leading furniture-building company, and a number of local businesses **use** Pilia for their interior. Its furniture **has become** famous around the region. Now is your chance to join this growing company. Pilia Furniture is looking for a Web designer to manage the store's Web site. This is a permanent position with benefits. The working hours are **flexible** and may be different from week to week. The successful candidate must have a bachelor's degree in graphic design or a related field. **However, equivalent work experience will also be accepted.** To apply, please submit a résumé, cover letter, and portfolio with at least three design samples to piliahr@piliafurniture.com.

웹사이트 디자이너를 찾습니다.

필리아 퍼니처 사는 이 지역의 선두적인 가구 제조 회사로, 많은 지역 사업체가 내부에 필리아 제품을 **사용하고** 있습니다. 필리아 사의 가구는 이 지역에서 유명해져 **왔습니다**. 지금이 이 성장하고 있는 기업과 함께 할 기회입니다. 필리아 퍼니처 사는 매장의 웹사이트를 관리할 웹 디자이너를 찾고 있습니다. 이것은 복리 후생이 포함된 정규직 자리입니다. 근무 시간은 **유동적이며**, 주마다 다를 수 있습니다. 합격자는 그래픽 디자인 또는 관련 분야의 학사 학위를 가지고 있어야 합니다. **그러나 그에 상응하는 업무 경력도 인정될 것입니다.** 지원하려면 이력서, 자기 소개서 그리고 최소 세 개의 디자인 샘플이 포함된 포트폴리오를 piliahr@piliafurniture.com으로 제출해 주세요.

어휘 | manage 관리하다, 운영하다　bachelor's degree 학사 학위　related 관련된　equivalent 동등한

9 Pilia Furniture is the area's leading furniture-building company, / and a number of local businesses <u>use</u> Pilia / for their interior.

(A) uses   **(B) use**   (C) using   (D) to use

해설 | **동사 자리 + 수일치**

and가 이끄는 절에 동사가 없으므로 빈칸은 동사 자리이다. 따라서 동사인 (A)와 (B)가 정답 후보이다. 빈칸 앞의 복수 명사 a number of local businesses가 주어이므로 복수 동사 (B)가 정답. 수량 표현 안의 부정관사 a를 보고 단수 주어라고 생각해서 단수 동사를 고르지 않도록 한다.

---

10 Its furniture **has become** famous / around the region.

(A) to become   (B) have become   **(C) has become**
(D) becoming

해설 | **동사 자리 + 수일치**

문장에 동사가 없으므로 빈칸은 문장의 동사 자리이다. 따라서 동사인 (B)와 (C)가 정답 후보. 빈칸 앞 주어가 Its furniture로 단수 명사이므로 동사도 단수 동사를 써야 한다. 그러므로 (C)가 정답.

---

11 The working hours are <u>flexible</u> / and may be different from week to week.

(A) flexible   (B) essential   (C) qualified   (D) capable
(A) 유연성 있는 (B) 필수적인 (C) 자격이 있는 (D) ~을 할 수 있는

해설 | **형용사 어휘 flexible**

근무 시간이 '유동적이고' 주마다 다를 수 있다는 내용이 가장 자연스러우므로 (A)가 정답.

---

12 (A) We are pleased to offer you the position.
(B) The program will prepare you for the job market.
(C) However, equivalent work experience will also be accepted.
(D) Therefore, we cannot process your application.

(A) 저희는 당신에게 일자리를 제안하게 되어 기쁩니다.
(B) 그 프로그램은 당신을 인력 시장에 대비시켜 줄 것입니다.
(C) 그러나 그에 상응하는 업무 경력도 인정될 것입니다.
(D) 그러므로, 저희는 당신의 지원서를 처리할 수 없습니다.

해설 | **알맞은 문장 고르기**

빈칸 앞에서 합격자는 그래픽 디자인이나 관련 분야의 학사 학위를 가지고 있어야 한다며 지원 자격을 이야기했다. 빈칸 다음에는 바로 지원 방법에 대해 설명하고 있으므로 두 문장 사이에는 합격자의 예외적인 지원 자격에 대해 설명하는 문장인 (C)가 들어가는 것이 가장 적절하다. However이라는 '대조'의 접속부사가 예외적인 채용 조건을 설명하기 위해 쓰였다.

오답 | 지문은 구인광고인데, (A)는 합격자에게 보내는 이메일에 어울리는 문장이므로 오답. (B)는 구직자에게 권하는 프로그램을 광고하는 글에 어울리는 내용이므로 오답. (D) Therefore(그러므로)은 앞 문장에 추가적인 설명을 덧붙일 때 쓰는 접속부사인데, 지원서를 처리할 수 없다는, 앞 문장과 정반대의 내용이 나오므로 오답이다.

UNIT 05 시제

1 단순 시제

1 conducts **2** returned **3** leave **4** are going **5** (C) **6** (A) **7** (A) **8** (C)

---

1 Dr. Jones currently (**conducts** / conducted) research / at Gosho Pharmaceutical Company.

해석| 존스 박사는 현재 고쇼 제약회사에서 연구를 한다.

해설| currently(현재)라는 시간 표현을 통해 문장이 현재의 상태를 나타냄을 알 수 있다. 따라서 현재 시제 conducts가 정답이다.

---

2 Ms. Anderson recently (**returned** / will return) / from a business trip to Brazil.

해석| 앤더슨 씨는 최근에 브라질 출장에서 돌아왔다.

어휘| return 돌아오다

해설| recently(최근에)를 통해 과거에 일어난 일임을 알 수 있다. 따라서 정답은 과거 시제인 returned.

---

3 A few international flights now (**leave** / will leave) the airport / every day.

해석| 이제 매일 몇 대의 국제선 여객기가 공항에서 출발한다.

어휘| international flight 국제선 여객기

해설| now(지금)와 every day(매일)라는 시간 표현을 통해 현재 반복적으로 일어나고 있는 일임을 알 수 있다. 따라서 현재 시제인 leave가 정답.

---

4 Several of the company's programmers / (went / **are going**) to attend an IT workshop / tomorrow.

해석| 회사의 프로그래머 몇 명이 내일 IT 워크숍에 참가할 것이다.

해설| tomorrow(내일)를 통해 미래에 대한 계획을 나타내고 있음을 알 수 있다. 미래 시제는 will 또는 be going to를 써서 나타내야 하므로 정답은 are going.

---

5 To prevent accidents, / the factory **suggested** a new set of safety procedures / last month.
(A) suggests (B) suggestion (C) **suggested**
(D) suggesting

해석| 사고를 방지하기 위해, 공장은 지난 달에 새로운 일련의 안전수칙을 제안했다.

어휘| prevent 방지하다, 막다 suggest 제안하다 a set of 일련의 safety procedure 안전수칙

해설| 문장에 동사가 없으므로 빈칸은 동사 자리이다. 따라서 현재 시제 동사 (A)와 과거 시제 동사 (C)가 정답 후보. 시제를 묻는 문제의 경우 문장에서 재빨리 시간 표현부터 찾아야 한다. 과거를 나타내는 last month가 있으므로 (C)가 정답.

---

6 Next fall, / the Metro Art Museum **will exhibit** local and national artists.
(A) **will exhibit** (B) exhibit (C) exhibiting (D) exhibited

해석| 내년 가을에, 메트로 미술관은 지역 및 전국의 화가들의 작품을 전시할 것이다.

어휘| exhibit 전시하다 national 전국의

해설| 빈칸은 동사 자리이므로 동사인 (A), (B), (D)가 정답 후보. Next fall(내년 가을)이라는 미래를 나타내는 표현이 있으므로 미래 시제인 (A)가 정답.

---

7 Usually, every editor of *Weekly Issue* **is** busy / on Fridays.
(A) **is** (B) been (C) will be (D) being

해석| 보통 〈위클리 이슈〉 지의 모든 편집자는 금요일에 바쁘다.

어휘| editor 편집자

해설| 문장에 동사가 없으므로 빈칸은 동사 자리이다. 따라서 동사인 (A)와 (C)가 정답 후보. 맨 앞의 시간 표현 Usually(대개, 보통)를 통해 반복되는 일임을 알 수 있다. 그러므로 정답은 현재 시제인 (A). 참고로 수량 형용사 every는 항상 뒤에 단수 명사와 단수 동사를 취한다는 것을 기억하자.

---

8 The general manager **visited** China / two weeks ago / for the regular factory inspection.
(A) will visit (B) visits (C) **visited** (D) visit
해석| 본부장은 공장 정기 점검을 위해 2주 전에 중국을 방문했다.
어휘| regular 정기적인

해설| two weeks ago(2주 전에)라는 시간 표현을 통해 과거에 일어난 일에 대해 설명하고 있음을 알 수 있다. 따라서 과거 시제 visited가 정답.

<table>
<tr><td>**2**</td><td>**완료 시제**</td><td>교재 95쪽</td></tr>
</table>

1 has operated **2** obtained **3** had finished **4** will have paid **5** (B) **6** (B) **7** (A) **8** (D)

---

1 The Barnes family (operates / **has operated**) Barnes Manufacturing Company / for seventy years.
해석| 반즈 가는 반즈 제조 회사를 70년 동안 운영해왔다.

해설| for seventy years(70년 동안)에서 전치사 for는 '~ 동안'이라는 의미로 기간을 나타내는 시간 표현이다. 따라서 특정 기간 동안 계속되었음을 나타내는 현재완료 has operated가 정답.

---

2 Yesterday, Avant Office Supplies (**obtained** / has obtained) the government's approval / to open a new branch.
해석| 어제 아반트 오피스 서플라이즈 사는 새 지점을 여는 것에 대한 정부 승인을 얻었다.
어휘| obtain 얻다

해설| yesterday(어제)는 명백한 과거 시점을 나타내기 때문에 현재완료를 쓸 수 없고, 과거 시제를 써야 한다. 따라서 정답은 obtained.

---

3 Ms. Hanson (finishes / **had finished**) filling out the application / before the doctor was ready.
해석| 핸슨 씨는 의사가 준비를 마치기 전에 신청서 작성을 완료했다.
어휘| fill out (서식을) 작성하다 application 신청(서)

해설| 문맥상 '의사가 준비되기 전에 이미 신청서 작성을 완료했다'라는 의미가 적절하다. 따라서 before절의 시제인 과거(was)보다 더 이전 시제가 주절에 와야 적절하므로 과거완료인 had finished가 정답.

---

4 By three o'clock tomorrow, / the manager (paid / **will have paid**) the building's utility bill.
해석| 내일 3시까지 관리자가 건물의 공과금을 납부할 것이다.
어휘| utility bill (가스·수도·전기 등의) 공공요금 (고지서)

해설| By three o'clock tomorrow(내일 3시까지)처럼 미래의 특정 시점까지 완료될 일을 나타낼 때 미래완료 〈will have+*p.p.*〉를 쓴다.

---

5 Due to limited funding, / the traffic lights on Preston Street / have not **yet** been upgraded.
(A) early (B) **yet** (C) enough (D) ever
해석| 한정된 자금 때문에, 프레스톤 가의 신호등은 아직 개선되지 않았다.
(A) 일찍 (B) 아직 (C) 충분히 (D) ~한 적
어휘| due to ~로 인해 limited 제한된, 부족한 funding 자금 traffic light 신호등

해설| 선택지를 보니 빈칸에 어울리는 부사를 고르는 문제로, 문맥상 가장 자연스러운 것을 골라야 한다. 빈칸 앞 부정어 not과 함께 쓰여, '아직 개선되지 않았다'는 의미를 나타내는 (B)가 정답. (D) ever도 현재완료와 어울려 쓰이지만 여기서는 문맥상 어색하다.

---

6 Rounders, Inc., a furniture retailer, / **had inquired** about the prices / before it placed an order.
(A) inquires (B) **had inquired** (C) will have inquired
(D) would be inquiring
해석| 가구 소매업체인 라운더즈 주식회사는 주문을 하기 전에 가격에 대해 문의했다.
어휘| inquire about ~에 대해 문의하다 place an order 주문하다

해설| 선택지를 보니, 빈칸에 알맞은 시제의 동사를 고르는 문제. 접속사 before를 통해 '가격 문의'가 '주문'보다 먼저 일어난 일임을 알 수 있다. 주문한 것은 과거 시점(placed)이고 문의한 것은 과거보다 더 이전에 일어난 일이므로 과거완료 (B)가 정답이다.

7 Since he was hired ten years ago, / Mr. Horton **has transferred** to new departments / several times.
(A) has transferred (B) is transferring (C) transfers
(D) transfer

해석 | 10년 전에 입사한 이래로, 호튼 씨는 새로운 부서로 여러 차례 옮겼다.

해설 | since는 '~ 이래로'라는 뜻의 접속사로, 특정 과거 시점부터 현재까지의 기간을 나타낸다. 따라서 과거부터 현재까지 계속의 의미를 나타내는 현재완료 (A)가 정답.

8 Stan Doering **will have completed** his first major film production / by the end of next year.
(A) completed (B) completes (C) had completed
(D) will have completed

해석 | 스탠 도어링 씨는 내년 말까지 자신의 첫 번째 주류 영화 제작을 완료할 것이다.
어휘 | graduate from ~를 졸업하다

해설 | by the end of는 '~ 말까지'라는 뜻의 시간 표현으로, 어떤 행위의 완료 시점을 나타낸다. 문맥상 미래의 특정 시점까지 완료될 것임을 표현하고 있으므로 미래완료 시제가 적절하다. 따라서 정답은 (D).

3 진행 시제

교재 97쪽

1 is meeting **2** are merging **3** will be sending **4** has been offering **5** (B) **6** (A) **7** (B) **8** (D)

1 Ms. Harper (met / **is meeting**) with the clothing distributor / now.

해석 | 하퍼 씨는 지금 의류 유통업자와 만나고 있다.
어휘 | clothing 의류 distributor 유통업체, 배급업자

해설 | 시간 표현 now를 통해 현재의 일을 나타내고 있음을 알 수 있으므로 현재진행형인 is meeting이 정답.

2 The two departments (**are merging** / were merging) / sometime next month.

해석 | 다음 달 중에 두 부서가 통합될 것이다.
어휘 | sometime 언젠가

해설 | sometime next month(다음 달 언젠가에)를 통해 미래의 일을 나타냄을 알 수 있지만, 괄호에는 미래 시제가 없다. 대신 현재진행형이 가까운 미래의 일을 나타내기도 하므로 are merging이 정답.

3 The marketing team (has sent / **will be sending**) out questionnaires / soon.

해석 | 마케팅 팀이 조만간 설문지를 발송할 것이다.
어휘 | send out 발송하다 questionnaire 설문지

해설 | soon은 '곧, 조만간'이란 뜻으로 앞으로의 일을 나타내는 미래 시제와 어울린다. 따라서 will be sending이 정답. 미래진행형은 미래에 진행 중일 동작이나 사건을 나타낸다.

4 Pike Sports Store (**has been offering** / will be offering) special deals on tents / for the past week.

해석 | 파이크 스포츠 스토어는 지난 한 주 동안 텐트에 대해 특가를 제공하고 있었다.

해설 | 시간 표현 for the past week(지난 한 주 동안)를 통해 이전부터 지금까지의 일을 나타내는 문장임을 알 수 있다. 따라서 과거부터 지금까지 동작이 진행되어 왔음을 강조하는 현재완료진행인 has been offering이 정답.

5 Presently, / the director of Sodes Co. **is addressing** the issue / of the company's factory emissions.
(A) addressed (B) **is addressing** (C) has addressed
(D) was addressing

해석 | 현재, 소드즈 사의 이사는 회사 공장의 배출물에 대한 문제를 처리하는 중이다.
어휘 | address 다루다, 대처하다 emission 배출(물), 배기가스

해설 | 시간 표현 presently(현재)를 통해 현재의 일을 나타내는 문장임을 알 수 있다. 따라서 현재진행형인 (B)가 정답.

6 The lawyer **was having** trouble establishing contract terms / during the previous meeting.
(A) was having (B) has (C) will have had (D) will have
해석| 이전 회의에서 그 변호사는 계약 조건을 정하는 데 어려움을 겪었다.
어휘| have trouble *doing* ~하는 데 어려움을 겪다   establish 정하다, 수립하다
contract terms 계약 조건

해설| during the previous meeting(이전 회의 동안)은 과거 시점을 나타내는 말이므로 빈칸에는 과거 시제가 들어가야 한다. 따라서 선택지 중에서는 과거진행형인 (A)가 정답. 이 문장에서는 과거진행형이 회의라는 특정한 기간 동안 진행된 일을 나타내어 쓰였다.

---

7 A real estate agent **is coming** / to appraise the building / next week.
(A) came (B) is coming (C) coming (D) had come
해석| 다음 주에 부동산 중개업자가 건물을 감정하러 올 것이다.
어휘| real estate agent 부동산 중개업자   appraise 감정하다, 평가하다

해설| 빈칸은 문장의 동사 자리로 (C)를 제외하고 모두 정답 후보이다. 시간 표현 next week를 보자마자 미래 시제를 찾아야 한다. 선택지에 미래 시제가 없으므로 가까운 미래의 일을 나타낼 수 있는 현재진행이 답이다. 따라서 답은 (B).

---

8 R&H Motors **will be celebrating** its company foundation anniversary / next Friday.
(A) celebrated (B) had been celebrating
(C) has celebrated (D) will be celebrating
해석| R&H 모터즈 사는 다음 주 금요일에 회사의 창립 기념일을 축하하고 있을 것이다.
어휘| foundation 창립, 설립

해설| next Friday를 보자마자 선택지에서 미래 시제를 찾아야 한다. 정답은 미래에 진행 중일 동작을 나타내는 미래진행형 (D).

REVIEW 핵심 POINT 다시 보기   교재 99쪽

1 (D) **2** (B) **3** (D) **4** (C) **5** (C) **6** (A)

---

1 Ms. Stanley **started** her new position / as head of finances / last Monday.
(A) is starting (B) to start (C) will start (D) started
해석| 스탠리 씨는 지난주 월요일에 재무 부장으로써 그녀의 새로운 직무를 시작했다.
어휘| finance 재무, 재정

해설| 빈칸은 문장의 동사 자리로 동사인 (A), (C), (D)가 정답 후보. 시간 표현 last Monday(지난주 월요일)를 보고 과거의 일임을 알 수 있다. 따라서 정답은 과거 시제인 (D).

---

2 Over the past year, / residents of Linsville **have donated** more than $10,000 / to local charities.
(A) is donating (B) have donated (C) donate (D) will donate
해석| 지난해 동안, 린스빌의 주민들은 지역 자선 단체들에 만 달러 이상을 기부해왔다.
어휘| resident 주민, 거주자   donate 기부하다

해설| 선택지를 보니, 알맞은 시제의 동사를 고르는 문제. Over the past year는 '지난해 동안'의 의미로, 전치사 over는 과거부터 현재까지의 일을 나타내어 현재완료 시제와 자주 어울려 쓰인다. 정답은 (B).

---

3 The hotel manager routinely **gives** employee evaluations / to all the workers.
(A) has given (B) giving (C) to give (D) gives
해석| 그 호텔 매니저는 모든 직원들에게 정기적으로 인사 평가를 한다.
어휘| employee evaluation 직원 평가(서)

해설| routinely(일상적으로)라는 시간 표현을 통해 반복적으로 일어나는 일임을 알 수 있다. 따라서 반복되는 일을 나타내는 현재 시제를 쓰는 것이 알맞다. 정답은 (D).

---

4 Currently, / the restaurant **is dealing** with its sanitary problem / in preparation for an inspection.
(A) dealt (B) will deal (C) is dealing (D) to deal
해석| 현재, 그 레스토랑은 단속에 대비하여 위생 문제를 처리하는 중이다.
어휘| sanitary 위생의   in preparation for ~의 대비[준비]로

해설| 문장의 동사 자리이므로 (A), (B), (C)가 정답 후보. currently는 '현재'라는 의미의 부사로, 주로 현재나 현재진행 시제와 함께 쓰인다. 따라서 빈칸에 들어갈 말로 적절한 것은 선택지에 있는 현재진행 시제인 (C).

5-6

To: Nautus Clinic Employees
From: Claudine Morask
Subject: Lobby Renovations
Date: January 18

We have decided to add new light fixtures to the waiting room. Workers **will be arriving** around 10 a.m. Friday. Expect some noise and other disturbances. The work should be complete by 1 p.m. The front desk staff has been notified of the plans **already** and has tried to schedule as few appointments as possible during those times, but we might still get some walk-ins. Thank you for your cooperation.

수신: 노터스 클리닉 직원들
발신: 클로딘 모라스크
제목: 로비 개조
날짜: 1월 18일

우리는 대기실에 새로운 조명 설비를 추가하기로 결정했습니다. 작업자들은 금요일 오전 10시쯤에 **도착할 것입니다.** 약간의 소음과 다른 피해들이 예상됩니다. 작업은 오후 1시까지 완료될 것입니다. 프런트 데스크 직원은 **이미** 작업 계획에 대해 통보받았고, 그 시간 동안 가능한 한 거의 예약을 잡지 않으려고 노력했습니다만, 아마 예약하지 않고 오는 손님을 받게 될 수도 있을 것입니다. 협조해 주셔서 감사드립니다.

어휘 | add 추가하다, 덧붙이다 **light fixture** 조명 설비 **disturbance** 방해, 소란 **complete** 완료된, 완성된 **notify** 알리다 **appointment** 예약, 약속 **walk-in** 예약 없이 오는 손님 **cooperation** 협조, 협력

---

5 Workers **will be arriving** / around 10 a.m. Friday.
(A) have arrived (B) to arrive **(C) will be arriving** (D) arrived

해설 | 지문은 앞으로 있을 공사에 대한 메모로, 10 a.m. Friday로 미래의 시점을 나타내고 있으므로 미래진행형인 (C)가 정답.

---

6 The front desk staff has been notified of the plans **already** / and has tried to schedule as few appointments as possible / during those times, / but we might still get some walk-ins.
(A) already (B) soon (C) anytime (D) next
(A) 벌써, 이미 (B) 곧 (C) 언제든지 (D) 다음에

해설 | 선택지를 보니 시제와 어울리는 시간 표현을 찾는 문제이다. 문장의 동사가 has been notified로 현재완료이므로 정답은 '벌써, 이미'라는 의미의 (A). 나머지 선택지는 모두 문맥상 어울리지 않아 오답이다.

VOCABULARY   **회사 어휘(2)**   교재 101쪽

1 offers 2 ensures 3 results 4 obtained 5 (B) 6 (C) 7 (A) 8 (B)

---

1 The company (proceeds / **offers**) free workshops / to all of its employees.
해석 | 그 회사는 모든 직원에게 무료 워크숍을 제공한다.

해설 | 괄호 앞뒤의 주어와 목적어만 보면 선택지로 주어진 '진행하다', '제공하다'로 모두 가능해 보인다. 그러나 문맥상 '모든 직원에게 워크숍을 제공한다'는 내용이 자연스러우므로 정답은 offers. offer A to B는 'A를 B에게 제공하다'라는 뜻임을 기억하자.

---

2 Careful market research (**ensures** / achieves) / that the company stays up-to-date / on current trends.
해석 | 면밀한 시장 조사는 회사가 현재 동향에 대한 최신 정보를 유지하게 한다.
어휘 | up-to-date 최신의 **trend** 동향, 추세

해설 | 내용상 '면밀한 조사가 회사로 하여금 최신 정보를 유지하게 한다'는 내용이 되어야 자연스러우므로 정답은 ensures.

3 The survey (commitments / **results**) indicate a clear improvement / in customer satisfaction.

해석 | 그 설문 조사 결과는 고객 만족에 있어서의 뚜렷한 향상을 보여준다.

어휘 | improvement 향상, 개선 satisfaction 만족(감)

해설 | 바로 앞의 명사 survey와 어울리는 명사를 골라야 한다. 문맥상 '설문 조사 결과가 고객 만족의 향상을 보여준다'는 내용이 자연스러우므로 정답은 '결과'라는 뜻의 results.

---

4 The restaurant (collaborated / **obtained**) a permit / to expand its dining area.

해석 | 그 식당은 식사 공간을 확장하기 위한 허가를 받았다.

어휘 | permit 허가(증) dining 식사, 정찬

해설 | 괄호 뒤의 목적어 a permit(허가)과 어울리는 동사는 '얻다, 획득하다'라는 의미의 동사 obtain이다. 따라서 정답은 obtained. collaborate는 자동사로, 뒤에 목적어를 취하려면 on 등의 전치사와 호응하여 쓰이기 때문에 답이 될 수 없다.

---

5 Mr. Greggs plans to **conduct** a meeting / with Japanese clients / using videoconferencing equipment.

(A) respond **(B) conduct** (C) proceed (D) accompany

해석 | 그렉스 씨는 화상회의 장비를 사용해서 일본 고객들과 회의를 할 계획이다.

(A) 응답하다 (B) 수행하다 (C) 진행하다 (D) 동반하다

어휘 | client 고객 videoconferencing 화상회의

해설 | 빈칸 뒤 목적어로 a meeting이 나오므로 '회의를 하다'라는 뜻이 되어야 자연스럽다. 어떤 활동을 '수행하다'라는 뜻으로 동사 conduct를 쓰므로 (B)가 정답이다. (C) proceed는 자동사이므로, 뒤에 목적어가 오려면 전치사 with 등이 함께 쓰여야 하므로 오답이다.

---

6 The personnel manager will soon **negotiate** new contracts / with exceptional employees.

(A) present (B) cooperate **(C) negotiate** (D) achieve

해석 | 인사팀장은 조만간 특출한 직원들과 새로 계약을 협상할 것이다.

(A) 수여하다 (B) 협동하다 (C) 협상하다 (D) 성취하다

어휘 | personnel manager 인사팀장 exceptional 특출한

해설 | 빈칸에 어울리는 동사를 고르는 문제로, 빈칸 뒤의 목적어와 자연스럽게 어울리는 것을 골라야 한다. '새 계약을 협상한다'는 내용이 자연스러우므로 정답은 (C)이다. (B) cooperate은 자동사라 in, on 등의 전치사와 함께 써야 하므로 오답이다.

---

7 To increase productivity, / Sulley Textiles Company has **implemented** an employee incentive plan.

(A) **implemented** (B) protected (C) collected (D) separated

해석 | 생산성을 높이기 위해서, 설리 섬유 사는 직원 성과급 제도를 시행했다.

(A) 시행하다 (B) 보호하다 (C) 수집하다 (D) 분리하다

어휘 | productivity 생산성 incentive plan 성과급 제도

해설 | 빈칸 뒤의 목적어 an employee incentive plan(직원 성과급 제도)과 어울리는 동사 어휘를 고르는 문제. 정식으로 채택된 제도나 정책을 '시행하다'의 의미를 가진 (A)가 정답. implement a plan[policy/measure]의 표현을 익혀두자.

---

8 Jasper Cocker will receive an award / for his **outstanding** performance / this year.

(A) increased **(B) outstanding** (C) urgent (D) determined

해석 | 제스퍼 카커 씨는 올해 뛰어난 실적으로 상을 받을 것이다.

(A) 늘어난 (B) 뛰어난 (C) 긴급한 (D) 단호한

해설 | 빈칸 뒤 명사를 수식하는 형용사를 고르는 문제. for 이하는 상을 받는 이유에 해당하므로 실적(performance)이 좋다는 뜻이 되어야 알맞다. 따라서 '뛰어난, 탁월한'이란 뜻의 (B)가 정답. (A) increased의 경우 수량이 증가한 경우를 의미할 뿐, 실적의 좋고 나쁜 상태를 나타낼 수 없으므로 오답이다.

ACTUAL TEST 실전 문제에 적용하기

교재 102쪽

1 (D) **2** (C) **3** (D) **4** (B) **5** (C) **6** (A) **7** (C) **8** (C) **9** (D) **10** (A) **11** (B) **12** (C)

1 With great excitement, / Mr. Thompson **announced** yesterday / that the company's stocks are at an all-time high.
(A) announce (B) announces (C) announcing
(D) announced

해석 | 몹시 흥분해서 톰슨 씨는 회사 주식이 사상 최고치에 이르렀다고 어제 발표했다.

어휘 | excitement 흥분 stock 주식 at an all-time high 사상 최고치인

해설 | **동사 자리+과거 시제**
문장에 빈칸 뒤쪽의 that절을 목적어로 취하는 동사가 없으므로 빈칸은 동사 자리이다. 따라서 동사인 (A), (B), (D)가 정답 후보. 빈칸 뒤에 yesterday라는 과거 시점을 나타내는 시간 표현이 있으므로 정답은 과거 시제인 (D).

2 Hanto Electronics plans to **acquire** Dobby Digital Company / because of its successful range of digital cameras.
(A) arrive (B) perform **(C) acquire** (D) generate

해석 | 한토 일렉트로닉스 사는 도비 디지털 사의 성공적인 디지털 카메라 제품군 때문에 그 회사를 인수할 계획이다.
(A) 도착하다 (B) 수행하다 (C) 인수하다 (D) 생성하다

어휘 | range 제품군

해설 | **동사 어휘 acquire**
빈칸 다음에 나오는 목적어인 Dobby Digital Company는 회사 이름이므로, 문맥상 특정 회사를 '인수하다'라는 뜻이 되어야 알맞다. 따라서 정답은 (C). acquire는 '(노력해서) 얻다, 취득하다'라는 뜻과 함께 회사를 '인수하다'라는 의미도 가진다.

3 Since its launch last year, / the van **has risen** / to the top of the domestic market.
(A) will rise (B) will be rising (C) rises **(D) has risen**

해석 | 지난해 출시 이후로, 그 화물차는 내수 시장의 정상에 올랐다.

어휘 | domestic 국내의, 가정(용)의

해설 | **현재완료 시제**
전치사 since는 현재완료와 자주 쓰이는 대표적인 시간 표현이다. 지난해 출시 이후부터 현재까지의 상황을 이야기하고 있으므로, 현재완료형을 써야 한다. 따라서 정답은 (D).

4 According to an article in *Business Monthly*, / MGV Inc. **will be merging** with Paula Corp. / next year.
(A) merging **(B) will be merging** (C) has merged
(D) to merge

해석 | 〈비즈니스 먼슬리〉 지의 기사에 따르면, 내년에 MGV 주식회사는 파울라 사와 합병하는 중일 것이다.

해설 | **동사 자리+미래진행 시제**
문장의 동사가 없으므로 빈칸은 동사 자리이다. 따라서 동사인 (B)와 (C)가 정답 후보. next year(내년에)라는 표현으로 미루어 보아, 미래의 일을 나타내고 있음을 알 수 있다. 따라서 미래진행 시제인 (B)가 정답.

5 Risk management specialists **determine** the best strategy / for investment / to avoid losses.
(A) purchase (B) move **(C) determine** (D) confess

해석 | 손실을 피하기 위해서 위험 관리 전문가들이 투자를 위한 최상의 전략을 결정한다.
(A) 구입하다 (B) 이동하다 (C) 결정하다 (D) 자백하다

어휘 | risk management 위험 관리 loss 손실

해설 | **동사 어휘 determine**
빈칸에 알맞은 동사를 고르는 문제. 빈칸 뒤 목적어 the best strategy(최상의 전략)과 어울리는 동사는 '결정하다, 판단하다'라는 의미의 (C)이다. 정답은 (C).

6 Government agencies **regularly** check the quality / of the city's drinking water.
(A) regularly (B) yet (C) recently (D) formerly

해석 | 정부 기관들은 정기적으로 그 도시 식수의 질을 검사한다.
(A) 정기적으로 (B) 아직 (C) 최근에 (D) 이전에

어휘 | agency 기관 drinking water 식수

해설 | **부사 어휘 regularly**
선택지를 보니 적절한 부사를 고르는 문제. 빈칸 뒤 동사 check가 현재 시제인 것으로 보아 가장 잘 어울리는 부사는 '정기적으로'의 뜻으로, 반복되는 일을 나타내는 (A)이다.
오답 | (B) yet은 주로 현재완료와 함께 쓰이고 (C) recently와 (D) formerly는 과거의 일을 의미하므로 모두 오답.

UNIT 05

7 Before he asked to speak to the manager, / the client **had requested** a refund / from the cashier.
(A) requests (B) will request (C) **had requested**
(D) is requesting

해석 | 고객은 매니저와 이야기해 보겠다고 요청하기 전에, 계산원에게 환불을 요구했다.

어휘 | refund 환불 cashier 계산원

해설 | **과거완료 시제**
선택지를 보니, 빈칸에 어울리는 동사의 시제를 고르는 문제. 문맥상 고객이 환불을 요청한 것은 매니저와 이야기하겠다고 요청하기 전에 일어난 일이므로, 과거보다 더 이전의 일을 나타내는 과거완료 시제를 써야 한다. 정답은 (C).

---

8 By the time his next novel is released, / Juan Fuentes **will have published** five children's books.
(A) published (B) has published (C) **will have published**
(D) is publishing

해석 | 후안 푸엔테스의 다음 소설이 발표될 때까지, 그는 어린이 대상 도서 다섯 권을 출간했을 것이다.

어휘 | release 발표하다 publish 출간하다

해설 | **미래완료 시제**
by the time은 '~할 때까지'의 뜻으로 미래의 기한을 나타내는 시간 표현이다. 따라서, 책이 출간되는 미래 시점까지 완료될 일을 나타내는 미래완료 시제를 쓰는 것이 적절하다. 정답은 (C). 오답 | 현재진행형인 (D)도 가까운 미래의 일을 나타낼 수 있으나, 특정 시점까지 완료될 일을 나타낼 수는 없으므로 오답이다.

9-12

Dan Morrow
133 Strathern Road
Dundee, DD4 7PW, UK

Mr. Morrow,

I'm afraid a mistake I made may have caused some confusion. Please ignore my previous request to see samples of your work. I didn't realize you **had sent** your portfolio already. I reviewed your pictures, and *Living Well* magazine would be delighted to employ you as a contributing photographer. We are currently writing a **contract** for you. You'll receive it later this week. Please sign and return it to us.

After you are officially hired, your first task will be to visit the Montrose Flower Show, which starts on April 22. Gail Halliwell **will be reporting** on this year's entries in the competition. We would like you to go with her to take pictures of the winning flowers.

We look forward to working with you.

Sincerely,

Kathy Burke, *Living Well* magazine

댄 모로우 씨
스트래선 로 133번지
영국, DD4 7PW 던디

모로우 씨께,

제가 한 실수로 혼란을 끼쳐드려 죄송합니다. 귀하의 작품 샘플을 보게 해 달라고 한 제 이전 요청은 무시해 주십시오. 귀하께서 이미 포트폴리오를 보내셨다는 것을 몰랐습니다. 귀하의 사진들을 검토했으며, 〈리빙 웰〉 지는 귀하를 저희 회사에 사진을 기고하는 사진작가로 채용하게 된다면 기쁠 것입니다. 저희는 현재 귀하의 **계약서**를 작성 중입니다. 이번 주 후반에 이것을 받으실 것입니다. 그것에 서명해서 저희에게 보내 주세요.

공식적으로 채용되신 후의 첫 번째 업무는 4월 22일에 시작하는 몬트로즈 꽃 박람회를 방문하는 것입니다. 게일 홀리웰 씨가 올해의 경연 출품작들에 대해 **보도할 것입니다.** 그녀와 함께 가서 우승한 꽃들의 사진을 찍어 주시기를 바랍니다.

함께 일하게 되기를 고대하고 있습니다.

〈리빙 웰〉 지, 캐시 버크 드림

어휘 | confusion 혼란 ignore 무시하다 realize 깨닫다 review 검토하다 be delighted to *do* ~하게 되어 기쁘다 contribute 기고하다 officially 공식적으로 entry 출품작, 참가작 winning 우승한

9 (A) I would like to apologize for the damage to your photos.
(B) Your annual subscription to *Living Well* has been renewed.
(C) Thank you for taking the time to review my résumé.
(D) I'm afraid a mistake I made may have caused some confusion.

(A) 귀하의 사진에 손상을 입힌 것에 대해 사과드리고 싶습니다.
(B) 고객님의 〈리빙 웰〉 지 연간 구독이 연장되었습니다.
(C) 시간을 내서 제 이력서를 검토해 주셔서 감사드립니다.
(D) 제가 한 실수로 혼란을 끼쳐드려 죄송합니다.

해설 | 알맞은 문장 고르기
빈칸 뒤로 자신이 상황을 잘 몰라서 실수를 했음을 설명하고, 자신의 이전 요청을 무시하라고 하고 있으므로 그 실수에 대해 사과하는 내용이 들어가야 알맞다. 따라서 I'm afraid로 시작하는 (D)가 정답이다.
오답 | 이어지는 내용상 수신자의 사진에 손상을 입힌 것은 아니므로 (A)는 오답. (B)는 잡지 구독을 갱신한 구독자에게, (C)는 이력서를 검토한 인사 담당자에게 보내는 편지에 어울리는 내용이므로 오답.

---

10 I didn't realize / you **had sent** your portfolio already.
(A) **had sent** (B) send (C) were sending (D) will send

해설 | 과거완료 시제
선택지를 보니 적절한 시제의 동사를 고르는 문제로, 문장이나 문맥상의 시간 관계를 파악해야 한다. already(이미, 벌써)를 통해 과거의 일임을 알 수 있고 문맥상 '(발신자가) 알아차리기 전에 이미 보냈다'는 뜻이 되어야 하므로, 주절의 과거 시제 didn't realize보다 더 앞선 시제를 나타내는 과거완료 (A)가 정답이다.

---

11 We are currently writing a **contract** / for you.
(A) negotiation **(B) contract** (C) dialogue (D) meeting

(A) 협상 (B) 계약(서) (C) 대화 (D) 회의

해설 | 명사 어휘 contract
채용되었음을 알리는 편지이므로 '(발신자가) 현재 계약서를 작성 중'이라고 하는 것이 가장 적절하다. 따라서 정답은 (B). 다음 문장의 sign and return it을 통해서도 contract가 답임을 유추할 수 있다.

---

12 Gail Halliwell **will be reporting** / on this year's entries in the competition.
(A) was reporting (B) reported **(C) will be reporting**
(D) has been reporting

해설 | 미래진행 시제
빈칸에 알맞은 시제의 동사를 고르는 문제. 빈칸 앞 문장에서 채용 후 업무에 대해 말하면서 미래 시제를 사용했으므로 빈칸이 포함된 문장도 미래 시제로 서술되어야 한다. 따라서 정답은 (C). 미래진행형의 경우 미래의 특정 시점에 동작이 진행되고 있음을 강조한다는 면에서 단순 미래 시제와 차이가 있다.

UNIT 06 태

1 The traffic law was (passing / **passed**) / by members of Congress / without much trouble.

해석| 그 교통법안은 큰 문제 없이 국회의원들에 의해 통과되었다.

어휘| traffic law 교통법(안)   member of Congress 국회의원   without trouble 문제[어려움] 없이

해설| 주어 traffic law(교통법안)는 통과시키는 주체가 아니라 '통과되는' 대상이므로 수동태를 써야 옳다. 괄호 앞에 be동사가 있으므로 be동사와 수동태 동사를 이루는 과거분사인 passed가 정답.

2 The constructions at Bello Beach Resort / will (complete / **be completed**) next week.

해석| 벨로 비치 리조트의 건설은 다음 주에 완료될 것이다.

해설| 주어 constructions(건설)가 '완료되는' 대상이므로 수동태를 써야 한다. 따라서 be completed가 정답. 〈will be+p.p.〉는 미래 시제 수동태이다.

3 The plane tickets for Ms. Taylor's business trip / are provided / (**by** / for) the company.

해석| 테일러 씨의 출장을 위한 비행기 티켓은 회사로부터 제공된다.

해설| 문장의 동사 are provided로 보아 이는 수동태 문장이다. 수동태 뒤의 알맞은 전치사를 묻는 문제이므로 혹여 〈by+목적격〉 형태의 행위자를 묻는 문제는 아닌지 의심해 본다. 문맥상 '회사로부터 제공되다'라는 의미가 적절하므로 정답은 by.

4 A new convention hall has (built / **been built**) / in the center of Springfield.

해석| 새 회의장이 스프링필드의 중심지에 지어지고 있다.

어휘| convention hall 회의장

해설| 주어 convention hall(회의장)이 '지어지는' 대상이므로 수동태가 와야 한다. 따라서 괄호 앞 has와 함께 완료 시제의 수동태 〈have been+p.p.〉 형태를 이루도록 괄호에는 been built가 들어가야 한다.

5 In accordance with the company policy, / refunds are **guaranteed** / for all defective products.
(A) guarantee   **(B) guaranteed**   (C) having guaranteed
(D) guaranteeing

해석| 회사 규정에 따라, 모든 불량품에 대해 환불이 보장된다.

어휘| in accordance with ~에 따라   guarantee 보장[보증]하다

해설| 주어 refunds(환불)가 규정에 의해 '보장되는' 대상이므로 수동태가 되어야 한다. 따라서 빈칸 앞 be동사인 are와 함께 수동태를 이루는 p.p. 형태인 (B)가 정답.

6 The raw materials were **tested** / by quality experts / before the production stage.
(A) test   (B) testing   **(C) tested**   (D) tests

해석| 원자재들은 생산 단계 전에 품질 전문가에 의해 검사되었다.

어휘| raw 원자재의, 가공되지 않은   expert 전문가

해설| 주어 raw materials(원자재)가 '검사되는' 대상이고, 빈칸 뒤에 by와 함께 행위자가 나오는 것으로 보아 문장의 동사는 수동태가 되어야 한다. 따라서 정답은 빈칸 앞 be동사인 were과 함께 수동태를 이루는 과거분사 (C).

7 Please try to avoid using the front doors / while the sidewalk **is being renovated**.
(A) is renovating   (B) renovates   **(C) is being renovated**
(D) has renovated

해석| 보도가 보수되는 동안 정문 이용을 자제해 주십시오.

어휘| front door 정문   sidewalk 보도

해설| 선택지를 보니 빈칸에 알맞은 동사의 형태를 고르는 문제. 주어 sidewalk(보도)가 '보수되는' 대상이므로 수동태가 되어야 한다. 따라서 수동태인 (C)가 정답. 일정 기간 동안 진행되는 일이므로 〈be being+p.p.〉 형태의 진행형 수동태를 썼다.

8 Because the merger **has been approved**, / the labor union wants to discuss contracts.

(A) approve (B) has approved (C) will approve

(D) has been approved

해석| 합병이 승인되었으므로, 노조는 계약에 관해 논의하기를 원하고 있다.

어휘| approve 승인하다 labor union 노조 discuss 논의하다

해설| 주어 merger(합병)는 '승인되는' 대상이므로 수동태를 써야 한다. 동사만으로 이뤄진 선택지에서 수동태로 쓰인 것은 (D)뿐이다. 나머지 선택지는 모두 능동태이므로 오답. 정답은 (D).

---

2 4문형·5문형 동사의 수동태

교재 109쪽

1 asked **2** been sent **3** is considered **4** be named **5** (C) **6** (B) **7** (C) **8** (C)

1 For the interviews, / applicants were (**asked** / asking) ten questions each.

해석| 그 인터뷰에서 지원자들은 각각 열 개의 질문을 받았다.

어휘| applicant 지원자 each 각각

해설| 괄호 뒤에 명사 ten questions를 목적어로 생각하여 능동태 문장이라고 생각하면 안 된다. 주어인 applicants(지원자)가 '질문을 받는' 대상이므로 수동태를 써야 한다. 괄호 앞의 be동사와 수동태를 이루는 과거분사 asked가 정답.

---

2 The annual fiscal reports have (sent / **been sent**) / to the board of directors.

해석| 연간 회계 보고서가 이사회에 보내졌다.

어휘| fiscal 회계의, 재정의 board of directors 이사회

해설| 주어 reports(보고서)는 사람에 의해 '보내지는' 대상이므로 정답은 앞의 have와 함께 완료시제의 수동태를 이루는 been sent.

---

3 Harvey Electric (considers / **is considered**) the best manufacturer / in the country.

해석| 하비 일렉트릭 사는 국내 최고의 제조업체로 여겨진다.

어휘| manufacturer 제조업체

해설| 동사 자리인 괄호 뒤의 명사구 the best manufacturer을 목적어로 생각하여 능동태 동사를 고르면 안 된다. 5문형 동사인 consider은 수동태일 때, 동사 뒤에 목적격 보어가 남아 목적어처럼 보일 수 있다. 주어 Harvey Electric은 '최고라고 여겨지는' 대상이므로 정답은 수동태 is considered.

---

4 According to the newsletter, / Ms. Johns will (name / **be named**) branch manager / by the CEO.

해석| 사보에 따르면, 존스 씨는 CEO에 의해 지점장으로 임명될 것이다.

어휘| newsletter 사보, 회보

해설| 괄호 뒤의 명사 branch manager만 보고 능동태로 착각해 name을 정답으로 고르면 안 된다. 동사 name은 '~를 …로 임명하다'란 뜻으로 목적어와 목적격 보어를 취하는데, 수동태로 쓸 때, 동사 뒤에 목적격 보어가 남게 된다. 내용상 주어 Mr. Johns가 '임명되는' 대상이므로 수동태인 be named가 정답.

---

5 Special awards are **given** / to members of the board / who have served the company / for more than ten years.

(A) give (B) gave **(C) given** (D) giving

해석| 10년 넘게 회사에 근무한 이사들에게는 특별상이 수여된다.

해설| Special awards(특별상)는 '수여되는' 대상이므로 수동태를 써야 한다. 따라서 be동사와 함께 수동태를 만드는 과거분사 (C)가 정답. give는 4문형 동사로, 직접 목적어인 special awards가 주어로 쓰였고, 간접 목적어인 members 앞에는 전치사 to가 붙었다.

6 Jaxen Supermart **offers** customers a 10 percent discount / for every purchase over $100.
(A) is offered (B) offers (C) will be offered (D) offering
해석| 잭슨 슈퍼마트는 손님들에게 100달러 이상의 모든 구매에 대해 10% 할인을 제공한다.

해설| 문장에 동사가 없으므로 빈칸은 문장의 동사 자리이다. 즉, 동사인 (A), (B), (C)가 정답 후보. 빈칸 뒤에 간접 목적어 customers와 직접 목적어 a 10 percent discount가 나란히 등장하므로 4문형 동사가 능동태로 쓰인 문장임을 알 수 있다. 따라서 답은 (B).

---

7 Tixian Telecomms **was left** bankrupt / by its risky investment / in a start-up smartphone manufacturer.
(A) left (B) will leave (C) **was left** (D) leaves
해석| 티샨 텔레콤스 사는 신생 스마트폰 제조업체에 위험한 투자를 하는 바람에 파산 상태에 처했다.
어휘| bankrupt 파산한 start-up 신생의

해설| 5문형 동사 leave는 '~을 …한 상태에 처하게 하다'라는 의미로, 〈leave+목적어+목적격 보어〉의 구조로 쓰이는데, 수동태 문장에서는 목적격 보어였던 형용사나 명사가 동사 뒤에 남게 된다. 이 문장에서도 빈칸 뒤에 형용사인 bankrupt가 남아있으므로 수동태 문장이다. 따라서 답은 (C).

---

8 Ms. Wade **was appointed** chief finance officer of Manthu Fragrances / last month.
(A) appoints (B) appointing (C) **was appointed**
(D) appointed
해석| 웨이드 씨는 지난 달에 만수 프레그런스 사의 최고 재무 책임자로 임명되었다.
어휘| chief finance officer 최고 재무 책임자

해설| 빈칸은 문장의 동사 자리이므로 동사인 (A), (C), (D)가 정답 후보. 내용상 주어 Ms. Wade는 '임명되는' 대상이므로 수동태인 (C)가 정답이다. appoint는 '~를 …로 임명하다'의 뜻으로 쓰이는 5문형 동사로, 수동태 동사 뒤에 목적어처럼 보이는 명사(목적격 보어)가 따라온다.

---

3 주의해야 할 수동태

교재 111쪽

1 concerned **2** frustrated **3** by **4** to watch **5** (D) **6** (B) **7** (C) **8** (A)

---

1 The CEO is (**concerned** / concerning) about the drop in sales revenue / this past quarter.
해석| 그 CEO는 지난 분기의 매출액 하락에 대해 걱정한다.
어휘| revenue 수익, 수입 quarter 사분기, 4분의 1

해설| 빈칸 앞의 be동사와 뒤의 전치사 about을 보면 '~에 대해 걱정하다'라는 의미로 수동태인 be concerned about이 쓰였음을 알 수 있다. 따라서 정답은 concerned.

---

2 Users of the Web site / were (frustrating / **frustrated**) / with the complicated registration procedure.
해석| 웹사이트 사용자들은 복잡한 등록 절차에 짜증이 났다.
어휘| complicated 복잡한 procedure 절차, 과정

해설| 문장의 주어인 '사용자'가 짜증이 나는 감정을 느끼는 대상이므로 수동태로 쓴다. 괄호 뒤의 with와 함께 be frustrated with(~에 짜증 나다)의 형태로 쓰인다. 따라서 정답은 frustrated.

---

3 The marketers are overwhelmed / (in / **by**) the massive amount of paperwork.
해석| 마케터들은 엄청난 양의 서류 작업에 압도당했다.
어휘| massive 거대한 paperwork 서류 작업

해설| '~에 압도되다'라는 의미의 be overwhelmed by를 평소에 암기했다면 바로 답을 고를 수 있는 문제이다. 수동태 동작의 행위자를 나타내는 전치사 by는 감정의 원인을 나타내어 쓰이기도 한다. 정답은 by.

---

4 Visitors to the park are advised (**to watch** / watching) their belongings / at all times.
해석| 공원 방문객들은 항상 소지품을 살피도록 조언받는다.
어휘| belongings 소지품, 소유물

해설| advise는 목적격 보어로 to부정사를 취하는 동사이다. advise가 수동태로 쓰이면 목적격 보어인 to부정사가 동사 뒤에 위치하게 되어 be advised to do 형태로 '~하라고 조언받다'라는 의미로 쓰인다. 동사 are advised를 보면 수동태 문장임을 알 수 있으므로 정답은 to watch.

---

5 Candidates / who are **interested** in this position / should fill out an application form.
(A) interesting　(B) interest　(C) interests　(D) **interested**

해석| 이 자리에 관심이 있는 지원자들은 지원서를 작성해야 합니다.

해설| 빈칸 앞의 be동사 are과 빈칸 뒤의 전치사 in을 보면 수동태 be interested in 형태로 쓰였음을 알 수 있다. 이 표현은 '~에 흥미가 있다'는 의미로 자주 쓰이므로 잘 기억해두자.

---

6 If the high-speed rail is built, / it will be used **for** transporting commuters.
(A) to　**(B) for**　(C) on　(D) over

해석| 만약 고속철도가 지어지면, 그것은 통근자들을 수송하는 데에 사용될 것이다.

어휘| high-speed rail 고속철도　transport 수송하다　commuter 통근자

해설| 문맥상 '그것(고속철도)이 통근자들을 수송하는 데에 사용될 것이다'라는 뜻이 되어야 자연스럽다. 따라서 '~을 위해서'라는 뜻의 전치사 for가 들어가야 알맞다. be used for(~에 사용되다)를 하나의 표현으로 암기해두자.

---

7 All of the tourists **are satisfied** with the explanations / the tour guide provided.
(A) satisfied　(B) are satisfying　**(C) are satisfied**
(D) will satisfy

해석| 그 관광객 모두는 여행 가이드가 제공한 설명에 만족한다.

어휘| explanation 설명

해설| 선택지를 보니 동사 satisfy의 알맞은 시제와 태를 고르는 문제이다. 문맥상 '관광객들이 설명에 만족한다'라는 의미이므로 '~에 만족하다'라는 의미의 be satisfied with을 떠올려야 한다. 선택지 중 수동태는 (C)뿐이므로 정답은 (C).

---

8 The construction of the new highway / is expected **to last** / until the end of June.
(A) to last　(B) lasted　(C) will last　(D) lasting

해석| 새로운 고속도로의 건설은 6월 말까지 계속될 예정이다.

어휘| highway 고속도로

해설| 문장의 동사가 is expected로 수동태이다. expect는 목적격 보어로 to부정사를 취하는 동사이므로, 수동태로 쓰일 경우 be expected to *do* 형태로 쓰여 '~할 것으로 기대되다, ~할 예정이다'라는 뜻을 나타낸다. 따라서 정답은 (A).

교재 113쪽

REVIEW	핵심 POINT 다시 보기

1 (B)　**2** (C)　**3** (A)　**4** (A)　**5** (A)　**6** (D)

---

1 The prestigious journalism award **was given** to Mr. Angus / following his recent article / on environmental policy.
(A) give　**(B) was given**　(C) will give　(D) has given

해석| 앵거스 씨의 환경 정책에 대한 최근 기사의 결과로 그 권위 있는 언론상이 그에게 주어졌다.

어휘| prestigious 권위 있는, 명망 높은　journalism 언론

해설| 빈칸에 알맞은 동사의 형태를 고르는 문제. 주어인 award(상)는 특정 인물에게 '주어지는' 대상이므로 수동태로 써야 한다. 따라서 정답은 (B). 동사 give는 4문형 동사로 간접 목적어와 직접 목적어를 모두 취하는데, 여기서는 직접 목적어인 명사구 The prestigious journalism award가 수동태 문장의 주어로 쓰여 동사 뒤에 전치사 to와 함께 간접 목적어 Mr. Angus가 남은 형태이다.

---

2 Elaine Sturrock has recently **been promoted** / to head of personnel / at Bacary Pharmaceuticals, Inc.
(A) promoting　(B) promoted　**(C) been promoted**
(D) to promote

해석| 일레인 스터로크 씨는 최근에 바카리 제약회사의 인사팀장으로 승진했다.

해설| 빈칸 앞 부사 recently와 동사 has로 보아 빈칸에는 현재완료 시제를 이루는 과거분사가 들어가야 한다. 과거분사 (B)와 (C)가 정답 후보. 주어인 Elaine Sturrock은 '승진된' 대상이므로, 〈have been+*p.p.*〉의 형태인 현재 완료 시제 수동태로 나타내야 한다. 따라서 (C)가 정답.

3 All board members **will be involved** in drafting the offer / for the acquisition of Gerlife Insurance.
(A) will be involved (B) have involved (C) are involving
(D) will be involving

해석| 모든 이사들은 제라이프 인슈어런스 사의 인수를 위한 제안서의 초안을 작성하는 일에 참여할 것이다.

어휘| involve 참여시키다, 관여시키다 draft 초안을 작성하다

해설| 선택지를 보니 빈칸에 알맞은 동사를 고르는 문제이다. 주어인 board members(이사들)가 초안 작성에 '참여되는' 대상이므로 수동태를 써야 한다. 선택지에서 수동태는 (A)뿐이므로 정답은 (A). be involved in(~에 참여하다[관련되다])은 하나의 표현으로 자주 쓰이므로 기억해 두자.

---

4 The employees in the sales department / always **perform** their duties properly.
(A) perform (B) to perform (C) are performed
(D) performance

해석| 영업 부서의 직원들은 언제나 그들의 업무를 제대로 해낸다.

해설| 문장의 동사가 없으므로, 빈칸은 동사 자리이다. 따라서 동사 (A)와 (C)가 정답 후보. 주어인 employees(직원들)가 '직무를 수행하는' 주체이므로 능동태로 써야 한다. 또한 빈칸 뒤에 목적어 their duties도 있으므로 능동태인 (A)가 정답.

5-6

To: Accounting Department
Subject: Software Upgrade

As we discussed in the meeting, all computers in the department are going to be equipped **with** state-of-the-art software. The new software will simplify how financial claims are processed and billing statements are submitted.

With our current software, bills for various categories **are kept** separate. As a result, the billing process is too complex. I think you will all save a lot of time with the new software.

수신: 회계 부서
안건: 소프트웨어 업그레이드

회의에서 논의했듯이, 부서의 모든 컴퓨터들에 최첨단 소프트웨어가 **구비될** 예정입니다. 신규 소프트웨어는 재정 청구가 처리되는 방식과 청구서가 제출되는 방식을 간소화해 줄 것입니다.

현재의 소프트웨어로는 여러 종류의 청구서들이 **분리되어 있습니다**. 그 결과, 청구서 처리 절차가 너무 복잡합니다. 새로운 소프트웨어로 여러분 모두가 많은 시간을 절감할 수 있으리라 생각합니다.

어휘| accounting 회계 state-of-the art 최첨단의 simplify 간소화하다 financial claim 재정 청구 process 처리하다 billing statement 청구서 separate 별도의, 따로의 complex 복잡한

5 As we discussed in the meeting, / all computers in the department / are going to be equipped **with** / state-of-the-art software.
(A) with (B) in (C) for (D) to

해설| 동사 equip이 수동태로 쓰일 때 전치사 with와 함께 be equipped with 형태로 쓰인다는 것을 알고 있다면 바로 풀 수 있는 문제이다. be equipped with ~은 '~을 갖추다'라는 의미임을 기억해두자.

---

6 With our current software, / bills for various categories / **are kept** separate.
(A) keep (B) kept (C) keeping **(D) are kept**

해설| 주어 bills의 동사가 없으므로 빈칸은 동사 자리이고, 동사가 아닌 (C)는 바로 오답으로 제외. 문맥상 '분리된 상태로 유지된다'는 의미가 적절한데 keep이 '~를 …의 상태로 유지하다'의 뜻으로 쓰일 때는 〈keep+목적어+목적격 보어〉의 형태로 쓰인다. 여기서는 목적어 없이 목적격 보어인 형용사 separate만 남은 형태이므로 수동태로 쓰였음을 알 수 있다. 따라서 수동태인 (D)가 정답.

1 representative **2** colleagues **3** encouraged **4** oversees **5** (A) **6** (B) **7** (D) **8** (C)

1 A (**representative** / contribution) of Hyan Corp. / confirmed the firm's plans to relocate.

해석 | 하이언 사의 대표는 회사의 이전 계획이 사실임을 인정했다.

어휘 | confirm 사실이라고 인정하다[확인하다]

해설 | 회사의 이전 계획 등이 사실임을 인정할 수 있는 주체는 회사의 '대표'가 되는 것이 자연스러우므로 답은 representative이다.

---

2 Henry Pilner and Daisy Smith are (boards / **colleagues**) / at a publishing company.

해석 | 헨리 필너 씨와 데이지 스미스 씨는 출판 회사의 동료이다.

어휘 | publishing company 출판사

해설 | 문맥상 출판 회사의 두 사람이 '동료'인 것이 자연스러우므로 정답은 colleagues이다.

---

3 All office workers are (allocated / **encouraged**) / to attend a workshop.

해석 | 모든 사무직 직원들이 워크숍에 참가하도록 권장된다.

해설 | 주어인 직원들이 워크숍에 참가하도록 '권장된다'는 내용이 자연스러우므로 정답은 encouraged. encourage는 to부정사를 보어로 취하는 5문형 동사로, 수동태로 be encouraged to do의 형태로 자주 쓰인다.

---

4 Each leader (**oversees** / transfers) a team / of eight to ten members.

해석 | 각 팀장들은 여덟 명에서 열 명의 팀원으로 구성된 팀 하나를 감독한다.

해설 | 문맥상 팀장이 한 팀을 '감독하는 것'이 자연스러우므로 oversees가 들어가는 것이 알맞다.

---

5 On January 1, / Rob's Burgers will hold a training program / at its **headquarters**.
(A) **headquarters** (B) residences (C) procedures (D) promotions

해석 | 1월 1일에, 롭스 버거 사는 본사에서 연수 프로그램을 개최할 것이다.

(A) 본사 (B) 거주지, 주택 (C) 절차 (D) 승진, 홍보

어휘 | hold 열다, 개최하다

해설 | 기업의 연수 프로그램이 개최된다는 내용인데, '~에서'라는 뜻의 전치사 at 이하에서 그 장소를 나타내고 있다. 문맥상 그 기업의 '본사'에서 연수가 진행되는 것이 자연스러우므로 정답은 (A).

---

6 The **spokesperson** for Garrido Electronics / announced / that the company will hire a new director of sales.
(A) outcome (B) **spokesperson** (C) patron (D) reputation

해석 | 가리도 일렉트로닉스 사의 대변인은 회사가 새로운 영업 이사를 고용할 것이라고 발표했다.

(A) 결과 (B) 대변인 (C) 단골손님, 후원자 (D) 명성

어휘 | director of sales 영업 이사

해설 | 빈칸은 문장의 주어 자리로, 동사가 announced(발표하다)이므로 사람을 나타내는 말이 들어가야 알맞다. 기업의 향후 계획에 대해 발표하는 사람은 '대변인'이 되어야 자연스러우므로 빈칸에는 (B)가 적절하다.

---

7 Ms. Dawson will be **transferring** / to the factory in Chengdu next year / to oversee its expansion.
(A) placing (B) assessing (C) calculating (D) **transferring**

해석 | 도슨 씨는 공장의 확장을 감독하기 위해 내년에 청두에 있는 그 공장으로 전근 갈 예정이다.

(A) 놓다, 두다 (B) 평가하다 (C) 계산하다 (D) 전근 가다

해설 | 빈칸 뒤 to the factory라는 방향을 나타내는 표현과 함께 쓰일 수 있는 어휘를 골라야 한다. 문맥상 다른 지역에 있는 공장으로 '전근을 가다'라는 뜻이 되어야 하므로 (D)가 알맞다. 옮기는 장소를 나타내어 전치사 to와 함께 쓰인다는 점에 주의한다.

8 All employees must comply with the restaurant's new health and safety <u>regulations</u>.
(A) admissions (B) contributions **(C) regulations**
(D) observations
해석| 모든 직원은 식당의 새로운 보건 및 안전 규정을 준수해야 한다.
(A) 입장 (B) 공헌, 기여 (C) 규정 (D) 관찰

해설| 빈칸은 동사 comply with(~을 따르다)의 목적어 자리이므로 따를 수 있는 대상이 와야 한다. 정답은 (C).

ACTUAL TEST 실전 문제에 적용하기   교재 116쪽

1 (B) **2** (D) **3** (B) **4** (C) **5** (B) **6** (C) **7** (A) **8** (D) **9** (B) **10** (D) **11** (C) **12** (B)

---

1 Clients **will be contacted** / by customer service representatives / about pending concerns / within one day.
(A) have contacted **(B) will be contacted**
(C) will contact (D) are contacting
해석| 고객들은 미결건에 대해 하루 안에 고객 서비스 직원의 연락을 받게 될 것이다.
어휘| pending 미결의 concern 일 within 이내에

해설| **수동태**
선택지가 모두 동사로 알맞은 시제와 태의 동사를 고르는 문제. 내용상 빈칸 앞 주어인 '고객'은 고객 서비스 직원에 의해 '연락받는' 대상이므로 수동태를 골라야 한다. 선택지에서 수동태는 (B) 뿐이므로 정답은 (B).

---

2 Sherman and Lopez's law team is **dedicated** / to providing exceptional legal advice.
(A) satisfied (B) distributed (C) supportable **(D) dedicated**
해석| 셔먼 앤 로페즈 사의 법률팀은 뛰어난 법적 조언을 제공하는 데에 전념한다.
(A) 만족하는 (B) 분포된 (C) 지지할 수 있는 (D) 전념하는
어휘| legal 법률의

해설| **동사 어휘 dedicate**
문맥상 어울리는 것은 '전념하다[헌신하다]'라는 뜻의 (D). dedicate는 be dedicated to *doing*, dedicate *oneself* to *doing*의 형태로 자주 쓰인다는 것을 기억해두자.

---

3 In light of the national recall, / customers **may return** any Gilmore product / without proof of purchase.
(A) to be returned **(B) may return** (C) returning
(D) should be returned
해석| 전국적인 제품 회수라는 점을 고려할 때, 소비자들은 구매에 대한 증명이 없어도 길모어 사의 제품을 반품할 수 있다.
어휘| in light of ~을 고려할 때 recall 제품 회수, 리콜 return 반품하다 proof 증명, 증거

해설| **동사 자리+능동태**
문장에 동사가 없는 것으로 보아 빈칸은 동사 자리이므로 (B)와 (D)가 정답 후보이다. 빈칸 뒤에 any Gilmore product라는 목적어가 있고, 주어인 customers가 '반품을 하는' 주체이므로 능동태가 와야 옳다. 따라서 정답은 (B). 조동사 may가 동사 앞에 쓰여 '~할 수 있다'라는 허가의 의미를 부여하고 있다.

---

4 After the old coffee machine broke down, / a new coffee maker **was ordered** / for the employees / on the second floor.
(A) orders (B) were ordered **(C) was ordered** (D) order
해석| 오래된 커피 머신이 고장 난 후, 새로운 커피 기계가 2층에 있는 직원들을 위해 주문되었다.
어휘| break down 고장 나다, 와해되다

해설| **수동태**
선택지를 보니 동사 order(주문하다)의 알맞은 형태를 묻는 문제이다. 주어인 '커피 기계'는 '주문되는' 대상이므로 수동태가 되어야 자연스럽다. 수동태 형태인 (B)와 (C)가 정답 후보인데, 주어가 단수 명사인 a new coffee maker이기 때문에 정답은 (C).

---

5 Business First **is considered** the best nonprofit group / for assisting entrepreneurs.
(A) considered **(B) is considered** (C) consider
(D) to consider
해석 | 비즈니스 퍼스트 사는 기업가들을 지원함에 있어 최고의 비영리단체로 여겨진다.
어휘 | nonprofit organization 비영리단체 assist 지원하다, 돕다
entrepreneur 기업가, 사업가

해설 | **동사 자리+수동태**
문장에 동사가 없기 때문에 빈칸은 동사 자리이다. 선택지 중 동사인 (A), (B), (C)가 정답 후보. 문맥상 특정 조직이 '최고의 비영리단체로 여겨지는' 대상이므로 수동태로 써야 한다. 따라서 정답은 (B). 동사 consider는 목적어와 목적격 보어를 취하는 5문형 동사로, 여기서는 목적격 보어인 the best nonprofit group이 동사 뒤에 와서 목적어처럼 보일 수 있다. 이를 보고 능동태 문장으로 생각하고 (A)나 (C)를 고르지 않도록 한다.

6 Since last year, / most of the negotiations with our partners / **have been conducted** / by Bogart International.
(A) will be conducted (B) have conducted
(C) have been conducted (D) was conducting
해석 | 작년부터 우리 파트너들과의 협상 대부분은 보가트 인터내셔널 사가 수행해왔다.
어휘 | negotiation 협상

해설 | **수동태**
선택지를 보니 적절한 시제와 태의 동사를 묻는 문제이다. 동사 conduct는 목적어가 필요한 3문형 동사인데, 빈칸 뒤에 목적어가 없다. 따라서, 수동태 문장임을 알 수 있으므로 (A)와 (C)가 정답 후보. Since last year라는 시간 표현으로 과거부터 현재까지 계속됨을 나타내고 있으므로, 현재완료형 수동태인 (C)가 적절하다.

7 The marketing team is **pleased** / with the feedback / customers have given.
(A) pleased (B) pleasing (C) pleasure (D) pleasant
해석 | 마케팅 팀은 고객이 제공한 피드백에 만족한다.

해설 | **수동태**
빈칸 앞의 be동사 is와 빈칸 뒤의 전치사 with를 보면 be pleased with의 형태로 쓰였음을 알 수 있다. 따라서 정답은 (A). be pleased with은 '~에 기뻐하다'라는 뜻으로 하나의 표현처럼 쓰이므로 기억해두자.

8 The winner of the presidential election / **will be announced** / promptly at six o'clock tomorrow night.
(A) is announcing (B) has been announced
(C) will announce **(D) will be announced**
해석 | 대통령 선거의 당선자가 지체 없이 내일 저녁 6시에 발표될 것이다.
어휘 | presidential election 대통령 선거 promptly 지체 없이, 신속히

해설 | **수동태**
선택지를 보니 알맞은 시제와 태의 동사를 고르는 문제. 시간 표현 tomorrow night을 통해 미래 시제인 (C)와 (D)가 정답 후보임을 알 수 있다. 또한 주어인 The winner(당선자)는 '발표되는' 대상이므로 수동태인 (D)가 정답이다.

9-12
From: George Jameson, General Manager
To: All New Staff
Subject: Re: Training Sessions

We **are starting** a new skills-improvement program. On Friday morning, a senior sales representative will lead a mandatory training session.

This session will include information on the structure of our organization. You'll also learn about the best techniques for managing your time. The class will take at least three hours. **The final thirty minutes will consist of a short written test.** Once you pass it, you **will be given** an official document for completing the program. We believe that this training will help us **assess** your needs

발신: 본부장, 조지 제임슨
수신: 모든 신입 직원
제목: 회신: 교육 프로그램

우리는 새로운 능력 개발 프로그램을 **시작합니다.** 금요일 오전에 선임 영업 사원이 필수 교육 프로그램을 이끌 것입니다.

이 교육은 우리 회사의 조직 구조에 대한 내용을 포함할 것입니다. 또한 시간을 관리하는 최고의 기술에 관해서도 배우게 될 것입니다. 수업은 최소 세 시간이 소요됩니다. **마지막 30분은 간단한 필기 시험으로 이루어질 것입니다.** 시험을 통과하자마자, 프로그램 이수에 대한

and skills and that it will be highly beneficial to the company.

Thank you.

공식적인 문서를 **받게 될 것입니다**. 이 교육이 우리로 하여금 당신의 요구와 자질을 **가늠하는** 데 도움이 되고, 이것이 기업에 매우 이득이 될 것이라고 믿습니다.

감사합니다.

어휘| training session 교육 프로그램   senior 선임의, 상급자의   organization 단체, 조직   technique 기술, 기법   consist of ~으로 이루어지다[구성되다]   beneficial (to) (~에) 이득이 되는

9 We **are starting** a new skills-improvement program.
   (A) are started **(B) are starting** (C) will be started
   (D) were starting

해설| 능동태

선택지를 보니 동사의 알맞은 시제와 태를 고르는 문제이다. 빈칸 앞 주어인 '우리'가 새로운 프로그램을 '시작하는' 주체가 되는 것이 자연스러우므로 능동태를 써야 한다. 선택지에서 능동태는 (B)와 (D)인데, 다음 문장에서 금요일부터 프로그램이 시작된다고 했으므로, 가까운 미래의 일을 나타내는 현재진행 시제로 써야 한다. 따라서 답은 (B).

10 (A) I hope you have enjoyed this workshop.
   (B) Please let us know whether you can participate.
   (C) Some customers have complained that this is too long.
   (D) The final thirty minutes will consist of a short written test.
   (A) 여러분에게 이 워크숍이 즐거웠기를 바랍니다.
   (B) 참석하실 수 있는지 여부를 저희에게 알려주시기 바랍니다.
   (C) 일부 고객들이 이것이 너무 길다고 불평했습니다.
   (D) 마지막 30분은 간단한 필기 시험으로 이루어질 것입니다.

해설| 알맞은 문장 고르기

빈칸 바로 다음의 문장의 Once you pass it,에서 대명사 it이 가리키는 것이 빈칸의 문장에 등장해야 한다. 동사 pass가 쓰였으므로, 통과할 수 있는 대상에 대한 내용이 되어야 자연스럽다. 선택지 중에서 3인칭 단수 대명사 it으로 받을 수 있으면서 '통과'할 수 있는 대상은 '시험'뿐이기 때문에 정답은 (D).
오답| (A)는 워크숍이 끝난 후에 할 만한 말이므로 오답. (B)는 첫 번째 문단에서 이 교육은 필수 교육이라고 했는데 이와 반대되는 내용이라 오답이다. 교육은 직원을 대상으로 하는 것인데 (C)는 고객이 과정의 길이에 대해 불평했다고 했으므로 관련이 없는 내용이라 오답.

11 Once you pass it, / you **will be given** an official document / for completing the program.
   (A) are giving (B) will give **(C) will be given** (D) have given

해설| 수동태

빈칸에 알맞은 시제와 태의 동사를 고르는 문제. 주어인 you가 가리키는 것은 메모의 수신자인 '교육에 참가하게 될 신입 직원'으로 수료증을 '받는' 대상이기 때문에 수동태를 써야 한다. 선택지에서 유일한 수동태인 (C)가 정답.

12 We believe / that this training will help us **assess** your needs and skills / and that it will be highly beneficial to the company.
   (A) allocate **(B) assess** (C) command (D) contribute
   (A) 할당하다 (B) 평가하다 (C) 명령하다 (D) 기여하다

해설| 동사 어휘 assess

문맥상 기업의 교육 프로그램이 직원들의 요구와 자질을 '가늠하는 데' 도움이 된다는 내용이 자연스러우므로 정답은 '평가하다, 판단하다'의 의미인 (B).

1 형용사의 개념과 쓰임

교재 121쪽

1 Comfortable **2** functional **3** special **4** cautious **5** (B) **6** (C) **7** (B) **8** (A)

---

1 (Comfort / **Comfortable**) chairs help employees maintain proper posture / at their desks.

해석| 편안한 의자는 직원들이 책상에서 적절한 자세를 유지하도록 도와 준다.

어휘| posture 자세

해설| 괄호는 뒤에 나온 명사 chairs를 수식하므로, 형용사가 들어갈 자리이다. 따라서 형용사 어미 -able이 붙은 Comfortable이 정답.

---

2 The new theater will be (function / **functional**) / by October 5.

해석| 새로운 극장은 10월 5일까지는 제 기능을 할 수 있게 될 것이다.

어휘| theater 극장 functional 가동되는, 기능하는

해설| 괄호는 동사 will be의 보어 자리로, 주어의 성질을 나타내는 주격 보어 자리이다. 따라서 명사 또는 형용사가 들어가야 하는데, 문맥상 '극장이 제 기능을 하다'와 같이 주어의 성질이나 상태를 나타내는 것이 자연스러우므로 형용사인 functional이 정답.

---

3 Ms. Garcia didn't do anything (**special** / specially) / during her time off.

해석| 가르시아 씨는 쉬는 동안 특별한 일을 하지 않았다.

어휘| time off 휴일, 휴식

해설| -thing이나 -body로 끝나는 명사는 형용사가 뒤에서 수식한다. 따라서 괄호에는 anything을 수식하는 형용사 special이 들어가야 한다.

---

4 The recent drop in the stock market / made investors (**cautious** / cautiously).

해석| 최근 주식 시장의 하락은 투자자들을 신중하게 만들었다.

어휘| drop 하락 stock market 주식 시장 cautious 신중한, 조심스러운

해설| 동사 make는 목적어와 목적격 보어를 취하는 5문형 동사로, 괄호는 목적어의 상태를 나타내는 목적격 보어 자리이다. 따라서 형용사 cautious가 들어가야 알맞다. 우리말로는 부사처럼 '신중하게'로 해석되지만, 보어 자리에는 부사가 올 수 없다는 것을 잊지 말자.

---

5 The client was impressed / with Mr. Miller's **creative** ideas / for the television commercial.
(A) creatively **(B) creative** (C) creativeness (D) create

해석| 고객은 텔레비전 광고에 대한 밀러 씨의 창의적인 생각에 깊은 인상을 받았다.

어휘| be impressed with ~에 깊은 인상을 받다 creative 창의적인 commercial 광고 (방송)

해설| 빈칸 앞의 소유격과 빈칸 뒤 명사로 보아, 〈한정사+형용사+명사〉의 구조이며, 빈칸에는 형용사가 쓰여야 함을 알 수 있다. 따라서 형용사인 (B)가 정답. (A)는 -ly로 끝나는 부사, (C)는 -ness로 끝나는 명사, (D)는 동사이므로 오답이다.

---

6 With its aggressive marketing tactics, / Zalbrec is quite **successful** in selling its newest laptop.
(A) succeed (B) success **(C) successful** (D) succeeded

해석| 공격적인 마케팅 전략으로, 잘브렉 사는 자사의 최신형 노트북 판매에 있어 꽤 성공적이다.

어휘| aggressive 공격적인 tactic 전술, 책략

해설| 빈칸은 동사 is 뒤의 주격 보어 자리이다. 주격 보어로는 명사 또는 형용사가 쓰일 수 있으므로 명사 (B)와 형용사 (C)가 정답 후보이다. 이 문장에서는 보어가 주어인 Zalbrec과 동격이 아니라 주어의 상태(잘브렉 사는 성공적이다)를 나타내고 있으므로 형용사인 (C)가 정답.

7 During winter, / transport authorities consider the slippery roads very **dangerous**.
(A) dangers **(B) dangerous** (C) danger (D) dangerously
해석 | 겨울 동안, 교통 당국은 미끄러운 길을 매우 위험하다고 여긴다.
어휘 | transport authority 교통 당국 slippery 미끄러운

해설 | 문장의 동사인 consider은 목적어와 목적격 보어를 취하는 5문형 동사이다. 따라서 빈칸이 동사의 목적어 slippery roads를 수식하는 목적격 보어 자리임을 알 수 있는데, 명사와 형용사만이 보어로 쓰일 수 있으므로 부사인 (D)는 정답에서 제외. 내용상 목적어 slippery roads의 '위험한' 성질을 나타내는 것이 자연스러우므로 빈칸에는 형용사 (B)가 들어가야 한다.

8 The educational programs at the community center / have had a beneficial **impact** / on residents.
(A) impact (B) impacted (C) impacting (D) to impact
해석 | 지역문화센터의 교육 프로그램들은 주민들에게 좋은 영향을 미쳤다.
어휘 | educational 교육의 community center 커뮤니티 센터, 지역문화센터 have an impact on ~에 영향을 주다

해설 | 빈칸 앞에 관사 a와 형용사 beneficial이 있는 것으로 보아 〈한정사+형용사+명사〉의 형태로 쓰였음을 알 수 있다. 따라서 빈칸에는 명사가 들어가야 하므로 정답은 (A). 참고로 빈칸은 동사 have had의 목적어로 쓰였다.

---

2 주의해야 할 형용사

교재 123쪽

1 economic **2** sensible **3** missing **4** useful **5** (B) **6** (B) **7** (C) **8** (D)

1 It is not easy to sustain (**economic** / economical) growth / over a long period.
해석 | 오랜 기간 동안 경제 성장을 지속하는 것은 쉽지 않다.
어휘 | sustain 지속하다 growth 성장

해설 | 괄호 뒤의 명사 growth와 어울려 '경제 성장'이라는 말이 되어야 알맞다. 둘 다 형용사지만 문맥상 '경제의'라는 뜻의 economic이 들어가야 한다. economical은 '알뜰한, 경제적인'이란 뜻으로 어울리지 않는다.

2 The management team took (**sensible** / sensitive) measures / to protect the fragile goods.
해석 | 관리팀은 깨지기 쉬운 제품들을 보호하기 위해서 현명한 조치를 취했다.
어휘 | management team 관리팀 take measures 조치를 취하다 fragile 깨지기 쉬운

해설 | 괄호 뒤에 나오는 명사 measures(조치, 대책)와 어울려 의미가 통하는 형용사를 골라야 한다. '현명한[합리적인] 조치'라는 뜻을 이루는 sensible이 정답. sensitive는 '민감한'이란 뜻으로 적절하지 않다.

3 The manager noticed something (miss / **missing**) / from Ms. Austin's sales report.
해석 | 그 관리자는 오스틴 씨의 매출 보고서에서 무언가 누락되었다는 것을 알아차렸다.
어휘 | notice 알아차리다, 눈에 띄다 sales report 매출 보고서

해설 | -thing으로 끝나는 명사는 형용사가 뒤에서 수식한다는 사실을 기억한다면 괄호가 형용사 자리임을 쉽게 알 수 있다. 괄호에는 something을 꾸밀 수 있는 형용사가 들어가야 하므로, 현재분사 형태로 쓰이는 형용사 missing이 정답.

4 The brochure about cultural heritage sites / is (using / **useful**) / to tourists.
해석 | 문화 유적지에 대한 안내책자는 관광객들에게 유용하다.
어휘 | brochure 안내책자 cultural heritage 문화 유산 site 장소, 현장

해설 | 괄호 앞의 be동사 is와 괄호 뒤의 전치사 to를 보고 바로 be useful to를 떠올려야 한다. be useful to(~에 유용하다)는 하나의 표현으로 자주 쓰이므로 기억해두자.

5 Numerous companies spend money / on protecting their <u>confidential</u> trade strategies / from competitors.
(A) confidence **(B) confidential** (C) confident
(D) confidentially

해석| 많은 기업들이 경쟁사로부터 자신들의 기밀 영업 전략을 지키는 데에 많은 비용을 들인다.

어휘| numerous 많은 spend ~ on *doing* …하는 데 ~을 쓰다 protect 지키다, 보호하다 trade 거래, 교역 strategy 계획

해설| 빈칸 앞의 소유격 인칭대명사와 빈칸 뒤 명사로 보아, 〈한정사＋형용사＋명사〉의 구조로, 빈칸에는 형용사가 쓰여야 함을 알 수 있다. 따라서 형용사인 (B)와 (C)가 정답 후보. 내용상 '기밀 영업 전략'이라는 뜻이 자연스러우므로 정답은 (B). (C)는 '확신하는'이라는 의미이므로 적절하지 않다.

---

6 Lyon Shipping is not <u>responsible</u> for delivery delays / due to poor weather conditions.
(A) responsibility **(B) responsible** (C) responding
(D) responsibly

해석| 라이온 택배 사는 악천후로 인한 배송 지연에는 책임을 지지 않습니다.

어휘| delivery 배송 delay 지연, 연기 weather condition 기상 상태

해설| 빈칸은 동사 is의 보어가 들어갈 자리인데, 빈칸 앞의 be동사, 빈칸 뒤의 전치사 for와 어울려 '~에 대해 책임을 지다'라는 뜻이 되어야 한다. 따라서 정답은 (B). be responsible for를 하나의 표현으로 알아두자.

---

7 The manager prepared a <u>detailed</u> product description / of the newly released vehicles.
(A) detailing (B) details **(C) detailed** (D) detail

해석| 그 매니저는 새롭게 출시된 차량의 상세한 제품 설명을 준비했다.

어휘| description 서술, 묘사

해설| 빈칸 바로 앞의 관사 a와 빈칸 뒤의 명사 product description으로 보아, 빈칸은 〈한정사＋형용사＋명사〉의 구조의 형용사 자리임을 알 수 있다. 따라서 형용사인 (A)와 (C)가 정답 후보이나, '상세한'이라는 의미의 detailed가 과거분사 형태로 굳어져 쓰이는 형용사이므로 정답은 (C)이다.

---

8 The conference hall is <u>capable</u> / of accommodating over one thousand people.
(A) capability (B) capably (C) capabilities **(D) capable**

해석| 그 회의장은 천 명 이상의 사람들을 수용하는 것이 가능하다.

어휘| accommodate 수용하다

해설| 빈칸은 동사 is 뒤의 주격 보어 자리로, 형용사나 명사만 들어갈 수 있으므로 부사인 (B)는 정답 후보에서 제외. 빈칸 앞의 be동사와 빈칸 뒤 of와 함께 '~을 할 수 있다'의 의미로 쓰이는 형용사 구문 be capable of를 안다면 바로 풀 수 있는 문제이다. 정답은 (D).

3	**부사의 개념과 쓰임**	교재 125쪽

1 expensive **2** permanently **3** strongly **4** steadily **5** (B) **6** (A) **7** (A) **8** (D)

---

1 The Victoria Hotel was too (expenses / **expensive**) / for our travel budget.

해석| 빅토리아 호텔은 우리 여행 예산에 비해 너무 비쌌다.

어휘| expensive 비싼 budget 예산

해설| 괄호는 동사 was의 보어 자리이다. 따라서 명사 expenses와 형용사 expensive 모두 들어갈 수 있는데, 괄호 앞의 부사 too의 수식을 받을 수 있는 것은 형용사뿐이다. 따라서 정답은 expensive.

---

2 Several teams in the existing factory / will relocate / to the new facility (permanent / **permanently**).

해석| 기존 공장의 몇몇 팀들은 새로운 시설로 영구히 이동하게 될 것이다.

어휘| existing 기존의 permanently 영구히

해설| 괄호의 내용 없이도 문장이 완전하므로 괄호에는 부사가 들어가야 한다. 따라서 정답은 부사인 permanently.

---

3 The new staff members are (strong / **strongly**) encouraged / to participate in the workshop.

해석 | 신입 직원들은 워크숍에 참석하도록 강력히 장려된다.

어휘 | strongly 강력히 be encouraged to *do* ~하도록 장려되다 participate in ~에 참석하다

해설 | 수동태 동사를 이루는 괄호 앞뒤의 be동사 are와 과거분사 encouraged 사이에 올 수 있는 것은 부사뿐이다. 따라서 -ly로 끝나는 부사 strongly가 정답.

---

4 Redwood Furnishings' operations are envisioned to grow (**steadily** / steady) / for five years.

해석 | 레드우드 퍼니싱 사의 영업 활동은 5년 동안 꾸준히 성장할 것으로 보여진다.

어휘 | operations 영업 활동 envision 마음속에 그리다, 상상하다

해설 | 괄호 없이도 문장이 완전하므로 괄호는 부사가 들어갈 자리이다. 괄호 앞의 동사 grow를 꾸며 줄 수 있는 부사인 steadily가 정답.

---

5 Ms. Thomas **personally** reviews each article / in the newspaper every morning.
(A) personal (B) **personally** (C) personable (D) personalize

해석 | 매일 아침 토마스 씨는 신문에 있는 각각의 기사를 직접 검토한다.

어휘 | personally 직접, 개인적으로 review 검토하다

해설 | 주어 Ms. Thomas와 동사 reviews 사이에 올 수 있는 것은 동사를 수식하는 부사이다. 따라서, -ly로 끝나는 (B)가 정답.

---

6 Most visitors to the Vinita Gallery / are **particularly** interested / in the sculpture collection.
(A) **particularly** (B) particularity (C) particular (D) particulars

해석 | 비니타 갤러리에 오는 대부분의 방문객들은 조각품 컬렉션에 특히 관심이 있다.

어휘 | particularly 특히 be interested in ~에 관심이 있다 sculpture 조각품 collection 수집품, 소장품

해설 | 수동태 동사를 이루는 be동사 are와 과거분사 interested 사이의 빈칸에 들어갈 수 있는 것은 부사뿐이다. 따라서 정답은 (A).

---

7 Delma Shipping has **generously** awarded college scholarships / to numerous deserving students.
(A) **generously** (B) most generous (C) generous
(D) generosity

해석 | 델마 쉬핑 사는 도움이 필요한 많은 학생들에게 대학 장학금을 아낌없이 주어왔다.

어휘 | award 주다, 수여하다 scholarship 장학금 deserving (경제적으로) 도움이 필요한

해설 | 완료 시제의 동사를 이루는 have동사 has와 과거분사 awarded 사이에 올 수 있는 것은 부사뿐이다. 따라서 -ly로 끝나는 부사 (A)가 정답.

---

8 The company is becoming **increasingly** reliant / on a few key markets in Asia and Europe.
(A) increased (B) increase (C) increasing (D) **increasingly**

해석 | 그 회사는 아시아와 유럽의 몇몇 주요 시장에만 점점 의존하게 되고 있다.

어휘 | increasingly 점점, 더욱 더 reliant on ~에 의지하는

해설 | 빈칸 없이도 문장이 완전하므로 빈칸은 부사 자리임을 알 수 있다. 따라서 부사인 (D)가 정답. increasingly는 주격 보어로 쓰인 형용사 reliant를 수식하기 위해 쓰였다.

---

4 **주의해야 할 부사**   교재 127쪽

1 closely **2** shortly **3** hardly **4** already **5** (D) **6** (D) **7** (D) **8** (A)

---

1 Investors (close / **closely**) monitor the stock market / for any changes in stock prices.

해석 | 투자자들은 주가에 어떤 변화라도 있는지 (알기 위해) 주식 시장을 면밀히 관찰한다.

해설 | 괄호에 알맞은 부사를 고르는 문제. 문맥상 '면밀히 관찰하다'라는 의미가 되어야 자연스러우므로 정답은 closely이다. close는 '가깝게'라는 의미이므로 적절하지 않다.

2 The agenda for Grande Bank's next board meeting / will be announced / (short / **shortly**).

해석| 그랜드 은행의 다음 이사회 안건이 곧 발표될 것이다.

해설| short와 shortly 모두 동사 announced를 꾸밀 수 있는 부사이지만, 문맥상 '곧 발표될 것이다'라는 의미가 되어야 하므로 정답은 shortly. short은 '짧게'라는 의미이므로 오답.

---

3 Audience members in the back row / could (hard / **hardly**) hear the speaker.

해석| 뒷줄에 있는 청중들은 연사의 말을 거의 들을 수 없었다.

어휘| audience 청중, 관객 row 줄, 열 speaker 연사

해설| 문맥상 '거의 들을 수 없었다'라는 부정의 뜻이 되어야 내용이 자연스럽다. hardly는 형용사 hard(열심히 하는)의 부사형처럼 보이지만, '거의 ~ 않는'이라는 전혀 다른 뜻으로 쓰이는 부사이다. hard는 형용사와 부사 둘 다로 쓰이지만 여기서는 문맥상 알맞지 않으므로 정답은 hardly.

---

4 The departure of the flight to Atlanta / has (**already** / mostly) been delayed / by the severe weather.

해석| 애틀랜타행 비행편의 출발이 악천후로 인해 이미 지연되었다.

어휘| departure 출발, 떠남 flight 비행(편) severe 극심한, 가혹한

해설| 완료 시제를 이루는 have동사 has와 과거분사 delayed 사이에 들어갈 수 있는 것은 부사뿐이다. already와 mostly 모두 부사인데, 문맥상 '비행기가 이미 지연되었다'라는 의미가 자연스럽다. 따라서 already가 정답.

---

5 The weekend's free concert was attended / by **nearly** five thousand people.
(A) near (B) nearer (C) nearest (D) **nearly**

해석| 주말의 무료 콘서트에는 거의 5천 명의 사람들이 참석했다.

해설| 빈칸 없이도 문장이 완전하고, 빈칸 뒤에 five thousand라는 수량 표현이 있으므로 빈칸은 수량 표현을 수식할 수 있는 부사 자리임을 알 수 있다. 문맥상 '거의 5천 명의 사람들이 참석했다'는 내용이 자연스러우므로 '거의'라는 의미의 nearly가 정답. nearly는 '가까이'라는 의미의 부사 near과는 전혀 다른 의미의 부사이므로 주의해야 한다.

---

6 The writers of controversial articles / **seldom** reveal the sources of their information.
(A) less (B) very (C) not (D) **seldom**

해석| 논란이 되는 기사의 저자들은 좀처럼 정보의 출처를 밝히지 않는다.

(A) 더 적은 (B) 매우 (C) ~ 않은 (D) 거의 ~ 않는

어휘| controversial 논란이 되는 reveal 밝히다 source 출처

해설| 선택지를 보니 알맞은 부사를 고르는 문제. 문맥상 '거의 드러내지 않는다'는 부정의 의미가 되어야 하므로 정답은 (D). (C) not도 부정을 의미하는 부사지만 일반동사 앞에서 단독으로 쓰이지 않고 do not, does not의 형태로 쓰인다.

---

7 The research and development team will **soon** finish the automobile's engine design.
(A) still (B) yet (C) already (D) **soon**

해석| 연구 개발팀은 곧 그 자동차의 엔진 디자인을 끝낼 것이다.

(A) 아직도 (B) 아직, 이미 (C) 이미 (D) 곧

어휘| research and development(=R&D) 연구 개발 automobile 자동차

해설| 미래 시제 will finish가 쓰였으므로 정답은 (D). (B)는 주로 부정문이나 의문문에서 쓰인다. (C)는 완료 시제 문장과 어울려 쓰인다. 빈출 부사들은 예문을 중심으로 정확한 쓰임을 알아두자.

---

8 Due to the road widening project, / most of the employees arrived very **late** for work.
(A) **late** (B) lately (C) latest (D) later

해석| 도로 확장 사업 때문에 대부분의 직원들이 매우 늦게 회사에 도착했다.

어휘| widening 확장, 넓히는 것

해설| 내용상 빈칸 앞의 부사 very가 그 앞의 동사 arrived를 꾸미는 것이 아니므로, 빈칸에는 동사 arrived를 꾸미면서 동시에 부사 very의 꾸밈을 받는 부사가 들어가야 한다. 선택지의 (A), (B), (D)가 정답 후보. 문맥상 '늦게 회사에 도착했다'는 의미가 되어야 하므로 부사 late가 정답. lately는 '최근에', later는 '나중에'라는 의미로 문맥상 어울리지 않아 오답이다.

1 (A) **2** (D) **3** (A) **4** (C) **5** (D) **6** (D)

1 The staff at *In Our World Magazine* is dedicated / to publishing <u>informative</u> articles.
(A) informative (B) informs (C) to inform (D) has informed
해석 | 〈인 아워 월드 매거진〉 지의 직원은 유익한 기사를 발행하는 데에 전념한다.
어휘 | dedicate 전념하다, 헌신하다 informative 유익한

해설 | 선택지를 보니 빈칸에 들어갈 알맞은 품사를 고르는 문제. 빈칸은 뒤에 있는 명사 articles를 수식하는 형용사 자리이므로 선택지 중 형용사인 (A)가 정답.

2 Those / who plan to attend seminars abroad / need to get permission / from their <u>respective</u> supervisors.
(A) respectably (B) respect (C) respecting **(D) respective**
해석 | 해외 세미나에 참석할 계획인 사람들은 각자의 상사로부터 승인을 받아야 한다.
어휘 | permission 허락, 허가

해설 | 빈칸 앞뒤를 보고 〈한정사+형용사+명사〉 구조임을 파악하면, 빈칸이 형용사 자리임을 쉽게 알 수 있다. 따라서 정답은 형용사 (D).

3 Film critics have <u>highly</u> recommended the World War II movie / *Pacific Soldiers*.
(A) highly (B) highest (C) high (D) higher
해석 | 영화 평론가들은 세계 2차 대전 영화 〈퍼시픽 솔져스〉를 적극 추천했다.
어휘 | critic 평론가, 비평가 recommend 추천하다

해설 | 완료 시제를 이루는 have동사와 과거분사 recommended 사이에 올 수 있는 것은 부사뿐이다. 문맥상 '적극 추천하다'라는 의미가 자연스러우므로 '아주, 매우'라는 의미의 highly가 정답. 참고로, high는 부사로 '높게'의 의미이다.

4 The building for the headquarters of V&V Inc. / is <u>completely</u> new.
(A) completed (B) complete **(C) completely** (D) completing
해석 | V&V 주식회사의 본사 건물은 완전히 새것이다.
어휘 | completely 완전히

해설 | 빈칸이 없어도 완전한 문장이므로 빈칸은 부사 자리. 따라서 -ly 형태의 부사 (C)가 정답이다. 참고로 부사 completely는 빈칸 뒤 형용사 new를 수식하기 위해 쓰였다.

5-6

Thank you for choosing Bassell Tours. We've been operating exciting bus tours across the country for **approximately** thirty years, so we know how to make your trip perfect. We know you will enjoy your upcoming tour of Riverwell National Park. Enclosed you will find your ticket and information about your tour. As there is <u>limited</u> space for luggage, please follow the enclosed guidelines carefully so that everyone can place their belongings.

배슬 투어를 선택해 주셔서 감사합니다. 저희는 **약** 30년간 흥미로운 버스 투어를 전국적으로 운영해왔기에, 여러분의 여행을 완벽하게 하는 방법을 알고 있습니다. 저희는 여러분이 다가오는 리버웰 국립공원 투어를 즐기실 것이라고 확신합니다. 여러분의 표와 여행에 관한 정보를 동봉합니다. 수화물을 위한 공간이 **제한되어** 있기 때문에, 모두가 각자의 소지품을 둘 수 있도록 동봉된 지침을 꼼꼼히 따라 주시기 바랍니다.

어휘 | exciting 흥미로운 upcoming 다가오는, 곧 있을 Enclosed you will find ~을 동봉합니다 guideline 지침

5 We've been operating exciting bus tours / across the country for <u>approximately</u> thirty years, / so we know how to make your trip perfect.
(A) approximate (B) approximated (C) approximation
(D) approximately

해설 | 빈칸 없이도 문장이 완전하고 빈칸 뒤의 수량 표현 thirty로 보아 빈칸은 수량 표현을 수식하는 부사 자리임을 알 수 있다. 따라서 '대략'이라는 의미로 수량 표현과 자주 쓰이는 부사 approximately가 정답.

6 As there is <u>limited</u> space for luggage, / please follow the enclosed guidelines carefully / so that everyone can place their belongings.
(A) limit (B) limits (C) to limit **(D) limited**

해설 | 빈칸은 〈there+be동사〉 구조의 주어인 명사 space를 수식하는 형용사 자리이다. 따라서 과거분사형 형용사인 (D)가 정답.

VOCABULARY | 업무 어휘(1)   교재 131쪽

1 developments **2** alternative **3** demonstrated **4** responded **5** (C) **6** (C) **7** (B) **8** (A)

---

1 The article explains some of the latest (**developments** / analysts) / in technology.
해석 | 그 기사는 기술 영역의 몇몇 최근 발전에 대해 설명한다.

해설 | 괄호 앞의 형용사 latest와 어울릴 수 있는 명사를 골라야 한다. '기술 영역의 최근 발전'이라는 표현이 자연스러우므로 정답은 developments.

---

2 Finding an (**alternative** / preferred) supplier will reduce the restaurant's costs.
해석 | 대안이 될 만한 공급업체를 찾는 것이 그 식당의 비용을 감소시켜 줄 것이다.

해설 | 괄호 뒤 명사 supplier를 수식하여 문맥에 어울리는 형용사를 찾아야 한다. '대안이 될 업체를 찾는 것이 비용을 줄여 줄 것'이라는 내용이 자연스러우므로 정답은 alternative.

---

3 A sales representative (modified / **demonstrated**) the product's various functions / to customers.
해석 | 한 영업 사원이 손님들에게 제품의 다양한 기능에 대해 설명했다.
어휘 | various 다양한 function 기능

해설 | 괄호 뒤의 목적어인 the product's various functions와 어울리는 동사를 골라야 한다. '기능을 설명했다'라는 내용이 자연스러우므로 정답은 demonstrated.

---

4 A number of people (researched / **responded**) / to the customer satisfaction survey.
해석 | 많은 수의 사람들이 고객 만족 설문 조사에 응답했다.

해설 | 괄호 뒤의 전치사 to와 호응하여 목적어 the customer satisfaction survey를 취하는 동사를 골라야 한다. '설문 조사에 응답했다'는 내용이 자연스러우므로 정답은 responded.

---

5 Product developers set the <u>deadline</u> of April 22 / for unveiling a prototype.
(A) advice (B) income **(C) deadline** (D) possibility
해석 | 제품 개발자들은 시제품을 공개하는 마감일을 4월 22일로 설정했다.
(A) 조언 (B) 수입 (C) 마감일, 기한 (D) 가능성
어휘 | unveil 공개하다 prototype 시제품

해설 | 빈칸 뒤에 '동격'을 의미하는 전치사 of와 함께 구체적인 날짜 April 22가 등장한다. 동사 set의 목적어이면서 특정 날짜와 동격이 될 수 있는 명사는 '마감일'이라는 의미의 (C)이다.

---

6 Fillmore Couture hopes to <u>expand</u> its customer base / by creating a range of men's clothing.
(A) refer (B) require **(C) expand** (D) arrive
해석 | 필모어 쿠튀르 사는 다양한 남성 의류를 만들어서 고객층을 확대하고 싶어 한다.
(A) 언급하다 (B) 필요로 하다 (C) 확대하다 (D) 도착하다
어휘 | customer base 고객층 by *doing* ~함으로써

해설 | 문맥상 '다양한 남성 제품을 만듦으로써 고객층을 확대한다'는 내용이 자연스럽다. 따라서, '확대하다, 확장하다'라는 뜻의 (C)가 정답.

---

7 Once our new laptop computer has been developed, / it will be **available** / in all major electronics stores.
(A) responsible (B) available (C) desirable (D) flexible

해석| 우리 새로운 노트북 컴퓨터가 일단 개발되기만 하면, 모든 주요 전자제품점에서 구입할 수 있을 것이다.

(A) 책임 있는 (B) 구입할 수 있는 (C) 바람직한 (D) 융통성 있는

어휘| once 일단 ~하기만 하면 electronics 전자제품

해설| 빈칸이 포함된 문장의 주어인 it이 가리키는 것은 our new laptop computer이므로 신제품이 매장에서 '구입 가능하다'는 뜻으로 (B)가 알맞다. available은 '이용 가능한, 구매 가능한'이란 뜻으로, 사람을 주어로 하여 '시간이 나는'의 의미로도 쓰인다.

---

8 The market research team is **investigating** possible reasons / why the product does not appeal to customers.
(A) investigating (B) contacting (C) preferring (D) removing

해석| 시장 조사팀은 그 제품이 고객들의 관심을 끌지 못하는 이유로 가능한 것들을 조사하고 있다.

(A) 조사하다 (B) 연락하다 (C) 선호하다 (D) 없애다

어휘| appeal to ~의 관심을 끌다

해설| 선택지를 보니 빈칸 앞 is와 함께 진행시제로 쓰이는 알맞은 동사를 고르는 문제. 빈칸 뒤 명사 reasons와 어울려 '문제의 이유를 조사하다'라는 뜻이 되어야 알맞으므로 (A)가 정답.

ACTUAL TEST 실전 문제에 적용하기   교재 132쪽

1 (C) **2** (A) **3** (D) **4** (D) **5** (D) **6** (B) **7** (A) **8** (B) **9** (B) **10** (C) **11** (B) **12** (A)

---

1 The steps for replacing the air purifier's filter / are explained quite **clearly** / in the user manual.
(A) clearing (B) clearable (C) clearly (D) clearest

해석| 공기청정기의 필터를 교체하는 순서는 사용설명서에 꽤 명확하게 설명되어 있다.

어휘| step 단계 air purifier 공기청정기 clearly 명확하게 user manual 사용설명서

해설| **부사 자리**
빈칸은 부사 quite의 수식을 받으면서 동시에 동사 are explained를 꾸며 주는 부사가 들어가야 알맞으므로 (C)가 정답.

---

2 Mr. Peterson has **analyzed** the consumer survey data / and is satisfied with the results.
(A) analyzed (B) regarded (C) required (D) vacated

해석| 피터슨 씨는 소비자 설문 조사 자료를 분석했고 그 결과에 만족한다.

(A) 분석하다 (B) 간주하다 (C) 필요로 하다 (D) (건물을) 비우다

어휘| analyze 분석하다 be satisfied with ~에 만족하다 result 결과

해설| **동사 어휘 analyze**
and 뒤에 이어지는 문장에서 결과(the results)에 만족한다고 했는데, 이는 설문 조사를 분석한 결과라고 보는 게 타당하므로 '분석하다'라는 뜻의 (A)가 정답.

---

3 Immigrants are eligible for citizenship / after they have lived in the country **continuously** / for four years.
(A) continue (B) continued (C) continuous (D) continuously

해석| 이민자들은 4년 동안 계속해서 그 나라에 거주한 이후에 시민권을 받을 자격이 된다.

어휘| immigrant 이민자 be eligible for ~의 자격이 있다 citizenship 시민권 continuously 계속해서

해설| **부사 자리**
빈칸이 없어도 완전한 문장이므로 빈칸은 부사 자리일 확률이 높다. 문맥상 동사 have lived를 수식하는 말이 들어가야 하므로 빈칸에 들어갈 수 있는 것은 부사인 continuously뿐이다.

---

4 Conference fees are fully **refundable** / to participants / who cancel their registration / by May 30.
(A) refunding (B) refund (C) refunds (D) refundable

해석| 학회 참가비는 5월 30일까지 등록을 취소한 참가자들에게 전액 환불 가능하다.

어휘| fee 요금 fully 완전히 refundable 환불 가능한 cancel 취소하다

해설| **형용사 자리**
빈칸은 be동사 are의 보어 자리이자, 빈칸 앞의 부사 fully의 수식을 받는 형용사 자리이다. 따라서 (D)가 정답이다.

---

5 Security cameras were **strategically** placed / in the building's main hallways.
(A) strategy (B) strategic (C) strategize (D) **strategically**

해석| 감시 카메라는 전략적으로 건물의 중앙 복도에 배치되었다.

어휘| strategically 전략적으로 hallway 복도

해설| **부사 자리**
빈칸 앞뒤의 be동사 were와 과거분사 placed는 수동태 동사의 형태로, 이 사이에 올 수 있는 것은 부사뿐이다. 따라서 선택지 중 -ly 형태로 끝나는 부사 (D)가 정답.

---

6 Management wants to find a **lasting** solution / to the fast employee turnover / at the company.
(A) lastly (B) **lasting** (C) lasts (D) lasted

해석| 경영진은 회사에서의 빠른 직원 이직률에 대한 지속적인 해결 방법을 찾길 원한다.

어휘| solution 해법, 해결책 turnover 이직률

해설| **형용사 자리**
빈칸 앞뒤를 보면 〈한정사+형용사+명사〉 구조이다. 빈칸은 빈칸 뒤 명사 solution을 수식하는 형용사 자리. 그러므로 -ing 형태로 굳어져 형용사로 쓰이는 lasting이 정답.
오답| (D) lasted도 마찬가지로 p.p. 형태이지만, 단독으로 형용사로 쓰이지는 않으므로 답이 될 수 없다.

---

7 Family members of the play's performers / are **exempt** from admission fees / on opening night.
(A) **exempt** (B) distinct (C) ready (D) delayed

해석| 그 연극에 나오는 배우들의 가족들은 개막일 밤에 입장료가 면제된다.
(A) 면제되는 (B) 뚜렷한 (C) 준비된 (D) 지연된

어휘| performer 연기자 admission fee 입장료

해설| **형용사 어휘 exempt**
문맥상 '배우의 가족들은 입장료에서 면제된다'는 의미가 자연스러우므로 정답은 빈칸 뒤 from과 어울려 be exempt from 형태로 '~에서 면제되다'라는 뜻으로 쓰이는 (A).
오답| (B) distinct도 뒤에 전치사 from과 함께 쓰이는데, be distinct from은 '~와 다르다, ~와 구별되다'라는 뜻으로 문맥상 적절하지 않다.

---

8 The sales figures for this month / are **remarkably** similar / to expectations.
(A) remarks (B) **remarkably** (C) remarked (D) remark

해석| 이번 달 매출수치는 기대치와 매우 유사하다.

어휘| sales figure 매출수치, 매출액 remarkably 매우, 현저히 expectation 기대

해설| **부사 자리**
빈칸이 없어도 완전한 문장이므로 빈칸은 부사 자리. 문맥상 빈칸은 뒤의 형용사 similar를 꾸며 '매우 유사한'이라는 의미를 나타내야 한다. 따라서 정답은 (B).

9-12

Male Skincare Products Gaining Popularity

In a recent study, close to 75 percent of males in the nation responded that they **regularly** use some kind of skin-treatment product. **This study was conducted by *Lyke Monthly*.** The full findings will be published in the magazine's next issue.

After examining the data, many cosmetics companies now plan to carry out their own **investigative** studies. They want to determine the needs and **expectations** of men who purchase and use skincare products.

남성 스킨케어 제품, 인기를 얻다

최근 조사에서 국내 남성의 약 75%가 **정기적으로** 피부관리 제품 종류를 사용한다고 응답했다. **이 연구는 〈라이크 먼슬리〉 지에서 실시되었다.** 전체 결과 내용은 잡지의 다음 호에 게재될 예정이다.

데이터를 검토한 후에, 많은 화장품 회사들은 현재 직접 **조사** 연구를 시행할 계획이다. 그들은 피부관리 제품을 구입해서 사용하는 남성들의 요구와 **기대를** 알아낼 수 있기를 바라고 있다.

Industry leader NTS Cosmetics says it could expand its skincare lines for men by up to 20 percent this year. Other companies are likely to do the same if the decision proves profitable.

시장 선두업체인 NTC 코스메틱스 사는 남성용 피부관리 제품을 올해 최대 20%까지 확대할 수도 있다고 말한다. 이 결정이 수익성이 있다고 판명되면 다른 업체들도 똑같이 할 가능성이 높다.

어휘 | gain 얻다 regularly 정기적으로, 자주 conduct 실시하다 issue (정기 간행물의) 호 examine 조사하다 cosmetics 화장품 carry out (조사 등을) 수행하다 determine 알아내다 expand 확대하다 up to 최대 ~까지 be likely to *do* ~할 가능성이 있다 prove 증명하다

9 In a recent study, / close to 75 percent of males in the nation / responded / that they <u>regularly</u> use some kind of skin-treatment product.
(A) regular **(B) regularly** (C) regulation (D) regulating

해설 | 부사 자리
빈칸이 없어도 문장이 완전하므로 빈칸은 뒤의 동사 use를 꾸며주는 부사 자리이다. 따라서 -ly로 끝나는 부사인 (B)가 정답.

10 (A) If you wish to participate, please respond to the survey.
(B) The most popular product is a moisturizing lotion.
(C) This study was conducted by *Lyke Monthly*.
(D) Nevertheless, several problems were discovered.
(A) 참가하고 싶으면, 설문 조사에 응하면 된다.
(B) 가장 인기 있는 제품은 수분 공급 로션이다.
(C) 이 연구는 〈라이크 먼슬리〉 지에서 실시되었다.
(D) 그럼에도 불구하고, 몇몇 문제들이 발견되었다.

해설 | 알맞은 문장 고르기
빈칸 다음 문장에서 설문 조사의 전체 결과가 '잡지의 다음 호'에 실린다고 했으므로 이 연구가 잡지사에 의해 시행되었음을 알 수 있다. 따라서 그러한 내용을 담고 있는 문장 (C)가 정답.

11 After examining the data, / many cosmetics companies now plan to carry out their own <u>investigative</u> studies.
(A) investigate **(B) investigative** (C) investigated
(D) to investigate

해설 | 형용사 자리
빈칸 앞의 소유격 their와 빈칸 뒤의 명사 studies를 보면 〈한정사+형용사+명사〉의 구조임을 알 수 있다. 따라서 빈칸에는 형용사인 (B)가 들어가는 것이 적절하다.
오답 | 과거분사 형태인 (C) investigated도 '조사된'의 의미를 가지는 형용사로 쓰일 수 있지만, 문맥상 '조사된 연구를 시행하다'는 어색하므로 정답이 될 수 없다.

12 They want to determine the needs and <u>expectations</u> of men / who purchase and use skincare products.
(A) expectations (B) invitations (C) variations (D) relations
(A) 기대 (B) 초대, 초청 (C) 변화, 차이 (D) 관계

해설 | 명사 어휘 expectation
잡지사에서 시행한 설문 조사 결과를 보고, 각 화장품 회사에서 시행할 조사 연구의 목적을 밝히고 있는 문장이다. 따라서 소비자들의 제품에 대한 수요와 함께 '기대'를 알아내는 것이 조사 연구의 목적으로 자연스러우므로 정답은 (A)이다.

UNIT 08 전치사

1 전치사의 개념과 쓰임

교재 137쪽

1 complaints **2** us **3** for **4** after **5** (B) **6** (D) **7** (B) **8** (C)

---

1 The staff members of ABK Appliances / respond to (complain / **complaints**) / from its customers / promptly.

해석| ABK 가전회사의 직원들은 고객들의 불만에 즉시 대응한다.

해설| 전치사 to 뒤에는 명사나 대명사, 동명사 등이 들어가야 한다. 따라서 명사인 complaints가 정답. 참고로 문장의 동사 respond는 자동사라 전치사 to와 어울려 목적어를 취한다.

---

2 Feel free to leave your luggage / with (we / **us**) during the tour.

해석| 투어를 하시는 동안 얼마든지 짐은 저희에게 맡겨두세요.

어휘| feel free to *do* 마음대로 ~하다

해설| 전치사 뒤에 나오는 명사는 전치사의 목적어로 취급한다. 따라서 전치사 with 다음에는 목적격 대명사인 us를 써야 한다. we는 주격이므로 빈칸에 들어갈 수 없다.

---

3 A large room (some / **for**) hosting parties / is located / at the back of the restaurant.

해석| 파티를 열기 위한 대형 룸은 식당 뒤편에 있습니다.

어휘| be located at ~에 위치해 있다

해설| hosting parties는 주어인 A large room을 수식하는 어구가 되어야 한다. 동명사와 함께 쓰여 명사를 수식하는 형용사 역할을 할 수 있는 것은 전치사이므로 for가 정답.

---

4 The office building will be sold / (**after** / later) the holiday season.

해석| 그 사무실용 빌딩은 휴가철 이후에 팔릴 것이다.

어휘| holiday 휴가, 휴일

해설| 괄호 앞 동사 will be sold는 수동태로 목적어를 취할 수 없으므로 괄호에는 괄호 뒤의 명사 the holiday season과 어울려 부사구 역할을 할 수 있는 전치사가 들어가야 한다. 따라서 '~ 후에'를 뜻하는 전치사 after가 정답.

---

5 Several methods of **payment** / can be used / when making purchases / at the festival's booths.
(A) pays **(B) payment** (C) payable (D) pay

해석| 축제 부스에서 구매를 할 때 몇 가지 지불 방식을 사용할 수 있다.

어휘| payment 지불 make a purchase 물건을 사다

해설| 전치사 of 뒤에는 명사 역할을 하는 말이 올 수 있다. 따라서 명사인 (B)와 (D)가 정답 후보. 문맥상 '몇 가지 지불 방식을 이용할 수 있다'는 의미가 되어야 하므로 '지불'이라는 뜻의 명사 (B)가 정답. pay는 '급료, 보수'라는 의미이다.

---

6 The west parking lot will be closed / **until** Friday due to maintenance work.
(A) already (B) those (C) some **(D) until**

해석| 서쪽 주차장은 보수 작업으로 인해 금요일까지 폐쇄될 것이다.

(A) 이미 (B) 그것들 (C) 일부의, 몇몇의 (D) ~까지

어휘| parking lot 주차장 close 폐쇄하다

해설| 빈칸 앞이 완전한 문장이므로 빈칸 이하는 수식어구가 되는 것이 적절하다. Friday라는 명사 앞에 붙어 '금요일까지'의 의미인 수식어구를 이루는 것은 전치사인 (D)이다. 여기서 until Friday는 동사 will be closed를 수식하는 부사 역할을 한다.

---

7 The company's profits have increased dramatically / **over** the last few years.
(A) more **(B) over** (C) about (D) further

해석| 그 기업의 수익은 지난 몇 년간 극적으로 증가했다.

(A) 더 많은 (B) ~ 동안 (C) ~에 대해 (D) 더 멀리

어휘| profit 수익, 이익

해설| 선택지가 전치사와 부사로 구성되어 있다. 빈칸 앞이 완전한 문장이므로, 빈칸 이하는 수식어구가 되어야 함을 알 수 있다. the last few years라는 명사구를 이끌어 부사구로 만들 수 있는 것은 전치사이므로 (B)와 (C)가 정답 후보. 문맥상 '지난 몇 년간'이라는 의미가 되어야 하므로 '~ 동안'이라는 의미의 (B)가 정답.

8 The building contractor is still far / from **completing** the lobby renovation.
(A) completed (B) will complete (C) completing
(D) to complete

해석│ 그 건설업자는 로비 개조공사를 끝내려면 아직 한참 멀었다.

어휘│ contractor 도급업자, 계약자

해설│ 빈칸 앞에 전치사 from이 있으므로, 빈칸은 전치사의 목적어에 해당하는 명사, 대명사 또는 동명사가 들어갈 자리이다. 따라서 동명사인 (C)가 정답.

---

2 시점·기간을 나타내는 전치사

교재 139쪽

1 in **2** for **3** by **4** throughout **5** (A) **6** (C) **7** (B) **8** (A)

---

1 Mr. Andrews went to London / (in / on) December for a business trip.

해석│ 앤드루스 씨는 12월에 출장으로 런던에 갔다.

해설│ 괄호 안의 전치사 in과 on 모두 시간을 나타내는 말 앞에서 '~에'라는 뜻으로 쓰인다. December와 같이 상대적으로 긴 시간인 월 앞에 쓰이는 전치사는 in이다. on은 주로 날짜와 요일 같은 상대적으로 짧은 시간을 나타내는 명사 앞에 쓰인다.

---

2 The engineer is going to stay in the city / (**for** / during) three days / to inspect the factory.

해석│ 그 기술자는 공장을 시찰하기 위해서 3일 동안 그 도시에 머무를 것이다.

해설│ '~ 동안'이란 뜻의 for와 during의 쓰임을 구별하는 문제이다. for는 뒤에 숫자를 동반한 구체적 기간이 오고, during 뒤에는 특정한 행사, 사건을 나타내는 명사가 온다는 차이점이 있다. 이 경우에는 뒤에 three days라는 숫자 표현을 동반한 기간이 나오므로 for를 써야 한다.

---

3 Ms. Morgan must submit the leave form / to her supervisor / (**by** / until) tomorrow morning.

해석│ 모건 씨는 내일 오전까지 그녀의 상사에게 휴가 신청서를 제출해야 한다.

어휘│ leave 휴가; 떠나다

해설│ '~까지'라는 의미의 전치사 by와 until을 구별하는 문제이다. by는 동작의 완료에 초점을 두고 until은 동작의 계속되는 상태를 강조한다. 이 경우에는 신청서 제출이 내일 오전까지 '완료' 되어야 한다는 내용이므로 by를 써야 한다.

---

4 Sitio Resort offers free scuba diving lessons to its guests / (on / **throughout**) the summer.

해석│ 시티오 리조트는 여름 내내 투숙객들에게 무료 스쿠버 다이빙 강습을 제공한다.

해설│ the summer라는 기간을 나타내는 말 앞에 올 수 있는 전치사는 '~ 동안 죽, 내내'라는 뜻의 throughout이다. '여름에'라고 할 때는 전치사 in을 써서 in summer로 쓴다.

---

5 The interest rate on home mortgages has remained steady / **over** the past year.
(A) **over** (B) to (C) out (D) from

해석│ 지난해 동안 주택담보 대출 이자율이 일정하게 유지되었다.

(A) ~ 동안 (B) ~로 (C) ~ 밖으로 (D) ~에서

어휘│ interest rate 이율 home mortgage 주택담보 대출 steady 일정한, 안정된

해설│ 빈칸은 the past year를 목적어로 취해서 동사 has remained를 꾸미는 부사구를 만드는 전치사 자리이다. '지난해 동안에 이자율이 그대로였다'는 의미가 되어야 자연스러우므로 '~동안'이라는 뜻의 (A)가 정답. 참고로 over는 현재완료 시제와 주로 어울려 쓰인다.

---

6 The store employees discussed window display ideas / for the products / **during** the meeting.
(A) about (B) into (C) **during** (D) along

해석│ 그 가게의 직원들은 회의 시간 동안 제품의 창가 진열 방법에 대해 논의했다.

(A) ~에 대해 (B) ~ 안으로 (C) ~ 동안 (D) ~을 따라

어휘│ window display 창가 진열

해설│ 선택지를 보니 빈칸에 알맞은 전치사를 고르는 문제. 문맥상 '회의 시간 동안'이라는 뜻이 되어야 알맞다. the meeting이라는 행사를 나타내는 명사가 나왔으므로 (C)가 정답.

---

7 Each application for renewing a driver's license / is processed / **within** two weeks.
(A) around **(B) within** (C) through (D) behind

해석 | 운전면허증 갱신을 위한 각각의 신청은 2주 내에 처리된다.
(A) ~ 근처에 (B) ~ 이내에 (C) ~ 동안 죽 (D) ~ 뒤에

어휘 | renew 갱신하다

해설 | 빈칸에 알맞은 전치사를 고르는 문제. 빈칸 뒤 two weeks는 신청을 처리하는 데 소요되는 기간을 의미하는 것이 자연스러우므로 '~ 이내에'라는 뜻인 (B)가 알맞다.

---

8 Visitors are required to pass through metal detectors / **before** entering Panthec Towers.
(A) before (B) across (C) around (D) until

해석 | 방문객들은 팬텍 타워스에 입장하기 전에 금속 탐지 장치를 통과하도록 요구된다.
(A) ~ 전에 (B) ~을 가로질러 (C) ~의 주위에 (D) ~까지

어휘 | be required to *do* ~하도록 요구되다 pass through 거쳐[지나]가다 metal detector 금속 탐지 장치

해설 | 빈칸에 적절한 전치사를 고르는 문제. 문맥상 타워에 입장하기 '전에' 금속 탐지 장치를 통과하는 것이 자연스러우므로 적절한 전치사는 '~ 전에'를 뜻하는 (A)이다. 빈칸 뒤의 entering은 전치사 before의 목적어 역할을 하는 동명사이다.

---

3 장소·방향을 나타내는 전치사　　　　　　　　　교재 141쪽

1 at　**2** between　**3** above　**4** toward　**5** (C)　**6** (C)　**7** (D)　**8** (B)

1 Ms. Bingley arrives (on / **at**) the office / before 9:00 A.M. every day.

해석 | 빙글리 씨는 매일 사무실에 오전 9시 이전에 도착한다.

해설 | 괄호 뒤의 명사 the office와 어울려 '사무실'이라는 의미를 나타낼 수 있는 것은 전치사 at이다. on은 '~의 위에[표면에]'라는 의미이므로 적절하지 않다.

---

2 Diners / who order the lunch set / can choose (**between** / among) soup and salad.

해석 | 런치 세트를 주문한 식사 손님들은 수프와 샐러드 중에서 선택할 수 있다.

어휘 | diner 식사 손님 choose 선택하다

해설 | between과 among은 둘 다 '~ 사이에, ~ 중에'라는 뜻이지만, between은 대상이 둘일 때, among은 대상이 불특정 다수일 때 쓰인다는 차이점이 있다. 이 경우는 대상이 soup와 salad 두 개이므로 between을 써야 한다.

---

3 Security placed a surveillance camera / (under / **above**) the entrance of every office.

해석 | 보안 부서는 모든 사무실의 입구 위에 감시 카메라를 설치했다.

어휘 | surveillance camera 감시 카메라

해설 | 문맥상 '감시 카메라를 입구 위에 설치했다'는 것이 자연스러우므로 '~보다 위쪽에'라는 의미의 전치사 above가 정답. under은 '~보다 아래쪽에'라는 의미이므로 적절하지 않다.

---

4 Shoppers in the supermarket / rushed / (**toward** / throughout) the exit / when the fire alarm went off.

해석 | 화재 경보가 울리자 슈퍼마켓 안의 쇼핑객들이 출구를 향해 달려갔다.

어휘 | rush 서두르다 exit 출구 fire alarm 화재 경보 go off (경보가) 울리다

해설 | 문맥상 '출구를 향해 달려갔다'는 말이 되어야 자연스럽다. '~을 향해'라는 뜻으로 방향을 나타낼 때 전치사 toward를 쓴다. throughout은 '~의 도처에'라는 뜻이므로 문맥상 어울리지 않는다.

---

5 The name and address of the recipient / should be clearly written / **on** the outside of the package.
(A) with (B) to **(C) on** (D) for

해석 | 수령인의 이름과 주소가 소포 바깥쪽에 분명하게 쓰여져 있어야 한다.
(A) ~와 함께 (B) ~로 (C) ~ 위에 (D) ~을 위해, ~을 향해

어휘 | recipient 수령인 outside 겉, 바깥쪽

해설 | 선택지를 보니 빈칸에 알맞은 전치사를 고르는 문제. 소포 겉면에 수령인의 이름과 주소를 적으라는 내용으로, '~ 위에[표면에]'라는 뜻의 전치사 (C)가 정답이다.

6 Medical history files for all the patients / should be kept / <u>in</u> this cabinet.
(A) into   (B) through   **(C) in**   (D) at
해석ㅣ 모든 환자의 의료기록 파일은 이 캐비닛에 보관되어야 한다.
(A) ~ 안으로 (B) ~의 도처에 (C) ~ 안에 (D) ~에
어휘ㅣ medical history 의료기록   patient 환자

해설ㅣ 빈칸 뒤의 명사구 this cabinet은 파일들이 보관되는 장소를 나타낸다. 따라서 캐비닛 '안에' 보관되어야 한다는 말이 되어야 하므로 전치사 in이 정답.

7 Sheila Colton <u>from</u> Dhalster Network / was a speaker / at the mass media summit.
(A) about   (B) by   (C) to   **(D) from**
해석ㅣ 달스터 네트워크 사의 셰일라 콜튼 씨는 대중매체 회담의 발표자였다.
(A) ~에 대해 (B) ~에 의해 (C) ~까지 (D) ~로부터
어휘ㅣ mass media 대중매체   summit 정상 회담

해설ㅣ 빈칸 앞뒤 말의 관계를 살펴보면, 문맥상 '달스터 네트워크 사 소속의 셰일라 콜튼 씨'라는 의미가 되어야 함을 알 수 있다. 따라서 빈칸에는 '~로부터'의 의미로 출신, 출처 등을 나타내는 전치사 (D)가 들어가는 것이 알맞다.

8 Ancient Egyptian artifacts are on display / <u>throughout</u> the museum.
(A) against   **(B) throughout**   (C) onto   (D) toward
해석ㅣ 고대 이집트의 유물들은 박물관 도처에 전시되어 있다.
(A) ~에 기대어 (B) ~의 도처에 (C) ~로 (D) ~을 향해
어휘ㅣ ancient 고대의   Egyptian 이집트의   artifact 유물, 인공물

해설ㅣ 문맥상 '유물들이 박물관 도처에 전시되어 있다'는 내용이 자연스러우므로 '~의 도처에[전역에]'의 의미를 가진 (B)가 정답.

---

4 그 외 주요 전치사
교재 143쪽

1 by   **2** without   **3** on   **4** Despite   **5** (D)   **6** (A)   **7** (C)   **8** (A)

1 Many travelers were attracted / (**by** / of) the airline's generous rewards program.
해석ㅣ 항공사의 후한 보상 프로그램에 의해 많은 여행객들이 유치되었다.
어휘ㅣ reward 보상

해설ㅣ '항공사의 후한 보상 프로그램'은 많은 여행객들을 유치하기 위한 수단에 해당하므로, '~에 의해'라는 의미로 수단을 나타내는 전치사 by가 들어가야 알맞다.

2 Applicants (except / **without**) at least three years of experience / will not be considered.
해석ㅣ 최소한 3년의 경력이 없는 지원자는 대상자로 고려되지 않을 것이다.
어휘ㅣ consider 고려하다, 숙고하다

해설ㅣ 문맥상 '경력이 없는 지원자는 고려 대상이 되지 않는다'는 의미가 되어야 하므로 '~ 없이'라는 의미의 전치사 without이 정답. except는 '~을 제외하고'라는 뜻으로 어울리지 않아서 오답.

3 The seminar (**on** / by) good leadership / will be held / this Thursday.
해석ㅣ 좋은 리더십에 대한 세미나가 이번 주 목요일에 열릴 것이다.

해설ㅣ will be held가 문장의 동사이므로 괄호부터 leadership까지는 주어인 seminar를 꾸며주는 수식어구이다. 따라서 '~에 대해'라는 의미로 관련 주제를 나타내는 전치사 on이 적절하다.

4 (**Despite** / Throughout) the bad weather, / management did not cancel the anniversary party.
해석ㅣ 궂은 날씨에도 불구하고, 경영진은 기념 파티를 취소하지 않았다.
어휘ㅣ management 경영진

해설ㅣ 문맥상 '궂은 날씨에도 불구하고 행사를 취소하지 않았다'라는 내용이 되어야 자연스럽다. 따라서 '~에도 불구하고'라는 양보의 의미를 가진 전치사 Despite가 정답. throughout은 '~ 동안 죽' 또는 '~도처에[전역에]'라는 의미.

5 All waterproof clothes <u>except</u> ski jackets / are eligible for a substantial discount / this week.
(A) between   (B) along   (C) before   **(D) except**
해석 | 스키 재킷을 제외한 모든 방수 의류는 이번 주에 상당한 할인이 주어진다.
(A) ~ 사이에 (B) ~을 따라 (C) ~ 전에 (D) ~을 제외하고
어휘 | waterproof 방수의 substantial 상당한

해설 | 빈칸 뒤의 ski jackets는 빈칸 앞 clothes의 한 종류이다. 문맥상 '스키 재킷을 제외한 모든 의류에 할인이 주어진다'는 내용이 자연스러우므로 '~을 제외하고'라는 뜻의 (D)가 정답.

---

6 The plant manager requested additional machines / <u>for</u> sealing product packages.
(A) for   (B) within   (C) through   (D) into
해석 | 공장 관리자는 제품 포장을 밀봉하기 위한 추가 기계를 요구했다.
(A) ~을 위해 (B) ~ 이내에 (C) ~ 동안 (D) ~ 안으로
어휘 | additional 추가적인

해설 | 빈칸 이하는 빈칸 앞의 명사 machines의 목적에 대해 설명하고 있으므로 '~을 위해'라는 뜻을 가진 전치사 (A)가 정답이다.

---

7 The Tourism Department collaborated <u>with</u> the Environment Bureau / to promote the Maishee Caves.
(A) out   (B) up   **(C) with**   (D) at
해석 | 관광청은 메이쉬 동굴을 홍보하기 위해 환경부와 협력했다.
(A) ~ 밖에 (B) ~ 위로 (C) ~와 함께 (D) ~에
어휘 | collaborate 협력하다. 공동으로 작업하다 bureau 부서[국] promote 홍보하다 cave 동굴

해설 | 문맥상 '관광청이 환경부와 협력했다'는 의미가 되는 것이 적절하므로 '~와 함께'라는 의미의 전치사 with가 정답이다. 참고로 with는 '~으로'라는 도구, 수단의 의미도 갖는다.

---

8 The manager of the Laurel building / told Mr. Patterson / <u>about</u> the repaving of the parking lot.
(A) about   (B) between   (C) only   (D) as
해석 | 로렐 빌딩의 관리자는 패터슨 씨에게 주차장을 다시 포장하는 것에 대해 말했다.
(A) ~에 대해 (B) ~ 사이에 (C) 오직 (D) ~로서
어휘 | repave 다시 포장하다

해설 | 빈칸 이하가 관리자가 패터슨 씨에게 말해 준 내용이므로, '~에 대해'라는 뜻으로 관련 주제를 나타내는 전치사 (A)가 정답. (C) only는 부사이므로 답이 될 수 없다.

---

5 | **특별한 형태의 전치사와 관용 표현**   교재 145쪽
1 because of **2** regardless of **3** considering **4** Following **5** (C) **6** (B) **7** (D) **8** (B)

---

1 Budrow Books published more of the author's novels / (**because of** / instead of) high demand.
해석 | 버드로우 출판사는 높은 수요 때문에 그 작가의 소설을 더 많이 출판했다.
어휘 | author 작가, 저자

해설 | 빈칸 이하에서 출판사가 소설을 더 많이 출판하게 된 이유에 대해 설명하고 있으므로 '~ 때문에'라는 의미를 가진 구전치사 because of가 정답. instead of는 '~ 대신에'라는 의미이다.

---

2 Mr. Young wants to purchase the antique desk / (on behalf of / **regardless of**) the price.
해석 | 영 씨는 가격에 상관없이 그 골동품 책상을 구입하기를 원한다.
어휘 | antique 골동품(의)

해설 | the price는 물건 구매를 결정하는 요소 중 하나이므로 문맥상 '~에 상관없이'라는 뜻의 regardless of가 알맞다. on behalf of는 '~을 대신[대표]해서'라는 뜻이다.

---

3 You'll probably arrive at the station late, / (**considering** / considered) the heavy traffic.
해석 | 교통 혼잡을 고려하면, 당신은 아마도 역에 늦게 도착할 것이다.
어휘 | probably 아마도

해설 | 괄호 앞이 완전한 문장이므로 괄호부터 문장 끝까지는 문장을 꾸미는 수식어구가 되어야 한다. 괄호 뒤의 명사와 함께 부사구를 이루는 전치사인 considering이 정답. considering은 -ing 형태의 전치사임을 기억해두자.

---

4 (Following / Follow) an interview with supervisors, / the most qualified applicant will be hired.

해석| 관리자와의 면접 후에, 가장 적격인 지원자가 채용될 것이다.

어휘| qualified 자격이 있는

해설| 빈칸부터 콤마까지가 문장 전체를 수식하는 수식어구 역할을 하고 있으므로, 빈칸은 빈칸 뒤 명사구를 이끌어 부사구를 이루는 전치사가 와야 한다. 따라서 -ing로 끝나는 형태의 전치사인 Following이 정답.

---

5 **Instead of** distributing paper copies of the monthly newsletter, / the company will post it online.
(A) Due to (B) Beyond **(C) Instead of** (D) Among

해석| 회사는 월간 사보의 종이본을 배포하는 대신, 온라인에 그것을 게시할 것이다.

(A) ~로 인해 (B) ~ 너머에 (C) ~ 대신에 (D) ~ 사이에

해설| 선택지를 보니 빈칸에 알맞은 전치사를 고르는 문제. 사보의 종이본을 배포하는 (distributing paper copies)것과 그것을 온라인에 게재하는(post it online)것은 서로 대치될 수 있는 것이므로, 빈칸에는 '~ 대신에'라는 뜻의 (C)가 적절하다.

---

6 Please speak to Dr. Walsh / about any concerns / **regarding** the medical treatment.
(A) regards **(B) regarding** (C) regarded (D) regard

해석| 의료 처치에 관해 우려되는 점은 무엇이든 월시 박사님께 말씀하세요.

어휘| concern 《pl.》 걱정, 염려 medical treatment 의학적 치료[처치]

해설| 빈칸 이하가 없어도 문장이 완전하므로, 빈칸은 빈칸 뒤 명사를 이끌어 수식어구를 만드는 전치사 자리. regarding은 -ing의 형태이지만 '~에 관해'라는 뜻의 전치사로 쓰이므로 (B)가 정답.

---

7 **According to** a survey, / 16 percent of office workers ride bikes to work.
(A) In addition to (B) Instead of (C) In front of **(D) According to**

해석| 설문 조사에 따르면, 사무직 근로자의 16%가 회사에 자전거로 출근한다.

(A) ~ 외에 (B) ~ 대신에 (C) ~ 앞에 (D) ~에 따르면

해설| 의미상 알맞은 구전치사를 고르는 문제이다. 빈칸 뒤 '설문 조사'는 구체적인 수치의 출처이므로, '~에 따르면'이라는 뜻의 구전치사 (D)가 정답.

---

8 YanTech creates software programs, / **including** quality-assurance applications, / for manufacturing companies.
(A) below **(B) including** (C) between (D) regarding

해석| 얀테크 사는 품질 보증 애플리케이션을 포함한, 제조업체용 소프트웨어를 만든다.

(A) ~ 보다 아래쪽에 (B) ~을 포함해서 (C) ~ 사이에 (D) ~에 관해

어휘| quality-assurance 품질 보증 application 응용 프로그램

해설| 선택지를 보니 알맞은 전치사를 고르는 문제이다. 빈칸 이하에서 얀테크 사가 제공하는 소프트웨어에 포함된 애플리케이션을 언급하고 있으므로 빈칸에는 '~을 포함해서'라는 의미의 -ing 형태의 전치사 including이 들어가는 것이 알맞다.

REVIEW 핵심 POINT 다시 보기 교재 147쪽

1 (D) **2** (D) **3** (D) **4** (C) **5** (C) **6** (A)

---

1 Visit the nearest bank / in person to get more information **about** small business loans.
(A) out (B) around (C) to **(D) about**

해석| 소기업 대출에 대해 더 자세한 정보를 얻으시려면 가까운 은행을 직접 방문하세요.

(A) ~ 밖에 (B) ~ 근처에 (C) ~로 (D) ~에 대해

어휘| in person 직접 loan 대출

해설| 빈칸 이하가 information을 수식하여 '무엇에 관한' 정보인지를 나타내고 있으므로 관련 주제를 나타내는 전치사 (D)가 정답.

2 The new books' titles must be entered into the database / **with** the product bar codes.
(A) by (B) onto (C) at **(D) with**

해석│ 신규 도서의 제목은 제품 바코드와 함께 데이터베이스에 입력되어야 한다.

(A) ~까지 (B) ~ 위에 (C) ~에 (D) ~와 함께

어휘│ title 제목, 표제 enter into ~에 입력하다

해설│ 문맥상 책의 제목과 책의 바코드가 '함께' 데이터베이스에 입력되는 것이 자연스러우므로 '~와 함께'라는 의미의 전치사 (D)가 들어가야 한다.

---

3 A significant amount of air pollution / comes **from** private cars.
(A) after (B) for (C) down **(D) from**

해석│ 엄청난 양의 대기 오염이 자가용 자동차로부터 발생된다.

(A) ~ 후에 (B) ~을 위해 (C) ~ 아래로 (D) ~로 부터

어휘│ significant 커다란, 중요한 air pollution 대기 오염 come from ~에서 나오다 private 사유의, 개인 소유의

해설│ 문맥상 '대기 오염이 자가용 자동차로부터 발생된다'라는 것이 자연스러우므로 빈칸에는 출처, 기원을 나타내는 전치사 from이 들어가는 것이 적절하다. 따라서 정답은 (D).

---

4 The board met several times / **before** approving the company's new logo design.
(A) beyond (B) among **(C) before** (D) within

해석│ 이사회는 회사의 새로운 로고 디자인을 승인하기 전에 몇 차례 만났다.

(A) ~ 너머 (B) ~ 사이에 (C) ~ 전에 (D) ~ 내에

어휘│ logo 로고, 상징

해설│ 선택지를 보니 빈칸에 알맞은 전치사를 고르는 문제. 문맥상 '디자인을 승인하기 전에 만났다'는 내용이 되어야 자연스러우므로 정답은 (C).

5-6

New Exhibition at the Toscano Gallery

April 28—The Toscano Gallery has announced plans to host an exhibition of paintings by Luisella DeRose that will start **on** May 2. Ms. DeRose is among the nation's top artists, and she has won numerous awards for her work.

The exhibition will feature watercolor paintings of the Italian countryside. Museum visitors can take advantage of the informative signs located throughout the exhibition. **In addition to** explanations about the background of each painting, these feature original poems written by the artist.

토스카노 갤러리의 새로운 전시회

4월 28일—토스카노 갤러리는 5월 **2일에** 시작되는 루이셀라 드로즈의 그림 전시회를 개최할 계획을 발표했다. 드로즈 씨는 국내 최정상의 미술가 중 하나이며, 자신의 작품으로 수많은 상을 수상했다.

전시회는 이탈리아의 전원 풍경을 담은 수채화를 주로 다룰 것이다. 미술관 방문객들은 전시회 곳곳에 위치한 안내판을 이용할 수 있다. 이것들은 각각의 그림들에 대한 설명 **외에도** 화가가 쓴 시의 원본도 보여 준다.

어휘│ exhibition 전시회 watercolor painting 수채화 countryside 전원, 시골 take advantage of ~을 이용하다 informative sign 안내판 explanation 설명 original 원래의 poem (한 편의) 시

---

5 The Toscano Gallery has announced plans / to host an exhibition of paintings by Luisella DeRose / that will start / **on** May 2.
(A) for (B) until **(C) on** (D) to

(A) ~ 동안에 (B) ~까지 (C) ~에 (D) ~까지

해설│ 빈칸 뒤에 May 2라는 특정한 날짜가 등장했다. 날짜 앞에서 '~에'라는 의미를 갖는 전치사는 on이므로 정답은 (C). 빈칸 이하의 전치사구가 동사 will start를 수식하는 말이므로, '~까지'라는 의미의 (D) until은 정답이 될 수 없다.

---

6 **In addition to** explanations about the background of each painting, / these feature original poems / written by the artist.
(A) In addition to (B) Because of (C) Despite
(D) Regardless of

(A) ~ 외에 (B) ~ 때문에 (C) ~에도 불구하고 (D) ~와 상관없이

해설│ 안내판이 '각 그림들에 대한 설명 이외에 화가가 쓴 시의 원본도 보여 준다'는 내용이 자연스러우므로 '~ 외에'라는 의미의 구전치사 In addition to가 빈칸에 들어가야 한다.

1 reductions **2** reviewed **3** detailed **4** refund **5** (A) **6** (B) **7** (D) **8** (C)

---

1 Price (installments / **reductions**) have helped attract more people / to the store.

해석 | 가격 인하는 더 많은 사람들을 가게로 끌어 모으도록 도왔다.

해설 | 괄호 앞의 명사 Price와 어울려 주어로 쓸 수 있는 단어를 골라야 한다. 문맥상 '가격 인하가 사람을 끌어 모으다'라는 내용이 적절하므로 정답은 reductions.

---

2 Several editors (**reviewed** / satisfied) the advertisement / before its publication.

해석 | 몇몇 편집자들이 발행 전에 그 광고를 검토했다.

어휘 | publication 발행, 출판

해설 | 편집자가 발행 전에 광고에 대해 할 수 있는 것은 '검토'이다. 따라서 reviewed가 정답.

---

3 The manual provides (permanent / **detailed**) instructions / for the book shelf's construction.

해석 | 그 설명서는 책꽂이 조립에 대한 자세한 설명을 제공한다.

어휘 | book shelf 책꽂이

해설 | 괄호 뒤의 명사 instructions를 알맞게 꾸며 줄 형용사를 골라야 한다. 설명서가 제공할 수 있는 것은 '자세한 설명'이므로 detailed가 정답.

---

4 The store manager immediately offered a (policy / **refund**) / for the broken item.

해석 | 지점장은 고장 난 물품에 대해 곧바로 환불을 제공했다.

어휘 | broken 고장 난, 깨진

해설 | 괄호 앞쪽의 동사 offered의 목적어인 명사로 적절한 것을 골라야 한다. 고장 난 물건에 대해 제공할 수 있는 것으로는 '환불'이 자연스러우므로 refund가 정답.

---

5 The restaurant at Guzman Hotel offers a variety of dishes / at **reasonable** prices.

(A) **reasonable** (B) cautious (C) temporary (D) durable

해석 | 구즈만 호텔의 레스토랑은 다양한 요리를 합리적인 가격에 제공한다.

(A) 합리적인 (B) 조심스러운 (C) 일시적인 (D) 내구성이 있는

어휘 | a variety of 여러 가지의

해설 | 빈칸 뒤의 명사 prices를 꾸며주는 적절한 형용사를 골라야 한다. 문맥상 '음식을 합리적인 가격에 제공하다'라는 내용이 되어야 자연스러우므로 정답은 (A).

---

6 Ms. Jordan is in charge of dealing with customer **complaints** / about product defects.

(A) purchases (B) **complaints** (C) satisfaction
(D) requirements

해석 | 조던 씨는 제품 결함에 대한 고객 불만 처리를 담당한다.

(A) 구입 (B) 불만 (C) 만족 (D) 요건

어휘 | defect 결함

해설 | 빈칸은 뒤의 전치사구 about product defects의 수식을 받는 명사이다. 관련 주제를 나타내는 전치사 about이 쓰였으므로 '제품 결함에 관한' 무언가가 되어야 하므로, 정답은 (B). customer complaints는 '고객 불만'의 뜻으로 하나의 표현처럼 쓰인다.

---

7 The warranty on your Zolo X50 stereo system / **expires** two years from the date of purchase.

(A) recalls (B) requires (C) confirms (D) **expires**

해석 | 귀하의 졸로 X50 스테레오 시스템의 품질보증서는 구입일로부터 2년 후에 만료됩니다.

(A) (제품을) 회수하다 (B) 요구하다 (C) 확인하다 (D) 만료되다

어휘 | warranty 품질보증서

해설 | 주어가 The warranty(품질보증서)이고 빈칸 다음에 기간(two years)이 나오므로 문맥상 '품질보증서가 2년 후에 만료된다'는 의미가 되어야 자연스럽다. 따라서 정답은 (D)이다.

8 We can **guarantee** one-hour processing of your photographs / if you pay ten cents per picture.
(A) notice   (B) afford   **(C) guarantee**   (D) display
해석| 사진 당 10센트를 지불하시면 한 시간 내 인화를 보장해 드릴 수 있습니다.
(A) 알아차리다 (B) 여유가 있다 (C) 보장하다 (D) 전시하다
어휘| per ~당

해설| 비용을 받고 제공하는 사항에 대해 약속하는 말로, '한 시간 내에 인화해 주는 것을 보장한다'는 내용이 자연스러우므로 (C)가 정답. guarantee는 어떤 일이 확실하도록 '보장하다'라는 뜻이며, 명사로는 '품질보증서'라는 뜻도 있다.

---

1 Hawthorne Hotels provides upscale accommodations / at fifty locations **across** North America.
(A) behind   (B) among   (C) over   **(D) across**
해석| 호손 호텔은 북아메리카 전역에 걸쳐 50군데에서 최고급 숙박시설을 제공한다.
(A) ~ 뒤에 (B) ~ 사이에 (C) ~ 위에 (D) ~에 걸쳐
어휘| upscale 고급의 accommodation 《pl.》 숙박시설

해설| **전치사 across**
선택지를 보니 빈칸에 알맞은 전치사를 고르는 문제. 문맥상 '북아메리카 전역에 걸쳐 있는 50개의 지점'이라는 의미가 되어야 자연스러우므로 정답은 (D).
오답| (C) over의 경우 뒤에 장소를 나타내는 말이 오면 '~ (바로) 위에 걸쳐서'라는 의미이므로 적절하지 않다.

---

2 **As** the special guest, / Ms. Jacobs will give the opening remarks / for Perchatown's founding celebration.
(A) As (B) Except (C) Off (D) Along
해석| 특별 초청 손님으로서, 제이콥스 씨는 페르카타운의 건립 기념식의 개회사를 하게 될 것이다.
(A) ~로서 (B) ~을 제외하고 (C) 벗어나서 (D) ~을 따라
어휘| opening remark 개회사 found 설립하다

해설| **전치사 as**
문맥상 '특별 초대 손님으로서 개회사를 하다'라는 것이 자연스러우므로 '~로서'라는 자격을 나타내는 전치사 As가 정답이다.

---

3 Our technical support team responds to all **inquiries** / within thirty minutes.
(A) refunds **(B) inquiries** (C) discounts (D) positions
해석| 저희의 기술 지원팀은 30분 내에 모든 문의에 응답합니다.
(A) 환불 (B) 문의 (C) 할인 (D) 직위, 자리
어휘| technical support 기술 지원 respond to ~에 응답하다

해설| **명사 어휘 inquiry**
빈칸 앞 동사 responds to와 어울려, 문맥상 '문의에 응답하다'라는 뜻이 되어야 자연스러우므로 (B)가 들어가야 알맞다.

---

4 The winding mountain roads are cleared regularly **throughout** the winter / to ensure greater safety for motorists.
(A) throughout (B) without (C) among (D) down
해석| 구불구불한 산길은 운전자들에게 더 안전하도록 겨울 내내 정기적으로 치워진다.
(A) ~ 내내 (B) ~ 없이 (C) ~ 사이에 (D) ~ 아래에
어휘| winding 구불구불한 motorist 자동차 운전자

해설| **전치사 throughout**
the winter라는 시간을 나타내는 말과 어울리는 것은 '~ 내내'라는 뜻의 (A)이다. throughout은 장소를 나타내는 말 앞에서는 '~ 도처에'라는 뜻으로 쓰인다.

---

5 Using the telecommunication technology, / employees can complete their assignments / without **leaving** home.
(A) leaves **(B) leaving** (C) leave (D) left
해석| 원격통신 기술을 이용하여, 직원들은 집을 나서지 않고도 업무를 완수할 수 있다.
어휘| telecommunication 원격통신 assignment 업무, 과제

해설| **전치사의 목적어**
빈칸은 전치사 without의 목적어 자리이므로 명사, 대명사, 동명사 등이 들어가야 한다. 따라서 정답은 동명사인 (B). without doing은 '~하지 않고'라는 뜻이다.

6 The production of the company brochures / is handled **by** the creative department.

(A) about (B) by (C) of (D) during

해석| 기업 홍보 책자의 제작은 크리에이티브 부서에서 담당한다.

(A) ~에 대하여 (B) ~에 의해 (C) ~의 (D) ~ 동안

해설| **전치사 by**

빈칸에 알맞은 전치사를 고르는 문제. '홍보 책자 제작이 크리에이티브 부서에 의해 처리된다'는 내용이 자연스러우므로 '~에 의해'라는 의미로 수단을 나타내는 전치사 by가 정답이다.

---

7 The labor minister will answer questions / **concerning** the proposed minimum wage increase.

(A) excluding (B) since (C) further (D) concerning

해석| 노동부 장관은 제안된 최저 임금 인상에 대한 질문에 대답할 것이다.

(A) ~을 제외하고 (B) ~ 이래로 (C) ~보다 더 (D) ~에 관해

어휘| labor 노동, 근로 minister 장관, 각료 minimum 최저의 wage 임금

해설| **전치사 concerning**

빈칸 앞 문장이 완전하므로 빈칸 이하는 부사구이다. 빈칸 뒤의 명사구와 어울려 부사구를 이루는 전치사가 빈칸에 들어가야 하므로 정답 후보에서 부사 (C)는 제외. 문맥상 '최저 임금 인상에 관한 질문에 답변한다'는 내용이 되어야 하므로 '~에 관해'라는 뜻의 (D)가 정답이다.

---

8 The air-conditioning unit in the conference room / needs to be **replaced** / because it makes too much noise.

(A) replaced (B) requested (C) worked (D) coordinated

해석| 회의실에 있는 에어컨은 소음이 너무 많이 나기 때문에 교체해야 한다.

(A) 교체하다 (B) 요청하다 (C) 작동하다 (D) 조정하다

어휘| air-conditioning unit 에어컨 제품 make noise 소음이 나다

해설| **동사 어휘 replace**

소음이 너무 많이 나는 것은 에어컨을 '교체해야' 하는 이유가 된다. 따라서, '교체하다, 대신하다'라는 뜻의 replaced가 정답.

9-12

From: Swann Auto Shop <jsnow@swann.com>
To: Mary Robinson <mrobinson@mymail.com>
Date: November 2
Subject: Re: Damage to your car

Dear Ms. Robinson,

I'm sorry about the damage caused to your vehicle by our staff. **According to** our policy, you are entitled to a refund for the recent work on your car. **Please return to our shop to claim it.**

As a token of goodwill, we would also like to offer you a fifty percent **discount**. It will be applied to your next visit for maintenance work conducted by our company.

We would like to remind you that we really do value you as a customer. **Furthermore**, we guarantee our prices will always be lower than those of our competitors.

Regards,

James Snow, Swann Auto Shop

발신: 스완 정비소 〈jsnow@swann.com〉
수신: 메리 로빈슨 〈mrobinson@mymail.com〉
날짜: 11월 2일
제목: 회신: 귀하의 차량 손상

로빈슨 씨께,

저희 직원이 귀하의 차량에 입힌 손상에 대해 사과드립니다. 저희 규정에 따라, 고객님의 차량에 했던 최근의 작업에 대해 환불을 받으실 수 있습니다. 환불을 청구하기 위해 저희 가게에 다시 들려 주십시오.

선의의 표시로, 저희는 또한 귀하에게 50% 할인을 제공하고자 합니다. 이것은 저희 회사에서 하는 정비 작업을 받기 위해 다음에 방문하셨을 때에 적용될 것입니다.

저희는 귀하를 진심으로 소중한 고객으로 모시고 있다는 점을 다시 한 번 알려 드리고 싶습니다. 뿐만 아니라, 저희 가격은 경쟁사의 가격들보다 항상 저렴할 것을 보장합니다.

스완 정비소, 제임스 스노우 드림

어휘| auto shop 정비소 damage 손상, 피해 vehicle 차량 entitle 자격[권리]를 주다 as a token of ~의 표시로 goodwill 선의 remind A that A에게 ~임을 상기시키다 value 소중히 여기다

9 <u>According to</u> our policy, / you are entitled to a refund / for the recent work on your car.
(A) On behalf of (B) Compared to **(C) According to**
(D) Instead of
(A) ~을 대신[대표]해서 (B) ~와 비교해서 (C) ~에 따라 (D) ~ 대신에

해설 | **구전치사 according to**
문맥상 알맞은 구전치사를 고르는 문제. 환불 등의 조치를 취할 때는 '규정에 따라' 결정하는 것이 자연스러우므로 '~에 따라'라는 의미의 (C)가 정답.

10 (A) We offer a wide range of services.
(B) Please return to our shop to claim it.
(C) Your car requires a new coat of paint.
(D) We recommend changing your engine's oil.
(A) 저희는 다양한 종류의 서비스를 제공합니다.
(B) 환불을 청구하기 위해 저희 가게에 다시 들려 주십시오.
(C) 고객님의 차량에 새로운 도색이 필요합니다.
(D) 엔진 오일을 교환하실 것을 권합니다.

해설 | **알맞은 문장 고르기**
빈칸 앞 문장에서 고객에게 최근의 차량 작업에 대해 환불해 주겠다고 했고, 다음 문단에서는 또 다른 보상(할인)에 대해 이야기하고 있으므로, 빈칸에서 환불에 대한 이야기를 마무리 짓는 것이 자연스럽다. 따라서 환불금을 청구(claim)하려면 가게로 방문해 달라는 내용의 (B)가 가장 적절하다.
오답 | 빈칸이 포함된 문단은 사과와 환불에 대해 이야기하고 있으므로 다양한 서비스 제공에 대한 (A)는 어울리지 않아 오답. (C)와 (D) 모두 정비를 권하는 내용이므로 고객에게 사과하고 있는 지문과는 어울리지 않아서 오답이다.

11 As a token of goodwill, / we would also like to offer you a fifty percent **discount**.
(A) profit (B) satisfaction **(C) discount** (D) warranty
(A) 이익 (B) 만족 (C) 할인 (D) 품질보증서

해설 | **명사 어휘 discount**
문맥상 선의의 표시로 제공할 수 있는 것은 '50% 할인'이 되어야 자연스러우므로 정답은 (C).

12 **Furthermore**, / we guarantee our prices will always be lower than / those of our competitors.
(A) Furthermore (B) Nevertheless (C) Otherwise
(D) By contrast
(A) 뿐만 아니라 (B) 그럼에도 불구하고 (C) 그렇지 않으면 (D) 그에 반해서

해설 | **접속부사 furthermore**
선택지는 모두 접속부사로, 문맥상 알맞은 연결어를 골라야 한다. 빈칸 바로 앞 문장에서 이메일 수신자를 소중한 고객으로 생각하고 있음을 밝혔고, 빈칸 뒤 문장에서 저렴한 가격도 보장하고 있다고 말했으므로 두 문장은 대조나 양보가 아닌 '추가'의 의미를 갖는 연결어로 이어져야 한다. 따라서 '뿐만 아니라'의 뜻인 (A)가 정답.
오답 | (B)와 (C)는 양보, (D)는 대조의 의미이다.

1 to부정사의 개념과 형태

교재 155쪽

1 To place **2** to advertise **3** to apply **4** to exceed **5** (B) **6** (D) **7** (D) **8** (B)

---

1 (Place / **To place**) an order after 6 P.M., / please visit our Web site at www.cosetimarket.com.

해석 | 오후 6시 이후에 주문을 하려면, 저희 웹사이트인 www.cosetimarket.com을 방문해 주세요.

해설 | 콤마 뒤에 please로 시작하는 명령문이 나왔다. 따라서 콤마 앞부분은 문장을 수식할 수 있는 수식어구 역할을 해야 하므로 빈칸에 들어갈 말로 to부정사인 To place가 적절하다. 문장에 이미 동사 visit이 있으므로 Place는 쓰일 수 없다.

---

2 We want (**to advertise** / advertisement) our products / in a popular weekly magazine.

해석 | 우리는 유명한 주간지에 우리 제품을 광고하기를 원한다.

어휘 | advertise 광고하다　weekly 주간, 주의

해설 | 동사 want의 목적어로 명사 역할을 하는 동시에 뒤에 있는 our products를 목적어로 취할 수 있는 것은 to부정사이다. 명사인 advertisement는 뒤에 나오는 명사 our products와 바로 연결될 수 없다.

---

3 Mr. Walton is ready (applied / **to apply**) for the researcher position / at JAX Pharmaceuticals.

해석 | 월튼 씨는 JAX 제약회사의 연구직에 지원할 준비가 되어 있다.

어휘 | apply for ~에 지원하다　researcher 연구원

해설 | 괄호 앞에 있는 형용사 ready를 수식할 수 있는 것은 부사처럼 쓸 수 있는 to부정사이다. be ready to do(~할 준비가 되다)라는 표현을 통째로 알아두자.

---

4 The architect has promised / not (exceed / **to exceed**) the construction budget.

해석 | 건축가는 공사 예산을 초과하지 않겠다고 약속했다.

어휘 | exceed 초과하다

해설 | 괄호는 동사 promise의 목적어가 들어갈 자리이다. 따라서 명사처럼 쓰일 수 있는 to부정사가 답. to부정사의 부정은 앞에 not을 붙여서 만든다는 것도 함께 알아두자.

---

5 The number of online banking customers / is likely to increase <u>steadily</u> / over the next five years.
(A) steady　(B) **steadily**　(C) steadied　(D) steadiness

해석 | 인터넷 뱅킹 고객의 숫자가 향후 5년간 꾸준히 증가할 것 같다.

어휘 | the number of ~의 수　steadily 꾸준히

해설 | to부정사인 to increase 뒤에 올 수 있는 말을 묻는 문제이다. to부정사는 동사의 성질을 가지므로 뒤에 목적어, 보어, 수식어를 가질 수 있다. 문맥상 '꾸준히 증가하다'라는 의미가 되어야 하므로 increase를 꾸미는 부사인 (B)가 정답.

---

6 Isis Biomedical claims <u>to have discovered</u> an effective cure / for a major disease.
(A) to discover　(B) discover　(C) discovered
(D) **to have discovered**

해석 | 이시스 바이오메디컬 사는 주요 질병에 대해 효과적인 치료제를 발견했다고 주장한다.

어휘 | claim 주장하다　discover 발견하다　effective 효과적인　cure 치료제[법]

해설 | 빈칸은 동사 claims의 목적어 자리이므로 명사 역할을 하는 to부정사가 올 수 있다. 따라서 (A)와 (D)가 정답 후보. '치료제를 발견한 것'은 '주장하는 것'보다 이전에 일어난 일이므로 완료형 to부정사 〈to+have p.p.〉 형태인 (D)가 정답.

---

7 Mr. Geller has contacted the personnel manager / to obtain <u>approval</u> for the order of office supplies.
(A) approve　(B) approved　(C) approves　(D) **approval**

해석 | 갤러 씨는 사무용품의 주문에 대해 승인을 받기 위해서 인사부장에게 연락했다.

해설 | 빈칸은 to부정사 to obtain의 목적어 자리로 명사인 (D)가 정답이다. to부정사는 동사의 성질을 가지고 있어 뒤에 목적어나 수식어가 따라올 수 있다.

---

8 Poor ticket sales caused the concert **to be rescheduled** / for a later date.
(A) is rescheduling **(B) to be rescheduled**
(C) will be rescheduled (D) to reschedule
해석 | 저조한 티켓 판매는 콘서트가 나중 날짜로 연기되게 만들었다.
어휘 | poor 빈약한, 부족한

해설 | 문장에 이미 동사 caused가 있으므로 빈칸에는 완전한 동사의 형태를 한 선택지들은 들어갈 수 없다. 따라서 to부정사 (B)와 (D)가 정답 후보. to부정사의 수식을 받는 the concert는 '연기되는' 대상이므로 수동형인 (B)가 정답.

---

2 to부정사의 쓰임

교재 157쪽

1 to resolve **2** to suspend **3** meet **4** to include **5** (D) **6** (C) **7** (D) **8** (B)

---

1 The goal is (**to resolve** / resolved) the problems / in our production line.
해석 | 목표는 우리 생산 라인의 문제들을 해결하는 것이다.
어휘 | goal 목표 resolve 해결하다 production line 생산 라인

해설 | The goal이 주어, is가 동사이므로 괄호는 주격 보어가 들어갈 자리이다. '해결하는 것'이란 뜻으로 명사 역할을 할 수 있는 to부정사인 to resolve가 들어가야 한다. 괄호 뒤 명사 the problems는 to resolve의 목적어이다.

---

2 Mr. Smith made the decision (**to suspend** / suspends) the renovation work / due to budget issues.
해석 | 스미스 씨는 예산 문제 때문에 수리 작업을 유예하기로 결정했다.

해설 | 괄호 앞의 문장이 완전하므로 괄호 이후는 수식어구이다. 괄호는 앞의 명사 the decision을 수식하는 형용사 역할을 하므로 명사를 뒤에서 수식할 수 있는 to부정사가 들어가야 한다. 정답은 to suspend. to부정사는 명사를 수식할 때 뒤에서 수식함을 기억하자.

---

3 The marketing department must work late / in order to (**meet** / meeting) the deadline.
해석 | 마케팅 부서는 마감을 맞추기 위해 야근해야 한다.
어휘 | meet the deadline 마감을 맞추다

해설 | in order to *do*(~하기 위해서)라는 to부정사 구문을 알고 있는지 묻는 문제. to 다음에 동사원형이 이어져야 하므로 답은 meet. 이와 같은 뜻을 지닌 표현으로 so as to *do*도 있다.

---

4 It is important for job applicants / (**to include** / including) all their qualifications / on their résumés.
해석 | 구직자들은 이력서에 그들의 모든 자격 요건을 포함시키는 것이 중요하다.

해설 | 완전한 문장 형태를 이룬 It is important 다음에 길게 이어지고 있으므로 가주어가 쓰인 문장일 확률이 높다. for 다음에 나오는 job applicants는 to부정사의 의미상 주어이고, 괄호에는 진주어인 to부정사가 나와야 하므로 to include가 정답.

---

5 The CEO of the investment firm / plans **to purchase** stock / in at least three corporations.
(A) purchased (B) purchases (C) are purchasing
(D) to purchase
해석 | 그 투자회사의 CEO는 최소한 세 개 회사의 주식을 매입할 계획이다.
어휘 | investment firm 투자회사 corporation 기업

해설 | plans가 문장의 동사이므로 빈칸은 동사의 목적어가 들어갈 자리이다. 따라서, 명사인 (B)와 명사 역할을 할 수 있는 to부정사 (D)가 정답 후보. 빈칸 뒤 명사 stock을 목적어로 취할 수 있는 것은 to부정사이므로 (D)가 정답이다.

---

6 Ms. Samson received an invitation / **to attend** the twelfth Annual Green Planet Convention / next month.
(A) is attending (B) attends **(C) to attend** (D) attend
해석 | 샘슨 씨는 다음 달에 열리는 제12차 연례 녹색 지구 총회에 참석해 달라는 초대장을 받았다.

해설 | 빈칸 앞이 〈주어+동사+목적어〉로 이루어진 완전한 문장이므로, 빈칸 이하는 수식어구가 되어야 한다. 문맥상 빈칸 앞 명사 an invitation을 수식하는 형용사 역할을 할 수 있는 to부정사가 들어가야 알맞다. 따라서 정답은 (C).

7 It is essential for sales representatives / **to send** the daily figures to the head office.
(A) send (B) is sending (C) will send **(D) to send**
해석| 영업 사원들이 일일 매출 수치를 본사에 보내는 것은 필수적이다.
어휘| figure 《pl.》 수치 head office 본사

해설| 문장의 주어인 It은 앞에 가리키는 대상이 없으므로 가주어로 쓰였음을 알 수 있다. 따라서 빈칸에는 진주어가 될 수 있는 to부정사 (D)가 와야 한다. 빈칸 앞 for sales representatives는 to부정사의 의미상 주어를 나타낸다.

---

8 **To encourage** cooperation, / the operations manager has placed employees / in diverse project teams.
(A) Encouragement **(B) To encourage** (C) To be encouraged
(D) Encouraged
해석| 협동을 장려하기 위해서, 업무 관리자는 직원들을 다양한 프로젝트 팀에 배치했다.
어휘| encourage 장려하다 operation 업무, 운영 place 배치하다, 두다 diverse 다양한

해설| 콤마 이하에 완전한 문장이 나오고 있으므로, 콤마 앞부분은 수식어구가 되어야 한다. 선택지로 보아 '~하기 위해서'라는 뜻의 to부정사 (B)와 (C)가 정답 후보. 빈칸 뒤 명사 cooperation을 목적어로 취할 수 있는 능동형 to부정사인 (B)가 정답. (C)는 수동형이므로 뒤에 목적어가 올 수 없다.

---

3 to부정사와 함께 쓰이는 표현
교재 159쪽

1 to raise **2** to create **3** to submit **4** to transform **5** (A) **6** (B) **7** (B) **8** (D)

---

1 The Caring Hands Organization hopes (raise / **to raise**) / over $10,000 / from the benefit event.
해석| 케어링 핸드 재단은 자선행사를 통해 만 달러 이상을 모으기를 희망한다.
어휘| benefit event 자선 행사

해설| 빈칸은 동사 hopes의 목적어 자리이다. hope는 to부정사를 목적어로 취하는 동사이므로 정답은 to raise.

---

2 Mr. Garland reminded me (**to create** / creating) a banner / for the new sports shoes.
해석| 갈랜드 씨는 나에게 새로운 스포츠 신발을 위한 현수막을 만들 것을 상기시켰다.
어휘| banner 현수막

해설| remind는 〈remind+목적어+to do〉의 형태로, '~에게 …할 것을 상기시키다'라는 뜻을 나타낸다. 따라서, 빈칸에는 to부정사인 to create가 들어가야 한다.

---

3 The contractor was able / (**to submit** / submitted) the design for the renovation / on time.
해석| 그 도급업자는 개조를 위한 설계도를 제시간에 제출할 수 있었다.
어휘| on time 정시에, 제때에

해설| 괄호 앞의 able을 보는 순간 to부정사와 자주 쓰이는 형용사임을 떠올려야 한다. 따라서 괄호에는 to부정사인 to submit이 들어가야 한다. be able to do는 '~할 수 있다'라는 의미임을 기억하자.

---

4 The shareholders approved the proposal / (**to transform** / transform) the building / into a hotel.
해석| 주주들은 그 건물을 호텔로 바꾸자는 제안을 승인했다.
어휘| transform 변형시키다

해설| 빈칸은 앞의 명사 the proposal을 수식하는 형용사 자리이다. 따라서 형용사 역할을 할 수 있는 to부정사가 들어가야 알맞다. 정답은 to transform.

---

5 The TMC foundation chose **to honor** Professor Yates / for his dedication to helping others.
(A) to honor (B) will honor (C) to be honored
(D) would honor
해석| TMC 재단은 다른 사람들을 도운 예이츠 교수의 헌신에 대해 그에게 상을 주기로 했다.
어휘| foundation 재단 honor 영예[상]을 주다 dedication 헌신, 전념

해설| 빈칸은 동사 chose의 목적어 자리이므로 명사 역할을 하는 to부정사가 들어가야 한다. to부정사 (A)와 (C) 중에서 빈칸 뒤의 명사 Professor Yates를 목적어로 취할 수 있는 것은 능동형인 (A)이다. 수동형인 (C)는 뒤에 목적어를 취할 수 없다.

6 Ms. Wilson asked her assistant / <u>to prepare</u> for the job fair.
   (A) prepare **(B) to prepare** (C) prepares (D) preparation
   해석 | 윌슨 씨는 그녀의 비서에게 취업 박람회를 준비할 것을 요청했다.
   어휘 | **assistant** 비서, 조수 **job fair** 취업 박람회

해설 | 빈칸 앞 문장이 완전해 보이나, 동사 ask가 '~에게 …을 요청하다'라는 의미로 쓰일 때 〈ask+목적어+to do〉 형태로 쓰인다. 따라서 목적어인 her assistant 뒤에 ask의 목적격 보어가 들어가야 하므로 빈칸에는 to부정사 (B)가 알맞다.

---

7 The global economic slowdown is expected **to present** challenges / for major businesses.
   (A) presents **(B) to present** (C) presenting (D) presentation
   해석 | 전 세계의 경기 둔화는 주요 사업들에 도전을 던져 줄 것으로 예상된다.
   어휘 | **slowdown** (사업·경제 등의) 둔화 **present** 주다 **challenge** 도전, 과제

해설 | 빈칸은 동사 expected의 목적어 자리이다. expect는 to부정사를 목적어로 취하는 동사이므로 빈칸에 들어갈 말로 적절한 것은 (B).

---

8 The internship at M&K Accounting / is a good opportunity / <u>to learn</u> useful information / about the industry.
   (A) learn (B) learning (C) has learned **(D) to learn**
   해석 | M&K 회계 사무소에서 인턴십을 하는 것은 업계의 유용한 정보를 배우는 좋은 기회이다.
   어휘 | **industry** 산업

해설 | 빈칸 앞의 명사 opportunity가 문제를 푸는 단서가 된다. 명사 opportunity는 to부정사와 어울려 쓰이는 대표적인 명사이다. 따라서 답은 (D). opportunity to do(~할 기회)라는 표현을 기억하자.

| REVIEW | 핵심 POINT 다시 보기 | 교재 161쪽 |

1 (D) **2** (A) **3** (C) **4** (B) **5** (D) **6** (B)

---

1 Bob Hilditch has the ability / <u>to perform</u> his core tasks more efficiently / than the other customer service representatives.
   (A) perform (B) performing (C) be performed **(D) to perform**
   해석 | 밥 힐디치 씨는 다른 서비스 담당자들보다 더 효율적으로 핵심 과업을 수행하는 능력을 가지고 있다.

해설 | 빈칸 앞 완전한 문장이므로 빈칸 이하는 수식어구가 들어가야 한다. 빈칸 앞 ability는 to부정사의 수식을 받아 ability to do의 구조로 자주 쓰인다. 따라서 정답은 (D). to부정사는 형용사처럼 쓰일 때 명사를 뒤에서 수식하며 '~할, ~하는'으로 해석된다.

---

2 It is standard procedure / <u>to send</u> defective appliances / back to manufacturers.
   (A) to send (B) sent (C) sends (D) will send
   해석 | 결함이 있는 기기는 제조사에 돌려 보내는 것이 표준 절차이다.
   어휘 | **defective** 결함이 있는 **appliance** 기기

해설 | 빈칸 앞 완전한 문장 형태를 이룬 It is standard procedure이므로 가주어가 쓰인 문장일 확률이 높다. 이미 문장의 동사 is가 앞에 있으므로 빈칸에는 완전한 동사의 형태를 가진 선택지 (B), (C), (D)는 들어갈 수 없다. 진주어로 쓸 수 있는 to부정사가 나와야 하므로 정답은 (A).

---

3 Management policies are likely **to differ** / from one business unit to another.
   (A) differing (B) difference **(C) to differ** (D) differ
   해석 | 경영 정책은 각 사업 단위별로 다를 것이다.
   어휘 | **management** 경영[운영/관리] **unit** 구성 단위, 한 개

해설 | 빈칸 앞의 are likely를 보고 to부정사와 함께 어울려 자주 쓰이는 형용사 구문임을 떠올려야 한다. be likely to do는 '~할 것 같다'라는 의미로 자주 함께 쓰인다. 따라서 정답은 to부정사인 (C).

---

4 Supervisors do not allow their employees / **to remove** confidential materials / from the premises.
(A) remove **(B) to remove** (C) removing (D) removed

해석| 관리자들은 직원들이 기밀 문서를 건물 밖으로 가지고 나가는 것을 허용하지 않는다.

어휘| remove A from B A를 B 밖으로 가지고 나가다[옮기다] premises 건물, 부지

해설| allow는 〈동사+목적어+to부정사〉 형태로 쓰이는 동사이다. 문장에서 allow 뒤의 their employees가 목적어이므로 빈칸에는 목적격 보어인 to부정사가 들어가야 한다. 따라서 정답은 (B).

5-6

Dear Ms. Chandler,

As you may remember, we met at the recent fundraising gala at Caird Hall. You were understaffed, and it was my pleasure **to have assisted** you with the setting up of the food tables.

Afterwards, I mentioned that I needed to find a caterer for an upcoming event, and you said you could handle the job.

Could you let me know what your rates are? We need to serve approximately fifty people. I would be happy **to arrange** a phone meeting to discuss the options further.

챈들러 씨께,

기억하실지 모르겠지만, 우리는 최근에 케어드 홀에서 열린 모금 행사에서 만났어요. 당신이 일손이 부족했고, 저는 식사 테이블 준비하는 **일을 도와 드리게 되어** 기뻤죠.

그 후에, 제가 곧 있을 행사에 출장요리업체가 필요하다고 말했더니, 당신이 그 일을 맡아줄 수 있다고 하셨어요.

비용이 어떻게 되는지 알려 주시겠어요? 우리는 50명 정도 접대해야 해요. 선택사항에 대해 더 논의하기 위해 전화상으로 회의할 시간을 **정했으면** 좋겠네요.

어휘| fundraising gala 모금 행사 understaffed 인원이 부족한 pleasure 기쁨, 즐거움 set up 설치하다 caterer 출장요리업체 rate 요금, 비용 serve 접대하다 arrange 마련하다 option 선택사항

5 You were understaffed, / and it was my pleasure **to have assisted** you / with the setting up of the food tables.
(A) assists (B) assisted (C) to be assisted
(D) to have assisted

해설| 내용상 주어 it이 가리키는 명사가 없으므로 it이 가주어임을 알 수 있다. 따라서 진주어로 쓰일 수 있는 to부정사인 (C)와 (D)가 정답 후보. 빈칸 뒤에 you라는 목적어가 있으므로 능동형인 (D)가 정답이다. 문맥상 '당신을 도운 것'이 '즐거웠다'는 것보다 먼저 일어난 일이므로 완료형을 썼다.

---

6 I would be happy **to arrange** a phone meeting / to discuss the options further.
(A) arranged **(B) to arrange** (C) would arrange
(D) to be arranged

해설| 빈칸 앞이 완전한 문장이므로 빈칸 이후는 수식어구이다. 선택지에서 빈칸 앞의 형용사 happy를 수식하는 부사구를 이끌 수 있는 것은 to부정사인 (B)와 (D). 빈칸 뒤의 명사 a phone meeting을 목적어로 취할 수 있는 것은 능동태이므로 정답은 능동형인 (B)이다.

1 limit **2** postponed **3** attended **4** restrictions **5** (A) **6** (B) **7** (D) **8** (C)

---

1 The host of the contest has decided to (implement / **limit**) / the number of entries.

해석| 대회 주최측은 응모작의 수를 제한하기로 결정했다.

어휘| host 주최자, 주인 contest 대회

해설| 괄호는 앞의 전치사 to와 함께 동사 decided의 목적어로 쓰인 to부정사의 일부이다. 문맥상 주최측이 응모작의 수에 대해 한 행동으로 '제한'하는 것이 가장 자연스러우므로 정답은 limit이다.

---

2 The meeting was (addressed / **postponed**) / until further notice.

해석| 그 회의는 추후 공지가 있을 때까지 연기되었다.

어휘| further notice 추후 공지[통보]

해설| 괄호 앞의 was와 함께 수동태로 쓰인, 적절한 동사를 고르는 문제. 주어인 meeting이 '연기되는 것'이 자연스러우므로 정답은 postponed이다.

---

3 More than twenty people (**attended** / settled) the seminar.

해석| 스무 명 이상의 사람들이 세미나에 참석했다.

해설| 괄호는 문장의 동사 자리로, 앞뒤의 주어, 목적어와 어울리는 동사를 골라야 한다. 세미나에 스무 명 이상의 사람들이 '참석하는 것'이 자연스러우므로 정답은 attended.

---

4 The reception hall has (**restrictions** / ceremonies) / on event type, number of people, and other elements.

해석| 그 피로연장은 행사의 종류, 사람의 수, 그리고 다른 요소들에 대한 제한이 있다.

어휘| reception hall 피로연장 element 요소

해설| 괄호에는 앞의 동사 has와 어울리는 말이 들어가야 한다. 그 피로연장이 행사 종류나 사람 수 등에 대한 '제한'이 있다는 내용이 자연스러우므로 정답은 restrictions.

---

5 Ms. Spencer will go over each item / on the **agenda** / in detail.

(A) **agenda** (B) process (C) function (D) presentation

해석| 스펜서 씨는 의제의 각 항목을 검토할 것이다.

(A) 의제, 안건 (B) 과정, 절차 (C) 기능 (D) 발표

어휘| go over 검토하다

해설| 빈칸 앞의 전치사 on과 함께, 그 앞의 item을 수식하고 있으므로 그에 어울리는 명사가 빈칸에 들어가야 한다. '의제의 각 항목을 검토하다'라는 내용이 자연스러우므로 '의제, 안건'이라는 뜻의 (A)가 정답.

---

6 Organizers are still trying to reserve a suitable **venue** / for the Annual Broadcasting Awards Dinner.

(A) candidate (B) **venue** (C) promotion (D) benefit

해석| 주최자들은 아직도 연례 방송 시상식 만찬을 열 적당한 장소를 예약하려고 애쓰고 있다.

(A) 후보 (B) (행사) 장소 (C) 홍보, 승진 (D) 혜택

어휘| organizer 주최자 reserve 예약하다

해설| 빈칸은 동사 reserve의 목적어가 되므로 예약할 수 있는 대상을 나타내는 말이 들어가야 알맞다. 시상식 등의 행사를 위해 예약할 수 있는 것으로는 '장소'를 뜻하는 (B)가 적절하다.

---

7 Front desk receptionists must **complete** the hotel's training program / before they work alone.

(A) cooperate (B) consent (C) participate (D) **complete**

해석| 안내 데스크의 접수원은 혼자서 일하기 전에 호텔의 교육 프로그램을 완료해야 한다.

(A) 협동하다 (B) 동의하다 (C) 참여하다 (D) 완료하다

어휘| receptionist 접수원 alone 혼자

해설| 문맥상 혼자 일하기 전에 '교육 프로그램을 완료해야 한다'라는 뜻이 되어야 알맞으므로 '완료하다, 끝마치다'라는 뜻의 (D)가 정답. (C) participate는 '~에 참여하다'라는 뜻으로 쓰려면 뒤에 전치사 in을 필요로 하는 자동사이므로 오답.

---

8 Do not make any travel plans / until you receive **approval** / from your supervisor.

(A) materials (B) admission **(C) approval** (D) comments

해석 | 상사에게서 승인을 받을 때까지는 어떤 여행 계획도 세우지 마십시오.

(A) 재료, 자료 (B) 입장, 입학 (C) 승인 (D) 논평

해설 | 빈칸은 동사 receive의 목적어로, 이와 어울리는 명사를 골라야 한다. 여행 계획은 상사의 '승인'을 받은 후에 세워야 하므로 정답은 (C).

ACTUAL TEST **실전 문제에 적용하기**

교재 164쪽

1 (D) **2** (A) **3** (B) **4** (D) **5** (B) **6** (C) **7** (B) **8** (D) **9** (C) **10** (D) **11** (B) **12** (A)

---

1 The employees started a carpool program / as an attempt **to commute** to work / in a more environmentally friendly way.

(A) commute (B) commutes (C) commuted **(D) to commute**

해석 | 직원들은 더 친환경적인 방법으로 회사까지 출근하려는 시도로 카풀 제도를 시작했다.

어휘 | commute 통근하다 environmentally friendly 친환경적인

해설 | **to부정사 형용사 역할**

빈칸 앞 문장이 완전해 보이므로, 빈칸에는 수식어구가 들어가야 한다. 구조상으로는 완전해 보이나, 내용상 직원들이 무엇을 하는 '시도'를 시작한 것인지 알 수 없으므로 빈칸 앞 명사 attempt를 수식할 수 있는 to부정사가 빈칸에 필요하다. 정답은 (D).

---

2 The branch manager must give **consent** / prior to any personnel changes, / including department transfers.

(A) consent (B) evidence (C) attention (D) influence

해석 | 부서 이동을 포함하여 어떠한 인사 변경이 있기 전에 지점장이 동의해야 한다.

(A) 동의 (B) 증거 (C) 주의 (D) 영향

어휘 | prior to ~ 이전에 personnel 인사 (담당 부서) transfer 이동, 전근

해설 | **명사 어휘 consent**

직원들의 인사 변경이 있기에 앞서 지점장이 이에 '동의해야 한다'는 내용이 되어야 자연스럽다. consent는 '동의(하다)'라는 뜻의 명사와 동사 둘 다로 쓰이며, give consent는 '동의하다'라는 뜻이다. 따라서 정답은 (A).

---

3 Mr. Sawyer is **too** busy to answer the phone / at the moment.

(A) now **(B) too** (C) very (D) not

해석 | 소이어 씨는 지금 너무 바빠서 전화를 받을 수 없다.

어휘 | at the moment (바로) 지금

해설 | **to부정사 부사 역할**

빈칸 뒤의 형용사 busy와 to부정사 to answer, 그리고 선택지의 too를 보면 to부정사 구문 〈too+형용사[부사] +to do〉를 떠올릴 수 있어야 한다. 문맥상 '너무 바빠서 전화를 받을 수 없다'는 의미가 되어야 자연스러우므로 정답은 too.

---

4 It is necessary **to sign** this form / for advanced classes registration.

(A) signature (B) to be signed (C) signing **(D) to sign**

해석 | 상급반을 신청하기 위해 이 양식에 서명하는 것이 필수이다.

어휘 | sign 서명하다, 계약하다 advanced 상급의, 고급의

해설 | **가주어 it과 진주어 to부정사**

It is necessary로 시작하는 문장은 대개 가주어 it을 이용한 구문으로, 진짜 주어는 뒤에 나온다. 선택지 중에서 to부정사 형태인 (B)와 (D)가 정답 후보인데, 빈칸 뒤에 있는 this form을 목적어로 취할 수 있으려면 능동형인 (D)가 들어가야 한다.

---

5 In an effort **to simplify** the hiring process, / the HR department will set up a new job application Web site.

(A) simplify **(B) to simplify** (C) simplifies (D) simplification

해석 | 채용 절차를 간소화하려는 노력으로, 인사부서는 새 입사 지원 웹사이트를 구축했다.

어휘 | job application 입사 지원(서)

해설 | **to부정사 형용사 역할**

콤마 뒤는 완전한 문장으로, 콤마 앞은 〈전치사+명사〉 구조의 수식어구로 볼 수 있다. 빈칸에는 빈칸 뒤의 명사구 the hiring process를 이끌어, 빈칸 앞 명사 effort를 수식하는 말이 와야 한다. 따라서 명사를 수식하는 형용사처럼 쓸 수 있는 to부정사인 (B)가 정답.

---

6 The information pamphlet **outlines** the steps / for applying for a loan at Havana Bank.
(A) approves (B) produces **(C) outlines** (D) allows

해석 | 안내 책자에는 하바나 은행에 대출을 신청하기 위한 절차가 요약되어 있다.
(A) 승인하다 (B) 생산하다 (C) 요약하다 (D) 허락하다

어휘 | information pamphlet 안내 책자

해설 | **동사 어휘 outline**
빈칸 앞 The information pamphlet을 주어로, 빈칸 뒤 the steps를 목적어로 하여 자연스럽게 어울리는 동사를 고르는 문제. 안내 책자에 대출 신청 절차가 나와 있다는 뜻이므로 '요약하다, 간추리다'라는 의미의 (C)가 들어가야 알맞다.

---

7 **To enhance** image quality, / Altrox redesigned its smartphone's high-resolution camera.
(A) Enhances **(B) To enhance** (C) To be enhanced
(D) Enhanced

해석 | 이미지의 품질을 향상시키기 위해서, 알트록스 사는 자사 스마트폰의 고해상도 카메라를 다시 디자인했다.

어휘 | enhance 향상시키다, 높이다 high-resolution 고해상도

해설 | **to부정사 부사 역할**
콤마 이하에 완전한 문장이 나오고 있으므로, 콤마 앞부분은 수식어구가 되어야 한다. 수식어로 쓸 수 있는 to부정사인 (B)와 (C)가 정답 후보. 빈칸 뒤의 명사 image quality를 목적어로 취하므로 능동형인 (B)가 정답.

---

8 Museum visitors were eager **to examine** some Egyptian artifacts / in the main exhibition hall.
(A) to have examined (B) examine (C) examined
(D) to examine

해석 | 박물관 방문객들은 주 전시장에서 이집트 공예품들을 살펴보고 싶어한다.

어휘 | eager 열심인, 열렬한 exhibition hall 전시장

해설 | **to부정사와 자주 쓰이는 형용사**
빈칸 앞의 eager를 보고 to부정사와 자주 쓰이는 형용사임을 떠올려야 한다. 따라서 to부정사인 (A)와 (D)가 정답 후보. 의미상 주절보다 이전 시제를 나타내는 완료형 (A)는 정답이 아니다. 따라서, (D)가 정답. be eager to do는 '몹시 ~하고 싶다'라는 의미임을 기억하자.

9-12

To: Ericka J. Flores <florese@wayneinc.com>, Rita Sheppard <sheppardr@wayneinc.com>
From: Dennis Bickley <bickleyd@wayneinc.com>
Date: June 8
Subject: Conference room booking

Ms. Flores and Ms. Sheppard,

Due to a system error, the conference room has been double-booked for June 16. Unfortunately, both of you need to meet with clients at the same time. It is important to **settle** this problem as soon as possible.

Here's what I propose. **Please decide who will take the original date between you.** Then, the other person can select a new date. To **reserve** the new time slot, that person should also cancel the current one in the system.

수신: 에리카 J. 플로레스<florese@wayneinc.com>, 리타 셰퍼드 <sheppardr@wayneinc.com>
발신: 드니스 비클리<bickleyd@wayneinc.com>
날짜: 6월 8일
제목: 회의실 예약

플로레스 씨와 셰퍼드 씨께,

시스템 오류로 인해, 6월 16일에 회의실이 이중으로 예약되었습니다. 유감스럽게도, 두 분 모두 같은 시간에 고객을 만나셔야 합니다. 가능한 한 빨리 이 문제를 **해결하는** 것이 중요합니다.

제가 제안하는 바는 다음과 같습니다. **누가 원래의 예약 날짜를 취하실지 두 분께서 결정하십시오.** 그런 후에, 나머지 분은 새로운 날짜를 선택하면 됩니다. 새로운 시간을 **예약하기** 위해, 그분은 또한 시스템에서 현재의 예약을 취소해 주셔야 합니다.

이로 인해 야기될 불편에 대해 죄송하게 생각하며, 두 분 중 한 분은 일정상 **조정이** 가능하기를 바랍니다.

행정 부서, 드니스 비클리 드림

어휘 | double-book 이중으로 예약을 하다   settle 해결하다   inconvenience 불편   administration 행정, 경영

9 It is important to <u>settle</u> this problem / as soon as possible.
(A) attend (B) maintain (C) settle (D) predict
(A) 참석하다 (B) 유지하다 (C) 해결하다 (D) 예측하다

해설 | 동사 어휘 settle
빈칸 뒤 문장을 보면 빈칸 앞쪽에서 서술된 문제에 대한 해결 방안을 제시하고 있다. 따라서 빈칸 뒤 명사 this problem과 어울려, '이 문제를 해결하다'라는 의미가 문맥상 가장 자연스럽다. 따라서 '해결하다'의 의미를 가진 (C)가 정답.

10 (A) I'll fix the problem with the site soon.
(B) The room can be shared because of its spaciousness.
(C) The room's available times are posted online.
(D) **Please decide who will take the original date between you.**
(A) 사이트의 문제를 곧 고치겠습니다.
(B) 회의실은 넓기 때문에 함께 쓰셔도 됩니다.
(C) 회의실 사용 가능 시간은 온라인에 게시되어 있습니다.
(D) 누가 원래의 예약 날짜를 취하실지 두 분께서 결정하십시오.

해설 | 알맞은 문장 고르기
Here's what I propose.라는 문장 뒤에 빈칸이 이어지고 있으므로, 빈칸에는 두 사람에게 제안하는 해결책이 들어가야 한다. 빈칸 뒤에서 the other person(나머지 한 명)은 새로운 날짜를 선택하라고 했으므로, 둘 중 한 명은 원래 날짜에 회의실을 쓸 수 있다는 내용이 빈칸에 들어가야 알맞다. 따라서 (D)가 정답이다.
오답 | 사이트를 고치겠다는 (A)나 회의실을 공유하라는 (B)는 빈칸 뒤의 문장인 '다른 한 명이 다른 날짜를 고르라'는 내용과 어울리지 않으므로 오답. (C)는 회의실 이용 안내에 어울리는 문장이므로 오답.

11 To <u>reserve</u> the new time slot, / that person should also cancel the current one / in the system.
(A) reserving (B) reserve (C) have reserved (D) reservation

해설 | to부정사 부사 역할
콤마 뒤의 문장이 완전한 것으로 보아, 콤마 앞은 수식어구이다. 빈칸 앞의 To가 수식어구를 이끄는 전치사인지, To부정사를 이끄는 말인지 문맥으로 확인해야 한다. '새 시간을 예약하기 위하여'의 의미가 자연스러우므로 부사적 용법의 to부정사가 쓰여야 함을 알 수 있다. 따라서 to부정사를 구성하는 (B)와 (C)가 정답 후보. '새 시간을 예약하는 것'과 '기존의 예약을 취소하는 것'은 동시에 일어나야 하므로 앞선 시제를 의미하는 완료형 to부정사는 쓸 수 없다. 따라서 정답은 (B).

12 I'm sorry for any inconvenience this may cause, / and I hope that one of you will be able **to change** her schedule.
(A) **to change** (B) changing (C) changed (D) change

해설 | to부정사와 자주 쓰이는 형용사
빈칸 앞의 형용사 able을 보고 to부정사와 자주 함께 쓰이는 형용사임을 알아야 한다. 따라서 빈칸은 to부정사가 들어갈 자리이다. 정답은 (A). be able to *do*는 '~할 수 있다'라는 의미임을 기억하자.

UNIT 10 동명사

1 동명사의 개념과 형태

교재 169쪽

1 Maintaining **2** working **3** allows **4** her **5** (A) **6** (D) **7** (C) **8** (D)

---

1 (Maintained / **Maintaining**) the trust of its customers / is important / to Fidelis Industries.

해석| 고객들의 신뢰를 유지하는 것은 피델리스 인더스트리스 사에게 중요하다.

어휘| maintain 유지하다, 지속하다 trust 신뢰, 신임

해설| 괄호에 들어갈 말은 the trust를 목적어로 취하면서 문장의 주어가 되어야 한다. 따라서 명사의 역할을 하면서 목적어를 가질 수 있는 동명사 Maintaining이 적절하다.

---

2 The intern denied (**working** / worked) for the company's competitor / in the past.

해석| 그 인턴은 과거에 그 회사의 경쟁사에서 일했다는 것을 부인했다.

어휘| deny 부인하다 in the past 과거에

해설| 괄호 앞 동사 denied의 목적어 자리에 어울리는 것을 고르는 문제이다. 문장에 동사가 이미 있으므로 동사의 과거형 worked는 정답이 될 수 없다. 동명사는 명사처럼 목적어 역할을 하므로 정답은 working.

---

3 Conducting customer surveys (allow / **allows**) companies / to obtain valuable feedback.

해석| 소비자 설문 조사를 실시하는 것은 기업들이 귀중한 의견을 얻을 수 있게 해 준다.

어휘| conduct 실시하다 allow A to do A가 ~하도록 해 주다 obtain 얻다 valuable 귀중한

해설| 동사의 수를 묻는 문제이므로 주어를 정확히 파악하는 것이 관건이다. 주어는 괄호 바로 앞에 있는 surveys가 아니라 동명사인 Conducting이다. 동명사 주어는 단수 취급하므로 단수 동사인 allows가 정답.

---

4 Despite Ms. Howson's lack of experience, / Mr. Gibbs approves of (she / **her**) leading the project team.

해석| 호슨 씨의 경험 부족에도 불구하고, 깁스 씨는 그녀가 프로젝트 팀을 이끄는 데 찬성한다.

어휘| despite ~에도 불구하고 lack 부족 approve of ~에 동의하다[승인하다]

해설| 괄호 뒤의 leading은 괄호 앞에 있는 전치사 of의 목적어로 쓰인 동명사이다. 따라서 그 사이에 들어갈 수 있는 것은 동명사의 행위 주체를 나타내는 소유격 또는 목적격인 her이다.

---

5 Ms. Lang's main responsibility is **handling** the promotion / of the company's latest products.
(A) handling (B) handle (C) handlers (D) handled

해석| 랭 씨의 주요한 임무는 기업의 최신 제품들의 홍보를 처리하는 것이다.

어휘| main 주된 responsibility 책임, 책무 latest 최신의

해설| 빈칸 앞 동사 is로 보아 빈칸은 문장의 보어 자리이다. 그런데 동시에 빈칸 뒤 명사 the promotion을 목적어로 취하는 자리이므로 동명사인 handling이 정답이다. 이때 〈be동사+doing〉이 진행 시제를 나타내는 것이 아님에 주의하자. (D) handled를 쓰면 수동태가 되어 뒤의 목적어를 취할 수 없으므로 답이 될 수 없다.

---

6 Ms. Wilkie was congratulated / for **having passed** the first interview.
(A) passes (B) will pass (C) passed (D) having passed

해석| 윌키 씨는 첫 번째 면접을 통과한 것에 대해 축하를 받았다.

어휘| congratulate for ~에 대해 축하하다 pass 통과하다

해설| 빈칸은 전치사 for의 목적어 자리이면서 뒤의 명사구 the first interview를 목적어로 갖는 자리이다. 따라서 명사의 역할을 하면서 동시에 목적어를 가질 수 있는 동명사가 빈칸에 들어가는 것이 적절하다. 선택지 중 유일한 동명사인 (D)가 정답. 시험에 통과한 것은 축하를 받은 것보다 더 먼저 일어난 일이므로 〈having p.p.〉의 완료형을 썼다.

---

7 Mr. Walters plans on **outlining** the firm's sales goals / for the coming year / at the shareholders meeting.
(A) outline (B) outliner **(C) outlining** (D) being outlined
해석 | 월터즈 씨는 주주 회의에서 내년도 회사 매출 목표를 간략히 설명할 계획이다.
어휘 | plan on *doing* ~할 계획이다 outline 요약하다 coming 다가오는, 이번의 shareholder 주주

해설 | 명사인 (A), (B)와 동명사인 (C), (D) 모두 빈칸 앞 전치사 on의 목적어로 쓰일 수 있으나, 빈칸 뒤 명사구 the firm's sales goals를 목적어로 취할 수 있는 것은 능동형 동명사 (C)뿐이다. (D)도 동명사이지만 수동형이므로 뒤에 목적어를 취할 수 없다.

---

8 In addition to **managing** his own catering firm, / Mr. Borrell also gives lectures at Grimley College.
(A) manage (B) manageable (C) manages **(D) managing**
해석 | 자기 소유의 출장요리업체를 경영하는 것 외에, 보렐 씨는 그림리 대학에서 강의도 한다.
어휘 | in addition to ~ 이외에 manage 경영하다 catering 출장요리 give a lecture 강의하다

해설 | 빈칸은 빈칸 뒤 his own catering firm을 목적어로 취하면서 빈칸 앞의 구전치사 in addition to의 목적어로 쓰이므로 빈칸에는 동명사가 들어가야 한다. 따라서 (D)가 정답. 이때 in addition to의 to는 부정사가 아니라 전치사임을 기억하자.

---

2 동명사와 함께 쓰이는 표현

교재 171쪽

1 purchasing **2** operating **3** dealing **4** analyzing **5** (C) **6** (A) **7** (B) **8** (A)

---

1 Mr. Quinn recommends (**purchasing** / purchase) recycled products / to help protect the environment.
해석 | 퀸 씨는 환경 보호를 돕기 위해 재활용된 제품을 구매하는 것을 추천한다.
어휘 | recommend 추천하다 recycled 재활용된, 재생의

해설 | 괄호 앞의 동사 recommends는 동명사를 목적어로 취한다. 따라서 동명사인 purchasing이 정답. 명사 purchase도 동사 recommend의 목적어로 쓰일 수 있으나, 괄호 뒤 명사 recycled products를 목적어로 취할 수 없어서 오답이다.

---

2 To prevent accidents, / avoid (**operating** / operate) the machine / near water or wet surfaces.
해석 | 사고를 예방하기 위해 그 기계를 물이나 젖은 바닥 근처에서 사용하는 것을 피하세요.
어휘 | prevent 예방하다, 막다 accident 사고, 재해 near 가까운 wet 젖은 surface 표면

해설 | 괄호 앞의 avoid는 동명사를 목적어로 취하는 동사이다. 따라서 동명사인 operating이 정답. 문장에 이미 동사가 있으므로 동사 operate는 그 뒤에 나올 수 없다.

---

3 Ms. Traynor is used to (dealt / **dealing**) with customer complaints / over the phone.
해석 | 트레이너 씨는 전화상으로 고객 불만을 처리하는 것에 익숙하다.
어휘 | deal with ~을 다루다[처리하다]

해설 | 문장에 동사 is가 있으므로 괄호에는 과거 시제의 동사 dealt는 쓸 수 없다. 대신 괄호 앞의 전치사 to의 목적어로 쓸 수 있는 동명사인 dealing이 답으로 알맞다. 괄호 앞에 쓰인 be used to는 동명사와 함께 쓰여 '~하는 것에 익숙하다'의 의미로 쓰인다.

---

4 Ms. Bora was busy (analyze / **analyzing**) the survey results / all week.
해석 | 보라 씨는 한 주 내내 설문 조사 결과를 분석하느라 바빴다.

해설 | 괄호 앞 was busy를 보고 동명사 관용 표현인 be busy *doing*을 떠올렸다면 바로 맞출 수 있는 문제이다. be busy는 뒤에 동명사를 취해 '~하느라 바쁘다'의 의미로 쓰인다. 따라서 정답은 analyzing.

5 The board delayed **relocating** the advertising firm's headquarters / to New York.
(A) relocate　(B) has relocated　**(C) relocating**
(D) is relocating
해석| 이사회는 광고 회사의 본사를 뉴욕으로 옮기는 것을 연기했다.
어휘| delay 연기하다, 미루다　firm 회사

해설| 빈칸은 동사 delayed의 목적어 자리로 명사나 명사 역할을 할 수 있는 선택지를 골라야 한다. 선택지 중 명사 역할을 하면서 빈칸 뒤 명사 headquarters를 목적어로 취할 수 있는 동명사 (C)가 정답이다. 참고로 delay는 동명사를 목적어로 취하는 동사이다.

---

6 The construction team finished **building** a new subway exit / on Forester Road.
(A) building　(B) will build　(C) build　(D) builds
해석| 건설 팀은 포레스터 로에 새 지하철 출구 건설을 마쳤다.
어휘| exit 출구

해설| 빈칸은 동사 finished의 목적어 자리로, 선택지 중 동사의 목적어로 쓸 수 있는 동명사 (A)가 정답이다. finish는 목적어로 동명사를 취하는 동사이다. 나머지 선택지는 모두 동사라 빈칸에 들어갈 수 없다.

---

7 Breetowne's government officials are committed to **serving** the people / to their fullest capacity.
(A) served　**(B) serving**　(C) services　(D) serves
해석| 브리타운의 공무원들은 최선을 다해서 주민들을 위해 일하는 것에 전념한다.
어휘| government 정부, 정권　official 공무원, 임원　capacity 능력, 용량

해설| 빈칸 앞에 전치사 to가 있으므로 전치사의 목적어로 쓸 수 있는 동명사 (B)와 명사 (C)가 정답 후보. 그 중 빈칸 뒤의 명사 the people을 목적어로 취할 수 있는 동명사 (B)가 정답이다. 또한 be committed to doing은 '~하는 것에 전념하다'라는 뜻의 동명사 관용 표현이다.

---

8 Mr. Park had some difficulty **adjusting** to his new job, / as he had never worked in the field.
(A) adjusting　(B) adjustment　(C) adjust　(D) adjusted
해석| 박 씨는 그 분야에서 일해 본 적이 전혀 없기 때문에 새 일자리에 적응하는 데 어려움을 겪었다.
어휘| adjust to ~에 적응하다　field 분야

해설| have (some) difficulty는 '~하는 데 어려움을 겪다'라는 뜻을 나타내기 위해 동명사와 함께 쓰이는 관용 표현이다. 따라서 정답은 (A).

---

3 동명사 vs. 명사 vs. to부정사
교재 173쪽

1 replacing　**2** development　**3** hiring　**4** to check　**5** (A)　**6** (B)　**7** (C)　**8** (C)

---

1 Management should consider / (**replacing** / replacement) the company's old computers / with new ones.
해석| 경영진은 회사의 오래된 컴퓨터들을 새것으로 바꾸는 것을 고려해야 한다.

해설| 괄호 안의 동명사와 명사 둘 다 괄호 앞 동사 consider의 목적어가 될 수 있다. 하지만 괄호 뒤의 명사를 목적어로 취할 수 있는 것은 동명사뿐이다. 따라서 정답은 replacing. 참고로 consider은 목적어로 동명사를 취하는 동사이다.

---

2 Every day, / the investor reads articles / about new (**development** / developing) / in modern technology.
해석| 매일 그 투자가는 최신 기술의 새로운 발전에 대한 기사를 읽는다.
어휘| investor 투자자　modern 최신의, 현대적인

해설| 괄호는 전치사 about의 목적어 자리이므로 동명사와 명사 모두 괄호에 들어갈 수 있다. 그러나 괄호 앞의 형용사 new의 수식을 받을 수 있는 것은 명사이다. 따라서 정답은 development.

3 Diona Textiles, Inc., is accused of (**hiring** / to hire) unqualified workers / to save on labor costs.

해석| 디오나 텍스타일 주식회사는 인건비를 절감하기 위해 자격이 없는 직원들을 채용한 혐의를 받고 있다.

어휘| be accused of ~라는 혐의를 받다 unqualified 자격이 없는 save on ~을 절약하다 labor cost 인건비

해설| 괄호는 전치사 of의 목적어 자리인데, to부정사는 전치사의 목적어로 쓰일 수 없으므로 동명사를 써야 한다. 따라서 hiring이 정답.

---

4 Airline employees must not forget (**to check** / checking) the validity / of each passenger's passport.

해석| 항공사 직원들은 승객 각각의 여권 유효 여부를 잊지 말고 확인해야 한다.

어휘| validity 유효함 passenger 승객 passport 여권

해설| 괄호는 동사 forget의 목적어 자리로, to부정사일 때와 동명사일 때 의미가 달라진다. to부정사를 쓰면 '(앞으로) ~할 것을 잊다'라는 뜻이고, 동명사를 쓰면 '(이전에) ~했던 것을 잊다'라는 뜻이다. 문맥상 앞으로 해야 할 일을 나타내고 있으므로 to부정사를 써야 한다. 따라서 to check가 정답.

---

5 The county government depends on donations / from local businesses / for **maintaining** historical buildings.
(A) maintaining (B) maintain (C) maintains (D) maintenance

해석| 주 정부는 역사적 건물들을 유지 관리하는 데 지역 사업체들의 기부에 의존하고 있다.

어휘| depend on ~에 의존하다 donation 기부 historical 역사적인

해설| 빈칸 앞에 전치사 for가 있으므로 동명사인 (A)와 명사인 (D)가 정답 후보가 된다. 둘 중에서 뒤에 있는 historical buildings를 바로 목적어로 취할 수 있는 동명사 (A)가 정답. (D) maintenance는 '유지 관리'라는 뜻의 명사로 뒤에 목적어를 바로 취할 수 없어 오답이다.

---

6 Starting in May, / the program updates will begin **supporting** / the newest version of the software.
(A) supportive (B) supporting (C) supported (D) support

해석| 5월부터 시작하여 프로그램 업데이트는 그 소프트웨어의 최신 버전에 대한 지원을 시작할 것입니다.

해설| 빈칸은 빈칸 앞 동사 begin의 목적어 자리이므로 동명사인 (B)와 명사인 (D)가 정답 후보. 빈칸 뒤에 있는 명사 the newest version을 전치사의 도움 없이 목적어로 취할 수 있는 것은 동명사이므로 (B)가 정답. 참고로 동사 begin은 동명사와의 의미 구분 없이 to부정사도 목적어로 취할 수 있다.

---

7 Applicants should submit three letters of **recommendation** / with their application forms.
(A) to recommend (B) recommended (C) recommendation (D) recommending

해석| 지원자들은 본인의 지원서와 함께 추천서 세 통을 제출해야 한다.

어휘| recommendation 추천(서) application form 지원서, 신청서

해설| 전치사 of 뒤에는 목적어로 명사인 (C)와 동명사인 (D)가 올 수 있다. 동사 recommend는 타동사로, 동명사로 쓰이면 빈칸 뒤에 전치사 없이 목적어가 따라와야 하는데 빈칸 뒤에 목적어가 없으므로 (D)는 답이 될 수 없다. 따라서 (C)가 정답. to부정사 (A)는 명사 역할은 할 수 있지만 전치사의 목적어로 쓰일 수 없어서 오답이다. 참고로 letter of recommendation은 '추천서'라는 뜻으로 자주 사용된다.

---

8 A front desk employee's duties include **confirming** guest room reservation / in the hotel's database.
(A) confirmation (B) confirms (C) confirming (D) confirmed

해석| 접수대 직원의 업무에는 호텔의 데이터베이스에서 손님의 객실 예약을 확인하는 것이 포함된다.

어휘| duty 업무, 임무 include 포함하다 confirm 확인하다 reservation 예약

해설| 빈칸은 빈칸 앞 동사 include의 목적어 자리이므로 명사인 (A)와 동명사인 (C)가 정답 후보. 빈칸 뒤에 있는 guest room reservation을 바로 목적어로 취할 수 있는 것은 동명사이므로 (C)가 정답.

1 <u>Recovering</u> deleted files is sometimes possible / if you contact the IT department.
(A) Recover (B) Recovery (C) Recovered **(D) Recovering**

해석| IT 부서에 연락하면 삭제된 파일을 복구하는 것이 가끔 가능할 때도 있다.

어휘| recover 되찾다, 회복하다 delete 삭제하다 contact 연락하다 recovery 회복, 복구

해설| 문장의 동사가 is인 것으로 보아, is 앞의 복수 명사 files는 문장의 주어가 아니다. 따라서 빈칸에는 files를 수식하는 말이 아니라 문장의 주어가 되는 말이 들어가야 한다. 빈칸 뒤 deleted files를 목적어로 취하면서 문장의 주어로 쓸 수 있는 것은 동명사이므로 정답은 (D). 참고로 동명사(구)가 주어로 쓰일 때 단수 취급한다.

2 The directors postponed **appointing** an additional member / to their board.
(A) to appoint **(B) appointing** (C) appointed (D) appoint

해석| 임원들은 이사회에 추가 임원을 임명하는 것을 연기했다.

어휘| director 임원, 중역 additional 추가의

해설| 빈칸은 동사 postponed의 목적어 자리이므로 선택지 중 목적어 자리에 올 수 있는 to부정사 (A)와 동명사 (B)가 정답 후보. 동사 postpone은 동명사를 목적어로 취하므로 정답은 (B).

3 Ms. Peters will receive the **payment** / for her magazine article / next Monday.
(A) paying (B) pays **(C) payment** (D) paid

해석| 피터스 씨는 그녀의 잡지 기사에 대한 보수를 다음 주 월요일에 받을 것이다.

해설| 빈칸은 동사 receive의 목적어 자리이다. 따라서 동명사인 (A)와 명사인 (C)가 정답 후보. 빈칸 앞의 the 같은 한정사와 함께 쓰일 수 있는 것은 명사이므로 정답은 (C).

4 Employees expressed interest in <u>learning</u> a foreign language / in preparation for business trips overseas.
(A) learning (B) learn (C) to learn (D) be learned

해석| 직원들은 해외 출장에 대비하여 외국어를 배우는 것에 관심을 표했다.

어휘| express 표하다, 나타내다 foreign 외국의 in preparation for ~의 대비 [준비]로

해설| 빈칸은 전치사 in의 목적어 자리이므로 명사 또는 동명사가 들어갈 수 있다. 따라서 정답은 (A). to부정사인 (C)도 명사처럼 쓰여 목적어 역할을 할 수 있지만, 전치사의 목적어로는 쓰일 수 없다.

5-6

Dear Mr. Hayes,

I appreciate your **having ordered** our organically-grown fruit and vegetables.

My business partner informed me that you would like to meet with us at 9 A.M. on Tuesday because you are interested in stocking our produce in your supermarket. We look forward to **seeing** you on Tuesday. Let's use this time for discussing ways that our businesses can help each other.

하예즈 씨께,

저희 유기농 재배 과일과 채소를 **주문해 주셔서** 감사드립니다.

고객님의 슈퍼마켓에 저희 농산물을 보유하는 데 관심이 있으신 까닭에, 화요일 오전 9시에 저희와 만나기를 원한다고 제 사업 파트너가 알려 주더군요. 저희는 고객님을 화요일에 **뵙기를** 고대하고 있습니다. 이번 기회를 서로의 회사가 서로에게 도움이 될 수 있는 방법에 대해 논의하는 시간으로 삼도록 하죠.

어휘| organically-grown 유기농으로 재배된 inform A that A에게 ~을 알리다 stock (상품을) 보유하다

UNIT 10

5 I appreciate / your **having ordered** our organically-grown fruit and vegetables.
(A) ordered **(B) having ordered** (C) order (D) orders

해설| 빈칸 앞 your의 수식을 받을 수 있는 것은 동명사인 (B)와 명사인 (C), (D)이다. 그 중 빈칸 뒤 명사구 our organically-grown fruit and vegetables를 바로 목적어로 취할 수 있는 것은 동명사뿐이므로 정답은 (B). 참고로 '고마워하는 것'보다 '주문한 것'이 먼저이므로 완료형 〈having *p.p.*〉로 쓰였다.

6 We look forward to **seeing** you on Tuesday.
(A) see (B) being seen **(C) seeing** (D) saw

해설| 빈칸 앞쪽의 look forward to는 동명사와 어울려 '~하기를 고대하다'라는 뜻으로 쓰이는 관용 표현이다. 따라서 동명사인 (B)와 (C)가 정답 후보. 빈칸 뒤 인칭대명사 you를 목적어로 삼을 수 있는 능동형 (C)가 정답이다. 빈칸 앞 to만 보고 to부정사를 떠올려 동사원형인 (A)를 답으로 고르지 않도록 주의해야 한다.

VOCABULARY 사회 어휘(1)   교재 177쪽

1 issue 2 period 3 adequate 4 steady 5 (C) 6 (A) 7 (C) 8 (B)

---

1 The next (forecast / **issue**) of *Mirror Magazine* / will feature an interview / with a famous chef.
해석| 〈미러 매거진〉 지의 다음 호는 유명 요리사와의 인터뷰를 특집으로 다룰 것이다.
어휘| feature 특집으로 다루다, 보여주다

해설| 괄호 뒤의 전치사구 of *Mirror Magazine*이 괄호를 수식하고 있으므로 괄호에는 '(잡지·신문 등의) 호'라는 의미의 issue가 들어가는 것이 알맞다.

---

2 The subscription will expire / after a (**period** / figure) of twelve months.
해석| 그 정기 구독은 12개월의 기간 후에 만료될 것이다.
어휘| expire 만료되다

해설| 괄호 뒤 전치사구 of twelve months가 괄호를 수식하여 '12개월의 기간 후에 만료된다'는 내용이 자연스러우므로 '기간'이라는 뜻의 명사 period가 정답.

---

3 Without (**adequate** / published) funding, / the project will have to be abandoned.
해석| 충분한 자금 제공이 없다면, 그 프로젝트는 폐기되어야 할 것이다.
어휘| funding 자금 제공, 자금 abandon 버리다, 방치하다

해설| 문맥상 프로젝트가 폐기될 만한 조건으로는 '충분한' 자금 제공이 없다는 것이 자연스러우므로 정답은 adequate이다.

---

4 Mr. Newman makes a (**steady** / confidential) income / by writing articles for newspapers.
해석| 뉴먼 씨는 신문에 기사를 투고해서 안정적인 수입을 만든다.
어휘| income 수입, 소득

해설| 괄호 뒤 명사 income을 수식하여 자연스러운 형용사를 골라야 한다. 문맥상 '안정적인 수입'이라는 뜻이 되어야 하므로 steady가 정답.

---

5 Professor Johnson will soon **publish** his research paper / in a popular medical journal.
(A) admit (B) generate **(C) publish** (D) broadcast
해석| 존슨 교수는 조만간 유명 의학 잡지에 자신의 연구 논문을 게재할 것이다.
(A) 인정하다 (B) 발생시키다 (C) 게재하다 (D) 방송하다
어휘| research paper 연구 논문 medical journal 의학 잡지

해설| 빈칸 뒤 목적어인 명사구 his research paper와 호응하여 '연구 논문을 게재하다'라는 뜻이 되어야 자연스럽다. 따라서 '출판하다, 게재하다'라는 뜻의 동사 (C)가 정답.

---

6 CCTV cameras have been set up / for **security** reasons in the neighborhood.

(A) security (B) efficiency (C) recognition (D) diversity

해석| CCTV 카메라가 인근 지역에 보안상의 이유로 설치되었다.

(A) 보안 (B) 효율성 (C) 인정 (D) 다양성

어휘| set up 설치하다 neighborhood 근처, 이웃

해설| for 이하가 CCTV를 설치한 이유에 해당하므로 '보안'이라는 뜻의 (A)가 알맞다. for security reasons는 '보안상의 이유로, 보안 목적으로'라는 의미로 자주 쓰인다.

---

7 Loretta Laing gained international **recognition** / for reducing poverty in the region.

(A) indicator (B) standard (C) recognition (D) council

해석| 로레타 랭 씨는 그 지역의 빈곤을 감소시킨 것에 대해 세계적인 인정을 받았다.

(A) 지표 (B) 표준, 기준 (C) 인정 (D) 의회

어휘| international 세계적인 poverty 빈곤 region 지역

해설| 문맥상 '세계적인 인정을 받다'라는 뜻이 자연스러우므로 '인정'의 의미인 (C)가 빈칸에 들어가야 알맞다. gain recognition(인정을 받다)을 하나의 표현으로 알아두자.

---

8 ABB Network received an award / for its **extensive** coverage of the presidential election.

(A) tentative (B) extensive (C) potential (D) illegal

해석| ABB 네트워크 사는 대통령 당선에 대한 폭넓은 보도로 상을 받았다.

(A) 잠정적인 (B) 폭넓은, 광범위한 (C) 잠재적인 (D) 불법적인

어휘| coverage 보도, 취재 presidential 대통령의 election 당선, 선거

해설| for 이하는 상을 받은(received an award) 이유에 해당된다. '폭넓은' 보도를 했다는 내용이 가장 적절하므로 (B)가 정답이다.

ACTUAL TEST 실전 문제에 적용하기　　　　　교재 178쪽

1 (B)　**2** (C)　**3** (A)　**4** (D)　**5** (C)　**6** (A)　**7** (B)　**8** (A)　**9** (C)　**10** (A)　**11** (A)　**12** (D)

---

1 As a travel agent, / Thomas Wilkinson's job involves **reviewing** itineraries / to check for scheduling problems.

(A) to reviewing (B) reviewing (C) reviewed (D) review

해석| 여행사 직원으로서, 토마스 윌킨슨 씨의 업무는 일정상의 문제를 확인하기 위해 여행 일정표를 검토하는 것을 포함한다.

어휘| travel agent 여행사 직원 itinerary 여행 일정표

해설| **동명사 vs. 명사**

빈칸은 동사 involves의 목적어가 들어갈 자리이므로 동명사 (B)와 명사 (D)가 정답 후보. 목적어로 쓰이면서 동시에 빈칸 바로 뒤에 오는 itineraries를 목적어로 취할 수 있는 동명사 (B)가 정답이다.

---

2 Only upper management employees have access / to **confidential** documents / related to criminal backgrounds.

(A) cautious (B) surrounding (C) confidential (D) limiting

해석| 고위 경영진 직원들만 범죄 전력과 관련된 기밀 문서에의 접근 권한을 가지고 있다.

(A) 조심스러운 (B) 주변의 (C) 기밀의 (D) 제한하는

어휘| upper 고위의, 위(쪽)의 access 접근 (권한) criminal 범죄의

해설| **형용사 어휘 confidential**

빈칸 뒤 명사 documents를 수식하는 형용사를 고르는 문제. 범죄 전력과 같은 정보는 보통 비밀에 부쳐 관리되므로 빈칸에는 '기밀의'를 뜻하는 (C)가 들어가야 한다. confidential documents(기밀 문서), confidential information(기밀 정보)과 같은 표현을 통째로 알아두자.

3 Underline: Corrections to articles from past issues / are handled by the science journal's chief editor, Mr. Kang.
(A) Corrections (B) Correct (C) Correcting (D) Corrected
해석| 과월호 기사의 수정은 과학 잡지의 편집장인 강 씨가 처리한다.
어휘| correction 수정 chief editor 편집장

해설| **동명사 vs. 명사**
문장의 동사가 are handled이고 빈칸은 주어 자리이다. 따라서 명사인 (A)와 동명사인 (C)가 정답 후보인데, 뒤에 전치사구 to articles from past issues의 수식을 받고 복수 동사 are와 호응하여 쓰이므로 복수 명사 (A)가 정답이다.
오답| 동명사가 주어가 되면 단수 동사를 써야 하므로 (C)는 오답.

---

4 Whizz Electronic Goods will continue stocking its e-reader / despite the item's increasingly poor sales.
(A) is stocking (B) stock (C) has stocked (D) stocking
해석| 휘즈 전자제품 사는 전자책 리더의 판매가 점점 저조해지는데도 불구하고 이 제품을 계속 구비할 것이다.
어휘| despite ~에도 불구하고 increasingly 점점 더

해설| **동명사 vs. 명사**
빈칸은 동사 will continue의 목적어가 들어갈 자리이므로 명사 (B)와 동명사 (D)가 정답 후보. 빈칸 뒤 명사 its e-reader를 목적어로 취할 수 있는 동명사 (D)가 정답이다. 참고로 continue는 의미 차이 없이 목적어로 동명사와 to부정사를 모두 취하는 동사이다.

---

5 Mr. Rooney was given the responsibility / of finding an ideal venue / for the company banquet.
(A) find (B) to find (C) finding (D) found
해석| 루니 씨에게 회사 연회에 가장 적합한 장소를 찾는 책임이 주어졌다.
어휘| responsibility 책임, 책무 ideal 이상적인 banquet 연회

해설| **동명사 vs. to부정사**
빈칸은 전치사 of의 목적어 자리. 전치사 of 뒤에 올 수 있고 빈칸 뒤 명사구 an ideal venue라는 목적어를 취할 수 있는 것은 동명사인 (C)이다. to부정사는 전치사의 목적어로 쓰일 수 없으므로 (B)는 오답.

---

6 According to several studies, / high levels of unemployment / are clear indicators / of economic decline.
(A) indicators (B) operators (C) contractors (D) instructors
해석| 몇몇 연구에 따르면, 높은 수준의 실업률은 경제 쇠퇴의 명확한 지표이다.
(A) 지표 (B) 기사, 운영자 (C) 계약자 (D) 강사
어휘| unemployment 실업(률)

해설| **명사 어휘 indicator**
빈칸은 주격 보어 자리로, 주어와 동격의 명사가 와야 한다. 의미상 '높은 수준의 실업률이 경제 쇠퇴의 지표이다'라는 의미가 자연스러우므로 빈칸에는 '지표, 척도'를 의미하는 명사 (A)가 와야 한다.

---

7 Before the end of the year, / the supervisors must spend time / evaluating each worker's contribution / to the company.
(A) evaluate (B) evaluating (C) evaluated
(D) being evaluated
해석| 연말 전에 상사들은 직원들의 회사 기여도에 대해 평가하는데 시간을 할애해야 한다.
어휘| contribution to ~에의 기여[공헌]

해설| **동명사 관용 표현**
spend time *doing*은 '~하는 데 시간[돈]을 쓰다'라는 의미의 동명사 구문이다. 따라서 빈칸에는 동명사인 evaluating이 들어가야 알맞다.

---

8 Due to having received negative feedback about the product, / Mr. Lee wants to change its design.
(A) having received (B) received (C) be receiving
(D) has received
해석| 제품에 대해 부정적인 반응을 받았기 때문에, 리 씨는 제품의 디자인을 바꾸고 싶어 한다.

해설| **동명사의 시제**
빈칸 앞 Due to는 '~ 때문에'라는 뜻의 전치사이므로 빈칸에는 명사나 동명사가 와야 한다. 따라서 정답은 동명사 (A). '제품에 대한 반응을 받은 것'은 '원하는 것'보다 더 먼저 일어난 일이므로 완료형 〈having p.p.〉으로 나타냈다.

9-12

From: Frank Milano
To: Karl Lovett
Subject: Hospital Renovations
Date: July 2

Dear Mr. Lovett,

As you requested, I have attached the estimated cost for our upcoming project. The **figure** includes the total price of the materials and the wages of all workers. This will cost a lot but it is **worth** investing that amount for our hospital.

Along with the installation of new facilities, our contractor suggested **upgrading** our existing machinery. Some machinery will be serviced by engineers next week.

These changes will increase the number of patients we can serve. The work is expected to take six months to fully complete.

Please let me know if you have any questions about the cost.

Frank Milano
General Operations Manager, Chapman Hospital

발신: 프랭크 밀라노
수신: 칼 로베트
제목: 병원 보수
날짜: 7월 2일

로베트 씨께,

요청하신 대로, 곧 있을 우리 공사에 대한 예상 경비를 첨부했습니다. 이 **수치**에는 자재의 총 비용과 인부 전원의 임금이 포함되어 있습니다. 이것은 많은 비용이 들겠지만, 병원을 위해 그만큼의 비용을 투자할 **가치가** 있습니다.

새로운 설비의 설치와 함께, 하청업체에서 기존의 기계를 **업그레이드하는 것을** 제안했습니다. 일부 기계는 다음 주에 기사들의 점검을 받을 예정입니다.

이러한 변화로 우리가 서비스를 제공할 수 있는 환자의 수가 늘어날 것입니다. 작업은 완전히 마치는 데에 6개월이 걸릴 것으로 예상됩니다.

비용에 대해 문의가 있으면 알려 주시기 바랍니다.

채프먼 병원,
경영 총책임자 프랭크 밀라노 드림

UNIT 10

어휘| renovation 개조 attach 첨부하다 estimate (비용·가치 등을) 예상하다 wage 임금 worker 인부 invest 투자하다 along with ~와 함께 contractor 하청업체 service 점검[정비]하다 patient 환자

9 The **figure** includes / the total price of the materials / and the wages of all workers.
(A) connection (B) problem **(C) figure** (D) procedure
(A) 연결 (B) 문제 (C) 수치 (D) 절차, 과정

해설| 명사 어휘 figure
빈칸이 포함된 문장과 앞 문장을 확인하면, 빈칸이 가리키는 것은 앞 문장에 언급된 the estimated cost(예상 경비)인 것을 알 수 있다. 다시 말해, 금액을 뜻하므로 금액을 가리키는 말로 '수치'라는 뜻의 (C)가 알맞다.

10 This will cost a lot / but it is **worth** investing that amount / for our hospital.
(A) **worth** (B) forward (C) use (D) spent
(A) 가치 (B) 앞쪽으로 (C) 사용 (D) 이미 쓴

해설| 동명사 관용 표현
빈칸 앞의 be동사 is와 빈칸 뒤의 동명사 investing을 보고 동명사 구문이 쓰인 것이 아닌지 의심해 보아야 한다. be worth *doing*은 '~할 가치가 있다'라는 의미의 동명사 구문이다. 따라서 빈칸에는 worth가 들어가야 한다.

11 Along with the installation of new facilities, / our contractor suggested <u>upgrading</u> our existing machinery.
(A) upgrading (B) will upgrade (C) to be upgraded
(D) are being upgraded

12 (A) Feel free to send copies to my office for review.
(B) I look forward to hearing from you about our service.
(C) Your help in recruiting volunteers was essential.
(D) Please let me know if you have any questions about the cost.

(A) 제가 검토할 수 있도록 제 사무실로 언제든지 복사본을 보내 주십시오.
(B) 저희의 서비스와 관련하여 귀하의 연락을 기다리고 있겠습니다.
(C) 자원봉사자들을 모집하는 데 있어 귀하의 도움은 꼭 필요한 것이었습니다.
(D) 비용에 대해 문의가 있으면 알려 주시기 바랍니다.

분사의 개념과 쓰임　　　　　　　　　　　　　　　　교재 183쪽

1 preferred　**2** beginning　**3** challenging　**4** published　**5** (D)　**6** (B)　**7** (B)　**8** (A)

---

1 Clients can choose their (**preferred** / prefer) means of communication / between telephone and e-mail.
해석 | 고객들은 전화와 이메일 중에 선호되는 통신 수단을 선택할 수 있다.

해설 | 괄호에는 괄호 뒤 명사 means를 수식할 수 있는 어휘가 들어가야 한다. 분사는 형용사처럼 명사를 수식할 수 있으므로 preferred가 정답. 분사가 수식하는 명사 means는 '선호되는' 대상이므로 수동의 관계라서 과거분사를 썼다.

---

2 Mr. Davids will attend an international economics conference / (begin / **beginning**) next Monday.
해석 | 데이비드 씨는 다음 주 월요일에 시작하는 국제 경제 학회에 참가할 것이다.

해설 | 괄호 앞 부분이 완전한 문장이므로, 괄호 이하는 수식어구이다. 괄호 뒤에 목적어 next Monday가 있으므로 괄호 앞의 명사 conference를 수식하며 뒤에 목적어를 취하는 분사 beginning을 써야 한다.

---

3 Selling the product will become (challenged / **challenging**) / when the advertising campaign ends.
해석 | 광고 활동이 끝나면 제품을 판매하는 것이 어려워질 것이다.
어휘 | advertising campaign 광고 활동

해설 | 괄호는 동사 become의 보어 자리로 명사나 형용사가 들어갈 수 있다. 형용사처럼 주격 보어 역할을 할 수 있는 분사 challenging이 정답. challenging은 '어려운, 도전적인'이라는 뜻의 형용사로 굳어져 쓰이는 표현이다.

---

4 Mr. Pirelli had his consumer study (publishes / **published**) / last week.
해석 | 피렐리 씨는 지난 주에 자신의 소비자 연구가 출간되도록 했다.

해설 | 동사 had는 '~을 …하도록 하다'라는 의미로, 〈목적어+목적격 보어〉가 뒤따른다. 따라서 had의 목적어는 his consumer study이고 괄호는 목적격 보어 자리. 따라서 형용사처럼 쓸 수 있는 분사 published가 정답이다. 분사가 수식하는 명사 study는 '출간되게 하는' 대상이므로 수동의 관계라서 과거분사를 썼다.

---

5 After correcting some errors, / Bennet Advertising Inc. sent the **revised** proposal / to all of its clients.
(A) revise　(B) revises　(C) revising　**(D) revised**
해석 | 베넷 광고사는 몇 가지 오류 사항을 수정한 후, 수정된 제안서를 자사의 모든 고객들에게 보냈다.
어휘 | revise 수정하다

해설 | 정관사 the와 명사 proposal 사이에 위치한 것으로 보아 빈칸은 형용사 자리. 따라서 형용사처럼 쓰이는 분사인 (C)와 (D)가 정답 후보이다. 문맥상 '수정된 제안서'란 뜻이 되어야 하므로 수동 관계를 나타낼 수 있는 과거분사 (D)가 정답.

---

6 Management is considering holding training sessions / **focusing** on customer service skills.
(A) focus　**(B) focusing**　(C) have focused　(D) will focus
해석 | 경영진은 고객 응대 기술에 초점을 둔 연수를 개최할 것을 고려 중이다.

해설 | 빈칸 앞 문장이 완전하므로 빈칸 이후는 수식어구가 되어야 한다. 선택지에서 수식어구로 쓸 수 있는 것은 형용사처럼 명사를 수식할 수 있는 분사 focusing뿐이므로 (B)가 정답. 분사에 목적어나 수식어가 붙어 길어지면 수식하는 명사 뒤에 놓인다.

7 The city's traffic laws have become **complicated** / over the past few years.
(A) is complicated   (B) **complicated**   (C) complicates
(D) to complicate
해석| 그 도시의 교통 법규는 지난 몇 년간 복잡해졌다.

해설| 빈칸은 동사 have become의 보어가 들어갈 자리이므로 형용사 또는 명사가 들어가야 한다. 선택지에서 (B)만이 형용사의 역할을 할 수 있는 분사이므로 정답은 (B). complicated 는 '복잡한'의 의미로 형용사처럼 굳어져 쓰이는 분사임을 기억하자.

8 Alfresco Craftwork, / a furniture maker **specializing** in outdoor furnishings, / will open another branch.
(A) **specializing**   (B) specializes   (C) will specialize
(D) is specializing
해석| 옥외 가구에 특화된 가구 제조업체인 알프레소 크래프트워크 사는 또 다른 지점을 낼 것이다.
어휘| outdoor 야외의 furnishing 가구, 비품

해설| 문장의 주어는 Alfresco Craftwork, 동사는 will open이므로 a부터 furnishings까지는 주어와 동격인 어구가 되어야 한다. 따라서 빈칸 이하가 빈칸 앞의 명사구 a furniture maker를 수식할 수 있어야 하므로 뒤에서 명사를 수식할 수 있는 분사 (A)가 정답.

---

2 현재분사 vs. 과거분사

교재 185쪽

1 contributing **2** anticipated **3** operating **4** surprised **5** (D) **6** (C) **7** (A) **8** (A)

1 The new advertising campaign is a (**contributing** / contributed) factor / to Hinxon's recent success.
해석| 새로운 광고 선전은 하인슨의 최근의 성공에 기여한 요소이다.
어휘| contribute 기여하다, 이바지하다 factor 요소, 요인

해설| 수식받는 명사와 분사의 관계가 능동이면 현재분사를, 수동이면 과거분사를 쓴다. 분사가 수식하는 괄호 뒤의 명사 factor는 '성공에 기여하는' 주체이므로 능동의 관계가 성립한다. 따라서 정답은 현재분사 contributing.

2 The figures released by the firm / were lower than the (anticipating / **anticipated**) annual earnings.
해석| 회사가 발표한 수치는 예상했던 연간 수입보다 낮았다.
어휘| anticipate 예상하다 annual 연간의 earnings 소득, 수입

해설| 괄호의 분사는 괄호 뒤의 명사구 annual earnings를 수식하여 쓰였으므로 수식받는 명사와 분사의 관계를 확인해야 한다. 연간 소득은 '예상되는' 대상이므로 수동의 관계를 나타내는 과거분사 anticipated가 정답이다.

3 The foreman noticed him (**operating** / operated) the factory machinery / in the wrong way.
해석| 공장장은 그가 잘못된 방식으로 공장 기계를 가동하고 있음을 알아차렸다.
어휘| foreman 공장장 notice 알아차리다 operate 가동[작동]하다
in a ~ way ~한 방식으로

해설| 동사 notice는 뒤에 〈목적어+목적격 보어〉를 취해서 '~가 …하는 것을 알아차리다'라는 의미를 나타낸다. 동사 뒤 him이 목적어이고, 괄호는 목적격 보어 자리. '그'는 공장 기계를 '가동하는' 주체이므로, 능동을 나타내는 현재분사 operating이 적절하다.

4 The publisher is (surprising / **surprised**) / by the increasing number of *Planters Magazine* subscribers.
해석| 그 출판사는 〈플랜터즈 매거진〉 지의 증가하는 구독자 수에 놀랐다.
어휘| subscriber 구독자

해설| 선택지를 보니 surprise의 알맞은 분사 형태를 찾는 문제이다. 감정을 나타내는 동사는 분사 형태로 자주 쓰이는데, 수식 받는 명사가 감정을 느끼는 대상이면 과거분사를, 감정을 유발하는 주체이면 현재분사를 주로 쓴다. 여기서는 publisher가 '놀라움을 느끼는 대상'이므로 과거분사 surprised를 쓰는 것이 알맞다.

5 Chairman Park will review the **proposed** budget / for the petroleum firm's expansion program.
(A) propose (B) proposing (C) proposes **(D) proposed**
해석 | 박 회장은 석유 회사의 확장 프로그램을 위해 제안된 예산을 검토할 것이다.
어휘 | petroleum 석유

해설 | 빈칸 앞의 한정사 the와 빈칸 뒤 명사 budget으로 보아 빈칸은 budget을 수식하는 형용사 자리이므로, 형용사처럼 쓸 수 있는 분사 (B)와 (D)가 정답 후보. 수식을 받는 명사인 budget은 '제안되는' 대상이므로 수동의 관계를 나타내는 과거분사 (D)가 정답.

---

6 The Odeon Theater is pleased to announce a new film festival / **featuring** the work of local filmmakers.
(A) feature (B) features **(C) featuring** (D) featured
해석 | 오데온 극장에서는 지역 영화제작자들의 작품이 상영되는 새로운 영화 축제를 알려드리게 되어 매우 기쁘게 생각합니다.
어휘 | be pleased to *do* ~해서 기쁘다

해설 | 빈칸 앞 문장이 완전하므로 빈칸 이하는 수식어구이다. 선택지 중 수식어구로 쓸 수 있는 것은 빈칸 앞 명사 festival을 수식할 수 있는 분사 (C)와 (D)뿐이다. 빈칸 뒤의 명사 the work를 목적어로 취하면서 동시에 빈칸 앞 명사를 수식할 수 있는 것은 현재분사이므로 정답은 (C).

---

7 Dominic Weston won the Independent Cinema Award / for his **fascinating** documentary.
(A) fascinating (B) fascinated (C) fascinate (D) fascination
해석 | 도미닉 웨스턴 씨는 그의 매혹적인 다큐멘터리로 독립영화상을 수상했다.

해설 | 빈칸 앞 한정사인 소유격 인칭대명사 his와 빈칸 뒤 명사 documentary로 보아, 빈칸은 명사를 수식하는 형용사 자리. 따라서 형용사 역할을 하는 분사 (A)와 (B)가 정답 후보이다. 수식되는 명사 documentary는 '매혹되는 감정을 일으키는' 주체이므로 현재분사인 (A)가 정답이다.

---

8 The staff of the production department / is **satisfied** with / the new equipment.
(A) satisfied (B) satisfy (C) to satisfy (D) satisfying
해석 | 생산 부서의 직원들은 신규 장비에 만족했다.

해설 | 빈칸은 동사 is의 보어 자리로, 명사 역할의 to부정사 (C)와 형용사 역할의 분사 (A), (D)가 정답 후보. to부정사 (C)는 '만족하는 것'이라는 의미로 주어인 '직원들'과 동격으로 쓰일 수 없는 내용이라 오답이다. 주어인 '직원들'은 '만족하는 감정을 느끼는' 대상이므로 정답은 과거분사 (A)이다.

---

3 분사구문

교재 187쪽

1 Creating **2** discussing **3** Repaired **4** Having provided **5** (B) **6** (D) **7** (C) **8** (D)

---

1 (Creation / **Creating**) several new dishes, / Chef Gordon hopes to improve the restaurant's menu.
해석 | 몇몇 새로운 메뉴를 개발해 냄으로써, 요리사 고든 씨는 식당의 메뉴를 개선시키기를 희망한다.

해설 | 콤마 이하가 완전한 문장이므로 콤마 앞부분은 부사 역할을 해야 한다. 괄호 안의 분사인 Creating이 분사구문을 이끌어 부사 역할을 할 수 있다. 따라서 Creating이 정답.

---

2 While (**discussing** / discussed) the library renovation, / Mr. Norris suggested / that the budget is too low.
해석 | 도서관 보수 작업에 대해 논의하는 동안, 노리스 씨는 예산이 너무 적다는 것을 시사했다.
어휘 | suggest 시사하다, 제안하다 low 적은, 낮은

해설 | 접속사 While 다음에 주어와 동사가 없으므로, 접속사를 생략하지 않은 분사구문으로 보아야 한다. 주절의 주어인 Mr. Norris가 '논의를 하는' 주체이므로 능동을 나타내는 현재분사 discussing이 정답.

3 (Repairing / **Repaired**) only last week, / the photocopier should be working perfectly.

해석| 기껏해야 지난주에 수리받기 때문에, 복사기는 완벽하게 작동할 것이다.

어휘| photocopier 복사기 perfectly 완벽하게

해설| 분사구문의 분사는 주절의 주어와의 관계가 능동이면 현재분사를, 수동이면 과거분사를 쓴다. 주절의 주어인 the photocopier(복사기)가 '수리되는' 대상이므로 수동의 관계에 있다. 따라서 과거분사 Repaired가 정답.

---

4 (Provided / **Having provided**) good service / to our company for five years, / Ettrick Office Supplies will remain / as our main supplier.

해석| 5년 동안 우리 회사에 좋은 서비스를 제공해 왔기 때문에, 에트릭 오피스 서플라이즈 사는 앞으로도 우리의 주요 공급업체일 것이다.

어휘| remain 계속 ~이다, 남다

해설| 괄호 속 선택지를 보니, 분사구문의 시제를 묻는 문제이다. 분사구문의 시제가 주절의 시제보다 앞설 때, 분사구문의 형태는 완료형인 〈having p.p.〉가 된다. 문맥상 분사구문은 과거부터 현재까지 5년 동안의 일을 나타내고, 주절은 미래의 일을 나타내므로 Having provided가 정답.

---

5 **Employing** more than one thousand salespeople nationwide, / Altus Telecom is the largest firm / in its field.
(A) Employ (B) **Employing** (C) Employed (D) Employment

해석| 전국적으로 천 명이 넘는 영업 사원을 고용하고 있어서, 알투스 텔레콤 사는 그 분야에서 가장 큰 회사이다.

어휘| nationwide 전국적으로

해설| 콤마 뒷부분이 완전한 문장을 이루고 있고, 콤마 앞뒤를 잇는 연결어가 없으므로 콤마 앞부분은 분사구문이 됨을 알 수 있다. 주절의 주어인 통신사(Altus Telecom)가 '고용하는' 주체이므로 능동을 나타내는 현재분사 Employing을 써야 한다. 따라서 정답은 (B).

---

6 **Instructed** to work over the weekend, / the project team was able to finish the proposal / before the deadline.
(A) Instruct (B) Instructs (C) Instructing (D) **Instructed**

해석| 주말 동안 일하라는 지시를 받았기 때문에, 그 프로젝트 팀은 기한 전에 제안서를 끝낼 수 있었다.

어휘| instruct A to do A에게 ~하라고 지시하다

해설| 콤마 뒤 문장이 완전하므로, 빈칸이 포함된 콤마 앞부분은 수식어구가 되어야 한다. 빈칸 뒤 내용을 이끌어 수식어구로 쓸 수 있는 분사 (C)와 (D)가 정답 후보. 〈주어+동사〉 없이 분사가 부사처럼 콤마로 연결되어 있는 경우 분사구문이므로, 주절의 주어와 분사의 관계를 먼저 파악한다. 내용상 프로젝트 팀은 주말에 일하도록 '지시받은' 대상이므로 수동의 관계이다. 따라서 과거분사인 (D)가 정답.

---

7 **When** inspecting the contents prior to shipping, / our staff always checks / for damaged items.
(A) Because (B) Despite (C) **When** (D) Yet

해석| 배송 전에 내용물을 검사할 때, 저희 직원은 항상 파손 물품에 대해 확인합니다.
(A) ~ 때문에 (B) ~에도 불구하고 (C) ~할 때 (D) 그러나

어휘| inspect 검사하다 contents 내용물 prior to ~ 전에

해설| 빈칸 뒤 inspecting이 동명사이면 전치사 (B)도 정답 후보이고, 분사이면 나머지 접속사들도 함께 쓰여 분사구문을 이룰 수 있으므로 정답 후보이므로 문맥상 알맞은 의미의 선택지를 고른다. '내용물을 검사할 때 파손 물품에 대한 확인을 한다'는 내용이 자연스러우므로 '~할 때'의 의미인 접속사 (C)가 정답. 의미를 명확하게 전달하기 위해 접속사를 남긴 분사구문 문장이다.

---

8 **Having introduced** the new member to the council, / the chairperson began discussing the first item on the agenda.
(A) Introduced (B) Will introduce (C) Has introduced (D) **Having introduced**

해석| 의회에 신규 회원을 소개한 후, 의장은 안건의 첫 번째 항목에 대해 논의하기 시작했다.

어휘| chairperson 의장

해설| 콤마 이하는 완전한 문장이므로 콤마 앞은 이를 수식하는 부사구 역할을 해야 한다. 따라서 부사구를 이끌 수 있는 분사 (A)와 (D)가 정답 후보. 둘 중 빈칸 뒤 명사구 the new member를 목적어로 삼을 수 있는 것은 현재분사인 (D)이다. 참고로, '신규 회원을 소개한 것'과 '안건에 대해 논의하기 시작한 것'은 함께 일어날 수 있는 일이 아니라 시제의 차이를 나타내는 완료형 〈having p.p.〉가 쓰였다.

1 (D) **2** (B) **3** (A) **4** (B) **5** (C) **6** (D)

---

1 The new audio equipment was severely **damaged** / during the delivery.
(A) damage (B) damaging (C) damages (D) damaged
해석ㅣ 새 오디오 장비가 배송 중에 심하게 파손되었다.
어휘ㅣ severely 심하게, 혹독하게

해설ㅣ 빈칸은 was의 보어 자리로, 빈칸 앞의 부사 severely의 수식을 받는 형용사가 들어가야 한다. 형용사처럼 보어 역할을 할 수 있는 분사 (B)와 (D)가 정답 후보. 주어인 equipment가 '파손된' 대상이므로 수동의 관계이다. 따라서 과거분사인 (D)가 정답.

---

2 Before **scheduling** a physical therapy session, / a patient must first be examined / by a doctor.
(A) will schedule **(B) scheduling** (C) scheduled
(D) is scheduling
해석ㅣ 물리 치료 시간의 일정을 잡기 전에, 환자는 의사에게 먼저 진찰받아야 한다.
어휘ㅣ physical therapy 물리 치료 examine 진찰[검사]하다

해설ㅣ 접속사 Before 뒤에 주어와 동사가 없으므로 접속사를 생략하지 않은 분사구문이다. 주절의 주어인 patient가 '일정을 잡는' 주체이므로 능동의 관계이다. 따라서 현재분사인 (B)가 정답.

---

3 The marketing team's survey received an **overwhelming** number of responses / from potential customers.
(A) overwhelming (B) overwhelmed (C) overwhelms
(D) overwhelm
해석ㅣ 마케팅 팀의 설문 조사는 잠재적 고객들로부터 압도적인 수의 응답을 받았다.
어휘ㅣ overwhelming 압도적인 potential 잠재적인, 가능성이 있는

해설ㅣ 빈칸 앞에 관사 an, 뒤에 명사 number이 있으므로 〈한정사+형용사+명사〉 구조임을 알 수 있다. 따라서 빈칸은 형용사 자리이므로 형용사 역할을 하는 분사 (A)와 (B)가 정답 후보. 수식을 받는 명사 number는 '압도되는 감정을 느끼게 하는' 주체이므로 능동을 나타내는 현재분사 (A)가 정답.

---

4 Once **confirmed**, your order of mechanical components / will be delivered to your premises.
(A) confirm **(B) confirmed** (C) confirming (D) to confirm
해석ㅣ 일단 확인이 되면, 귀하가 주문하신 기계 부품들은 자택으로 배송될 것입니다.

해설ㅣ Once가 접속사임에도 불구하고 뒤에 주어와 동사가 없으므로, 접속사를 생략하지 않은 분사구문임을 알 수 있다. 따라서 분사인 (B)와 (C)가 정답 후보. 주절의 주어인 your order가 '배송되는' 대상이므로 수동의 의미인 과거분사 (B)가 정답.

5-6

Hillman Apartments Makes Changes after Fire

Due to last week's fire at Hillman Apartments, the building owners have decided to implement stricter safety measures. As indicated in the safety officer's report, the owners must conduct regular fire drills and improve the signs **directing** people to exits.

Tenants are **concerned** as they are still unsure which route to take in case of a fire. These new measures should help them feel safer.

힐만 아파트가 화재 후에 탈바꿈하다

지난주 힐만 아파트의 화재로 인해, 건물주들은 더 엄격한 안전 조치를 취하기로 결정했다. 안전 관리자의 보고서에 나온 대로, 건물주들은 정기적인 소방 훈련을 실시하고 사람들을 출구로 **안내하는** 표지판들을 개선해야 한다.

세입자들은 화재가 발생할 경우 어떤 길로 가야 할지 여전히 확신할 수 없기 때문에 **걱정한다**. 이 새로운 조치들은 그들이 더 안전하다고 느끼게 해 줄 것이다.

어휘ㅣ make a change 변화시키다 conduct 시행하다 regular 정기적인 fire drill 소방 훈련 direct 지시하다, 안내하다 tenant 세입자 unsure 확신하지 못하는 route 길, 경로 in case of ~ ~이 발생할 시에는

5 As indicated in the safety officer's report, / the owners must conduct regular fire drills / and improve the signs <u>directing</u> people to exits.
(A) director　(B) directed　**(C) directing**　(D) direct

해설| 빈칸 앞 문장이 완전하므로 빈칸 이하는 수식어 역할을 한다. 선택지 중 수식어로 쓸 수 있는 것은 빈칸 앞 명사구 the signs를 꾸미는 형용사 역할의 분사 (B)와 (C)이다. 수식받는 명사 signs는 '출구로 안내하는' 주체이므로 능동의 관계를 나타내는 현재분사 (C)가 정답.

---

6 Tenants are <u>concerned</u> / as they are still unsure / which route to take in case of a fire.
(A) concerning　(B) concern　(C) concerns　**(D) concerned**

해설| 빈칸은 빈칸 앞 be동사 are의 보어 자리이다. 따라서 분사 (A)와 (D), 명사 (B)와 (C) 모두 빈칸에 올 수 있다. 그러나 명사는 주어와 동격이어야 하므로 내용상 어색하기 때문에 오답. 주어인 Tenants는 '걱정하는 감정을 느끼는' 대상이므로 과거분사 (D)가 정답이다.

VOCABULARY　　**사회 어휘(2)**　　　　　　　　　教材 191쪽

1 conventional　**2** government　**3** comply　**4** charged　**5** (A)　**6** (C)　**7** (D)　**8** (C)

---

1 The Reika Organization holds more fundraising events / than (compliant / **conventional**) charities.
해석| 레이카 단체는 일반적인 자선 단체보다 모금 행사를 더 많이 한다.

해설| 괄호 뒤의 명사 charities와 잘 어울리는 형용사를 고르는 문제. '기존의 일반적인 자선 단체보다 모금 행사를 더 많이 한다'는 내용이 자연스러우므로 정답은 '관습적인, 관례적인'의 의미인 conventional.

---

2 The road development project was paid for / by (delegate / **government**) funds.
해석| 그 도로 개발 프로젝트는 정부 자금으로 비용이 지불되었다.

해설| 괄호는 전치사 by와 함께 수동태 동사인 was paid for의 행위자를 나타내고 있다. 문맥상 도로 개발과 같은 프로젝트는 '정부 자금'으로 지불되는 것이 자연스러우므로 정답은 government.

---

3 Workers must (**comply** / constitute) with the safety regulations / of the factory floor.
해석| 작업자들은 반드시 작업 현장의 안전 규정을 따라야 한다.
어휘| safety regulation 안전 규정　factory floor 작업 현장

해설| 괄호 뒤 전치사 with와 어울려 그 뒤의 명사를 목적어로 취하는 동사를 골라야 한다. constitute는 타동사로 전치사의 도움 없이 목적어를 취할 수 있으므로 오답. 따라서 comply가 정답이다.

---

4 The lawyer's client was not (**charged** / enforced) / for the first consultation.
해석| 그 변호사의 고객은 첫 번째 상담에 대해서는 비용을 청구받지 않았다.
어휘| consultation 상담

해설| 문맥상 고객이 변호사에게 비용을 '청구받다'라는 의미가 되어야 자연스러우므로 charged가 정답.

---

5 The local government has <u>declared</u> a state of emergency / in the town / due to the flooding.
(A) declared　(B) reformed　(C) enlarged　(D) prohibited
해석| 지역 정부는 그 홍수 때문에 지역에 비상 사태를 선포했다.
(A) 선언하다 (B) 개선하다 (C) 확장하다 (D) 금지하다
어휘| state of emergency 비상 사태　flooding 홍수

해설| 빈칸 뒤의 명사구 a state of emergency와 어울려 '비상 사태를 선포하다'의 의미가 자연스러우므로 '선언하다'라는 뜻의 동사 declare가 빈칸에 들어가야 알맞다. 따라서 정답은 (A).

6 The mayor of Garrity has gained a **reputation** / for listening closely to the concerns of citizens.

(A) destination (B) renewal **(C) reputation** (D) transfer

해석| 개리티 시의 시장은 시민들의 걱정을 주의 깊게 경청하는 것으로 명성을 얻었다.

(A) 목적지 (B) 갱신, 재개 (C) 명성, 평판 (D) 이동

어휘| closely 주의 깊게   concern 《*pl.*》 걱정, 관심사   citizen 시민

해설| 빈칸 앞 동사 gained와 잘 어울리는 명사 어휘를 고르는 문제. '명성을 얻었다'는 의미가 가장 잘 어울리므로 '명성, 평판'이라는 뜻의 (C)가 정답.

---

7 The city council tried to resolve a **conflict** / between local homeowners and Wickham Construction.

(A) combination (B) prevention (C) following **(D) conflict**

해석| 시의회는 지역 주택 소유주들과 위컴 건설사 간의 갈등을 해결하려고 노력했다.

(A) 조합 (B) 예방 (C) 추종자, 다음 (D) 갈등

어휘| council 시의회   homeowner 주택 소유주

해설| 빈칸 앞 to부정사 to resolve와 어울려 '갈등을 해결하다'라는 의미가 자연스러우므로 '갈등'을 뜻하는 (D)가 정답. conflict는 갈등을 빚는 두 대상을 나타내기 위해 전치사 between과 함께 쓸 수 있다.

---

8 Castleford locals largely **support** the plan / to transform the parking lot into a park.

(A) suppose (B) propose **(C) support** (D) reform

해석| 캐슬포드 지역민들은 그 주차장을 공원으로 바꾸는 계획을 대체로 지지한다.

(A) 가정하다 (B) 제안하다 (C) 지지하다 (D) 개선하다

어휘| local 지역 주민, 현지인   largely 대체로, 크게   transform 바꾸다

해설| 문맥상 '계획을 지지하다'라는 뜻이 되어야 자연스러우므로 (C)가 정답이다. '계획을 제안하다'라는 뜻으로 (B) propose도 가능해 보이지만 largely(대체로)라는 부사의 수식을 받기에 어울리지 않으므로 오답.

ACTUAL TEST 실전 문제에 적용하기   교재 192쪽

1 (D) **2** (C) **3** (B) **4** (A) **5** (B) **6** (A) **7** (D) **8** (B) **9** (D) **10** (B) **11** (C) **12** (C)

---

1 The **enclosed** warranty card / must be completed and registered / within thirty days of purchase.

(A) enclosing (B) to enclose (C) be enclosed **(D) enclosed**

해석| 동봉된 보증서 카드는 구매로부터 30일 내에 작성되고 등록되어야 합니다.

어휘| complete 작성하다, 기입하다   register 등록하다

해설| **과거분사**

빈칸 앞 한정사 the와 빈칸 뒤 명사 warranty card로 보아, 빈칸은 빈칸 뒤 명사를 수식하는 형용사 자리이다. 형용사처럼 쓰일 수 있는 분사 (A)와 (D)가 정답 후보인데, 수식을 받는 명사 warranty card가 '동봉된' 대상으로 수동의 관계이므로 과거분사 (D)가 정답이다.

---

2 The governor expressed his **concern** / about the high level of pollution / in the area.

(A) stability (B) intrigue **(C) concern** (D) need

해석| 주지사는 그 지역의 높은 오염 수준에 대해 우려를 표했다.

(A) 안정성 (B) 계략 (C) 우려 (D) 필요(성)

어휘| governor 주지사   express 표현하다, 나타내다   pollution 오염

해설| **명사 어휘 concern**

문맥상 '우려를 표명하다'란 내용이 자연스러우므로 '우려, 근심'이란 뜻의 명사 (C)가 정답. 보통 전치사 about과 함께 concern about[over](~에 대한 우려)의 형태로 많이 쓰인다.

---

3 Unfortunately, / the exercise machine was shipped without some vital parts, / **making** it useless.

(A) made **(B) making** (C) will make (D) has made

해석| 유감스럽게도 그 운동 기구는 일부 중요한 부품들이 빠진 채 배송되었는데, 그렇게 되면 그 기구는 쓸모없게 된다.

어휘| unfortunately 유감스럽게도   vital 필수적인   part 부품   useless 쓸모없는

해설| **분사구문**

빈칸 이하는 콤마 앞의 완전한 문장과 접속사 없이 이어지고 있으므로 분사구문임을 알 수 있다. 분사구문을 이끌 수 있는 분사 (A)와 (B) 중에서 빈칸 뒤의 대명사 it을 목적어로 취할 수 있는 현재분사 (B)가 정답이다.

4 Ms. Arnett was **disappointed** / by the lack of features on the digital camera, / considering the price / that she paid.
(A) disappointed (B) disappointedly (C) disappointing
(D) disappoint

해석 | 아네트 씨는 자신이 지불한 가격을 고려할 때, 디지털 카메라의 기능 부족에 실망했다.

어휘 | lack 부족, 부실 feature 기능 considering ~을 고려할 때

해설 | **과거분사**
빈칸은 동사 was의 보어 자리이다. 따라서 보어로 쓸 수 있는 형용사 또는 명사가 들어가야 하므로, 형용사 역할을 할 수 있는 분사 (A)와 (C)가 정답 후보. 감정을 나타내는 동사 disappoint가 쓰였는데, 주어인 Ms. Arnett이 '실망한 감정을 느끼는' 대상이므로 과거분사인 (A)가 정답이다.
오답 | 부사 (B)와 동사 (D)는 형용사 역할을 할 수 없으므로 오답이다.

---

5 By following the guidelines / **outlined** in the user manual, / you can prolong the life / of the product.
(A) outlining (B) outlined (C) outline (D) outlines

해석 | 사용설명서에 요약된 지침을 따름으로써, 제품의 수명을 연장시킬 수 있습니다.

어휘 | outline 요약하다 prolong 연장하다

해설 | **과거분사**
빈칸부터 콤마까지 없어도 문장이 완전하므로 해당 부분은 수식어구이다. 선택지 중 수식어로 쓸 수 있는 것은 빈칸 앞 명사구 the guidelines를 꾸밀 수 있는 형용사 역할의 분사 (A)와 (B)이다. 수식받는 명사 guideline은 '요약되는' 대상이므로 수동의 의미를 나타내는 과거분사 (B)가 정답.

---

6 In order to provide the local community with a greater sense of identity, / the Winterborne Historical Society was **constituted** in 1946.
(A) constituted (B) limited (C) explored (D) diminished

해석 | 지역 사회에 더욱 강한 정체성을 부여하기 위해 1946년 윈터본 역사 학회가 설립되었다.

(A) 설립하다, 구성하다 (B) 제한하다 (C) 탐험하다 (D) 줄이다, 감소시키다

어휘 | provide A with B A에게 B를 제공하다 identity 정체성, 본질

해설 | **동사 어휘 constitute**
주절의 주어 the Winterborne Historical Society와 어울리는 동사를 고르는 문제. 따라서 빈칸에는 '(조직·집단을) 설립하다, 구성하다'라는 뜻의 (A)가 들어가야 한다.

---

7 Staff members are reminded to turn off the air conditioning / when **exiting** the meeting room.
(A) exit (B) exited (C) exits (D) exiting

해석 | 직원들은 회의실을 나갈 때 에어컨을 끄라는 말을 다시 한 번 듣게 된다.

어휘 | remind A to do A가 ~하도록 다시 말해주다[상기시키다] turn off (전원을) 끄다 exit 나가다, 떠나다

해설 | **분사구문**
when이 접속사임에도 불구하고 뒤에 주어와 동사가 없다. 따라서 접속사를 남겨둔 분사구문으로 볼 수 있으며, 분사인 (B)와 (D)가 정답 후보이다. 주절의 주어 Staff members가 '밖으로 나가는' 주체이므로 능동을 나타내는 현재분사 (D)가 적절하다.

---

8 Due to an increase in thefts, / tourists are **advised** to watch their belongings / at all times.
(A) advising (B) advised (C) advisor (D) advise

해석 | 절도의 증가로 인해, 여행객들은 항상 본인의 소지품을 조심하라는 조언을 듣는다.

어휘 | theft 절도 watch 조심하다 at all times 항상, 상시

해설 | **과거분사**
빈칸 앞에 be 동사 are가 있으므로 빈칸에 들어갈 수 있는 것은 보어로 쓸 수 있는 분사 (A), (B)와 명사 (C)이다. (C)는 빈칸에 들어가면 '여행객은 조언자들이다'라는 의미로 어색하므로 오답. 주어인 '여행객들'은 '조언을 듣는' 대상이므로 수동의 의미를 나타내는 과거분사 (B)가 정답. be advised to do(~하라는 조언을 듣다)라는 표현을 꼭 기억해두자.

Harington Set to Begin Local Clean-up

10 May—Harington Council has announced the launch of a new environmental project, Clean Up Harington. This project aims to improve the facilities of the town for all residents. It will be carried out by community members through **voluntary** work.

Workers will first turn their attention to Blighty Park, where they will focus on trash removal from the pond and **surrounding** area. This park used to be a beautiful, clean area **enjoyed** by many Harington residents. **However, it has become dirty due to the lack of regular maintenance.**

In a recent interview, the mayor told of his delight at receiving local support for the project. He said, "We consider providing the town with these services extremely important."

해링턴, 지역 정화에 착수하다

5월 10일—해링턴 의회는 새로운 환경 사업인 '해링턴 정화 사업'의 착수를 발표했다. 이 사업은 주민 모두를 위해 지역의 시설을 개선하는 것을 목표로 한다. 이는 지역민들의 **자발적인** 작업을 통해 실행될 것이다.

작업자들은 먼저 블라이티 공원으로 주의를 돌려, 연못 및 **주변** 지역의 쓰레기 제거에 중점을 둘 것이다. 이 공원은 예전에는 많은 해링턴 주민들이 **즐기는** 아름답고 깨끗한 구역이었다. **하지만, 정기적인 관리의 부족으로 인해 점점 더러워졌다.**

최근의 인터뷰에서, 시장은 프로젝트에 대한 지역 주민들의 지지를 받는 것이 기쁘다고 말했다. "저희는 도시에 이러한 편익을 제공하는 것을 대단히 중요하게 생각합니다."라고 그는 말했다.

어휘| clean-up 정화, 정비 aim to *do* ~할 것을 목표로 하다 turn *one's* attention to ~로 주의를 돌리다 focus on ~에 중점을 두다 [주력하다] trash 쓰레기 removal 제거 pond 연못 surrounding 주변의 used to *do* (예전에)~했었다[였다] delight 기쁨, 즐거움

9 It will be carried out by community members / through **voluntary** work.
(A) consistent (B) conventional (C) previous (D) voluntary
(A) 한결같은, 일관된 (B) 관습적인 (C) 이전의 (D) 자발적인

해설| 형용사 어휘 voluntary
빈칸 뒤에 work라는 명사와 어울리는 형용사를 골라야 한다. 빈칸 앞 문장들의 내용을 봤을 때, 환경 정화 사업이 주민들의 '자발적인 작업'에 의해 실행된다는 것이 자연스러우므로 정답은 (D).

10 Workers will first turn their attention to Blighty Park, / where they will focus on trash removal / from the pond and **surrounding** area.
(A) surround (B) **surrounding** (C) surrounded
(D) have surrounded

해설| 현재분사
빈칸은 뒤의 명사 area를 수식하는 형용사 자리이다. 선택지에서 형용사 역할을 할 수 있는 것은 분사인 (B)와 (C)이다. 여기서 현재분사 surrounding은 '인근의'라는 뜻으로 굳어져 쓰이는 형용사임을 알아야 한다. 따라서 정답은 (B).

11 This park used to be a beautiful, clean area / **enjoyed** by many Harington residents.
(A) enjoy (B) enjoying (C) **enjoyed** (D) to enjoy

해설| 과거분사
빈칸 앞 문장이 완전하므로, 빈칸 이하는 앞의 명사 area를 수식하는 어구가 되어야 한다. 따라서 형용사 역할을 하는 분사 (B), (C)와 to부정사 (D)가 빈칸에 들어갈 수 있는데, 문맥상 지역이 사람들에 의해 '즐겨지는' 대상이므로 수동의 관계이다. 정답은 (C).
오답| to부정사 (D)도 능동의 의미라 오답이다.

12 (A) Safety is a top priority for the city's park.

(B) The department is considering planting flowers.

(C) However, it has become dirty due to the lack of regular maintenance.

(D) Alternatively, there are indoor spaces for various activities.

(A) 안전이 도시 공원의 최우선 과제이다.

(B) 그 부서에서는 꽃을 심는 것을 고려하고 있다.

(C) 하지만, 정기적인 관리의 부족으로 점점 더러워졌다.

(D) 그 대신에, 다양한 활동을 위한 실내 공간들이 있다.

해설 | **알맞은 문장 고르기**

빈칸 앞에서 공원이 아름답고 깨끗했던 것을 과거 시제(used to be)로 나타낸 것으로 보아, 현재에는 공원 상태가 좋지 않음을 알 수 있다. 따라서 이러한 현재의 공원 상태를 언급하는 (C)가 들어가야 알맞다. used to(한때 ～했었다)는 역접의 접속사 however와 대구를 이루어 과거와 현재를 비교하여 쓰이니 알아두자.

오답 | (A)는 공원 안전, (B)는 꽃 심기, (D)는 실내 활동 공간에 대한 내용으로 빈칸 앞뒤 흐름과 전혀 어울리지 않아 오답이다.

1 접속사의 개념과 종류

교재 197쪽

1 and **2** or **3** but **4** that **5** (C) **6** (D) **7** (B) **8** (D)

---

1 Vero Insurance promotes its products / through e-mails (of / **and**) calls.

해석| 베로 보험사는 자사의 상품을 이메일과 전화로 홍보한다.

어휘| insurance 보험

해설| 괄호에는 괄호 앞뒤의 명사 e-mails와 calls를 연결하는 접속사인 and가 들어가야 알맞다. 전치사 of는 수식 기능을 하므로 내용상 적절하지 않다.

---

2 He suggested meeting at the concert venue (its / **or**) at the nearest station.

해석| 그는 공연장이나 가장 가까운 역에서 만날 것을 제안했다.

해설| 괄호 앞뒤에 장소를 나타내는 전치사구인 at the concert venue와 at the nearest station이 나열되었으므로 둘을 연결하는 접속사가 필요하다. 따라서 or이 정답.

---

3 We wanted to attend the lecture, / (**but** / to) the tickets were sold out.

해석| 우리는 강의에 참석하기를 원했지만, 입장권이 매진되었다.

어휘| lecture 강의 sold out 매진된, 다 팔린

해설| 괄호 앞으로 완전한 문장이 있으므로 괄호에는 두 문장을 연결하는 접속사가 들어가야 한다. 따라서 접속사인 but이 정답. but은 '대조'를 의미하는 접속사로 '그러나, 하지만'의 의미이다. 전치사 to는 절과 절을 연결하는 기능을 하지 못하므로 오답.

---

4 New supervisors think / (**that** / but) managing people in organizations / is a challenging task.

해석| 새로운 관리자는 조직 내의 사람들을 관리하는 것이 어려운 일이라고 생각한다.

어휘| manage 운영하다, 관리하다 organization 조직, 단체 challenging 도전적인 task 일, 과업

해설| 내용상 괄호 이하가 동사 think의 목적어가 되어야 한다. 괄호에는 목적어 역할의 명사절을 이끌 수 있는 종속접속사 that이 들어가야 한다. 등위접속사 but은 명사절을 이끌어 주절에 연결할 수 없다.

---

5 Ms. Smith applied for a home loan, / **and** her application was approved / by the bank.

(A) during (B) through **(C) and** (D) over

해석| 스미스 씨는 주택 자금 융자를 신청했고, 그녀의 신청이 은행에 의해 승인되었다.

(A) ~ 동안에 (B) ~ 내내 (C) 그리고 (D) ~의 위에

어휘| home loan 주택 자금 융자

해설| 빈칸 앞뒤로 완전한 절이 있으므로 빈칸에는 두 절을 연결하는 접속사가 들어가는 것이 알맞다. 선택지 중 접속사는 and뿐이므로 정답은 (C). 나머지는 모두 전치사로 두 절을 연결할 수 없으므로 오답.

---

6 Please sign up online / **or** go to the HR department / to register for the training.

(A) ever (B) though (C) at **(D) or**

해석| 교육에 등록하려면 온라인으로 신청하거나 인사부서로 가세요.

(A) 언젠가 (B) ~이지만 (C) ~에 (D) 또는

어휘| sign up 신청하다, 등록하다

해설| 빈칸에는 빈칸 앞뒤로 위치한 동사구 sign up online과 go to the HR department를 연결하는 등위접속사가 들어가는 것이 알맞으므로 '또는'의 의미인 등위접속사 (D)가 정답. 부사 (A), 종속접속사 (B), 전치사 (C)는 동사구를 연결할 수 없으므로 오답.

---

7 Market research shows / **that** young consumers are spending more on travel / these days.

(A) this **(B) that** (C) for (D) and

해석| 시장 조사에서 젊은 소비자들이 요즘 여행에 더 많은 돈을 쓰는 것으로 나타났다.

(A) 이것 (B) ~라는 것 (C) 왜냐하면 (D) 그리고

어휘| these days 요즘에는

해설| 빈칸은 뒤에 나온 절을 이끌 수 있어야 하므로 접속사인 (B), (C), (D)가 정답 후보. 그러나 빈칸 이하는 빈칸 앞 동사 shows의 목적어가 되어야 하므로 목적어 역할을 할 수 있는 명사절을 이끄는 것은 '~라는 것'이라는 뜻의 등위접속사 that뿐이다. 따라서 답은 (B).

8 Ms. Wu didn't want to take the medication / **because** she was concerned / about its side effects.
(A) just   (B) following   (C) from   **(D) because**

해석 | 우 씨는 부작용이 걱정되어서 그 약을 먹는 것을 원하지 않았다.
(A) 방금, 막 (B) ~ 이후에 (C) ~로부터 (D) ~ 때문에
어휘 | medication 약, 약물   be concerned about ~에 대해 걱정하다   side effects 부작용

해설 | 빈칸 앞뒤로 〈주어＋동사〉로 이루어진 완전한 절이 나오고 있다. 따라서 빈칸에는 절과 절을 연결하는 접속사가 들어가야 하므로 (D)가 정답. (A)는 부사로 수식 기능만 할 수 있고, (B)와 (C)는 전치사로 절과 절을 연결할 수 없어서 오답이다.

---

2 등위접속사

교재 199쪽

1 recycled   **2** so   **3** both   **4** locks   **5** (A)   **6** (B)   **7** (A)   **8** (C)

---

1 The town's household trash is collected and (recycling / **recycled**) / properly.

해석 | 그 도시의 생활 쓰레기는 제대로 수거되어 재활용된다.
어휘 | household 가정의   collect 모으다, 수집하다

해설 | 괄호는 괄호 앞의 과거분사 collected와 등위접속사 and로 연결되어 병렬 구조를 이루어야 한다. 즉, 등위접속사 앞뒤로 대등한 요소가 들어가야 하므로 괄호에도 과거분사 recycled가 들어가야 알맞다.

---

2 Mr. Lee's flight arrived late, / (but / **so**) he missed the ceremony.

해석 | 이 씨의 비행기가 늦게 도착해서, 그는 식에 참석하지 못했다.

해설 | 비행기가 늦게 도착한 것이 식에 참석하지 못한 이유가 되므로 '그래서'라는 뜻으로 결과를 나타내는 so가 들어가야 알맞다.

---

3 Quality inspections must be conducted / (either / **both**) closely and consistently.

해석 | 품질 검사는 면밀하고 지속적으로 이루어져야만 한다.
어휘 | inspection 점검   closely 면밀하게   consistently 지속적으로

해설 | 선택지에 상관접속사 either와 both가 있으므로 뒤에 어떤 접속사가 쓰였는지 확인해야 한다. 접속사 and가 쓰였으므로 'A와 B 둘 다'라는 의미의 both A and B가 쓰였음을 알 수 있다. 따라서 정답은 both.

---

4 Either the security guards or the manager (lock / **locks**) the main entrance / so that no one enters / after 6 p.m.

해석 | 저녁 6시 이후에는 아무도 들어오지 못하도록 경비원들이나 관리인이 중앙 출입구를 잠근다.
어휘 | security guard 경비원   main entrance 중앙 출입구

해설 | 주어가 either A or B의 형태로 이루어져 있을 때, 동사의 수는 B에 일치시킨다. 이 문장의 경우에는 the manager에 일치시켜야 하므로 3인칭 단수형에 맞는 locks를 써야 한다.

---

5 In most stores in Lilletowne Outlet, / customers can pay / in cash **or** with credit cards.
(A) or   (B) up   (C) nor   (D) if

해석 | 릴타운 아웃렛의 대부분의 상점에서 고객들은 현금 또는 신용카드로 결제할 수 있다.
(A) 또는 (B) ~ 위로 (C) ~도 아닌 (D) 만약 ~라면
어휘 | credit card 신용카드

해설 | 빈칸은 빈칸 앞뒤의 전치사구 in cash와 with credit cards를 대등하게 연결하는 말이 들어가야 한다. 따라서 전치사인 (B)와 종속접속사 (D)는 정답 후보에서 제외. 등위접속사 (A)와 (C) 중 (C)는 앞쪽에 다른 부정어가 있어야 쓸 수 있으므로 정답은 '또는'을 의미하는 (A).

---

6 The reading club usually meets / in **either** the employee lounge or the cafeteria.
(A) still   **(B) either**   (C) both   (D) neither

해석 | 독서 클럽은 대개 직원 휴게실이나 구내 식당에서 모인다.
(A) 여전히 (B) 어느 것 (C) 둘 다 (D) 어느 것도 ~ 아니다
어휘 | employee lounge 직원 휴게실

해설 | 빈칸 뒤쪽으로 명사구 the employee lounge와 the cafeteria가 등위접속사 or로 연결되어 있는 것으로 보아, or와 짝을 이루어 쓰이는 (B)가 정답. either A or B는 'A나 B 둘 중 하나'라는 뜻의 상관접속사이다.

7 Mr. Nelson's position involves / **revising** news articles and generating original content / for the magazine.
(A) revising (B) revised (C) revise (D) to revise
해석 | 넬슨 씨의 일자리는 잡지에 들어갈 새로운 기사를 수정하고 독창적인 내용을 만들어내는 일을 포함한다.
어휘 | involve 포함하다 generate 만들어내다 original 독창적인, 원래의
content 내용

해설 | 빈칸은 동사 involves의 목적어가 들어갈 자리로 뒤에 and로 연결되는 동명사 generating과 문법적으로 동등한 병렬 구조를 이루어야 한다. 따라서 동명사인 (A)가 정답.

---

8 Neither audio recording equipment nor video cameras / **are allowed** in the theater.
(A) allowing (B) is allowed **(C) are allowed** (D) to allow
해석 | 극장 안에서는 오디오 녹음 장비와 비디오 카메라 둘 다 허용되지 않는다.
어휘 | allow 허용하다

해설 | 문장에 동사가 없는 것으로 보아 빈칸은 동사 자리이므로, 동사의 형태를 갖춘 (B)와 (C)가 정답 후보이다. neither A nor B 구문이 주어 자리에 쓰였으므로 동사의 수는 B에 일치시킨다. 이 문장의 경우에는 복수 명사 video cameras에 일치시켜야 하므로 복수 동사 are를 쓴 (C)가 정답.

---

3 종속접속사 – 명사절 접속사

교재 201쪽

1 that **2** that **3** if **4** whether **5** (A) **6** (B) **7** (C) **8** (B)

---

1 The delivery company assured / (and / **that**) the equipment would arrive / at the client's office tomorrow.
해석 | 배송 회사는 그 장비가 내일 고객의 사무실로 도착할 것이라고 장담했다.
어휘 | assure 장담하다

해설 | 괄호 이하는 동사 assured의 목적어가 되는 절이므로, 명사절을 이끌 수 있는 종속접속사 that이 정답이다. and도 접속사이나, 문법적으로 대등한 두 단어나 구, 절을 연결하는 등위접속사이다.

---

2 The belief of the chairman of the board is / (**that** / if) more foreign investment is needed.
해석 | 이사회 의장의 생각은 더 많은 해외 투자가 필요하다는 것이다.
어휘 | belief 생각, 믿음 chairman 의장 investment 투자

해설 | 괄호 이하는 동사 is의 보어가 된다. that과 if 둘 다 보어 역할을 하는 명사절을 이끌 수 있다. 문맥상 괄호 이하가 '~라는 것'이라는 특정 사실을 나타내므로, that이 적절하다. if는 '~인지 아닌지'라는 뜻의 불확실한 상황을 나타내므로 적절하지 않다.

---

3 Mr. Tao wonders / (that / **if**) buying a house is better / than renting one.
해석 | 타오 씨는 집을 구매하는 것이 임대하는 것보다 나은지 궁금해한다.
어휘 | wonder 궁금해하다 rent 빌리다, 세내다

해설 | 괄호 이하는 동사 wonders의 목적어가 되는 부분이다. that과 if 모두 목적어 역할을 하는 명사절을 이끌 수 있는데, 문맥상 '집을 사는 것이 나은지, 임대하는 것이 나은지'라는 뜻으로 불확실한 상황에 대해 궁금해하고 있으므로 '~인지 아닌지'라는 의미의 if가 적절하다.

---

4 Wayne cannot decide / (**whether** / if) to enroll in online courses / or study at a local institute.
해석 | 웨인 씨는 온라인 강좌에 등록할지 아니면 지역 교육 기관에서 공부할지 결정하지 못하고 있다.
어휘 | enroll 등록하다 institute (교육) 기관

해설 | whether과 if는 둘 다 '~인지 아닌지'라는 뜻으로 불확실한 상황에 대한 명사절을 이끌 수 있지만, 뒤에 to부정사(구)를 취할 수 있는 것은 whether뿐이다. 따라서 답은 whether.

5 The secretary will ask / **if** the director can join the video conference / tomorrow afternoon.
(A) if (B) despite (C) to (D) however
해석 | 그 비서가 국장이 내일 오후의 화상 회의에 참가할 수 있는지 물어볼 것이다.
(A) ~인지 아닌지 (B) ~에도 불구하고 (C) ~에 (D) 그러나

해설 | 빈칸 이하는 완전한 문장이고 빈칸 앞 동사 ask는 목적어가 필요하다. 따라서 빈칸에는 '~인지 아닌지'라는 뜻으로 명사절을 이끄는 종속접속사 (A)가 들어가는 것이 알맞다. (B)와 (C)는 전치사, (D)는 부사의 일종이므로 오답.

6 Members of the homeowners association will discuss / **whether** to plant some trees / around the parking lot.
(A) about (B) whether (C) after (D) that
해석 | 주택 소유주 협회 회원들은 주차장 주변에 나무를 좀 심을지에 대해 논의할 것이다.
(A) ~에 대해 (B) ~인지 아닌지 (C) ~ 후에 (D) ~라는 것
어휘 | association 협회

해설 | 빈칸 이하는 동사 discuss의 목적어여야 한다. 빈칸 뒤 to부정사를 취하여 명사 역할을 할 수 있는 것은 (B)뿐이다. (D)도 명사절을 이끌 수 있으나, 바로 뒤에 to부정사를 취할 수 없다.

7 It is imperative / **that** workers wear protective gear / at all times / on the project site.
(A) whether (B) beyond (C) that (D) each
해석 | 작업자들이 건설 현장에서 항상 보호 장비를 착용하는 것은 필수이다.
(A) ~인지 아닌지 (B) ~ 너머에 (C) ~라는 것 (D) 각각의
어휘 | imperative 필수적인, 꼭 필요한 protective gear 보호 장비 site 현장

해설 | 빈칸 앞뒤로 완전한 문장이며, 문맥상 주어인 It이 가리키는 내용이 빈칸 뒤에 오는 절이라고 볼 수 있다. 즉 가주어 it을 이용한 구문으로, 빈칸 이하가 진짜 주어이다. 따라서 '~라는 것'이란 뜻으로 명사절을 이끄는 접속사 (C)가 정답. (A) whether도 명사절을 이끌 수 있으나, '~인지 아닌지'라는 뜻으로 문맥상 적절하지 않다.

8 A poll conducted by the newspaper / indicates / **that** most voters are in favor of the proposal.
(A) like (B) that (C) but (D) them
해석 | 신문사에서 실시한 여론조사에서 대부분의 유권자가 그 제안에 찬성인 것으로 나타났다.
(A) ~ 처럼 (B) ~라는 것 (C) 그러나 (D) 그것들
어휘 | poll 여론조사 voter 유권자 be in favor of ~에 찬성하다

해설 | 빈칸 이하는 동사 indicates의 목적어가 되는 절이므로, 명사절을 이끌 수 있는 접속사 (B)가 정답. (C) but도 접속사이나 명사절을 이끌어 목적어 역할을 하지는 못한다. (A)는 전치사, (D)는 대명사로 오답.

REVIEW | 핵심 POINT 다시 보기
교재 203쪽

1 (B) **2** (D) **3** (C) **4** (A) **5** (D) **6** (C)

1 Rice **and** corn are the two main agricultural products / exported by ACM Corporation.
(A) other (B) and (C) either (D) likewise
해석 | 쌀과 옥수수는 ACM 사에 의해 수출되는 주요 농산물 두 가지이다.
(A) 다른 하나의 (B) ~와 (C) 어느 것 (D) 마찬가지로
어휘 | agricultural 농업의 export 수출하다

해설 | 문장의 동사가 are이고 그 앞부분이 주어에 해당하므로 빈칸에는 Rice와 corn이라는 두 명사를 연결하는 접속사가 필요하다. 병렬 구조의 단어와 단어를 연결하는 등위접속사 (B)가 정답.

2 Doeville Repairs will temporarily shut down, / **for** the business is relocating / to the commercial district.
(A) or (B) through (C) behind (D) for
해석 | 도빌 리페어즈 사는 사업체가 상업지구로 이전할 것이기 때문에 일시적으로 문을 닫는다.
(A) 또는 (B) ~을 통해 (C) ~의 뒤쪽에 (D) 왜냐하면
어휘 | temporarily 일시적으로 shut down 문을 닫다, 폐업하다 commercial district 상업지구

해설 | 빈칸 앞뒤로 주어와 동사를 하나씩 가진 완전한 절이 있으므로 빈칸에는 두 절을 연결할 수 있는 접속사가 들어가야 한다. 따라서 등위접속사인 (A)와 (D)가 정답 후보인데, 문맥상 '왜냐하면'이라는 이유를 나타내는 for이 들어가는 것이 알맞다. 따라서 정답은 (D). 참고로 접속사 for은 절과 절만 연결할 수 있다는 것을 기억하자.

3 Doctors recommend **both** walking and biking / as ways to have a healthier lifestyle.
(A) neither (B) alike **(C) both** (D) none

해석 | 의사들은 걷기와 자전거 타기 둘 다 더 건강한 생활방식을 갖기 위한 방법으로 추천한다.
(A) 어느 것도 ~ 아닌 (B) 비슷한 (C) 둘 다 (D) 아무(것)도 ~ 않은

해설 | 빈칸 뒤쪽에서 접속사 and로 연결된 walking과 biking은 둘 다 동사 recommend의 목적어로 쓰인 동명사이다. 따라서 상관접속사 both A and B(A와 B둘 다)를 이루는 (C)가 빈칸에 들어가야 알맞다.

---

4 Clients must specify / **whether** they will pay for the magazine subscription / annually or quarterly.
(A) whether (B) but also (C) both (D) neither

해석 | 고객들은 잡지 구독료를 일년에 한 번 결제할지 분기별로 결제할지 명시해야만 한다.
(A) ~인지 아닌지 (B) 또한 (C) 둘 다의 (D) 어느 것도 ~ 아닌

어휘 | specify 명시하다 quarterly 분기별의

해설 | 빈칸 이하는 완전한 문장으로, 동사 specify의 목적어가 되는 절이다. 따라서 빈칸에는 명사절을 이끄는 접속사가 와야 하므로 선택지 중 명사절 접속사 (A)가 적절하다.

5-6

Dear Ms. Hernandez,

As you know, there has been a series of avoidable accidents at our company recently. To address this issue, not only the president but also the directors **have agreed** to form a workplace health and safety committee.

We believe **that** a group of members should meet regularly to assess current conditions and give recommendations for improving the working environment.

Please let me know how we can start organizing this.

헤르난데즈 씨께,

아시다시피, 최근에 우리 회사에 피할 수도 있었던 일련의 사고들이 있었습니다. 이 문제를 해결하기 위해서, 사장님뿐만 아니라 임원들도 직장 보건 및 안전 위원회를 만드는 데 **동의했습니다.**

저희는 단체의 구성원들이 현재 상황을 평가하고 근무 환경 개선을 위한 권고를 하기 위해 정기적으로 만나야 **한다고** 생각합니다.

이것을 어떻게 준비하기 시작해야 할지 알려 주시기 바랍니다.

어휘 | a series of 일련의 avoidable 피할 수 있는 address 다루다, 처리하다 president 회장 form 형성하다 workplace 직장 assess 평가하다 recommendation 추천, 권고 working environment 근무 환경 organize 조직하다

5 To address this issue, / not only the president but also the directors **have agreed** / to form a workplace health and safety committee.
(A) agrees (B) to agree (C) agreeable **(D) have agreed**

해설 | 문장에 동사가 보이지 않으므로 빈칸은 동사 자리이고 선택지 중 동사인 (A)와 (D)가 정답 후보. 빈칸 앞 주어를 보면 'A뿐만 아니라 B도'라는 의미의 상관접속사 not only A but also B가 쓰였음을 알 수 있다. 따라서 동사 자리인 빈칸은 B에 해당하는 the directors에 수일치시켜야 한다. 복수 주어에는 복수 동사를 써야 하므로 정답은 (D).

---

6 We believe **that** a group of members should meet regularly / to assess current conditions / and give recommendations / for improving the working environment.
(A) if (B) so **(C) that** (D) what
(A) ~인지 아닌지 (B) 그래서 (C) ~라는 것 (D) 무엇

해설 | 빈칸 뒤에 완전한 절이 나오고 빈칸 앞 동사 believe의 목적어가 없다. 따라서 빈칸 이하는 동사 believe의 목적어가 되는 절이므로 빈칸에는 명사절을 이끌 수 있는 접속사가 들어가야 한다. 그러므로 '~라는 것'이라는 의미의 명사절 접속사 (C)가 정답.

1 cooperation　2 factors　3 immediately　4 excessive　5 (B)　6 (D)　7 (B)　8 (C)

1 Several companies worked in (property / **cooperation**) / to organize this technology convention.

해석 | 몇몇 기업들이 이 기술 총회를 조직하기 위해 협력하여 일했다.

어휘 | organize 조직하다, 준비하다

해설 | 문맥상 몇몇 기업들이 총회를 조직하기 위해 '협력'하여 일했다는 내용이 되어야 하므로 cooperation이 정답.

---

2 Many (**factors** / customizations) contributed / to triggering the current economic crisis.

해석 | 많은 요소들이 현재의 경제 공황을 촉발하는 원인이 되었다.

어휘 | contribute 기여하다　trigger 촉발하다, 일으키다　economic crisis 경제 공황

해설 | 괄호 뒤 동사 contributed로 보아, 괄호가 문장의 주어에 해당하므로, 동사와 어울리는 명사를 찾아야 한다. 경제 공황의 촉발에 원인이 될 수 있는 것으로 많은 '요소들'이 적절하므로 정답은 factors.

---

3 Mago Corp.'s market shares (**immediately** / competitively) plunged / following the CEO's announcement.

해석 | 마고 사의 시장 점유율은 CEO의 발표 후에 즉시 폭락했다.

어휘 | market share 시장 점유율　plunge 폭락하다, 급감하다

해설 | 괄호의 선택지를 보니 괄호 뒤 동사 plunged를 수식하는 부사를 고르는 문제이다. 기업의 시장 점유율이 CEO의 발표 후에 '즉시' 폭락했다는 내용이 되어야 자연스러우므로 답은 immediately이다.

---

4 To limit (**excessive** / remarkable) spending, / the city council has decided to review the budget.

해석 | 과도한 지출을 제한하기 위해, 시의회는 예산을 재검토하기로 결정했다.

해설 | 괄호 뒤의 명사 spending과 호응할 수 있는 형용사를 고르는 문제이다. 시의회가 예산을 재검토하는 것은 '과도한 지출'을 막기 위함일 것이므로 정답은 excessive이다.

---

5 Mr. Tetley's initial **investment** entitles him / to a thirty percent share of the company.
(A) delivery　(B) investment　(C) delay　(D) consumption

해석 | 테틀리 씨는 초기 투자로 회사 지분의 30%를 가질 자격이 있다.

(A) 배달 (B) 투자 (C) 지연 (D) 소비

어휘 | initial 초기의　entitle A to B A에게 B의 자격을 주다　share 지분

해설 | 빈칸은 테틀리 씨가 회사 지분의 30%를 갖게 해 준 '원인'이 된다. 따라서, 지분 소유의 원인으로 자연스러운 '투자'를 의미하는 (B)가 알맞다.

---

6 Even though much of Europe has suffered a recession, / the economic situation is **stable** in Belgium.
(A) coupled　(B) mutual　(C) excessive　(D) stable

해석 | 유럽 대부분이 경기 침체를 겪었지만, 벨기에에서는 경제 상황이 안정적이다.

(A) 연결된 (B) 상호의 (C) 과도한 (D) 안정적인

어휘 | recession 경기 후퇴, 불황　economic 경제의

해설 | even though라는 접속사는 '비록 ~이지만'이라는 뜻으로, 해당 접속사로 연결된 콤마 앞뒤의 문장이 서로 상반되는 내용임을 알 수 있다. 따라서 앞에서 언급된 '경기 침체 (recession)'와 대조적으로 경제가 '안정적'이라는 말이 되어야 알맞으므로 (D)가 정답.

---

7 Following the merger with the Chinese firm, / we experienced **significant** growth / in Asian markets.
(A) complete　(B) significant　(C) correct　(D) approximate

해석 | 중국 기업과의 합병 후에, 우리는 아시아 시장에서 상당한 성장을 경험했다.

(A) 완전한 (B) 상당한 (C) 올바른 (D) 대략의

해설 | 내용상 빈칸 뒤의 '성장(growth)'이라는 명사와 어울리는 것은 '상당한'이란 뜻의 형용사 significant이다. 따라서 답은 (B).

8 Due to the **consistent** decline in exports, / the government has encouraged citizens to buy domestic goods.

(A) strategic (B) enhanced **(C) consistent** (D) competitive

해석| 수출의 지속적인 감소로 인해, 정부는 시민들에게 국산 제품을 사도록 장려했다.

(A) 전략적인 (B) 향상된 (C) 지속적인 (D) 경쟁적인

어휘| export 수출(품) encourage A to *do* A가 ~하도록 장려하다 domestic 국산의

해설| 빈칸 뒤의 명사 decline(감소)을 수식해 의미가 통하는 형용사를 골라야 한다. '지속적인 감소'라는 뜻이 되어야 자연스러우므로 (C)가 정답.

ACTUAL TEST 실전 문제에 적용하기

교재 206쪽

1 (B) **2** (C) **3** (A) **4** (B) **5** (B) **6** (D) **7** (A) **8** (D) **9** (A) **10** (B) **11** (A) **12** (A)

---

1 We couldn't have been successful / without the team's strong support and full **cooperation**.

(A) cooperator **(B) cooperation** (C) cooperated

(D) cooperate

해석| 우리는 그 팀의 든든한 지원과 전폭적인 협조가 없었다면 성공할 수 없었을 것이다.

어휘| without ~ 없이 support 지원 cooperation 협조

해설| **등위접속사**

빈칸 앞쪽의 and를 보고 무엇이 연결되었는지 먼저 파악한다. without의 목적어인 the team's strong support와 병렬 구조를 이루어 〈형용사+명사〉 구조가 and 뒤에 와야 한다. 빈칸은 명사 자리에 해당하므로 명사인 (A)와 (B)가 정답 후보. 내용상 '팀의 든든한 지원과 전폭적인 협조'가 자연스러우므로 정답은 (B).

---

2 The HR department's problem is / **that** the employees and management refuse to compromise / on the additional benefits.

(A) while (B) this **(C) that** (D) since

해석| 인사부의 문제는 직원들과 경영진이 추가 복지에 대해 타협하기를 거부한다는 것이다.

(A) ~하는 동안 (B) 이것 (C) ~라는 것 (D) ~ 이래로

어휘| refuse 거부하다, 거절하다 compromise 타협하다 additional 추가의

해설| **명사절 접속사**

빈칸 이하는 빈칸 앞 동사 is의 보어 자리이고, 빈칸 뒤에 완전한 절이 나오는 것으로 보아, 빈칸에는 명사절을 이끌어 보어 역할을 하도록 하는 명사절 접속사가 들어가야 한다. 따라서 정답은 명사절 접속사인 (C).

오답| (A)와 (D)도 접속사라 절을 연결할 수 있지만, 명사절이 아닌 부사절만 이끌 수 있다.

---

3 To meet the particular requirement of each client, / every product of Wein & Gaber is individually **customized**.

(A) customized (B) resolved (C) preferred (D) invested

해석| 각 고객의 특정 요구 사항을 만족시키기 위해, 웨인 앤 가버 사의 모든 상품은 개별적으로 맞춤제작된다.

(A) 맞춤제작하다 (B) 해결하다 (C) 선호하다 (D) 투자하다

어휘| meet a requirement 요구 사항을 만족시키다, 충족시키다 particular 특정한 individually 개별적으로

해설| **동사 어휘 customize**

콤마 앞에서 '개별 고객의 요구 사항을 만족시키기 위해서'라는 '이유'를 밝혔으므로, 모든 물품이 '맞춤제작된다'는 내용이 자연스럽다. 따라서 '맞춤제작하다'라는 의미의 동사 (A)가 정답.

---

4 The patient had health insurance, / **but** the policy did not cover medical treatment / while out of the country.

(A) or **(B) but** (C) if (D) then

해석| 그 환자는 건강보험이 있었지만, 그 보험은 해외에 있는 동안의 의료 처치는 보장하지 않았다.

(A) 또는 (B) 그러나 (C) ~인지 아닌지 (D) 그 다음에

어휘| health insurance 건강보험 cover (보험으로) 보장하다 medical treatment 의학적 치료

해설| **등위접속사**

빈칸 앞뒤로 완전한 두 개의 절이 연결되어 있으므로, 접속사인 (A), (B), (C)가 정답 후보. 이 중 문맥에 맞는 접속사를 골라야 한다. 건강보험이 있지만 보장을 받지 못했다는 내용이므로, '그러나, 하지만'이라는 뜻의 대조 관계를 나타내는 (B)가 알맞다.

오답| (C) if는 명사절을 이끄는 종속접속사로 완전한 두 절을 연결할 수 없다.

5 Ticket holders of the postponed concert / will be refunded / or **provided** with vouchers.
(A) providing (B) provided (C) provide (D) provides
해석| 연기된 콘서트의 입장권 구매자들은 환불을 받거나 할인권을 제공받을 것이다.
어휘| ticket holder 입장권 구매자 voucher 상품권, 할인권

해설| **등위접속사**
빈칸 앞에 등위접속사 or가 있으므로 빈칸과 or로 연결되어 병렬 구조를 이루는 것을 or 앞에서 찾아야 한다. or 앞에 수동태 동사를 이루는 과거분사 refunded가 있으므로 이와 문법적으로 동등한 과거분사 (B)가 정답이다.

---

6 The magazine gives useful tips / for **both** saving money and staying organized.
(A) many (B) neither (C) few (D) both
해석| 그 잡지는 돈을 절약하는 것과 계획성 있게 지내는 것에 대한 유용한 조언을 해 준다.
(A) 많은 (B) 어느 것도 ~ 아닌 (C) 거의 없는 (D) 둘 다, 양쪽
어휘| organized 계획성 있는, 체계적인

해설| **상관접속사**
빈칸 뒤에 saving과 staying은 둘 다 전치사 for의 목적어로 쓰인 동명사이다. 두 동명사가 and로 이어지고 있으므로, 빈칸에는 both A and B(A와 B 둘 다) 구문을 이루는 (D)가 들어가야 알맞다.

---

7 The CEO congratulated the entire staff / on the **remarkable** sales figures / this month.
(A) **remarkable** (B) forceful (C) sensible (D) deliverable
해석| CEO는 이번 달의 두드러진 매출액에 대해 전 직원에게 축하의 말을 전했다.
(A) 두드러진 (B) 주장이 강한 (C) 분별 있는 (D) 완제품
어휘| congratulate 축하하다 entire 전체의 sales figures 매출액

해설| **형용사 어휘 remarkable**
빈칸 뒤의 명사구 sales figures를 수식하는 형용사를 고르는 문제. 문맥상 '두드러진 매출액'이라는 표현이 되어야 자연스러우므로 정답은 (A). 오답| (D)는 -able의 형태로 형용사처럼 생겼으나 '완제품'이라는 명사이고 내용상으로도 어울리지 않아 오답.

---

8 In the event of the manager's absence, / the receptionist usually asks / **whether** the caller would like to leave a message or try again later.
(A) for (B) either (C) despite (D) **whether**
해석| 매니저가 부재 중인 경우, 접수원은 대개 전화를 건 사람에게 메시지를 남길 것인지 아니면 나중에 다시 전화할 것인지를 묻는다.
(A) ~ 동안 (B) 어느 것 (C) ~에도 불구하고 (D) ~인지 아닌지
어휘| in the event of ~의 경우에는 absence 부재 receptionist 접수원 would like to *do* ~하고 싶다

해설| **명사절 접속사**
빈칸 뒤는 완전한 절이고 빈칸 앞 asks의 목적어가 없으므로 빈칸에는 절을 이끌어 목적어인 명사절이 되도록 하는 명사절 접속사가 들어가야 한다. 따라서 '~인지 아닌지'의 의미인 명사절 접속사 (D)가 정답.
오답| (A)는 등위접속사로 절과 절을 연결하여 쓰이고, (C)는 전치사라 뒤에 절을 이끌 수 없고, (B)는 빈칸 뒤쪽의 or와 짝을 이루어 쓰일 수 있지만 연결하는 내용이 병렬 구조가 아니라 오답이다.

9-12

Speedy Trak Partners with Competitor

Two rivals in the rail industry announced **that** they are planning to form one company. After having competed with each other for many years, the two largest rail firms in the country, Speedy Trak and FastLink, have decided to merge and operate under the name FastTrak.

Industry experts expect that, in doing so, they will be able to produce trains equipped with the most modern technology. Speedy Trak and FastLink have both expressed their goal as not only improving speed and comfort, **but also** developing more eco-friendly trains.

스피디 트랙, 경쟁사와 협력하다

철도업계의 두 경쟁사가 하나의 회사를 이룰 계획이라고 발표했다. 수년간 서로 경쟁한 끝에, 국내 최대 규모의 두 철도 회사 스피디 트랙 사와 패스트링크 사는 합병하여 패스트트랙이라는 이름으로 운영하기로 결정했다.

업계 전문가들은 그렇게 함으로써 그들이 가장 최신의 기술을 갖춘 기차를 생산할 수 있을 것이라고 예상한다. 스피디 트랙 사와 패스트링크 사 두 업체 모두 속도와 안락함을 증진시키는 것뿐만 아니라 더 환경 친화적인 기차를 만들어 내는 것 **또한** 그들의

A spokesperson for FastTrak stated that they hope to **enhance** the experience of rail travel through the purchase of more modern vehicles and the renovation of train stations. **This is great news for travelers tired of outdated amenities**.

목표라고 말해왔다.

패스트트랙 사의 대변인은 더 현대적인 열차의 구매와 기차역의 보수를 통해 철도 여행의 경험을 **향상시키기를** 바란다고 말했다. **이것은 낡은 편의시설이 지겨운 여행객들에게 아주 좋은 소식이다.**

어휘 | **partner with** ~와 협력하다 **rival** 경쟁자 **form** 이루다, 형성하다 **equipped with** ~을 갖춘 **spokesperson** 대변인 **state** 말하다 **outdated** 오래된, 낡은 **amenity** ((*pl.*)) 편의시설

9 Two rivals in the rail industry announced / **that** they are planning to form one company.
(A) that (B) moreover (C) as for (D) despite
(A) ~라는 것 (B) 게다가 (C) ~에 대해 말하자면 (D) ~에도 불구하고

해설 | **명사절 접속사**
빈칸 뒤에 완전한 절이 있고 빈칸 앞 동사 announced의 목적어가 없으므로 빈칸에는 절을 이끌어 목적어처럼 쓸 수 있게 하는 명사절 접속사가 들어가야 한다. 따라서 '~라는 것'이라는 뜻의 명사절 접속사 (A)가 정답.
오답 | (B)는 접속부사라 구조적으로 절을 연결할 수 없어서 오답이다. (C)와 (D)는 전치사로 뒤에 절을 이끌 수 없으므로 오답.

10 Speedy Trak and FastLink have both expressed their goal / as not only improving speed and comfort, / **but also** developing more eco-friendly trains.
(A) only if **(B) but also** (C) along with (D) and then
(A) ~해야만 (B) ~ 또한 (C) ~에 덧붙여 (D) 그런 다음

해설 | **상관접속사**
문장 안에서 not only를 보는 순간 but also를 떠올려야 한다. not only와 짝을 이루어 쓰이는 but also가 정답. Not only A but also B는 'A뿐만 아니라 B도'라는 의미이다.

11 A spokesperson for FastTrak stated / that they hope to **enhance** the experience of rail travel / through the purchase of more modern vehicles and the renovation of train stations.
(A) enhance (B) describe (C) illustrate (D) accelerate
(A) 향상시키다 (B) 묘사하다 (C) 설명하다 (D) 가속화하다

해설 | **동사 어휘 enhance**
문맥상 빈칸 뒤 목적어인 the experience of rail travel(철도 여행의 경험)을 좋은 쪽으로 개선한다는 의미가 되어야 하므로 '향상시키다, 질을 높이다'라는 뜻의 (A)가 알맞다.

12 (A) This is great news for travelers tired of outdated amenities.
(B) Mergers are common in the energy production industry.
(C) The competition was at its maximum a few years ago.
(D) Research indicates that consumers are looking for cheaper tickets.
(A) 이것은 낡은 편의시설이 지겨운 여행객들에게 아주 좋은 소식이다.
(B) 합병은 에너지 생산 업계에서 흔한 일이다.
(C) 그 경쟁은 몇 년 전에 최고조에 달했다.
(D) 조사에 따르면 소비자들은 더 저렴한 표를 찾고 있는 것으로 나타난다.

해설 | **알맞은 문장 고르기**
빈칸 앞에 두 철도 회사의 합병으로 인해 철도 여행의 질이 향상될 거라는 내용이 나온다. 따라서 이는 철도 여행객들이 반길 소식이라며 반응을 소개하는 (A)가 빈칸에 들어갈 내용으로 가장 자연스럽다. 여기서 지시대명사 this가 앞의 문장 전체를 가리킬 수 있다는 것도 기억해두자.
오답 | (B)는 지문과 같이 합병에 대한 내용이나, 철도 업계가 아니라 타업계에 대한 내용이므로 오답. (C)는 두 업체의 경쟁에 대한 내용으로 지문의 첫 번째 단락에 어울리는 문장이라 오답이다. (D)는 소비자 선호에 대해 이야기하고 있으나 빈칸 앞의 열차 구매나 역 보수와 관계가 없으므로 연결이 자연스럽지 않아 오답이다.

UNIT 12

1 시간·이유의 부사절 접속사

교재 211쪽

1 when　**2** after　**3** since　**4** now that　**5** (D)　**6** (B)　**7** (B)　**8** (A)

---

1 Please turn off the lights in the conference room / (**when** / because) you leave.

해석┃ 나갈 때 회의실 불을 꺼주세요.

어휘┃ **turn off** (전원을) 끄다 (⊞ **turn on** 켜다)　**conference room** 회의실

해설┃ 괄호 앞뒤의 두 절을 하나의 문장으로 연결하는 접속사로 알맞은 것을 고르는 문제. 문맥상 '회의실을 나갈 때 불을 끄라'는 내용이 되어야 하므로 '~할 때'라는 뜻의 when이 알맞다.

---

2 The corrected invitations will be distributed / (**after** / before) they are reprinted.

해석┃ 교정된 초대장은 재인쇄된 후에 사람들에게 배포될 것이다.

어휘┃ **correct** 교정하다, 고치다　**distribute** 배포하다, 배분하다

해설┃ 괄호 앞뒤 내용의 전후 관계를 파악해야 한다. 문맥상 교정된 초대장이 재인쇄된 '후에' 배포될 것이라는 내용이 자연스러우므로 after가 알맞다.

---

3 Mr. Whelan didn't get the job / (while / **since**) he didn't have the proper qualifications.

해석┃ 웰런 씨는 적합한 자격 요건을 갖추지 못했기 때문에 그 일자리를 얻지 못했다.

어휘┃ **proper** 적절한　**qualification** 《pl.》 자격 (요건)

해설┃ 문맥상 괄호 뒤의 절이 일자리를 얻지 못한 '이유'에 해당하므로 '~ 때문에'라는 뜻의 since가 알맞다. since가 '~한 이래로'라는 뜻으로 시간을 나타내는 접속사로도 쓰인다는 점을 기억해두자.

---

4 Traffic is flowing smoothly / (as soon as / **now that**) the new bridge has been opened.

해석┃ 새로운 다리가 개통되어서 교통 흐름이 원활하다.

어휘┃ **flow** 흐르다, 이동하다　**smoothly** 원활하게

해설┃ 새로운 다리 개통은 교통 흐름이 원활해진 '이유'에 해당하므로 '~이므로, ~이기 때문에'라는 뜻의 now that이 알맞다.

---

5 Pharmaceutical companies cannot sell medicine or supplements / <u>until</u> the products pass an inspection.
(A) by　(B) even　(C) during　(D) until

해석┃ 제약 회사들은 제품이 검사를 통과할 때까지 약품이나 보충제를 판매할 수 없다.
(A) ~까지　(B) 훨씬　(C) ~동안　(D) ~할 때까지

어휘┃ **medicine** 약품, 약　**supplement** 보충(물)　**inspection** 검사, 점검

해설┃ 빈칸 앞뒤로 완전한 절이 나오므로 빈칸은 두 절을 연결하는 접속사가 들어갈 자리이다. 따라서 전치사인 (A)와 (C), 부사인 (B)는 오답이다. '검사를 통과할 때까지 판매할 수 없다'는 의미가 되어야 하므로 알맞은 접속사는 '~할 때까지'의 의미인 (D)이다.

---

6 Employees must get approval from a supervisor / at least one week / <u>before</u> they plan to use vacation time.
(A) from　(B) before　(C) later　(D) about

해석┃ 직원들은 휴가를 쓸 계획을 세우기 적어도 일주일 전에 상사의 승인을 받아야 한다.
(A) ~로부터　(B) ~ 전에　(C) 나중에　(D) ~에 대해

해설┃ 빈칸 뒤에 완전한 절이 나오므로 절을 연결할 수 있는 접속사가 정답이다. 문맥상 '휴가 계획을 세우기 전에 승인을 받아야 한다'고 해야 하므로 (B)가 정답. 절을 연결할 수 없는 전치사 (A), (D)와 부사 (C)는 오답이다.

---

7 The town council rejected the proposal / for a community park / <u>because</u> the project was expensive.
(A) so　(B) because　(C) then　(D) however

해석┃ 시의회는 비용이 많이 든다는 이유로 근린 공원을 건설하자는 제안을 거부했다.
(A) 그래서　(B) ~ 때문에　(C) 그때　(D) 그러나

어휘┃ **town council** 시의회　**reject** 거부하다　**community park** 근린 공원

해설┃ 빈칸 앞뒤의 완전한 절을 연결할 수 있는 접속사 (A)와 (B)가 정답 후보. 빈칸 뒷부분이 근린 공원 건설을 거부한 '이유'에 해당하므로 '~ 때문에'라는 뜻의 (B)가 정답. (C)와 (D)는 부사라서 절을 연결할 수 없으므로 오답이다.

---

8 Mr. Hall no longer handles questions from the press / <u>as</u> he transferred to another department last month.

(A) as (B) when (C) yet (D) before

해석│ 홀 씨는 지난달에 다른 부서로 옮겨서 더 이상 언론사에서 오는 질문을 처리하지 않는다.

(A) ~ 때문에, ~할 때 (B) ~할 때 (C) 아직 (D) ~ 전에

어휘│ no longer 더 이상 ~ 않는 the press 언론사

해설│ 선택지를 보니 빈칸에 알맞은 접속사를 고르는 문제. 빈칸 이하가 홀 씨가 더 이상 언론의 질문을 처리하지 않는 '이유'에 해당한다. 따라서 이유를 나타내는 접속사 (A)가 정답. as는 이유뿐만 아니라 시간을 나타내어 '~할 때'라는 의미도 갖는다.

---

2 **조건·양보의 부사절 접속사**　　　　　　　　　교재 213쪽

1 if **2** in case **3** even though **4** so **5** (B) **6** (A) **7** (D) **8** (C)

---

1 Customers can return a defective product / (if / unless) they have a receipt.

해석│ 고객들은 영수증이 있으면 불량품을 반품할 수 있다.

어휘│ defective 결함이 있는 receipt 영수증

해설│ 영수증이 있어야 물품을 반품할 수 있다고 해야 자연스러우므로 '(만약) ~라면'이라는 뜻의 if가 알맞다. unless는 '~가 아니라면'이라는 뜻이다.

---

2 The team members have their supervisor's personal phone number/ (in case / so that) they encounter a problem / on a weekend.

해석│ 팀원들은 주말에 문제가 발생할 경우에 대비해 상사의 개인 연락처를 가지고 있다.

어휘│ personal 개인의 encounter 맞닥뜨리다

해설│ in case는 '~한 경우에 (대비하여)', so that은 '~하기 위해서'라는 뜻이다. 문맥상 '문제가 발생할 경우에 대비하여 연락처를 가지고 있다'는 의미가 자연스러우므로 in case가 정답.

---

3 The film failed at the box office / (as long as / **even though**) it was a high-budget movie.

해석│ 그 영화는 고예산 영화임에도 불구하고 관객 동원에는 실패했다.

어휘│ fail 실패하다 at the box office 관객 동원에서, 흥행 면에서

해설│ '관객 동원에 실패한 것'은 '고예산 영화라는 것'의 예상치 못한 결과이므로 양보를 나타내는 접속사로 '(비록) ~이지만, ~에도 불구하고'란 뜻의 even though가 알맞다. as long as는 '~하는 한'이란 뜻이다.

---

4 The vase is (so / such) fragile / that it must be shipped / in special packaging.

해석│ 그 꽃병은 매우 깨지기 쉬우므로 특별 포장으로 운송해야 한다.

어휘│ fragile 깨지기 쉬운

해설│ '매우 ~해서 …하다'라는 뜻으로 결과를 나타내는 〈so/such ~ that〉 구문을 쓴다. 이때 부사 so 뒤에는 형용사나 부사가 오고, 형용사 such 뒤는 명사가 온다. 괄호 뒤에 fragile이라는 형용사가 나오므로 부사인 so를 써야 한다.

---

5 The project cannot progress any further / <u>unless</u> the board approves the proposed budget increase.

(A) otherwise **(B)** unless (C) if (D) because

해석│ 이사회가 증액 제안된 예산을 승인하지 않으면 프로젝트는 더 이상 진행될 수 없다.

(A) 그렇지 않으면 (B) ~가 아니라면 (C) ~라면 (D) ~ 때문에

어휘│ progress 진행하다, 나아가다

해설│ 빈칸 앞뒤에 완전한 절이 있으므로 빈칸에는 두 절을 연결할 수 있는 접속사가 들어가야 한다. 따라서 부사인 (A)는 정답 후보에서 제외. 내용상 '이사회가 승인하지 않으면 프로젝트를 진행할 수 없다'는 뜻이므로 '~가 아니라면'이란 의미의 unless가 정답.

---

6 The video presentation was brief, / <u>although</u> it explained the marketing plan / in detail.

(A) although (B) also (C) in case (D) so that

해석│ 영상 발표는 마케팅 전략을 상세히 설명했지만, 시간은 짧았다.

(A) ~에도 불구하고 (B) 또한 (C) ~한 경우에 (D) ~하기 위해서

어휘│ brief 짧은, 간략한 explain 설명하다 in detail 상세히

해설│ 빈칸에는 빈칸 앞뒤의 절을 연결할 수 있는 접속사가 들어가야 하므로 부사인 (B)는 정답이 될 수 없다. '발표 시간이 짧았다는 것'과 '상세히 설명했다는 것'은 예상치 못한 결과이므로 '~에도 불구하고'란 뜻의 양보를 나타내는 부사절 접속사 (A)가 정답이다.

7 The company's finances are managed by the accounting department / <u>while</u> salaries are handled by Mr. Hardy.
(A) despite   (B) unless   (C) through   **(D) while**

해석| 회사 재정은 회계부에서 관리하는 반면에, 임금은 하디 씨가 처리한다.
(A) ~임에도 불구하고 (B) ~가 아니라면 (C) ~을 통해 (D) ~ 인 반면
어휘| finances 재정 (상태)   salary 급여

해설| 빈칸 앞뒤로 절이 나오므로 전치사인 (A)와 (C)는 정답 후보에서 제외. 문맥상 앞뒤 절이 '대조'의 의미를 가지고 있으므로 '~인 반면'의 뜻인 부사절 접속사 (D)가 정답. (B)는 '~가 아니라면'의 의미로 내용상 자연스럽지 않아 오답.

---

8 The writing in the article must be clear / <u>so that</u> all readers can understand the complex issue.
(A) while   (B) as though   **(C) so that**   (D) neither

해석| 신문 기사의 글은 모든 독자들이 그 복잡한 문제를 이해할 수 있도록 명확해야 한다.
(A) ~ 동안, ~ 반면에 (B) 마치 ~처럼 (C) ~하기 위해서 (D) 어느 것도 ~ 아닌
어휘| complex 복잡한

해설| 빈칸 앞뒤로 완전한 절이 있으므로 빈칸에는 두 절을 연결하는 접속사가 들어가야 한다. 한정사 (D)는 빈칸 뒤에 짝을 이루어 쓰이는 nor가 있어야만 상관접속사로 쓰일 수 있으므로 정답 후보에서 제외. 내용상 '독자들이 이해할 수 있도록 하기 위해 글이 명확해야 한다'는 내용이 자연스러우므로 '~하기 위해서'의 의미를 가진 부사절 접속사 (C)가 정답.

---

3   접속사 vs. 전치사 vs. 접속부사
교재 215쪽

1 because of   **2** although   **3** by the time   **4** nevertheless   **5** (A)   **6** (D)   **7** (A)   **8** (B)

---

1 The historical artwork was not properly preserved / (since / **because of**) the museum's lack of equipment.

해석| 미술관의 장비 부족으로, 역사적인 예술 작품이 제대로 보존되지 못했다.
어휘| historical 역사적인, 역사와 관련된   artwork 미술품   preserve 보존하다, 보호하다   lack 부족, 결핍

해설| 의미가 같은 접속사와 전치사 중에 정답을 고르는 문제. 접속사인 since 다음에는 〈주어+동사〉로 이루어진 절이 오고, 전치사인 because of 다음에는 명사(구)가 온다. 괄호 뒤에 명사구가 나오므로 because of를 써야 한다.

---

2 This year's music festival had a low turnout / (despite / **although**) it had a lot of publicity.

해석| 올해의 음악 축제는 많은 홍보가 있었음에도 불구하고 참석자 수가 저조했다.
어휘| turnout 참석자 수   publicity 홍보

해설| 전치사 despite와 접속사 although는 둘 다 (비록) ~이지만'이라는 뜻. 하지만 괄호 뒤에 〈주어+동사〉의 절이 나오므로 접속사인 although가 정답이다. despite는 전치사이므로 뒤에 명사(구, 절)가 나와야 한다.

---

3 The post office was already closed / (by / **by the time**) Ms. Simpson arrived.

해석| 심슨 씨가 도착했을 때는 우체국은 이미 문을 닫았다.

해설| by와 by the time은 둘 다 '~(할 때)까지'라는 뜻이지만, 각각 전치사와 접속사라는 점에서 다르다. 괄호 뒤에 주어와 동사로 이루어진 절이 나오므로 접속사인 by the time이 정답이다.

---

4 Silverware at Bon Appétit is extremely expensive; / (**nevertheless** / although), many customers still visit the shop.

해석| 본 아페티의 은식기류는 매우 비싼데도 불구하고, 많은 사람들이 여전히 가게를 방문한다.
어휘| silverware 은식기류, 은제품   extremely 극히, 극도로

해설| nevertheless와 although는 뒤에 절이 올 수 있다는 점은 같다. 하지만 절을 이끌어 다른 절과 연결시켜 한 문장으로 만드는 부사절 접속사 although와 달리 접속부사 nevertheless는 두 절을 한 문장으로 만들지는 못한다. 두 문장을 연결한 것은 and의 의미로 쓰인 ;(세미콜론)이므로 '그럼에도 불구하고'라는 의미의 연결만 해 주는 접속부사 nevertheless가 정답이다.

5 While the air conditioner is in operation, / please keep the door closed / securely.
(A) While   (B) Throughout   (C) Within   (D) During
해석 | 에어컨이 작동하는 동안에는 문을 꽉 닫아 주세요.
(A) ~ 동안 (B) ~ 내내 (C) ~ 이내에 (D) ~ 동안
어휘 | air conditioner 에어컨   in operation 작동 중인   securely 꽉, 단단히

해설 | 문맥상 '에어컨이 작동하는 동안에 문을 닫아 달라'는 내용이 자연스러우므로 '~ 동안에' 라는 의미의 (A)와 (D)가 정답 후보. 콤마 앞뒤로 완전한 절이 나오므로 빈칸은 두 절을 연결하는 접속사 자리이다. 선택지 중에서 접속사는 (A)뿐 이므로 (A)가 정답이다.

---

6 The picnic has been postponed / until next week / **due to** a forecast of heavy rain.
(A) because   (B) although   (C) instead of   **(D) due to**
해석 | 소풍은 폭우가 온다는 일기예보 때문에 다음 주로 연기되었다.
(A) ~ 때문에 (B) ~에도 불구하고 (C) ~ 대신에 (D) ~ 때문에
어휘 | postpone 연기하다   forecast 일기예보

해설 | 빈칸 뒤의 '일기예보'는 빈칸 앞 '소풍이 연기되었다는 것'의 원인이므로 이유를 나타내는 접속사 (A)와 전치사 (D)가 정답 후보. 빈칸 뒤에 명사구가 나왔으므로 정답은 전치사 (D)이다. (C)도 전치사이나, 의미상 적절하지 않아 오답이 다.

---

7 Kellenvue Repair contacts clients / **as soon as** their watches are ready for pickup.
(A) as soon as   (B) until   (C) upon   (D) ahead of
해석 | 켈렌뷰 리페어 사는 고객들의 시계가 찾아갈 준비가 되면 바로 고객들에게 연락한다.
(A) ~하자마자 (B) ~까지 (C) ~하자마자 (D) ~의 앞에
어휘 | pickup (물건을) 찾으러 감

해설 | 의미상 '시계가 준비되자마자 고객에게 연 락한다'는 내용이 자연스러우므로 '~하자마자'의 의미인 (A)와 (C)가 정답 후보. 빈칸 앞뒤에 완전 한 절이 있어서 빈칸에는 절을 연결하는 접속사 as soon as가 들어가야 한다. 따라서 정답은 (A). (C)와 (D)는 전치사라 절을 연결할 수 없고 뒤에 명사(구, 절)나 동명사와 함께 쓰이므로 오 답이다.

---

8 Mr. Gorash landed more than an hour late in Philadelphia / and **therefore** he missed his connection.
(A) because   **(B) therefore**   (C) whereas   (D) however
해석 | 고라시 씨는 필라델피아에 한 시간 이상 늦게 도착했고 그래서 연결편 비행기를 놓 쳤다.
(A) ~ 때문에 (B) 그러므로 (D) ~하는 반면에 (D) 그러나
어휘 | land 도착하다   miss 놓치다   connection (비행기 등의) 연결편

해설 | 빈칸 앞에 완전한 절이 나오고 빈칸 바로 앞에 두 절을 연결하는 접속사 and가 있다. 빈칸이 없어도 문장이 완전하므로 빈칸은 부사 자리이다. 선택지 중 부사는 (B)와 (D)인데, and 앞 내용 '늦은 도착'과 빈칸 뒤의 내용 '연결편을 놓친 것'은 인과 관계이므로, 결과를 나타내는 접 속부사 (B)가 정답이다. (D)는 '그러나'의 의미로 대조를 나타내는 접속부사라 오답.

UNIT 13

교재 217쪽

REVIEW   핵심 POINT 다시 보기

1 (C)   **2** (B)   **3** (A)   **4** (C)   **5** (A)   **6** (D)

---

1 Your travel expenses will not be reimbursed / **unless** official receipts are submitted.
(A) providing   (B) that   **(C) unless**   (D) as long as
해석 | 공식적인 영수증을 제출하지 않으면 귀하의 출장 경비는 변제되지 않을 것입니다.
(A) ~한다면 (B) ~라는 것 (C) ~가 아니라면 (D) ~하는 한
어휘 | travel expense 출장비   reimburse 변제[배상]하다   official 공식적인

해설 | 빈칸 앞뒤로 완전한 절이 왔으므로 빈칸에 는 두 절을 연결하는 부사절 접속사가 들어가야 한다. 따라서 명사절 접속사 (B)는 정답 후보에 서 제외. 나머지 선택지 모두 조건을 나타내는 부 사절 접속사인데, 내용상 '공식적인 영수증을 제 출하지 않으면, 변제되지 않는다'는 내용이 자연 스러우므로 정답은 '~가 아니라면'의 뜻인 (C)가 정답.

2 Customers can track the shipment of their purchases online / **while** the goods are in transit.

(A) during **(B) while** (C) in case (D) without

해석│ 고객들은 물품들이 수송되는 동안, 그들의 온라인 구매한 물품들의 수송을 추적할 수 있다.

(A) ~ 동안에 (B) ~ 동안에 (C) ~한 경우에 (D) ~ 없이

어휘│ track 추적하다 transit 수송

해설│ 의미상 '물품이 수송되는 동안 추적할 수 있다'는 내용이 자연스러우므로 '~ 동안에'의 의미인 전치사 (A)와 접속사 (B)가 정답 후보. 빈칸 앞뒤에 완전한 절이 나오므로 빈칸에는 절을 연결하는 접속사가 들어가야 한다. 따라서 정답은 (B). (A)는 전치사라 절을 연결할 수 없고 명사나 동명사와 함께 쓰이므로 오답이다.

---

3 Keyace Motors only sells pre-owned cars / **whereas** other dealerships carry new and used vehicles.

(A) whereas (B) in case (C) as soon as (D) unlike

해석│ 다른 대리점이 새 차와 중고차를 취급하는 반면에, 키야스 모터스 사는 오직 중고차만 판매한다.

(A) 반면에 (B) ~한 경우에 (C) ~하자마자 (D) ~와 다른

어휘│ pre-owned 중고의 dealership (승용차) 대리점

해설│ 빈칸이 완전한 두 절을 연결하고 있으므로 접속사가 들어가야 할 자리이다. '키야스 모터스 사는 중고차만 취급한다'는 앞 부분의 내용은 '다른 대리점들은 새 차와 중고차 모두 취급한다'는 뒷 내용과 반대되므로, 대조를 나타내는 접속사 whereas가 적절하다. (D) unlike는 '~와 다른'이라는 뜻의 전치사로 절을 연결할 수 없고 뒤에 명사가 뒤따르므로 오답.

---

4 More moviegoers went to see *Crovella* / **after** the film received an award.

(A) following (B) next to **(C) after** (D) regarding

해석│ 〈크로벨라〉가 상을 받은 후에, 더 많은 영화 관람객들이 그 영화를 보러 갔다.

(A) ~ 후에 (B) ~ 옆에 (C) ~ 후에 (D) ~에 관해

어휘│ moviegoer 영화 관람객, 영화 팬

해설│ 빈칸 앞의 내용인 '영화 관람객들이 그 영화를 보러 간 것'이 빈칸 뒤의 내용인 '영화가 상을 받은 것'보다 더 나중에 일어난 일이므로 '~ 후에'를 의미하는 (A)와 (C)가 정답 후보. 빈칸 뒤는 〈주어+동사〉 구조의 절이므로 절을 이끌 수 있는 접속사 (C)가 정답. (A)는 전치사라 뒤에 명사(구, 절)를 이끌 수 있으므로 오답.

5-6

Dear Mr. Bowers,

I am writing **because** the elevator in the west wing is out of order. Despite numerous requests to the maintenance team, this problem has not been resolved.

I realize that there is another elevator available on the east side of the building. **Nevertheless**, we need the west wing elevator fully functioning.

As the owner of the building, you are responsible for all repairs. I ask that you take care of this matter as soon as possible.

바워즈 씨께,

서관에 있는 엘리베이터가 고장이 났기 **때문에** 메일을 드립니다. 관리팀에 수차례 요청했음에도 불구하고, 이 문제가 해결되지 않았습니다.

건물 동쪽에 이용할 수 있는 엘리베이터가 하나 더 있다는 것을 알고 있습니다. **그렇기는 해도**, 서관 엘리베이터가 완전하게 기능해야 할 필요가 있습니다.

건물주로서, 바워즈 씨께 모든 수리의 책임이 있습니다. 가능한 한 빨리 이 문제를 처리해 주실 것을 부탁드립니다.

어휘│ out of order 고장 난 numerous 수많은 maintenance 관리, 보수 fully 완전히 be responsible for ~에 책임이 있다 take care of ~을 처리하다

5 I am writing / **because** the elevator in the west wing / is out of order.

(A) because (B) even if (C) however (D) not only

(A) ~ 때문에 (B) 비록 ~일지라도 (C) 그러나 (D) 뿐만 아니라

해설│ 빈칸 앞뒤로 절이 위치하고 있으므로, 빈칸에는 접속사가 들어가야 해서 접속사 (A)와 (B)가 정답 후보. 문맥상 서관의 고장 난 엘리베이터가 화자가 편지를 쓰는 '이유'이므로 '~ 때문에'라는 의미의 (A)가 정답.

6 <u>Nevertheless,</u> / we need the west wing elevator fully functioning.

(A) While (B) Whereas (C) For example **(D) Nevertheless**

(A) ~하는 동안에 (B) ~인 반면에 (C) 예를 들어 (D) 그럼에도 불구하고

해설 | 빈칸이 없어도 문장이 완전한 것으로 보아 빈칸은 부사 자리이다. 선택지 중 문장의 의미를 자연스럽게 연결하기 위해 사용되는 접속부사 (C)와 (D)가 정답 후보. 내용상 빈칸 앞 문장의 '건물 동쪽에 엘리베이터가 있는 것을 알고 있다'는 내용과 뒤 문장의 '서관 엘리베이터도 완전히 기능해야 한다'는 내용이 상반되므로 '대조'를 나타내는 접속부사 (D)가 정답. (A)와 (B)는 부사절 접속사로 오답이다.

VOCABULARY	생활 어휘(1)	교재 219쪽

1 notify **2** Participation **3** exhibition **4** celebration **5** (A) **6** (D) **7** (A) **8** (B)

---

1 Tenants must (intend / **notify**) the landlord / before doing any repairs / in a housing unit.

해석 | 세입자들은 주택 내의 어떤 수리라도 진행하기 전에 집주인에게 알려야만 한다.

어휘 | tenant 세입자, 임차인 landlord 주인, 임대주

해설 | 문맥상 세입자가 집을 수리하기 전에 집주인에게 '알려야 한다'는 내용이 자연스러우므로 정답은 notify.

---

2 (**Participation** / Disposal) in this year's arts festival / was much higher / than anticipated.

해석 | 올해의 아트 페스티벌에의 참가는 예상했던 것보다 훨씬 더 많다.

어휘 | anticipate 예상하다, 예측하다

해설 | 페스티벌에의 '참가'가 예상했던 것보다 많다는 내용이 자연스러우므로 정답은 Participation이다.

---

3 The museum is featuring a special (**exhibition** / individual) / on ancient art.

해석 | 그 미술관은 고대 미술에 대한 특별 전시회를 개최 중이다.

해설 | 미술관이 전시하여 보여줄 수 있는 것은 특별 '전시'가 되는 것이 알맞다. 따라서 정답은 exhibition.

---

4 The city held a (**celebration** / rental) / to mark the one hundredth anniversary of its founding.

해석 | 그 도시는 건립 100주년을 기념하기 위해 기념 행사를 열었다.

어휘 | mark 기념하다, 표시하다 anniversary 기념일 found 설립하다, 세우다

해설 | 동사 held의 목적어로 적절한 명사 어휘를 고르는 문제이다. hold(개최하다)라는 동사에 어울리는 목적어로는 '축하[기념] (행사)'라는 의미의 celebration이 가장 적절하다.

---

5 As a long-time **resident** of Watson City, / Edwin Anderson was familiar / with its historical sites.

(A) resident (B) gathering (C) foundation (D) community

해석 | 왓슨 시의 오랜 주민으로서, 에드윈 앤더슨 씨는 그곳의 유적지를 잘 알고 있었다.

(A) 주민 (B) 모임, 수집 (C) 재단, 토대 (D) 지역 사회

어휘 | long-time 오랜 be familiar with ~을 잘 알고 있다 historical site 유적지

해설 | 전치사 As가 '~로서'라는 자격을 나타내므로, 빈칸에는 주어인 Edwin Anderson이라는 사람의 자격을 나타내는 어휘가 들어가야 한다. 선택지 중에서 사람을 나타내는 것은 '주민'이라는 뜻의 resident뿐이다. 따라서 정답은 (A).

---

6 Stratford Towers is **conveniently** located / within walking distance of a shopping center and Regina Beach.

(A) previously (B) commonly (C) increasingly

(D) conveniently

해석 | 스트래트포드 타워즈는 쇼핑 센터와 레지나 해변까지 걸어갈 수 있는 거리에 편리하게 위치하고 있다.

(A) 이전에 (B) 일반적으로 (C) 점점 더 (D) 편리하게

어휘 | be located 위치해 있다 walking distance 걸어서 갈 수 있는 거리

해설 | 쇼핑 센터와 해변가까지 걸어갈 수 있는 곳이라고 했으므로 문맥상 '편리하게 위치해 있다, 편리한 위치이다'라는 뜻이 되어야 한다. 따라서 conveniently가 알맞다. 정답은 (D).

7 The corporation plans to host a small **reception** / to honor Mr. Kohl's thirty years of service.
(A) reception (B) completion (C) establishment
(D) accomplishment

해석 | 회사에서는 콜 씨의 30년 근속을 기념하기 위해서 작은 축하연을 주최할 계획이다.
(A) 축하연, 환영회 (B) 완성 (C) 설립, 기관 (D) 업적, 성취
어휘 | corporation 회사, 기업 honor 기념하다

해설 | 동사 host는 '주최하다, 열다'라는 뜻으로 목적어로 주로 meeting(회의), party 등 사람들이 모이는 행사가 온다. 따라서 '축하연, 환영회'라는 뜻의 (A)가 알맞다.

---

8 The **appliance** scheduled to be delivered on Saturday / requires installation / by a skilled technician.
(A) invoice **(B) appliance** (C) address (D) directory

해석 | 토요일에 배송되기로 한 가전제품은 숙련된 기술자의 설치를 필요로 한다.
(A) 송장, 명세서 (B) (가정용) 기기, 전기제품 (C) 주소 (D) (건물 내의) 안내판
어휘 | scheduled to *do* ~하기로 예정된 installation 설치 skilled 숙련된

해설 | 선택지 중에서 숙련된 기술자의 설치를 필요로 할 만한 것을 고른다. 가정에서 사용하는 냉장고, 세탁기, 청소기 등의 '(가정용) 기기, 전기제품'을 뜻하는 (B)가 알맞다.

ACTUAL TEST 실전 문제에 적용하기   교재 220쪽

1 (B) **2** (D) **3** (A) **4** (D) **5** (C) **6** (C) **7** (B) **8** (D) **9** (B) **10** (A) **11** (C) **12** (A)

---

1 **When** Jaspoint Restaurant first started, / it had a lot of positive reviews / online.
(A) For **(B) When** (C) Through (D) Until

해석 | 제스포인트 식당이 처음 개업했을 때, 그곳은 온라인상에서 많은 호평을 받았다.
(A) 왜냐하면 (B) ~할 때 (C) ~을 통해 (D) ~할 때까지

해설 | **부사절 접속사 when**
콤마 앞뒤로 완전한 절이 있으므로 빈칸은 절과 절을 연결하는 접속사가 들어갈 자리이다. 따라서 전치사인 (C)는 정답에서 제외. 문맥상 식당이 개업했을 '때' 온라인상에서 호평을 얻었다는 내용이 되어야 하므로 정답은 When.

---

2 The Winter Hills Hotline provides citizens with **reliable** information / about the city's attractions.
(A) residential (B) portable (C) approximate **(D) reliable**

해석 | 윈터 힐스 핫라인은 시민들에게 시의 명소에 대한 믿을 만한 정보를 제공한다.
(A) 주거의 (B) 휴대용의 (C) 대략의 (D) 믿을 만한
어휘 | provide A with B A에게 B를 제공하다 attraction 명소

해설 | **형용사 어휘 reliable**
문맥상 어울리는 형용사를 고르는 문제로, 빈칸 뒤의 명사 information과 어울리는 것은 '믿을 만한'이란 뜻의 reliable이다. 따라서 정답은 (D).

---

3 The effects of the new strategy can be determined / **once** the figures have been analyzed.
(A) once (B) almost (C) so that (D) away

해석 | 일단 수치를 분석하면 새로운 전략의 결과를 판단할 수 있다.
(A) 일단 ~하면 (B) 거의 (C) ~하기 위해서 (D) 떨어져서
어휘 | strategy 전략 figure 수치 analyze 분석하다

해설 | **부사절 접속사 once**
빈칸 앞뒤로 절이 나오므로 접속사인 (A)와 (C)가 정답 후보가 된다. 문맥상 '수치를 분석하면'이라는 뜻이 되어야 알맞으므로 (A)가 정답. once는 '일단 ~하면'이라는 뜻이다.
오답 | (B)와 (D)는 부사이므로 오답.

---

4 **While** the other manufacturing companies experienced a slowdown last year, / Milltown Industries profits increased.
(A) Except for (B) Besides (C) Only if **(D) While**

해석 | 다른 제조사들이 지난 해 사업 둔화를 겪은 반면에, 밀타운 인터스트리즈 사의 수익은 증가했다.
(A) ~을 제외하고 (B) ~ 외에 (C) ~해야만 (D) ~ 반면에
어휘 | slowdown 둔화 profit 수익, 이익

해설 | **부사절 접속사 while**
콤마 앞뒤로 완전한 절이 나왔으므로 빈칸은 두 절을 연결하는 접속사 자리이다. 선택지 중 (A)와 (B)는 전치사로 정답 후보에서 제외. '다른 제조사들은 사업 둔화를 겪었다'는 콤마 앞부분 내용은 '수익이 증가했다'는 콤마 뒷부분 내용과 반대되므로, 대조를 나타내는 접속사 (D)가 적절하다.

5 <u>Provided</u> the director approves the proposal / from the security department, / employees will be issued electronic key cards.
(A) Provide   (B) Provides   **(C) Provided**   (D) Provision
해석| 이사가 보안부서의 제안을 승인하면, 직원들에게 전자 카드키가 발급될 것이다.
어휘| director 이사   issue 발급[발부]하다   electronic 전자의

해설| **부사절 접속사 provided (that)**
선택지를 보니, 동사 provide의 적절한 형태를 고르는 문제이다. 콤마 앞뒤로 완전한 절이 나오는 것으로 보아, 빈칸은 두 절을 연결하는 접속사 자리이다. 동사 provide는 과거분사의 형태로 '~한다면'을 뜻하여 '조건'을 나타내는 부사절 접속사로 쓰인다. 따라서 정답은 (C). 참고로 supposed[supposing](~라고 가정하면)과 given(~을 고려하면)도 분사 형태의 부사절 접속사이다.

---

6 The video game system includes only one wireless controller, / but extra controllers can be purchased <u>separately</u>.
(A) suddenly   (B) loosely   **(C) separately**   (D) accidentally
해석| 그 비디오 게임 시스템에는 무선 조종 장치가 하나만 포함되어 있지만, 추가 조종 장치를 별도로 구입할 수 있다.
(A) 갑자기 (B) 헐겁게 (C) 별도로 (D) 우연히
어휘| wireless 무선의   controller 조종 장치

해설| **부사 어휘 separately**
'대조'를 나타내는 접속사 but을 통해 콤마 앞뒤 문장이 서로 상반된 내용임을 알 수 있다. 문맥상 무선 조종 장치가 하나만 들어있지만 '별도로' 구입 가능하다라는 뜻이 되어야 알맞으므로 (C)가 정답.

---

7 Golden Ferry still allows motorcycles on its vessels / <u>even though</u> larger vehicles are temporarily banned / on board.
(A) owing to   **(B) even though**   (C) whether   (D) despite
해석| 큰 운송 수단은 선상에 싣는 것이 일시적으로 금지되었음에도 불구하고, 골든 페리 사는 여전히 오토바이를 자사의 선내에 실을 수 있게 한다.
(A) ~ 때문에 (B) 비록 ~이지만 (C) ~인지 아닌지 (D) 비록 ~이지만
어휘| motorcycle 오토바이   vessel 선박, 배   ban 금하다

해설| **부사절 접속사 even though**
문맥상 '큰 운송 수단을 선내에 싣는 것이 금지되었음에도 골든 페리 사에서는 실었다'는 내용이 자연스러우므로 '(비록) ~이지만'의 의미인 접속사 (B)와 전치사 (D)가 정답 후보. 빈칸 앞뒤로 완전한 절이 나오므로 절을 연결하는 접속사 (B)가 정답.
오답| (A)와 (D)는 명사구가 뒤따르는 전치사이므로 오답. (C)는 명사절을 이끄는 명사절 접속사이므로 오답.

---

8 All merchandise can be returned / within thirty days of purchase / <u>unless</u> it was a custom order.
(A) in case   (B) during   (C) instead   **(D) unless**
해석| 모든 상품은 주문제작품이 아니라면 구입한 지 30일 이내에 반품 가능하다.
(A) ~한 경우에 (B) ~ 동안 (C) 대신 (D) ~가 아니라면
어휘| merchandise 상품   custom 주문제작한, 맞춤의

해설| **부사절 접속사 unless**
빈칸은 절과 절을 잇는 접속사 자리로 (A)와 (D)가 가능하다. 주문제작품이 '아니라면' 반품이 가능하다는 내용이 자연스러우므로 '~가 아니라면'이라는 뜻의 (D)가 알맞다.
오답| (C) instead는 부사, (B)는 전치사이므로 오답.

9-12

Let Sherman Realty Help You

Since it was **established** nearly ten years ago, Sherman Realty has become a trusted source for high-quality real estate in Maryville.

After our real estate brokers are selected to work for us, we provide them with an intensive in-house training program. **This equips staff with a high degree of professionalism.** So we're confident you'll be fully satisfied with your experience working with us.

셔먼 부동산에서 여러분을 도와드리겠습니다

거의 10년 전에 **설립된** 이래로, 셔먼 부동산은 메리빌에서 입지가 좋은 부동산을 제공하는 것으로 신뢰받는 정보원이 되었습니다.

저희 부동산 중개업자들이 저희와 일하도록 선발된 **후에**, 저희는 이들에게 집중적인 사내 교육 프로그램을 제공합니다. **이 덕분에 직원들은 높은 수준의 전문성을 갖추고**

Furthermore, we do a high volume of business and have more listings than any other realtor in the region. That means you'll have more properties to view and to choose from. From residential homes to commercial buildings, Sherman Realty is your number one resource.

있습니다. 그래서, 저희와 함께하는 경험에 여러분이 충분히 만족하시리라 확신합니다.

게다가 저희는 거래량이 많고 지역의 다른 어떤 중개업체보다 더 많은 목록을 보유하고 있습니다. 다시 말하자면 여러분이 둘러보고 선택할 수 있는 부동산이 더 많다는 말입니다. 주거용 주택에서 상업용 건물에 이르기까지, 셔먼 부동산은 여러분의 최고의 정보원입니다.

어휘| realty 부동산 nearly 거의 trusted 신뢰받는 source 정보원, 출처 real estate 부동산 broker 중개인 intensive 집중적인 in-house 사내의 equip A with B A에게 B를 갖게 하다[제공하다] a high degree of 높은 수준의 professionalism 전문성 confident 확신하는 be satisfied with ~에 만족해하다 high volume 다량 realtor 부동산업자 property 부동산, 토지 residential 주거용의 commercial 상업의

9 Since it was <u>established</u> nearly ten years ago, / Sherman Realty has become a trusted source / for high-quality real estate in Maryville.
(A) settled **(B) established** (C) arranged (D) produced
(A) 정착하다 (B) 설립하다 (C) 마련하다 (D) 생산하다

해설| **동사 어휘 establish**
주어인 it이 가리키는 것은 주절의 주어인 Sherman Realty(셔먼 부동산)이므로 이를 주어로 해서 의미상 가장 자연스러운 것을 고른다. 업체가 '설립되다'라는 뜻으로 (B)가 들어가야 알맞다.

10 <u>After</u> our real estate brokers are selected / to work for us, / we provide them with an intensive in-house training program.
(A) After (B) During (C) Rather (D) So that
(A) ~ 후에 (B) ~ 동안에 (C) 꽤 (D) ~이 되도록

해설| **부사절 접속사 after**
콤마 앞뒤로 완전한 절이 있으므로, 빈칸에는 절과 절을 연결하는 접속사가 들어가야 한다. 선택지에서 접속사는 (A)와 (D)뿐인데, 문맥상 직원을 채용한 '후에' 그들을 위한 사내 교육을 제공한다는 의미가 되어야 자연스러우므로 정답은 (A)이다.
오답| (B)는 전치사, (C)는 부사이므로 오답.

11 (A) The training sessions are usually held in the mornings.
(B) We recommend registering for the program as early as possible.
(C) This equips staff with a high degree of professionalism.
(D) If you have experience, feel free to apply to work with us.
(A) 교육은 대개 오전에 진행됩니다.
(B) 최대한 일찍 프로그램에 등록할 것을 권합니다.
(C) 이 덕분에 직원들은 높은 수준의 전문성을 갖추고 있습니다.
(D) 당신이 경력을 갖고 있다면, 망설이지 말고 지원하세요.

해설| **알맞은 문장 고르기**
지문은 부동산 중개소를 광고하는 내용으로, 빈칸 앞에서 직원들을 자체적으로 교육하고 있다는 내용이 나온다. 따라서 그로 인해 얻을 수 있는 장점을 이야기하는 (C)가 들어가면 자연스럽게 연결된다. 여기서 대명사 This는 앞 문장 전체를 가리키고 있다.
오답| (A) 바로 앞에 나온 자체 교육에 대한 이야기를 이어가고 있지만, 교육 시간은 빈칸 뒤에 언급되는 고객의 만족도와 관계가 없으므로 오답이다. (B) 빈칸 앞에 나온 program이라는 단어를 이용한 함정이다. 고객에게 부동산의 사내 교육 프로그램에 등록하라고 권하는 내용은 어울리지 않으므로 오답. (D) 지문은 부동산 중개소의 광고이지, 채용 광고가 아니므로 지원을 유도하는 내용은 지문과 어울리지 않는다.

12 <u>Furthermore</u>, we do a high volume of business and have more listings / than any other realtor in the region.

(A) **Furthermore** (B) Otherwise (C) Supposing (D) Because

(A) 게다가 (B) 그렇지 않으면 (C) 만약 ～라면 (D) 왜냐하면

해설| **접속부사 furthermore**
빈칸 없이도 문장이 완전하고 빈칸이 빈칸 뒤 문장과 콤마로 연결되므로, 접속부사 (A)와 (B)가 정답 후보. 빈칸 앞까지 업체의 전문성 있는 부동산 중개업자들에 대한 이야기를 했고, 빈칸 뒤에서는 많은 물량을 강조하고 있다. 빈칸 앞뒤 모두 부동산 업체의 강점에 대해 설명하고 있으므로 '첨가'의 뜻을 가진 접속부사 Furthermore가 적절하다.

UNIT 14 관계사

1 Mr. Hunt hired a lawyer / (he / **who**) is an expert / in corporate law.

해석| 헌트 씨는 회사법에 전문가인 변호사를 선임했다.

어휘| lawyer 변호사 corporate 회사[기업]의

해설| 괄호 앞이 완전한 문장이고, 괄호 뒤의 절에 주어 없이 바로 동사가 나오고 있다. 따라서 괄호는 접속사와 주어의 역할을 동시에 하는 관계대명사가 들어가야 한다. 따라서 정답은 who. 주격 인칭대명사인 he는 두 문장을 연결하는 접속사 역할을 할 수 없어서 오답이다.

2 Conchi Incorporated should develop a recycling program, / (and / **which**) would reduce its industrial waste.

해석| 콘치 주식회사는 그것의 산업 폐기물을 줄여줄 수 있는 재활용 프로그램을 개발해야 한다.

어휘| Incorporated 주식회사 recycle 재활용하다 industrial 산업의 waste 폐기물, 쓰레기

해설| 괄호 앞은 완전한 문장이고, 괄호 뒤에 접속사와 주어 없이 동사로 시작되는 불완전한 절이 이어지고 있으므로, 괄호는 주격 관계대명사가 들어갈 자리이다. 따라서 which가 정답. and는 절을 연결해 줄 수 있으나 and 뒤의 절에 없는 주어(명사)를 대신할 수는 없어서 오답이다.

3 Ms. Hall explained the benefits of the merger / to shareholders, / (who / **and**) they discussed the matter.

해석| 홀 씨는 주주들에게 합병의 이점을 설명했고, 그들은 그 문제에 대해 논의했다.

어휘| benefit 이점, 혜택 merger 합병

해설| 괄호 앞뒤로 완전한 두 문장이 나오므로, 두 절을 잇는 접속사가 들어가야 한다. 따라서 정답은 and. who는 〈접속사+대명사〉 역할을 하므로 괄호 뒤에 완전한 절이 올 수 없다.

4 The newspaper listed the (**residents** / residences) / who participated in the local clean-up drive.

해석| 그 신문은 지역 정화 작업에 참여한 주민들의 이름을 열거했다.

어휘| list 열거하다 participate 참가하다 clean-up 정화, 청소 drive 운동, 캠페인

해설| 괄호 뒤 who가 이끄는 관계대명사절이 수식하는 알맞은 선행사를 고르는 문제이다. 사람을 가리키는 관계대명사 who가 사용되었으므로 선행사는 사람 명사인 residents가 정답. residences는 '저택, 거주'의 의미이므로 내용상으로도 어색하므로 오답이다.

5 Ms. Wanda recently met the artist / <u>who</u> painted the portrait of a famous musician.
(A) who (B) so (C) they (D) few

해석| 완다 씨는 인기 있는 음악가의 초상화를 그린 예술가를 최근에 만났다.

어휘| portrait 초상화 musician 음악가

해설| 빈칸 앞이 완전한 절이고, 빈칸 뒤의 절이 주어 없이 동사로 시작하고 있다. 따라서 빈칸에는 두 절을 연결하는 접속사와 주어의 역할을 동시에 하는 관계대명사가 들어가야 한다. 선택지에서 관계대명사는 who뿐이므로 정답은 (A).

6 In *Crusaders*, / Ben Porter played the lead role, / <u>which</u> required him to learn another language.
(A) who (B) **which** (C) whom (D) whose

해석| 〈크루세이더〉에서 벤 포터 씨는 주인공 역을 맡았는데, 그 역할로 그는 다른 언어를 배워야 했다.

어휘| lead role 주연

해설| 빈칸 앞이 완전한 절이고 빈칸 다음에 바로 동사가 이어지므로, 빈칸에는 주격 관계대명사가 필요하다. 따라서 (A)와 (B)가 정답 후보. 선행사 the lead role이 사물이므로 (B)가 정답. (C)는 목적격 관계대명사이고, (D)는 소유격 관계대명사라 오답이다.

7 The company has a new attendance policy, / and **this** will be implemented / next month.
(A) who (B) these (C) this (D) which

해석| 그 기업에는 새로운 출근 규정이 있는데, 이것은 다음 달에 시행될 것이다.

어휘| attendance 출석, 참석

해설| 콤마 앞이 완전한 절이고 콤마 뒤에 접속사 and가 있으므로 빈칸 이하가 완전한 문장이어야 한다. 빈칸은 동사 will be implemented 앞으로 주어 자리이다. 따라서 관계대명사 (A)와 (D)는 정답 후보에서 제외. 주어 역할을 할 수 있는 대명사 (B)와 (C) 중 앞서 나온 단수 명사 a new attendance policy를 가리킬 수 있는 단수 대명사 (C)가 정답이다.

---

8 The long-running musical features **performers** / who have delighted audiences across the globe.
(A) performance (B) perform (C) performers (D) performing

해석| 장기 공연 중인 그 뮤지컬은 전세계 관객들을 즐겁게 하는 배우들이 출연한다.

어휘| long-running 오래 지속되는 feature ~을 출연시키다 performer 배우 delight 즐겁게 하다 across the globe 전세계에서

해설| 빈칸은 빈칸 앞 동사 features의 목적어로 동사 (B)는 정답 후보에서 제외되고 나머지 명사 선택지들이 정답 후보. 빈칸 뒤 관계대명사 who는 사람 선행사를 수식할 때 쓰이므로 정답은 '배우'의 의미인 (C).

<table>
<tr><td rowspan="2">**2**</td><td colspan="2">**주격·목적격·소유격 관계대명사**</td><td>교재 227쪽</td></tr>
<tr><td colspan="3">**1** wish **2** whose **3** which **4** whom **5** (C) **6** (B) **7** (D) **8** (B)</td></tr>
</table>

1 All employees / who (**wish** / wishes) to retire early / must submit a formal letter / to their managers.

해석| 조기 퇴직을 하고 싶어 하는 모든 직원들은 그들의 매니저에게 공식 서신을 제출해야 한다.

어휘| retire 은퇴[퇴직]하다 formal 공식적인, 정식의

해설| who 이하에 주어가 없고 괄호가 동사 자리이므로 who는 접속사와 주어의 역할을 동시에 하는 주격 관계대명사이다. 주격 관계대명사 뒤의 동사는 선행사에 수일치 시켜야 한다. 선행사인 All employees는 복수 명사이므로 이에 맞는 복수 동사 wish가 정답.

---

2 Borsa and Associates is a law firm / (**whose** / who) lawyers specialize in corporate conflicts.

해석| 보르사 앤 어소시어츠 사는 소속 변호사들이 기업 분쟁을 전문으로 하는 법률 사무소이다.

어휘| specialize 전문적으로 다루다, 전공하다 conflict 갈등, 충돌

해설| 괄호 안에 알맞은 관계대명사를 고르는 문제. 괄호 앞 선행사 a law firm과 괄호 뒤 lawyers가 소유 관계이므로 소유격인 whose가 정답. 주격 관계대명사 who는 괄호 뒤에 동사가 바로 따라와야 하므로 오답. who가 목적격 관계대명사라 해도 괄호 뒤 문장은 목적어 자리에 명사 corporate conflicts가 있으므로 오답.

---

3 The Sandyport beach resort has airport shuttles / (whose / **which**) guests can ride for free.

해석| 샌디포트 비치 리조트에는 손님들이 무료로 탈 수 있는 공항 셔틀 버스가 있다.

어휘| for free 무료로, 공짜로

해설| 선행사인 airport shuttles가 관계대명사절에서 동사 can ride의 목적어 역할을 하므로, 선행사가 사물인 경우에 쓰는 목적격 관계대명사 which가 정답이다.

---

4 I have not met the assistant / (**whom** / whose) the general manager hired last week.

해석| 나는 총지배인이 지난주에 채용한 조수를 만난 적이 없다.

해설| 선행사인 assistant가 관계대명사절에서 동사 hired의 목적어 역할을 하므로, 선행사가 사람일 때 쓰는 목적격 관계대명사 whom이 정답.

5 Anyone / **who** collects vintage cars / must attend the tenth Mewshire Classica Auto Show.
(A) whom (B) whose **(C) who** (D) which

해석| 빈티지 자동차를 수집하는 사람이라면 누구든지 제10회 뮤샤이어 클래식 자동차 전시회에 참가해야 한다.

어휘| collect 수집하다, 모으다

해설| 선택지를 보니 빈칸에 알맞은 관계대명사를 고르는 문제. 빈칸 뒤에 주어 없이 동사가 나오므로 빈칸은 접속사와 주어의 역할을 동시에 하는 주격 관계대명사 자리이다. 따라서 (C)와 (D)가 정답 후보. 선행사가 Anyone이므로 사람 선행사인 경우에 쓰는 주격 관계대명사 (C)가 정답.

---

6 Mr. Daniels paid $50 extra / for the overdue SUV / **which** he rented from Union Cars.
(A) through **(B) which** (C) thus (D) who

해석| 다니엘스 씨는 유니온 카즈 사에서 빌렸다가 반납 기한이 지난 SUV 차량에 대해 50달러를 추가로 지불했다.

어휘| overdue 기한이 지난

해설| 빈칸 앞이 완전한 절이고, 빈칸 뒤에 불완전한 절이 나오는 것으로 보아 빈칸은 관계대명사 자리이다. 따라서 전치사 (A)와 접속부사 (C)는 정답 후보에서 제외. 빈칸 앞 선행사가 사물인 the overdue SUV이므로 사물 선행사와 어울려 쓰이는 목적격 관계대명사 (B)가 정답이다.

---

7 A singer / **whose** most recent album sold more than one million copies / will give a live concert / in Pembroke Park tomorrow.
(A) that (B) which (C) their **(D) whose**

해석| 가장 최근 앨범이 백만 장 이상 팔린 가수 한 명이 내일 펨브로크 공원에서 라이브 공연을 할 것이다.

해설| 빈칸 앞의 명사 A singer가 문장의 주어이고 동사가 will give이다. 그 사이의, 빈칸부터 copies까지는 빈칸 앞 명사를 수식하는 관계대명사절이므로 빈칸에는 관계대명사 (A), (B), (D)가 들어갈 수 있다. 괄호 앞뒤의 명사가 소유 관계(가수의 최근 앨범)이므로 정답은 소유격 관계대명사 (D)가 정답이다. (A)와 (B)는 주격, 목적격 관계대명사로 쓰이고 소유격으로는 쓰일 수 없으므로 오답이다.

---

8 The main tunnel / that **connects** the national zoo and the art museum / will be out of service / this weekend.
(A) connection **(B) connects** (C) connect (D) connecting

해석| 국립 동물원과 미술관을 연결하는 주요 터널이 이번 주말에 운영되지 않을 것이다.

어휘| connect 연결하다 out of service 사용되지 않는, 고장 난

해설| 주어인 The main tunnel을 수식하는 관계대명사 that절에 주어와 동사가 없으므로 that이 주격 관계대명사이고, 빈칸은 관계대명사절의 동사 자리이다. 따라서 동사 (B)와 (C)가 정답 후보. 관계대명사절의 동사는 선행사에 수 일치 시키는데, 선행사인 The main tunnel이 단수이므로 단수 동사 (B)가 정답이다.

---

3 관계대명사 that과 what   교재 229쪽

1 which **2** that **3** What **4** what **5** (B) **6** (B) **7** (A) **8** (D)

---

1 The Louvre is the museum / in (**which** / that) Leonardo da Vinci's *Mona Lisa* is displayed.

해석| 루브르는 레오나르도 다빈치의 〈모나리자〉가 전시되어 있는 미술관이다.

어휘| display 전시하다

해설| 괄호 앞의 전치사 in으로 보아 괄호는 전치사의 목적어로 쓰이면서 괄호 앞뒤의 절을 연결할 수 있는 목적격 관계대명사가 들어가야 한다. 따라서 전치사의 목적어로 쓸 수 있는 관계대명사 which가 정답. which나 who(m) 자리를 대신하여 that을 쓸 수 있으나, 전치사 뒤에는 쓸 수 없다는 것을 기억하자.

2 A research study indicates / (**that** / whom) Questo Bank offers the country's most convenient online banking service.

해석| 한 연구는 퀘스토 은행이 국내에서 가장 편리한 온라인 은행업무 서비스를 제공한다는 것을 보여 준다.

어휘| indicate 보여 주다, 나타내다   convenient 편리한, 간편한

해설| 괄호 이하는 괄호 앞 동사 indicates의 목적어이다. 괄호 앞에 선행사가 없고, 괄호 뒤 절이 완전하므로 관계대명사 whom을 쓸 수 없다. 따라서 정답은 that. 여기서 that은 관계대명사가 아니라, 괄호 뒤의 완전한 절을 이끌어 명사절을 만드는 명사절 접속사이다.

---

3 (Which / **What**) the brochure mainly describes / is a practical way to reduce household waste.

해석| 안내책자에서 주로 설명하는 것은 가정용 쓰레기를 줄이는 실제적인 방법이다.

어휘| brochure 안내책자   mainly 주로   describe 설명하다   practical 실제적인   household 가정

해설| 문장의 동사는 is이며, 그 앞부분이 문장의 주어이다. 괄호 안의 선택지 중 명사절을 이끌어 문장에서 주어 역할을 할 수 있는 것은 선행사를 포함한 관계대명사 what이다. which는 선행사를 필요로 하는 관계대명사인데 괄호 앞에 아무 명사도 없어서 오답이다.

---

4 The supervisor explained / (that / **what**) employees should do / in case of emergency.

해석| 그 감독관은 비상 상황이 발생할 경우 직원들이 어떻게 해야 하는지를 설명했다.

어휘| in case of ~의 경우   emergency 비상

해설| 괄호 이하는 괄호 앞 동사 explained의 목적어이다. 괄호 뒤 절에 목적어가 없이 불완전하고 괄호 앞에 선행사도 없다. 따라서 괄호에 알맞은 것은 명사절 접속사 that이 아니라, 선행사를 포함하는 관계대명사 what이다. 따라서 정답은 what. that을 관계대명사로 보더라도 괄호 앞에 선행사가 없으므로 괄호에는 쓸 수 없다.

---

5 The server / **that** takes your order / will make recommendations / for a variety of menu selections.
(A) neither **(B) that** (C) each (D) what

해석| 고객님의 주문을 받는 종업원이 다양한 메뉴 선택을 위한 추천을 해 줄 것입니다.

어휘| server 종업원   make a recommendation 추천하다   a variety of 다양한   selection 선택

해설| 빈칸 앞 명사 The server가 주어이고 will make가 동사이므로, 빈칸부터 order까지는 주어를 수식하는 수식어구이다. 따라서 빈칸에 들어갈 수 있는 것은 빈칸 뒤 동사 takes와 목적어 your order를 이끌어 선행사 The server를 수식하는 주격 관계대명사 (B)이다. (D)는 선행사를 포함한 관계대명사라, 빈칸 앞 The server와 함께 쓸 수 없으므로 오답.

---

6 **What** we allocated for the retirement dinner / was not enough / to cover the unexpected expenses.
(A) Those **(B) What** (C) Therefore (D) Which

해석| 우리가 은퇴식을 위해 배정한 것은 예기치 않은 비용을 치르기에 충분하지 않았다.

어휘| allocate 배정하다   cover 비용을 치르다   unexpected 예기치 않은   expense 비용, 경비

해설| was가 문장의 동사이므로 그 앞부분이 주어이다. 빈칸 뒤에 주어와 동사가 있으나 목적어가 없는 불완전한 절이므로 빈칸에는 관계대명사가 들어가야 한다. 따라서 (B)와 (D)가 정답 후보. (D)는 절을 이끌어 선행사를 수식하도록 하는 관계대명사인데 빈칸 앞에 선행사가 없으므로 오답이고, 선행사를 포함한 관계대명사 (B)가 정답이다. (A)는 지시대명사, (C)는 접속부사라 절을 연결할 수 없으므로 오답이다.

---

7 The quality control staff selected / **what** needed to be sent back / to the manufacturer.
(A) what (B) this (C) that (D) who

해석| 그 품질 관리 직원은 제조사로 돌려보내져야 하는 것들을 골라냈다.

어휘| quality control 품질 관리   send back ~을 돌려보내다

해설| 빈칸 이하는 동사 selected의 목적어가 되는 명사절이다. 선택지 중에서 빈칸 뒤의 불완전한 절을 이끌 수 있는 것은 관계대명사인 (A), (C), (D). 빈칸 앞에 선행사가 없으므로 선행사를 포함한 관계대명사 what을 써야 한다. 따라서 정답은 (A).

8 The latest research suggests / **that** vitamin supplements from EZ-Med prevent colds.
(A) to (B) what (C) you (D) that

해석 | 최근 연구에서 이지-메드에서 나온 비타민 보충제가 감기를 예방한다는 점을 시사한다.

어휘 | supplement 보충제 prevent 예방하다

해설 | 빈칸 이하는 suggests의 목적어가 되는 명사절이다. 빈칸 뒤에 주어 vitamin supplements와 동사 prevent, 목적어 colds가 다 갖춰진 완전한 절이 나오므로 명사절을 이끄는 접속사 (D)가 빈칸에 들어가야 한다. (B) what은 선행사를 포함한 관계대명사로 불완전한 절을 이끌어야 하므로 오답.

---

4 관계부사와 복합관계사

교재 231쪽

1 where **2** why **3** whatever **4** whenever **5** (B) **6** (B) **7** (C) **8** (D)

---

1 Police officers examined the intersection / (which / **where**) the accident occurred.

해석 | 경찰관들이 사고가 발생한 교차로를 조사했다.

어휘 | examine 조사하다 intersection 교차로 occur 발생하다

해설 | 괄호 앞이 완전한 절이므로 괄호 이하는 the intersection을 수식하는 절이다. 그런데 괄호 뒤 역시 완전한 절이 이어지므로 관계대명사가 아닌 관계부사 where가 괄호에 들어가야 한다. 관계대명사 다음에는 불완전한 절이, 관계부사 다음에는 완전한 절이 나온다는 것을 기억하자.

---

2 The publisher didn't explain the reason / (**why** / how) the manuscript was rejected.

해석 | 출판사는 원고를 거절한 이유를 설명해 주지 않았다.

어휘 | publisher 출판사 manuscript 원고 reject 거절하다

해설 | 괄호 안에 알맞은 관계부사를 고르는 문제. 선행사인 the reason이 '이유'를 나타내므로 관계부사 why를 써야 한다.

---

3 Employees can sign up / for a workshop / in (**whatever** / whose) they prefer.

해석 | 직원들은 그들이 선호하는 것과 관련된 워크숍에 신청할 수 있다.

어휘 | sign up for ~에 신청하다[등록하다]

해설 | 괄호 앞의 전치사 in은 목적어를 필요로 하는데, 따라서 빈칸에는 명사절을 이끌 수 있는 복합관계대명사 whatever이 들어가야 한다. 관계대명사 whose는 명사절이 아니라 형용사절을 이끌므로 오답.

---

4 Customers may call the Halk Electronics technical support hotline / (**whenever** / which) they need help / with products.

해석 | 고객들은 제품에 대한 지원이 필요하면 언제든 호크 일렉트로닉스 사의 기술 지원 상담 전화로 전화할 수 있다.

어휘 | technical support 기술 지원

해설 | 괄호 앞이 완전한 절이기 때문에 괄호 이하는 수식어구임을 알 수 있다. 괄호 뒤에 완전한 절이 왔으므로 불완전한 절을 이끄는 관계대명사 which는 괄호에 들어갈 말로 적절하지 않다. 따라서 뒤에 완전한 절을 이끌어 부사절의 역할을 할 수 있는 복합관계부사 whenever가 정답.

---

5 From 8 A.M. to 11 A.M., / parking is prohibited / on the street / **where** the parade is scheduled / to take place.
(A) until **(B) where** (C) beside (D) near

해석 | 오전 8시부터 오전 11시까지, 행진이 예정된 거리에서는 주차가 금지된다.
(A) ~할 때까지 (B) ~한 곳 (C) ~의 옆에 (D) ~ 가까이에

어휘 | prohibit 금지하다 parade 행진 be scheduled to *do* ~할 예정이다 take place 열리다

해설 | 빈칸 앞뒤로 완전한 절이 나오므로 두 절을 연결할 수 있는 접속사 (A)와 관계부사 (B)가 정답 후보. 내용상 빈칸 이하의 절이 빈칸 앞 선행사 the street을 꾸며서 '행진이 예정된 거리'라는 내용이 자연스러우므로 정답은 (B). (A)는 문맥상 어울리지 않으므로 오답.

6 Members of our rewards club / can receive substantial discounts / on the day / **when** the store celebrates its anniversary.
(A) whose (B) when (C) which (D) what

해석| 우리 고객 혜택 클럽의 회원은 매장에서 기념일을 축하하는 날에 상당한 할인을 받을 수 있다.

어휘| rewards club 리워즈 클럽(가입하는 고객에게 혜택을 주는 제도) substantial 상당한

해설| 빈칸 앞뒤로 완전한 절이 나오므로 두 절을 연결할 수 있는 관계부사 (B)가 정답이다. 나머지 선택지는 모두 불완전한 절이 뒤따르는 관계대명사이므로 오답. 빈칸 앞 선행사 the day는 시간을 가리키는 말이므로 시간을 나타내는 관계부사 when이 빈칸 뒤의 절을 이끌어 the day를 수식해 주는 구조이다.

---

7 Please send this letter / to **whoever** is in charge of handling mutual funds and investment / at your company.
(A) whatever (B) wherever (C) **whoever** (D) whichever

해석| 이 서신을 귀사에서 뮤추얼 펀드와 투자를 담당하고 있는 사람 누구에게든 보내 주십시오.

어휘| send A to B A를 B에게 보내다 be in charge of ~을 담당하다[맡고 있다]

해설| 빈칸은 전치사 to의 목적어 자리인데, 빈칸 뒤 절의 주어 역할을 하는 동시에 두 절을 연결하는 역할도 해야 한다. 이런 역할을 할 수 있는 복합관계대명사인 (A), (C), (D)가 정답 후보. 문맥상으로도 '담당하고 있는 사람 누구에게든'라는 뜻이 되어야 하므로 정답은 사람을 가리켜 쓰이는 복합관계대명사 (C)이다.

---

8 **However** limited the given time was, / the marketing team still produced a great advertising campaign.
(A) Whenever (B) Why (C) Which (D) **However**

해석| 주어진 시간이 아무리 한정되어 있어도, 마케팅 팀은 여전히 대단한 광고를 만들어 냈다.

어휘| limited 제한된

해설| 문장이 콤마로 구분되어 있고 콤마 이하가 완전한 절이므로 콤마 앞이 부사절이 되어야 함을 알 수 있다. 선택지 중 부사절을 이끌 수 있는 복합관계부사 (A)와 (D)가 정답 후보. 문맥상 '아무리 한정되어 있어도'라는 의미가 되어야 하므로 정답은 '아무리 ~한다 해도'의 의미인 (D)가 정답. (A)는 시간의 관계사 when에 -ever가 결합한 복합관계부사로 '언제든지'를 의미하므로 문맥상 어색하다.

---

1 Candidates / **who** meet the minimum requirements / will be contacted / for an interview and examination.
(A) **who** (B) they (C) which (D) when

해석| 최소 요구 조건을 충족하는 지원자들은 인터뷰와 시험을 위해 연락을 받게 될 것입니다.

어휘| minimum 최소의, 최저의 examination 시험

해설| 빈칸 앞 명사 Candidates는 주어이고, will be contacted가 동사이므로 빈칸부터 requirements까지는 주어를 수식하는 절이다. 그런데 이 절에 주어가 빠져 있으므로 빈칸에는 주격 관계대명사가 들어가야 한다. 따라서 (A)와 (C)가 정답 후보. 빈칸 앞 선행사 Candidates가 사람이므로 사람 선행사를 취하는 (A)가 정답이다. (C)는 사물 선행사와 어울려 쓰인다.

---

2 **What** attracts consumers to H-TEC Electronics / is its affordable prices.
(A) That (B) Both (C) **What** (D) Each

해석| 고객들을 에이치테크 일렉트로닉스 사로 이끄는 것은 그 회사의 저렴한 가격이다.

어휘| affordable 저렴한, 살 만한 가격의

해설| is가 문장의 주어이므로, 그 앞부분은 주어이다. 주어 역할을 하는 명사절을 이끌 수 있는 것은 명사절 접속사 (A)와 선행사를 포함한 관계대명사 (C)인데, 빈칸 뒤는 주어가 빠져 있는 불완전한 절이므로 명사절 접속사가 올 수 없고, 관계대명사는 올 수 있다. 따라서 정답은 (C).

UNIT 14

3 Telcom Inc. promoted Ms. Dumas, / **whose** excellent market analysis helped / to foresee several trend changes.
(A) who (B) whom (C) which **(D) whose**

해석| 텔콤 주식회사는 탁월한 시장 분석으로 몇몇 트렌드 변화를 예측할 수 있게 도와 주었던 뒤마 씨를 승진시켰다.

어휘| analysis 분석 foresee 예견하다

해설| 선택지를 보니 빈칸에 알맞은 관계대명사를 고르는 문제. 빈칸 뒤에 주어 excellent market analysis와 동사 helped가 있는 것으로 보아 빈칸에는 목적격이나 소유격 관계대명사가 들어가야 한다. 빈칸 앞 명사 Ms. Dumas와 빈칸 뒤 excellent market analysis가 소유 관계이므로 소유격 관계대명사인 (D)가 정답. (A)와 (C)는 주격, 목적격 관계대명사로 모두 쓰일 수 있고, (B)는 목적격 관계대명사이므로 오답.

4 Customer service representatives are trained / to deal with **whatever** customers report / about products and services.
(A) whoever **(B) whatever** (C) whomever (D) whichever

해석| 고객 서비스 직원은 물품과 서비스에 대해 고객이 신고하는 것은 무엇이든지 처리하도록 교육을 받는다.

어휘| deal with ~을 처리하다[다루다] report 신고[보고]하다

해설| 선택지를 보니 빈칸에 알맞은 복합관계대명사를 고르는 문제. 문맥상 고객 서비스 직원은 고객이 신고하는 '무엇이든지' 처리한다는 내용이 자연스러우므로 '~하는 것은 무엇이나'를 뜻하는 복합관계대명사 (B)가 정답.

5-6

The editorial meeting for next month's issue of the magazine has been moved. It was originally scheduled to take place in the conference room **where** last month's meeting was held. However, the ceiling has started leaking.

While repairs are being made, the room will be off limits. Therefore, please come to my office instead. As usual, we will try to choose a theme **that** readers will find interesting. Please think of some unique and exciting topics in advance.

잡지의 다음 호를 위한 편집 회의가 옮겨졌습니다. 회의는 원래 지난달 회의가 열렸던 **회의실에서** 열릴 예정이었습니다. 그러나 천장에서 물이 새기 시작했습니다.

수리가 진행되는 동안, 회의실은 출입이 금지될 것입니다. 따라서, 대신 제 사무실로 오십시오. 평소대로 우리는 독자들이 흥미롭게 생각할 만한 **주제를** 선정하는 데 힘쓸 것입니다. 독특하고 흥미로운 주제들을 미리 생각해 보시기 바랍니다.

어휘| editorial 편집의 originally 원래 ceiling 천장 leak (액체가) 새다 off limits 출입금지인 as usual 평소대로 theme 주제 unique 독특한 exciting 흥미로운

5 It was originally scheduled / to take place in the conference room / **where** last month's meeting was held.
(A) which **(B) where** (C) when (D) whose

해설| 빈칸 앞뒤에 나오는 절이 완전하므로 관계부사 (B)와 (C)가 정답 후보. 빈칸 앞 선행사 the conference room이 장소를 나타내므로 (B)가 정답이다. 관계대명사인 (A)와 (D)는 불완전한 절이 뒤따르므로 오답.

6 As usual, / we will try to choose a theme / **that** readers will find interesting.
(A) of which (B) such as (C) what **(D) that**

해설| 빈칸 앞은 완전한 절이고 빈칸 뒤는 동사 find의 목적어가 빠진 불완전한 절이 나오므로, 접속사와 목적어 역할을 동시에 하는 목적격 관계대명사가 빈칸에 들어가야 한다. 따라서 정답은 (D). 선행사 a theme과 관계대명사절의 주어 readers가 소유 관계가 아니므로 소유격 관계대명사 (A)는 오답. 빈칸 앞에 선행사가 있으므로 선행사를 포함한 관계대명사 (C)도 오답이다.

1 exchange 2 pharmacy 3 coverage 4 claim 5 (C) 6 (D) 7 (A) 8 (A)

---

1 The customer asked to (lease / **exchange**) the shirt / for a bigger size.

해석| 그 고객은 셔츠를 더 큰 사이즈로 교환해 달라고 요청했다.

해설| 괄호에 알맞은 동사를 고르는 문제인데, 동사의 목적어인 the shirt 뒤의 전치사 for에 주목한다. for는 '~로'라는 대상을 나타내어 '셔츠를 더 큰 사이즈로 교환하다'라는 의미가 되어야 자연스럽다. 따라서 정답은 exchange. 참고로 exchange A for B는 'A를 B와 교환하다[맞바꾸다]'라는 의미이다.

---

2 Ms. Edmonds went to the (**pharmacy** / treatment) to pick up a prescription.

해석| 에드먼드 씨는 처방약을 타러 약국에 갔다.

어휘| pick up a prescription 처방약을 타다

해설| 문장 안의 관련 어휘 prescription만 보아도 답을 금방 찾을 수 있다. 문맥상 처방약을 타러 '약국에 갔다'는 내용이 되어야 자연스러우므로 정답은 pharmacy.

---

3 Pia Insurance provides more (injury / **coverage**) / than its competitors at a lower price.

해석| 피아 보험사는 경쟁 업체보다 더 낮은 가격에 더 넓은 보장을 제공한다.

해설| 보험사가 고객에게 그것의 경쟁 업체보다 더 많이 제공할 수 있는 것은 '보장'이 되는 것이 자연스럽다. 따라서 정답은 coverage.

---

4 Mr. Flinch filed a (**claim** / refund) / with his insurance company / for the roof repairs.

해석| 플린치 씨는 지붕 수리에 대해 그의 보험회사에 청구 신청을 했다.

어휘| file 신청을 하다, 제출하다 repair 수리, 보수

해설| 괄호 앞 동사 filed의 목적어로 어울리는 명사 어휘를 고르는 문제. 보험 회사에 수리 비용에 대한 '청구 신청'을 제출했다는 의미가 자연스러우므로 정답은 claim이다.

---

5 If the clerk doesn't accept the discount coupon, / Ms. Morgan cannot **afford** the watch.
(A) rearrange (B) verify **(C) afford** (D) exchange

해석| 점원이 할인 쿠폰을 받아 주지 않으면, 모건 씨는 그 시계를 살 여유가 없다.

(A) 재배열하다, 재조정하다 (B) 확인하다 (C) 여유가 되다 (D) 교환하다

어휘| clerk 점원 accept 받아들이다

해설| 문맥상 '그 시계를 살 수 없다'라는 뜻이 알맞으므로 '여유가 있다'는 의미의 동사 (C)가 알맞다. afford는 주로 조동사 can[cannot]과 함께 쓰여 '~을 살[할] 여유가 있다[없다]'라는 뜻으로 쓰인다. 목적어로 명사를 취하거나 afford to do의 형태를 취한다.

---

6 The **expense** of repairing the wall will be fully covered / by the moving company.
(A) premiums (B) wage (C) advantage **(D) expense**

해석| 벽을 수리하는 비용은 이삿짐업체가 전부 치를 것이다.

(A) 보험료, 추가 요금 (B) 임금 (C) 장점 (D) 비용

어휘| cover (돈을) 충당하다, 대다 moving company 이삿짐업체

해설| 문맥상 벽을 수리하는 데 드는 '비용'이라는 뜻이 되어야 알맞으므로 (D)가 정답이다. expense는 어떤 일에 드는 돈, 즉 '비용, 경비'를 뜻한다.

---

7 Ms. Teller read the insurance **policy** carefully / before signing it.
(A) policy (B) payment (C) method (D) lease

해석| 텔러 씨는 보험 증서에 서명하기 전에 그것을 주의 깊게 읽었다.

(A) (보험) 증서 (B) 지불 (C) 방법 (C) 임대차 계약

해설| 빈칸 앞의 명사 insurance와 어울려 쓰일 수 있는 어구가 들어가야 한다. insurance policy는 '보험 증서[증권]'을 뜻하므로 (A)가 정답.

UNIT 14

8 Patients can make decisions / about their treatment / after the initial <u>consultation</u>.
(A) consultation (B) activity (C) machine (D) information
해석| 환자들은 첫 진찰 후에 치료에 대한 결정을 내릴 수 있다.
(A) 상담, 진찰 (B) 행동 (C) 기계 (D) 정보
어휘| treatment 치료   initial 처음의, 최초의

해설| 치료에 대한 결정을 내리는 것은 첫 '진찰' 후에 할 수 있는 일이므로 (A)가 정답.

ACTUAL TEST **실전 문제에 적용하기**   교재 236쪽

1 (C) **2** (B) **3** (A) **4** (D) **5** (A) **6** (B) **7** (C) **8** (C) **9** (A) **10** (D) **11** (C) **12** (B)

---

1 Celebrax is a company / <u>that</u> supplies a wide range of party products / for all types of events.
(A) who (B) whoever **(C) that** (D) whichever
해석| 셀러브렉스 사는 모든 종류의 행사를 위한 다양한 파티 용품을 제공하는 회사이다.
어휘| supply 공급하다   wide 넓은   range 다양성, 범위

해설| **관계대명사 that**
빈칸 앞은 완전한 절이고, 빈칸 뒤는 주어가 빠진 불완전한 절이므로 접속사와 주어의 역할을 동시에 하는 주격 관계대명사가 빈칸에 들어가야 한다. 따라서 (A)와 (C)가 정답 후보. 선행사가 사물인 a company이므로 (C)가 정답.
오답| 복합관계대명사 (B)와 (D)도 부사절을 이끌어 빈칸에 들어갈 수 있으나 내용상 어색해서 오답.

---

2 Ms. Everton spent months trying to find an effective <u>treatment</u> / for her medical condition.
(A) involvement **(B) treatment** (C) injury (D) origin
해석| 에버튼 씨는 자신의 병에 효과적인 치료법을 찾으려 애쓰는 데에 몇 달을 보냈다.
(A) 관련, 관여 (B) 치료(법) (C) 부상 (D) 기원
어휘| effective 효과적인   medical condition 질병

해설| **명사 어휘 treatment**
빈칸은 뒤에 나온 for her medical condition의 수식을 받고 있으므로, 질병과 관련된 것이어야 한다. 문맥상 '질병에 효과적인 치료법을 찾기 위해서'라는 뜻이 되어야 하므로 (B)가 정답.

---

3 Junior executives / who <u>need</u> to attend seminars abroad / must get clearance from their supervisors / two weeks in advance.
(A) need (B) is needing (C) needs (D) to need
해석| 해외 세미나에 참석해야 하는 중견 간부들은 2주 전에 그들의 상사에게 승인을 받아야 한다.
어휘| clearance 승인

해설| **관계대명사절 동사의 수일치**
who부터 abroad까지는 문장의 주어인 Junior executives를 수식하는 관계대명사절로, 빈칸은 그 안의 동사 자리이다. 관계대명사절의 동사는 선행사에 수일치 시켜야 하므로, 선행사인 복수 명사 executives와 어울리는 복수 동사인 (A)가 정답.
오답| (B)와 (C)는 단수 동사, (D)는 to부정사라 오답이다.

---

4 Seaside Restaurant, / <u>whose</u> chef underwent intensive training in Italy, / received positive reviews from food critics.
(A) which (B) who (C) whatever **(D) whose**
해석| 씨사이드 레스토랑은 그곳의 주방장이 이탈리아에서 집중 교육을 받았는데, 음식 평론가들로부터 호평을 받았다.
어휘| chef 주방장   undergo 겪다, 경험하다   intensive 집중적인

해설| **관계대명사 whose**
콤마로 삽입된, 빈칸부터 Italy까지는 주어인 Seaside Restaurant을 수식하는 절인데, 그 안에 주어(chef)와 목적어(training)가 갖춰져 있으므로 빈칸에는 주격, 목적격 관계대명사는 올 수 없다. 선행사인 Seaside Restaurant과 절의 주어인 chef 사이에 '씨사이드 레스토랑의 주방장'이란 뜻으로 소유 관계가 성립하므로 소유격 관계대명사인 (D)가 정답.

---

5 The caterer sends updates / to his regular customers / **whenever** he adjusts the prices of the packages.
(A) whenever (B) however (C) moreover (D) whoever

해석| 그 출장 음식 제공 업자는 그가 패키지의 가격을 바꿀 때마다 자기 단골 손님들에게 업데이트된 내용을 발송한다.

어휘| regular customer 단골 손님 adjust 조정하다

해설| **복합관계부사 whenever**
빈칸 앞뒤에 모두 완전한 절이 나오므로, 선택지 중에서는 빈칸에는 접속사의 역할을 하면서 부사절을 이끄는 관계부사가 들어가야 한다. 문맥상 '~할 때마다'라는 의미이므로 복합관계부사 (A)가 정답이다.
오답| (C) moreover은 '게다가, 더욱이'라는 의미의 부사이므로 오답.

---

6 The shipment requested by local customers / was **delivered** / to the Marks & Vaughn warehouses in Slough / yesterday.
(A) connected (B) delivered (C) observed (D) afforded

해석| 현지 고객들이 요청한 화물은 슬로우에 있는 막스 앤 본 창고로 어제 배송되었다.
(A) 연결하다 (B) 배송하다 (C) 관찰하다 (D) (살) 여유가 있다

어휘| shipment 화물, 선적물

해설| **동사 어휘 deliver**
선택지를 보니, 빈칸 앞 be동사 was와 함께 수동태를 이루는 동사 어휘를 고르는 문제. 문맥상 주어인 The shipment(화물)가 '배송되는' 것이 자연스러우므로 정답은 (B)이다.

---

7 Its poor business model is / **what** caused the software developer to go bankrupt.
(A) whose (B) who (C) what (D) which

해석| 빈약한 사업 계획이 그 소프트웨어 개발업체를 파산하게 만들었다.

어휘| go bankrupt 파산하다

해설| **관계대명사 what**
선택지를 보니 알맞은 관계대명사를 고르는 문제. 빈칸 이하는 동사 is의 보어가 되는 명사절이다. 빈칸 앞에 선행사가 없으므로 선행사를 포함한 관계대명사 (C)가 정답.

---

8 The admission ticket shows the time / **when** the performance begins.
(A) which (B) how (C) when (D) their

해석| 입장권에 공연이 시작하는 시간이 나와 있다.

어휘| admission ticket 입장권

해설| **관계부사 when**
빈칸 앞뒤에 완전한 절이 있으므로 선택지 중에서는 두 절을 연결할 수 있는 관계부사 (B)와 (C)가 정답 후보. 빈칸 앞 선행사 the time이 시간을 나타내므로 (C)가 정답.
오답| (A)는 관계대명사로 뒤에 불완전한 절이 와야 하고, (D)는 소유격 인칭대명사로 절을 연결할 수 없으므로 오답.

9-12

Stylish Living at City Suites

Be a part of the energy and excitement of downtown! City Suites is a luxury apartment complex **which** is located in the heart of Toronto. Units of various sizes are available now, and tenants have the option of signing a one- or two-year **lease**.

City Suites is the ideal home for anyone who **wants** to enjoy urban life. In addition, it has easy access to shopping and dining.

Stop by our rental office on the first floor of City Suites, at 142 Avenue Road, for a tour. **We are even able to provide a contract on the same day.** So please have your financial documents ready. This will allow us to accept your initial payment quickly and get you into your new home as soon as possible.

We look forward to seeing you!

시티 스위트에서의 멋진 생활

도심의 열정과 흥분에 빠져 보세요! 시티 스위트는 토론토 중심가에 위치한 고급 아파트 **단지입니다.** 다양한 크기의 아파트를 지금 이용하실 수 있으며, 세입자들은 1년 혹은 2년 **임대 계약을** 선택할 수 있습니다.

시티 스위트는 도시 생활을 즐기고 **싶어하는** 사람이라면 누구에게나 이상적인 주택입니다. 게다가, 쇼핑 센터와 식당가에 접근하기도 쉽습니다.

구경하시려면 애버뉴 로 142번지, 시티 스위트 1층에 있는 저희 임대 사무실에 들러 주세요. **저희는 또한 당일에 계약서를 제공할 수도 있습니다.** 그러니, 여러분의 재정 관련 서류를 준비해오시기 바랍니다.

그렇게 하면 저희가 여러분의 초기 납입금을 빨리 수령하여 가능한 한 빨리 여러분을 새 주택에 입주하도록 해 드릴 수 있습니다.

만나 뵙기를 고대하고 있겠습니다!

어휘| excitement 흥분 complex (건물) 단지 be located in ~에 위치하다 unit (공동주택의) 한 가구 tenant 세입자 ideal 이상적인 urban 도시의 have access to ~에 접근할 수 있다 dining 식사 stop by ~에 잠깐 들르다 financial 재정의 initial 초기의, 처음의

9 City Suites is a luxury apartment complex / **which** is located / in the heart of Toronto.
(A) **which** (B) where (C) what (D) whenever

해설| 관계대명사 which
선택지를 보니 알맞은 관계사를 고르는 문제이다. 빈칸은 앞은 완전한 절이고, 빈칸 뒤는 주어가 없는 불완전한 절이므로, 빈칸에는 접속사와 주어의 역할을 동시에 하는 주격 관계대명사가 들어가야 한다. 따라서 정답은 사물 선행사와 어울려 쓰이는 관계대명사 (A).
오답| (C)는 절의 주어로 쓰일 수 있지만 선행사를 포함한 관계대명사라 빈칸 앞의 선행사 a luxury apartment complex와 함께 쓸 수 없으므로 오답이다.

10 Units of various sizes are available now, / and tenants have the option / of signing a one- or two-year **lease**.
(A) license (B) budget (C) subscription (D) **lease**
(A) 면허(증) (B) 예산 (C) 구독 (D) 임대 계약

해설| 명사 어휘 lease
세입자(tenants)가 선택할 수 있는 것이므로 '임대 계약'이라는 뜻의 (D)가 알맞다.

11 City Suites is the ideal home / for anyone / who **wants** to enjoy urban life.
(A) wanting (B) to want (C) **wants** (D) want

해설| 관계대명사절 동사의 수일치
빈칸은 빈칸 앞 관계대명사 who가 이끄는 관계대명사절의 동사 자리이다. 따라서 동사인 (C)와 (D)가 정답 후보. 관계대명사절의 동사는 선행사에 수일치 시켜야 하는데, 선행사 anyone이 단수 명사이므로 단수 동사인 (C)가 정답이다.

12 (A) You can visit www.city-suites.com to view photos.
(B) **We are even able to provide a contract on the same day.**
(C) There is a free parking area for guests in the underground.
(D) Many of our tenants have lived here for a long time.
(A) www.city-suites.com을 방문하셔서 사진을 보실 수 있습니다.
(B) 저희는 또한 당일에 계약서를 제공할 수도 있습니다.
(C) 지하에는 손님들을 위한 무료 주차 구역이 있습니다.
(D) 많은 저희 세입자들이 오랫동안 이곳에 살고 있습니다.

해설| 알맞은 문장 고르기
빈칸 뒤에 결과를 나타내는 연결사 So가 나온다. 따라서 빈칸 내용은 뒷문장 내용의 원인이나 이유에 해당하는 내용이 나와야 한다. 재정 관련 서류를 준비해야 하는 이유로는 임대 계약을 체결할 수도 있다는 내용의 (B)가 가장 알맞다.
오답| 빈칸 앞에서 직접 구경을 하러 오라고 하고 있으므로 사진 열람을 안내하는 (A)는 어울리지 않는다. 빈칸 앞 방문 안내와는 (C)의 내용이 어울리나 빈칸 뒤 재정 서류와는 무관하므로 오답이다. (D)는 아파트 광고인 지문에 어울리는 문장이나 빈칸 앞뒤 흐름과 어울리지 않아 오답이다.

1 원급·비교급·최상급과 원급 비교   교재 241쪽

1 more rapidly   **2** strongest   **3** competent   **4** many   **5** (A)   **6** (B)   **7** (A)   **8** (B)

---

1 Big Travels is growing (rapidly / **more rapidly**) / than any of its competitors.

해석 | 빅 트래블스 사는 경쟁사들 중 어느 업체보다도 더 빠르게 성장하고 있다.

어휘 | rapidly 빠르게

해설 | 괄호 바로 뒤에 '어느 업체보다'라는 비교 대상이 나오므로 비교급인 more rapidly가 어울린다.

---

2 A recent study said / Praville had the (stronger / **strongest**) economy in the region / last year.

해석 | 최근 한 연구는 작년에 프라빌이 그 지역에서 가장 튼튼한 경제를 가지고 있었다는 것을 보여 주었다.

해설 | 괄호 안을 보니 비교급과 최상급 중 알맞은 것을 고르는 문제이다. 문장 뒤쪽에 in the region을 통해 두 대상만 비교하는 게 아니라는 것을 알 수 있다. 따라서 비교급은 알맞지 않고, 여럿 중에 '가장 ~한'이라는 뜻을 나타내는 최상급이 알맞다. 정답은 strongest.

---

3 The design team's newest member is as (**competent** / more competent) / as some of the older members.

해석 | 디자인 팀의 가장 새로 들어온 팀원은 몇몇 오래된 팀원들만큼이나 능숙하다.

해설 | 괄호가 두 as 사이에 위치하고 있는 것으로 보아, 원급 비교 표현인 〈as+형용사[부사]+as〉의 형용사나 부사 자리이다. 괄호에는 원급이 들어가야 하는데 competent는 형용사의 원급이고 more competent는 비교급이므로 정답은 competent.

---

4 Interns work as (**many** / much) hours / as full-time staff members.

해석 | 인턴 사원도 정규직 사원만큼 오랜 시간 일한다.

어휘 | full-time 정규직의

해설 | as ~ as 사이에 〈형용사+명사〉 형태가 나오고 있다. many와 much 둘 다 형용사의 원급인 것은 맞지만, 괄호 뒤의 셀 수 있는 명사인 hours를 수식해야 하므로 many가 정답.

---

5 The convention will be attended / by some of the <u>most prominent</u> politicians in the country.
(A) most prominent   (B) prominence   (C) more prominently
(D) prominently

해석 | 그 총회에는 국내에서 가장 유명한 정치인들 몇 명이 참석할 예정이다.

어휘 | convention 총회   prominent 유명한   politician 정치인

해설 | 관사 the와 명사 politicians 사이에 올 수 있는 형태는 형용사이다. 선택지 중에서 형용사는 최상급의 형태인 (A)뿐이므로 정답은 (A). (B)는 명사, (C)와 (D)는 각각 부사의 비교급, 부사의 원급이므로 오답.

---

6 Pillhurst Express is as <u>responsive</u> to client requests as / larger courier companies.
(A) most responsive   **(B) responsive**   (C) responsiveness
(D) responsively

해석 | 필허스트 익스프레스 사는 대형 택배 회사만큼이나 고객의 요청에 즉각 대응한다.

어휘 | responsive 즉각 반응하는   request 요청, 요구   courier 택배 회사

해설 | as ~ as 사이에 동사 is의 보어인 형용사구가 들어가야 한다. 빈칸 뒤의 to client requests는 수식어이므로 빈칸에는 핵심어인 형용사가 들어가야 한다. 선택지에서 형용사는 (A)와 (B)인데, as ~ as 사이에는 원급이 들어가야 하므로 정답은 (B)이다. (A)는 형용사의 최상급이라 오답.

7 The results of medical checkups are sent to patients / as <u>soon</u> as possible.
(A) as soon (B) so that (C) much to (D) as of
해석 | 건강 검진의 결과지는 가능한 한 빨리 환자에게 보내진다.
어휘 | medical checkup 건강 검진

해설 | 빈칸 뒤의 as possible을 보는 순간 '가능한 ~한[하게]'라는 의미의 〈as+원급+as possible〉 표현이 아닌지 의심해 보아야 한다. 문맥상 '결과지가 가능한 한 빨리 환자에게 보내진다'는 내용이 자연스러우므로 정답은 (A). as soon as possible은 '가능한 한 빨리'라는 뜻으로 시험에 자주 등장하므로 기억해두자.

---

8 Journalists from the *Montgomery Gazette* gathered **as much** information about the scandal / as the police department did.
(A) more than **(B)** as much (C) so many (D) the most
해석 | 〈몽고메리 가제트〉지의 기자들은 스캔들에 대한 정보를 경찰서만큼 많이 수집했다.
어휘 | journalist 기자 gather 모으다

해설 | as 이하에 '경찰서'라는 비교 대상이 나오고 있으므로 as ~ as 구문임을 알 수 있다. 빈칸 뒤의 셀 수 없는 명사 information와 어울리는 형용사의 원급이 as와 함께 빈칸에 들어가야 하므로 (B)가 정답.

2	**비교급·최상급 비교**	교재 243쪽

1 harder **2** more sensitive **3** greatest **4** busiest **5** (A) **6** (C) **7** (D) **8** (C)

---

1 No one on the team works (hard / **harder**) / than Mr. Murphy.
해석 | 팀원 중 누구도 머피 씨보다 더 열심히 일하는 사람은 없다.

해설 | 괄호 바로 뒤에 비교 대상을 나타내는 전치사 than이 나오므로 비교급인 harder가 들어가야 한다.

---

2 This experiment requires laboratory scales / that are much (sensitive / **more sensitive**).
해석 | 이 실험은 훨씬 더 민감한 실험용 저울을 필요로 한다.
어휘 | experiment 실험 laboratory 실험실 scale 저울 sensitive 민감한

해설 | 괄호 앞에 있는 부사 much가 단서. much는 비교급을 강조하는 부사이므로 괄호에는 비교급이 들어가야 한다. 2음절 이상인 sensitive는 앞에 more를 붙여서 비교급을 만든다. 따라서 정답은 more sensitive.

---

3 Mr. Tratoni is the (greater / **greatest**) designer / in the country.
해석 | 트라토니 씨는 국내에서 가장 훌륭한 디자이너이다.

해설 | 비교 범위를 나타내는 in the country라는 말이 나오고, 괄호 앞의 the도 있으므로 빈칸에는 최상급이 들어가야 함을 알 수 있다. 따라서 답은 greatest.

---

4 Aloya Station is the third (busier / **busiest**) station / in the city / at the moment.
해석 | 알로야 역은 현재 시에서 세 번째로 번화한 역이다.
어휘 | at the moment 현재, 지금

해설 | 괄호 앞의 the와 서수 third를 보면 〈the+서수+최상급〉 구문이 쓰였음을 알 수 있다. 따라서 괄호는 형용사 또는 부사의 최상급 자리이므로 정답은 busiest이다.

---

5 Some staff members from satellite offices / are <u>less</u> familiar / with the company's policies / than others.
(A) less (B) quite (C) so (D) fewer
해석 | 지사 출신의 몇몇 직원들은 다른 사람들보다 회사 정책에 덜 익숙하다.
(A) 덜 (B) 꽤 (C) 정말 (D) ~보다 적은
어휘 | satellite office 지사 familiar with ~에 익숙한[친숙한]

해설 | 빈칸 없이도 문장이 완전하므로 빈칸은 부사 자리이다. 따라서 형용사인 (D)는 정답 후보에서 제외. 문장 마지막에 than others라고 비교 대상을 밝히고 있으므로 비교급이 쓰여야 함을 알 수 있다. 빈칸 뒤에 형용사의 원급이 나왔으므로 more나 less처럼 비교급을 만드는 부사가 빈칸에 와야 한다. 선택지에 있는 것은 less이므로 정답은 (A).

6 Outsourcing the billing procedures is considerably cheaper / __than__ performing the work in-house.
(A) within   (B) between   **(C) than**   (D) to

해석| 청구서 발송 과정을 외부에 위탁하는 것이 사내에서 작업을 수행하는 것보다 훨씬 저렴하다.

(A) ~ 이내에 (B) ~ 사이에 (C) ~보다 (D) ~로

어휘| outsource 외부에 위탁하다, 외주로 하다   billing 청구서 발송   procedure 절차   considerably 상당히

해설| 빈칸에 알맞은 전치사를 고르는 문제이다. 빈칸 앞에 비교급인 cheaper가 있으므로 '~보다'라는 뜻으로 비교 대상을 나타내는 전치사 than이 들어가야 한다. 따라서 정답은 (C).

---

7 These days, / government inspectors examine factory machinery / even **more carefully** / than before.
(A) more careful   (B) most careful   (C) most carefully
(D) more carefully

해석| 요즘에는 정부 조사관들이 예전보다 훨씬 더 주의 깊게 공장 기계를 점검한다.

어휘| these days 요즘   inspector 조사관   examine 검사하다

해설| 빈칸 뒤에 than before라는 비교 대상이 있고, 빈칸 앞에 even이라는 비교급 강조 부사가 있다. 따라서 빈칸은 비교급이 들어갈 자리. '더 주의 깊게 점검하다'라는 뜻으로 동사인 examine을 수식하는 부사가 빈칸에 들어가야 하므로 부사 carefully의 비교급인 (D)가 정답.

---

8 Ravenbam Tower is the **highest** / of all structures in Attium City.
(A) higher   (B) high   **(C) highest**   (D) highly

해석| 레이븐밤 타워는 아티움 시의 모든 건축물 중 가장 높다.

어휘| structure 건축물, 구조물

해설| 빈칸 뒤 of all structures로 비교 범위를 나타내고 있고, 빈칸 앞에 관사 the가 있으므로 최상급을 쓰는 것이 알맞다. 따라서 최상급인 (C)가 정답.

---

3 **가정법의 종류와 쓰임**   교재 245쪽

1 lose   **2** were found   **3** have done   **4** see   **5** (A)   **6** (B)   **7** (D)   **8** (C)

---

1 If the company went bankrupt, / shareholders would (**lose** / have lost) large amounts of money.

해석| 회사가 파산한다면, 주주들은 큰 액수의 돈을 잃게 될 텐데.

어휘| go bankrupt 파산하다   amount 액수

해설| if절의 과거 시제 동사 went와 주절의 조동사 would로 보아 가정법 과거 문장이다. 따라서 주절에는 would 다음에 동사원형인 lose가 들어가야 한다.

---

2 If a suitable location (was found / **were found**), / Estus Enterprises would seriously consider relocating its headquarters.

해석| 적당한 장소를 찾으면, 에스투스 엔터프라이즈 사는 본사 이전을 진지하게 고려할 텐데.

어휘| suitable 적당한   seriously 진지하게

해설| 괄호 안의 동사는 if절의 동사인데, 과거 시제이고, 주절의 동사도 would consider인 것으로 보아 가정법 과거 문장이다. 가정법 과거의 if절에 be동사는 인칭에 상관 없이 were를 쓰므로 were found가 정답.

---

3 If the supervisor had known about the problem, / he could (**have done** / done) something / to solve it.

해석| 감독관이 문제에 대해 알았다면, 그것을 해결하려고 무언가를 할 수 있었을 텐데.

해설| if절의 과거완료시제의 동사 had known과 주절의 조동사 could로 보아 가정법 과거완료 문장이다. 따라서 괄호에는 have done이 들어가야 한다.

---

4 If you should (have seen / **see**) an error message on the printer, / check for a paper jam.

해석| 만일 프린터에서 에러 메시지를 보게 되면, 종이가 걸렸는지 확인하세요.

어휘| check for ~이 있는지 확인하다   paper jam 종이 걸림

해설| 문장이 if로 시작하고 주절이 명령문이므로 가정법 미래 문장이다. 따라서 종속절의 동사는 조동사 뒤에 동사원형인 see가 정답.

5 If the manager **had given** them enough time, / the staff could have prepared a presentation / for the potential investors.
(A) **had given** (B) gives (C) will give (D) gave

해석| 매니저가 직원들에게 충분한 시간을 주었다면, 그들은 잠재적 투자자들을 위한 발표를 준비했을 텐데.

어휘| potential 가능성이 있는

해설| 선택지를 보니 빈칸에 알맞은 동사 형태를 고르는 문제. 주절의 동사가 could have prepared이므로 가정법 과거완료 문장이다. 빈칸은 if절의 동사 자리로, 과거완료가 되어야 하므로 〈had p.p.〉의 (A)가 정답.

---

6 If the machine **were** capable / of producing more units per hour, / we might install it / in our factory.
(A) be (B) **were** (C) is (D) been

해석| 그 기계가 시간당 더 많은 제품을 생산할 수 있다면, 우리 공장에 그것을 설치할 수도 있을 텐데.

어휘| be capable of *doing* ~할 수 있다

해설| 선택지를 보니 if절에 알맞은 be동사의 형태를 고르는 문제. 주절의 동사가 might install이므로, 가정법 과거 문장이다. 따라서 if절의 빈칸에는 be동사의 과거형이 들어가야 하는데 가정법 과거 문장에서는 인칭에 상관 없이 주로 were를 쓰므로 (B)가 정답.

---

7 If Ms. Etherington had not made the payment on June 30, / ownership of the vehicle **would have reverted** to the original seller.
(A) will revert (B) being reverted (C) has reverted
(D) **would have reverted**

해석| 에더링턴 씨가 6월 30일에 대금을 지불하지 못했다면, 그 차의 소유권은 원래의 판매자에게 돌아갔을 텐데.

어휘| make payment 지불하다 ownership 소유권 revert to ~로 되돌아가다

해설| if절의 동사 형태가 〈had p.p.〉이므로 가정법 과거완료 문장이다. 빈칸은 주절의 동사 자리로, 〈would+have p.p.〉 형태의 (D)가 정답.

---

8 If you **should wish** to end your magazine subscription early, / send an e-mail / to our customer service department.
(A) had wished (B) have wished (C) **should wish** (D) wished

해석| 고객님의 잡지 정기 구독을 조기에 종료하기를 원하실 경우, 저희 고객 서비스 부서로 이메일을 보내 주십시오.

어휘| subscription 정기 구독

해설| 문장이 if절로 시작하고, 주절은 동사원형 send로 시작하는 명령문이다. 따라서 일어날 가능성이 낮은 미래의 일을 가정하는 가정법 미래 문장이다. 가정법 미래의 주절은 〈if+주어+should+동사원형〉 형태이므로 정답은 (C).

---

4 가정법 및 기타 구문의 도치

교재 247쪽

1 Were **2** Should **3** Had **4** will anyone **5** (C) **6** (C) **7** (A) **8** (D)

---

1 (**Were** / If) the invitations sent out earlier, / the event would be filled to capacity.

해석| 초대장을 더 일찍 보낸다면, 행사는 만원이 될 텐데.

어휘| send out 보내다, 발송하다 be filled to capacity 만원이다, 꽉 차다

해설| 주절의 동사가 〈would+동사원형〉이므로 가정법 과거 문장이다. 따라서 주절의 동사는 과거형이어야 한다. 그러므로, 주어 the invitations 뒤의 sent를 과거 동사라고 생각하고 접속사 if를 답으로 고를 수 있다. 하지만 the invitations는 누군가에 의해 '보내지는' 대상이므로 수동태 동사가 쓰여야 한다. 따라서, If the invitations were sent에서 If가 생략되고 were가 문장 맨 앞으로 도치된 형태가 적절하다. 따라서 were가 정답.

2 (**Should** / Although) you have any inquiries / about our products, / please call BirzaTech / at 800-1256.

해석| 저희 제품에 대해 문의가 있으시면, 버자테크 사에 800-1256번으로 전화 주세요.
어휘| inquiry 문의, 질문

해설| 괄호가 포함된 콤마 앞부분은 '저희 제품에 대해 문의가 있으시면'이라는 내용이 자연스러운데, 괄호 안 선택지 중에 if가 없으므로 도치된 문장인지 확인해 봐야 한다. 주절이 명령문이므로 접속사 if를 생략하고 조동사 should가 문장 맨 앞으로 나간 가정법 미래 문장임을 알 수 있으므로 정답은 Should. Although는 내용상 어울리지 않으므로 오답.

---

3 (Has / **Had**) Ms. Olsen studied harder, / she might have passed the computer proficiency test.

해석| 올슨 씨가 더 열심히 공부했더라면, 컴퓨터 능력 시험에 합격했을 텐데.
어휘| pass 통과하다   proficiency 숙달, 능숙

해설| 주절의 동사 형태가 〈조동사+have *p.p.*〉이므로 가정법 과거완료 문장이다. 따라서 if절의 동사 형태는 had *p.p.*가 되어야 한다. 구조상 접속사 if를 생략하고 주어와 동사가 도치된 문장이므로, 정답은 Had.

---

4 Never (**will anyone** / anyone will) be able to come into the office / under our surveillance system.

해석| 저희 감시 시스템 하에서는 어느 누구도 사무실에 들어올 수 없을 것입니다.
어휘| surveillance 감시

해설| 문장이 '결코 ~ 않다'라는 의미의 부정어 Never로 시작하고 있다. 부정어가 문장 앞으로 나오면 주어와 동사가 도치되므로 〈동사+주어〉 순서인 will anyone이 정답.

---

5 <u>Had</u> Brionext Graphics invested / in online game development, / it could have significantly grown its business.
(A) Have (B) Never (C) **Had** (D) Should

해석| 브리오넥스트 그래픽스 사가 온라인 게임 개발에 투자했다면, 자사의 사업을 상당히 성장시킬 수 있었을 텐데.
어휘| significantly 상당히

해설| 콤마 앞뒤로 완전한 절이 나오므로 빈칸은 접속사 자리로 볼 수 있다. 그런데 선택지에 조동사나 부정어가 나오는 것으로 보아, 도치구문임을 파악해야 한다. 콤마 뒤 주절의 동사 형태가 〈조동사+have *p.p.*〉이므로 가정법 과거완료 문장이다. 따라서 if절의 동사는 과거완료형인 had *p.p.*가 되어야 한다. 형태상 접속사 if를 생략하고 주어와 동사가 도치된 문장이므로 빈칸에 들어갈 수 있는 것은 (C)이다.

---

6 <u>Attached</u> is the invoice / for the completed Olevao Clubhouse landscaping project.
(A) To attach (B) Attach (C) **Attached** (D) Attaches

해석| 첨부된 것은 완료된 올레바오 클럽 회관 조경 프로젝트의 청구서입니다.
어휘| invoice 청구서, 송장   landscaping 조경

해설| 문장 맨 앞이 빈칸으로 시작하고 빈칸 뒤가 동사이므로 주어 자리라고 생각할 수 있으나, 선택지에서 attach를 보고, 문장의 맨 앞에 자리한 빈칸의 위치를 보면 보어를 강조하기 위한 도치에 대해 떠올릴 수 있어야 한다. 보어 Attached를 강조하기 위해 문장 맨 앞에 쓰고 주어와 동사를 도치시킨 문장으로, 정답은 (C)이다.

---

7 <u>Should</u> any machinery malfunction, / please report the incident / to the plant manager immediately.
(A) **Should** (B) Even so (C) As well as (D) Somewhere

해석| 만약 어떤 기계라도 제대로 작동하지 않으면, 그 일을 즉시 공장 관리자에게 보고해 주세요.
어휘| malfunction 제대로 작동하지 않다   incident 일, 사건   immediately 즉시, 즉각

해설| 콤마 뒤가 명령문이고, 내용상 콤마 앞은 '만약 어떤 기계라도 작동하지 않으면'의 의미가 되는 것이 자연스러우므로 콤마 앞쪽은 if절이어야 한다. 선택지에 if가 없고 빈칸 뒤 주어가 단수 명사인데 동사는 원형인 것으로 보아, 가정법 미래의 if절에서 if가 생략되고 주어 any machinery와 조동사 should가 도치된 문장임을 알 수 있다. 따라서 정답은 (A)이다.

8 **Seldom** does Veestan Hardware miss its monthly sales target / of $5,000.
(A) Still (B) While (C) Until (D) Seldom

해석| 베스탄 하드웨어 사가 5천 달러의 월 매출 목표를 놓치는 일은 거의 없다.

어휘| miss 놓치다, 빗나가다 target 목표, 대상

해설| 부정문도, 의문문도 아닌데 조동사 does 가 쓰였고, 동사 does와 miss 사이에 문장의 주어가 있는 것으로 보아 주어와 동사가 도치되었음을 알 수 있다. 주어와 동사가 도치되려면 강조하고자 하는 부정어나 보어, 조동사가 문장 맨 앞으로 나와야 한다. 선택지에 '거의 ~ 않다'라는 의미의 부정어 Seldom이 있으므로 정답은 (D)이다.

교재 249쪽

REVIEW | **핵심 POINT 다시 보기**

1 (A) **2** (D) **3** (D) **4** (A) **5** (B) **6** (C)

---

1 The northern part of Berpo City is **more densely** populated / than the southern area.
(A) **more densely** (B) most densely (C) more dense
(D) most dense

해석| 베르포 시의 북부 지역은 남부 지역보다 인구가 더 밀집되어 있다.

어휘| densely 빽빽하게, 조밀하게 (파) dense 빽빽한, 조밀한) populate 살다, 거주하다

해설| 빈칸 앞뒤로 수동태 동사를 구성하는 be 동사 is와 과거분사 populated가 있으므로 빈칸은 부사 자리이다. 따라서 비교급 부사 (A)와 최상급 부사 (B)가 정답 후보. 빈칸 뒤쪽으로 '~보다'의 의미로 비교급과 어울려 쓰이는 전치사 than이 나오므로 비교급인 (A)가 정답이다.

---

2 Ms. Davenport is considered the **most eloquent** senior executive / of Yanpro Insurance, Inc.
(A) eloquence (B) more eloquent (C) eloquently
(D) **most eloquent**

해석| 데번포트 씨는 얀프로 보험사에서 가장 언변이 좋은 고위 간부로 여겨진다.

어휘| eloquent 유창한 executive 간부, 임원

해설| 빈칸 앞의 관사 the와 빈칸 뒤 명사 senior executive로 보아 빈칸에는 뒤의 명사를 수식하는 형용사가 들어가야 한다. 따라서 비교급 형용사 (B)와 최상급 형용사 (D)가 정답 후보. 정관사 the와 빈칸 뒤쪽에 범위를 한정하는 표현인 of Yanpro Insurance, Inc.가 있으므로 정답은 최상급인 (D)이다.

---

3 If Emanti Ventures had provided better benefits, / many former employees **would have stayed** with the company.
(A) were staying (B) had stayed (C) be staying
(D) **would have stayed**

해석| 만약 에만티 벤처스 사가 더 나은 복지를 제공했다면, 많은 이전 직원들이 회사에 남았을 텐데.

어휘| former 이전의, 과거의

해설| 선택지를 보니 빈칸에 알맞은 동사를 고르는 문제. 빈칸은 콤마 뒤 절의 동사 자리로, if절의 동사 형태가 had p.p.이므로 빈칸에는 가정법 과거완료 문장의 주절 동사 형태인 〈조동사+have p.p.〉가 와야 한다. 따라서 (D)가 정답.

---

4 **Had** the store clerk been able to assist the shopper, / the customer's feedback would have been more positive.
(A) **Had** (B) Whenever (C) Although (D) In fact

해석| 만약 그 점원이 쇼핑객을 도울 수 있었더라면, 고객의 피드백이 더 긍정적이었을 텐데.

어휘| assist 돕다, 도움이 되다

해설| 콤마 이하의 절의 동사가 〈조동사+have p.p.〉인 것으로 보아 가정법 과거완료 문장이다. 콤마 앞이 if절이 되어야 하는데, if절에 동사도 없고 선택지에 if가 없으므로 if가 생략되고 주어와 동사가 도치된 경우로 생각해야 한다. 따라서 선택지 중 동사인 (A)가 정답. if절의 동사가 had, were, should인 경우에 주로 이렇게 도치된다.

5-6

To: All employees
From: Karen Spencer, Office Manager

Starting May 1, we will use a software program to track employees' days off. This program will allow us to process vacation requests twice **as fast** as we did with the paper system.

Instead of gathering signatures from multiple supervisors, employees will file requests centrally on the company's Web site.

Should you encounter any problems with the software, **contact** Klaus Meldon in the IT department.

수신: 전 직원
발신: 사무 관리자, 카렌 스펜서

5월 1일부터, 직원들의 휴가 내역을 기록하는 소프트웨어 프로그램을 사용할 예정입니다. 이 프로그램으로 우리는 서류로 하던 것보다 두 배 더 **빨리** 휴가 요청을 처리할 수 있게 될 것입니다.

다수의 관리자에게서 서명을 모으는 대신에, 직원들은 회사 웹사이트에서 중앙 집중적으로 요청서를 제출하게 됩니다.

소프트웨어 사용에 어떠한 문제가 생기면, IT 부서의 클라우스 멜든 씨에게 **연락하세요**.

어휘| track 추적 기록하다 process 처리하다 instead of ~ 대신에 signature 서명 multiple 다수의 file 제출하다 centrally 중앙 집중적으로 encounter 맞닥뜨리다

5 This program will allow us to process vacation requests / twice **as fast** as we did with the paper system.
(A) fastest　(B) as fast　(C) faster　(D) as faster

해설| 빈칸 뒤의 as와 선택지의 as를 보면 원급 비교 구문 〈as+형용사+as〉를 떠올려야 한다. 빈칸에는 as+형용사가 들어갈 수 있어서 (B)와 (D)가 정답 후보이나, as ~ as 사이의 형용사 자리에는 원급만 들어갈 수 있으므로 정답은 (B).

6 Should you encounter any problems with the software, / **contact** Klaus Meldon in the IT department.
(A) contacts　(B) contacted　(C) **contact**　(D) to contact

해설| 조동사 should가 문장 앞으로 나오고 주어가 그 뒤에 이어지는 형태이므로 접속사 if가 생략되어 주어와 동사가 도치된 가정법 미래 문장임을 알 수 있다. 따라서 주절의 동사는 〈조동사+동사원형〉의 형태이거나 동사원형으로 시작하는 명령문이 되어야 알맞다. 콤마 이하의 주절은 완전한 절이어야 하는데 주어, 동사가 없으므로, 빈칸에는 명령문을 이루는 동사원형이 들어가야 한다. 따라서 정답은 (C).

VOCABULARY　생활 어휘(3)　　　　　　교재 251쪽

1 views　2 expansion　3 extensive　4 accommodate　5 (C)　6 (D)　7 (A)　8 (C)

1 Rooms with (**views** / vehicles) on the sea / are more expensive.
해석| 바다의 경관이 보이는 방들은 더 비싸다.

해설| 괄호는 '~을 가진'의 뜻인 전치사 with의 목적어 자리로 문맥상 '바다 경관을 가진 방'이 되는 것이 자연스럽다. 따라서 정답은 views.

2 Orsus Co. is preparing / for an overseas (**expansion** / itinerary) of its business.

해석│ 오서스 사는 자사 사업의 해외 확장을 준비하고 있다.

어휘│ overseas 해외의

해설│ 괄호 앞의 형용사 overseas와 어울리는 명사를 찾아야 한다. 기업에서 사업에 대해 준비할 수 있는 것은 '해외로의 확장'이 될 수 있으므로 정답은 expansion. business expansion(사업 확장)은 하나의 표현으로 자주 쓰이므로 기억해두자.

---

3 All of our travel agents / have (**extensive** / upcoming) experience / customizing vacation packages.

해석│ 저희의 모든 여행사 직원들은 휴가 패키지를 맞춤 설계하는 많은 경험을 갖고 있습니다.

해설│ 빈칸 뒤의 명사 experience와 어울리는 형용사를 골라야 한다. 여행사 직원이 여행 패키지를 맞춤 설계하는 '많은 경험'을 갖고 있다는 내용이 자연스러우므로 정답은 extensive이다.

---

4 The hotel's event hall can (expand / **accommodate**) / up to seventy-five people.

해석│ 그 호텔의 행사장은 최대 75명까지 수용할 수 있다.

해설│ 빈칸은 문장의 동사 자리로 주어인 The hotel's event hall과 어울리는 동사를 찾아야 한다. 특정 장소가 사람을 '수용하다'는 의미가 되어야 하므로 정답은 accommodate이다.

---

5 Meadow Railways cannot process ticket changes / within one hour of the scheduled <u>departure</u>.
(A) baggage (B) direction **(C) departure** (D) location

해석│ 메도우 철도는 예정된 출발 시각 한 시간 이내에는 표 교환을 처리해 드릴 수 없습니다.

(A) 수하물 (B) 방향 (C) 출발 (D) 장소

어휘│ process 처리하다 scheduled 예정된

해설│ 표 교환이 불가한 것이 무엇을 기준으로 '한 시간 이내(within one hour)'일지 생각해 본다. '출발' 시각을 기준으로 하는 것이 자연스러우므로 (C)가 정답.

---

6 Please follow the boarding procedures / to ensure the flight can depart without <u>delay</u>.
(A) destination (B) favor (C) belongings **(D) delay**

해석│ 비행편이 지연 없이 출발할 수 있도록 탑승 절차를 따라 주십시오.

(A) 목적지 (B) 호의 (C) 소지품 (D) 지연

어휘│ boarding 탑승 procedure 절차 ensure (that) 확실히 ~하게 하다

해설│ 빈칸은 '~ 없이'라는 의미의 전치사 without의 목적어 자리로, 비행편이 '지연 없이' 출발할 수 있도록 해달라는 내용이 자연스러우므로 정답은 '지연'을 뜻하는 (D)이다.

---

7 Additional lanes will be built / in order to avoid <u>congestion</u> / during rush hour.
(A) congestion (B) transportation (C) climates
(D) pavement

해석│ 출퇴근 시간 동안 교통 혼잡을 피하기 위해서 추가 차선이 건설될 것이다.

(A) 혼잡 (B) 교통 (C) 기후 (D) 포장도로

어휘│ additional 추가의 in order to *do* ~하기 위해서 avoid 피하다
rush hour 출퇴근 시간, 러시 아워

해설│ 추가로 차선을 건설하는 이유는 '교통 혼잡을 피하기 위해서'라는 내용이 자연스러우므로 (A)가 정답. (traffic) congestion이나 traffic jam은 모두 '교통 혼잡, 교통 체증'을 뜻하는 표현이다.

---

8 Send an e-mail to the public relations department / to <u>arrange</u> a private tour of the facility.
(A) intend (B) arrive **(C) arrange** (D) communicate

해석│ 그 시설의 개인 견학을 예약하시려면 홍보부에 이메일을 보내 주세요.

(A) 의도하다 (B) 도착하다 (C) 정하다, 준비하다 (D) 의사소통하다

어휘│ public relations department 홍보부 private 개인적인

해설│ 빈칸 앞 to 이하는 홍보부로 이메일을 보내는 '목적'을 나타낸다. 문맥상 빈칸 뒤의 명사 a private tour와 어울려 '견학을 예약하다'라는 뜻이 되어야 알맞다. 따라서 '정하다'라는 의미의 (C)가 정답. 시간 약속을 잡거나 사전에 어떤 일을 준비한다고 할 때 동사 arrange를 쓴다.

1 (B) **2** (C) **3** (B) **4** (A) **5** (A) **6** (C) **7** (B) **8** (A) **9** (D) **10** (A) **11** (B) **12** (C)

---

1 If his video conference with investors finished earlier, / the CEO **would go** / to the product launch.
(A) go **(B) would go** (C) will go (D) gone

해석| 투자자들과의 화상 회의가 일찍 끝나면, CEO는 제품 출시 발표회에 갈 텐데.

어휘| video conference 영상[화상] 회의 launch 출시 (발표회)

해설| **가정법 과거**

부사절 접속사 if로 연결된 두 절 중, 콤마 뒤 주절에 동사가 없으므로 빈칸에는 동사가 필요하다. 따라서 동사가 아닌 (D)는 정답 후보에서 제외. 콤마 앞 if절의 동사가 과거 시제이므로 가정법 과거 문장이다. 따라서 주절의 동사는 〈조동사+동사원형〉이어야 하므로 정답은 (B).

---

2 The regional manager will explain the details / of the **upcoming** relocation to Fraize Lake.
(A) numerous (B) adjacent **(C) upcoming** (D) frequent

해석| 지역 담당 매니저는 곧 있을 프레이즈 레이크로의 이전에 대해 상세 정보를 설명할 것이다.

(A) 수많은 (B) 인접한 (C) 곧 있을 (D) 빈번한

해설| **형용사 어휘 upcoming**

빈칸 뒤 명사 relocation을 수식하는 알맞은 형용사를 고르는 문제. 문맥상 미래 시제와 어울려 '곧 있을 이전'이라는 내용으로 쓰일 수 있는 (C)가 정답.

오답| (B) adjacent은 거리상으로 '인접한, 가까운'이란 뜻이므로 의미상 적절하지 않다.

---

3 If the promotional displays **had been placed** in a more visible spot, / a greater number of customers would have purchased the products.
(A) place **(B) had been placed** (C) has placed
(D) are placed

해석| 홍보용 전시물이 더 눈에 띄는 장소에 놓였더라면, 더 많은 고객들이 제품을 구입했을 텐데.

어휘| promotional 홍보의 display 전시 place 놓다, 두다 visible 눈에 띄는 a great number of 많은

해설| **가정법 과거완료**

선택지를 보니 알맞은 동사의 형태를 고르는 문제. 주절의 동사가 would have purchased이므로 가정법 과거완료 문장이다. 따라서 if절의 동사는 〈had *p.p.*〉 형태가 되어야 하므로 (B)가 정답. 주어인 the promotional displays는 특정 장소에 '놓이는' 대상이므로 수동태가 쓰였다.

---

4 Experts say that employees / who receive **more precise** feedback / perform better than others.
(A) more precise (B) precisely (C) most precise
(D) as precise

해석| 전문가들은 더 정확한 피드백을 받은 직원들이 다른 사람들보다 일을 더 잘한다고 말한다.

어휘| precise 정확한, 정밀한

해설| **비교급 비교**

빈칸은 빈칸 뒤의 명사 feedback을 수식하는 형용사 자리이다. 따라서 형용사인 (A)와 (C), (D)가 정답 후보. 문장 맨 끝에 '~보다'의 뜻을 가진 전치사 than과 함께 비교대상이 나오므로 비교급인 (A)가 정답.

오답| (D) as precise는 as ~ as 구문의 일부인데, 빈칸 뒤에 as가 없으므로 쓸 수 없다.

---

5 Please **confirm** your appointment with Mr. Walsh / by calling his assistant / no later than June 12.
(A) confirm (B) remind (C) agree (D) comply

해석| 늦어도 6월 12일까지는 월시 씨의 비서에게 전화해서 그와의 약속을 확인해 주세요.

(A) 확인하다 (B) 상기시키다 (C) 동의하다 (D) 따르다

어휘| confirm 확인하다 appointment (만날) 약속 assistant 비서 no later than 늦어도 ~까지는

해설| **동사 어휘 confirm**

빈칸 뒤의 목적어 your appointment와 어울리는 동사 어휘를 고르는 문제. 문맥상 '약속을 확인하다'라는 내용이 자연스러우므로 (A)가 정답.

오답| (B)는 '~에게 …을 상기시키다'라는 의미로는 〈remind+사람+about[of]〉의 형태로 쓰이므로 오답이다.

6 Ms. Scott's speech at the technology conference / was **even** longer than the keynote address.
(A) too (B) so **(C) even** (D) more

해석 | 기술 회담에서 스캇 씨의 연설은 기조 연설보다 훨씬 더 길었다.
(A) 너무 (B) 매우 (C) (비교급 앞에서) 훨씬 (D) 더
어휘 | speech 연설 keynote address 기조 연설

해설 | 비교급 강조 부사
선택지를 보니 빈칸에 어울리는 부사를 고르는 문제. 빈칸 뒤에 형용사의 비교급 longer가 있으므로 빈칸에는 비교급 강조 부사로 '훨씬'의 의미인 (C)가 들어가는 것이 알맞다. 참고로 even, still, far, a lot과 같은 부사들이 비교급을 강조하여 쓰인다.
오답 | 나머지도 모두 부사이지만 이들은 원급의 형용사를 수식한다.

---

7 Mr. Burnage may contact some successful local business owners / **should** extra funding be required / to start his new restaurant.
(A) when **(B) should** (C) in fact (D) through

해석 | 버니지 씨는 새 식당을 차리기 위해 추가 자금이 필요하다면, 몇몇 성공한 지역 사업주들에게 연락할지도 모른다.

해설 | 가정법 미래
빈칸 앞의 절이 완전하고 빈칸 뒤도 절을 이루므로 빈칸을 접속사 자리라고 생각할 수도 있다. 그러나 빈칸 뒤 절의 동사가 원형인 be required인 것을 보고 if절에서 접속사 if가 생략되고 주어, 동사가 도치된 문장임을 알아야 한다. 따라서 빈칸은 도치되어 주어 앞으로 이동한 동사 자리. 선택지의 유일한 동사 (B)가 정답.

---

8 Freetelecomm's revenue has increased / continuously over the year, / but Internet bundles sales grew / **most quickly** last June.
(A) most quickly (B) quickness (C) more quickly (D) quick

해석 | 프리텔레콤 사의 이익은 일 년 동안 지속적으로 증가해 왔는데, 인터넷 묶음 상품의 판매는 지난 6월에 가장 급속하게 증가했다.
어휘 | revenue 수익 bundle 묶음, 꾸러미

해설 | 최상급 비교
빈칸이 없어도 문장이 완전하므로 빈칸은 부사 자리이다. 따라서 최상급 부사 (A)와 비교급 부사 (C)가 정답 후보. 문장 내에 비교 대상도 없고, 문맥상 '지난 6월에 가장 급속하게 증가했다'는 내용이 자연스러우므로 최상급이 들어가야 한다. 따라서 (A)가 정답.
오답 | (B) quickness는 명사, (D) quick은 형용사이므로 오답.

9-12

Irene Reynolds
318 Saint Francis Way
Brookfield, WI 53005

Dear Ms. Reynolds,

Thank you for your interest in our European Summer Tour, one of our **most popular** tour packages so far. The trip is fully booked at this time, but I have added you to the waiting list. If a spot **should open** up, I will let you know right away.

In the event of a last-minute cancellation, I'd like you to be fully prepared. All tour participants must possess a **valid** passport with at least one blank page remaining.

The trip package includes all hotel stays, travel costs, and admission fees to sites for the duration of the tour. However, please keep in mind that you will be responsible for transportation to the starting point, which is in Paris.

이렌느 레이놀즈
세인트 프랜시스 대로 318번지
53005 위스콘신 주, 브룩필드

레이놀즈 씨께,

지금까지 저희의 **가장 인기 있는** 투어 패키지 중 하나인 유럽 여름 투어에 대한 고객님의 관심에 감사드립니다. 이번에는 여행 예약이 다 찬 상태지만, 고객님을 대기 명단에 넣어 드렸습니다. 빈 자리가 **나면**, 바로 알려 드리겠습니다.

마지막 순간에 취소가 생길 경우를 대비해, 고객님께서는 완벽하게 준비를 해 주시기 바랍니다. 모든 투어 참가자들은 최소한 한 페이지의 공란이 남아 있고 **유효한** 여권을 소지해야 합니다.

여행 패키지에는 투어 기간 동안의 호텔 숙박비와 이동 경비, 방문지 입장료가 모두 포함됩니다. 하지만 파리에 있는 출발지까지의 교통

We hope you will be able to travel with us soon.

Tamara Indell
Customer Service Agent, Go Abroad Tours

편은 본인이 책임져야 한다는 점을 유념하시기 바랍니다.

조만간 저희와 함께 여행하실 수 있기를 바랍니다.

고우 어브로드 투어즈 사, 고객 서비스 담당자
타마라 인델 드림

어휘 | so far 지금까지 be fully booked 예약이 다 차다 waiting list 대기 명단 spot 자리, 장소 in the event of ~의 경우에 last-minute 마지막 순간의 cancellation 취소 possess 소지하다 valid 유효한 blank 공백의 remaining 남아 있는 admission free 입장(료) duration 지속 기간 keep in mind that ~을 유념하다 be responsible for ~에 책임이 있다 transportation 수송, 이동

---

9 Thank you for your interest in our European Summer Tour, / one of our **most popular** tour packages so far.
(A) popular (B) more popular (C) popularity
(D) most popular

해설 | 최상급 비교

빈칸 앞 한정사 our와 빈칸 뒤의 명사 tour packages로 보아, 빈칸은 형용사가 들어갈 자리이므로 명사인 (C)는 정답 후보에서 제외. 빈칸 뒤의 복수 명사 tour packages와 빈칸 앞의 one of라는 단어를 보고 〈one of the+최상급+복수 명사〉 구문을 떠올려야 한다. 따라서 빈칸은 형용사의 최상급 자리이므로 정답은 (D)이다.

---

10 If a spot **should open** up, / I will let you know right away.
(A) should open (B) had opened (C) opened (D) to open

해설 | 가정법 미래

빈칸이 포함된 콤마 앞 부분은 접속사 If로 연결된 절이나, 동사가 없으므로 빈칸은 동사 자리이다. 따라서 to부정사인 (D)를 제외한 모든 선택지가 정답 후보. 주절의 동사가 will let이므로 가정법 미래 문장임을 알 수 있다. 이때, if절의 동사는 〈should+동사원형〉 형태로 쓰여야 하므로 정답은 (A).

---

11 All tour participants must possess a **valid** passport / with at least one blank page remaining.
(A) domestic **(B) valid** (C) distinctive (D) relevant
(A) 국내의, 가정의 (B) 유효한 (C) 독특한 (D) 관련 있는

해설 | 형용사 어휘 valid

빈칸 뒤의 passport(여권)와 의미가 자연스럽게 연결되는 형용사를 골라야 한다. 입출국시 스탬프를 찍을 공간이 있는 '유효한 여권'을 소지해야 한다는 내용이 자연스럽다. 따라서 (B)가 정답.

---

12 (A) The hotels we have reserved have excellent service.
(B) Paris is well-known for its many tourist attractions.
(C) We hope you will be able to travel with us soon.
(D) Please send in your application in a timely manner.
(A) 저희가 예약한 호텔들은 뛰어난 서비스를 갖추고 있습니다.
(B) 파리는 그곳의 많은 관광지들로 잘 알려져 있습니다.
(C) 조만간 저희와 함께 여행하실 수 있기를 바랍니다.
(D) 제때에 당신의 신청서를 보내 주십시오.

해설 | 알맞은 문장 고르기

빈칸이 편지의 마지막 인사말에 해당하므로 편지의 단락 구조만 알고 있다면 쉽게 정답을 예측할 수 있다. 마지막 인사말로 기대나 요청을 나타내는 (C)와 (D)가 적절한데, 앞의 내용을 생각했을 때, 빈 자리가 나서 여행에 합류하게 되기를 바란다는 내용의 (C)가 가장 자연스럽다.
오답 | (A)와 (B)는 빈칸 바로 앞 문단에 언급한 호텔과 파리를 각각 반복한 함정으로, 지문의 흐름과 관계가 없다. 이미 여행을 신청한 상태이므로 (D)는 오답이다.

UNIT 15

UNIT 16 문제 유형

1 일반적 내용을 묻는 유형

교재 258쪽

Q (C) / 1 (A) 2 (D) 3 (C)

To: Joel Swanson <j_swanson@acefoods.com>
From: ABC Supplies <service@abcsupplies.com>
Date: January 18
Ⓠ Subject: Your order

Ⓠ Order number 2894-4029 for Joel Swanson will not arrive on January 19. Unfortunately, **Ⓠ** our delivery trucks are behind schedule due to heavy snow. Your merchandise is now scheduled to arrive on January 22. **Ⓠ** We're pleased to offer you a coupon for 10 percent off your next order as an apology for the inconvenience.

Sincerely,

The ABC Supplies Team

수신: 조엘 스완슨
〈j_swanson@acefoods.com〉
발신: ABC 서플라이즈
〈service@abcsupplies.com〉
날짜: 1월 18일
Ⓠ 제목: 귀하의 주문

Ⓠ 조엘 스완슨 씨의 주문 번호 2894-4029 물품이 1월 19일에 도착하지 못할 것입니다. 공교롭게도 **Ⓠ** 저희의 배송 트럭이 폭설 때문에 예정보다 늦어지고 있습니다. 귀하의 상품은 이제 1월 22일에 도착할 예정입니다. **Ⓠ** 불편함에 대한 사과로 다음번 주문을 위한 10% 할인 쿠폰을 기꺼이 드리도록 하겠습니다.

ABC 서플라이즈 팀 드림

어휘 | unfortunately 공교롭게도, 불행하게도 be behind schedule 예정보다 늦어지다 due to ~ 때문에 heavy snow 폭설
merchandise 상품, 물품 be scheduled to *do* ~할 예정이다 apology 사과, 사죄 inconvenience 불편

Q What is the purpose of the e-mail?
(A) To advertise a sale
(B) To request a payment
(C) To report a delivery delay
(D) To place an order

이메일의 목적은?
할인 판매를 광고하기 위해서
지불을 요청하기 위해서
배송 지연을 보고하기 위해서
주문을 하기 위해서

어휘 | advertise 광고하다 payment 지불 delay 지연
해설 | 단서 **Ⓠ**에서 지문이 고객의 주문과 관련된 이메일이고, 주문 번호에 해당하는 물건이 예정일에 도착하지 못할 것이며 이에 대한 이유와 보상책에 대해 알 수 있으므로 이 글의 목적은 배송 지연에 대해 알려 주는 것이다. 정답은 (C).
패러프레이징 | 단서 behind schedule → 정답 delay

On behalf of Worldwind Travel, **❶** I'd like to inform you that you are eligible for 25 percent off any travel package booked between February 1 and March 31. This includes cruises, guided tours, and luxury vacations. This discount is available to preferred members only.

월드윈드 여행사를 대표하여, **❶** 귀하께서는 2월 1일과 3월 31일 사이에 예약되는 모든 여행 패키지에 대해 25% 할인받을 자격을 갖추셨음을 알려 드립니다. 여기에는 유람선 여행, 가이드 여행, 그리고 호화스러운 휴가가 포함됩니다. 이 할인은 우대 고객들만 이용 가능합니다.

어휘 | on behalf of ~을 대표하여, ~ 대신에 be eligible for ~의 자격을 갖추다 cruise 유람선 여행 luxury 호화스러운 available 이용 가능한 preferred 우대되는, 선호되는

1 Why was this letter written?
(A) To introduce a special offer
(B) To correct an error in a bill
(C) To send a travel itinerary
(D) To recommend a travel destination

편지가 쓰여진 이유는?
특별 할인을 소개하려고
청구서 내의 오류를 정정하려고
여행 일정표를 보내려고
여행지를 추천하려고

어휘| offer 할인, 제공 itinerary 일정표 bill 청구서 destination 목적지

해설| 글의 목적을 묻는 문제의 단서는 주로 앞부분의 주제문에서 바로 노출되는 점을 잊지 말자. 단서 **1**에서 고객에게 할인 자격이 된 다는 것을 알려 주고 있으므로 정답은 (A)이다.

오답| 단서의 travel package(여행 패키지) 부분만 보고 여행과 관련된 (C)나 (D)를 답으로 선택하지 않도록 주의하자.

Announcement	공지
2 3 The lease on our office here in the Utica Building will expire soon, so we are moving to a new place. A real estate agent has finally found a space that is suitable for our needs. The office is newly built, and it can accommodate all of our staff. **3** Employees will be responsible for packing their personal belongings. If you need any materials such as boxes or tape, please talk to your supervisor. **3** I'm sure everyone will enjoy the spacious new office. Regards, Donna Harris	**2 3** 이곳 유티카 건물에서의 우리 사무실 임대가 조만간 만기되므로, 우리는 새로운 장소로 이전할 예정입니다. 부동산 중개인이 마침내 우리의 요구에 적합한 장소를 발견했습니다. 그 사무실은 새로 지어진 것이고, 우리 전 직원을 수용할 수 있습니다. **3** 직원들은 책임지고 자신의 개인 소지품을 꾸려야 합니다. 만약 박스나 테이프와 같은 재료들이 필요하시다면, 관리자에게 이야기하세요. **3** 저는 모든 직원들이 넓은 새 사무실을 좋아할 것이라 확신합니다. 도나 해리스 드림

어휘| lease 임대 expire (계약·보증 등이) 만기되다[끝나다] real estate agent 부동산 중개인 be suitable for ~에 적합하다
accommodate 수용하다 be responsible for ~을 책임지다 pack 꾸리다, 포장하다 belongings 소지품 materials 재료, 물질
spacious (공간이) 넓은

2 What is the purpose of the announcement?
(A) To show appreciation to staff
(B) To describe job responsibilities
(C) To explain a new policy
(D) To announce a location change

공지의 목적은?
직원들에게 감사를 표하려고
직무를 설명하려고
새로운 정책을 설명하려고
위치 변경을 발표하려고

어휘| appreciation 감사 describe 설명[묘사]하다 job responsibility 직무 policy 정책 location 위치

해설| 글의 목적을 묻는 문제 유형. 단서 **2**에서 사무실 임대 만기와 새로운 장소로의 이전에 대해 설명하고 있으므로 정답은 (D).

오답| 본문은 임대(lease)와 관련된 내용으로 정책(policy)과는 무관하므로 (C)는 오답.

패러프레이징| **단서** moving to a new place → **정답** a location change

---

3 For whom is the announcement intended?
(A) Project supervisors
(B) Job applicants
(C) Staff members
(D) Apartment tenants

공지가 의도하고 있는 대상은?
프로젝트 관리자들
구직자들
직원들
아파트 세입자들

해설| 글의 대상을 묻는 문제는 앞부분의 주제문 파악과 함께 지문 전체를 훑어 읽어 내려가는 기술(skimming)을 활용해야 한다. 단서 **3**에서 사무실이 이전할 것이므로 소지품을 꾸리라고 요구하고 있으며, 모두 새 사무실을 좋아할 것이라고 하는 것으로 보아 공지의 대상자들은 회사 직원들임을 알 수 있다. 정답은 (C).

Dear Ms. Zimmerman,

Jeanette Robinson is highly recommended for the position of manager of the human resources department. She has given a strong performance during her five years at Fritz Financial. **Q** Management is especially impressed with her ability to keep her work organized despite working on multiple projects at the same time.

Regards,

Paul Dreher

짐머맨 씨께,

지넷 로빈슨을 인사부 부장 직위에 적극 추천합니다. 그녀는 프릿츠 파이낸셜 사에서 5년 동안 훌륭한 업무 수행을 했습니다. **Q** 경영진은 특히 동시에 다양한 프로젝트를 해야 함에도 불구하고 자신의 업무를 체계적으로 하는 그녀의 능력에 감명받았습니다.

폴 드레어 드림

어휘| highly 매우, 대단히 human resources department 인사부 be impressed with ~에 감명[감동]받다 ability to do ~하는 능력 organize 체계화[조직]하다 despite ~에도 불구하고 multiple 다양한 at the same time 동시에

Q Why is management impressed with Ms. Robinson?
(A) She worked as a project leader.
(B) She can finish the work quickly.
(C) She developed a good financial plan.
(D) She has excellent organizational skills.

경영진이 로빈슨 씨에게 감명받은 이유는?
그녀는 프로젝트 리더로 일했다.
그녀는 일을 빨리 끝낼 수 있다.
그녀는 좋은 재무 계획을 개발했다.
그녀는 훌륭한 체계화 기술을 가졌다.

어휘| financial 재무[재정]의 organizational 체계화 능력의, 조직의

해설| 질문의 키워드인 impressed(감명을 받은)란 표현을 염두에 두고, 지문에서 찾아 보자. 단서 **Q**에서 impressed 뒤로 업무를 체계적으로 하는 그녀의 능력에 감명받았다고 했으므로 정답은 (D)이다.

패러프레이징| **단서** her ability to keep her work organized → **정답** excellent organization skills

We have recently signed a contract with Prime Co. to advertise the Carter-360 washing machine. We're confident that the campaign designed by Prime Co. will be a success, **1** as the company specializes in promoting products that are new to the market.

우리는 최근 카터-360 세탁기를 광고하기 위해 프라임 사와 계약을 체결했습니다. **1** 그 회사는 시장에 처음 나오는 제품들의 홍보를 전문으로 하기 때문에, 우리는 프라임 사가 만드는 캠페인이 성공할 것임을 확신합니다.

어휘| sign a contract 계약을 체결하다 advertise 광고하다 washing machine 세탁기 confident 확신하는, 자신 있는 specialize in ~을 전문으로 하다 promote 홍보하다, 촉진시키다

1 What is Prime Co.'s specialty?
(A) Repairing washing machines
(B) Manufacturing electronics
(C) Advertising new products
(D) Transporting merchandise

프라임 사의 전문 분야는?
세탁기 수리하기
전자기기 제조하기
신제품 광고하기
제품 운송하기

어휘| specialty 전문 (분야) repair 수리하다 electronics 전자기기 transport 운송하다

해설| 질문의 키워드 specialty를 지문에서 찾아보니 단서 **1**의 specializes in(~을 전문으로 하다)이 패러프레이징된 표현이다. 여기에서 프라임 사가 시장에 처음 나오는 제품의 홍보를 전문으로 한다고 했으므로 신제품 광고가 전문 분야임을 알 수 있다. 따라서 정답은 (C).

패러프레이징| **단서** promoting products that are new to the market → **정답** Advertising new products

Etta Stuart
Knight Apartments, #302
1791 Columbia Road
Philadelphia, PA 19108

Dear Ms. Stuart,

The maintenance team has reviewed your request for renovation work on September 19. The apartment owner approved it on September 23. ② A crew is going to start the renovation at 10 A.M. on Saturday, September 27, and it will be completed in around four hours. ③ A crew member will pick up the key from the rental office, so you don't have to be home at that time. Someone from the rental office will stop by the following day to make sure you are satisfied with the finished result.

Sincerely,

The Knight Apartments Staff

에타 스튜어트
나이트 아파트 302호
콜롬비아 가 1791번지
19108 펜실베이니아 주 필라델피아

스튜어트 씨께,

유지보수팀이 귀하의 9월 19일자 보수 공사 요청을 검토했습니다. 아파트 소유주는 9월 23일에 그것을 승인했습니다. ② **직원이 9월 27일 토요일 오전 10시에 보수를 시작할 것이고, 4시간 정도 후에 완료될 것입니다.** ③ **직원이 임대 사무실에서 열쇠를 가져갈 것이니,** 이 때 집에 꼭 계셔야 할 필요는 없습니다. 임대 사무실의 누군가가 그 다음 날 귀하께서 완료된 결과에 만족하시는지 확인하기 위해서 들를 것입니다.

나이트 아파트 직원 드림

어휘 | maintenance 유지보수 review 검토하다 crew 직원 complete 완료하다, 끝내다 pick up ~을 찾아오다[집어 들다] stop by (잠깐) 들르다 be satisfied with ~에 만족하다 result 결과

2 When will the renovation be finished?
(A) On September 19
(B) On September 23
(C) On September 27
(D) On September 28

보수 공사가 끝나는 때는?
9월 19일
9월 23일
9월 27일
9월 28일

해설 | 질문의 키워드인 finished를 지문에서 찾아서 그 주변을 자세히 읽어 보자. 단서 ②에서 9월 27일 오전 10시에 보수 공사를 시작해서 4시간 정도 후에 끝난다고 했으므로 공사는 당일에 끝난다. 따라서 정답은 (C). 질문의 finished라는 키워드는 단서의 completed를 바꿔 쓴 것이다.

3 Where will a crew member get the key?
(A) From Ms. Stuart
(B) From the rental office
(C) From the crew supervisor
(D) From the maintenance office

직원이 열쇠를 받을 장소는?
스튜어트 씨
임대 사무실
작업감독관
유지보수 사무실

해설 | 단서 ③에서 직원이 임대 사무실에서 열쇠를 가져갈 것이라고 명시했으므로 정답은 (B). 단서의 pick up the key를 질문에서는 get the key라고 표현했다.

Q (A) / **1** (D) **2** (A) **3** (B)

Managers should prepare the factory for the inspection tomorrow. **QB** Please check the machinery, **QC** give safety goggles and gloves to your employees, **QD** and throw away all boxes and containers that we are not using. Let's work together to improve our score compared to last year.

관리자들은 내일 점검을 위해서 공장을 준비해야 합니다. **QB** 기계를 확인하시고, **QC** 보안경과 장갑들을 직원들에게 나눠 주시고 **QD** 사용하지 않는 모든 상자들과 용기들을 버려 주세요. 작년에 비해 점수가 향상되도록 힘을 합칩시다.

어휘| inspection 점검　safety goggles 보안경　throw away ~을 버리다　container 용기　compared to ~에 비해

Q What is NOT mentioned as a task that managers should do?
(A) **Posting a safety notice**
(B) Checking some equipment
(C) Giving workers protective gear
(D) Throwing away unnecessary items

관리자들이 해야 할 일로 언급되지 않은 것은?
안전 공지 게시하기
장비 확인하기
직원들에게 보호 장비 주기
불필요한 물건 버리기

어휘| post (공지·글 등을) 게시하다　protective gear 보호 장비

해설| 관리자들이 공장 점검을 위해 해야 할 일에 대한 지문에서 언급되지 않은 내용을 고르는 문제. 단서 **QB**, **QC**, **QD**의 내용들이 각각 선택지에 패러프레이징되어 나오므로 언급되지 않은 (A)가 정답이다. 지문 안의 safety란 단어가 (A)의 함정으로 사용되었다.

Ms. Hutchinson would be an excellent candidate for the hotel manager position. She has **1C** nearly ten years of experience in the tourism industry, **1A** and she planned training programs at her former job. In addition, she is **1B** proficient in three languages, which would be useful for communicating with international travelers.

허친슨 씨는 호텔 매니저직에 훌륭한 후보자일 것입니다. 그녀는 **1C** 거의 10년간의 관광업계 경험이 있으며, 이전 직장에서 **1A** 연수 프로그램을 기획했습니다. 게다가 그녀는 **1B** 3개 언어에 능통한데, 이는 해외 여행객들과 의사소통 하는 데 유용할 것입니다.

어휘| tourism industry 관광업계　in addition 게다가　proficient in ~에 능숙한[숙련된]　communicate with ~와 의사소통 하다

1 What is NOT indicated as one of Ms. Hutchinson's qualifications?
(A) The ability to plan training
(B) Proficiency in multiple languages
(C) Work history in the tourism industry
(D) **Experience in international business**

허친슨 씨의 자격 요건 중 하나로 언급되지 않은 것은?
연수 계획 능력
다중 언어 능숙도
관광업계에서의 이력
해외 사업 경험

해설| 각 선택지의 키워드가 등장하는 부분을 자세히 살펴 보자. 단서 **1A**에서 연수 프로그램을 기획했다고 했고, 단서 **1B**에서 3개국어에 능통하다고 했으며, 단서 **1C**에서 관광업계에서 거의 10년의 경험이 있다고 했으므로, 선택지에서 언급되지 않은 (D)가 정답이다. 지문 마지막의 international이라는 어휘를 단순 반복 사용한 함정이므로 주의한다.

At the Lakeville Community Center meeting on April 2, upcoming activities for local residents were announced. Participants can take classes in **2C** watercolor painting, **2B** yoga, **2D** choir singing, and more.

Sign up for any activity **3A** by clicking on the "Registration" button on our homepage. **3B** Community members of all ages are invited to participate. **3C** The deadline for registration for the summer session is May 15. Remember, because of generous financial support from the community, **3D** all classes are offered free of charge.

4월 2일 레이크빌 지역 문화 센터 회의에서 지역 주민들을 위한 향후 활동들이 발표되었습니다. 참가자들은 **2C** 수채화 그림 그리기, **2B** 요가, **2D** 합창단에서 노래하기 등의 수업을 들을 수 있습니다.

3A 저희 홈페이지에서 '등록' 버튼을 클릭해서 어떤 활동이든지 신청하세요. **3B** 모든 연령대의 지역 사회 구성원들이 참여하실 수 있습니다. **3C** 여름 학기 등록 마감 기한은 5월 15일입니다. 기억하세요, 지역 사회의 넉넉한 재정 후원 덕분에 **3D** 모든 수업이 무료로 제공됩니다.

어휘 | community center 지역 문화 센터 take a class 수업을 듣다 watercolor 수채화 choir 합창단 sign up for ~을 신청하다 registration 등록 be invited to *do* ~하도록 초대되다 deadline 마감 기한 session 학기, 기간 generous 넉넉한, 후한 financial 재정[재무](상)의 free of charge 무료로

2 What is NOT an activity residents can do at the center?
   (A) Take swimming classes
   (B) Practice yoga
   (C) Learn to paint
   (D) Participate in a choir

주민들이 센터에서 할 수 있는 활동에 포함되지 않는 것은?
수영 강습 받기
요가 연습하기
그림 배우기
합창단 참여하기

해설 | 지역 문화 센터에서 제공할 수업을 나열하고 있는 단서 **2B** 요가, **2C** 수채화 그림 그리기, **2D** 합창단에서 노래하기를 하나씩 비교 대조하여 소거하면, (A)의 '수영 강습 받기'는 등장하지 않았음을 알 수 있다. 따라서 (A)가 정답.

---

3 What is NOT true about the registration?
   (A) It can be done online.
   (B) It is open only to adults.
   (C) It ends on May 15.
   (D) It is offered at no cost.

등록에 대해서 사실이 아닌 것은?
온라인으로 할 수 있다.
성인들에게만 개방된다.
5월 15일에 끝난다.
무료로 제공된다.

어휘 | open 개방된, 열려 있는 at no cost 무료로

해설 | 선택지의 문장들을 지문에서 하나씩 대조 소거해야 하는 문제 유형. 단서 **3A**, **3C**, **3D**에서 등록에 대한 내용이 선택지와 같이 언급되었지만, 단서 **3B**에서는 모든 연령의(of all ages) 주민들이 참석 가능하다고 했으므로 (B)는 지문과 다르다. 따라서 정답은 (B).

4 추론 유형

교재 264쪽

Q (D) / **1** (C) **2** (C) **3** (B)

Please join us for personnel manager Valerie Wiley's retirement dinner on August 13. All employees are invited, and it will be a great opportunity for everyone to meet Travis Harding. **Q** Mr. Harding will be in charge of all personnel and administrative employees after the departments are combined next month.

8월 13일에 있을, 인사팀 팀장인 발레리 와일리 씨의 은퇴 기념식에 함께해 주십시오. 모든 직원들이 초대되며, 모두에게 트래비스 하딩 씨를 만나게 될 좋은 기회가 될 것입니다. **Q** 하딩 씨는 다음 달에 부서들이 통합되고 난 후 모든 인사팀과 행정팀 직원들을 맡을 것입니다.

어휘 | retirement 은퇴, 퇴직 opportunity 기회 in charge of ~을 맡는[책임지는] administrative 행정의 combine 통합[연합]하다

Q What is implied about the company?
(A) It is moving to a new location.
(B) It currently has a job opening.
(C) It has recently hired Valerie Wiley.
(D) It plans to restructure its departments.

회사에 대해 암시하는 바는?
새로운 곳으로 옮겨갈 것이다.
현재 공석이 있다.
최근에 발레리 와일리 씨를 고용했다.
부서들을 재구성할 계획이다.

어휘 | restructure ~을 재편성하다

해설 | 추론 유형도 지문에서 정확한 단서를 찾아서 답을 골라야 한다. 마지막 문장인 단서 ⓓ에 '부서들이 다음 달에 통합된다'는 내용이 있으므로 부서에 일종의 재구성이 있음을 시사한다. 정답은 (D).

패러프레이징 | 단서 the departments are combined → 정답 restructure its departments

---

Movie fans are highly anticipating the release of *Space Dust II*. ❶ Its fantastic special effects are certain to make it even more popular than the original, which was a box-office hit. This action film from director Ryan Ressler is the second in a series of three.

영화 팬들은 〈스페이스 더스트 II〉의 개봉을 매우 기대하고 있다. ❶ **그 영화의 환상적인 특수 효과가 그것을 박스 오피스 히트작이었던 원작보다 훨씬 더 인기 있게 만들 것이 분명하다.** 라이언 레슬러 감독의 이번 액션 영화는 세 개의 시리즈 중 두 번째이다.

어휘 | anticipate 기대하다 release 개봉 special effect 특수 효과 be certain to *do* ~하는 것이 분명하다 original 원작 director 감독

1 What can be inferred about *Space Dust II*?
(A) It stars a popular actor.
(B) It was recently released.
(C) It will get many viewers.
(D) Its director won an award.

〈스페이스 더스트 II〉에 대해 추론할 수 있는 것은?
인기 있는 배우가 주연을 맡는다.
최근에 개봉했다.
많은 관람객을 끌 것이다.
감독이 상을 받았다.

어휘 | star (배우에게) 주연을 맡기다 win an award 상을 받다

해설 | 원작과 비교하는 내용이 담긴 단서 ❶에서, 이 작품이 원작보다 훨씬 더 인기가 있을 것(even more popular)이라고 했으므로 많은 관람객을 끌 것임을 추론할 수 있다. 따라서 정답은 (C)이다.

오답 | 지문 첫 번째 문장에서 개봉을 기대하고 있다(are anticipating the release)고 했으므로 최근에 개봉했다는 진술의 (B)는 오답이다.

Over the past few months, our company has experienced a decrease in sales. ❷ Since other companies have cut their prices significantly, it has been difficult for us to maintain our previous sales volume. While our sales representatives are doing their best, we need to develop a new strategy. Therefore, ❸ we will be adding more staff to the marketing team and investing more in this side of the business. We want to show customers that our high-quality goods are well worth the price.

지난 몇 달 동안에 우리 회사는 매출 감소를 겪었습니다. ❷ **다른 회사들이 가격을 상당히 낮췄기 때문에, 우리가 이전 매출 규모를 유지하기가 어렵게 되었습니다.** 우리 영업 사원들이 최선을 다하고는 있지만, 우리는 새로운 전략을 개발할 필요가 있습니다. 따라서, ❸ **우리는 마케팅 팀에 더 많은 직원을 추가하고 사업의 이런 측면에 더 많이 투자할 것입니다.** 우리는 고객들에게 우리의 고품질의 제품이 가격 만큼의 충분한 가치가 있음을 보여줄 것입니다.

어휘 | decrease 감소 significantly 상당히 maintain 유지하다 previous 이전의 do *one's* best 최선을 다하다 strategy 전략 add 추가하다 invest in ~에 투자하다 worth ~의 가치가 있는

2 What is implied about the decrease in sales?
(A) It was predicted by the sales representatives.
(B) It was due to inexperienced employees.
(C) It was influenced by other companies.
(D) It was stopped by reducing prices.

판매량 감소에 대해 암시하는 바는?
영업 사원들에 의해 예측되었다.
경험이 없는 직원들 때문이었다.
다른 회사들로부터 영향을 받았다.
가격을 낮춰서 감소가 멈췄다.

해설 | 단서 ❷에서 이전의 매출 규모를 유지하기 어려웠던 이유가 다른 회사들이 가격을 상당히 낮췄기(other companies have cut their prices significantly) 때문이라고 언급했다. 이를 통해서 매출 감소가 타사의 영향을 받았음을 알 수 있으므로 정답은 (C).

오답 | 가격을 낮춘 것은 경쟁사에 대한 내용이므로 (D)는 오답이다.

3 What is probably true about the company's plan?
(A) It will be tested with some customers.
(B) It will focus on marketing the products.
(C) It will be based on a previous strategy.
(D) It will involve hiring more sales employees.

회사 계획에 대해 아마도 사실인 것은?
일부 소비자가 테스트할 것이다.
제품 마케팅에 집중할 것이다.
이전 전략을 기반으로 할 것이다.
더 많은 영업 직원 고용이 수반될 것이다.

어휘 | focus on ~에 집중하다 involve 수반하다

해설 | 단서 **3**을 보면, 마케팅 부문에의 직원 추가(adding more staff to the marketing team)와 사업적 투자(investing more in this side of the business)에 대한 내용이 드러나고 있으므로 회사가 제품 마케팅에 집중할 예정임을 알 수 있다. 정답은 (B).
오답 | 지문에서 새로운 전략이 필요하다고 했으므로 이전 전략을 기반으로 할 거라는 (C)는 오답이다.

---

5 동의어 찾기 유형   교재 266쪽

Q (C) / **1** (A) **2** (D) **3** (A)

The Norcross Museum is proud to present the early **Q** pieces of painter Marco Pirozzi. Visitors are asked to follow all museum guidelines. Do not bring food or beverages into the gallery. You may take pictures of the paintings, but please remember that flash photography is not allowed.

노크로스 미술관은 화가 마르코 피로치 씨의 초기 **Q** 작품들을 보여드리게 되어 자랑스럽게 생각하고 있습니다. 방문객들은 미술관의 모든 규정을 따를 것이 요청됩니다. 음식이나 음료를 갤러리 안으로 가져오시면 안 됩니다. 여러분들께서는 그림의 사진을 찍을 수는 있으나 플래시를 사용한 사진 촬영은 허락되지 않는다는 점을 기억해 주세요.

어휘 | be proud to *do* ~을 자랑스럽게 생각하다 present 보여주다, 제시하다 be asked to *do* ~하도록 요청되다 beverage 음료 allow 허락하다

Q The word "pieces" in paragraph 1, line 2, is closest in meaning to
(A) belongings
(B) duties
(C) artworks
(D) careers

첫째 단락 두 번째 줄의 "pieces"와 의미상 가장 가까운 단어는?
소지품
의무
예술품
직업

해설 | 지문의 문맥에 맞는 어휘의 뜻을 묻는 문제. piece는 '(한) 조각'이라는 뜻 이외에 '예술품'이란 뜻으로도 쓰인다. 지문에서 미술관(museum)과 화가(painter)라는 단어들이 등장하므로 정답은 (C)임을 알 수 있다.

Enroll in BizCo's business seminars and see excellent results! Our specially designed courses will give you an **1** edge in the market. You will learn how to manage others effectively and address customer needs. This will help you increase production and experience company growth.

비즈코 사의 비즈니스 세미나에 등록하시고 훌륭한 결과를 확인하세요! 특별히 설계된 저희 과정들이 당신에게 시장에서의 **1** 우위를 제공할 것입니다. 당신은 다른 사람들을 효과적으로 관리하는 방법과 고객의 요구에 대처하는 방법을 배우게 될 것입니다. 이것은 당신이 생산성을 증가시키고 회사의 성장을 경험할 수 있도록 도와줄 것입니다.

어휘 | enroll in ~에 등록하다 effectively 효과적으로 address (일·문제 등에) 대처하다 production 생산(량) growth 성장

1 In the advertisement, the word "edge" in paragraph 1, line 3, is closest in meaning to
(A) advantage
(B) side
(C) profit
(D) change

광고에서, 첫째 단락 세 번째 줄의 "edge"와 의미상 가장 가까운 단어는?
강점
측면
수익
변경

해설| 문맥상 '세미나에 등록하는 사람들에게 시장에서의 우위를 제공한다'는 의미로, 여기에서 해당 어휘 **1**은 '우위, 우세'의 의미로 사용되었음을 알 수 있다. 따라서 이와 가장 유사한 '강점'이라는 뜻을 가진 (A)가 정답. edge는 '가장자리'란 뜻 외에도 상대적인 '우위'의 의미가 있으니 알아두자.

Tower Communications and Telelinx, Inc., have announced plans for joint operations. Beginning March 1, the two companies will merge in order to use each other's strengths to serve customers better. The companies will be able to **2** reach more customers in Glenwood and the surrounding areas. According to William Howell, the CEO of Telelinx, plans are **3** set for an expansion of the telecommunications network. "With the population increase in Glenwood, it is necessary to install more telephone lines," Howell said.

타워 커뮤니케이션즈 사와 텔레링스 주식회사는 공동 운영에 대한 계획을 발표했다. 3월 1일부터 두 회사는 고객들에게 더 나은 서비스를 제공할 수 있는 서로의 강점을 이용하기 위해서 합병할 것이다. 두 회사는 글렌우드와 그 주변 지역들의 더 많은 고객들에게 **2** 닿을 수 있을 것이다. 텔레링스 사의 CEO인 윌리엄 하웰 씨에 따르면, 원격 통신 네트워크의 확장을 위한 계획들이 **3** 준비되어 있다고 한다. "글렌우드 지역의 인구 증가와 관련해 더 많은 전화선을 설치하는 것은 필수적입니다."라고 하웰 씨는 말했다.

어휘| joint 공동의 operation 운영 strength 장점, 강점 reach 닿다, 도착하다 surrounding 주변의 according to ~에 따르면 set 준비된, 계획된 expansion 확장 install 설치하다

2 The word "reach" in paragraph 1, line 3, is closest in meaning to
(A) arrive
(B) stretch
(C) aim
(D) serve

첫째 단락 세 번째 줄의 "reach"와 의미상 가장 가까운 단어는?
도착하다
펴다
목표하다
제공하다

어휘| serve 서비스를 제공하다

해설| reach는 '닿다, 도착하다'라는 의미로 자주 쓰이는 단어이지만, 지문의 맥락에서는 다른 의미로 사용되었다. 해당 어휘 **2**의 앞 내용에서 두 회사의 공동 운영의 목적이 고객들에게 더 나은 서비스를 제공하는 것이라고 했으므로 정답은 '서비스를 제공하다'란 뜻의 (D) serve가 정답.

3 The word "set" in paragraph 1, line 5, is closest in meaning to
(A) ready
(B) useful
(C) agreed
(D) unusual

첫째 단락 다섯 번째 줄의 "set"과 의미상 가장 가까운 단어는?
준비된
유용한
합의된
예외적인

해설| set이란 단어를 '고정된'이란 의미로 많이 알고 있지만, 해당 지문에서는 다른 의미로 쓰인 점에 주의하자. 해당 어휘 **3** 앞뒤 내용을 통해서 '확장을 위한 계획들이 준비되어 있다'는 문맥적 의미를 파악할 수 있다. 따라서 정답은 (A). 어휘 문제는 원래 뜻보다는 문맥을 통해 어떤 의미로 쓰였는지 잘 파악해야 한다.

6 화자의 의도를 묻는 유형

Q (C) / **1** (D) **2** (D) **3** (B)

GEORGIA HUGHES	6:41 P.M.	**조지아 휴즈**	오후 6:41
Have you left for the banquet hall yet?		벌써 연회장으로 출발했어요?	
ANTHONY PEREIRA	6:42 P.M.	**앤서니 페레이라**	오후 6:42
No. Why?		아뇨. 왜요?	
GEORGIA HUGHES	6:44 P.M.	**조지아 휴즈**	오후 6:44
I'm here setting up, but I left the storage device on my desk.		저는 여기서 연회 준비를 하고 있는 데, 제 책상 위에 저장장치를 놓고 왔어요.	
GEORGIA HUGHES	6:45 P.M.	**조지아 휴즈**	오후 6:45
Q Can you grab it and bring it with you?		**Q** 그것을 집어서 제게 가져다 주실 수 있나요?	
ANTHONY PEREIRA	6:49 P.M.	**앤서니 페레이라**	오후 6:49
You bet. **Q** I'll be there in twenty minutes.		물론이죠. **Q** 20분 후에 도착할 거예요.	

어휘 | banquet hall 연회장 set up 준비하다, 설치하다 storage device 저장장치 grab 집다

Q At 6:49 P.M., what does Mr. Pereira mean when he writes, "You bet"?
(A) He will buy a storage device.
(B) He will leave as soon as possible.
(C) He will take a forgotten item with him.
(D) He will meet Ms. Hughes outside a venue.

오후 6시 49분에, 페레이라 씨가 "물론이죠"라고 한 것에서 그가 의도한 것은?
저장장치를 살 것이다.
가능한 한 빨리 출발할 것이다.
잊은 물건을 가지고 갈 것이다.
행사장 밖에서 휴즈 씨를 만날 것이다.

해설 | You bet.은 '물론이다. 바로 그거다'라는 뜻으로 쓰이는 표현이다. 따라서 그 앞에 나온 단서 **Q**에서 Can you grab it and bring it with you?의 요지를 파악해야 한다. '잊고 온 물건을 가져다 줄 수 있느냐'는 요청이므로 이를 수락한다는 의미인 (C)가 정답. You bet.이 수락의 표현임을 몰랐다고 해도 그 뒤의 단서 **Q**를 보니 곧 도착할 거라고 했으므로 해당 표현이 수락의 의미임을 유추할 수 있다.

오답 | You bet은 앞의 요청에 대한 수락의 의미로, 앞의 요청이 빨리 와 달라는 것은 아니었으므로 (B)는 오답.

TERRANCE KOLB	3:26 P.M.	**터렌스 콜브**	오후 3:26
I'm at the eye doctor's. Apparently I need to have surgery.		제가 안과에 있는데요. 보아하니 수술을 받아야 할 것 같아요.	
MICAELA PAYNE	3:28 P.M.	**미카엘라 페인**	오후 3:28
Oh, really? When?		아, 정말요? 언제요?	
TERRANCE KOLB	3:29 P.M.	**터렌스 콜브**	오후 3:29
Tomorrow morning. **1** I won't be able to attend the meeting at 11 A.M. tomorrow. Can you do that for me?		내일 아침이요. **1** 내일 오전 11시 회의에 참석하지 못할 것 같아요. 저 대신 참석해 줄 수 있을까요?	
MICAELA PAYNE	3:32 P.M.	**미카엘라 페인**	오후 3:32
Definitely. Where is the information I need for the meeting?		물론이죠. 회의에 필요한 자료는 어디 있나요?	
TERRANCE KOLB	3:35 P.M.	**터렌스 콜브**	오후 3:35
There is a file on my desk. Thanks.		제 책상 위에 파일이 있어요. 고마워요.	

어휘 | apparently 보아하니, 분명히 have surgery 수술 받다

1 At 3:32 P.M., what does Ms. Payne mean when she writes, "Definitely"?
(A) She will give a speech for Mr. Kolb.
(B) She is agreeing to distribute some files.
(C) She is allowing Mr. Kolb to take time off.
(D) She will be present at a meeting.

오후 3시 32분에 페인 씨가 "물론이죠"라고 한 것에서 그녀가 의도한 것은?
콜브 씨 대신 연설을 하겠다.
파일들을 배포하는 데 동의하고 있다.
콜브 씨가 휴가를 내는 것을 허락하고 있다.
회의에 참석하겠다.

어휘 | distribute 배포하다, 나누어 주다   take time off 휴가를 내다   be present 참석하다

해설 | 상대방의 말에 대해 Definitely라고 응답하면, '물론이지, 그렇고 말고'라는 강한 긍정을 나타낸다. 이는 단서 **1**에서 콜브 씨가 한 '회의에 대신 참석해 줄 수 있겠냐'는 부탁에 대한 '긍정'의 응답이므로 (D)가 정답이다.

Heather Nelsen	[2:25 P.M.]	헤더 넬슨	[오후 2:25]
Good morning. Does anyone have the revised program for the conference?		좋은 아침이네요. 수정된 회의 일정표를 갖고 계신 분이 있나요?	
Carlos Palmer	[2:26 P.M.]	카를로스 파머	[오후 2:26]
The head of HR was supposed to send it to the department managers, but I didn't get any e-mail yet.		인사팀장님이 부서장들에게 보내 주시기로 되어있었는데, 저는 아직 어떤 이메일도 받지 못했네요.	
Carlos Palmer	[2:27 P.M.]	카를로스 파머	[오후 2:27]
He should send it soon. The conference is in less than three weeks, and **2** I'm not sure when my team is scheduled to give the marketing presentation.		그걸 빨리 보내주셔야 할 텐데요. 회의가 3주도 안 남았어요. 그리고 **2** 저는 저희 팀이 언제 마케팅 발표를 하기로 예정되어 있는지 확실히 모르겠어요.	
Katrina Burnings	[2:28 P.M.]	카트리나 버닝즈	[오후 2:28]
3 You can find the schedule on the company's Web site. HR decided to post it there so that everyone could easily see it.		**3** 회사의 웹사이트에서 일정표를 찾아 보실 수 있어요. 인사팀에서 모든 사람이 쉽게 볼 수 있도록 그걸 거기에 게시하기로 했어요.	
Heather Nelsen	[2:29 P.M.]	헤더 넬슨	[오후 2:29]
3 Oh, I didn't think to check the Web site. I see it now. Thanks.		**3** 오, 웹사이트를 확인해 볼 생각을 못 했네요. 이제 보이네요. 고마워요.	

어휘 | revised 수정[개정]된   HR 인사팀 (= Human Resources)   be supposed to *do* 하기로 되어 있다, 해야 한다   be scheduled to *do* ~하기로 예정되어 있다   post 게시하다

2 Which department does Mr. Palmer most likely work for?
(A) Web design
(B) Customer service
(C) Human Resources
(D) Marketing

파머 씨가 일할 것 같은 부서는?
웹 디자인
고객 서비스
인사팀
마케팅

해설 | 여러 명의 화자가 등장하는 온라인 채팅 지문에서는 이름과 시간대를 잘 보면서 내용을 파악해야 한다. 단서 **2**에서 파머 씨가 자기 팀이 언제 마케팅 발표를 하는지 모르겠다고 했으므로, 이를 통해 파머 씨는 마케팅 팀에서 일하고 있음을 알 수 있다. 따라서 정답은 (D).

오답 | (A), (C)는 각각 지문의 Web과 HR을 반복한 함정이다.

3 At 2:29 P.M., what does Ms. Nelsen mean when she says, "I see it now"?
(A) She has updated the Web site.
(B) She has found a schedule online.
(C) She has just received an e-mail.
(D) She has met with a coworker.

오후 2시 29분에, 넬슨 씨가 "이제 보이네요"라고 했을 때, 그녀가 의도한 것은?
웹사이트를 업데이트했다.
일정표를 온라인에서 찾았다.
막 이메일을 받았다.
동료와 만났다.

어휘 | coworker 동료

해설 | 해당 표현 앞쪽의 단서 **3**에서 버닝즈 씨의 '인사팀이 웹사이트에 일정표를 게시하기로 했다'는 말에 넬슨 씨가 '웹사이트를 확인해 볼 생각을 못 했다'고 했다. 그 뒤에 이어 해당 표현을 말했으므로 넬슨 씨가 일정표를 웹사이트에서 찾고 한 말임을 알 수 있다. 따라서 정답은 (B)이다.

패러프레이징 | 단서 find the schedule on the company's Web site → 정답 has found a schedule online

7 문장의 적절한 위치를 묻는 유형

Q (D) / **1** (C) **2** (C) **3** (D)

Hello all,

—[1]— . Motivational speaker Glenn Castor will be delivering several talks in the city next month. —[2]— . I attended his presentation in New York last year, and I highly recommend that you go and hear him speak. —[3]— . **Q** I advise you to book in advance because tickets are selling out quickly. —[4]— . So act fast if you want to go.

Best regards,

Bailey Ruffolo

안녕하세요, 여러분,

—[1]— . 동기 부여 전문 강사인 글렌 캐스터 씨가 다음 달에 우리 시에서 몇 차례 강연을 할 예정입니다. —[2]— . 저는 작년에 뉴욕에서 그의 강연에 참석했는데 여러분도 가셔서 그의 강연을 들으실 것을 매우 권장합니다. —[3]— . **Q** 티켓은 빠르게 매진될 것이기 때문에 사전 예매를 권해드립니다. —[4]— . 그러니 가기를 원하시는 분은 서둘러 주십시오.

베일리 러폴로 드림

어휘| deliver a talk 강연을 하다

Q In which of the positions marked [1], [2], [3], and [4] does the following sentence best belong?
"Apparently, half of them have been sold already."
(A) [1]
(B) [2]
(C) [3]
(D) [4]

[1], [2], [3], [4]번으로 표시된 위치들 중 다음 문장이 들어가기에 가장 적절한 곳은?
"그 중 절반이 이미 다 팔렸을 것임이 분명합니다."

해설| 지문은 직원들에게 강연을 들을 것을 권하는 내용이고, 주어진 문장은 '팔릴 수 있는 상품'에 대한 것이다. 문장 간의 연결 관계를 파악할 때, 대명사에 주목하면 힌트를 얻을 수 있다. 주어진 문장 속 대명사 them이 가리킬 만한 것으로 적절한 것은 단서 **Q**의 tickets이므로 주어진 문장은 그 뒤에 있는 [4]번에 들어가야 알맞다. 따라서 (D)가 정답.

Join the Costello, Inc., Team!

—[1]— . Costello, Inc. is seeking a public relations manager. —[2]— . Your primary role will be to supervise a team of marketing and media specialists. **1** We are looking for someone who is capable of working with diverse personalities and thrives under pressure. —[3]— . If you think you match this description, then we want to hear from you! Applications must be submitted by February 23. —[4]— .

코스텔로 주식회사의 일원이 되세요!

—[1]— . 코스텔로 주식회사에서는 홍보 담당 관리자를 찾고 있습니다. —[2]— . 주요 업무는 마케팅 및 미디어 전문가들로 이루어진 팀을 관리하는 일이 될 것입니다. **1** 우리는 다양한 개성을 지닌 사람들과 협력하고, 압박감 속에서도 잘 해낼 수 있는 사람을 찾고 있습니다. —[3]— . 귀하가 이러한 설명에 부합한다고 생각하시면, 저희에게 연락 주시기 바랍니다! 지원서는 2월 23일까지 제출해야 합니다. —[4]— .

어휘| public relations 홍보 primary 주요한, 주된 supervise 관리[감독]하다 specialist 전문가 be capable of *doing* ~할 수 있다 diverse 다양한 personality 개성, 인물 thrive 잘 해내다, 번창하다 under pressure 압박감 속에서 match 부합하다, 들어맞다 description 설명, 묘사

1 In which of the positions marked [1], [2], [3], and [4] does the following sentence best belong?

"Willingness to travel is also necessary."

(A) [1]
(B) [2]
(C) [3]
(D) [4]

[1], [2], [3], [4]번으로 표시된 위치들 중 다음 문장이 들어가기에 가장 적절한 곳은?

"출장을 기꺼이 감수하는 것 또한 필요합니다."

어휘| willingness 기꺼이 하려는 마음

해설| 지문은 홍보 담당 관리자 구인 광고로, 주어진 문장은 지원자가 지녀야 할 태도에 대한 내용이다. 주어진 문장의 also로 보아 태도가 나열된 문장 뒤에 내용을 첨가하여 쓰인 문장이므로 해당 내용을 지문에서 찾아야 한다. 단서 **①**에서 '다양한 사람들과 협력할 수 있고 압박감 속에서도 잘 해낼 수 있는' 태도에 대해 말하고 있으므로 그 뒤인 [3]번에 오는 것이 자연스럽다. 따라서 정답은 (C).

Attention Staff

—[1]— . With the temperature getting colder, many people are using personal heaters at their desks. —[2]— . Recently, it has been noted that several staff members consistently forget to turn their heaters off before going home. **②** It is a fire hazard to leave unattended heaters running throughout the night. —[3]— . **③** Therefore, we would like all staff members to be more careful when they leave. —[4]— . We can address this issue by working together.

Thank you,

Management

직원 여러분께 알립니다

—[1]— . 기온이 낮아지면서, 많은 사람들이 책상에서 개인 난방기를 사용하고 있습니다. —[2]— . 최근에 몇몇 직원들이 퇴근하기 전에 난방기를 끄는 것을 지속적으로 잊어버리는 것이 목격되었습니다. **②** 밤새 난방기가 혼자 작동하도록 두는 것은 화재의 위험이 있습니다. —[3]— . **③** 따라서 모든 직원들은 퇴근 시에 더 주의해 주시기를 바랍니다. —[4]— . 우리는 서로 협력함으로써 이 문제를 해결할 수 있습니다.

관리부 드림

어휘| consistently 지속적으로 turn off (전원을) 끄다 hazard 위험 unattended 방치된, 지켜보는 사람이 없는 throughout 내내, ~동안 쭉 therefore 따라서

---

2 What is the problem with personal heaters?
(A) They are difficult to move around.
(B) They increase the utility costs.
(C) They could cause a fire.
(D) They raise the temperature too much.

개인 난방기의 문제점은?
옮기기가 어렵다.
공공요금을 증가시킨다.
화재를 유발할 수 있다.
기온을 너무 많이 올린다.

어휘| move around 옮기다 utility cost (가스·수도·전기 등의) 공공요금

해설| 단서 **②**에서 밤새 난방기가 작동하도록 두는 것은 화재의 위험(a fire hazard)이 있다고 했으므로 (C)가 정답.

패러프레이징| 단서 a fire hazard → 정답 cause a fire

---

3 In which of the positions marked [1], [2], [3], and [4] does the following sentence best belong?

"If someone near you has accidentally left their heater running, please shut it down."

(A) [1]
(B) [2]
(C) [3]
(D) [4]

[1], [2], [3], [4]번으로 표시된 위치들 중 다음 문장이 들어가기에 가장 적절한 곳은?

"여러분 주변의 누군가가 실수로 난방기를 켜놓은 채로 두었을 경우, 꺼주십시오."

어휘| accidentally 실수로, 우연히 shut down 끄다, 정지시키다

해설| 주어진 문장은 누가 난방기를 켜두었을 경우, 꺼달라는 구체적인 당부의 내용이므로 당부의 말을 하고 있는 부분을 지문에서 찾아야 한다. 단서 **③**에서 '퇴근 시에 주의하라'고 했으므로, 이 뒤에 위치하여 구체적으로 퇴근 시에 '주변 난방기를 확인하라'는 흐름이 되는 것이 자연스럽다. 따라서 주어진 문장은 [4]번에 들어가는 것이 알맞기 때문에 정답은 (D).

1 (A) **2** (A) **3** (B) **4** (A) **5** (B) **6** (B) **7** (A) **8** (A) **9** (A)

---

1 inspect the machinery → check the **equipment**
(A) **equipment** (B) merchandise

기계를 검사하다 → 장비를 검사하다
(A) 장비 (B) 상품

---

2 visit the production plant → stop by the manufacturing **facility**
(A) **facility** (B) headquarters

생산 공장을 방문하다 → 제조 시설에 들르다
(A) 시설 (B) 본사

---

3 go over an instruction manual → **review** an instruction booklet
(A) produce (B) **review**

사용 설명서를 살펴보다 → 설명 책자를 검토하다
(A) 생산하다 (B) **검토하다**

---

4 become more efficient → increase **productivity**
(A) **productivity** (B) demand

더 효율적이게 되다 → 생산성을 높이다
(A) **생산성** (B) 요구

---

5 These items are breakable and must be handled with care.
(A) These items are broken and need to be changed soon.
(B) You must be careful when handling these fragile items.

이 물건들은 깨질 수 있으므로 반드시 주의해서 취급해야 한다.
(A) 이 물건들은 깨졌으므로 곧 교체되어야 한다.
(B) 이 부서지기 쉬운 물건들을 다룰 때는 반드시 주의해야 한다.

---

6 The facilities are temporarily closed because of renovations.
(A) State-of-the-art equipment was installed at the warehouse.
(B) Due to construction, the place is provisionally shut down.

시설들은 보수 작업 때문에 임시로 닫는다.
(A) 최신식 장비가 창고에 설치되었다.
(B) 공사 때문에, 그 장소는 잠정적으로 휴업한다.

---

7 Some of the machine's components need to be replaced.
(A) The device has parts that should be changed.
(B) The factory must produce new computer products.

기계의 부품 중 일부가 교체되어야 한다.
(A) 기기에는 교체되어야 할 부품들이 있다.
(B) 공장은 반드시 새로운 컴퓨터 제품을 생산해야만 한다.

8-9

On July 7, **8** we will start to manufacture a new product. We already produce many tools and machines to be used in hospitals and by doctors. However, there is a lot of demand for clothing that is specially designed for nurses. Thus, **9** this new line of clothing will be tailored to the needs of medical workers and feature pants, scrubs, masks, and hats. More information will be sent out soon.

7월 7일에, **8** 우리는 새 제품을 생산하기 시작할 것입니다. 우리는 이미 병원과 의사들이 사용하는 많은 도구들과 기계들을 생산하고 있습니다. 그러나 간호사들을 위해 특별 제작된 의류에 대한 요구가 많이 있습니다. 그러므로 **9** 이 새로운 의상 라인은 의료 직원들의 요구에 맞춰질 것이며, 바지, 스크럽, 마스크, 모자를 특징으로 갖출 것입니다. 조만간 더 많은 정보가 발송될 예정입니다.

어휘ㅣ tool 도구, 기구 **demand** 요구 **specifically** 특별히, 특히 **nurse** 간호사 **thus** 그러므로 **be tailored to** ~에 맞춰지다 **medical** 의료의 **feature** 특징으로 하다 **scrub** 수술복

8 What is being announced?
(A) The company will produce some new merchandise.
(B) Some tools will be redesigned by medical workers.

공지되고 있는 것은?
(A) 회사는 새로운 상품을 생산할 것이다.
(B) 몇몇 도구들은 의료 직원들에 의해 다시 고안될 것이다.

해설| 지문의 앞부분에 주제가 정확히 드러나고 있다. 단서 **8**에서 '새 제품을 생산하기 시작할 것'이라고 했으므로 이 글은 신제품 생산에 대한 내용이다. 정답은 (A).

패러프레이징| **단서** manufacture a new product → **정답** produce new merchandise

---

9 What will be special about the line of clothing?
(A) It will be customized for medical workers.
(B) It will be produced using new technology.

새로운 의상 라인의 특별한 점은?
(A) 의료 직원들을 위해 맞춤제작될 것이다.
(B) 신기술을 이용해서 생산될 것이다.

해설| 단서 **9**에서 새 의류 라인은 의료 직원의 요구에 맞춘 것이 될 것이라고 했다. 따라서 정답은 (A).

패러프레이징| **단서** be tailored to → **정답** be customized for

ACTUAL TEST 실전 문제에 적용하기 교재 274쪽

1 (C) **2** (A) **3** (C) **4** (A) **5** (A) **6** (D) **7** (C) **8** (B) **9** (D) **10** (C) **11** (C)

Cloud Nine Airlines
1264 Hyde Park Road, Los Angeles, CA 90017
Phone: 310-341-3870

January 14

Jason Welkins
519 Nields Street
El Monte, CA 91731

Dear Mr. Welkins,

❶ Your application to become a member of the Cloud Nine Airlines frequent flyer program has been approved. When you book a flight with us or any of our partners, you will now earn points. These points can be used for discounts on seat upgrades, airport purchases, and airfare. Enclosed with this letter is your membership card. The next time you fly with us, ❷ please show it to the airport staff when you check in. This will ensure that your account receives the appropriate number of points. If you have any questions, visit our Web site at www.cloudnineairlines.com/frequentflyers.

We look forward to your next flight with us.

Sincerely,

Peggy Marcos
Cloud Nine Airlines, Frequent Flyer Program Manager

클라우드 나인 에어라인즈
90017 캘리포니아 주, 로스앤젤레스
하이드 파크 가 1264번지
전화번호: 310-341-3870

1월 14일

제이슨 웰킨스
니일즈 가 519번지
91731 캘리포니아 주, 엘몬트

웰킨스 씨께,

❶ 클라우드 나인 에어라인즈 사의 상용 고객 우대 프로그램의 회원이 되기 위한 고객님의 신청이 승인되었습니다. 저희나 저희 협력사의 비행편을 예약하실 때, 고객님께서는 이제 포인트를 받으시게 됩니다. 이 포인트는 좌석의 업그레이드, 공항에서의 구매, 그리고 항공 요금의 할인에 사용될 수 있습니다. 이 편지에 고객님의 회원 카드가 동봉되어 있습니다. 다음번에 저희 항공기를 이용하시면, ❷ 탑승 수속을 하실 때 공항 직원에게 그것을 보여 주세요. 이것은 귀하의 계정이 적절한 포인트를 받을 수 있도록 해 줄 것입니다. 질문이 있으면, 저희 웹사이트인 www.cloudnineairlines.com/frequentflyers로 방문해 주세요.

다음 비행을 저희와 함께 하시길 고대합니다.

클라우드 나인 에어라인즈 사
상용 고객 우대 프로그램 매니저
페기 마르코스 드림

어휘| frequent 빈번한 flyer 비행기 승객 earn 얻다 airfare 항공 요금 enclosed 동봉된 check in (공항에서) 탑승 수속을 하다 account 계정 appropriate 적절한

1 For whom is the letter intended?
(A) A flight attendant
(B) A travel agent
(C) A new member
(D) An airline manager

편지가 의도하고 있는 대상은?
승무원
여행사 직원
신규 회원
항공사 매니저

해설| 단서 **1**에서 항공사의 상용고객 우대 프로그램의 회원이 되기 위한 신청이 승인되었다고 했으므로 (C)가 정답.
오답| (A)와 (D)는 항공 관련 어휘를 통한 오답 함정이다.

---

2 How can Mr. Welkins make sure he gets points on his account?
(A) By presenting his card to a staff member
(B) By purchasing some goods at the airport
(C) By upgrading his seat at the check-in desk
(D) By logging into the Cloud Nine Airlines Web site

웰킨스 씨가 그의 계정에 포인트를 확실히 받을 수 있는 방법은?
그의 카드를 직원에게 제시함으로써
공항에서 물건을 구매함으로써
탑승 수속대에서 좌석을 업그레이드함으로써
클라우드 나인 에어라인즈 사 웹사이트에 로그인함으로써

어휘| check-in desk 탑승 수속대
해설| 단서 **2**를 보면, 탑승 수속 시 직원에게 카드를 제시하면, 계정에 적절한 포인트를 확실히 받을 수 있다고 했다. 정답은 (A).
패러프레이징| 단서 show it to the airport staff → 정답 presenting his card to a staff member

---

https://www.cometcourse.com/reviews/

Home	Classes	Teachers	Fees	**Reviews**

홈	과정	강사	요금	**후기**

Great class!
Review by Aurora Harrison

I highly recommend attending a Comet program. I took the public speaking course over the summer. I had heard good things about it, but it was even better than I had expected. The instructor gave **3** practical advice and provided many opportunities for hands-on practice. The class size was small, so the professor could give feedback to each of us individually.

Before the class, **4** every time I presented my company's products to potential clients, I would have difficulty explaining things, and the clients would seem bored. Thanks to this class, my speech is now organized and clear. I can tell that, as a result, my audience is interested. In fact, my sales have gone up by several percentage points since I completed the course. I have no doubt that this is due to my improved public-speaking skills. **5** The only criticism I have about the class is that it is quite expensive. Despite this, I would advise anyone trying to improve their skills to join a Comet program.

훌륭한 과정!
오로라 해리슨의 후기

저는 코밋 프로그램에 참석하는 것을 강력 추천합니다. 저는 여름 동안 대중 연설 과정을 들었어요. 그 과정에 대한 좋은 이야기들을 들었었는데, 제 기대보다도 훨씬 더 좋았어요. 강사님은 **3** 실용적인 조언을 해 주시고 실제 연습을 위한 많은 기회들을 제공해 주셨어요. 수업의 규모가 작아서, 교수님이 저희 각각에게 개별적으로 피드백을 주실 수 있었어요.

그 과정을 듣기 전에는, **4** 잠재적인 고객들에게 저희 회사 제품을 소개할 때마다 설명하는 데 어려움을 겪었고, 고객들도 지루해 보였어요. 이 과정 덕분에 제 말하기가 이제는 체계적이고 명확해요. 결과적으로 저는 제 청중이 흥미로워 한다고 말할 수 있어요. 실제로, 이 수업을 이수하고 난 이후로 제 판매 실적이 몇 퍼센트 포인트 상승했어요. 이것이 제 향상된 대중 연설 기술 때문이라는 것에 의심의 여지가 없어요. **5** 제가 그 과정에 대해 가지는 유일한 비판은 꽤 비싸다는 점이에요. 이런 사실에도 불구하고 저는 기술을 향상시키려고 하는 모두에게 코밋 프로그램에 참여하라고 조언하고 싶어요.

어휘| take a course 과정을 듣다 instructor 선생님. 강사 practical 실용적인 hands-on 실질적인 individually 개별적으로 present 보여주다. 발표하다 potential 잠재적인 bored 지루한 thanks to ~ 덕분에[때문에] organized 체계적인 as a result 결과적으로 audience 청중. 관객 doubt 의심하다 criticism 비판 quite 꽤. 매우

3 In paragraph 1, line 3, the word "practical" is closest in meaning to

(A) cheap

(B) comfortable

(C) useful

(D) complex

첫째 단락 세 번째 줄의 단어 "practical"과 의미상 가장 가까운 단어는?

싼

편안한

유용한

복잡한

해설 | 단서 **3**의 해당 단어 뒷부분을 보면, 실제 연습을 위한 많은 기회들(many opportunities for hands-on practice)이 주어졌다고 했다. 문맥을 통해 해당 단어가 '실용적인'이라는 뜻으로 쓰였음을 알 수 있다. 정답은 이와 가장 유사한 의미인 (C).

---

4 What is probably true about Ms. Harrison?

(A) She regularly gives presentations for her work.

(B) She teaches public speaking.

(C) She is the best salesperson at her company.

(D) She recently started a new job.

해리슨 씨에 대해서 아마 사실인 것은?

그녀는 일 때문에 정기적으로 발표를 한다.

그녀는 대중 연설을 가르친다.

그녀는 회사에서 최고의 영업 사원이다.

그녀는 최근에 새로운 일을 시작했다.

어휘 | regularly 정기적으로　recently 최근에

해설 | 질문의 probably로 보아 추론 유형이다. 단서 **4**에서 '잠재적인 고객에게 회사 제품을 소개할 때마다'라고 했으므로 해리슨 씨는 직업상 발표를 종종 한다는 것을 알 수 있다. 정답은 (A).

오답 | 해리슨 씨는 수업을 추천하는 수강생이므로 (B)는 오답. 영업 실적이 올라갔다고 했으나, 최고의 영업 사원인지는 알 수 없으므로 (C)도 오답.

패러프레이징 | **단서** presented my company's products → **정답** gives presentations

---

5 What does Ms. Harrison criticize about the Comet program?

(A) Its price

(B) Its topic

(C) Its class size

(D) Its instructor

해리슨 씨가 코밋 프로그램에 대해 비판한 것은?

가격

주제

수업 크기

강사

어휘 | criticize 비판하다

해설 | 단서 **5**에서 '그 과정에 대한 유일한 비판은 꽤 비싸다는 점'이라고 했으므로 해리슨 씨가 과정에 대해 비판한 것은 '과정의 가격'이다. 따라서 정답은 (A). 지문의 The only criticism I have about the class가 질문에서 criticize about the Comet program으로 패러프레이징되었다.

오답 | (C) 수업 크기에 대해 언급하였으나, 수업 규모가 작아서 개별 피드백을 받는 것을 장점으로 꼽았으므로 오답이다.

Victor Santini [1:58 P.M.]

Hi, Polly. I'm sorry, but I'm running late to pick you up. A client called to change an order, and I haven't been able to leave my desk. Did your train already arrive?

Polly Dupont [2:00 P.M.]

Yes, it arrived a little early. **6** I was walking to the parking lot to meet you.

Victor Santini [2:01 P.M.]

Actually, I have to call the warehouse now before they ship out the order. So it will be a few more minutes before I leave. **7** If you prefer, I'll pay for a cab to go pick you up instead.

빅터 산티니 [오후 1:58]

안녕하세요, 폴리 씨. 죄송하지만 제가 당신을 태우러 가야 하는데 늦어지고 있어요. 고객이 주문을 변경하려고 전화를 해서 제가 책상을 떠날 수가 없었어요. 열차가 벌써 도착했나요?

폴리 뒤퐁 [오후 2:00]

네, 열차가 좀 일찍 도착했네요. **6** 저는 당신을 만나려고 주차장으로 걸어가고 있던 중이었어요.

빅터 산티니 [오후 2:01]

사실은 창고에서 주문 제품을 발송하기 전에 제가 지금 창고로 전화를 해야 해요. 그래서 떠나기 전에 몇 분이 더 걸릴 것 같아요. **7** 만약에 괜찮으시다면, 제가 당신을 태우러 가는 택시비를 대신 내드릴게요.

Polly Dupont [2:03 P.M.] That's not necessary. **7** I'm not in a hurry. **Victor Santini** [2:04 P.M.] OK. I'll contact you again when I leave.		**폴리 뒤퐁** [오후 2:03] 그럴 필요 없어요. **7** 저는 바쁘지 않아요. **빅터 산티니** [오후 2:04] 알았어요. 출발할 때 다시 연락 드릴게요.

어휘 | be running late 늦어지다 parking lot 주차장 ship out ~을 발송하다[보내다] pay for ~에 대해 돈을 지불하다 cab 택시 instead 대신에 in a hurry 바쁜; 서둘러

6 Where did Mr. Santini and Ms. Dupont plan to meet?
   (A) At an office
   (B) In a train station
   (C) At a warehouse
   (D) In a parking lot

산티니 씨와 뒤퐁 씨가 만나기로 계획한 장소는?
사무실
기차역
창고
주차장

해설 | 단서 **6**에서 뒤퐁 씨가 산티니 씨를 만나려고 주차장으로 걸어가고 있었다고 했으므로 두 사람이 주차장에서 만나기로 했음을 알 수 있다. 정답은 (D).
오답 | (B)와 (C)는 본문에 등장한 단어인 train과 warehouse를 각각 반복한 오답 함정이다.

---

7 At 2:03 P.M., what does Ms. Dupont most likely mean when she writes, "That's not necessary"?
   (A) She will take a taxi to the office.
   (B) She can call the warehouse herself.
   (C) She will wait for Mr. Santini.
   (D) She doesn't need to pay for the shipment

오후 2시 3분에, 뒤퐁 씨가 "그럴 필요 없어요"라고 할 때, 그녀가 의도한 바는?
그녀가 사무실로 택시를 타고 갈 것이다.
그녀가 직접 창고로 전화할 수 있다.
그녀는 산티니 씨를 기다릴 것이다.
그녀가 배송비를 지불할 필요가 없다.

해설 | 반드시 해당 표현 앞뒤의 문맥을 이해해야 한다. 해당 표현 바로 앞의 단서 **7**에서 산티니 씨가 뒤퐁 씨를 '데리러 가는 택시비를 대신 내준다'고 한 제안에 대해 바쁘지 않다며 거절했다. 따라서 해당 표현을 바쁘지 않으니 산티니 씨를 기다리겠다는 뜻으로 받아들일 수 있다. 정답은 (C).
오답 | 그럴 필요가 없다는 건 택시 타는 것을 거절하는 의미이므로 (A)는 오답. (B) 창고로 전화하는 것은 산티니 씨가 할 일이므로 오답. 대화체 지문에서는 발화자를 잘 확인해야 한다.

A New Turn for Portsmouth

PORTSMOUTH (18 November)— **8** A recent report on Portsmouth's economic status shows that the city's retailers and restaurants have had a high increase in business over the past year. —[1]— . **9A** While the city has seen steady growth for about a decade, the last few months mark a sharp rise. —[2]— .

11 Economists believe that this sudden growth is due to the opening of a new manufacturing plant right outside the city. —[3]— . As a result, unemployment in the area is at an all-time low, and **9B** the average income of local residents has increased. **10** "With job security and higher incomes, consumers are more willing to spend money," explains Maria Denton, who helped write the report.

—[4]— . Moreover, experts agree that the growth will continue well into the upcoming year. Real estate companies have noticed the trend and the resulting population increase. **9C** They have already started building new apartments with

포츠머스를 위한 새로운 전환

포츠머스 (11월 18일)— **8** 포츠머스의 경제 상황에 관한 최근 보고서는 도시의 소매업체들과 식당들이 지난 한 해 동안 높은 사업 성장세를 누렸음을 보여준다. —[1]— . **9A** 도시가 10여 년간 꾸준한 성장을 보였던 반면에, 지난 몇 달은 급격한 증가가 눈에 띈다. —[2]— .

11 경제학자들은 이러한 갑작스러운 성장이 도시 바로 외곽의 신규 제조 공장의 개업 때문이라고 믿는다. —[3]— . 결과적으로, 지역의 실업률은 역대 최저치이며, **9B** 지역 주민들의 평균 수입이 증가했다. **10** "고용 안정과 더 높아진 소득으로, 소비자들은 기꺼이 더 많은 돈을 쓰려고 합니다."라고 그 보고서 작성에 일조한 마리아 덴턴 씨가 설명했다.

—[4]— . 게다가 전문가들은 다음 해에도 성장이 잘 지속될 것이라는 것에 동의한다. 부동산 업체들은 그런 경향과 이로 인한 인구 증가를 이미 알아챘다. **9C** 그들은 이미 최신 설비를 갖춘 새 아파트를

up-to-date appliances, and ⑨ᴰ property prices in Portsmouth are increasing. It is thus safe to assume that the city will keep developing.

짓기 시작하였고, ⑨ᴰ 포츠머스의 부동산 가격은 증가하고 있다. 그러므로 이 도시가 계속 발전될 것이라고 생각해도 무방하다.

어휘| turn 전환   status 상태   retailer 소매업체   while 반면에   steady 꾸준한   decade 10년   mark 눈에 띄게 하다, 나타내다   plant 공장   unemployment 실업률   average 평균(의)   income 소득, 수입   job security 고용 안정   be willing to do 기꺼이 ~하다   moreover 게다가   trend 추세, 경향   population 인구   up-to-date 최신신의   appliance 기구, 도구   property 부동산   assume 가정하다

8 What is the purpose of the article?
(A) To encourage consumers to spend money
(B) To discuss an economic trend
(C) To announce new job openings
(D) To recommend some business strategies

기사의 목적은?
소비자들에게 돈을 쓰도록 권장하기 위해서
경제 동향을 논하기 위해서
새로운 공석들을 발표하기 위해서
몇몇 사업 전략을 추천하기 위해서

어휘| encourage A to do A가 ~하도록 격려하다   strategy 전략
해설| 첫 문장인 단서 **8**의 내용을 시작으로 포츠머스 지역의 경제 변화와 상태에 대해 설명하고 있으므로 이 글의 목적은 (B)이다.
오답| (C) 새로운 제조 공장의 개업(the opening of a new manufacturing plant)에서 일자리 창출을 연상시키는 오답 함정이다.
패러프레이징| 단서 Portsmouth's economic status → 정답 an economic trend

9 What is NOT indicated about Portsmouth?
(A) Business had been increasing continuously for ten years.
(B) Residents of the city are earning higher salaries.
(C) Apartments with state-of-the-art appliances are being built.
(D) Real estates in Portsmouth have become more affordable.

포츠머스에 대해 시사되지 않은 것은?
경기가 10년 동안 지속적으로 좋아졌다.
그 도시의 거주자들이 더 높은 급여를 받고 있다.
최신 설비가 있는 아파트가 지어지고 있다.
포츠머스의 부동산들이 더 저렴해졌다.

해설| NOT이 들어간 문제는 선택지 키워드를 지문과 대조하여 소거하는 방식으로 답을 찾아야 한다. 단서 **9ᴬ**에서 도시가 10여년 동안 꾸준히 성장세를 보였다고 했고, 단서 **9ᴮ**에서 지역 주민의 평균 소득이 높아졌다고 했다. 단서 **9ᴄ**에서는 이미 최신식 설비를 갖춘 아파트를 짓기 시작했다고 했다. 그러나 단서 **9ᴰ**에서 포츠머스의 부동산 가격은 증가하고 있다고 했으므로 선택지가 지문의 내용과 일치하지 않는다. 따라서 정답은 (D).

10 Who most likely is Ms. Denton?
(A) A real estate owner
(B) A factory worker
(C) An economist
(D) A job seeker

덴턴 씨의 신분은?
부동산 주인
공장 직원
경제학자
구직자

해설| 질문의 most likely로 보아 이 문제는 추론 유형이다. 단서 **10**에서 덴턴 씨는 지문 맨 앞에 나온 포츠머스의 경제 상황에 대한 보고서 작성에 일조한 인물로 소개되었다. 따라서 경제 상황에 대한 보고서를 작성할 수 있는 해당 분야의 전문가로 유추할 수 있으므로 정답은 (C).
오답| (A)는 지문의 real estate, (D)는 job을 반복 사용한 오답이다. (B)는 manufacturing plant에서 연상되는 단어를 이용한 오답 함정이다.

11 In which of the following positions marked [1], [2], [3], and [4] does the following sentence best belong?

"This new facility has created more than a thousand new jobs."

(A) [1]

(B) [2]

(C) [3]

(D) [4]

[1], [2], [3], [4]번으로 표시된 위치들 중 다음 문장이 들어가기에 가장 적절한 곳은?

"이 새로운 시설은 천 개 이상의 새 일자리를 창출해냈다."

해설 | 주어진 문장의 this라는 지시형용사를 힌트로 접근해야 한다. '이 새로운 시설'이 가리킬 만한 단어가 주어진 문장 앞에 등장해야 한다. 단서 ⑪에서 도시 외곽에 있는 새로운 제조 공장에 대한 내용이 등장하므로 그 뒷자리인 [3]번에 주어진 문장이 들어가야 한다. 따라서 정답은 (C). 주어진 문장에서 This new facility는 단서 ⑪의 a new manufacturing plant를 가리키는 말이다.

1 **이메일/편지** E-mail/Letter 교재 281쪽

1 (B) **2** (A) **3** (A) **4** (C) **5** (C)

To: Bernie Collins <bcollins@collinssupplies.com>
From: Margaret Ling <mling@webmail.com>
Date: October 18
Subject: Recent order

Dear Mr. Collins,

I'm writing to report a problem with a recent delivery.
I purchased a photocopier from your store, and it was
delivered yesterday. The machine is in perfect working order,
and I am pleased with it.

However, I also ordered a box of extra ink cartridges for the
machine, and that was not included with the delivery.
I checked the invoice later and saw that I was charged for the
cartridges. Please let me know by e-mail what the problem is
and when I can expect the delivery.

We are going to need the cartridges very soon, so I hope to
receive them as quickly as possible. I have attached a copy of
my invoice for your reference.

Sincerely,

Margaret Ling
Appleton Office

수신: 버니 콜린즈
〈bcollins@collinssupplies.com〉
발신: 마거릿 링 〈mling@webmail.com〉
날짜: 10월 18일
제목: 최근의 주문

콜린스 씨께,

저는 최근 배송에 대한 문제를 알리기 위해 이메일을 쓰고 있습니다. 저는 귀하의 매장에서 복사기를 구매했고, 그것은 어제 배송되었습니다. 그 기계는 완벽하게 정상적으로 작동했고, 저는 그것에 만족합니다.

그러나 저는 그 기계에 쓸 추가 잉크 카트리지 한 상자도 주문을 했는데, 그것은 배송품에 포함되어 있지 않았습니다. 나중에 송장을 확인하고 카트리지 가격이 청구된 것을 보았습니다. 무엇이 문제인지 그리고 언제 배송을 받을 수 있을지를 이메일로 알려 주세요.

조만간 카트리지가 필요할 예정이므로, 가능한 한 빨리 받고 싶습니다. 참고하실 수 있도록 송장 한 부를 첨부합니다.

애플턴 사무실
마거릿 링 드림

어휘| **photocopier** 복사기 **in working order** 정상적으로 작동하는 **be pleased with** ~에 만족하다[기쁘다] **extra** 추가의 **cartridge** 카트리지 **invoice** 송장 **be charged for** ~에 대한 요금이 부과되다 **attach** 첨부하다 **a copy of** ~ 한 부 **reference** 참고

Angela Manzo
445 Maven Avenue
Boston, MA 02210

Dear Ms. Manzo,

1 I am sending you this letter to officially offer you the job
of regional branch manager. I was very impressed with your
qualifications and experience. The job will start on May 3. **2**
Please let me know as soon as possible if you would like to
accept our offer. You can call me at (508) 555-0283 anytime
between 9 A.M. and 5 P.M. Enclosed are a copy of the
contract and a copy of our employee handbook. These outline
the terms and conditions of the position.

안젤라 맨조
마빈 로 445번지
02210 매사추세츠 주, 보스턴

맨조 씨께,

1 저는 공식적으로 당신에게 지점장직을 제안하기 위해 이 편지를 보냅니다. 저는 당신의 자격 요건과 경력에 깊은 인상을 받았습니다. 업무는 5월 3일에 시작할 것입니다. **2** 당신이 우리의 제안을 받아들일 것인지 가능한 한 빨리 알려 주세요. 저에게 오전 9시와 오후 5시 사이에 언제든 (508) 555-0283번으로 전화 주세요. 당신의 계약서 사본 한 부와 저희 직원 안내서 한 부를 동봉합니다. 이것들은 그 직위의 계약 조건을 서술합니다.

I look forward to meeting you again soon.

Gary Carter
Director of Personnel, LTV Electronics

곧 다시 만날 수 있기를 고대합니다.

LTV 일렉트로닉스 사, 인사부장
개리 카터 드림

어휘| **officially** 공식적으로 **offer** 제공[제안]하다 **regional** 지역의 **branch** 지점 **accept** 받아들이다 **contract** 계약(서) **terms and conditions** 계약 조건

1 Why did Mr. Carter write the letter?
(A) To schedule a job interview
(B) **To offer a position to Ms. Manzo**
(C) To request an employee handbook
(D) To apply for a job at LTV Electronics

카터 씨가 편지를 쓴 이유는?
면접 일정을 잡기 위해서
맨조 씨에게 일자리를 제안하기 위해서
직원 안내서를 요청하기 위해서
LTV 일렉트로닉스 사에 지원하기 위해서

어휘| **schedule** 일정을 잡다 **apply for** ～에 지원하다

해설| 편지를 쓴 이유를 단서 **1**에서 I'm sending you this letter to *do*(～하기 위해서 편지를 보내다)란 표현을 통해 드러냈다. 지점장직을 제안하기 위해 편지를 보내고 있다고 했으므로 정답은 (B)이다.

오답| 일자리 지원은 수신자인 맨조 씨가 했으므로 (D)는 오답이다.

패러프레이징| **단서** offer you the job → **정답** offer a position

- -

2 What does Mr. Carter ask Ms. Manzo to do?
(A) **Inform him of her decision**
(B) Come in for a meeting
(C) Revise a handbook
(D) Send some contact information

카터 씨가 맨조 씨에게 요청하는 것은?
그에게 그녀의 결정을 알려 주기
회의에 오기
안내서를 수정하기
연락처 정보를 보내기

어휘| **inform A of B** A에게 B를 알려 주다 **revise** 수정하다

해설| 요청 사항은 Please let me know(～을 알려 주세요)라는 표현이 나오는 단서 **2**에서 찾아볼 수 있다. '일자리 제안을 받아들일지 알려 달라'고 했으므로 정답은 (A)이다.

To: Rover Rentals <reservations@roverrentals.com>
From: Ronald Lloyd <ronald@buzzmail.com>
Subject: Rental request
Date: June 9

Dear Sir or Madam,

A colleague of mine visited Auckland recently and recommended your agency to me. **3** I'm writing to inquire if you have a minivan available that seats six people. **4** My family and I will be arriving in Auckland on July 2 for our summer vacation. We will be staying in the city for six days and will need the vehicle during that time. If a minivan is unavailable, I will need a list of the other options you have. In addition, I'll also need to know how much you charge per day and if you offer any weekly rental packages.

You can respond to this e-mail or call me at (082) 555-8823. **5** My current insurance plan has coverage for vehicle rentals, so I have included a copy of my policy in an attachment for reference. Thanks for your time, and I hope to hear from you soon.

수신: 로버 렌탈즈 〈reservations@roverrentals.com〉
발신: 로날드 로이드 〈ronald@buzzmail.com〉
제목: 임대 요청
날짜: 6월 9일

관계자 분께,

제 동료 중 한 명이 최근에 오클랜드에 방문했었고 저에게 당신의 대리점을 추천해 주었습니다. **3** 저는 6개의 좌석이 있는 미니밴을 빌릴 수 있는지 문의하려고 이메일을 씁니다. **4** 제 가족과 저는 여름 휴가 차 오클랜드에 7월 2일에 도착할 예정입니다. 저희는 6일 동안 도시에 머무를 것이며 그 시간 동안 차량이 필요합니다. 만약 미니밴을 이용할 수 없다면, 당신이 갖고 있는 다른 선택항의 목록이 필요합니다. 또한 저는 하루당 얼마가 청구되는지와 주 단위의 임대 상품을 제공하는지도 알고 싶습니다.

이 이메일에 회신하거나 (082) 555-8823번으로 전화 주셔도 됩니다. **5** 제 현재 보험은 임대 차량에 대해서도 보장해서, 참고하시라고 첨부 파일에 제 보험 증서 사본을 포함시켰습니다. 시간을 내주

어휘| colleague 동료 agency 대리점 inquire 문의하다 seat 좌석이 있다. 앉히다 vehicle 자동차 option 선택 항목 charge 청구하다 weekly 주 단위의 respond to ~에 응답하다 current 현재의 insurance plan 보험 계획[계약] coverage (보험의) 보상 범위 policy (보험) 증서[계약] attachment (이메일의) 첨부 파일 for reference 참고로

3 What is the purpose of the e-mail?

(A) To inquire about renting a vehicle
(B) To make reservations for a hotel
(C) To request changes to a trip itinerary
(D) To ask about city attractions

이메일의 목적은?

자동차 임대에 대해 문의하기 위해서
호텔 예약을 하기 위해서
여행 일정에 변경을 요청하기 위해서
도시의 관광지에 대해 문의하기 위해서

어휘| make a reservation 예약하다 attraction 관광지, 명소

해설| 글의 목적은 대개 지문 도입부에 제시된다. 단서 **3**의 I'm writing to do(저는 ~하기 위해서 글을 씁니다)에서 미니밴을 빌릴 수 있는지를 문의하기 위해서 이메일을 쓴다고 명시하였다. 따라서 정답은 (A)이다.

오답| (B), (C), (D)는 모두 여행 관련 상황에서 연상될 수 있는 것들로 오답이다.

4 What does Mr. Lloyd mention about his trip?

(A) It will last for more than a week.
(B) It will include stops in numerous cities.
(C) It will be with members of his family.
(D) It will be paid for by his company.

로이드 씨가 여행에 대해 언급한 것은?

일주일 이상 지속될 것이다.
수많은 도시에 경유하는 것도 포함될 것이다.
가족 구성원과 함께일 것이다.
회사에서 지불할 것이다.

어휘| last 지속하다 stop 경유, 들르기 numerous 수많은

해설| 로이드 씨는 이메일의 목적을 밝힌 후, 자신의 여행 일정에 대해서 설명하고 있다. 단서 **4**에서 가족과 자신이 휴가 차 오클랜드로 간다고 했으므로 정답은 (C)이다.

오답| 6일 동안 그 도시에 머무를 것(staying in the city for six days)이라고 했으므로 (A)와 (B)는 모두 오답이다.

5 What is included with the e-mail?

(A) A rental application form
(B) A hotel information brochure
(C) A copy of an insurance policy
(D) A receipt for an upcoming trip

이메일에 포함된 것은?

임대 신청서
호텔 정보 안내 책자
보험 증서 사본
다가올 여행에 대한 영수증

어휘| application form 신청서 brochure 안내 책자

해설| 단서 **5**를 통해 (C)가 정답임을 알 수 있다. (insurance) policy란 '보험 증서'를 뜻하는 말로, insurance plan(보험 정책)도 비슷한 표현으로 사용된다.

2 기사/정보문 Article/Information   교재 285쪽

1 (B) **2** (A) **3** (C) **4** (B) **5** (C)

Ingram Properties' Building Project

On July 8, international property developer Ingram Properties will begin construction of a shopping mall in Calgary. In a recent press release, the company said the facility will contain units for 200 retailers, parking facilities, and 20 restaurants.

인그램 프로퍼티즈 사의 건축 프로젝트

7월 8일에, 국제 부동산 개발사인 인그램 프로퍼티즈 사가 캘거리에 쇼핑몰 건축을 시작할 것이다. 최근의 언론 발표에서, 회사는 이 시설이 200개의 소매업체, 주차 시설, 20개의 식당을 포함할 것이라고 말했다.

Work will last for three years at a cost of $380 million. Ingram will provide nearly 60 percent of the funding, while the city will provide the rest as an investment. The company chose to build the mall to offer residents a convenient shopping venue.

Ingram Properties also plans to add an upscale hotel to the mall in the future. However, that project would not begin for at least four years.

작업은 3억 8천만 달러의 비용으로 3년 동안 지속될 것이다. 인그램 사는 자금의 거의 60%를 제공하며 시에서 투자로서 나머지를 제공할 것이다. 회사는 주민들에게 편리한 쇼핑 장소를 제공하기 위해 쇼핑몰을 건축하기로 선택했다.

인그램 프로퍼티즈 사는 또한 향후 그 쇼핑몰에 고급 호텔도 추가할 계획이다. 그러나, 그 프로젝트는 최소 4년 동안은 시작되지 않을 것이다.

어휘| construction 건축 release 언론 발표 facility 시설 contain 포함하다 funding 자금 rest 나머지 investment 투자 convenient 편리한 venue 장소 upscale 고급의, 상급의

LEVITTOWN, December 5 — **1** Tourism in Levittown and its suburbs has decreased this past year. In response to this, Mayor Rodham announced at a recent press conference that he would launch a campaign aimed at emphasizing Levittown's artistic attractions. As part of the campaign, he plans to talk to several contractors about building a new convention hall. He hopes this will encourage performers and artists from various fields to organize more events in Levittown rather than go to the neighboring city of Sillaville, and thus **1** attract audience members from around the country. "Levittown is a city full of diversity," Mayor Rodham explained. "We want people to come see the wonderful art that can be produced by this diversity." **2** For further details on the plan, you can visit Levittown's Web site at www.levittownnews.net.

레빗타운, 12월 5일—**1** 지난해 레빗타운과 그 근교에서의 관광 사업이 감소했다. 이에 대한 대응으로 로드햄 시장은 최근 기자 회견에서 레빗타운의 예술적 볼거리를 강조하는 것을 목표로 하는 캠페인을 시작하겠다고 발표했다. 캠페인의 일환으로, 그는 여러 하청 업체에 새로운 대회장 건축에 관해 이야기할 계획이다. 그는 이것이 다양한 분야의 공연인들과 예술가들에게 인근 도시인 실라빌로 가는 것 대신에 레빗타운에서 더 많은 행사를 계획하도록 장려하기를 바라며, 그렇게 해서 전국에서 **1** 관객들을 끌어 모으기를 바란다. "레빗타운은 다양함으로 가득한 도시입니다." 로드햄 시장이 설명했다. "우리는 사람들이 이러한 다양성에 의해 만들어질 수 있는 훌륭한 예술을 보러 오기를 바랍니다." **2** 그 계획에 대한 더 많은 정보를 알아보려면, 레빗타운의 웹사이트인 www.levittownnews.net을 방문하면 된다.

어휘| tourism 관광 (사업) suburbs 《집합적》 근교, 교외 in response to ~에 대응, 응답 press conference 기자 회견 launch 시작하다 aim ~을 목표로 하다 emphasize 강조하다 artistic 예술적인 attraction 볼거리, 명소 contractor 계약 업체 convention hall 대회장, 전시회장 various 다양한 field 분문, 분야 A rather than B B보다는 A하다 neighboring 인근[근처]의 diversity 다양(성)

1 Why is Mayor Rodham launching a campaign?
(A) To encourage citizens to vote
(B) To attract more visitors to the city
(C) To raise funds for a construction project
(D) To advertise artists and musicians

로드햄 시장이 캠페인을 시작하려는 이유는?
시민들에게 투표를 권장하려고
도시로 더 많은 관광객을 끌려고
건축 프로젝트를 위한 자금을 모으려고
예술가들과 음악가들을 홍보하려고

어휘| citizen 시민 vote 투표하다 attract 끌다 raise (돈을) 모으다
해설| 캠페인의 내용이 등장하는 단서 **1**에서, 지난 해 관광 사업이 감소했고, 이에 대한 대응으로 캠페인을 시작할 것이라고 했다. 또한 기사 중반부 이후의 단서 **1**에서도 캠페인을 통해 관객들을 끌기(attract audience members)를 바란다고 했으므로 정답은 (B).
패러프레이징| 단서 audience members → 정답 visitors

2 What can readers find at the Levittown Web site?
(A) More information about a project
(B) A performance schedule
(C) Contract terms and conditions
(D) A map to a new convention hall

독자들이 레빗타운 웹사이트에서 찾을 수 있는 것은?
프로젝트에 대한 더 많은 정보
공연 일정
계약 조건
새로운 대회장으로 가는 지도

해설| 추가 정보에 대한 내용은 보통 기사의 마지막 부분에 등장한다. 단서 **2**에서, 그 계획에 대한 더 많은 정보를 알아보려면(For further details on the plan), 웹사이트를 방문하라고 했으므로 정답은 (A)이다.

오답| (C)는 본문에 등장한 contractors에서 연상되는 어휘를 이용한 오답 함정. (D)는 convention hall을 반복 사용한 오답 함정이다.

패러프레이징| **단서** further details on the plan → **정답** More information about a project

---

Study Results Show Surprising Findings

3 At a press conference on Monday morning, professors from Billington University announced the findings of a study comparing the health of residents in large cities and rural areas. The research project started a decade ago, with scientists gathering information from 500 urban residents and 500 participants who live in rural areas. **4** Both groups filled out health information surveys four times a year for the past ten years. The results were obtained from the data gathered through the surveys.

Many experts were surprised that the health of country residents was poorer than that of city residents. Nearly 70 percent of city residents reported good health, with the figure only at 62 percent for country participants. Experts say there are several reasons for this, including the lack of healthcare facilities and educational programs in rural areas. **5** The study also showed that those living in cities had healthier diets.

However, country residents did show fewer signs of stress. Of the city participants, 43 percent said they had stressful lives, while the rate was only 22 percent for country residents.

연구 결과가 놀라운 발견을 보여 주다

3 월요일 오전 기자 회견에서, 빌링턴 대학의 교수진은 대도시 거주자들과 시골 지역의 거주자들의 건강을 비교한 연구 결과를 발표했다. 그 연구는 10년 전에 시작했으며, 과학자들이 500명의 도시 거주자들과 500명의 시골 지역에 살고 있는 참가자들로부터 정보를 모았다. **4** 두 집단은 지난 10년간 일 년에 네 번 건강 정보 설문지를 작성했다. 그 결과는 설문 조사를 통해 모은 데이터로부터 얻어졌다.

많은 전문가들은 시골 지역 거주자들의 건강이 도시 지역에 사는 거주자들보다 더 좋지 못하다는 것에 놀랐다. 도시 거주자들의 약 70%가 건강이 양호하다고 보고하였으나, 시골 참가자들은 62%만이 그 수치를 보였다. 전문가들은 여기에는 시골 지역의 건강 관리 시설 및 교육 프로그램의 부족을 포함한 몇 가지 이유가 있다고 했다. **5** 그 연구는 또한 도시 지역에 사는 사람들이 더 건강한 음식들을 섭취한다는 것을 보여 주었다.

그러나, 시골 거주자들은 더 적은 스트레스의 징후를 보였다. 도시 참가자들 중 43%가 그들이 스트레스가 많은 삶을 살고 있다고 말한 반면에, 시골 거주자들에 대한 비율은 단지 22%였다.

어휘| study 연구 finding (*pl.*) 발견, 결과 compare 비교하다 rural 시골의 gather 모으다, 축적하다 urban 도시의 fill out ~을 기입하다 obtain 얻다 expert 전문가 lack 부족, 결핍 healthcare 건강 관리 educational 교육적인 diet 음식 rate 비율

3 What was the study conducted by Billington University mainly about?
(A) Improved healthcare facilities
(B) Rising rates of urban populations
(C) The health of two groups of residents
(D) Increasing levels of medical problems

빌링턴 대학에 의해 수행된 연구의 주제는?
개선된 건강 관리 시설
도시 인구의 증가율
두 거주자 집단의 건강
의료 문제의 증가 수치

해설| 단서 **3**의 At a press conference(기자 회견에서)라는 표현 다음에 이 글 전체의 주제가 등장한다. 대도시 거주자들과 시골 지역 거주자들의 건강을 비교한 연구 결과(the findings of a study comparing the health of residents in large cities and rural areas)라는 직접적인 표현이 있으므로 정답은 (C).

패러프레이징| **단서** residents in large cities and rural areas → **정답** two groups of residents

---

4 What is indicated about the results of the study?
(A) They are not completely accurate.
(B) They are based on several surveys.
(C) They were not surprising to experts.
(D) They will be updated at a later time.

연구 결과에 대해 시사된 것은?
완전히 정확하지는 않다.
몇몇 설문 조사에 근거한다.
전문가들에게는 놀랍지 않았다.
나중에 업데이트될 것이다.

---

5 What does the article mention about people living in cities?
(A) They have poorer medical care facilities.
(B) They are dissatisfied with educational programs.
(C) They eat healthier food than country residents.
(D) They have less stressful lives.

도시에 사는 사람들에 대해 기사에서 언급된 것은?
더 열악한 의료 관리 시설을 갖고 있다.
교육 프로그램에 불만족스러워 한다.
시골 거주자보다 더 건강에 좋은 음식을 먹는다.
스트레스가 더 적은 삶을 살고 있다.

---

3 제품/서비스 광고 Product/Service Advertisement   교재 289쪽

1 (D) **2** (C) **3** (B) **4** (A) **5** (D)

Pangea! Always a smooth flight!

Are you looking for an airline with fewer flight delays and cancellations? With Pangea International Airlines, you can stop worrying about those problems and enjoy your trip. We are known for having the lowest rates of delays and cancellations of all airlines, and we will take you safely to one of more than 100 destinations worldwide. We've been the winner of the Customer Service Award from the Global Airline Organization for the past two years.

So why not book your next flight by visiting our Web site at www.pangeaintairlines.com and experience our excellent service for yourself?

We hope to see you aboard one of our flights soon!

팡지아! 언제나 원활한 비행!

항공편 연착과 취소가 더 적은 항공사를 찾고 계십니까? 팡지아 인터내셔널 에어라인즈 사와 함께 하시면, 이런 문제들에 대한 걱정을 하지 않고 여행을 즐기실 수 있습니다. 저희는 모든 항공사 중 가장 낮은 연착률 및 취소율로 알려져 있으며, 여러분들을 전 세계 100개 이상의 목적지 중 하나로 안전하게 모셔 드릴 것입니다. 저희는 지난 2년간 세계 항공 기구의 고객 서비스상의 수상 업체였습니다.

그러니 저희 웹사이트인 www.pangeaintairlines.com으로 방문하셔서 여러분의 다음 항공편을 예약하시고, 저희의 훌륭한 서비스를 직접 경험해 보시는 게 어떨까요?

저희는 조만간 여러분이 저희 비행기 중 한 대에 탑승하신 것을 보고 싶습니다!

EASY-BACK 2300!

Do you need a comfortable office chair that supports your back? Then look no further than the all-new Easy-Back 2300! This chair was created by a team of designers and medical experts who developed a structure that supports the back.

이지-백 2300!

여러분의 등을 지탱해 줄 편한 사무실 의자가 필요하십니까? 그렇다면 완전히 새로운 이지-백 2300 외에 더 보실 필요가 없습니다! 이 의자는 등을 지탱해 주는 구조를 개발한 디자이너와 의학 전문가

1 Unlike others, our chairs come equipped with a spinal support system which is ideal for office workers or those spending long periods sitting down.

Each chair is crafted from stainless steel and genuine leather. We also provide a money-back guarantee for one year. **2** You can find our chairs at Business-Co office supply stores nationwide, or at many office furniture retailers. For a list of outlets, visit our Web site at www.easybackchairs.com.

팀에 의해 만들어졌습니다. **1** 다른 것들과 달리, 저희 의자들은 척추를 지지해 주는 시스템을 갖추어 나오며 이는 사무직 근로자들이나 오랜 시간을 앉아서 보내는 분들께 이상적입니다.

각각의 의자는 스테인리스강과 천연 가죽으로 공들여 만들어졌습니다. 저희는 또한 일 년간 환불 보증도 제공합니다. **2** 여러분은 전국의 비즈니스-코 사무용품점이나 여러 사무용 가구 소매업체에서 저희 의자를 찾아보실 수 있습니다. 판매점의 목록을 원하시면, 저희 웹사이트인 www.easybackchairs.com을 방문하세요.

어휘| comfortable 편한, 기분 좋은 support 지탱하다, 지지하다 back 등 further than ~보다 더 medical expert 의학 전문가 structure 구조(물) come (제품 등이) 나오다, 생산되다 spinal 척추의 be ideal for ~에 이상적이다 period 시간, 기간 craft 공들여 만들다 stainless steel 스테인리스강[鋼] genuine 진짜의 leather 가죽 guarantee 품질 보증서 office supply 사무용품 outlet 판매점

1 What is a characteristic of the Easy-Back 2300?
(A) It has adjustable parts.
(B) It includes a lifetime guarantee.
(C) It is less expensive than similar items.
(D) **It comes with a unique support system.**

이지-백 2300의 특징은?
조절 가능한 부품들이 있다.
평생 보증서가 들어 있다.
비슷한 제품들보다 덜 비싸다.
독특한 지지 시스템을 갖추어 나온다.

어휘| adjustable 조절 가능한 lifetime 평생, 일생

해설| 광고하고 있는 제품의 특장점은 광고 지문의 가장 핵심적인 부분이라고 할 수 있다. 단서 **1**에서 다른 의자와는 다르게 척추 지지 시스템(a spinal support system)을 갖추었다고 했으므로 정답은 (D)이다.

2 How can the Easy-Back 2300 be purchased?
(A) By visiting a Web site
(B) By filling out a form
(C) **By going to a retail store**
(D) By placing a phone call

이지-백 2300을 구매할 수 있는 방법은?
웹사이트를 방문해서
서식을 작성해서
소매업체에 가서
전화 주문을 해서

해설| You can find(당신은 ~을 찾으실 수 있습니다)로 시작하는 단서 **2**에서 특정 업체의 사무용품 매장(office supply stores)이나 사무용 가구 소매업체(office furniture retailers)에서 물건을 살 수 있다고 했다. 따라서 정답은 (C)이다.
오답| (A) 웹사이트에서는 판매점의 목록을 제공하고 있다고 했으므로 오답.

3 Maharani's Kitchen Introduces
HOME DELIVERY SERVICE!

3 Are you tired of eating the same thing for dinner every day? Then add some spice to your life and order a home delivery meal from Maharani's Kitchen, located at 629 Bohemia Boulevard. We provide quality foods, using only the freshest ingredients, **4** at prices that anyone can afford. To promote this brand-new service, the following meals are offered at only $28:

- *Beef curry meal: includes curry, rice, flat bread, and salad*
- *Tandoori chicken meal: includes chicken, rice, and salad*

3 마하라니 키친에서 자택 배달 서비스를 소개합니다!

3 매일 저녁으로 똑같은 것을 먹는 것에 싫증 나셨나요? 그렇다면 여러분의 삶에 자극을 더하고, 보헤미안 대로 629번지에 위치한 마하라니 키친에서 자택 배달을 시켜 보세요. 저희는 가장 신선한 재료만을 이용한 질 좋은 음식을 **4** 누구나 지불할 수 있는 가격에 제공합니다. 이 신규 서비스를 홍보하고자, 다음의 식사류가 단돈 28달러에 제공됩니다:

- 쇠고기 카레 정식: 카레, 쌀밥, 난, 샐러드가 포함됩니다
- 탄두리 치킨 정식: 치킨, 쌀밥, 샐러드가 포함됩니다

• *Vegetable curry meal: includes curry, rice, and salad*

Take advantage of this special offer this week only from June 6 to 12. To place an order, simply call us at (604) 555-7676. This service is only available to residents of this city. Delivery time usually takes between 30 and 40 minutes. Orders will not be taken within 1 hour of our closing time of 10 P.M.

5B To learn about our other menu options and **5C** special offers, or **5A** to inquire about delivery services, visit the restaurant's Web site at www.maharaniskitchen.com.

• 채소 카레 정식: 카레, 쌀밥, 샐러드가 포함됩니다

6월 6일부터 12일까지, 오직 이번 주에만 이 특별한 혜택을 이용해 보세요. 주문하시려면, (604) 555-7676번으로 저희에게 전화만 주시면 됩니다. 이 서비스는 이 도시의 거주자에 한해 이용 가능합니다. 배달 시간은 보통 30분에서 40분 소요됩니다. 오후 10시인 폐점 시각 한 시간 이내에는 주문을 받지 않습니다.

5B 저희의 다른 선택 메뉴와 **5C** 특별 혜택에 대해 알고 싶으시거나, **5A** 배달 서비스에 대해 문의하시려면, 레스토랑 웹사이트인 www.maharanis kitchen.com을 방문하세요.

어휘| be tired of ~에 싫증나다   spice 자극, 흥미   located at ~에 위치하다   boulevard 대로, 도로   quality 질 좋은, 고급의   ingredient 재료   afford ~할 여유가 있다   promote 홍보하다   brand-new 새로운   beef 쇠고기   vegetable 채소   take advantage of ~을 이용하다

3 What is being advertised?
(A) Added menu items
(B) A new service
(C) Extended business hours
(D) A banquet event

광고되고 있는 것은?
추가된 메뉴
신규 서비스
연장된 영업 시간
연회 행사

어휘| extended (시간 등이) 연장된

해설| 광고의 특성상 광고되고 있는 대상은 지문 초반에 직접적으로 드러난다. 제목에서 HOME DELIVERY SERVICE(자택 배달 서비스)를 확인할 수 있고, 단서 **3**에서 자택 배달을 권하고 있다. 배달은 서비스의 일종이므로 정답은 (B).

4 What is mentioned about Maharani's Kitchen?
(A) It has affordable prices.
(B) It only uses local ingredients.
(C) It accepts orders any time of day.
(D) It opened for business a week ago.

마라하니 키친에 대해 언급된 것은?
가격이 저렴하다.
지역의 재료만을 사용한다.
하루 중 언제든 주문을 받는다.
일주일 전에 가게를 열었다.

어휘| affordable 저렴한, 알맞은

해설| 단서 **4**에서 누구나 지불할 수 있는 가격이라고 했다. 따라서 정답은 (A).
오답| (B)는 지역의(local) 재료가 아니고 가장 신선한(freshest) 재료를 쓴다고 했으므로 오답. (D)는 폐점 시각인 오후 10시의 한 시간 전부터는 주문을 받지 않는다고 했으므로 오답.

패러프레이징| 단서 prices that anyone can afford → 정답 affordable prices

5 What is NOT available on the Web site?
(A) Details on delivery services
(B) A list of other food offerings
(C) Information on special promotions
(D) An online order form

웹사이트에서 볼 수 없는 것은?
배달 서비스의 세부 사항
다른 식사 제공 목록
특별 홍보에 대한 정보
온라인 주문 양식서

해설| NOT 유형 문제이므로 선택지의 핵심어들을 파악한 다음, 지문 내용과 대조해가며 하나씩 소거해 보자. 웹사이트에서 살펴 볼 수 있는 내용들은 지문 후반부에 나온다. 단서 **5B**의 다른 메뉴 선택 사항(other menu options)이나 단서 **5C**의 특별 혜택(special offers)은 선택지 (B)와 (C)로 패러프레이징 되었고, 단서 **5A**의 delivery service(배달 서비스)에 대한 내용은 선택지 (A)에서 등장하였다. 따라서 언급되지 않은 선택지인 (D)가 정답이다.

POSITION NOW AVAILABLE:
Edward Regency Hotel

The Edward Regency Hotel is currently looking for two new members for its housekeeping staff. The selected applicants will start the job on May 20. A minimum of two years of housekeeping experience is required, but training will be provided. Knowledge of cleaning equipment is also an asset. Candidates should be willing to work some weekend shifts. We offer good salaries with a generous benefits package. Employees are provided two weeks of annual vacation and receive insurance coverage.

To apply for a position, drop off a copy of your résumé at the hotel's administrative office, located at 443 Ninth Avenue. Only selected candidates will be contacted for interviews, which will take place on May 16.

현재 지원 가능한 자리:
에드워드 리젠시 호텔

에드워드 리젠시 호텔에서 현재 새로운 청소 직원 두 명을 구하고 있습니다. 선택된 지원자들은 5월 20일에 업무를 시작하게 될 것입니다. 최소 2년의 호텔 청소 경력이 요구되지만, 교육이 제공될 것입니다. 청소 장비에 대한 지식 역시 유용합니다. 지원자들은 주말 교대에도 기꺼이 일할 수 있어야 합니다. 저희는 후한 복리후생 제도와 함께 넉넉한 급여를 제공합니다. 직원들은 2주일의 연차 휴가를 제공받고, 보험 보장도 받게 됩니다.

일자리에 지원하시려면, 이력서를 9번가 443번지에 위치한 호텔의 행정실에 갖다 내세요. 선정된 지원자들만이 5월 16일에 있을 면접을 위해 연락받을 것입니다.

어휘| currently 현재　housekeeping (호텔·병원 등의) 청소 (업무)　minimum 최소의　require 요구하다　knowledge 지식　asset 자산, 유용한 것　shift 교대[근무조]　salary 급여, 봉급　benefits package (회사 등의) 복리후생 제도　drop off ~을 갖다 놓다　take place 일어나다, 발생하다

Appleton Bakery, located at 913 Vineyard Avenue, is a family-run business that has been in operation for forty years. ❶ We currently have a vacant position for a morning shift sales clerk. Some weekend shifts may also be required on occasion, but overtime pay will be provided. We offer competitive salaries and a standard benefits package. Applicants should have at least one year of experience in retail.

❷ Please send a résumé, cover letter, and at least one reference to anitachoi@appletonbakery.com. Make sure to include your contact information so that we may call you for an interview. Only those who meet the requirements for the position will be contacted.

바인야드 로 913번지에 위치한 애플턴 베이커리는 40년간 운영되어 온 가족 경영 사업체입니다. ❶ **저희는 현재 오전 근무 시간의 판매원 자리가 비어 있습니다.** 경우에 따라 주말 근무도 약간 필요할 수 있지만, 초과 근무 수당이 제공될 것입니다. 저희는 경쟁력 있는 급여와 표준 복지 혜택을 제공합니다. 지원자들은 소매업에 최소 1년의 경력이 있어야 합니다.

❷ **이력서, 자기 소개서, 그리고 최소 한 부의 추천서를 anitachoi@appletonbakery.com으로 보내 주세요.** 면접을 위해 저희가 전화할 수 있도록 연락처를 꼭 포함시켜 주세요. 요구 조건을 충족하는 사람에게만 연락이 갈 것입니다.

어휘| family-run 가족이 운영하는　in operation 운영 중인　vacant (자리가) 빈　on occasion 때때로　overtime pay 초과 근무 수당　competitive 수준 높은, 경쟁력 있는　cover letter 자기 소개서　meet requirements 요구 조건을 충족시키다

1　Who is the business looking to hire?
(A) A full-time baker
(B) A sales assistant
(C) A delivery person
(D) A kitchen cook

가게가 고용하려고 찾는 사람은?
정규직 제빵사
판매 점원
배달원
주방 요리사

해설| 단서 **1**의 We currently have a vacant position for(저희는 현재 ~에 공석이 있습니다)라는 부분을 통해 어떤 사람을 구인하는지를 알 수 있다. 오전 근무 시간의 판매원 자리가 공석이라고 했으므로 정답은 (B)이다.

오답| (A)는 광고를 낸 가게가 제과점인 것에서 연상할 수 있는 오답이다.

패러프레이징| 단서 sales clerk → 정답 sales assistant

---

2 What should people interested in the position do?
(A) E-mail the bakery
(B) Fill out the provided forms
(C) Visit an establishment
(D) Call the business's owner

이 자리에 관심 있는 사람들이 해야 할 일은?
제과점에 이메일 보내기
제공된 양식 작성하기
시설에 방문하기
사업주에게 전화 걸기

어휘| establishment 시설, 기관

해설| 단서 **2**에서 명시된 이메일 주소로 이력서, 자기 소개서, 그리고 최소 한 부의 추천서를 보내 달라고 했다. 따라서 정답은 (A).

오답| (B) 제공된(provided) 양식은 언급된 바 없으므로 오답이다.

패러프레이징| 단서 send a résumé, ~ to anitachoi@appletonbakery.com → 정답 E-mail the bakery

---

Heathcliff Savings Bank
POSITION AVAILABLE

3 Heathcliff Savings Bank has a job opening for a full-time manager for a team of bank tellers and customer service associates. A university degree in management or a related field is required. Only those with at least five years of previous bank managerial experience will be considered. The successful candidate will report directly to the branch manager.

The selected applicant will be responsible for **4A** providing training, **4B** scheduling work shifts, handling payroll, **4C** dealing with vacation requests, and making sure the employees maintain high levels of service in the bank.

It is necessary for applicants to send a résumé, cover letter, and two references to: Adam Lewis, Branch Manager, Heathcliff Savings Bank, 3388 Sullivan Street, Edgewood, WI 53072. **5** Telephone interviews will be conducted first, and then final candidates will be invited to visit our offices to meet with a panel of bank executives.

히드클리프 저축 은행
지원 가능한 자리

3 히드클리프 저축 은행은 은행 창구 직원들과 고객 서비스 직원들로 구성된 팀의 정규직 관리자 자리에 공석이 있습니다. 경영이나 관련 분야의 학사 학위가 요구됩니다. 이전에 최소 5년의 은행 관리 경력을 가진 사람들만이 대상으로 고려될 것입니다. 합격한 후보자는 지점장에게 직접 업무 보고를 하게 될 것입니다.

선택된 지원자는 **4A** 연수 제공하기, **4B** 교대 근무조 일정 정하기, 급여 처리하기, **4C** 휴가 요청 처리하기, 직원들로 하여금 은행에서 높은 수준의 서비스를 확실히 유지시키기의 책임을 맡게 될 것입니다.

지원자들은 필수적으로 이력서, 자기 소개서, 그리고 추천서 2부를 53072 위스콘신 주, 에지우드, 설리번 가 3388번지 히드클리프 저축 은행의 지점장, 아담 루이스 씨에게 보내야 합니다. **5** 먼저 전화 면접이 있은 후, 최종 후보자들은 은행 경영진 패널을 만나기 위해 저희 사무실로 방문하도록 요청될 것입니다.

어휘| bank teller 은행원 associate 직원, 동료 degree 학위 related 관련된 managerial 관리(상)의 consider 고려[숙고]하다 successful 합격한, 성공한 directly 직접 training 연수, 훈련 deal with ~을 처리하다 final 최종의 executive 경영진

3 What position is Heathcliff Savings Bank looking to fill?
(A) Bank teller
(B) Branch manager
(C) Team leader
(D) Customer service employee.

히드클리프 저축 은행이 충원하려고 찾는 직책은?
은행원
지점장
팀장
고객 서비스 직원

해설 | 단서 **3**에서 a job opening for(~을 위한 공석)라는 표현 뒤에 광고되고 있는 직책이 등장한다. 은행 창구 직원들과 고객 서비스 직원들의 팀을 위한 정규직 관리자가 필요하다고 했으므로 정답은 (C)이다.

패러프레이징 | 단서 a full-time manager for a team of bank tellers and customer service associates → 정답 Team leader

4 What is NOT mentioned as a responsibility of the selected applicant?
(A) Training employees
(B) Making schedules
(C) Handling vacation requests
(D) Dealing with customers

선택된 지원자의 책무로 언급되지 않은 것은?
직원 연수시키기
일정 정하기
휴가 요청 처리하기
고객들 대하기

해설 | NOT이 포함된 문제이므로 지문에서 be responsible for(~의 책임을 맡다)라는 표현 뒤에 열거된 단서를 하나씩 대조해서 살펴본다. 단서 **4A**에서 연수 제공하기(providing training), **4B**에서 교대 근무조 일정 정하기(scheduling work shifts), **4C**에서 휴가 요청 처리하기(dealing with vacation requests)가 각각 등장한다. 따라서 언급되지 않은 (D)가 정답.

5 What is suggested about the hiring process?
(A) It takes at least a week.
(B) It involves more than one interview.
(C) It is conducted twice a year.
(D) It requires e-mailed documents.

채용 과정에 관해서 암시된 바는?
최소 일주일이 걸린다.
한 개 이상의 면접이 포함된다.
일 년에 두 번 시행된다.
이메일로 보낸 서류들이 필요하다.

해설 | 마지막 문장인 단서 **5**에서 먼저 전화 면접이 있고 나서, 최종 후보자들이 경영진 패널을 만나기 위해 사무실에 오게 될 것이라고 했으므로 두 번의 면접이 있을 것임을 추론할 수 있다. 따라서 정답은 (B).

PARAPHRASING 패러프레이징(2)　　　　교재 296쪽

1 (A) **2** (A) **3** (B) **4** (B) **5** (A) **6** (B) **7** (B) **8** (A) **9** (A)

1 difficult to reject the offer → hard to **turn down** the proposal
(A) **turn down** (B) discuss

제안을 거절하기 어려운 → 제안을 거절하기 어려운
(A) 거절하다 (B) 토론하다

2 frequently work together on advertisements → often **collaborate** on commercials
(A) **collaborate** (B) negotiate

빈번하게 광고에 대해 협력하다 → 자주 광고를 <u>공동 작업하다</u>
(A) 협력하다[공동 작업하다] (B) 협상하다

3 the start day of a job → the first day in a **position**
(A) membership **(B) position**

일의 시작일 → 직위의 첫 날
(A) 회원권 **(B) 직위**

4 show ID → **present** some identification
(A) display **(B) present**

신분증을 보여 주다 → 신분증을 제시하다
(A) 전시하다 **(B) 제시하다**

5 The company met with the supplier in order to discuss a contract.
(A) The company and the provider gathered to negotiate some terms.
(B) The supplier signed a contract that the company proposed.

계약에 대해 논의하기 위해서 회사는 공급업체와 만났다.
(A) 조건을 협상하기 위해 회사와 공급업체가 모였다.
(B) 공급업체는 회사가 제안한 계약서에 서명을 했다.

6 The human resources manager has interviewed some candidates.
(A) People are interested in the interview for the human resources position.
(B) Some applicants were interviewed by the department manager.

인사부 부장은 몇몇 후보자들을 면접했다.
(A) 사람들은 인사팀 자리를 위한 면접에 관심이 있다.
(B) 몇몇 지원자들은 부장에 의해 면접을 보았다.

---

7 The department head will attach a revised work schedule to the e-mail.
(A) The department head will send a new job advertisement by e-mail.
(B) An updated shift timetable will be attached to the e-mail by the team leader.

부서장은 수정된 작업 일정을 이메일에 첨부할 것이다.
(A) 부서장은 이메일로 새로운 구인 광고를 보낼 것이다.
(B) 최신 교대근무 시간표가 팀장에 의해 이메일에 첨부될 것이다.

8-9

I am writing to let you know that I have reserved the Rosehill Convention Center for the Marketing Strategies Conference on June 1. It was the **8** venue for the awards ceremony last year. **9B** The main room there can accommodate a hundred people. Tables and chairs are provided, and **7A** we will hire a catering service to have some refreshments during the event. You asked whether you would be able to show some slides for your presentation, and I did get confirmation that the room has a projector.

저는 6월 1일 마케팅 전략 회의를 위해 로즈힐 컨벤션 센터를 예약했다는 것을 귀하에게 알려 드리기 위해 글을 쓰고 있습니다. 그곳은 지난 해의 시상식 **8** 장소였습니다. **9B** 그곳의 본실은 100명을 수용할 수 있습니다. 탁자들과 의자들은 제공될 것이며, **7A** 저희는 행사 동안 간단한 음식을 먹기 위해서 출장 요리 서비스를 고용할 것입니다. 귀하의 발표를 위해 슬라이드를 보여 줄 수 있을지 문의하셨었는데, 제가 그 방에 프로젝터가 있다는 것을 확인받았습니다.

어휘| reserve 예약하다 catering 출장 요리 refreshments 다과, 간단한 음식 confirmation 확인

8 The word "venue" in paragraph 1, line 2, is closest in meaning to
(A) location
(B) reservation

첫째 단락 두 번째 줄의 "venue"와 의미상 가장 가까운 단어는?
(A) 장소
(B) 예약

해설| 단서 **8**로 표시된 해당 어휘 바로 앞 문장에서 로즈힐 컨벤션 센터를 예약했다고 했으므로 해당 어휘와 동격인, 문장의 주어 It이 가리키는 것은 행사를 위한 '장소'임을 알 수 있다. 따라서 정답은 (A).

---

9 What is NOT indicated about the main room?
(A) It provides free catering services.
(B) It has seating for a hundred people.

본실에 대해 시사되지 않은 것은?
(A) 무료 음식 제공 서비스를 공급한다.
(B) 100명의 사람을 위한 자리가 있다.

해설| NOT 유형 문제이므로 지문과 같은 내용의 선택지를 소거한다. 단서 **9B**에서 본실은 100명을 수용할 수 있다고 했으므로 (B)는 옳은 내용. 단서 **7A**에서 간단한 음식을 먹기 위해 출장 요리 서비스를 고용할 것(hire a catering service)이라고 했으므로 무료가 아님을 알 수 있다. 따라서 정답은 (A).

1 공지/메모 Announcement/Memorandum

교재 301쪽

1 (D) **2** (A) **3** (B) **4** (A) **5** (C)

NOTICE: Entrance Closure

This notice is for all tenants in Westerly Towers. Please be reminded that the building's main entrance on Carlin Avenue will be closed tomorrow, April 29. The floors in the main lobby will undergo repairs, and the entrance will be closed for the convenience of the work crew.

We request that all tenants use the rear entrance of the building or the side doors on Leighton Avenue instead. The main entrance will be available for use again from April 30. Please contact us if you have any questions. We apologize for the inconvenience and thank you for your cooperation in this matter.

Westerly Towers Building Administration

공지: 입구 폐쇄

이 공지는 웨스터리 타워즈의 모든 세입자를 위한 것입니다. 칼린 로 쪽의 건물 중앙 출입구가 내일 4월 29일에 폐쇄될 예정이라는 것을 기억하세요. 중앙 로비에 있는 바닥이 수리될 것이며, 출입구는 작업자들의 편의를 위해 폐쇄될 것입니다.

저희는 대신에 모든 세입자들이 건물의 후문이나 라이튼 로 쪽의 옆문을 이용하시기를 요청합니다. 중앙 출입구는 4월 30일부터 다시 사용이 가능하게 될 것입니다. 질문이 있으시면 저희에게 연락 주세요. 불편함에 사과드리며, 이 일에 협조해 주셔서 감사드립니다.

웨스터리 타워즈 건물 관리팀

어휘| entrance 입구 closure 폐쇄, 닫음 undergo 겪다, 받다 convenience 편의 rear 뒤의 instead 대신에 apologize for ~에 대해 사과하다 cooperation 협조, 협력 administration 관리, 행정

MEMO

To: Front desk staff
From: Elena Klum, Hotel Manager
Subject: Holiday work schedule
Date: December 18

The holiday season is coming, so ❶ I want to let you know about some opportunities to earn some extra income. As this is a busy time of year at the hotel, we are looking for people to work additional shifts on December 24 and 25. Those of you who choose to work on those days will be eligible for overtime pay. Moreover, you will receive two additional vacation days to use in the future. ❷ Please send me an e-mail by Friday with your availability and preferred shifts. If you require further information, feel free to contact me anytime. Thank you for your cooperation.

메모

수신: 프런트 데스크 직원들
발신: 호텔 매니저 엘레나 클룸
제목: 공휴일 업무 일정
날짜: 12월 18일

휴가 시즌이 다가오고 있어서 ❶ **여러분께 추가 소득을 얻을 수 있는 기회에 관해 알려 드리고 싶습니다.** 이때는 호텔에서 일 년 중 바쁜 시기이므로, 우리는 12월 24일과 25일에 추가 근무를 할 사람들을 찾고 있습니다. 여러분 중 이날들에 일하기로 결정한 분들은 초과 근무 수당을 받을 수 있습니다. 게다가 여러분은 나중에 사용할 추가 휴가도 이틀 받게 될 것입니다. ❷ **여러분의 업무 가능 여부와 선호 근무 시간을 금요일까지 저에게 이메일로 보내 주세요.** 추가 정보가 필요하시면, 저에게 아무 때나 연락해 주세요. 협조해 주셔서 감사합니다.

어휘| overtime 시간 외의, 초과근무의 availability (시간) 가능성 feel free to do 마음껏 ~하다

---

1 What is the main purpose of the memo?
(A) To thank employees for their hard work
(B) To request payment for a hotel reservation
(C) To invite personnel to an end-of-year party
(D) To announce a chance to get additional pay

메모의 주된 목적은?
직원들에게 그들의 노고에 대해 감사하려고
호텔 예약에 대한 지불을 요청하려고
직원들을 연말 파티에 초대하려고
추가 보수를 얻을 수 있는 기회를 알리려고

어휘| personnel 직원들, 인원

해설| 단서 **1**의 I want to let you know(저는 당신에게 ~을 알려드리고 싶습니다) 뒷부분에서 메모의 주제가 언급되고 있다. 추가 소득을 얻을 기회를 알려 주겠다고 했으므로 정답은 (D).

오답| (B) hotel에서 연상할 수 있는 어휘 reservation을 이용한 오답. (C) 12월 24일과 25일에서 연상할 수 있는 어휘 end-of-year를 이용한 오답이다.

패러프레이징| 단서 some opportunities to earn some extra income → 정답 a chance to get additional pay

2 What do front desk employees need to do by Friday?
(A) Send a response by e-mail
(B) Update a reservations list
(C) Fill out a vacation request form
(D) Provide their contact details

프런트 직원들이 금요일까지 해야 할 일은?
이메일로 답장 보내기
예약 목록 업데이트하기
휴가 요청서 작성하기
본인의 상세 연락처 제공하기

어휘| response 응답

해설| 요청하는 내용을 묻는 질문은 메모 양식에서 단골로 등장하는 유형이다. 단서 **2**의 요청 표현인 Please(~해 주세요) 이하의 내용을 통해 그들에게 금요일까지 업무 가능 여부와 선호 근무 시간을 이메일로 보내달라고 하는 것을 알 수 있다. 정답은 (A).

패러프레이징| 단서 send me an e-mail → 정답 Send a response by e-mail

IMPORTANT ANNOUNCEMENT:
Dellacourt City Transit Authority

3 This is to notify all passengers of the Dellacourt City subway system that the regular hours of operation will be changed for the upcoming long weekend. Train service will be offered from 7 A.M. to 10 P.M. from Saturday, July 2 to Monday, July 4. In addition, trains will arrive at stations every fifteen minutes rather than every eight minutes. **4** Subway service will return to the regular hours of operation on July 5. The airport line's schedule will remain the same during this time, departing every thirty minutes.

5 You are advised to check the holiday service schedules posted at ticketing counters in each station for further details. You may also log on to our Web site at www.dellacourttransit.com to view the modified timetables or call us at 555-0097. We thank you for your cooperation and understanding and hope you enjoy the holiday.

중요 공고: 델라코트 시 교통 당국

3 이것은 델라코트 시 지하철 시스템의 모든 승객들에게 곧 있을 긴 주말 연휴 동안 정기 운행 시간이 변경될 것임을 알려 주기 위함입니다. 열차 서비스는 7월 2일 토요일에서부터 7월 4일 월요일까지 오전 7시부터 오후 10시까지 제공될 것입니다. 또한, 열차들은 8분마다 도착하는 것 대신에 15분마다 역에 도착할 것입니다. **4** 지하철 서비스는 7월 5일에 정기 운행 시간으로 돌아올 것입니다. 공항선 일정은 이 시기 동안 그대로 유지되어 매 30분마다 출발할 것입니다.

5 추가 정보를 위해서 각 역의 매표소에 게시된 휴일 서비스 일정을 확인하시길 권해드립니다. 수정된 시간표를 보시려면 저희의 웹사이트인 www.dellacourttransit.com에 로그인하시거나 555-0097번으로 저희에게 전화 주세요. 여러분들의 협조와 이해에 감사드리며, 여러분들이 휴일을 즐겁게 보내시기를 바랍니다.

어휘| transit 교통, 운송 authority 당국 passenger 승객 return to ~로 되돌아가다 remain ~인 채로 남다 depart 출발하다 ticketing counter 매표소 log on (접속하여) 로그인하다 modified 수정된 thank A for B A에게 B에 대해 감사하다

3 What is the announcement mainly about?
(A) Employee work timetables for a holiday
(B) Scheduling changes for a transit service
(C) New policies for requesting a transport pass
(D) Upcoming maintenance work on a subway system

공고의 주제는?
휴일 동안의 직원 근무 시간표
교통 서비스의 일정 변경
교통 승차권 요청에 대한 새로운 정책들
지하철 시스템의 향후 유지보수 작업

어휘ㅣ transport pass 교통 승차권

해설ㅣ 공지의 주제는 앞부분에 보통 언급된다. 단서 **3** 에서 지하철 승객들을 위해 주말 연휴 동안 정기 운행 시간이 변경됨을 알려 주고 있으므로 정답은 (B)이다.

오답ㅣ (C)의 지하철을 탈 수 있는 승차권에 관련된 내용과 (D)의 지하철에 유지보수를 한다는 내용은 전혀 언급이 되지 않았으므로 오답 이다.

패러프레이징ㅣ 단서 the regular hours of operation will be changed → 정답 Scheduling changes

4 What will take place on July 5?
(A) Regular hours of operation will resume.
(B) A subway system will shorten its hours.
(C) An airport train will stop its services.
(D) Departure schedules will be posted.

7월 5일에 있을 일은?
정규 운행 시간이 재개될 것이다.
지하철 시스템이 운영 시간을 줄일 것이다.
공항 철도가 서비스를 중단할 것이다.
출발 일정이 게시될 것이다.

어휘ㅣ resume 재개되다

해설ㅣ 세부 내용을 묻는 유형의 문제로 질문의 키워드인 7월 5일을 지문에서 찾아보니 단서 **4** 부분이다. 여기서 7월 5일에 정기 운행 시간으로 돌아온다고 했으므로 정답은 (A)이다.

오답ㅣ (B) 7월 2일부터 4일까지 휴일 동안에만 지하철 운영 시간이 변경되는 것이므로 오답이다.

패러프레이징ㅣ 단서 return to the regular hours of operation → 정답 Regular hours of operation will resume

5 What are people asked to do?
(A) Purchase tickets in advance
(B) Make reservations online
(C) Check temporary schedules
(D) Apply for transit passes

사람들에게 요청된 일은?
미리 승차권 구매하기
온라인으로 예약하기
임시 일정 확인하기
교통 승차권 신청하기

어휘ㅣ in advance 미리 temporary 임시의

해설ㅣ 단서 **5** 의 조언 You are advised to ~ 이하의 부분을 살펴 보면, 각 역의 매표소에 게시된 휴일 서비스 일정을 확인하라고 했 다. 따라서 정답은 (C). 이 서비스 일정은 휴일 기간에만 한시적으로 적용되는 것이므로 정답에서 temporary(임시의)란 단어를 사용해 서 표현했다.

오답ㅣ (B) 웹사이트 주소가 나오는 것을 이용한 함정.

패러프레이징ㅣ 단서 check the holiday service schedules → 정답 Check temporary schedules

---

2 **대화체 지문** Text Message/Chat Discussion

교재 305쪽

1 (C) **2** (D) **3** (B) **4** (C) **5** (A)

LUIS ZIRINSKY	4:12 P.M.	루이스 지린스키	오후 4:12
There's a lot of traffic on the road, and I won't make it back to our office before the end of the day.		도로에 정체가 상당해서 퇴근 시간 전에 사무실로 돌아가지 못할 것 같아요.	
LUIS ZIRINSKY	4:13 P.M.	루이스 지린스키	오후 4:13
So I need you to do me a favor.		그래서 당신이 부탁 하나 들어줬으면 해요.	
ELISE KELLER	4:14 P.M.	엘리스 켈러	오후 4:14
Sure, what is it?		그럴게요, 뭐예요?	

LUIS ZIRINSKY	4:16 P.M.	루이스 지린스키	오후 4:16
I have an important package on my desk that needs to be mailed out today. Would you please send it for me?		제 책상에 오늘 발송해야 하는 중요한 소포가 있어요. 저 대신 소포를 보내 줄래요?	
ELISE KELLER	4:22 P.M.	엘리스 켈러	오후 4:22
OK. I'll take it over to the post office now.		알겠어요. 지금 우체국으로 가져갈게요.	
ELISE KELLER	4:24 P.M.	엘리스 켈러	오후 4:24
Do you want me to send it by regular mail?		일반 우편으로 보낼까요?	
LUIS ZIRINSKY	4:27 P.M.	루이스 지린스키	오후 4:27
Yes, that's fine. I really appreciate your help.		네, 그게 좋겠어요. 도와줘서 정말 고마워요.	

어휘 | traffic 교통(량), 차량 make it to ~에 도착하다 do A a favor A의 부탁을 들어주다 package 소포 mail out 발송하다
appreciate 고마워하다

BRENT DORRIAN	2:01 P.M.	브렌트 도리안	오후 2:01
Are you still at the stationery store?		아직 문구점에 있어요?	
LARISSA PERKINS	2:02 P.M.	라리사 퍼킨즈	오후 2:02
Yes, I'm here now.		네, 지금 여기 있어요.	
LARISSA PERKINS	2:03 P.M.	라리사 퍼킨즈	오후 2:03
I'm waiting in line to order the invitations for our fundraiser.		우리 모금행사에 쓸 초대장을 주문하려고 줄 서서 기다리고 있어요.	
BRENT DORRIAN	2:14 P.M.	브렌트 도리안	오후 2:14
Great. ❶ I've decided to add a few more agencies to the guest list. ❷ Can you change the size of our order?		잘 됐네요. ❶ 초대손님 목록에 몇몇 업체를 더 추가하기로 결정했거든요. ❷ 우리 주문량을 변경해 주겠어요?	
LARISSA PERKINS	2:19 P.M.	라리사 퍼킨즈	오후 2:19
How many more are you thinking?		얼마나 더 많이 생각하고 계신데요?	
BRENT DORRIAN	2:21 P.M.	브렌트 도리안	오후 2:21
❷ About twenty-five extra.		❷ 추가로 약 25장 정도요.	
LARISSA PERKINS	2:24 P.M.	라리사 퍼킨즈	오후 2:24
Got it.		알겠어요.	
LARISSA PERKINS	2:26 P.M.	라리사 퍼킨즈	오후 2:26
Is there anything else you need?		또 필요한 거 있으세요?	
BRENT DORRIAN	2:31 P.M.	브렌트 도리안	오후 2:31
No. Thanks.		아뇨. 고마워요.	

어휘 | stationery store 문구점 wait in line 줄 서서 기다리다 fundraiser 모금행사 agency 업체, 기관

1 Why did Mr. Dorrian contact Ms. Perkins?
(A) To remind her of a party's budget
(B) To ask to design event invitations
(C) To inform her of changes to an order
(D) To thank her for donating to a fundraiser

도리안 씨가 퍼킨즈 씨에게 연락한 이유는?
파티의 예산을 상기시켜 주려고
행사 초대장 디자인을 부탁하려고
주문 변경에 대해 알려주려고
모금행사에 기부해 준 것에 감사하려고

어휘 | remind A of B A에게 B를 상기시키다 donate 기부하다

해설 | 단서 ❶에서 도리안 씨는 문구점에서 초대장을 주문하려고 하는 퍼킨즈 씨에게 초대 손님을 늘리기로 했다는 결정을 알리면서 Can you change the size of our order?라고 '주문량 변경'을 요청하고 있다. 결국 주문 변경 내용을 알리기 위해 연락한 것이므로 (C)가 정답이다.

2 At 2:24 p.m., what does Ms. Perkins mean when she writes, "Got it"?

(A) She will stop by the stationery store again.
(B) She is confirming a project's budget.
(C) She received the guest list in advance.
(D) She will increase the number of invitations.

오후 2시 24분에 퍼킨즈 씨가 "알겠어요"라고 한 것에서 그녀가 의도한 것은?
문구점에 다시 들르겠다.
프로젝트의 예산을 확인 중이다.
초대손님 목록을 미리 받았다.
초대장 개수를 늘리겠다.

어휘 | confirm 확인하다

해설 | "Got it"은 I got it을 줄인 말로, 상대방이 뭔가를 설명하거나 요청할 때 '알겠다, 이해했다'라는 뜻으로 쓰이는 표현이다. 단서 **2** 에서 Can you change the size of our order?라는 요청에 대해 구체적으로 추가 주문량을 확인한 후, 그에 대한 응답으로 나온 것이므로, 결국 주문량 변경 요청에 대해 '알겠다'고 답한 것이 된다. 따라서 (D)가 정답.

Meredith Hawking [11:11 A.M.]

Hey, Vincent and Robert. **3** I'm overseeing the theater project, and we're almost out of bricks. It looks like we didn't order enough for the east wall.

Vincent Purcell [11:12 A.M.]

I checked the order. It seems that we ordered more than enough bricks according to the measurements. Something is not right.

Robert Schmidt [11:13 A.M.]

Ah, I forgot to tell you about this. **4** The supplier called us this morning and explained that they couldn't deliver all of the bricks at once. So there will be a second delivery. They said it would be made between 2 and 2:30. Is that a problem?

Meredith Hawking [11:14 A.M.]

Actually, I have to leave the site to meet another client at 2. So I won't be here when they make the delivery. Vincent, do you think you could stop by around that time?

Vincent Purcell [11:15 A.M.]

Sure, no problem. I can be there from 1:30 to 3. **5** When the delivery people arrive with the second part of the order, I'll go over it to make sure everything is correct.

Robert Schmidt [11:17 A.M.]

Thanks, Vincent. That would be great.

메레디스 호킹 [오전 11:11]

저기요, 빈센트와 로버트 씨. **3** 제가 극장 프로젝트를 감독하고 있는 중인데요. 벽돌이 거의 다 떨어졌어요. 동쪽 벽 작업용으로 충분히 주문하지 않은 것 같네요.

빈센트 퍼셀 [오전 11:12]

제가 주문을 확인해 봤어요. 측량한 치수에 따라 충분한 양 이상의 벽돌을 주문했던 것 같은데요. 뭔가 맞지 않네요.

로버트 슈미트 [오전 11:13]

아, 제가 이걸 여러분께 얘기하는 걸 잊었네요. **4** 공급업체가 오늘 아침에 전화해서 모든 벽돌들을 한 번에 배달할 수 없겠다고 설명을 했어요. 그래서 두 번째 배달이 있을 거예요. 그게 2시에서 2시 30분 사이가 될 거라고 말했어요. 그게 문제가 될까요?

메레디스 호킹 [오전 11:14]

사실, 저는 다른 고객을 만나기 위해서 2시에 현장을 떠나야 해요. 그래서 그들이 배달해 줄 때 제가 여기에 없을 거예요. 빈센트 씨, 혹시 그 시간쯤에 들르실 수 있을 것 같나요?

빈센트 퍼셀 [오전 11:15]

물론이죠. 문제없어요. 1시 30분부터 3시까지 거기에 있을 수 있어요. **5** 배달하는 사람들이 두 번째 배달 분을 가지고 도착하면, 제가 모든 게 확실히 맞는지 검토해 볼게요.

로버트 슈미트 [오전 11:17]

고마워요, 빈센트 씨. 그래 주면 좋겠어요.

어휘 | oversee 감독하다　out of ~가 떨어진　brick 벽돌　measurement 치수　site 현장　go over ~을 검토하다

3 Where most likely is Ms. Hawking?

(A) In an office building
(B) At a construction site
(C) In a performance hall
(D) At a supplier's headquarters

호킹 씨가 있을 것 같은 장소는?
사무실 건물
건축 현장
공연장
공급업체의 본사

해설| 호킹 씨가 대화를 나누는 중에 있을 것 같은 장소를 묻는 추론 문제. 단서 **3**을 보면, 현재 극장 프로젝트를 감독하고 있다(I'm overseeing the theater project)고 하며 벽돌이 부족한 상황에 대해 얘기하고 있으므로 건축 현장에 있음을 알 수 있다. 정답은 (B).

---

4 Why did a supplier make a phone call?
(A) To explain that an item is sold out
(B) To request that a fee be paid in full
(C) To warn that two deliveries would be made
(D) To confirm that an order amount was modified

공급업체가 전화를 했던 이유는?
물건이 다 팔렸음을 설명하기 위해서
요금의 전액 지불을 요청하기 위해서
두 번 배달이 될 것을 알려 주기 위해서
주문량이 수정되었음을 확인하기 위해서

어휘| fee 요금 in full 전액으로 warn 알려주다, 경고하다 amount 금액 modify 바꾸다

해설| 공급업체의 전화와 관련된 단서 **4**를 살펴보면, 주문품인 벽돌을 한 번에 배달할 수 없어서 두 번째 배달이 온다(there will be a second delivery)는 것을 확인할 수 있다. 정답은 (C). 지문의 called가 질문의 make a phone call로 패러프레이징되었다.

---

5 At 11:15 a.m., what does Mr. Purcell mean when he writes, "I'll go over it"?
(A) He will review a delivery.
(B) He will meet a client.
(C) He will change an order.
(D) He will set up an appointment.

오전 11시 15분에, 퍼셀 씨가 "제가 검토해 볼게요"라고 한 것에서 그가 의도한 바는?
그가 배달을 검토할 것이다.
그는 고객을 만날 것이다.
그는 주문을 변경할 것이다.
그는 약속을 잡을 것이다.

어휘| set up an appointment 약속을 정하다

해설| 단서 **5**에서 해당 표현의 앞뒤 문맥을 통해 배달부들이 두 번째 배달을 가지고 오면 그것이 맞는지 확실히 하기 위해 그것을 '검토한다'는 내용이 되어야 적절하므로 정답은 (A).

오답| (B) 고객을 만날 것은 호킹 씨이므로 오답이다.

패러프레이징| **단서** go over it → **정답** review a delivery

---

3 **웹페이지** Web Page 교재 309쪽

1 (C) **2** (A) **3** (C) **4** (D) **5** (B)

---

http://www.kalakafabrics.com/

| HOME | PRODUCTS | CART | CONTACT |

KALAKA FABRICS
Thank you for visiting Kalaka Inc.!

We are the area's leading apparel retailer. We've been around for more than ten years, and we can provide everything you need to stay warm in the winter and cool in the summer! We hold more items than any of our competitors, and now is a great time to shop! We offer the following deals every winter season:

30% off sweaters
20% off coats
10% off pants

| 홈 | 제품 | 장바구니 | 연락처 |

칼라카 패브릭스
칼라카 주식회사를 방문해 주셔서 감사합니다!

저희는 지역의 선도적인 의류 소매업체입니다. 저희는 약 10년 이상 이어져 왔으며 여러분들이 겨울에는 따뜻하게 지내고 여름에는 시원하게 지내기 위해 필요한 모든 것을 제공해 드릴 수 있습니다! 저희는 그 어떤 경쟁업체보다 더 많은 상품들을 확보하고 있으며 지금이 바로 물건을 구매할 좋은 기회입니다! 저희는 겨울철마다 다음의 혜택을 제공합니다.

스웨터 30% 할인
코트 20% 할인
바지 10% 할인

There is no need to download any coupon. When you check out, simply enter SNOWFLAKE in the code box. Hurry up before items become sold out! To browse our winter apparel, go to the "Products" page and enter a search term.

어떤 쿠폰도 다운로드를 하실 필요가 없습니다. 여러분이 계산을 할 때, 그저 SNOWFLAKE를 코드 란에 입력하기만 하면 됩니다. 물건이 다 팔리기 전에 서두르세요! 저희의 겨울 의상을 살펴보시려면, '제품' 페이지로 가서 검색어를 입력하세요.

어휘| **leading** 선도[주도]하는 **apparel** 의류, 의복 **hold** 확보[보유]하다 **deal** 거래 **term** 말, 용어

---

http://www.pietragallery.com/Exhibitions

| ABOUT | EXHIBITIONS | MEMBERSHIP | CONTACT |

PIETRA GALLERY EXHIBITIONS

We are proud to announce that our April exhibition theme is the sea. Here you can find the dates for each week-long exhibition. **①** As usual, we will host our monthly guest speaker lecture at the gallery on the first of the month from 6 to 8 P.M.

Dates	Artist	Exhibition Title
April 2 – 8	Paulina Smith	*Sailors of Tomorrow*
April 9 – 15	Ivan Lucas	*Underwater Worlds*
April 16 – 22	Noel Lee	*Deep Thoughts*
April 23 – 29	Mia Jackson	*Water Colors*

April 30, 7 P.M. to 9 P.M.: Closing event *
Join us for dinner at the Bruge Hotel. A five-course meal will be served for $45 per person.

*Due to limited space, advanced reservation is required, though payment can be made at the door. **②** Please click here to reserve a seat.

| 소개 | 전시 | 회원권 | 연락처 |

피에트라 미술관 전시

우리는 4월 전시 주제가 바다라는 것을 발표하게 되어 자랑스럽습니다. 여기서 여러분들은 각 일주일간의 전시 날짜를 찾아보실 수 있습니다. **①** 늘 그렇듯이 저희는 미술관에서 이번 달 1일 오후 6시부터 8시까지 월간 초청 인사 강연을 개최할 것입니다.

날짜	예술가	전시 제목
4월 2일–8일	폴리나 스미스	〈내일의 선원들〉
4월 9일–15일	이반 루카스	〈수중 세계〉
4월 16일–22일	노엘 리	〈깊은 사색〉
4월 23일–29일	미아 잭슨	〈물의 색〉

4월 30일, 오후 7시부터 9시까지: 폐막 행사 *
브러지 호텔에서의 저녁 식사에 참여하세요. 다섯 개의 음식이 나오는 코스 식사가 인당 45달러에 제공될 것입니다.

*제한된 공간 때문에, 지불은 현장에서 할 수 있지만, 사전 예약을 필요로 합니다. **②** 좌석을 예약하시려면 여기를 클릭하세요.

어휘| **exhibition** 전시 **be proud to** *do* ~해서 자랑스럽다 **theme** 주제 **week-long** 일주일간의 **lecture** 강연, 강의 **advanced** 사전의, 미리의 **though** ~일지라도

---

1 How often does Pietra Gallery invite guest speakers?
(A) Every day
(B) Every week
(C) Once a month
(D) Once a year

피에트라 미술관이 초청 인사들을 초대하는 빈도는?
매일
매주
한 달에 한 번
일 년에 한 번

해설| 질문의 키워드인 guest speakers가 나오는 부분을 집중해 보자. 단서 **①**을 보면, 늘 그렇듯이 이달 1일에 월간 초청 인사 강연(our monthly guest speaker lecture)을 열 것이라고 했다. monthly는 '한 달에 한 번'이라는 의미이므로 정답은 (C).
패러프레이징| 단서 monthly → 정답 Once a month

---

2 How can visitors sign up for the closing event?
(A) By following a link
(B) By going to the gallery
(C) By displaying their artwork
(D) By paying a fee

방문객들이 폐막 행사에 등록할 수 있는 방법은?
링크를 따라감으로써
미술관에 감으로써
예술작품을 전시함으로써
요금을 냄으로써

해설| 지문 마지막 부분에서 폐막 행사에 대한 구체적인 설명이 나오며, 단서 **②**의 Please ~ 이하 부분에서 좌석 예약을 원하면 링크를 클릭하라고 했다. 따라서 정답은 (A). 해당 단서는 웹페이지 지문에 자주 나오는 링크에 관련된 표현이므로 기억해두자.

| HOME | HOURS | WILDLIFE | HIKING TRAILS | LIVE CHAT |

Welcome to Mount Marjorie Park's Web site! **3A** Mount Marjorie is a mountain with wonderful views. It features many trails of different difficulties. **3D** Visit the "Hiking Trails" page to find a list of trails and explanations of their difficulty levels. Be sure to consult the "Hours" page before coming. You may not enter the park after the main center closes at 6 P.M.

In addition, **3B** Mount Marjorie Park is the home of diverse wildlife. Descriptions for all of the animals are on the "Wildlife" page. **4** Search for the creatures you want to see on this page by entering a keyword in the search box. The page will suggest the paths where you are most likely to see the animal.

Note that Mount Marjorie Park is a protected area, and visitors are asked to respect the environment at all times. If you wish to donate money to our efforts to protect the local wildlife, please call 555-8282.

Finally, **5** to find out more about the park, try a live chat with one of our park rangers. Simply click on "Live Chat" to write directly to staff members.

| 홈 | 운영 시간 | 야생 생물 | 등산로 | 실시간 대화 |

마운트 마조리 공원의 웹사이트에 오신 것을 환영합니다! **3A** 마운트 마조리는 훌륭한 전망을 지닌 산입니다. 그것은 각기 다른 난이도의 여러 등산로들을 특징으로 합니다. **3D** 등산로의 목록과 난이도에 대한 설명 정보를 찾으시려면 "등산로" 페이지를 방문해 주세요. 오시기 전에 "운영 시간" 페이지를 확실히 참고해 주세요. 중앙 센터가 닫히는 오후 6시 이후에는 공원에 입장하실 수 없습니다.

또한, **3B** 마운트 마조리 공원은 다양한 야생 동물의 서식지입니다. 모든 동물들에 대한 설명은 "야생 동물" 페이지에 있습니다. **4** 검색 상자에 키워드를 입력해서 보고 싶은 동물들을 이 페이지에서 검색해 보세요. 그 페이지에는 여러분들이 그 동물을 볼 가능성이 가장 큰 등산로가 제안될 것입니다.

마운트 마조리 공원은 보호 지역이라는 점을 유의해 주시고, 방문객들은 항상 환경을 존중해 주셔야 합니다. 지역의 야생 생물을 보호하려는 저희의 노력에 기부하길 원하신다면, 555-8282로 전화 주세요.

마지막으로, **5** 공원에 대해 더 많은 정보를 찾기 위해서는, 저희의 삼림 관리인 중 하나와 실시간 대화를 한번 해 보세요. 직원들에게 직접 대화를 쓰시려면 "실시간 대화"를 클릭하기만 하면 됩니다.

어휘 | trail 길 difficulty 난이도 consult 참조하다 creature 생물 path 경로, 길 protected 보호된 respect 존중[존경]하다 effort 노력 ranger 삼림 관리인

3 What is NOT mentioned about Mount Marjorie?
(A) It features beautiful scenery.
(B) It has many animals living in it.
(C) It is the highest mountain in the area.
(D) It has various paths with different difficulties.

마운트 마조리에 관해 언급되지 않은 것은?
아름다운 풍경을 특징으로 한다.
거기에 서식하는 많은 동물들이 있다.
지역에서 가장 높은 산이다.
여러 난이도의 다양한 길들이 있다.

어휘 | scenery 풍경

해설 | NOT이 들어간 유형의 문제이므로 선택지를 하나씩 대조 소거해보자. 단서 **3A**를 보면, 마운트 마조리는 훌륭한 전경(wonderful views)이 있다고 했으며, 단서 **3B**에서는 해당 공원이 다양한 야생 동물의 집(the home of diverse wildlife)이라고 했다. 또한 단서 **3D**에서는 길의 목록과 난이도의 설명 정보를 "등산로" 페이지("Hiking Trails" page to find a list of trails and explanations of their difficulty levels)에서 찾아 볼 수 있다고 했으므로, 지문에 언급되지 않은 (C)가 정답이다.

4 Why should visitors visit the "Wildlife" page?
(A) To report endangered species
(B) To register for a tour
(C) To make a donation
(D) To look up an animal

방문객들이 "야생 동물" 페이지를 방문할 이유는?
멸종 위기종들을 보고하기 위해서
여행을 신청하기 위해서
기부를 하기 위해서
동물을 찾아 보기 위해서

어휘| endangered 멸종 위기에 처한   species (공통 특성을 지닌) 종   register for ~을 등록하다   look up ~을 찾아보다

해설| 질문의 키워드인 "Wildlife" page가 등장하는 부분에 집중하자. 단서 **4**를 보면, 키워드를 입력해서 해당 페이지에서 보고 싶은 동물들을 검색하면, 해당 동물을 볼 수 있는 가능성이 큰 경로를 제안해 줄 것이라고 했다. 따라서 정답은 (D).

패러프레이징| **단서** search for the creatures → **정답** look up an animal

---

5 How can visitors learn more about Mount Marjorie Park?
(A) By calling a number
(B) By chatting online
(C) By going to another Web site
(D) By visiting the center after 6 P.M.

방문객들이 마운트 마조리 공원에 관해 더 알 수 있는 방법은?
전화를 걸어서
온라인으로 채팅을 해서
다른 웹사이트로 가서
오후 6시 이후에 센터를 방문해서

해설| 마무리 내용이 등장하는 단서 **5**를 보면, 공원에 대한 더 많은 정보를 원하면, 삼림 관리인 중 하나와 실시간 대화로 직접 대화를 하라고 했다. 정답은 (B). 지문의 find out more about the park가 질문에서 learn more about Mount Marjorie Park로 패러프레이징 되었다.

오답| (A) 전화를 거는 목적은 기부를 하기 위해서(donate money)이므로 오답. (D) 센터가 문 닫는 오후 6시를 이용한 오답.

패러프레이징| **단서** try a live chat → **정답** chatting online

---

4 양식 Form

교재 313쪽

1 (A) **2** (C) **3** (A) **4** (B) **5** (C)

Augustus Fitness Center

This form is for current members of Augustus Fitness Center who wish to renew or extend their membership.

The following information includes necessary details to be filled in. Please hand in the form to a staff member at the front desk after completing it.

NAME	Albert Brookside
ADDRESS	2119 Rosemont Crescent, Portland OR
PHONE	(503) 555-3847
PAYMENT METHOD	Credit card
EXTENSION OR RENEWAL REQUESTED	Annual membership renewal

If you have a question regarding our fees, packages, or services, please speak to a membership coordinator. Those renewing or extending their membership will receive a ten percent discount.

Thank you for your business.

아우구스투스 피트니스 센터

이 양식은 회원권을 갱신하거나 연장하기를 원하는 아우구스투스 피트니스 센터의 기존 회원들을 위한 것입니다.

다음은 기입하실 필수 세부 사항을 포함하고 있습니다. 작성하신 후에 프론트 데스크에 있는 직원에게 양식을 제출해 주세요.

이름	알버트 브룩사이드
주소	오리건 주 포틀랜드, 로즈몬트 크레센트 2119번지
전화번호	(503) 555-3847
지불 방법	신용 카드
연장 또는 갱신 요청	연간 회원권 갱신

저희의 요금, 패키지, 또는 서비스에 관해 문의 사항이 있으면, 회원권 조정 담당자에게 말씀해 주세요. 회원권을 갱신하거나 연장하시는 분들은 10% 할인을 받게 됩니다.

이용해 주셔서 감사합니다.

어휘| renew 갱신하다(**몡** renewal 갱신)   extend 연장하다   hand in ~을 제출하다   payment method 지불 방법   regarding ~에 관해
coordinator 조정(담당)자

Gryllis Stationery

2715 Granville Lane

Weehawken, NJ 07872

www.gryllisstationery.com

Invoice: 130259 Date placed: October 13	Ship to: Pedros Solex 1391 Shearwood Forest Drive Keene, NJ 07463

1 This is to confirm that we have received your online order. Your order number is 130259. Please submit a payment for the amount stated by transfer or credit card payment. We will then ship your order. **2** If we do not receive the due amount by October 20, the order will be canceled automatically. If you have a question regarding this order, please contact our customer service at 555-2957.

Item	Quantity	Unit Price	Total
Large Whiteboard	3	$80.00	$240.00
Scissors	5	$12.00	$60.00
Plastic Container	15	$10.00	$150.00
Subtotal			$450.00
Shipping			$30.00
AMOUNT DUE			$480.00

Once you receive your order, feel free to leave a comment in the review section of our Web site, www.gryllisstationery.com.

Thank you for shopping at Gryllis Stationery.

그릴리스 문구점

그랜빌 가 2715호

07872 뉴저지 주 위하켄

www.gryllisstationery.com

송장 번호: 130259 주문 날짜: 10월 13일	수신: 페드로스 솔렉스 쉬어우드 포레스트 드라이브 1391호 07463 뉴저지 주 킨

1 이것은 저희가 귀하의 온라인 주문을 받았음을 확인해 드리기 위함입니다. 귀하의 주문 번호는 130259번입니다. 계좌 이체나 신용 카드로 명시된 금액에 대한 지불을 해주십시오. 그러면 저희가 귀하의 주문품을 보내드릴 겁니다. **2** 만약 저희가 10월 20일까지 예정 금액을 받지 못하면, 주문은 자동으로 취소될 것입니다. 만약 이 주문에 관한 문의 사항이 있으시다면, 555-2957번의 저희 고객 서비스로 연락 주십시오.

상품	수량	개별 단가	총액
대형 화이트보드	3개	80달러	240달러
가위	5개	12달러	60달러
플라스틱 용기	15개	10달러	150달러
소계			450달러
배송비			30달러
지불해야 할 금액			480달러

주문품을 받으시면, 저희 웹사이트인 www.gryllisstationery.com의 후기란에 의견을 마음껏 남겨 주세요.

그릴리스 문구점에서 쇼핑해 주셔서 감사합니다.

어휘 | state 명시하다 transfer 계좌 이체 credit card 신용 카드 due 예정인 cancel 취소하다 automatically 자동으로 comment 의견, 논평

1 What can be inferred about Mr. Solex?

(A) He recently placed an order on a Web site.

(B) He has paid $450 using a credit card.

(C) He is a regular customer of Gryllis Stationery.

(D) He requested that an order be canceled.

솔렉스 씨에 대해 추론할 수 있는 것은?

그는 최근에 웹사이트에서 주문을 했다.

그는 신용 카드를 이용해서 450달러를 지불했다.

그는 그릴리스 문구점의 단골 고객이다.

주문이 취소되도록 요청했다.

어휘 | regular customer 단골 고객

해설 | 단서 **1**의 This is to confirm 이하의 내용을 보면, 이메일 발신자가 수신자인 솔렉스 씨의 온라인 주문을 받았다고(we have received your online order) 했으므로 솔렉스 씨가 최근 웹사이트에서 주문했음을 확인할 수 있다. 정답은 (A).

오답 | (B) 해당 금액을 계좌 이체나 신용 카드로 지불해 달라는 내용을 보아 아직 지불 전이며, 내야 할 금액 역시도 450달러가 아닌 배송비 포함 480달러이므로 오답. (C) 주문 고객인 것은 맞지만 단골 고객(regular customer)임을 확인할 단서는 찾을 수 없다.

패러프레이징 | 단서 your online order → **정답** an order on a Web site

2 What will happen if payment is not submitted by October 20?

  (A) A fee will be applied.
  (B) A reminder will be sent.
  (C) The order will be canceled.
  (D) The delivery will be delayed.

10월 20일까지 지불이 되지 않으면 발생할 일은?
수수료가 적용될 것이다.
독촉장이 보내질 것이다
주문이 취소될 것이다.
배달이 연기될 것이다.

어휘 | fee 수수료, 요금 apply 적용하다 reminder 독촉(장)

해설 | 질문의 키워드인 날짜 10월 20일이 나오는 부분인 단서 **2**를 집중적으로 살펴봐야 한다. 지불 예정 금액을 업체가 받지 못하면, 주문이 자동 취소된다(the order will be canceled automatically)고 했으므로 정답은 (C). 지문의 we do not receive the due amount가 질문에서 payment isn't submitted로 패러프레이징되었다.

SJJ Supermarket   **SURVEY FORM**

Thank you for agreeing to participate in our survey. **3** The following information will help us to improve our services and bring you better products. Please provide the following information and drop off the completed form at SJJ Supermarket.

FULL NAME	Cathy Tan
4A E-MAIL*	ctan@goal.com

4B How often do you shop for groceries?
About twice a week
4D How often do you shop at SJJ Supermarket?
Maybe four to five times a month
What products do you purchase every week?
Milk, bread, fruit, and vegetables
What suggestions do you have for SJJ Supermarket?
I would like to see a better produce section. **4C** I usually buy my fruits and vegetables from other markets, as the section is better.

4A *Please provide your e-mail address if you would like to receive information on upcoming promotions or sales.

5 Our employees are always here to assist you at the service counter. Please hand in this form to one of them when it is completed.

SJJ 슈퍼마켓   **설문 양식**

저희 설문에 참여하시는 데 동의해 주셔서 감사합니다. **3** 다음 정보는 저희가 서비스를 개선하고 여러분께 더 나은 제품들을 제공할 수 있도록 도와줄 것입니다. 다음 정보를 제공해 주시고 완성된 양식을 SJJ 슈퍼마켓으로 갖다 주세요.

이름	캐시 탠
4A 이메일*	ctan@goal.com

4B 식료품 쇼핑을 얼마나 자주 하시나요?
한 주에 약 두 번 정도
4D 얼마나 자주 SJJ 슈퍼마켓에서 쇼핑하시나요?
아마 한 달에 네다섯 번 정도
매주 어떤 제품을 구매하시나요?
우유, 빵, 과일과 채소
SJJ 슈퍼마켓에게 어떤 제안을 해 주시겠어요?
저는 더 나은 농산물 코너를 보고 싶습니다. **4C** 저는 보통 과일과 채소를 다른 마켓에서 구매하는데, 그 코너가 더 낫기 때문입니다.

4A *앞으로 있을 판촉 행사나 할인 판매에 관한 정보를 받고 싶으시면, 이메일 주소를 제공해 주세요.

5 저희 직원들은 항상 여기 서비스 카운터에 여러분들을 돕기 위해 있습니다. 이 양식을 다 작성하시면 직원 중 한 명에게 전달해 주세요.

어휘 | help A to do A가 ~하는 것을 돕다 grocery 식료품 produce 농산물 promotion 판촉 counter 카운터, 계산[판매]대

3 Why is SJJ Supermarket conducting a survey?

  (A) To help provide better items
  (B) To decide how to promote its products
  (C) To find out how to compete with other stores
  (D) To determine where new branches should be opened

SJJ 슈퍼마켓이 설문을 실시한 이유는?
더 나은 물품을 제공하려고
제품을 홍보할 방법을 결정하려고
다른 가게들과 경쟁하는 방법을 알아보려고
새로운 지점 위치를 결정하려고

어휘 | find out 알아내다 compete with ~와 경쟁하다 determine 결정하다

해설 | 단서 **3**에서 The following information will help us to ~(다음 정보는 저희가 ~하도록 도와줄 것입니다)라는 표현을 통해서 이 설문 조사 양식의 목적을 드러내고 있다. 서비스 개선과 더 나은 제품 제공을 위함이라고 명시했다. 정답은 (A).

패러프레이징 | 단서 bring you better products → 정답 provide better items

4 What is NOT indicated about Ms. Tan?
(A) She wants to receive information on sales.
(B) She only buys groceries once every week.
(C) She purchases vegetables at another store.
(D) She shops at SJJ Supermarket several times a month.

탠 씨에 관해 시사되지 않은 것은?
세일에 관한 정보를 얻고 싶어한다.
식료품을 매주 한 번씩만 구매한다.
다른 가게에서 채소를 구매한다.
SJJ 슈퍼마켓에서 매달 몇 번 쇼핑을 한다.

해설 | NOT이 포함된 유형으로 선택지를 하나씩 지문과 대조해서 살펴 보자. 단서 **4B**를 보면, 식료품을 한 주에 약 두 번 정도 구매한다고 했다. 따라서 (B)가 사실과 다른 내용으로 정답이다. (A) 단서 **4A**에서 탠 씨가 이메일 주소를 제공한 것을 통해 세일 정보를 받고 싶어 함을 알 수 있다. 표 아래 * 표시가 있는 참고 사항에서 단서를 찾을 수 있는 경우가 많으니 유의해야 한다. (C) 단서 **4C**에서 과일과 채소를 다른 가게에서 산다고 했으므로 맞는 내용이다. (D) 단서 **4D**에서 탠 씨가 한 달에 네다섯 번 정도 SJJ 슈퍼마켓에 간다고 했으므로 맞는 내용이다.

---

5 What is suggested about SJJ Supermarket?
(A) It is considering an expansion of its operations.
(B) It has numerous outlets across the country.
(C) It provides a customer service counter in the store.
(D) It sends out flyers with information on special promotions.

SJJ 슈퍼마켓에 대해 암시된 것은?
사업 확장을 고려하고 있다.
전국에 수많은 판매점이 있다.
매장에 고객 서비스 카운터가 있다.
특별 판촉에 대한 전단지를 보낸다.

어휘 | outlet 판매점 flyer 전단지

해설 | 지문 마지막에 등장한 단서 **5**를 보면, 고객들을 위해 서비스 카운터에 늘 도와줄 직원이 있다고 했다. 따라서 정답은 (C)임을 유추할 수 있다.

오답 | 판촉이나 세일에 관한 정보는 이메일을 통해 보낸다고 유추할 수 있으므로, 전단지를 보낸다는 (D)는 오답이다.

PARAPHRASING 패러프레이징(3) 교재 316쪽

1 (A) **2** (A) **3** (B) **4** (A) **5** (B) **6** (A) **7** (B) **8** (A) **9** (B)

1 reserve their tickets in advance → **book** their seats ahead of time
(A) book (B) print

미리 티켓을 예매하다 → 미리 좌석을 예약하다
(A) 예약하다 (B) 출력하다

2 struggling in the difficult economic times → having difficulties in the **economic crisis**
(A) economic crisis (B) dangerous circumstances

힘든 경제 시기에 분투하는 → 경제 위기 시에 어려움을 겪는
(A) 경제 위기 (B) 위험한 상황

3 loyal customers at this restaurant → **regular** patrons of the establishment
(A) first-time **(B) regular**

이 식당의 단골 고객들 → 점포의 단골 고객들
(A) 처음의 **(B) 정기적인**

4 have the authority to supervise the workers → have **permission** to oversee the employees
(A) permission (B) abilities

직원들을 감독할 권한을 가지다 → 직원들을 감독할 허가를 얻다
(A) 허가, 허락 (B) 능력

5 We will hold a press conference soon about the merger.
(A) A decision will be made soon about the merger.
(B) The merger will soon be announced to the public.

우리는 합병에 관해 조만간 기자 회견을 열 것이다.
(A) 합병에 관한 결정이 조만간 있을 것이다.
(B) 합병은 조만간 공표될 것이다.

UNIT 18

6 The CEO told Ms. Hertz to pick him up from the airport.
(A) The CEO asked Ms. Hertz to give him a ride from the airport.
(B) The CEO asked Ms. Hertz to reserve a plane ticket from the airport.

CEO는 허츠 씨에게 공항에서 그를 차로 태워와 달라고 말했다.
(A) CEO는 허츠 씨에게 공항에서 그를 차로 태워와 줄 것을 요청했다.
(B) CEO는 허츠 씨에게 공항으로부터 비행기 표를 예약해 줄 것을 요청했다.

---

7 Thanks to new building projects, the unemployment rate has gone down.
(A) Employers advertised fewer job openings despite the new projects.
(B) The number of unemployed people has decreased because of the construction.

신규 건축 프로젝트 덕분에, 실업률이 감소했다.
(A) 신규 프로젝트에도 불구하고 고용주들은 더 적은 채용 광고를 냈다.
(B) 건축 공사 때문에 실업자의 수가 감소했다.

8-9

Dear Ms. Manning,

Thank you for telling me about the Benson Arts Festival next month. Unfortunately, **8** I am taking that week off from work and will be out of the country until the following weekend. I booked my flight a month ago and cannot change my dates. It's a shame because the festival looks like it will be a lot of fun. I'm glad **9** it's an annual event so that I can go next year. I hope you enjoy it even though I can't go.

Sincerely,

Karen Carlson

매닝 씨께,

저에게 다음 달 벤슨 예술 축제에 관해 알려 주셔서 감사해요. 안타깝게도, **8** 저는 그 주에 회사에서 휴가를 내서 그 다음 주 주말까지 외국에 있을 거예요. 한 달 전에 비행기를 예약해서 날짜를 바꿀 수가 없어요. 축제가 엄청 재미있을 것 같아서 유감이에요. **9** 그게 매년 있는 행사라서 제가 내년에 갈 수 있는 건 기쁘게 생각되네요. 저는 갈 수 없지만 당신이 즐기고 오길 바래요.

카렌 칼슨 드림

어휘| shame 유감스러운[난처한] 일 even though ~일지라도

8 Why is Ms. Carlson unable to attend the festival?
(A) She is taking a vacation at that time.
(B) She has a lot of work to do that week.

칼슨 씨가 축제에 참석할 수 없는 이유는?
(A) 그 때 휴가를 갈 것이다.
(B) 그 주에 할 일이 많다.

해설| 단서 **8**을 보면, 축제가 있을 때 휴가를 내서 외국에 나가 있을 것이라고 했다. 따라서 정답은 (A).

패러프레이징| 단서 taking that week off → 정답 taking a vacation at that time

---

9 How often does the Benson Arts Festival take place?
(A) Quarterly
(B) Yearly

벤슨 예술 축제는 얼마나 자주 있는가?
(A) 1년에 네 번
(B) 1년에 한 번

해설| 해당 축제가 연례 행사라서 다음 해에 갈 수 있어 기쁘다는 단서 **9**의 내용을 통해 정답은 (B).

패러프레이징| 단서 annual → 정답 yearly

1 이메일/편지(E-mail/Letter) 이중 지문

교재 321쪽

Q (B) / 1 (B) 2 (A) 3 (D) 4 (B) 5 (C)

To: Metro Realty <info@metro-realty.net>
From: Diane Coleman <d.coleman@inbox4u.com>

To whom it may concern:

I am interested in the office space for rent on the fourth floor of the Frederickson Building. The location is convenient because it's within walking distance of the subway.

Q However, there are two different pieces of information detailing the moving-in dates for this space. The local newspaper said it is available from April 5 while your Web site says the moving-in date is April 28.

Please let me know which is correct. Also, I would like to schedule a time to view the office space. You can reply to this message or call my office at 555-2040 anytime before 6 P.M. today.

Regards,

Diane Coleman

수신: 메트로 부동산 〈info@metro-realty.net〉
발신: 다이앤 콜맨 〈d.coleman@inbox4u.com〉

담당자 분께,

저는 프레드릭슨 빌딩의 4층 임대용 사무실 공간에 관심이 있습니다. 그 장소는 지하철까지 걸어갈 수 있는 거리 내에 있기 때문에 편리합니다.

Q 그러나 이 공간에 입주하는 날짜가 설명된 두 개의 다른 정보가 있더군요. 귀사의 웹사이트에는 입주일이 4월 28일이라고 나와 있는 반면에, 지역 신문에는 4월 5일부터 이용 가능할 것이라고 나와 있었습니다.

어느 쪽이 올바른지 알려 주세요. 또한, 저는 사무실 공간을 구경할 시간을 정하고 싶습니다. 이 메시지에 답장을 보내 주시거나 제 사무실인 555-2040번으로 오늘 오후 6시 전에 아무 때나 전화 주세요.

다이앤 콜맨 드림

어휘| be interested in ~에 관심이 있다   rent 임대   within walking distance 걸어갈 수 있는 거리 내에   detail 자세히 설명하다, 구체화하다   moving-in date 입주 날짜   correct 올바른, 정확한   view 구경하다, 둘러보다   reply to ~에 응답하다

To: Diane Coleman <d.coleman@inbox4u.com>
From: Metro Realty <info@metro-realty.net>

Dear Ms. Coleman,

Thank you for pointing out the error. We hadn't noticed that two different dates had been listed. **Q** The correct moving-in date is April 28. I hope that will work out for your business.

I've attached a brochure to this e-mail that has lots of pictures of the office. As you can see, it is quite spacious. I can give you a tour on Tuesday afternoon at 3 P.M. If you're busy then, just let me know, and I'll try to rearrange my schedule.

Sincerely,

Fred Logan
Real Estate Agent, Metro Realty

수신: 다이앤 콜맨 〈d.coleman@inbox4u.com〉
발신: 메트로 부동산 〈info@metro-realty.net〉

콜맨 씨께,

오류를 지적해 주셔서 감사합니다. 저희는 두 개의 다른 날짜가 기재되었다는 걸 몰랐습니다. **Q** 올바른 입주일은 4월 28일입니다. 그 날짜가 귀하의 회사에 맞기를 바랍니다.

이 이메일에 그 사무실의 사진이 많이 들어 있는 안내 책자를 첨부했습니다. 보시다시피 공간이 꽤 넓습니다. 제가 화요일 오후 3시에 둘러보실 수 있게 해 드릴 수 있습니다. 만약 그때 바쁘시다면, 저한테 알려만 주세요. 그러면 제 일정을 재조정해 보도록 하겠습니다.

메트로 부동산, 부동산 중개인
프레드 로건 드림

어휘| point out 지적하다   notice 알아 차리다   list (목록에) 기재[기입]하다   work out 좋게 진행되다, 잘 풀리다   rearrange 재조정하다

Q Where can an error be found?
(A) In a previous e-mail
(B) In a newspaper listing
(C) On a Web site
(D) In a company brochure

오류가 발견될 수 있는 곳은?
이전 이메일
신문 목록
웹사이트
회사 안내 책자

To: Kevin Reilly <reillyk@inboxnow.net>
From: Rahul Kilam <rkilam@acrosstn.com>
Date: October 29
Subject: Open position

Dear Mr. Reilly,

Thank you for your interest in working for *Across the Nation*. ❶ Please note that our current full-time science writer is leaving on November 10. Therefore, her replacement should start three days before that. That way, she can train the new reporter.

This position has many benefits. ❷Ⓐ The salary is higher than average for our industry. ❷Ⓑ You will also get to choose when you work, as long as it adds up to forty hours per week. That means you are in charge of your own schedule. Finally, ❷Ⓒ we offer a bonus every December, which is based on your job performance.

Having looked at your submitted résumé, I would like to invite you for an interview at our headquarters at 10 A.M. on November 1. Please let me know if this is suitable for you. Also, ❸❶ could you please send a sample article so I can review your writing style before the interview?

Thanks,

Rahul Kilam
HR manager, *Across the Nation*

수신: 케빈 라일리 〈reillyk@inboxnow.net〉
발신: 라울 킬램 〈rkilam@acrosstn.com〉
날짜: 10월 29일
제목: 공석

라일리 씨께,

〈어크로스 더 네이션〉 지에서 일하는 것에 관심을 가져 주셔서 감사합니다. ❶ **우리의 현재 정규직 과학 작가가 11월 10일에 떠나는 점을 유념해 주십시오.** 그러므로 그녀의 후임자는 그보다 3일 전부터 일을 시작할 것입니다. 그렇게 하면 그녀가 새로운 기자를 교육시킬 수 있을 것입니다.

이 자리는 많은 혜택들이 있습니다. ❷Ⓐ **급여는 우리 업계의 평균보다 높습니다.** 근무 시간이 주당 40시간까지 채우기만 하면, ❷Ⓑ **당신이 일할 시간도 선택할 수 있게 될 것입니다.** 그것은 당신이 스스로의 일정을 관리할 수 있음을 의미합니다. 마지막으로 ❷Ⓒ **저희는 매년 12월마다 보너스를 제공하는데,** 그것은 당신의 업무 성과를 토대로 합니다.

당신이 제출한 이력서를 보고 나서, 저는 당신에게 11월 1일 오전 10시 저희 본사에서 하는 면접에 올 것을 요청하고자 합니다. 이 시간이 당신에게 괜찮은지 알려 주세요. 또한 면접 전에 당신의 문체를 검토할 수 있도록 ❸❶ **샘플 기사를 보내 주시겠어요?**

감사합니다.

〈어크로스 더 네이션〉 지, 인사부장
라울 킬램 드림

어휘 | replacement 후임자, 교체[대체] **train** 교육[연수]시키다 **benefit** (*pl.*) 혜택, 이익 **as long as** (오직) ~하는 한 **add up to** 총 ~가 되다 **be based on** ~을 토대로 하다

To: Rahul Kilam <rkilam@acrosstn.com>
From: Kevin Reilly <reillyk@inboxnow.net>
Date: October 29
Subject: RE: Open position

Dear Mr. Kilam,

Thank you for considering me for an interview. ❸❷ The file you requested is attached to this e-mail. I think I would make a great addition to your team because I have a lot of experience as a science writer. As you saw on my résumé, ❹ I spent

수신: 라울 킬램 〈rkilam@acrosstn.com〉
발신: 케빈 라일리 〈reillyk@inboxnow.net〉
날짜: 10월 29일
제목: 회신: 공석

킬램 씨께,

저를 면접 대상으로 고려해 주셔서 감사합니다. ❸❷ **요청하신 파일은 이 이메일에 첨부되어 있습니다.** 제 생각에, 저는 과학 작가로서 많은 경험이 있기 때문에 당신의 팀에 훌륭한 충원 인원이 될 것 같습

three years writing for the science and technology section of *Janesburg News*. It is no problem to meet on November 1 at 10 A.M. In fact, **⑤** my apartment is only a five-minute walk from your headquarters in the Madison Building. I look forward to meeting you and explaining my experience in greater detail.

Sincerely,

Kevin Reilly

니다. 제 이력서에서 보셨다시피, **④ 저는 〈제인스 버그 뉴스〉** 지의 과학기술란에 글을 쓰면서 3년을 보냈습니다. 11월 1일 오전 10시에 만나는 것은 문제 없습니다. 사실, **⑤ 제 아파트가 매디슨 빌딩에 있는 귀사의 본사에서부터 걸어서 고작 5분 거리에 있습니다.** 당신을 만나서 제 경력에 대해 더 상세하게 설명할 수 있기를 고대합니다.

케빈 라일리 드림

어휘| addition 추가, 부가 in detail 상세하게

1 When does the new position start?
(A) November 1
(B) November 7
(C) November 10
(D) November 11

새로운 일자리의 일이 시작되는 때는?
11월 1일
11월 7일
11월 10일
11월 11일

해설| 첫 번째 지문의 단서 **❶**에서 현재 작가가 11월 10일에 떠난다고 하고 후임자는 떠나기 3일 전부터 근무한다고 했으므로, 새로운 후임자가 일을 시작하는 날짜는 11월 7일이다. 정답은 (B). 단서의 replacement란 단어가 사람과 관련될 경우 '교체[대체]'라는 뜻 대신, '후임자'라는 뜻으로 쓰인다는 것을 알아두자.

오답| (C)는 현재 작가가 떠나는 날짜이므로 오답.

2 What is NOT mentioned as a benefit of the position?
(A) Many vacation days
(B) Flexible working hours
(C) A year-end bonus
(D) A generous salary

그 자리의 혜택으로 언급되지 않은 것은?
많은 휴가 일수
유연한 근무 시간
연말 보너스
많은 급여

어휘| flexible 유연한

해설| 질문의 키워드 benefit이 등장하는 곳은 첫 번째 지문의 두 번째 단락이다. 단서 **②B**의 언제 일할지를 선택할 수 있다는 내용이 (B)의 flexible(유연한, 탄력적인)이란 표현으로 함축되었고, 단서 **②C**의 December(12월)는 (C)에서 year-end(연말의)로 바꿔 표현되었다. 마지막으로 단서 **②D**의 higher than average(평균보다 높은)는 (D)의 generous(후한, 많은)로 바꿔 표현되었다. 따라서 정답은 언급되지 않은 (A).

3 What is attached to Mr. Reilly's e-mail?
(A) A work schedule
(B) An updated résumé
(C) A recommendation letter
(D) A writing sample

라일리 씨의 이메일에 첨부된 것은?
근무 일정표
업데이트된 이력서
추천서
글 견본

해설| 두 지문 연계 유형 문제. 첫 번째 지문의 단서 **❸-1**에서 샘플 기사를 요청했고, 이에 두 번째 지문의 단서 **❸-2**에서 요청한 파일이 이 이메일에 첨부되어 있다고 했다. 따라서 두 지문을 합쳐서 단서를 찾으면 정답은 (D).

오답| 구직 상황에서 연상할 수 있는 어휘를 이용한 함정인 (B)나 (C)를 답으로 고르지 않도록 주의하자.

4 How long has Mr. Reilly worked as a science writer?
(A) Two years
(B) Three years
(C) Five years
(D) Eight years

라일리 씨가 과학 작가로서 일한 기간은?
2년
3년
5년
8년

해설| 세부 정보 찾기 문제. 두 번째 지문에서 라일리 씨가 자신의 경력을 설명하는 단서 **④**를 보면, 〈제인스버그 뉴스〉 지에서 3년을 근무했다고 했다. 따라서 정답은 (B).

5 What can be inferred about Mr. Reilly?
(A) He has met Mr. Kilam before.
(B) He prefers to arrive before 10 A.M.
(C) He lives near the Madison Building.
(D) He studied science in college.

라일리 씨에 대해 추론할 수 있는 것은?
킬램 씨를 전에 만난 적이 있다.
오전 10시 전에 도착하는 것을 선호한다.
매디슨 빌딩 근처에 산다.
대학에서 과학을 공부했다.

해설| 두 번째 지문의 마지막 부분인 단서 **5**에서 라일리 씨의 아파트가 본사가 위치한 매디슨 빌딩과 걸어서 5분 거리라고 했다. 따라서 정답은 (C).

오답| (D)의 경우 라일리 씨가 과학 작가 자리에 지원했으므로 정답으로 착각할 수 있지만, 지문에서 등장하지 않은 내용이므로 오답이다.

---

2 공지(Announcement) 이중 지문   교재 325쪽

Q (C) / **1** (C) **2** (C) **3** (B) **4** (A) **5** (A)

To: Tri-State Cellular Customers
From: Tri-State Cellular Customer Service Department
Date: September 30

To offer more efficient service, Tri-State Cellular is separating its customer service department into four sections. Please contact the manager who is in charge of the section you need. You will receive a response within one working day.

Contract Details – Ann Dunigan <a.dunigan@tristate.com>
: For renewing or ending your contract with Tri-State Cellular

Payments and Invoices – Greg Foster <g.foster@tristate.com>
: For questions about current or past payments and invoices

Q Service Packages – Edward Fields <e.fields@tristate.com>
: For upgrading or changing your cell phone service package

Warranty Inquiries – Susan Dean <s.dean@tristate.com>
: For obtaining warranty information about your cell phone

수신: 트리-스테이트 휴대폰 고객들
발신: 트리-스테이트 휴대폰 고객 서비스 부서
날짜: 9월 30일

더 효율적인 서비스를 제공하기 위해서, 트리-스테이트 휴대폰은 고객 서비스 부서를 4개의 부문으로 나눌 것입니다. 여러분들이 필요한 부문을 담당하는 관리자에게 연락해 주세요. 여러분들은 영업일 하루 내로 응답을 받으실 것입니다.

계약 세부사항 – 앤 더니건 〈a.dunigan@tristate.com〉: 트리-스테이트 휴대폰과의 계약 갱신 및 종료

지불 및 명세서 – 그레그 포스터 〈g.foster@tristate.com〉: 현재 또는 과거의 지불과 명세서 관련 문의

Q 서비스 패키지 – 에드워드 필즈 〈e.fields@tristate.com〉: 휴대 전화 서비스 패키지의 업그레이드 및 변경

보증서 문의 – 수전 딘 〈s.dean@tristate.com〉: 휴대 전화에 관한 보증 정보 획득

어휘| efficient 효율적인   separate 나누다, 분리하다   section 부문, 구획   within ~ 이내에

Q To: Edward Fields <e.fields@tristate.com>
From: David McNeil <davidmc@inbox99.com>
Date: October 3
Subject: Inquiry

Hello,

I currently have a two-year contract with Tri-State Cellular. It is the Silver Package, which has 450 minutes per month. I got a new job, so now I use my phone a lot more than I used to. The past two months, I exceeded my monthly limit. **Q** Therefore,

Q 수신: 에드워드 필즈
〈e.fields@tristate.com〉
발신: 데이비드 맥닐 〈davidmc@inbox99.com〉
날짜: 10월 3일
제목: 문의사항

안녕하세요.

저는 현재 트리-스테이트 휴대폰 사와 2년 약정을 맺고 있습니다. 그것은 실버 패키지인데, 한 달에 450분짜리입니다. 제가 새로운 직업을 갖게 되어서 이제 전화를 예전보다 훨씬 더 많이 사용합니다.

I think it would be better to change to the Gold Package because it has unlimited minutes. Please e-mail me a copy of the forms I need in order to make this change. I'd like to do it as soon as possible.

Thank you,

David McNeil

지난 2개월 동안 저는 월 한도를 초과했습니다. **ⓠ** 그래서 제 생각에 골드 패키지로 바꾸는 게 나을 것 같은데, 그게 무제한이기 때문입니다. 이렇게 변경하기 위해서 필요한 서류들의 사본을 저에게 이메일로 보내 주세요. 가능한 한 빨리 변경하고 싶습니다.

감사합니다.

데이비드 맥닐 드림

어휘| exceed 초과하다 limit 제한, 한도 unlimited 무제한의

Q Which section did Mr. McNeil contact?
   (A) Contract Details
   (B) Payments and Invoices
   (C) Service Packages
   (D) Warranty Inquiries

맥닐 씨가 연락한 부서는?
계약 세부사항
지불 및 명세서
서비스 패키지
보증서 문의

Announcement from the Rose Foundation

❶ The Rose Foundation provides a variety of services to the underprivileged in our community. Please contact one of the following departments to get involved:

Financial Services
❷A Make a donation by check or bank transfer.
Contact Fang Shih at fshih@rosefd.org.

❸-2 Outreach Department
Plan your own event to raise funds for the Rose Foundation.
Contact Anna Soranen at asoranen@rosefd.org.

Volunteer Department
❷C We offer a free dinner every Sunday. Prepare food and serve the dinner.
Contact Jean Williams at jwilliams@rosefd.org.

Professional Services
❷D Provide health services to those in need at our on-site clinic. Medical professionals only.
Contact Raymond Carter at rcarter@rosefd.org.

로즈 재단에서의 공지

❶ 로즈 재단은 우리 지역 공동체의 빈곤한 사람들을 위해 다양한 종류의 서비스를 제공합니다. 참여하기 위해서는 다음의 부서 중 한 곳에 연락 주세요.

재무 서비스
❷A 수표나 은행 계좌 이체로 기부하세요.
fshih@rosefd.org로 팡 시 씨에게 연락하세요.

❸-2 봉사 활동 부서
로즈 재단을 위한 자금을 모으기 위해 당신만의 행사를 계획하세요.
asoranen@rosefd.org로 안나 소라넨 씨에게 연락하세요.

자원봉사자 부서
❷C 저희는 매주 일요일에 무료 저녁을 제공합니다. 음식을 준비하고 저녁을 차려 주세요.
jwilliams@rosefd.org로 진 윌리엄스 씨에게 연락하세요.

전문 서비스
❷D 저희 현장 진료소에서 도움이 필요한 사람들에게 공공 의료 서비스를 제공하세요. 의료 전문가만 가능.
rcarter@rosefd.org로 레이먼드 카터 씨에게 연락하세요.

어휘| a variety of 다양한 underprivileged 혜택을 못 받는, 빈곤한 get involved 참가하다, 연관되다 make a donation 기부하다 check 수표 outreach 봉사 활동 raise funds 자금을 모으다 on-site 현장의 clinic 진료소

8-1 To: Anna Soranen <asoranen@rosefd.org>

3-1 To: Anna Soranen <asoranen@rosefd.org>
From: Lauren Shafer <l_shafer@inboxtime.net>
Date: February 19
Subject: The Rose Foundation

Dear Ms. Soranen,

3-1 I am interested in assisting the Rose Foundation by hosting an event. The work your organization does for the community is necessary, and I know that many people have been helped by your services. As a local business owner, I would love the opportunity to support such important work. I 4 run a small coffee shop downtown, and I know a lot of customers who would be interested in attending an event for the Rose Foundation. My shop is located right next to 5 the Horner Gallery, which is where I'd like to hold the event. The gallery's owner has generously offered to provide the space for free.

My plan is to hold a formal party with drinks and appetizers. I've never planned an event like this before, so your advice would be quite useful to me. It would be easiest to meet in person. You could tell me about some of the previous fundraising events that others have held. 5 Could you visit the proposed venue sometime next week? Then we could discuss the plan.

Thank you,
Lauren Shafer

3-1 수신: 안나 소라넨 〈asoranen@rosefd.org〉
발신: 로렌 샤퍼 〈l_shafer@inboxtime.net〉
날짜: 2월 19일
제목: 로즈 재단

소라넨 씨께,

3-1 저는 행사를 열어 로즈 재단을 돕는 데 관심이 있습니다. 당신의 기관이 지역 공동체를 위해 하는 일은 꼭 필요한 일이며, 저는 많은 사람들이 당신의 서비스에 도움을 받은 것을 알고 있습니다. 지역 사업주로서 저는 그러한 중요한 일을 후원할 기회를 갖고 싶습니다. 저는 시내에서 작은 커피숍을 4 운영하고 있으며, 로즈 재단을 위한 행사에 참석하는 것에 관심을 가질 만한 고객들을 많이 알고 있습니다. 제 가게는 5 제가 행사를 열고 싶어하는 장소인 호너 갤러리 바로 옆에 위치해 있습니다. 그 갤러리의 주인이 관대하게도 장소를 무료로 제공할 것을 제안했습니다.

제 계획은 음료와 전채 요리가 있는 정식 파티를 여는 것입니다. 저는 전에 이러한 행사를 계획해 본 적이 없어서, 당신의 조언이 저에게 꽤 유용할 것 같습니다. 직접 만나는 게 가장 쉬울 것입니다. 저에게 다른 사람들이 개최했던 이전의 모금 행사들에 대해서 얘기해 주십시오. 5 다음 주 중으로 제안된 장소로 방문해 주시겠습니까? 그 때 우리가 계획을 논의할 수 있을 겁니다.

감사합니다.
로렌 샤퍼 드림

어휘| host 열다, 주최[개최]하다 community 지역 공동체 run 운영하다 generously 관대하게 for free 무료로, 공짜로 formal 정식의

1 What is the purpose of the announcement?
(A) To ask people to attend an annual event
(B) To promote an organization's opening
(C) To recruit people to help an organization
(D) To explain changes in a service

공지의 목적은?
사람들에게 연례 행사에 참석하라고 요청하려고
기관 개장을 홍보하려고
기관을 도울 사람들을 모집하려고
서비스 변경 사항을 설명하려고

해설| 공지글의 목적은 지문의 앞부분에 주로 노출된다. 단서 1을 보면 로즈 재단이 빈곤한 사람들(the underprivileged)을 위한 기관이며, 참여하기를(get involved) 원하는 사람들에게 연락을 달라고 권하고 있으므로 정답은 (C)이다.
오답| 지문을 잘못 이해할 경우 행사 참석을 요청하는 (A)를 정답으로 생각할 수 있으니 주의하자.

2 What is indicated about the Rose Foundation?
(A) It accepts donations by credit card.
(B) It receives funding from the government.
(C) It provides a free meal once a week.
(D) It is working with a nearby clinic.

로즈 재단에 대해 시사된 것은?
신용 카드로 기부를 받는다.
정부로부터 자금을 받는다.
한 주에 한 번 무료 식사를 제공한다.
근처 진료소와 함께 일한다.

어휘| nearby 근처의

해설| 로즈 재단의 각 부서에 대해 잘 읽어보면, 단서 2C에서 매주 일요일에 무료 저녁을 제공한다고 했다. 따라서 정답은 (C).
오답| (A) 단서 2A에서 재무 서비스 부서의 내용을 보면, 수표나 은행 계좌 이체로 기부하는 것을 알 수 있다. (B) 정부 관련 언급은 없었으며, (D) 단서 2D에서 저희 현장 진료소(our on-site clinic)라는 것으로 보아 직접 진료소를 운영한다는 것을 알 수 있으므로 오답.

3 Which department did Ms. Shafer contact?
(A) Financial Services
(B) Outreach Department
(C) Volunteer Department
(D) Professional Services

샤퍼 씨가 연락한 부서는?
재무 서비스
봉사 활동 부서
지원봉사자 부서
전문 서비스

해설| 두 지문 연계 유형 문제. 이메일의 단서 **3-1**에서 샤퍼 씨가 안나 소라넨 씨에게 이메일을 보내 자신이 행사를 주최하고 싶다는 것을 알리고 있으며, 공지의 단서 **3-2**에서는 봉사 활동 부서에서 지금 모금 행사 계획을 담당하고 있으며, 안나 소라넨 씨가 이 일을 맡고 있음을 알 수 있다. 두 내용을 토대로 정답은 (B)이다.

---

4 In the e-mail, the word "run" in paragraph 1, line 4, is closest in meaning to
(A) operate
(B) continue
(C) race
(D) compete

이메일에서, 첫째 단락 네 번째 줄의 "run"과 의미상 가장 가까운 단어는?
운영하다
계속하다
경주하다
경쟁하다

해설| 동의어 찾기 유형 문제는 문맥상 가장 어울리는 의미의 단어를 찾는 게 관건. 해당 단어 run 뒤에 작은 커피숍(a small coffee shop)이라는 목적어가 등장하므로 run은 '(가게 등을) 운영하다'란 뜻으로 쓰인 것을 알 수 있다. 따라서 유사한 의미의 (A)가 정답.

---

5 Where would Ms. Shafer like to meet?
(A) At a gallery
(B) At a charity
(C) At a coffee shop
(D) At a restaurant

샤퍼 씨가 만나고 싶어하는 장소는?
갤러리
자선 단체
커피숍
식당

해설| 두 번째 지문에서 단서가 두 위치에 등장하기 때문에 추론 능력이 필요한 문제. 두 번째 지문 첫 번째 단락의 단서 **5**에서 샤퍼 씨가 행사를 열고 싶어하는 장소가 호너 갤러리임을 알 수 있고, 이어 두 번째 단락의 단서 **5**에서는 이 제안된 장소로 와 주겠냐고 부탁하고 있으므로, 두 단서를 종합하면 만날 장소는 갤러리임을 알 수 있다. 따라서 정답은 (A).

---

3 양식(Form) 이중 지문   교재 329쪽

Q (B) / **1** (B) **2** (A) **3** (B) **4** (D) **5** (A)

Salinas Hotel

Refund Receipt

Customer: Orika Mori
Customer reservation number: CP396
Venue: Grand Ballroom
Reservation date: March 27
Q Payment received: $200
  Refund amount: $100

According to the hotel refund policy, the above amount will be refunded to the credit card that was used for the original reservation. If you do not receive the refund within 60 days, contact our booking department at reservations@salinashotel.com.

살리나스 호텔

환불 영수증

고객: 오리카 모리
고객 예약 번호: CP396
장소: 대연회장
예약 날짜: 3월 27일
Q 결제 금액: **200달러**
  환불 금액: **100달러**

호텔 환불 정책에 따라서 위의 금액은 최초 예약을 위해 사용된 신용 카드로 환불될 것입니다. 만약 60일 이내로 환불을 받지 못하시면, 저희의 reservations@salinashotel.com의 예약 부서로 연락해 주세요.

어휘| refund 환불 receipt 영수증 grand ballroom 대 연회장 booking 예약

To: Salinas Hotel <reservations@salinashotel.com>
From: Orika Mori <orikamori@edgeacct.com>
Date: April 20
Subject: Refund

To whom it may concern:

I recently canceled an event at Salinas Hotel. When I looked at my credit card statement, I saw that the wrong refund amount had been sent. At first, I thought that it was my mistake. However, after checking the contract, I discovered that the problem must be with your hotel. Because I gave more than two weeks' notice for the cancellation, **Q** my full payment should have been returned. Please e-mail me back to let me know how soon you can resolve this issue.

Thank you,

Orika Mori

수신: 살리나스 호텔
〈reservations@salinashotel.com〉
발신: 오리카 모리 〈orikamori@edgeacct.com〉
날짜: 4월 20일
제목: 환불

관계자분께,

저는 최근에 살리나스 호텔에서의 행사를 취소했습니다. 신용 카드 명세서를 보았을 때, 저는 잘못된 환불 금액을 받은 것을 알게 되었습니다. 처음에는 그것이 제 실수라고 생각했습니다. 그러나 계약서를 확인해 보고 난 후, 호텔 측에 문제가 있다는 점을 발견하게 되었습니다. 저는 취소에 대해 2주 이상 전에 통보했기 때문에, **Q** 전액이 환불되어야 합니다. 언제쯤 이 문제를 해결할 수 있을지 이메일로 회신해서 알려 주세요.

감사합니다
오리카 모리 드림

어휘| statement 명세서   resolve (문제 등을) 해결하다

Q   What is suggested about Ms. Mori?
(A) She attended an event on March 27.
(B) She expected to receive $200.
(C) She paid for a reservation in cash.
(D) She needs a new copy of a contract.

모리 씨에 대해 암시된 것은?
3월 27일 행사에 참석했다.
200달러를 받을 것을 예상했다.
현금으로 예약에 대해 지불했다.
새로운 계약서 사본 한 부가 필요하다.

어휘| expect 기대하다   in cash 현금으로

Itinerary from Jetset Travel	
Passenger: Sylvia Jenkins	
Confirmation code: 9304-3950	
Booking date: April 8	
Total charge: USD 856.00	

April 29	
Depart	Rica Airlines
Manila, Philippines 8:10 A.M.	Flight RZ993
Ninoy Aquino International Airport (MNL)	**2** Class: First
	Seat number: B2
Arrive	Flight duration: 2hrs 10min
Hong Kong, Hong Kong 10:20 A.M.	
Hong Kong Airport (HKG)	**1B** Meal: Breakfast

제트셋 여행사의 여행 일정표

승객: 실비아 젠킨스
확인 번호: 9304-3950
예약 날짜: 4월 8일
총 금액: 미화 856달러

4월 29일	
출발	리카 항공사
필리핀, 마닐라	편명 RZ993
오전 8시 10분	**2** 등급: 일등석
니노이 아키노 국제공항 (MNL)	좌석 번호: B2
도착	비행 시간: 2시간 10분
홍콩, 홍콩	
오전 10시 20분	**1B** 식사: 조식
홍콩 공항 (HKG)	

5-1 May 5	
Depart	Rica Airlines
Hong Kong, Hong Kong 7:25 P.M.	Flight RZ120
Hong Kong Airport (HKG)	2 Class: First
1C Arrive	Seat number: C1
Manila, Philippines 9:40 P.M.	Flight duration: 2hrs
Ninoy Aquino International Airport	15min
(MNL)	1B Meal: Dinner

Baggage allowance: 2 Two pieces of free checked luggage for first-class passengers. One piece of free checked luggage for economy passengers. Extra luggage will be charged at a rate of $30 per bag.

1D A fee of $20 will be charged for any changes to the above itinerary. Please note that this is a non-refundable ticket, so cancellations cannot be made without penalty.

Thank you for choosing Jetset Travel. To book another trip with us, call 1-800-555-4097.

5-1 5월 5일	
출발	리카 항공사
홍콩, 홍콩	편명 RZ120
오후 7시 25분	2 등급: 일등석
홍콩 공항 (HKG)	좌석 번호: C1
1C 도착	비행 시간: 2시간 15분
필리핀, 마닐라	1B 식사: 석식
오후 9시 40분	
니노이 아키노 국제공항	
(MNL)	

수화물 허용량: 2 일등석 승객들은 화물용 수화물 두 개 무료. 이코노미석 승객들은 화물용 수화물 한 개 무료. 추가 짐은 가방 하나당 30달러의 요금이 부과될 것입니다.

1D 위의 일정표를 변경하게 되면 20달러의 수수료가 청구될 것입니다. 이것은 환불할 수 없는 표이므로 위약금 없이 취소할 수 없다는 것에 유의하세요.

제트셋 여행사를 선택해 주셔서 감사합니다. 저희의 다른 비행을 예약하시려면, 1-800-555-4097번으로 전화 주세요.

어휘 | duration (지속) 시간, 기간 baggage allowance 수화물 허용량 checked luggage 화물용 수화물 first-class (여객기의) 일등석의 at a rate of ~의 요금으로 non-refundable 환불할 수 없는 penalty 위약금, 벌금

Jetset Travel
1332 Coral Way Avenue
Manila Bay, Manila, Philippines

To whom it may concern:

I received the itinerary for my upcoming trip. However, since I have to visit a manufacturing plant during my business trip, 3 I'd like to make one change. On April 29, I need to take the Rica Airlines 6:30 A.M. flight to Hong Kong instead of the one I booked. I hope you are able to accommodate this request. The return flight doesn't need any changes at all.

Additionally, the total cost of the trip was much higher than I expected. 1A I didn't realize that the 4 figure you told me over the phone did not include taxes. In the future, please let me know exactly how much will be charged to my credit card before it is processed.

5-2 The day before my return flight, I'll have quite a bit of free time in the afternoon. Can you recommend some famous places to visit? I'd love to see what the city has to offer. Any information you could share would be greatly appreciated. Please send my updated itinerary to my e-mail address at s_jenkins@athacorp.com.

제트셋 여행사
코랄 웨이 가 1332번지
필리핀 마닐라 마닐라 베이

담당자분께,

다가오는 여행에 대한 일정표를 받았습니다. 그러나 출장 동안에 제조 공장을 방문해야 하기 때문에, 3 한 가지 변경을 하고 싶습니다. 4월 29일에, 제가 예약했던 것 대신에 홍콩으로 가는 리카 항공사의 오전 6시 30분 비행편을 이용해야 합니다. 이 요청을 당신이 받아들여 주시기를 바랍니다. 되돌아오는 항공편은 전혀 변경할 필요가 없습니다.

또한, 여행의 전체 비용이 제가 예상했던 것보다 훨씬 비쌌습니다. 1A 저는 당신이 전화로 말씀해 주신 4 금액에 세금이 포함되지 않았다는 것을 몰랐습니다. 앞으로는 저에게 제 신용 카드로 정확히 얼마가 청구될지를 처리하기 전에 알려 주세요.

5-2 되돌아오는 비행 전날에 저는 오후에 자유 시간을 좀 가질 것입니다. 방문할 만한 유명한 장소들을 추천해 주시겠어요? 그 도시에 어떤 것들이 있을지를 보고 싶습니다. 어떤 정보라도 공유해 주시면 매우 감사하겠습니다. 업데이트된 일정표를 제 이메일

Thank you,

Sylvia Jenkins

주소인 s_jenkins@athacorp.com으로 보내 주세요.

감사합니다.

실비아 젠킨스 드림

어휘 | return flight 돌아오는[왕복] 항공편   additionally 추가적으로, 게다가   realize ~을 인식하다   figure 금액, 수치   exactly 정확하게   process 처리하다   share 공유하다

1 What is indicated about the trip?
(A) It was booked through a Web site.
(B) A meal will be served on both flights.
(C) The return flight will arrive at noon.
(D) It can be changed at no extra charge.

여행에 대해 시사된 것은?
웹사이트를 통해 예약되었다.
두 항공편 모두에서 식사가 제공될 것이다.
되돌아 오는 비행기는 정오에 도착할 것이다.
추가 비용 없이 변경될 수 있다.

해설 | 비행기 일정표인 첫 번째 지문의 단서 **1B**에서, 4월 29일과 5월 5일 양일의 항공편에서 조식과 석식이 각각 제공될 것임이 드러나 있다. 정답은 (B).

오답 | (A) 예약은 두 번째 지문의 단서 **1A**에서 전화로(over the phone) 되었음을 알 수 있고, (C) 첫 번째 지문의 단서 **1C**에서 돌아오는 비행편은 정오가 아닌 오후 늦게 도착함을 알 수 있다. (D) 첫 번째 지문의 단서 **1D**에서 일정 변경에는 20달러의 수수료가 청구된다고 했으므로 틀린 내용이다.

2 How much will Ms. Jenkins be charged if she checks two bags?
(A) $0.00
(B) $20.00
(C) $30.00
(D) $60.00

젠킨스 씨가 두 개의 가방을 부칠 경우 청구받을 비용은?
0달러
20달러
30달러
60달러

해설 | 단서 **2**를 보면, 젠킨스 씨는 왕복 항공편 모두에서 일등석 승객임을 알 수 있고, 일등석 승객은 가방을 두 개까지 무료로 부칠 수 있다는 것도 알 수 있다. 따라서 정답은 청구 비용이 없다는 의미의 (A)이다.

3 What is the purpose of Ms. Jenkins' letter?
(A) To cancel an upcoming trip
(B) To make an itinerary change
(C) To complain about an error
(D) To request payment information

젠킨스 씨 편지의 목적은?
다가오는 여행을 취소하기 위해서
일정표 변경을 하기 위해서
오류에 대해 불평하기 위해서
지불 정보를 요청하기 위해서

어휘 | complain 불평하다

해설 | 여행사에 보내는 편지의 단서 **3**에서 4월 29일에 예약했던 항공기 대신에 오전 6시 30분의 항공기를 타야 하기 때문에 일정 변경을 요청하고 있다. 정답은 (B).

오답 | (A) 비행 시간만을 바꾸는 것이지 여행 전체를 아예 취소하는 내용은 아니므로 오답.

4 In the letter, the word "figure" in paragraph 2, line 2, is closest in meaning to
(A) plan
(B) shape
(C) proposal
(D) amount

편지에서, 둘째 단락 두 번째 줄의 단어 "figure"와 의미상 가장 가까운 단어는?
계획
형태
제안
액수

해설 | 동의어 찾기 유형의 문제는 문맥상의 의미 파악을 위해 해당 단어의 전후 내용을 잘 읽어야 한다. 해당 단어인 단서 **4**가 포함된 문장에서 전화로 알려 준 figure가 세금이 포함되지 않은 것이었는지 몰랐다고 했으므로, figure는 여행사가 젠킨스 씨에게 청구한 '금액'임을 알 수 있다. 따라서 가장 유사한 어휘는 '액수', '총계'를 가리키는 (D)이다.

5 What will Ms. Jenkins most likely do on May 4?
(A) Go sightseeing in the city
(B) Visit a manufacturing plant
(C) Have a meeting with investors
(D) Return to her departure city

젠킨스 씨가 5월 4일에 할 것 같은 일은?
시내 관광 가기
제조 공장 방문하기
투자자와 회의하기
출발 도시로 되돌아 오기

어휘| sightseeing 구경, 관광

해설| 두 지문 연계 유형 문제. 일단 질문에서 묻고 있는 5월 4일이 등장하는 부분을 찾으니 정확히 일치하는 부분이 없다. 추론을 위해 지문에 등장하는 다른 날짜 부분을 찾으니, 첫 번째 지문의 단서 5-1에서 5월 5일이 되돌아 오는 날임을 알 수 있다. 또한 두 번째 지문의 단서 5-2에서 젠킨스 씨가 돌아오기 하루 전 날 자유 시간을 가질 것이고, 방문할 장소를 추천해 달라고 했으니 젠킨스 씨는 돌아오는 날(5월 5일) 하루 전인 5월 4일에 도시를 관광할 것임을 알 수 있다. 정답은 (A)이다.

1 **광고(Advertisement) 삼중 지문**

교재 335쪽

Q (B) / **1** (D) **2** (C) **3** (B) **4** (C) **5** (A)

Falleni's Restaurant Now Open!

Falleni's Restaurant is proud to announce that after months of construction, we are officially opening for business. In addition to amazing food, we have a contest-winning bartender on staff. Our grand opening will take place on Friday, June 19. **Q** And all groups with more than twenty diners will save ten percent on their bills as a special promotion that month.

팔레니 레스토랑이 이제 문을 엽니다!

팔레니 레스토랑은 수개월간의 공사 끝에, 공식적으로 영업을 개시함을 알려 드리게 되어 자랑스럽습니다. 멋진 음식뿐만 아니라, 직원 중에는 대회 수상 경력이 있는 바텐더도 있습니다. 저희 개점은 6월 19일 금요일에 있을 것입니다. **Q** 그리고 20명 이상의 손님으로 구성된 모든 단체는 그 달의 특별 행사로 계산서 가격에서 10% 할인을 받게 될 것입니다.

어휘| in addition to ~뿐만 아니라

How to Seat Tonight's Guests

Tonight's dinner service includes several bookings for large parties. All of these groups cannot be in the same section because there would be too many patrons for one server. Please distribute big groups evenly throughout the restaurant. Each server should have not only the same number of tables, but approximately the same number of customers as well.

금일 저녁 손님 좌석 배치 방법

오늘의 저녁 식사 서비스는 몇몇 대규모 단체 예약을 포함합니다. 이 단체들은 한 구역에 모두 배정될 수 없는데, 그러면 종업원 한 명이 너무 많은 손님들을 담당하게 되기 때문입니다. 각 대규모 단체들을 식당에 고르게 배치시켜 주세요. 각 종업원은 같은 수의 테이블뿐만 아니라 대략적으로 비슷한 수의 고객을 담당해야 합니다.

어휘| patron 손님, 고객 server 식당 종업원, 서버

Falleni's Restaurant	
Date: 21 / 06	Time: 8:57 P.M.
Q Guests: 25	Table #: 2
	Food Total 1147.43
	Q Discount 114.74
	Subtotal 1032.69
	Tip 25.00
	TOTAL 1057.69
SIGN X *Trisha Nakao*	

팔레니 레스토랑	
날짜: 6월 21일	시간: 오후 8시 57분
Q 손님: 25명	테이블 번호: 2
	음식 총액 1147.43
	Q 할인 **114.74**
	소계 1032.69
	팁 25.00
	합계 1057.69
서명 X 트리샤 나카오	

Q Why did Ms. Nakao receive a discount?
(A) She ate in the restaurant on opening night.
(B) She came as part of a large group.
(C) She presented a coupon to the hostess.
(D) She shared a table with other groups.

나카오 씨가 할인을 받은 이유는?
개업일 저녁에 레스토랑에서 식사했다.
대규모 단체의 일원으로 왔다.
직원에게 쿠폰을 제시했다.
다른 단체와 테이블을 공유했다.

어휘| hostess 직원, 주인

Convenient Cars is here for you!

Convenient Cars vehicles can be booked in advance or reserved at the last minute, depending on availability. Prices are based on vehicle category: compact, full size, and luxury. For an additional charge, **1B** larger vehicles are also available to move furniture.

To rent a car, drivers must be 21 years of age or older. **4-2** Renters 21 through 24 years of age are considered "young drivers". They can only rent compact through full-size cars and will be subject to a $20.00/day young-driver fee.

1A Convenient Cars sends staff members to pick up and drop off customers at their homes before and after rental car use. **1C** Also included in the rental fees is twenty-four hour roadside assistance in the case of an emergency.

여러분 곁엔 컨비니언트 카즈 사가 있습니다!

컨비니언트 카즈 사의 차량은 이용 가능 여부에 따라 미리 예약하실 수도 있고, 바로 직전에 예약하실 수도 있습니다. 비용은 소형차, 대형차, 고급차의 차량 종류를 기준으로 합니다. 추가 비용을 내시면, **1B** 가구를 옮기기 위해 더 큰 차량을 이용하실 수도 있습니다.

차를 대여하기 위해서는, 운전자가 21세 이상이어야 합니다. **4-2** 21세부터 24세까지의 대여자는 '청년 운전자'로 간주됩니다. 소형차부터 대형차까지만 대여할 수 있으며 하루 20달러의 청년 운전자 요금을 내게 됩니다.

1A 컨비니언트 카즈 사에서는 직원을 보내 렌터카 사용 전과 후에 고객의 자택으로 고객을 태우러 가고 다시 모셔다 드립니다. **1C** 또한 대여료에는 비상시에 대비하여 24시간 긴급출동 서비스도 포함되어 있습니다.

어휘| at the last minute 마지막 순간에, 임박해서 depending on ~에 따라 compact 소형의 luxury 고급의, 사치의 additional charge 추가 비용 renter 대여자 be subject to ~의 대상이다, ~의 적용을 받다 drop off 내려 주다 roadside assistance 긴급출동 서비스 emergency 비상(사태)

RETURN POLICY

Please follow these return instructions after our business hours. Simply park the car, lock its doors, and place the car keys inside the slot of this **2** sealed drop box. Before you return a vehicle, please verify that you have filled up the fuel tank.

Convenient Cars Business Hours:

Monday	7:30 A.M.–6:00 P.M.
Tuesday	7:30 A.M.–6:00 P.M.
Wednesday	7:30 A.M.–6:00 P.M.
Thursday	7:30 A.M.–6:00 P.M.
Friday	7:30 A.M.–6:00 P.M.
3 **5-2** Saturday	9:00 A.M.–12:00 P.M.
3 Sunday	CLOSED

반납 규정

저희 영업시간 이후에는 다음의 반납 지시사항을 따라 주십시오. 차를 주차하고 문을 잠그고 나서, 이 **2** 봉인된 투입함의 투입구 안에 자동차 열쇠를 넣으시면 됩니다. 차량을 반납하기 전에, 연료 탱크를 가득 채웠는지 확인해 주시기 바랍니다.

컨비니언트 카즈 사의 영업시간:

월요일	오전 7:30 – 오후 6:00
화요일	오전 7:30 – 오후 6:00
수요일	오전 7:30 – 오후 6:00
목요일	오전 7:30 – 오후 6:00
금요일	오전 7:30 – 오후 6:00
3 **5-2** 토요일	**오전 9:00 – 오후 12:00**
3 일요일	휴무

어휘| return 반납; 돌려주다, 반납하다 instruction (pl.) 지시사항 business hours 영업시간 slot 투입구, 구멍 sealed 봉인을 한 drop box 투입함 verify 확인하다 fill up 가득 채우다 fuel tank 연료 탱크

어휘| summary 개요 insurance fee 보험료 charge 비용

---

1 What is NOT a service provided by Convenient Cars?
(A) Customer pickup
(B) Large vehicles rental
(C) Roadside assistance
(D) Free GPS service

컨비니언트 카즈 사에서 제공하는 서비스가 아닌 것은?
고객 픽업
대형 차량 대여
긴급출동 서비스
무료 GPS 서비스

해설| 컨비니언트 카즈 사에 대한 광고인 첫 번째 지문에서 그 회사가 제공하는 서비스의 내용을 찾아볼 수 있다. (A) 단서 1️⃣A에서는 직원을 보내서 렌터카 사용 전후에 고객을 태워가고 온다고 했고, (B) 단서 1️⃣B에서 가구를 옮길 만한 큰 차량도 대여가 가능하다고 했으며, (C) 1️⃣C에서 24시간 긴급출동 서비스를 제공한다고 했다. (D)의 GPS에 대해서는 설명이 없지만, 세 번째 지문인 영수증의 단서 1️⃣D에서 GPS 대여료가 청구된 것으로 보아 무료가 아님을 알 수 있다. 따라서 (D)가 정답.

---

2 In the notice, the word "sealed" in paragraph 1, line 2, is closest in meaning to
(A) stamped
(B) authorized
(C) secured
(D) marked

공지에서, 첫째 단락 두 번째 줄의 "sealed"와 의미상 가장 가까운 단어는?
우표를 붙인
공인된
안전이 보장된
표시가 된

해설| 동의어 찾기 문제를 풀 때, 지문에서 해당 어휘 대신 넣어서 의미가 가장 자연스러운 것을 선택하는 것도 한 방법이다. sealed drop box는 렌터카 회사의 영업시간 이후에 자동차를 반납할 때, 자동차 열쇠를 넣는 함을 가리킨다. 다른 사람이 가져가지 못하도록 투입구를 제외한 나머지 부분을 '봉인한' 상자를 의미하므로, '안전이 보장된' 상자라는 말로 대신할 수 있다. 따라서 답은 (C).

---

3 What is indicated about service on weekends?
(A) Special rates are available.
(B) Office hours are shortened.
(C) Fewer vehicles are available.
(D) The pickup area is reduced.

주말 동안의 서비스에 대해 시사된 것은?
특별 요금을 이용할 수 있다.
영업시간이 단축된다.
이용할 수 있는 차량이 더 적다.
픽업 범위가 좁아진다.

어휘| office hours 영업시간 shorten 단축하다

해설| 두 번째 지문에 나오는 영업시간표의 단서 3️⃣에서 토요일에는 평일보다 더 늦게 열어 더 일찍 문을 닫고, 일요일은 휴무이다. 따라서 주말에는 영업시간이 단축되는 것을 알 수 있으므로 (B)가 정답이다.

4 Why was Mr. Hetzel charged a $20 fee?

(A) He kept a vehicle longer than specified.
(B) He requested additional driver's insurance.
(C) He is under the age of twenty-five.
(D) He did not refill the fuel tank.

헤젤 씨에게 20달러가 청구된 이유는?
명시된 것보다 차를 오래 가지고 있었다.
운전자 보험을 추가로 요청했다.
25세 미만이다.
연료 탱크를 다시 채우지 않았다.

어휘 | specified 명시된 under age of ~세 미만의 refill 다시 채우다

해설 | 연계 유형 문제이다. 영수증의 단서 ④-1에서 청구된 20달러는 운전자 요금(Driver Fee)으로, 하루 기본 요금이 20달러임을 알 수 있다. 이는 첫 번째 지문의 단서 ④-2에서 설명한 청년 운전자 요금(young-driver fee)임을 알 수 있다. 이 요금은 21세에서 24세까지의 운전자에게 부과되는 것이므로 (C)가 정답이다.

---

5 What can be inferred about Mr. Hetzel's rental car?

(A) It was returned after hours.
(B) It was reserved at the last minute.
(C) It was rented from an airport.
(D) It was the only vehicle available.

헤젤 씨의 대여 차량에 대해 추론할 수 있는 것은?
영업시간 이후에 반납되었다.
막판에 예약되었다.
공항에서 대여되었다.
이용 가능한 유일한 차량이었다.

해설 | 두 지문을 연계해야 풀 수 있는 문제. 영수증의 단서 ⑤-1을 보면 헤젤 씨의 렌터카는 금요일에 오후 5시에 픽업되었으며 대여 기간이 24시간이므로 토요일 오후 5시에 반납되었을 것이다. 두 번째 지문의 단서 ⑤-2에서는 토요일의 영업시간이 오전 9시부터 오후 12시까지라고 했으므로 헤젤 씨는 영업시간 이후인 오후 5시에 차를 반납했을 것임을 추론할 수 있다. 따라서 정답은 (A).

---

2 기사(Article) 삼중 지문

교재 339쪽

Q (B) / 1 (C) 2 (A) 3 (B) 4 (B) 5 (D)

Mahier Inc. Recalls Ceiling Fans
By *Anne Collier*

Last week, Mahier Inc. recalled forty-three ceiling fan models because of malfunctioning motors. This is the second time in three months that Mahier has recalled a potentially dangerous product. According to a Mahier spokesperson, customers should return fan model J45 to stores for a full refund.

마이어 주식회사, 천장 선풍기를 회수하다
앤 콜리어 작성

지난주에, 마이어 주식회사는 제대로 기능하지 않는 모터 때문에 43개의 천장 선풍기 모델을 회수했다. 마이어 사가 잠재적으로 위험한 제품을 회수한 것은 석 달 동안 이번이 두 번째이다. 마이어 사의 대변인에 따르면, 고객들은 전액 환불을 받으려면 매장에 J45 모델의 선풍기를 반납해야 한다.

어휘 | recall (결함이 있는 제품을) 회수[리콜]하다 ceiling fan 천장 선풍기 malfunctioning 제대로 기능하지 않는 potentially 잠재적으로

To: Customer Service <cs@mahier.com>
From: Mariah Reyes <mreyes@usernet.mail>
Date: May 14
Subject: Recall procedures

Hello,

I purchased the J45 ceiling fan a week ago. When taking it out of the box, ❶ I accidentally dropped and broke it. Since the product is being recalled anyway, am I entitled to a refund?

Kind thanks,

Mariah Reyes

수신: 고객 서비스 센터 ⟨cs@mahier.com⟩
발신: 머라이어 레이예스
⟨mreyes@usernet.mail⟩
날짜: 5월 14일
제목: 회수 절차

안녕하세요,

저는 일주일 전에 J45 천장 선풍기를 구입했습니다. 상자에서 제품을 꺼내다가, ❶ **제가 실수로 바닥에 떨어뜨려서 고장이 났습니다.** 어쨌든 그 제품이 회수 중이므로, 저도 환불 자격이 되나요?

머라이어 레이예스 드림

어휘 | procedure 절차 accidentally 실수로 anyway 어쨌든 be entitled to ~을 받을 자격이 있다

Mahier Coverage Policy for Recalled Products	
Condition of recalled item	Refund (%)
Broken during delivery (courier responsible for compensation)	0%
ⓠ Broken by customer	50%
Broken due to improper installation	75%
Unopened or intact	100%

회수 제품에 대한 마이어 사의 환불 정책	
회수 제품의 상태	환불 비율
배송 중 파손 (택배 회사에 보상의 책임이 있음)	0%
ⓠ 고객에 의한 파손	50%
부적절한 설치로 인한 파손	75%
미개봉 또는 온전한 상태	100%

어휘 | coverage 보상, 보장 courier 택배 회사 compensation 보상 improper 부적절한, 잘못된 installation 설치 intact 온전한 상태의, 손대지 않은

Q How much of a refund will Ms. Reyes receive?
(A) 0%
(B) 50%
(C) 75%
(D) 100%

레이예스 씨가 받게 될 환불 비율은?
0%
50%
75%
100%

Miami City Convention Center Finally Open

October 1—After nearly nine months of building, the City Convention Center has officially opened in downtown Miami. Construction plans for the convention center included a 47,000 square-foot ballroom; 88,300 square-foot public lobby, concourse, and registration area; and 151,100 square feet of exhibition space that can ❶ accommodate over 800 exhibit booths.

As a promotional incentive for organizations to start using the new space, ❷ rental fees will be lowered by 15% for any conferences before the end of the year.

마이애미 시립 컨벤션 센터, 드디어 개관하다

10월 1일—거의 9개월간의 공사 끝에, 마이애미 시내에 시립 컨벤션 센터가 정식으로 문을 열었다. 컨벤션 센터의 건축 계획서에는 4만 7천 평방 피트의 연회장과 8만 8천 3백 평방 피트의 공공 로비, 중앙 홀, 접수대 그리고 전시 부스 800개 이상을 ❶ 수용할 수 있는 전시 공간 15만 천 백 평방 피트가 포함되어 있었다.

이 새로운 공간을 사용하기 시작하는 단체들을 위한 홍보 장려책으로, ❷ 올 연말까지는 어떤 회의에 대해서든 대여료를 15% 낮춰 줄 것이다.

어휘 | downtown 시내에 concourse 중앙 홀 exhibit booth 전시 부스 promotional 홍보의 incentive 장려책

To: Adele Dresner <adele@employmentsolutions.com>
From: Bernard Pender <bernard@employmentsolutions.com>
Date: November 14
Subject: Management Seminar
Attachment: Seminar Agenda

Dear Adele,

Everything has been finalized for your seminar tomorrow. I've confirmed the arrangements with the convention center, and there are fifty participants in total. However, there's been a change. ❹ We won't have the discussion after all. We concluded that it would overlap too much with the previous period, and it makes the day too long. So we'll just end the event after the Q&A session. ❸ Then, you will need to make an announcement informing participants of the new schedule.

수신: 아델 드레스너
〈adele@employmentsolutions.com〉
발신: 버나드 펜더
〈bernard@employmentsolutions.com〉
날짜: 11월 14일
제목: 경영관리 세미나
첨부: 세미나 의제

아델 씨께,

내일 세미나를 위해 모든 것이 마무리되었습니다. 컨벤션 센터 측의 준비도 확인했는데, 참석자는 총 50명이었습니다. 그러나, 변경 사항이 하나 있습니다. ❹ 우리는 토론을 하지 않을 것입니다. 그것이 그 전 시간과 너무 많이 겹쳐서 일정이 너무 길어지게 될 것이라고 결론 내렸습니다. 그래서 행사를 질의응답 시간 이후에 그냥 끝낼 것입니다. ❸ 그러면, 아델 씨가 참석자들에게 새 일정을 알리는 공지를 하셔야 할 것 같습니다.

Thanks,
Bernard Pender

버나드 펜더 드림

어휘| agenda 의제 finalize 마무리짓다 **arrangement** 준비, 마련 in total 통틀어 conclude 끝내다, 끝나다 make an announcement 공지하다, 알리다

Management Seminar Agenda	
2-1 Miami City Convention Center, Miami, November 15 Conducted by Adele Dresner, Leadership Consultant, Employment Solutions	
MORNING AGENDA	**AFTERNOON AGENDA**
10:30 SESSION 1— EFFECTIVE BUDGETING TECHNIQUES	14:00 SESSION 3— WRITING REFERENCE LETTERS FOR FORMER EMPLOYEES
11:30 Coffee break	
5 11:45 SESSION 2— KEEPING YOUR STAFF MOTIVATED	15:00 SESSION 4—BEST INTERVIEW QUESTIONS TO ASK CANDIDATES
12:45 Lunch	4-2 16:00 Question & answer period
	16:30 Discussion
	17:00 End of event

경영관리 세미나 의제	
2-1 마이애미 시립 컨벤션 센터, 마이애미 11월 15일 임플로이먼트 솔루션즈 사, 리더십 컨설턴트, 아델 드레스너 진행	
오전 의제	**오후 의제**
10:30 세션 1–효과적인 예산 편성 기술	14:00 세션 3–이전 직원들을 위한 추천서 작성하기
11:30 휴식시간	15:00 세션 4–지원자들에게 하는 최고의 면접 질문
5 11:45 세션 2–직원들에게 지속적으로 동기 부여하기	4-2 16:00 질의응답 시간
12:45 점심	16:30 토론
	17:00 행사 종료

어휘| conduct 행하다 motivated 동기가 부여된 reference letter 추천서 former 이전의

1 In the article, the word "accommodate" in paragraph 1, line 9, is closest in meaning to
(A) submit
(B) arrange
(C) contain
(D) approve

기사에서, 첫째 단락 아홉 번째 줄의 "accommodate"와 의미가 가장 가까운 단어는?
제출하다
조율하다
포함하다
허락하다

해설| 동의어 찾기 유형의 문제는 문맥상 가장 어울리는 의미의 어휘를 찾는 것이 중요하다. 해당 단어인 accommodate 뒤에 800개가 넘는 전시 부스(over 800 exhibit booths)라는 목적어가 등장하므로 가장 잘 어울리는 어휘는 '포함하다'란 뜻의 (C).

2 What is probably true about Employment Solutions?
(A) It received a discount on a room reservation.
(B) It has a partnership with the Miami Convention Center.
(C) It limits seminar participation to only fifty attendees.
(D) It visits local businesses to provide leadership seminars.

임플로이먼트 솔루션즈 사에 대해서 사실일 것 같은 것은?
회의실 예약에 대해 할인을 받았다.
마이애미 컨벤션 센터와 제휴를 맺고 있다.
세미나 참석자를 단 50명으로 제한하고 있다.
리더십 세미나를 제공하기 위해 지역 사업체들을 방문한다.

어휘| have a partnership with ~와 제휴를 맺다 limit 제한하다 attendee 참석자

해설| 두 지문 연계 유형 문제이다. 세 번째 지문의 단서 2-1을 보면 세미나를 주최하는 곳이 임플로이먼트 솔루션즈 사이고 세미나 개최 장소는 마이애미 시립 컨벤션 센터이다. 세미나 개최일은 11월 15일인데, 첫 번째 지문인 기사의 단서 2-2에서 해당 장소에 대해 연말까지는 대여료를 낮춰 준다고 했으므로 할인을 받았다는 (A)가 정답이다.

3 What will Ms. Dresner make an announcement about? / 드레스너 씨가 공지할 내용은?
(A) The order of two sessions will be switched. / 두 세션의 순서가 바뀔 것이다.
(B) The program has been modified. / **프로그램이 수정되었다.**
(C) One of the seminars has been canceled. / 세미나 중 하나가 취소되었다.
(D) The question & answer session will be extended. / 질의응답 시간이 연장될 것이다.

어휘 | order 순서 switch 바꾸다 extend 연장하다

해설 | 두 번째 지문인 이메일의 단서 ③에서 드레스너 씨가 새 일정을 알리는 공지를 해야 한다고 했으므로 (B)가 정답이다.

---

4 What time will the seminar conclude? / 세미나가 끝날 시간은?
(A) At 16:00 / 16시
(B) At 16:30 / **16시 30분**
(C) At 17:00 / 17시
(D) At 17:30 / 17시 30분

해설 | 두 지문을 연계해야 풀 수 있는 문제이다. 두 번째 지문의 단서 ④-①에서 토론을 하지 않고 질의응답 시간 이후에 행사를 끝내겠다고 했다. 세 번째 지문의 단서 ④-②에서 질의응답이 4시에 시작해서 4시 30분에 끝나며, 그 이후가 토론 시간이므로, 토론을 하지 않으면 행사가 끝나는 시각이 이때이다. 따라서 (B)가 정답이다.

---

5 What will participants hear following the first refreshment break? / 첫 번째 다과 휴식시간 후에 참석자들이 듣게 되는 것은?
(A) Tips for managing a budget / 예산 관리에 관한 조언
(B) Information about writing a reference letter / 추천서 작성에 관한 정보
(C) Advice on asking good interview questions / 좋은 면접 질문하기에 관한 조언
(D) A talk about employee motivation strategies / **직원 동기 부여 전략에 관한 담화**

어휘 | refreshment break 간단한 다과가 제공되는 휴식시간 tip 조언

해설 | 질문의 refreshment break는 세 번째 지문에 나오는 coffee break와 비슷한 뜻이다. 따라서 세 번째 지문의 단서 ⑤에서 coffee break 뒤에 이어지는 11시 45분의 세션 2 내용을 달리 표현한 것을 선택하면 된다. 직원 동기 부여에 관한 것이므로 (D)가 정답이다.

오답 | (A)는 세션 1에, (B)는 세션 3에, (C)는 세션 4에 해당하는 내용이다.

패러프레이징 | 단서 KEEPING YOUR STAFF MOTIVATED → 정답 employee motivation strategies

---

3 웹페이지(Web Page) 삼중 지문
교재 343쪽

Q (A) / 1 (A) 2 (A) 3 (D) 4 (B) 5 (A)

www.arcoil.com/customersurvey

Tell us what you think!

Throughout January, customers who purchase gasoline from one of our stations will be asked to fill out a feedback survey. As a thank-you, Q two-dozen participants will be randomly selected from the responses. You could win a premium gas card, which will provide free gasoline for seven days. Those who aren't selected will also receive a car-wash coupon for $5 off. Don't miss out on this fantastic chance.

여러분의 생각을 말해 주세요!

1월 동안, 저희 주유소 중 한 곳에서 휘발유를 구입하시는 모든 고객분들께 설문 조사를 작성해 주실 것을 부탁드립니다. 감사의 뜻으로, Q 수거된 응답들 중에서 무작위로 24명의 참가자가 선정됩니다. 7일 동안 무료로 휘발유를 제공해 드리는 고급 주유 카드를 받으실 수 있습니다. 당첨되지 못한 분들도 세차 5달러 할인권을 받으실 수 있습니다. 이 멋진 기회를 놓치지 마세요.

어휘 | gasoline 휘발유 (gas) station 주유소 randomly 무작위로

Arc Oil Customer Survey	아크 오일 고객 설문 조사
Name: Christine Stout	이름: 크리스틴 스타우트
address: 72 Spinnaker Lane, Chicago	주소: 시카고, 스피나커 가 72번지
1. How much do you spend on gasoline each month? $100–$200	1. 매달 휘발유에 쓰는 액수는? 100달러에서 200달러
2. Why do you choose our gas station? It offers low prices, and it's close to work.	2. 저희 주유소를 선택하신 이유는? 가격이 저렴하고, 직장과 가까워서.

Ⓠ Christine Stout	**Ⓠ** 크리스틴 스타우트
72 Spinnaker Lane, Chicago, IL 60654	60654 일리노이 주, 시카고, 스피나커 가 72번지
Dear Ms. Stout:	스타우트 씨께,
Ⓠ Congratulations! Your name was randomly selected as one of our 24 prize winners. You should receive your thank-you gift through the mail within 4–6 weeks.	**Ⓠ** 축하드립니다! 귀하의 성함이 24명의 당첨자 중 하나로 무작위로 선정되었습니다. 4주에서 6주 내에 우편으로 감사 상품을 받으시게 될 것입니다.
Thank you once again for your participation,	참여해 주셔서 다시 한번 감사드립니다.
Arc Oil	아크 오일 드림

어휘 | prize winner 당첨자, 수상자

Q What will be mailed to Ms. Stout? 스타우트 씨에게 우편으로 발송될 것은?
(A) A gift card for complimentary gasoline **무료 휘발유 상품권**
(B) A detailed customer survey form 상세한 고객 설문 조사 양식
(C) A coupon for free oil changes 무료 엔진오일 교환 쿠폰
(D) A discount voucher for a vehicle cleaning 세차 할인권

어휘 | gift card 상품권 complimentary 무료의 detailed 상세한 discount voucher 할인권

www.platinumbank.com/onlineapplicationresults	축하드립니다, 콜튼 씨!
Congratulations, Ms. Coleton!	**❶** 플래티넘 은행 항공 마일리지 신용 카드에 대한 귀하의 온라인 신청이 승인되었습니다. **❷** 이미 항공 마일리지를 적립하고 계실 경우, 귀하의 계정으로 최초 2만 5천 항공 마일리지를 즉시 적립 받게 됩니다.
❶ Your online application for a Platinum Bank Air Miles credit card has been approved. **❷** If you are already an air miles collector, you will receive an initial 25,000 air miles credited to your account immediately.	
In 3 to 5 weeks, you will receive your new credit card at the address you submitted on the previous screen. Once it has arrived, you can activate it by calling 1-866-254-6486. After selecting a personalized code for your new card, you can use it right away.	3주에서 5주 후에, 귀하가 이전 화면에서 제출하신 주소로 새로운 신용 카드를 받게 되실 것입니다. 카드가 도착하면 1-866-254-6486번으로 전화하셔서 카드를 활성화시키실 수 있습니다. 신규 카드에 쓸 개인 비밀번호를 정한 후에 바로 카드를 사용하실 수 있습니다.

어휘 | air miles 항공 마일리지 collector 수집가 initial 처음의, 초기의 credit 입금[적립]하다 immediately 즉시 screen 화면
activate 활성화시키다 personalized 개인에 맞춘, 개별의

Platinum Bank Air Miles Credit Card Statement

Account Holder: Ruth Coleton
Account Number: 263-8934-985
②② Air Miles Number: 754-567-923
Statement Period: Dec. 1 to Dec. 31

Current Purchases: $815.00
⑤② Previous Balance: $400.00
Total Amount Due: $1,215.00

TRANSACTION DATE	PURCHASE	AMOUNT
December 06	③A Bambino Airport Café	$15.00
December 13	③C Express Fuel Gas Station	$50.00
December 16	Deckard Bookstore	$150.00
December 22	③B Golden's Grocery & Market	$600.00
	Total	$815.00

Minimum payment due: $40.00   **Payment due date:** January 7

For inquiries about this statement or your account, contact 1-866-254-5475, or write to Platinum Bank, Credit Card Services, 480 Hawthorne Avenue, Benton Harbor, Michigan 49022.

플래티넘 은행 항공 마일리지 신용 카드 명세서

계좌 소유자: 루스 콜튼
계좌 번호: 263-8934-985
②② 항공 마일리지 번호: 754-567-923
명세서 기간: 12월 1일부터 12월 31일

이달 구매 금액: 815달러
⑤② 전달 미납액: 400달러
총 결제 금액: 1,215달러

거래일	구매	금액
12월 6일	③A 밤비노 공항 카페	15달러
12월 13일	③C 익스프레스 퓨얼 주유소	50달러
12월 16일	데커드 서점	150달러
12월 22일	③B 골든 식료품점	600달러
	합계	815달러

최소 결제 금액: 40달러
결제 기한: 1월 7일

위 명세서나 귀하의 계좌에 대하여 문의하시려면, 1-866-254-5475번으로 연락하시거나, 49022 미시건 주 벤튼 하버, 호손 가 480번지, 플래티넘 은행, 신용 카드 서비스부로 우편을 보내십시오.

어휘| holder 소유자 balance 지불 잔액, 잔금 transaction 거래 minimum 최소한의 due date 지불 기일

Platinum Bank
480 Hawthorne Avenue
Benton Harbor, Michigan 49022
January 2

To whom it may concern,

④ I recently received my credit card statement in the mail, and I wanted to inform you of an error.

⑤① My statement says that I have a balance carried over from my previous statement. However, I paid this amount in full on December 2 and the payment has been received. I verified that the money was taken out of my bank account, so please update your records accordingly.

Sincerely,

Ruth Coleton

플래티넘 은행
호손 가 480번지
49022 미시건 주, 벤튼 하버
1월 2일

관계자분께,

④ 제가 최근에 우편으로 신용 카드 명세서를 받았는데, 오류를 알려 드리고자 합니다.

⑤① 제 명세서에는 전달 명세서에서 미납액이 이월되었다고 나와 있습니다. 하지만 저는 12월 2일에 이 금액을 전액 지불했고 결제가 완료되었습니다. 이 돈이 제 은행 계좌에서 인출된 것을 확인했으므로, 그에 맞춰 기록을 갱신해 주시기 바랍니다.

루스 콜튼 드림

어휘| pay in full 전액 지불하다 accordingly 그에 맞춰

1 How did Ms. Coleton obtain a new credit card?
   (A) By applying on a Web site
   (B) By filling out a form at an airport
   (C) By speaking with a bank teller
   (D) By reporting a stolen card

콜튼 씨가 새로운 신용카드를 얻게 된 방법은?
웹사이트에서 신청함으로써
공항에서 양식을 작성함으로써
은행원과 이야기를 나눔으로써
도난 카드를 신고함으로써

2 What is implied about Ms. Coleton?　　　　　　　콜튼 씨에 대해 암시된 것은?
(A) She earned additional air miles.　　　　　　　추가로 항공 마일리지를 얻었다.
(B) She activated her card at the bank.　　　　　　은행에서 카드를 활성화시켰다.
(C) She requested a credit limit increase.　　　　　신용 카드 한도액 상향을 요청했다.
(D) She lives in Benton Harbor.　　　　　　　　　벤튼 하버에 살고 있다.

어휘| earn 얻다　credit limit 신용 카드 한도액

해설| 두 지문 연계 유형 문제이다. 첫 번째 지문의 단서 **2-1**에서 이미 항공 마일리지를 적립하고 있다면 추가로 항공 마일리지를 적립받게 된다고 했는데, 두 번째 지문의 단서 **2-2**에서 콜튼 씨의 항공 마일리지 번호가 있는 것으로 보아 기존에 항공 마일리지를 적립하고 있었음을 유추할 수 있다. 따라서 콜튼 씨는 추가로 항공 마일리지를 얻었을 것이므로 (A)가 정답이다.

3 Where did Ms. Coleton NOT make a purchase?　　콜튼 씨가 구매를 한 장소가 아닌 곳은?
(A) At a coffee shop　　　　　　　　　　　　　커피숍
(B) At a grocery store　　　　　　　　　　　　식료품점
(C) At a fuel station　　　　　　　　　　　　　주유소
(D) At a pharmacy　　　　　　　　　　　　　　약국

어휘| make a purchase 구매를 하다　pharmacy 약국

해설| 콜튼 씨가 구매한 내역은 두 번째 지문의 단서 **3A**, **3B**, **3C**에서 확인할 수 있다. 차례로 카페, 식료품점, 주유소가 열거되고 있으며, 약국은 목록에 없으므로 (D)가 정답이다.

4 Why did Ms. Coleton send the letter?　　　　　콜튼 씨가 편지를 보낸 이유는?
(A) To mail a payment by check　　　　　　　　결제액을 수표로 부치려고
(B) To correct a mistake on a bill　　　　　　　명세서상의 오류를 바로잡으려고
(C) To close a credit card account　　　　　　　신용 카드 계좌를 해지하려고
(D) To request a lower interest rate　　　　　　더 낮은 이율을 요청하려고

어휘| check 수표　close an account 계좌를 해지하다　interest rate 이율

해설| 편지를 보낸 목적은 편지 첫 부분에서 밝히는 경우가 대부분이다. 세 번째 지문의 첫 문장인 단서 **4**에서 신용 카드 명세서상의 오류를 알리고 싶다고 했으므로 (B)가 정답이다.

패러프레이징| 단서 error → 정답 mistake / 단서 credit card statement → 정답 bill

5 According to Ms. Coleton, how much did she pay in
December?　　　　　　　　　　　　　　　　콜튼 씨에 따르면, 그녀가 12월에 결제한 금액은?
　　　　　　　　　　　　　　　　　　　　　400달러
(A) $400　　　　　　　　　　　　　　　　　600달러
(B) $600　　　　　　　　　　　　　　　　　815달러
(C) $815　　　　　　　　　　　　　　　　　1,215달러
(D) $1,215

해설| 두 지문을 연계해서 푸는 문제이다. 세 번째 지문의 단서 **5-1**에서에서 콜튼 씨는 명세서에 오류가 있다면서, 자신이 전달 미납액을 12월 2일에 이미 전액 결제했다고 주장하고 있다. 두 번째 지문인 명세서의 단서 **5-2**를 보면 전달 미납액(Previous Balance)이 400달러이다. 따라서 정답은 (A).

ANSWER KEY

교재 348쪽

101 (A)	**102** (D)	**103** (C)	**104** (A)	**105** (B)	**106** (D)	**107** (A)	**108** (A)	**109** (C)	**110** (C)
111 (B)	**112** (A)	**113** (D)	**114** (A)	**115** (D)	**116** (B)	**117** (B)	**118** (D)	**119** (B)	**120** (A)
121 (B)	**122** (C)	**123** (D)	**124** (A)	**125** (C)	**126** (A)	**127** (D)	**128** (A)	**129** (A)	**130** (C)
131 (C)	**132** (C)	**133** (A)	**134** (B)	**135** (B)	**136** (A)	**137** (C)	**138** (A)	**139** (A)	**140** (A)
141 (B)	**142** (D)	**143** (B)	**144** (A)	**145** (C)	**146** (D)	**147** (C)	**148** (B)	**149** (B)	**150** (D)
151 (A)	**152** (B)	**153** (A)	**154** (A)	**155** (D)	**156** (A)	**157** (B)	**158** (A)	**159** (B)	**160** (D)
161 (A)	**162** (C)	**163** (C)	**164** (D)	**165** (A)	**166** (B)	**167** (C)	**168** (A)	**169** (A)	**170** (D)
171 (C)	**172** (B)	**173** (C)	**174** (B)	**175** (B)	**176** (C)	**177** (D)	**178** (C)	**179** (C)	**180** (B)
181 (C)	**182** (A)	**183** (D)	**184** (A)	**185** (D)	**186** (D)	**187** (B)	**188** (A)	**189** (C)	**190** (A)
191 (C)	**192** (A)	**193** (A)	**194** (D)	**195** (D)	**196** (B)	**197** (D)	**198** (C)	**199** (A)	**200** (C)

101 The straps on this bag / are **adjustable** / to each person / simply by pulling on them.
(A) adjustable (B) adjustment (C) adjusting (D) adjust
해석| 이 가방의 끈은 잡아당기는 것만으로 각각의 사람들에 맞게 조절할 수 있다.
어휘| strap 끈, 줄 pull on 잡아당기다

해설| 빈칸은 be동사의 보어 자리이므로 동사인 (D)를 제외하고 형용사, 명사, 분사인 나머지가 모두 가능하다. 주어인 The straps(끈)와 의미상 자연스럽게 연결되어 '조절할 수 있는 끈'이라는 뜻이 되어야 하므로 정답은 (A).
오답| 명사인 (B)가 들어가면 The straps와 동격이 되어 '끈이 조절이다'라는 뜻이 되므로 의미상 적절하지 않다. 현재분사인 (C)는 뒤에 전치사가 아닌 목적어가 나와야 하므로 적절하지 않다.

102 Come to Melinka's special summer sale / and check out our many great **deals** / on shoes and accessories.
(A) dealer (B) dealing (C) deal (D) deals
해석| 멜린카의 특별 여름 세일에 오셔서 신발 및 액세서리들에 대한 다양한 특별 혜택을 확인해 보세요.
어휘| check out 확인하다

해설| 빈칸은 동사 check out의 목적어이면서 앞의 형용사 many와 great의 수식을 받는 자리이다. 따라서 명사가 들어가야 하는데, 복수를 나타내는 수량형용사 many의 수식을 받을 수 있는 것은 복수 명사인 deals이다. 따라서 정답은 (D).

103 Members must present both a membership card **and** photo ID / to receive the discount.
(A) but (B) through (C) and (D) or
해석| 회원들은 할인을 받기 위해서 회원 카드와 사진이 부착된 신분증을 둘 다 제시해야 한다.
(A) 그러나 (B) ~을 통해 (C) 그리고 (D) 또는
어휘| photo ID 사진이 부착된 신분증

해설| 빈칸 앞쪽의 both를 보고 바로 and를 떠올릴 수 있어야 한다. both A and B는 'A와 B 둘 다'라는 뜻의 상관접속사이다. 따라서 정답은 (C).

104 Audience members are asked to find their seats / **at least** ten minutes / before the start of the show.
(A) at least (B) so that (C) but also (D) no less
해석| 관객들은 공연 시작 최소 10분 전에 자기 자리를 찾도록 요청 받는다.

해설| 빈칸이 없어도 완전한 문장을 이루므로 빈칸 이하는 수식어구가 되어야 한다. '최소 10분 전에'라는 뜻으로 (A)가 적절하다.
오답| (B)는 '~하기 위해서'라는 뜻의 접속사, (C)는 not only와 함께 쓰이는 상관접속사이다. (D)는 뒤에 전치사 than을 붙여 no less than이라고 하면 '최소한'이란 뜻으로 at least 대신 쓸 수 있다.

105 By investing in stocks and bonds, / Zoe Harvey hopes **to earn** money / in the long run.
(A) earning **(B) to earn** (C) having earned
(D) to be earned

해석 | 주식 및 채권에 투자함으로써, 조 하비 씨는 장기적으로 수익을 얻기를 희망한다.

어휘 | stock 주식 bond 채권 in the long run 장기적으로

해설 | 빈칸은 동사 hopes의 목적어 자리로, hope는 to부정사를 목적어로 취하는 동사이다. 선택지의 (B)는 to부정사의 능동형, (D)는 to부정사의 수동형인데 빈칸은 뒤에 명사 money를 목적어로 취하므로 능동형 to부정사인 (B)가 정답이다.

---

106 The presenter's **clarifications** usually help the audience understand the graph / on the screen.
(A) clarification (B) clarify (C) clarified **(D) clarifications**

해석 | 발표자의 설명은 대개 청중이 화면의 그래프를 이해하는 데 도움이 된다.

어휘 | presenter 발표자 clarification 설명, 해명

해설 | 빈칸은 소유를 나타내는 The presenter's의 수식을 받는 주어 자리이므로 명사인 (A)와 (D)가 정답 후보이다. 빈칸 뒤의 동사가 복수 동사인 help이고 주어 자리에도 이에 일치하는 복수 명사가 들어가야 하므로 정답은 (D).

---

107 All trains to Stephenville depart from track 2 / unless **otherwise** noted on the display screen.
(A) otherwise (B) once (C) forward (D) each

해석 | 모든 스테판빌 행 기차는 알림 전광판에 달리 언급이 없으면 2번 트랙에서 출발합니다.

(A) 달리, 다르게 (B) 일단 ~하면 (C) 앞으로 (D) 각각

어휘 | unless ~하지 않는 한 note 언급하다 display screen 알림 전광판

해설 | 빈칸이 없어도 완전한 문장이므로 빈칸은 부사 자리이다. 알맞은 의미의 부사를 골라야 하는데, 빈칸 앞 접속사 unless가 이끄는 절에는 〈주어+동사〉에 해당하는 it is가 생략되어 있다. 문맥상 '전광판에 달리 언급되어 있지 않으면'이란 뜻이 되어야 자연스러우므로 '달리, 다르게'라는 뜻의 부사 (A)가 적절하다.

---

108 By switching suppliers for the raw materials, / Corofa Corp. was able to cut production **costs** / by a significant amount.
(A) costs (B) currency (C) origin (D) results

해석 | 원자재 공급업체를 변경함으로써, 코로파 사는 생산 비용을 상당액 줄일 수 있었다.

(A) 비용 (B) 통화 (C) 기원 (D) 결과

어휘 | raw material 원자재

해설 | 빈칸에는 앞에 있는 명사 production과 어울려 복합 명사를 이루면서 동사 cut과 어울리는 어휘가 들어가야 한다. 문맥상 절감(cut)할 수 있는 것은 '생산 비용'이므로 정답은 (A). 복합 명사 production cost가 '생산 비용'이라는 뜻임을 기억하자.

---

109 On the cruise, / tourists have to pay for drinks, / but they can order / **whatever** they want from the menu.
(A) another (B) them **(C) whatever** (D) some

해석 | 유람선에서 관광객들은 음료에 대한 비용은 지불해야 하지만, 메뉴에서 원하는 것은 무엇이든 주문할 수 있다.

어휘 | cruise 유람선

해설 | 빈칸 이하는 order의 목적어가 되는데, 빈칸 뒤에 나오는 절에 want의 목적어가 없으므로 빈칸에는 목적격 관계대명사가 필요하다. 그런데 앞에 선행사가 없으므로 선행사를 포함한 관계대명사, 즉 복합관계대명사인 (C)가 들어가야 한다. whatever는 '~하는 것은 무엇이나'라는 뜻으로 여기서는 명사절을 이끌고 있다.

---

110 The Reina Maritime Museum **requires** all visitors to check their bags / at the entrance.
(A) covers (B) opens **(C) requires** (D) decides

해석 | 레이나 해양 박물관은 모든 방문객들에게 입구에서 가방을 검사받을 것을 요구한다.

(A) 덮다 (B) 열다 (C) 요구하다 (D) 결정하다

어휘 | maritime 해양의 check 점검하다

해설 | 문맥상 '방문객들에게 가방을 검사받을 것을 요구하다'라는 뜻이 되어야 자연스러우므로 (C)가 정답이다. 동사 require는 to부정사를 목적격 보어로 취해 〈require+목적어+to부정사〉의 구조로 쓰인다는 것도 알아두자.

111 Cell phones must be turned off / **during** the concert / out of respect for the performers.
(A) upon **(B) during** (C) while (D) when
해석 | 콘서트 동안에는 공연하는 사람들을 존중하여 휴대폰을 꺼야 한다.
(A) ~하자마자 (B) ~ 동안에 (C) ~ 동안에 (D) ~할 때
어휘 | out of respect (for) (~을) 존중해서

해설 | 문맥상 '콘서트 동안에'라는 내용이 자연스러우므로, '~ 동안에'의 의미인 전치사 (B)와 접속사 (C)가 정답 후보. 빈칸 뒤에 the concert라는 명사가 나오므로 전치사 (B)가 정답이다.
오답 | 접속사 (C)는 〈주어+동사〉로 이루어진 절이 뒤따라야 하므로 오답이다.

---

112 By the time Mr. Cramer arrived / at the conference hall, / the first presentation had **already** started.
(A) already (B) yet (C) before (D) as soon as
해석 | 크레이머 씨가 회의장에 도착했을 때는, 이미 첫 번째 발표가 시작되었다.
(A) 이미 (B) 아직 (C) 전에 (D) ~하자마자
어휘 | by the time ~할 때 쯤에는

해설 | 빈칸 없이도 문장이 완전하므로 빈칸에는 부사가 들어가야 한다. 따라서 접속사인 (D)는 정답 후보에서 제외. 문맥상 크레이머 씨가 회의장에 도착했을 때는 '이미 발표가 시작되었다'라고 해야 자연스럽다. 따라서 빈칸에는 (A)가 들어가야 적절하다.

---

113 The runner managed to maintain a **steady** speed / throughout the course / and win the race.
(A) best (B) faulty (C) final **(D) steady**
해석 | 그 주자는 경주 코스 내내 일정한 속도를 유지하여 경주에서 우승했다.
(A) 최상의 (B) 잘못된 (C) 최종의 (D) 일정한

해설 | 선택지 중에서 빈칸 뒤의 명사 speed를 수식하여 의미상 자연스러운 형용사는 '일정한, 꾸준한, 한결같은'이란 뜻의 (D)이다.
오답 | '최고 속도'는 best가 아니라 highest speed라고 하므로 (A)는 적절하지 않다.

---

114 Yorta Automobiles sold over one million vehicles / this year, / **surpassing** all other years / by several hundred thousands.
(A) surpassing (B) surpass (C) surpasses (D) surpassed
해석 | 요타 오토모빌즈 사는 올해 백만 대 이상의 차량을 판매하여, 다른 해 대비 수십만 대를 초과했다.
어휘 | surpass 능가하다, 뛰어넘다

해설 | 빈칸 앞 절이 완전하고 빈칸 이하는 콤마로 연결된 것으로 보아, 빈칸 이하는 문장을 수식하는 수식어구가 되어야 한다. 선택지에서 수식어구가 될 수 있는 것은 분사인 (A)와 (D)뿐이다. 빈칸 뒤의 명사 all other years를 목적어로 취할 수 있는 것은 현재분사이므로 정답은 (A). 참고로, 문장에서 surpassing은 접속사와 주어가 생략된 분사구문으로 쓰여 문장을 수식한다.

---

115 This neighborhood houses a diverse population / and has the highest **concentration** / of immigrants in the city.
(A) difference (B) conference (C) variation
(D) concentration
해석 | 이 근방은 다양한 주민들에게 거처를 제공하며, 도시에서 가장 많은 이민자들이 밀집해 있다.
(A) 차이 (B) 회의 (C) 변형 (D) 밀집, 집중
어휘 | neighborhood 이웃, 근처 house 거처를 제공하다 immigrant 이민자

해설 | 접속사 and 앞의 다양한 사람들에게 거처를 제공하고 있다는 말과 이어지려면 '가장 높은 이민자 밀집도'라는 의미가 되도록 빈칸에 concentration이 들어가야 한다. highest concentration은 '가장 높은 밀집도', 즉 '가장 많이 모여 있다'는 의미이므로 답은 (D).

---

116 This year's year-end office party will have **fewer** attendants / than last year's / because of the venue's location.
(A) some **(B) fewer** (C) higher (D) as well
해석 | 올해의 회사 송년 파티는 행사 장소의 위치 때문에 작년보다 참석자가 더 적을 것이다.

해설 | 빈칸은 뒤의 명사 attendants를 수식하는 형용사 자리이므로 부사 (D)를 제외한 선택지 모두가 정답 후보. 뒤에 비교를 나타내는 전치사 than이 있으므로 비교급 형용사가 들어가야 한다. 문맥상 '더 적은 참석자'라는 뜻이 되어야 어울리므로 (B)가 정답이다.

117 People with disabilities and the elderly / may use the elevators / at the end of the hall / <u>rather than</u> walk up the stairs.

(A) instead **(B) rather than** (C) for instance (D) except for

해석| 장애가 있는 사람들과 고령자들은 계단을 걸어 올라가는 대신 복도 끝에 있는 엘리베이터를 이용할 수 있다.

(A) 대신에 (B) ~ 대신에 (C) 예를 들어 (D) ~을 제외하고

어휘| disability 장애 the elderly 고령자

해설| 빈칸은 문맥상 '~ 대신에'라는 뜻이 되어야 자연스러운데, 선택지 중에서 이런 뜻으로 쓰이면서 뒤에 명사, 동명사, 동사원형 등 다양한 품사가 올 수 있는 것은 (B)이다.

오답| (A)와 (C)는 접속부사이므로 적절하지 않다. (A)가 of를 수반하여 '~ 대신에'라는 뜻의 전치사로 쓰일 수 있지만, 이 경우 뒤에 동사원형이 아닌 명사나 동명사가 와야 한다. (D)는 전치사라 오답이다.

---

118 All of the interns performed <u>admirably</u> / in their temporary assignments, / and most were offered permanent positions.

(A) admire (B) admired (C) admirable **(D) admirably**

해석| 모든 인턴 사원들은 각자의 한시적인 업무를 훌륭히 수행했고, 대부분은 정규직을 제안받았다.

어휘| admirably 훌륭히 assignment 업무 permanent 영구적인

해설| 빈칸 없이도 문장이 완전하므로 빈칸은 부사 자리이다. 동사인 performed를 수식할 수 있는 부사 (D)가 정답. perform은 '수행하다'라는 뜻으로 자동사와 타동사 둘 다 쓰일 수 있다는 것도 알아두자.

---

119 Only managers / who are <u>authorized</u> to make changes to the payroll / can log into this computer.

(A) automated **(B) authorized** (C) avoided (D) postponed

해석| 급여를 변경할 수 있는 권한을 가진 관리자들만 이 컴퓨터에 로그인할 수 있다.

(A) 자동화하다 (B) 권한을 부여하다 (C) 피하다 (D) 연기하다

어휘| make changes to ~을 변경하다

해설| 빈칸이 포함된 관계대명사절 who부터 payroll까지가 앞의 선행사 managers를 수식하는 구조의 문장이다. 문맥상 급여를 변경할 수 있는 '권한을 가진 관리자'라는 뜻이 되어야 적절하다. authorize가 '권한을 부여하다, 허가하다'라는 뜻이므로 (B)가 정답이다.

---

120 The documentary was not as <u>attractive</u> / to the younger generation / as the book it was based on.

(A) attractive (B) attract (C) attracts (D) attractively

해석| 그 다큐멘터리는 그것의 토대가 된 책만큼 젊은 세대의 흥미를 끌지는 못했다.

어휘| attractive 매력적인 generation 세대

해설| 빈칸은 be동사 was의 보어 자리로 형용사가 들어가야 한다. 그리고 원급 비교 표현인 as ~ as 사이에 위치하고 있으므로 형용사의 원급인 (A)가 정답이다.

오답| (D)의 부사도 원급 비교 표현에 쓸 수 있으나 보어 자리에 올 수 없으므로 오답.

---

121 It is Alison Horton / who <u>customarily</u> greets clients / at the airport / when they come to visit the headquarters.

(A) momentarily **(B) customarily** (C) progressively (D) seemingly

해석| 고객들이 본사를 방문하러 올 때 관례적으로 공항에서 그들을 맞이하는 사람은 앨리슨 호튼 씨이다.

(A) 잠깐 (B) 관례적으로, 습관적으로 (C) 점진적으로 (D) 외견상으로

어휘| greet 맞이하다, 환영하다

해설| 빈칸에 알맞은 부사를 고르는 문제. 빈칸 뒤의 동사 greets를 수식하여 문맥상 '관례적으로 고객을 맞이하다'라는 뜻이 되어야 자연스러우므로 (B)가 정답이다. '관습, 습관'이란 뜻의 명사 custom에서 파생된 부사라는 것을 이해한다면, '관례적으로, 습관적으로'라는 부사의 의미를 짐작할 수 있다.

---

122 Henny Co. offered all of its employees <u>compensation</u> / for having them work on a holiday.

(A) compensate (B) compensating **(C) compensation** (D) compensates

해석| 헤니 사는 휴일에 근무하게 한 것에 대해 직원 모두에게 보상을 제공했다.

해설| 문장의 동사 offered는 '~에게 …를 제공하다'의 의미로 간접 목적어와 직접 목적어를 취하는 4문형 동사이다. 빈칸이 동사 offered의 간접 목적어 all of its employees 뒤에 나오므로, 빈칸은 직접 목적어에 해당하는 자리이다. 따라서 명사인 (C)가 정답이다.

123 The new coffee shop is offering a free cookie / to the first fifty customers each day / to **attract** customers.

(A) charge　(B) reject　(C) inform　**(D) attract**

해석 | 새로 생긴 커피숍은 고객을 끌어들이기 위해 매일 선착순 50명의 고객들에게 무료 쿠키를 제공하고 있다.

(A) 청구하다　(B) 거부하다　(C) 알리다　(D) 끌어들이다

해설 | 선택지의 동사 중 문맥상 빈칸 뒤 목적어인 customers와 호응하여 '고객을 끌어들이다'라는 뜻이 되어야 자연스러우므로 (D)가 정답이다. attract는 고객과 관련된 맥락에서 '(어디로) 끌어들이다, 유치하다'라는 뜻으로 쓰인다.

---

124 **Should** you wish to return this product for any reason, / please refer to the customer service desk.

(A) Should　(B) Whereas　(C) Anywhere　(D) Resulting in

해석 | 어떤 이유로든 이 제품을 반품하기를 원하실 경우, 고객 서비스 센터로 문의하시기 바랍니다.

어휘 | refer to ~로 문의하다

해설 | 콤마 앞뒤로 완전한 절이 연결되므로 빈칸에는 일단 접속사가 필요하다고 볼 수 있다. 그런데 유일한 접속사인 (B)는 '~하는 반면에'라는 뜻으로 문맥상 어울리지 않는다. 콤마 뒤에 명령문이 이어지고 있는 것을 보면 If가 생략된 가정법 미래 구문을 떠올려야 한다. 접속사 if를 생략하고 주어 you와 동사 should가 자리를 바꾼 도치구문이므로 정답은 (A)이다.

오답 | 부사 (C)와 전치사 (D)는 모두 절을 이끌 수 없다.

---

125 Jonathan Perkin's retirement party will be held in March, / and further details about the event will be given / as **it** approaches.

(A) he　(B) they　**(C) it**　(D) his

해석 | 조나단 퍼킨 씨의 은퇴 기념 파티가 3월에 열릴 예정이며, 행사에 관한 더 자세한 사항은 행사가 다가오면 알려 드리겠습니다.

어휘 | approach 다가오다

해설 | 선택지를 보니 빈칸에 알맞은 인칭대명사를 고르는 문제임을 알 수 있다. 빈칸에 들어갈 대명사가 가리키는 것은 앞에 나온 the event이다. 따라서 3인칭 단수인 사물 명사를 대신하는 (C)가 정답이다.

---

126 **Since** he was first hired / five years ago as an IT consultant, / Thomas Finslor has been promoted twice.

(A) Since　(B) Yet　(C) However　(D) When

해석 | IT 컨설턴트로 5년 전에 처음 채용된 이후로, 토마스 핀슬러 씨는 두 차례 승진했다.

(A) ~한 이후로　(B) 그렇지만　(C) 하지만　(D) ~할 때

해설 | 콤마 앞뒤에 완전한 두 개의 절이 연결어 없이 이어지고 있으므로, 빈칸에는 절을 연결하는 접속사가 들어가야 한다. 접속사 (B)는 두 절을 연결할 때 문장 맨 앞에 올 수 없고, 접속부사인 (C)는 절을 이끌어 다른 절과 연결시키는 역할을 할 수 없으므로 이 자리에 올 수 없다. 문장 맨 앞에서 두 절을 연결할 수 있는 접속사인 (A)와 (D) 중에서 문맥상 '~한 이후로'라는 뜻이 되어야 적절하므로 (A)가 정답이다.

---

127 After her company opened several new branches overseas, / Emily Elkins became interested / in the **prospect** of working abroad.

(A) routine　(B) supply　(C) rejection　**(D) prospect**

해석 | 회사가 해외에 몇 군데 새로 지점을 개설한 이후에, 에밀리 엘킨즈는 해외에서 일할 수 있는 가능성에 관심을 갖게 되었다.

(A) 일상　(B) 공급　(C) 거절　(D) 가능성

어휘 | overseas 해외에(윤 abroad)

해설 | 문맥상 '해외에서 일할 수 있는 가능성'이라는 뜻이 되어야 자연스러우므로 (D)가 정답이다. prospect는 '가능성, 가망, 전망'이라는 뜻으로 쓰인다.

128 The doctor provided the patient / with information on topics **beyond** the illness, / such as advice on lifestyle and eating habits.

(A) beyond   (B) against   (C) inside   (D) apart

해석| 의사는 그 환자에게 질병 외의 주제에 관한 정보, 예를 들어 생활 방식이나 식습관에 대한 조언을 제공했다.

(A) ～ 외에 (B) ～에 반대하여 (C) ～ 안에 (D) 떨어져

어휘| illness 질병 eating habit 식습관

해설| 빈칸 뒤의 목적어 the illness와 어울려 문맥상 '질병 외의 주제에 관한 정보'라는 뜻이 되어야 자연스럽다. '～ 이상, ～을 넘어, ～ 외에'라는 뜻으로 쓰이는 전치사 (A)가 정답이다.
오답| (D)는 (A)와 유사한 의미이나 전치사가 아니라 부사이므로 뒤에 명사가 따라오려면 전치사 from을 수반하여 apart from(～외에)의 형태가 되어야 한다.

---

129 *This Time*, a painting by Gertrude Mitchell, was **previously** revealed at the Stelton Gallery / before being moved to the Garata Museum.

(A) previously   (B) passively   (C) heavily   (D) essentially

해석| 거트루드 미첼의 그림인 〈이번에〉는 가라타 미술관으로 옮겨지기 전에 스텔턴 갤러리에서 미리 공개되었다.

(A) 미리, 이전에 (B) 수동적으로 (C) 심하게 (D) 근본적으로

어휘| reveal 드러내다

해설| 선택지를 보니, 빈칸에 알맞은 부사 어휘를 고르는 문제. 문맥상 다른 곳으로 옮겨지기 전에 '미리 공개되었다'라고 해야 자연스럽다. previously가 '미리, 이전에'라는 뜻이므로 정답은 (A).

---

130 Due to the difficult economic times, / by this time next year, / Stanic Electronics **will have closed** the majority of its factories.

(A) will be closed   (B) has been closed
(C) will have closed   (D) has closed

해석| 경제가 어려운 시기라서, 내년 이맘때쯤 스태닉 일레트로닉스 사는 공장 대부분의 문을 닫을 것이다.

어휘| majority 대다수

해설| 선택지를 보니 동사의 시제와 태를 묻는 문제이다. 빈칸 앞쪽에 미래를 나타내는 부사 next year가 있으므로 미래 시제가 되어야 한다. 따라서 (A)와 (C)가 정답 후보. 빈칸 뒤에 명사 the majority가 목적어로 나오므로 능동태 동사가 필요하다. (A)는 수동태라 오답이고 미래완료 시제인 (C)가 정답. by this time next year(내년 이맘때쯤)라는 미래의 특정 시점까지 완료되는 일을 나타내기 위해 미래완료를 썼다.

131-134

PRIMAVILLE, August 13—Primaville is quickly becoming the tourism capital of the area. **In fact**, the number of tourists to Primaville has more than doubled this year compared to last. **This rise in touristic appeal is largely due to the Primaville Arts Festival.** The event, which features various arts and crafts made of local **materials**, was launched two years ago and has been a huge success. Citizens of Primaville **see** this sudden spark in tourism as a great opportunity to increase business and make the city more dynamic.

프리마빌, 8월 13일—프리마빌은 빠르게 이 지역의 관광 중심지가 되어 가고 있다. **실제로,** 프리마빌의 관광객 수는 작년에 비해 올해 두 배 이상이 되었다. **이렇게 관광지로서의 매력이 증가한 것은 주로 프리마빌 예술 축제 때문이다.** 지역에서 나는 **재료로** 만든 다양한 미술품과 공예품들을 선보이는 이 행사는 2년 전에 시작되어 큰 성공을 거두고 있다. 프리마빌 시민들은 이런 갑작스러운 관광업의 활기를 사업을 확장하고 도시를 더 역동적으로 만들 좋은 기회로 **보고 있다.**

어휘| capital 수도, 중심지 rise 증가, 상승 touristic 관광의 appeal 매력 largely 주로 spark 촉발, 활기 dynamic 역동적인

131 In fact, the number of tourists to Primaville / has more than doubled this year / compared to last.
(A) However   (B) At first   (C) In fact   (D) Even so
(A) 하지만   (B) 처음에는   (C) 실제로   (D) 그렇기는 하지만

해설 | 알맞은 접속부사를 고르는 문제이므로 앞뒤 문장의 의미 관계를 파악하는 것이 중요하다. 앞 문장에서 프리마빌이 빠르게 관광 중심지가 되어 가고 있다고 하고 나서, 뒤 문장에서는 올해 관광객 수가 작년에 비해 두 배가 되었다고 덧붙이고 있다. 앞 문장에 대한 보충 설명이라고 볼 수 있으므로, '실제로, 실은'이라는 뜻으로 첨가를 나타내는 (C)가 적절하다.

132 (A) With many famous historic sites, Primaville is a fascinating place to visit.
(B) Information on tourist attractions is displayed throughout the city.
(C) **This rise in touristic appeal is largely due to the Primaville Arts Festival.**
(D) We would like to invite you to an event on August 20.
(A) 많은 유명한 역사 유적지가 있어, 프리마빌은 방문하기에 흥미로운 곳이다.
(B) 관광 명소에 대한 정보는 시 도처에서 보여 주고 있다.
(C) 이렇게 관광지로서의 매력이 증가한 것은 주로 프리마빌 예술 축제 때문이다.
(D) 8월 20일에 열리는 행사에 여러분을 초대하고자 합니다.

해설 | 빈칸 앞에서는 빠르게 성장하는 관광업에 대해 말하고 나서, 빈칸 뒤에서 갑자기 앞에서 언급되지 않은 행사에 대한 내용이 나오고 있다. 따라서 빈칸에는 이 행사에 대한 소개가 들어가야 자연스럽다. 선택지 중에서 프리마빌 예술 축제라는 행사를 언급하고 있는 (C)가 적절하다.
오답 | (A) 역사 유적지는 지문에 등장하지 않으므로 오답. (B) 관광 명소 정보에 대한 내용은 빈칸 뒤의 '그 행사'와 연관이 없으므로 오답. (D)는 초대장이나 전단지 도입부에 언급될 내용으로 빈칸 앞 내용인 관광객 수의 증가와는 연관이 없으므로 오답.

133 The event, / which features various arts and crafts made of local <u>materials</u>, / was launched two years ago / and has been a huge success.
(A) materials   (B) artists   (C) benefits   (D) residents
(A) 재료   (B) 예술가   (C) 혜택   (D) 주민

해설 | 빈칸 앞쪽의 made of는 '~로 만든'이란 뜻으로 앞에 있는 명사 arts and crafts를 수식하는 과거분사구이다. 따라서 빈칸에는 수공예품의 '재료'를 뜻하는 어휘가 들어가야 적절하므로, (A)가 정답이다.

134 Citizens of Primaville <u>see</u> this sudden spark in tourism / as a great opportunity / to increase business and make the city more dynamic.
(A) are seen   (B) see   (C) sees   (D) seeing

해설 | Citizens of Primaville이 주어이고, 뒤쪽에 동사가 없으므로, 빈칸은 동사 자리이다. 따라서 동사로 쓸 수 없는 동명사 (D)는 정답 후보에서 제외한다. 빈칸 뒤에 목적어 this sudden spark가 있으므로 능동태 동사인 (B)와 (C)가 정답 후보인데, 주어가 Citizens로 복수 명사이므로 복수 동사 (B)가 정답이다.

135-138

Thank you for purchasing the Scorpio X printer. <u>Please follow these directions for maintaining your printer.</u> Regularly remove dust and paper particles using compressed air and wipe down the paper-handling mechanism with a damp cloth. In case of a paper jam, open the drawer and ensure that the paper path is <u>free</u> from any obstructions. If you notice changes in colors or if some elements are not <u>correctly</u> aligned in your printouts, you may have to perform a head cleaning or print head alignment. <u>Look</u> for these functions in the system preferences of the accompanying software's main menu.

스콜피오 X 프린터를 구매해 주셔서 감사합니다. **프린터를 유지 관리하기 위해 다음 지시사항을 따라 주십시오.** 정기적으로 압축 공기를 이용하여 먼지 및 종이 부스러기를 제거하고 젖은 천으로 용지 관리 장치를 닦아 주십시오. 용지가 걸린 경우에는, 용지함을 열어 용지가 나오는 통로로 어떤 장애물도 **없도록** 해 주십시오. 색상 변화를 발견하거나 출력물에서 일부 요소가 **제대로** 맞지 않을 경우에는, 헤드 클리닝이나 프린트 헤드 조정을 실행해야 할 수도 있습니다. 함께 제공된 소프트웨어 메인 메뉴의 시스템 설정에서 이 기능을 **찾으세요.**

어휘 | direction ((*pl.*)) 사용법, 설명서 remove 제거하다 particle 입자 compressed air 압축 공기 wipe down 말끔히 닦다 mechanism 기계 장치 damp 젖은 in case of ~의 경우에 paper jam 종이 걸림 drawer 서랍, 함 ensure 반드시 ~하게 하다 obstruction 장애물 element 요소 correctly 바르게, 정확하게 align 조정하다, 나란히 만들다 printout 출력물 alignment 조정 accompany 함께 제공되다

135
(A) All of our devices are on sale for up to 60 percent off.
(B) Please follow these directions for maintaining your printer.
(C) We apologize for the issues with your equipment.
(D) However, your payment has not been processed properly.

(A) 모든 저희 기기는 최고 60%까지 세일하고 있습니다.
(B) 프린터를 유지 관리하기 위해 다음 지시사항을 따라 주십시오.
(C) 고객님의 기기에 발생한 문제에 대해 사과드립니다.
(D) 하지만 고객님의 결제가 아직 제대로 처리되지 않았습니다.

해설 | 빈칸 앞 문장에서 프린터 구입에 대해 감사하다고 하고 나서, 빈칸 뒤에서는 바로 프린터 관리법을 계속 열거하고 있다. 따라서 빈칸에도 프린터 관리와 관련된 내용이 들어가야 적절하므로 (B)가 정답이다.
오답 | 프린터를 이미 구매한 상황이므로 (A)와 (D)는 적절하지 않고, 프린터에 문제가 발생한 상황이 아니므로 (C)도 문맥상 어울리지 않는다.

136 In case of a paper jam, / open the drawer / and ensure that the paper path is <u>free</u> from any obstructions.
(A) free (B) absent (C) evident (D) trivial
(A) 없는 (B) 결석한, 부재의 (C) 분명한 (D) 사소한

해설 | 빈칸 뒤의 전치사 from과 호응할 수 있는 형용사가 들어가야 한다. be free from이 '~이 없다'라는 뜻으로 문맥상으로도 '장애물이 없다'라는 뜻이 되어 적절하므로 (A)가 정답이다.
오답 | (B) absent도 뒤에 from을 수반하여 be absent from의 형태로 쓰이지만 주로 사람을 주어로 하여 '~에 결석[결근]하다'라는 뜻으로 쓰이므로 적절하지 않다.

137 If you notice changes in colors / or if some elements are not <u>correctly</u> aligned in your printouts, / you may have to perform a head cleaning or print head alignment.
(A) corrected (B) correcting (C) correctly (D) correct

해설 | 빈칸은 수동태 동사를 구성하는 be동사 are과 과거분사 aligned 사이에 위치하고 있다. 이 사이에 올 수 있는 것은 부사뿐이므로 (C)가 정답이다.

138 <u>Look</u> for these functions / in the system preferences of the accompanying software's main menu.
(A) Look (B) Change (C) Accept (D) Call
(A) 보다 (B) 변경하다 (C) 받아들이다 (D) 부르다

해설 | 빈칸 뒤에 전치사 for가 있으므로 (A)를 제외한 나머지 타동사들은 모두 적합하지 않다. 따라서 정답은 (A). look은 타동사로 착각하기 쉬운 자동사로, 뒤에 목적어를 취할 때 다양한 전치사와 결합해 쓰인다. look for는 '~을 찾다'라는 뜻이다.

139-142

Two months ago, Veria Tech gathered data <u>from</u> hundreds of survey respondents about what functions they'd like to see in the next smartphone. Now, with only a few weeks left before the new Veria XD 5 smartphone hits the market, the company has <u>launched</u> an aggressive marketing campaign specifically targeting the needs expressed by these survey respondents. By highlighting the exact features people expressed the most interest in, Veria Tech has managed to build up excitement surrounding the new smartphone. <u>Indeed, it has exceeded all previous models in number of preorders.</u> Critics have high expectations for the Veria XD 5's

두 달 전에, 베리아 테크 사는 다음 스마트폰에서 어떤 기능을 보고 싶은지에 관해 수백 명의 설문 조사 **응답자들로부터** 데이터를 수집했다. 이제, 신제품 베리아 XD 5 스마트폰이 시장에 출시되기 전 불과 몇 주 남겨 놓고, 회사에서는 특히 이 설문 조사 응답자들이 드러낸 요구를 대상으로 하는 공격적인 마케팅 활동을 **개시했다.** 사람들이 가장 많은 관심을 나타낸, 바로 그 기능을 강조함으로써, 베리아 테크 사는 새로운 스마트폰을 둘러싼 흥미를 고조시키기 위해 애

interface, which was completely redesigned for the **optimal** user experience.

써 왔다. **실제로 그것은 선주문 수량에 있어서 모든 이전 모델들을 능가했다.** 평론가들은 베리아 XD 5의 인터페이스에 높은 기대감을 갖고 있는데, 이것은 **최적의** 사용자 경험을 위해 완전히 재디자인되었다.

어휘| hit the market 시장에 출시되다 **aggressive** 공격적인 **target** ~을 대상으로 하다 **highlight** 강조하다 **exact** 정확한 **build up** ~을 더 높이다 **preorder** 선주문 **critic** 평론가 **expectation** 기대 **redesign** 다시 디자인[설계]하다 **optimal** 최적의

---

139 Two months ago, / Veria Tech gathered data / **from** hundreds of survey respondents / about what functions they'd like to see / in the next smartphone.
(A) from　(B) above　(C) in　(D) since
(A) ~부터　(B) ~ 위에　(C) ~에　(D) ~ 이후로

해설| 빈칸에 알맞은 전치사를 고르는 문제이다. 문맥상 '수백 명의 응답자들로부터 데이터를 수집하다'라는 뜻이 되어야 자연스러우므로 '~로부터'라는 뜻의 (A)가 정답이다.

---

140 Now, with only a few weeks left / before the new Veria XD 5 smartphone hits the market, / the company has **launched** an aggressive marketing campaign / specifically targeting the needs / expressed by these survey respondents.
(A) launched　(B) advertised　(C) failed　(D) misplaced
(A) 개시하다　(B) 광고하다　(C) 실패하다　(D) 분실하다

해설| 빈칸 뒤의 an aggressive marketing campaign(공격적인 마케팅 활동)을 목적어로 취해 의미상 어울리는 동사는 '개시하다'라는 뜻의 (A)이다.

---

141 (A) This was in part due to the negative feedback from the survey.
(B) Indeed, it has exceeded all previous models in number of preorders.
(C) Unfortunately, this particular model is sold out at the moment.
(D) It is therefore imperative that more research be done in marketing.
(A) 이것은 부분적으로 설문조사의 부정적인 평가 때문이다.
(B) 실제로 그것은 선주문 수량에 있어서 모든 이전 모델들을 능가했다.
(C) 안타깝게도, 이 특정 모델은 현재 품절이다.
(D) 따라서 반드시 마케팅에서 더 많은 조사가 이루어져야 한다.

해설| 빈칸 앞에서는 베리아 테크 사가 공격적인 마케팅 활동을 펼쳐 스마트폰 신제품에 대한 흥미를 고조시켰다는 내용이 나오고, 빈칸 뒤에서는 평론가들이 제품에 대해 높은 기대를 하고 있다는 내용이 나온다. 신제품에 대한 긍정적인 내용이 이어지고 있으므로 빈칸에도 이와 이어지는 내용이 들어가야 적절하다. 선택지 중에서 신제품에 대해 긍정적인 내용을 담은 (B)가 정답이다.
오답| (A)는 빈칸 앞의 '기대감 고조'와 상반된 내용이므로 오답. (C)는 신제품이 아직 출시 전이므로 오답. (D)의 마케팅 조사는 지문에 언급되었지만 빈칸 앞뒤의 흐름과 어울리지 않아서 오답이다.

---

142 Critics have high expectations for the Veria XD 5's interface, / which was completely redesigned / for the **optimal** user experience.
(A) optimize　(B) optimization　(C) optimizes　**(D) optimal**

해설| 빈칸 앞의 한정사 the와 뒤에 나오는 복합명사 user experience로 보아 빈칸은 형용사 자리이고, 문맥상 '최적의 사용자 경험'이라는 의미가 되어야 자연스러우므로 (D)가 정답이다.

143-146

Visitors to the Taurus Gym may use the changing rooms located in the east wing of the building. Please do not leave <u>clothing</u> lying around in the changing rooms. <u>Instead, please place your items in one of the lockers.</u> These are secured by a code of your choosing and are large enough to hold all of your articles. <u>Each</u> requires a deposit of $1.00, which is returned to the user. If you forget your passcode, please report to the main desk, which is open from 8 A.M. to 9 P.M. daily. Note that it will take <u>approximately</u> thirty minutes to resolve the issue.

토러스 헬스클럽 방문객들은 건물 동관에 있는 탈의실을 이용할 수 있습니다. 탈의실에 **옷을** 늘어놓지 않도록 해 주시기 바랍니다. **대신에 여러분의 물품을 사물함 중 하나에 넣어 주십시오.** 사물함은 여러분이 고른 비밀번호로 보안되며 여러분의 소지품 전부를 보관할 정도로 큽니다. **각각의** 사물함은 1달러의 보증금이 필요한데, 이는 사용자에게 돌려 드립니다. 비밀번호를 잊어버렸을 경우에는, 안내 데스크에 알려 주십시오. 안내 데스크는 매일 오전 8시부터 오후 9시까지 엽니다. 문제를 해결하는 데 **약** 30분 정도 걸린다는 점에 주의하세요.

어휘| changing room 탈의실 located in ~에 위치한 lie around 아무렇게나 놓여 있다 secure 안전하게 지키다 code 비밀번호 (유password) article 물품 deposit 보증금 report 알리다 approximately 대략

---

143 Please do not leave <u>clothing</u> lying around / in the changing rooms.
  (A) machinery **(B) clothing** (C) facilities (D) locations
  (A) 기계 (B) 옷 (C) 시설 (D) 장소

해설| 문맥상 탈의실에 여기저기 늘어놓을 수 있는 것은 '옷'이므로 정답은 (B).

---

144 **(A) Instead, please place your items in one of the lockers.**
  (B) Once you're done changing, you may use equipment.
  (C) For directions, please check the floor plan on the wall.
  (D) We apologize for this temporary inconvenience.
  (A) 대신에 여러분의 물품을 사물함 중 하나에 넣어 주십시오.
  (B) 옷을 다 갈아입으시면, 장비를 이용하셔도 됩니다.
  (C) 길 안내를 원하시면, 벽에 있는 평면도를 확인하십시오.
  (D) 이렇게 일시적으로 불편을 끼쳐 드려 죄송합니다.

해설| 빈칸 앞 문장에서는 탈의실에 옷을 늘어놓지 말라고 당부하고, 빈칸 뒤에서는 사물함에 대해 안내하고 있다. 따라서 빈칸에는 소지품을 사물함에 보관하라는 내용이 들어갈 것임을 짐작할 수 있으므로 정답은 (A).
오답| (B)는 빈칸 앞뒤에서 사물함에 대해 설명하고 있으므로 흐름에 어울리지 않아 오답. (C)는 길 안내와 평면도가 지문과 관련이 없어서 오답. (D)의 불편(inconvenience)도 지문의 내용과 전혀 상관이 없으므로 오답.

---

145 <u>Each</u> requires a deposit of $1.00, / which is returned to the user.
  (A) Every (B) Another **(C) Each** (D) Either
  (A) 모든 (B) 또 하나의 (C) 각각 (D) (둘 중) 어느 하나

해설| 주어 자리에 들어갈 대명사를 고르는 문제이다. 앞에서 언급한 locker를 가리키는 대명사로, 문맥상 '각각, 개당'이라는 뜻이 되어야 적절하므로 (C)가 정답이다.
오답| 의미상 (A)도 가능해 보이지만, every는 뒤에 단수 명사를 필요로 하며, 단독으로 대명사처럼 쓰이지는 않으므로 적절하지 않다.

---

146 Note that it will take <u>approximately</u> thirty minutes / to resolve the issue.
  (A) approximate (B) approximated (C) approximation
  (D) approximately

해설| 빈칸이 없어도 완전한 문장을 이루고 있으므로 빈칸은 부사 자리이다. 따라서 정답은 부사인 (D).

147-148

www.meteorshowertrilogy.com/news/

The first trailer for director Tyler Morton's newest movie, *Comets*, was just released. As the last chapter of the *Meteor Shower* trilogy, *Comets* is the most anticipated science-fiction movie of the year. **147** It will be in theaters on July 1.

To view the trailer, click here: www.cometsmovie.com/trailer1

148 Share the trailer on any of your social media pages to be automatically entered to win two seats at the premiere! Contest winners will get to meet director Tyler Morton and lead actor Jed Barrings for a question-and-answer session! Winners will be contacted by e-mail on May 13.

타일러 모튼 감독의 신작 〈코멧〉의 첫 번째 예고편이 막 공개되었습니다. 〈유성우〉 3부작의 마지막 편인 〈코멧〉은 올해 가장 기대되는 SF 영화입니다. **147** 이 영화는 7월 1일에 개봉됩니다.

예고편을 보시려면, 여기: www.cometsmovie.com/trailer1를 클릭하십시오.

148 여러분의 소셜 미디어 어느 페이지에나 예고편을 공유하면 시사회 좌석 2장을 받을 수 있는 기회에 자동 응모됩니다! 당첨자들은 타일러 모튼 감독과 주연 배우인 제드 바링즈 씨를 만나 질의응답 시간을 갖게 됩니다! 당첨자들에게는 5월 13일에 이메일로 연락이 갈 것입니다.

어휘| trailer (영화 등의) 예고편 trilogy 3부작 premiere 시사회, 개봉 lead actor 주연 배우

147 What will happen on July 1?
(A) A participant will be chosen.
(B) A director will be interviewed.
(C) A movie will be released.
(D) A trailer will be shown.

7월 1일에 있을 일은?
참가자가 선정된다.
감독을 인터뷰한다.
영화가 개봉된다.
예고편이 상영된다.

해설| **세부 사항▶** 단서 **147**에서 영화 개봉일자가 7월 1일이라고 했으므로 정답은 (C).
패러프레이징| **단서** be in theaters → **정답** be released

148 How can people participate in the contest?
(A) By purchasing movie tickets
(B) By sharing a video
(C) By sending an e-mail
(D) By filling out a form

사람들이 콘테스트에 참여할 수 있는 방법은?
영화표를 구입함으로써
동영상을 공유함으로써
이메일을 보냄으로써
양식을 작성함으로써

어휘| participate in ~에 참여[참가]하다
해설| **세부 사항▶** 단서 **148**에서 소셜 미디어 페이지에 예고편을 공유하면 자동으로 응모된다고 했는데, 예고편은 일종의 동영상이므로 정답은 (B).
패러프레이징| **단서** the trailer → **정답** a video

149-150

To: Employees <customerservicestaff@jplusluggage.com>
From: Gerard Keaton <gkeaton@jplusluggage.com>
Subject: Web Site Change
Date: February 1

As you know, our Web site was recently updated, and you'll notice that **149** customers now go through a different procedure to leave comments about our products and services. These comments are now all made public, and customers must provide proof of

수신: 직원들 〈customerservicestaff@jplusluggage.com〉
발신: 제라드 키튼 〈gkeaton@jplusluggage.com〉
제목: 웹사이트 변경
날짜: 2월 1일

여러분도 아시다시피, 우리 웹사이트가 최근에 업데이트되어서, **149** 고객들이 이제는 우리 제

purchase to contribute. **150** If you notice a negative comment from a customer, please respond to the review by starting with a polite sentence using the person's name and acknowledging the issue. Then, please offer a solution or explanation. See the example below.

150 Meredith McGuire, we are very sorry to hear that the suitcase you received was not of the quality you expected. Please note that our products come with a warranty, and we'd be happy to replace your suitcase. You can fill out a request at this link: www.jplusluggage.com/exchangeform/.

If you have any questions, feel free to contact me.

Gerard Keaton
Customer Service Manager

품 및 서비스에 의견을 남기기 위해 다른 절차를 거치게 된다는 것을 알게 되실 겁니다. 이 의견들은 이제 모두 공개되고, 고객들은 의견을 작성하려면 구매의 증거를 제공해야 합니다.

150 만약 부정적인 고객 의견을 보게 되면, 그 사람의 이름을 넣은 정중한 문장으로 시작하여 문제점을 인지했음을 알리는 것으로 그 의견에 대응해 주십시오. 그리고 나서 해결책이나 설명을 제공하십시오. 아래 예시를 참고하세요.

150 메레디스 맥과이어 씨, 고객님께서 받으신 여행가방이 기대하셨던 품질이 아니었다고 하시니 정말 죄송합니다. 저희 제품은 보증서가 포함되어 있다는 점을 알려 드리며, 기꺼이 고객님의 여행가방을 교환해 드리겠습니다. 이 링크에서 요청서를 작성하시면 됩니다: www.jplusluggage.com/exchangeform/.

문의사항이 있으시면, 언제든지 저에게 연락 주십시오.

고객서비스 담당자
제라드 키튼 드림

어휘| go through 거치다 procedure 절차 make public 공개하다 contribute 기고하다 negative 부정적인 respond to ~에 대응하다 review 평가 polite 정중한 acknowledge (편지 등을) 받았다고 알리다 explanation 설명 replace 교환하다

---

149 What did the company recently change?
(A) Its return policy
(B) Its feedback process
(C) Its product prices
(D) Its Web site address

회사에서 최근에 변경한 것은?
반품 규정
피드백 과정
제품 가격
웹사이트 주소

해설| 세부 내용▶ 단서 **149** 에서 고객들이 의견을 남기는 절차가 달라졌다고 했으므로 정답은 (B).
오답| (D) 웹사이트 내용을 업데이트한 것이지 주소가 바뀐 것은 아니므로 오답.
패러프레이징| 단서 a different procedure to leave comments → **정답** Its feedback process

---

150 Who is Ms. McGuire?
(A) An airline agent
(B) A customer service representative
(C) A department manager
(D) A product reviewer

맥과이어 씨의 신분은?
항공사 직원
고객서비스 담당직원
부서장
제품 평가자

어휘| agent 직원 reviewer 평가자, 논평가
해설| 세부 내용▶ 맥과이어 씨는 고객 응대 예시로 든 글에 등장하는 이름으로, 단서 **150** 에서 의견을 제시한 고객의 이름을 넣은 문장으로 대응하라는 지침을 따른 것임을 알 수 있다. 따라서 맥과이어 씨는 제품을 평가한 고객에 해당하므로 정답은 (D).

151-153

From: GJ Bank <customerservice@gjbank.com>
To: Mary Princeton <m_princeton@theonemail.com>
Subject: Your GJ Bank Card
Date: January 3

Dear Ms. Princeton,

151 We've noticed that some irregular transactions were recently made with your GJ Bank card. To protect you from fraud, **153** we have frozen your account. —[1]— . To remove the freeze, you must call us at 5332-5726 or visit any GJ Bank branch. —[2]— . You will be asked to prove your identity and to verify some transactions. —[3]— .

We'd like to remind you that lost cards and unrequested transactions should be reported as soon as they are noticed in order to avoid funds being stolen. —[4]— . **152** We also recommend changing your password often to ensure that your account is protected.

Sincerely,

GJ Bank Customer Service

발신: GJ 은행
⟨customerservice@gjbank.com⟩
수신: 메리 프린스톤
⟨m_princeton@theonemail.com⟩
제목: 고객님의 GJ 은행 카드
날짜: 1월 3일

프린스톤 씨께,

151 최근에 고객님의 GJ 은행 카드로 비정상적인 거래가 이루어졌음을 알게 되었습니다. 고객님을 사기로부터 보호하기 위해, **153** 고객님의 계좌를 정지시켰습니다. —[1]— . 정지를 해지하시려면 5332-5726번으로 전화 주시거나 GJ 은행 지점을 방문하셔야 합니다. —[2]— . 고객님은 신분 증명과 거래 확인을 요청받으실 겁니다. —[3]— .

예금 도난을 방지하기 위해 카드 분실 및 요청하지 않은 거래는 알아차리신 즉시 신고하셔야 한다는 점을 다시 한번 알려드립니다. —[4]— . 또한 계좌가 확실히 보호될 수 있도록 **152** 고객님의 비밀번호를 자주 변경하실 것을 권해 드립니다.

GJ 은행 고객서비스부 드림

어휘| **irregular** 비정상적인, 불규칙한 **fraud** 사기 **freeze** (자산·예금 등을) 정지하다, 동결하다 **identity** 신분, 신원 **unrequested** 요청받지 않은

---

151 Why was the e-mail sent to Ms. Princeton?
(A) **To notify her of unusual activities**
(B) To request payment for a recent order
(C) To inform her of a new banking policy
(D) To thank her for being a loyal customer

프린스톤 씨에게 이메일을 보낸 이유는?
평소와 다른 거래 활동을 알리기 위해
최근 주문에 대한 지불을 요청하기 위해
새로운 금융 규정을 알리기 위해
우수 고객이 되어 준 것에 대해 감사하기 위해

어휘| **notify** 알리다 **loyal customer** 단골[우수] 고객
해설| **글의 목적▶** 이메일을 보내는 이유는 주로 글의 초반에 언급된다. 단서 **151** 에서 수신인인 프린스톤 씨의 카드로 비정상적인 거래가 이루어졌음을 알리고 있는데, 이것이 바로 이메일을 보낸 이유에 해당하므로 정답은 (A).
패러프레이징| 단서 some irregular transactions → 정답 unusual activities

---

152 What is Ms. Princeton advised to do?
(A) Open a new account
(B) **Modify security codes**
(C) Request transaction receipts
(D) Always carry an ID card

프린스톤 씨가 하도록 요청받은 것은?
새로운 계좌 개설하기
비밀번호 변경하기
거래 영수증 요청하기
항상 신분증 지참하기

어휘| **ID card** 신분증
해설| **세부 내용▶** 단서 **152** 에서 비밀번호를 자주 변경할 것을 권하고 있으므로 정답은 (B).
패러프레이징| 단서 changing your password → 정답 Modify security codes

153 In which of the positions marked [1], [2], [3], and [4] does the following sentence best belong?

"**Thus, no transaction can be done using your bank card.**"

(A) [1]

(B) [2]

(C) [3]

(D) [4]

[1], [2], [3], [4]번으로 표시된 위치들 중 다음 문장이 들어가기에 가장 적절한 곳은?

"따라서 고객님의 은행 카드를 이용하여 어떠한 거래도 할 수가 없습니다."

해설 | **문장 삽입 ▶** 주어진 문장이 '따라서, 그러므로'라는 의미의 Thus로 시작하고 있다. 어떤 일의 결과에 대해 말하고 있으므로, 원인이 되는 문장 뒤에 위치해야 함을 알 수 있다. 은행 카드를 이용하지 못하는 것은, 그 계좌가 정지되었기 때문일 것이므로 이러한 내용의 단서 **153** 다음인 [1]번에 주어진 문장이 들어가야 자연스럽다. 따라서 답은 (A).

154-155

Richard Webster [12:03 P.M.]

Hey, Helen and Tarah. I saw a listing for an office on Chestnut Street online.

Tarah Layman [12:05 P.M.]

I think I know which place you're talking about. **154** It looks perfect for our new law offices. It has everything we are looking for.

Richard Webster [12:05 P.M.]

Yes, so I contacted the landlord, and he said he's available now until two. Do you want to check it out?

Helen Nord [12:06 P.M.]

We were just about to go to lunch. Is it possible to visit it tomorrow instead?

Richard Webster [12:07 P.M.]

Well, it probably is, but it is really nice, and apparently, he's getting a lot of interest. So I think it's better for us to go see it as soon as possible.

Tarah Layman [12:08 P.M.]

OK. I guess we can just eat lunch later. You're not at the office, right? **155** Shall we meet at the subway station on Chestnut Street?

Richard Webster [12:09 P.M.]

I can pick you up. I'm only a couple of minutes from the office. I'm leaving now.

리처드 웹스터 [오후 12:03]

안녕하세요, 헬렌과 태라. 인터넷에서 체스넛 가에 있는 사무실이 실린 목록을 보았어요.

태라 레이먼 [오후 12:05]

어느 곳을 말씀하시는지 알 것 같아요. **154** 우리 새 법률 사무소로 적격일 것 같아요. 우리가 찾고 있는 모든 것이 갖춰져 있어요.

리처드 웹스터 [오후 12:05]

네, 그래서 제가 집주인에게 연락했는데, 지금 두 시까지 시간이 난대요. 확인해 보시겠어요?

헬렌 노드 [오후 12:06]

우린 막 점심을 먹으러 나가던 참이었어요. 대신 내일 가도 될까요?

리처드 웹스터 [오후 12:07]

그게, 가능할 것 같긴 하지만, 정말 좋은 곳이고 보아하니 그 사람이 관심을 많이 받고 있는 것 같더라고요. 그래서 우리가 가능한 한 빨리 가 보는 게 더 좋을 것 같아요.

태라 레이먼 [오후 12:08]

알겠어요. 점심은 나중에 먹어야겠네요. 지금 사무실에 있는 거 아니죠? **155** 체스넛 가에 있는 지하철역에서 만날까요?

리처드 웹스터 [오후 12:09]

제가 태우러 갈 수 있어요. 사무실에서 몇 분밖에 안 걸리는 곳에 있거든요. 지금 출발할게요.

어휘 | listing 목록 **landlord** 집주인 **available** 시간이 나는 **be about to** *do* 막 ~하려던 참이다

154 What is most likely true about the writers?

(A) **They are planning to move to another place.**

(B) They currently work on Chestnut Street.

(C) They are the owners of several properties.

(D) They have been trying to contact their landlord.

메시지 작성자들에 대해 사실일 것 같은 것은?

다른 장소로 이사할 계획이다.

현재 체스넛 가에서 일한다.

몇몇 건물을 소유하고 있다.

집주인에게 연락하려고 애쓰고 있다.

해설 | **내용 일치/사실 확인** ▶ 첫 번째 메시지의 단서 **154**에서 우리 새 법률 사무소(our new law offices)로 적격일 것 같다는 말에서, 세 사람이 사무실을 옮길 계획임을 알 수 있으므로 정답은 (A).

오답 | (B) 새로 옮기고자 하는 사무실 위치가 체스넛 가이므로 오답. (C) 세 사람이 건물을 소유하고 있다는 내용은 없으므로 오답. (D) 집주인에게 이미 연락을 취한 상태이므로 오답.

---

155 At 12:09 P.M., what does Mr. Webster mean when he writes, "I'm leaving now"?
(A) He is already on the subway.
(B) He has just finished eating lunch.
(C) He is taking the rest of the day off.
(D) He will meet his coworkers soon.

오후 12시 9분에, 웹스터 씨가 "지금 출발할게요"라고 말한 의미는?
이미 지하철을 탔다.
막 점심식사를 끝냈다.
오늘 나머지 시간은 쉴 것이다.
곧 동료들을 만날 것이다.

해설 | **의도 파악** ▶ 해당 표현은 단서 **155**에서 레이먼 씨가 지하철역에서 만나자고 제안한 것에 대해, 웹스터 씨가 자신이 태우러 가겠다고 말한 뒤, 지금 출발한다고 덧붙이는 말이다. 따라서 노드 씨와 레이먼 씨를 만나러 간다는 의미이므로 정답은 (D).

156-157

MEMO	메모
To: Customer Service Staff	수신: 고객서비스부 전 직원
From: Bianca Dargan	발신: 비앙카 다르간
Date: March 2	날짜: 3월 2일
Subject: Name Badges	제목: 명찰

A few months ago, we distributed name badges to all of our staff. **156** We'd like to emphasize once again that it is imperative that all customer service personnel have their names clearly visible. The badge must be worn on the left side of your shirt, right below the shoulder. We have noticed several customer service representatives not wearing a name badge or wearing it in the wrong place. Studies show that customers tend to respond in a much friendlier way and have a more positive view of an interaction when they know the customer service representative's name. We must therefore insist that you make every effort to follow this policy. **157** If you have misplaced your badge or if it is damaged, please immediately request a new one from human resources.

몇 달 전에, 우리 직원 모두에게 명찰을 나누어 드렸습니다. **156** 모든 고객서비스부 직원은 반드시 이름이 확실히 보이도록 해야 한다는 점을 다시 한번 강조하고자 합니다. 명찰은 셔츠 왼쪽, 어깨 바로 아래쪽에 달아야 합니다. 몇몇 고객서비스 담당 직원들이 명찰을 착용하지 않거나 엉뚱한 곳에 착용하고 있는 것을 보았습니다. 조사에 따르면 고객은 고객서비스 담당 직원의 이름을 알고 있을 때 훨씬 더 친근하게 반응하며, 대화에 있어 더 긍정적인 관점을 취하는 경향이 있다고 합니다. 따라서 우리는 여러분이 이 규정을 따르기 위해 모든 노력을 다 해야 한다고 생각합니다. **157** 명찰을 분실하거나 손상되었을 경우에는, 즉시 인사부에 새 것을 요청해 주십시오.

어휘 | **name badge** 명찰 **imperative** 반드시 해야 하는 **visible** 보이는, 알아볼 수 있는 **tend to** *do* ~하는 경향이 있다 **interaction** 대화, 상호작용 **misplace** 분실하다, 둔 곳을 잊어버리다 **damaged** 손상된 **human resources** 인사부

156 What is the purpose of the memo?
(A) To remind employees of a rule
(B) To inform staff of a recent study's results
(C) To announce the hiring of new members
(D) To report an increase in negative feedback

메모의 목적은?
직원들에게 규정을 상기시키기 위해
직원들에게 최근 조사 결과를 알리기 위해
신입 직원 채용을 발표하기 위해
부정적인 의견의 증가를 보고하기 위해

해설 | **글의 목적** ▶ 지문과 같은 메모의 목적은 대개 첫 부분에 언급된다. 단서 **156**에서 고객서비스부 직원들에게 반드시 이름이 확실히 보이도록 해야 한다는 것, 즉 반드시 명찰을 착용해야 한다는 규정을 상기시키고 있으므로 정답은 (A).

157 What should employees do if they have a problem with their badge?
(A) Tell customers their names
(B) Contact a department
(C) Check a policy manual
(D) Speak with their supervisors

직원들이 명찰에 문제가 있을 경우 해야 하는 것은?
고객에게 자신의 이름을 말해 주기
부서에 연락하기
규정 지침서를 확인하기
상사에게 말하기

어휘ㅣ manual 지침서

해설ㅣ **세부 내용 ▶** 마지막 문장인 단서 **157**에서 명찰을 분실하거나 손상되었을 경우에는, 인사부에 새 것을 요청하라고 했으므로 정답은 (B).

패러프레이징ㅣ **단서** request a new one from human resources → **정답** Contact a department

---

158-160

From: Pasha Beauty <customerservice@pashabeauty.com>
To: Mia Robert <miarobert@cleanmail.com>
Subject: Order 36694
Date: May 4

Dear customer,

Thank you for shopping at Pasha Beauty, your one-stop online store for all cosmetics and beauty products! **158** We are writing to inform you that your order has shipped. Your order number is 36694 and you may track the package by following this link: www.denverspeeddelivery.com/ordertracking/125a55.
Below is a summary of your order:

159 1 Tinty Hand Cream 225mL	$15.50
1 Tinty Hand Cream 50mL	$5.00
1 Laloo Eye Shadow Kit	$17.75
TOTAL	**$38.25**

For returns, exchanges, or any other issues, you may respond to this e-mail or call 494-8813 to speak to a customer service representative.

We hope you enjoy your Pasha Beauty items and shop with us again soon. After you receive your merchandise, **160** please review our products! We and other customers would love to hear what you think.

Sincerely,
Pasha Beauty Customer Service

발신: 파샤 뷰티 〈customerservice@pashabeauty.com〉
수신: 미아 로버트 〈miarobert@cleanmail.com〉
제목: 주문 36694
날짜: 5월 4일

고객님께,

모든 화장품 및 미용 제품을 한 곳에서 살 수 있는 온라인 매장인, 파샤 뷰티에서 구입해 주셔서 감사합니다! **158** 고객님의 주문 상품이 발송되었음을 알려드리고자 메일을 드립니다. 고객님의 주문 번호는 36694번이며 다음 링크에 들어가서 상품을 추적하실 수 있습니다. www.denverspeeddelivery.com/ordertracking/125a55
귀하의 주문 내역은 다음과 같습니다.

159 틴티 핸드크림 225ml 1개	15.50달러
틴티 핸드크림 50ml 1개	5.00달러
랄루 아이섀도우 키트 1개	17.75달러
합계	**38.25달러**

반품, 교환 및 기타 문제에 대해서는, 이 이메일에 회신을 주시거나 494-8813번으로 전화하셔서 고객서비스 담당 직원에게 말씀하시면 됩니다.

파샤 뷰티 제품에 만족하시기를 바라며 조만간 다시 구매해 주시기를 바랍니다. 제품을 받으신 후에, **160** 저희 제품에 대해 평가해 주십시오! 저희와 다른 고객들이 고객님의 의견을 듣고 싶어합니다.

파샤 뷰티 고객서비스부 드림

어휘ㅣ one-stop 한 곳에서 다 살[할] 수 있는 cosmetics 화장품 track 추적하다 exchange 교환 merchandise 상품

158 What is the purpose of the e-mail?
(A) To confirm shipment of a package
(B) To thank a shopper for a review
(C) To provide an update on item availability
(D) To inform a customer of a declined payment.

이메일의 목적은?
소포 발송을 확인해 주기 위해
쇼핑객의 평가에 감사하기 위해
제품 구매 가능 여부에 대해 업데이트해주기 위해
고객에게 결제 거부를 알리기 위해

어휘 | shipment 발송, 배송
해설 | **글의 목적** ▶ 단서 **158**의 We are writing to 이하에서 이메일을 보낸 목적을 밝히고 있다. 주문 상품이 발송되었음을 알리기 위해서라고 했으므로 정답은 (A).

패러프레이징 | 단서 inform you that your order has shipped → 정답 confirm shipment of a package

---

159 What is implied about the Tinty hand cream?
(A) It was on sale at the time of the order.
(B) It comes in more than one size.
(C) It is currently out of stock.
(D) It was shipped separately.

틴티 핸드크림에 대해 암시된 것은?
주문 당시 할인 중이었다.
한 가지 이상의 용량으로 나온다.
현재 품절이다.
따로 발송되었다.

어휘 | out of stock 품절인
해설 | **세부 내용** ▶ 주문 내역의 단서 **159**에서 틴티 핸드크림을 225ml와 50ml, 두 가지 용량으로 주문한 것으로 미루어 보아 이 핸드크림은 용량이 최소 두 가지로 나온다는 것을 알 수 있으므로 정답은 (B).

---

160 What is Ms. Robert asked to do?
(A) Contact customer service
(B) Refer a friend
(C) Return one of the items
(D) Provide some feedback

로버트 씨가 하도록 요청받은 것은?
고객서비스부에 연락하기
친구 추천하기
제품 한 가지를 반품하기
평가 제공하기

어휘 | refer 추천하다
해설 | **세부 내용** ▶ 이메일 끝부분의 단서 **160**에서 제품을 평가해 달라고 요청하고 있으므로 정답은 (D).
오답 | (A) 고객서비스부에 연락하는 것은 제품에 문제가 있을 경우의 해결 방법에 해당하는 것이므로 오답.

패러프레이징 | 단서 review our products → 정답 Provide some feedback

161-164

Tessa Museum is extending its hours starting in September. Come check out our newest artifacts and exhibitions!

161 Museum Hours
Tuesday to Thursday: 9 A.M. to 6 P.M.
Friday to Saturday: 10 A.M. to 8 P.M.
Sunday: 8 A.M. to 7 P.M.

Special Exhibit: *Metal in Art*
October 3 to October 31
The Tessa Museum of Art has a special exhibit on metal and its artistic value. **162B** The exhibit gives a history of metal and its use throughout history with chronologies, **162A** artifacts from a variety of countries and time periods, photographs of famous items, and **162D** videos showing art being made. It explains the role that metal has played in shaping our society and the way it has been used in art to convey a wide range of messages. The exhibit will also feature

테사 미술관은 9월부터 운영시간을 연장합니다. 오셔서 새로 들여온 유물 및 전시를 확인하세요!

161 미술관 운영시간
화요일부터 목요일: 오전 9시부터 오후 6시
금요일부터 토요일: 오전 10시부터 오후 8시
일요일: 오전 8시부터 오후 7시

특별 전시: 〈예술 속의 금속〉
10월 3일부터 10월 31일까지
테사 미술관에서는 금속과 그 예술적 가치를 주제로 하는 특별 전시를 하고 있습니다. **162B** 전시에서는 금속의 역사와 역사 속 금속의 사용을 연대표로 보여주고, **162A** 여러 국가 및 시대에서 비롯된 유물, 유명한 물품들의 사진, **162D** 미술품이 만들어지는 것을 보여주는 영상을 소개

many modern metal art pieces, contributions from **163** Gabriel Harrah's private collection.

In addition, the museum's curator, Dr. Dmitri Raja, will give a lecture on October 20 at 5:00 P.M. **164** Dr. Raja will talk about *Black Crystals*, artist Valery Borjes's most recent piece, which is featured in the exhibit. While the exhibit is free, the lecture costs $20.00 to attend. Reserve your seat by calling 555-3270.

합니다. 전시는 금속이 우리 사회를 형성하는 데에 수행한 역할과 다양한 메시지를 전달하기 위해 예술에서 사용되어온 방식을 설명해 줍니다. 또한 이 전시에는 많은 현대 금속 미술작품들도 소개되는데, 이는 **163** 가브리엘 하라 씨의 개인 소장품에서 기증된 것입니다.

그뿐만 아니라, 미술관 큐레이터인 드미트리 라자 박사가 10월 20일 오후 5시에 강연을 합니다. **164** 라자 박사는 미술가 발레리 보르예스의 가장 최근 작품이며 이번 전시에 소개되는 〈블랙 크리스털〉에 관해 이야기할 예정입니다. 전시는 무료이지만, 강연은 참가비가 20달러입니다. 555-3270으로 전화하셔서 자리를 예약하십시오.

어휘| artifact (인공) 유물 chronology 연대기 convey 전달하다 a wide range of 다양한 contribution 기증, 기부 collection 소장품, 수집품

---

161 What is indicated about the Tessa Museum of Art?
(A) It closes later on weekends.
(B) It first opened on October 3.
(C) It focuses on modern art.
(D) It charges an extra fee for exhibits.

테사 미술관에 대해 시사된 것은?
주말에는 더 늦게 문을 닫는다.
10월 3일에 처음 개관했다.
현대 미술에 중점을 두고 있다.
전시에 추가 요금을 청구한다.

어휘| charge 청구하다 extra fee 추가 요금
해설| 내용 일치/사실 확인▶ 단서 **161**의 미술관 운영시간을 보면 주중에는 6시, 토요일과 일요일에는 8시와 7시에 문을 닫는다고 나와 있으므로 주말에는 더 늦게 문을 닫는다는 것을 알 수 있다. 따라서 정답은 (A).
오답| (B) 10월 3일은 미술관이 처음 문을 연 날이 아니라 특별 전시가 시작하는 날짜이므로 오답. (D) 별도로 강연 참가비는 필요하지만, 전시는 무료라고 했으므로 오답.

---

162 What is NOT mentioned as featured in the *Metal in Art* exhibit?
(A) Examples of artwork
(B) Historical timelines
(C) **Pictures of artists**
(D) Educational films

〈예술 속의 금속〉 전시에서 소개되는 것으로 언급된 것이 아닌 것은?
미술품 예시
역사 연대표
미술가들의 사진
교육 영상

어휘| timeline 연대표 educational 교육적인
해설| 내용 일치/사실 확인▶ (A) 단서 **162A**에서 여러 국가와 시대의 유물이 소개될 것이라고 했고, (B) 단서 **162B**에서 금속의 역사를 연대표로 보여줄 것이라고 했으며, (D) 단서 **162D**에서 미술품이 만들어지는 영상을 보여준다고 했다. 그러나 미술가들의 사진에 대한 언급은 없으므로 정답은 (C).

---

163 Who is Mr. Harrah?
(A) A museum curator
(B) A world historian
(C) **An art collector**
(D) A metal artist

하라 씨의 신분은?
미술관 큐레이터
세계사 학자
미술품 수집가
금속 미술가

어휘| historian 역사학자
해설| 세부 내용▶ 단서 **163**에서 가브리엘 하라 씨의 개인 소장품(Gabriel Harrah's private collection)인 미술품들이 소개된다고 했으므로 하라 씨가 미술품 수집가라는 것을 알 수 있다. 따라서 정답은 (C).

164 What will the lecture on October 20 be about?
(A) Metal's history
(B) An artist's life
(C) Artistic methods
(D) A work of art

10월 20일자 강연에서 다룰 내용은?
금속의 역사
한 예술가의 일생
미술 기법들
하나의 미술작품

해설 | **세부 내용** ▶ 단서 **164**를 보면 강연에서 라자 박사는 *Black Crystals*라는 작품에 대해 이야기한다고 했으므로 정답은 (D).

165-168

Wilfried Parkson	[11:33 A.M.]

Hello. I'm with FFD Co. I was given this contact number for the retirement lunch. **165** I'm in charge of setting up the buffet and setting the tables.

Jessica Fern	[11:35 A.M.]

Hi. Yes, I'm the event organizer for today. Is there something I can help you with?

Wilfried Parkson	[11:36 A.M.]

166 I've just arrived at the venue, the Natalia room at Tran Ly Hotel. I've noticed that the room has only thirty chairs. I was told you have a party of thirty-five. I want to make sure you are aware of that.

Jessica Fern	[11:38 A.M.]

Oh, I didn't know. That is strange. The hotel had told us the room could accommodate thirty-five people. Anyway, is it possible for you to provide some?

Wilfried Parkson	[11:39 A.M.]

167 Well, that shouldn't be a problem. I have to make a couple more trips back to the headquarters anyway. **168** But chair rental is not free.

Jessica Fern	[11:40 A.M.]

Yes, I assumed so. That's fine. Just add it to the bill. We still have some room in the budget.

Wilfried Parkson	[11:41 A.M.]

OK. I'll go get those for you now. Everything should be ready by 1 P.M.

윌프리드 파크슨	[오전 11:33]

안녕하세요. 저는 FFD 사 직원입니다. 은퇴 기념 오찬과 관련해서 이 연락처를 받았습니다. **165** 제가 뷔페 준비와 테이블 세팅을 담당하고 있습니다.

제시카 펀	[오전 11:35]

안녕하세요. 네, 제가 오늘 행사 담당자입니다. 제가 뭐 도와드릴 일이 있나요?

윌프리드 파크슨	[오전 11:36]

166 제가 좀 전에 행사 장소인 트란 리 호텔의 나탈리아 룸에 도착했는데, 룸에 의자가 30개 밖에 없다는 것을 알았습니다. 귀사의 일행이 35명이라고 들었거든요. 그 점을 알고 계신지 확인하고 싶어서요.

제시카 펀	[오전 11:38]

아, 몰랐어요. 그거 이상하네요. 호텔에서는 그 공간에 35명을 수용할 수 있다고 말했거든요. 어쨌든, 의자를 좀 제공해 줄 수 있으신가요?

윌프리드 파크슨	[오전 11:39]

167 음, 그건 어렵지 않을 것 같습니다. 어쨌든 본사에 몇 번 더 다녀와야 합니다. **168** 하지만 의자 대여는 무료가 아닙니다.

제시카 펀	[오전 11:40]

네, 그렇게 예상했습니다. 괜찮습니다. 청구서에 추가해 주세요. 아직 저희 예산에 약간 여유가 있어요.

윌프리드 파크슨	[오전 11:41]

알겠습니다. 지금 가지러 가겠습니다. 오후 1시 까지는 모두 준비될 겁니다.

어휘 | **be in charge of** ~을 담당하다[맡다] **event organizer** 행사 기획자[담당자] **be aware of** ~을 알다 **make a trip to** ~에 가다 **rental** 사용료, 임대료 **room** 여유, 여지

165 Who most likely is Mr. Parkson?

(A) **A caterer**

(B) A hotel manager

(C) An event organizer

(D) A furniture store owner

파크슨 씨의 신분은?

출장음식 제공업자

호텔 매니저

행사 기획자

가구 매장 주인

어휘| caterer 출장음식 제공업재[업체]

해설| **세부 내용▶** 단서 **165**에서 파크슨 씨가 자신이 뷔페 준비와 테이블 세팅을 맡고 있다고 밝히고 있고, 이어지는 내용에서 파크슨 씨가 행사 음식 제공을 전문으로 하는 업체 소속임을 알 수 있으므로 정답은 (A).

---

166 What is mentioned about the Natalia room?

(A) It is already set up for a party.

(B) **It does not have enough seating.**

(C) It was double-booked.

(D) It does not have audiovisual equipment.

나탈리아 룸에 대해 언급된 것은?

이미 파티 준비가 되어 있다.

좌석이 충분하지 않다.

이중으로 예약되어 있다.

시청각 장비가 구비되어 있지 않다.

어휘| double-book 이중으로 예약을 받다 audiovisual 시청각의

해설| **내용 일치/사실 확인▶** 단서 **166**에서 나탈리아 룸에는 의자가 30개밖에 없는데 파티 일행은 35명이라고 했으므로 좌석이 충분하지 않음을 알 수 있다. 따라서 정답은 (B).

오답| (A) 뷔페 준비와 테이블 세팅을 맡은 파크슨 씨가 방금 전에 파티 장소에 도착했고, 오후 1시까지 다 준비될 거라는 마지막 메시지로 보아 이미 파티 준비가 되어 있다는 내용은 오답.

패러프레이징| 단서 chairs → 정답 seating

---

167 What is indicated about Mr. Parkson?

(A) He will be retiring soon.

(B) He has made a reservation.

(C) **He needs to go back to his company.**

(D) He is on a business trip.

파크슨 씨에 대해 시사된 것은?

조만간 은퇴할 예정이다.

예약을 했다.

회사로 돌아가야 한다.

출장 중이다.

어휘| on a business trip 출장 중인

해설| **내용 일치/사실 확인▶** 단서 **167**에서 파크슨 씨가 의자를 제공해 줄 수 있느냐는 펀 씨의 부탁을 수락하며 본사에 몇 번 더 다녀와야 한다고 했으므로 정답은 (C).

패러프레이징| 단서 make a couple more trips back to the headquarters → 정답 go back to his company

---

168 At 11:40 A.M., what does Ms. Fern mean when she writes, "I assumed so"?

(A) **She guessed that a service was not free.**

(B) She is aware of Mr. Parkson's tight budget.

(C) She had to return to the headquarters.

(D) She has already made a payment.

오전 11시 40분에 펀 씨가 "그렇게 예상했습니다"라고 말한 의미는?

서비스가 무료가 아님을 짐작했다.

파크슨 씨의 예산이 빠듯한 것을 알고 있다.

본사로 돌아가야만 했다.

이미 결제를 했다.

어휘| tight 빠듯한

해설| **의도 파악▶** I assumed so는 '그럴 줄 알았다, 그렇게 예상했다'라는 뜻으로, 해당 문장의 바로 앞 단서 **168**에서 파크슨 씨가 의자 대여가 무료가 아니라고 한 것에 대해 답한 것이다. 따라서 의자 대여 서비스가 무료가 아닐 것이라고 이미 짐작하고 있었다는 뜻이므로 정답은 (A).

오답| (C) 의자를 가지러 본사로 돌아가야 하는 사람은 파크슨 씨이지, 펀 씨가 아니라서 오답.

패러프레이징| 단서 chair rental → 정답 a service

169-171

From: Constance Milavich <constance@payapa.com>
To: Patrick Sienna <psienna@pjubusinessschool.edu>
Subject: International Business Lecture Series
Date: September 14

Dear Mr. Sienna,

169 I wish to register for one of the Communication Abroad seminars from the international business lecture series that your company is offering on September 22 at 5:00 P.M. I am a doctoral student writing a thesis on the subject of international relations, **170** so I believe I am entitled to a discount, as all events organized by PJU Business School are supposed to be discounted for doctoral students. Please remember to take this into account when you send me the bill for my attendance.

171 Also, the flyer I saw mentioned that the lecture would be held on PJU Campus, but that university has two campus locations, so I was wondering whether it will be on the North Campus or South Campus.

Thank you for your help.

Sincerely,

Constance Milavich

발신: 콘스탄스 밀라비치
〈constance@payapa.com〉
수신: 패트릭 시에나
〈psienna@pjubusinessschool.edu〉
제목: 국제 비즈니스 강의 시리즈
날짜: 9월 14일

시에나 씨께,

귀사에서 9월 22일 오후 5시에 제공하는 **169** 국제 비즈니스 강의 시리즈에서 해외 커뮤니케이션 세미나 중 하나에 등록하고 싶습니다. 저는 국제 관계를 주제로 하는 논문을 쓰고 있는 박사 과정 학생이라서 **170** 할인받을 자격이 된다고 생각합니다. PJU 경영 대학원에서 주최하는 모든 행사는 박사 과정 학생들에게 할인해 주는 것으로 되어 있으니까요. 제 참석에 대한 청구서를 보내실 때 잊지 말고 이 점을 고려해 주십시오.

171 또, 제가 본 전단지에서는 강의가 PJU 캠퍼스에서 열린다고 했는데, 그 대학에는 캠퍼스가 두 군데 있어서, 그것이 북측 캠퍼스에서 열리는지 남측 캠퍼스에서 열리는지 모르겠습니다.

도움에 감사드립니다.

콘스탄스 밀라비치 드림

어휘 | register 등록하다 doctoral 박사 과정의 thesis 논문 international relations 국제 관계 be supposed to *do* ~하기로 되어 있다 take ~ into account ~을 고려하다

---

169 What is the purpose of the e-mail?
(A) To reserve a seat for a lecture
(B) To suggest a topic for a class
(C) To inform of a venue change
(D) To request a partial refund

이메일의 목적은?
강의 좌석을 예약하기 위해
강의 주제를 제안하기 위해
장소 변경을 알리기 위해
일부 환불을 요청하기 위해

어휘 | partial 부분적인

해설 | 글의 목적 ▶ 이메일의 목적은 주로 첫 부분에서 드러난다. 첫 문장의 단서 **169**에서 세미나에 등록하고 싶다고 했다. 즉, 강의를 들으려고 좌석을 예약하기 위한 목적을 밝히고 있으므로 정답은 (A).

패러프레이징 | 단서 to register for one of the Communication Abroad seminars → **정답** To reserve a seat for a lecture

---

170 What does Ms. Milavich ask Mr. Sienna to do?
(A) Transfer some funds
(B) Hire a student worker
(C) Review her thesis
(D) Apply a discount

밀라비치 씨가 시에나 씨에게 요청하는 것은?
자금 이체하기
학생 신분의 직원 채용하기
자신의 논문 검토하기
할인 적용하기

어휘 | transfer 옮기다, 이동하다

해설 | 세부 내용 ▶ 단서 **170**에서 자신이 할인받을 자격이 된다고 청구서를 보낼 때 고려해 달라고 했다. 따라서 결국 할인을 해 달라는 말이므로 정답은 (D).

171 What does Ms. Milavich suggest about the flyer?

(A) It did not mention the lecture times.

(B) It featured inaccurate information.

(C) It did not include directions.

(D) It was designed for her thesis.

밀라비치 씨가 전단지에 대해 암시한 것은?

강의 시간에 대한 언급이 없었다.

잘못된 정보가 나와 있었다.

약도가 나와 있지 않았다.

자신의 논문을 위해 만든 것이다.

어휘 | inaccurate 잘못된, 부정확한 directions 약도, 방향

해설 | 추론▶ 단서 **171**에서 전단지 내용만으로는 강의가 열리는 캠퍼스가 어느 쪽인지 정확히 알 수 없다고 했으므로 전단지에 약도가 나와 있지 않음을 짐작할 수 있다. 따라서 정답은 (C).

오답 | (B) 장소에 대한 설명이 부족하다는 것이지 전단지 정보가 잘못된 것은 아니므로 오답.

172-175

HICKSVILLE, February 16—**172** Penny Stationery will be moving its store from the outskirts of the city to the center of Hicksville, in the heart of the commercial zone.

Since its opening three years ago, the stationery store has grown its business into a very healthy one, with profits increasing almost every month. —[1]— . This is all despite its relatively remote location, a good twenty-minute drive from the city. **173** The store has managed to make a name for itself simply by word of mouth. "Now that we've saved up enough money," says store owner Melanie Walker, "we can finally afford to move downtown, close to where our customers are."

175 There is no doubt that relocating to the center of town will bring more foot traffic to the store. —[2]— . **175** First, rent is much higher in the city, and profits need to be higher to offset the additional expense. —[3]— . One other concern is that Penny Stationery will no longer be in the large wooden cottage that it became renowned for. —[4]— . Indeed, when asked what they liked most about the store, customer Elizabeth Arroya said, "They have nice products. **174** But the biggest attraction is the atmosphere. I love the space, the wooden walls, and the rustic décor. I don't know any other store like that."

Penny Stationery is not likely to have the same look in its new home, as the downtown facilities will be modern and much smaller.

힉스빌, 2월 16일—**172** 페니 문구점이 시 외곽에서 힉스빌 중앙에 있는 상업지구의 중심지로 매장을 이전할 예정이다.

3년 전에 개점한 이후로, 이 문구점은 매우 건실한 사업체로 성장했으며, 거의 매달 수익이 증가해왔다. —[1]— . 이는 시내에서 차로 족히 20분은 걸리는, 상대적으로 외진 위치에도 불구하고 이루어낸 것이다. **173** 이 매장은 순전히 입소문으로 유명해졌다. "이제 돈을 충분히 모았기 때문에, 마침내 우리 고객들이 있는 곳과 가까운 시내로 옮길 수 있게 되었습니다."라고 매장 주인인 멜라니 워커 씨는 말한다.

175 시내 중심가로 이전하면 매장을 방문하는 사람들이 더 많아질 것에는 의심의 여지가 없다. —[2]— . **175** 우선, 시내는 임대료가 훨씬 비싸므로, 추가 비용을 상쇄하기 위해서는 수익이 더 많아야 한다. —[3]— . 또 다른 우려는 페니 문구점이 더 이상 그곳을 유명하게 만든 큰 목조 건물에 있는 것이 아니게 된다는 점이다. —[4]— . 실제로, 매장에 대해 어떤 점이 가장 마음에 들었는지를 물어보니, 고객인 엘리자베스 아로야 씨는 "그곳에는 멋진 제품들이 많아요. **174** 하지만 가장 큰 매력은 분위기예요. 저는 그 공간, 목조로 된 벽, 투박한 장식이 정말 좋아요. 그와 비슷한 다른 매장이 있는지 모르겠어요."라고 말했다.

도심의 시설은 더 현대적이고 훨씬 협소할 것이므로, 페니 문구점은 새로운 둥지에서 예전과 같은 모습을 유지할 것 같지 않다.

어휘 | outskirts 외곽, 변두리 commercial 상업의 profit 수익 relatively 상대적으로 remote 외진, 먼 make a name for *oneself* 유명해지다 by word of mouth 입소문으로 save up (돈을) 모으다 relocate 이전하다 foot traffic 방문자, 유동 인구 offset 상쇄하다 cottage 시골집 renowned for ～으로 유명한 atmosphere 분위기 rustic 투박한, 시골스러운 décor 장식 facility 《*pl.*》 시설, 설비

172 What is the purpose of the article?
(A) To review a new retailer
(B) To announce a relocation
(C) To explain a rise in rent prices
(D) To attract tourists to a city

기사의 목적은?
새로운 소매점을 평가하기 위해
이전을 알리기 위해
임대료 인상을 설명하기 위해
관광객들을 도시로 끌어들이기 위해

해설| **글의 목적 ▶** 기사에서 전달하고자 하는 핵심 내용은 주로 첫 문장에서 언급된다. 첫 문장의 단서 **172** 에서 문구점이 도시 외곽에서 도심으로 이전한다고 말하고 있으므로 정답은 (B).

패러프레이징| 단서 Penny Stationery will be moving its store → 정답 a relocation

---

173 How did Penny Stationery become famous?
(A) By its store being in a high traffic area
(B) By its owner creating some commercials
(C) By people talking to one another about it
(D) By a newspaper publishing an article on it

페니 문구점이 유명해지게 된 계기는?
매장이 유동 인구가 많은 지역에 있어서
주인이 광고 방송을 제작해서
사람들이 그것에 대해 서로 이야기해서
한 신문에서 그것에 관한 기사를 게재해서

어휘| high traffic 유동 인구가 많은 one another 서로 publish 게재하다

해설| **세부 내용 ▶** 단서 **173** 에서 페니 문구점이 순전히 입소문만으로 유명해졌다고 했으므로 정답은 (C). 지문의 make a name이 질문에서 become famous로 패러프레이징 되었다.

패러프레이징| 단서 by word of mouth → 정답 By people talking to one another about it

---

174 What does Ms. Arroya say she likes most about Penny Stationery?
(A) Its products are unique.
(B) Its interior design is appealing.
(C) Its facilities are modern.
(D) Its prices are reasonable.

아로야 씨가 페니 문구점에 대해 가장 좋아하는 점은?
제품이 독특하다.
실내 디자인이 매력적이다.
시설이 현대적이다.
가격이 저렴하다.

어휘| unique 독특한 appealing 매력적인 reasonable 가격이 저렴한

해설| **세부 내용 ▶** 직접 인용된 부분인 단서 **174** 에서 고객인 아로야 씨는 페니 문구점의 가장 큰 매력은 분위기라면서 공간, 목조 벽, 투박한 장식을 언급했는데, 이것은 실내 디자인에 해당하므로 정답은 (B).

패러프레이징| 단서 the wooden walls, and the rustic décor. → 정답 Its interior design

---

175 In which of the positions marked [1], [2], [3], and [4] does the following sentence best belong?
"Yet the move presents a few risks for the retailer."
(A) [1]
(B) [2]
(C) [3]
(D) [4]

[1], [2], [3], [4]번으로 표시된 위치들 중 다음 문장이 들어가기에 가장 적절한 곳은?
"하지만 이전은 그 업체에 몇 가지 위험을 야기한다."

어휘| present 야기하다 risk 위험

해설| **문장 삽입 ▶** 주어진 문장이 '하지만'이라는 의미의 역접의 접속사 Yet으로 시작하고 있다. 따라서 서로 반대되는 내용이 이어지는 부분을 찾으면 된다. [2]번의 앞뒤 문장인 단서 **175** 에서 '이전 후에 매장을 찾는 손님이 많아질 것이다'라는 긍정적인 내용 뒤에 바로 '시내는 임대료가 비싸므로 수익을 더 많이 내야 한다'는 부정적인 내용이 이어진다. 이 부분에 주어진 문장을 넣으면 자연스럽게 이어지므로 정답은 (B).

From: Burt Lincoln <b.lincoln@beautynow.com>
To: Colin Kinsley <c.kinsley@beautynow.com>
Subject: Image Editing Workshop
Date: August 21
Attachment: Workshop Flyer

Dear Mr. Kinsley,

176 I was wondering how much we are authorized to spend on workshops and how we can get funds for them. As you know, we have a few new workers on our team who started just a couple of weeks ago. While all of them are highly qualified, I think it would be beneficial for them to attend some workshops to ensure they feel confident in their new jobs.

I've attached a flyer about an upcoming workshop for image editing. It seems to be highly relevant to our work, **177** especially since we plan to start working on the advertisements for the new lipstick line soon. The individual cost is $120 per person, but we should be able to get a discount if all six of the new employees attend. There is limited seating, so **179-1** I think we should reserve now and simply cancel later if the budget isn't sufficient.

I look forward to hearing from you about this matter.

Sincerely,

Burt Lincoln
177 Marketing Department Manager

발신: 버트 링컨
〈b.lincoln@beautynow.com〉
수신: 콜린 킨슬리
〈c.kinsley@beautynow.com〉
제목: 이미지 편집 워크숍
날짜: 8월 21일
첨부파일: 워크숍 전단지

킨슬리 씨께,

176 우리가 워크숍에 쓸 수 있도록 승인된 액수가 얼마인지와 어떻게 자금을 받을 수 있는지 알고 싶습니다. 아시다시피, 우리 팀에는 불과 이삼 주 전에 일을 시작한 신입 직원들이 몇 명 있습니다. 그들 모두 훌륭한 자격을 갖추었지만, 그들이 새로운 직장에서 자신감을 갖기 위해서 몇몇 워크숍에 참석하는 것이 도움이 될 거라고 생각합니다.

곧 있을 이미지 편집 워크숍에 관한 전단지를 첨부했습니다. 우리 업무와 긴밀한 관련이 있어 보이는데, **177** 곧 새로운 립스틱 제품 라인의 광고 작업을 시작할 계획이기 때문에 특히 더 그렇습니다. 개인 비용은 한 사람당 120달러이지만, 신입 직원 여섯 명이 모두 참석할 경우 할인을 받을 수 있을 것 같습니다. 좌석이 한정되어 있어서, **179-1** 지금 예약하고 예산이 충분하지 않을 경우 나중에 취소하면 될 것 같습니다.

이 문제에 관해 연락을 기다리고 있겠습니다.

177 마케팅 부장, 버트 링컨 드림

어휘| editing 편집 authorize 허가하다 qualified 자격이 있는 beneficial 유익한, 이로운 relevant to ~에 관련된 per person 일인당 limited 제한된 sufficient 충분한

IMAGE EDITING WORKSHOP

Location: Piora Center, Room 120
Date: September 2
Time: 2 P.M. to 5 P.M.
Registration: August 20 to August 30
180 Instructor: Laura Goryl

This image editing workshop is for people with beginner to intermediate skills. You will learn to modify an image to achieve various goals. **180** Participants will be provided with four images of completely different genres and walked through the step-by-step processes to edit each in order to make it more appealing,

이미지 편집 워크숍

장소: 피오라 센터, 120호
날짜: 9월 2일
시간: 오후 2시부터 5시
등록: 8월 20일부터 8월 30일
180 강사: 로라 고릴

이번 이미지 편집 워크숍은 초보자부터 중급의 실력을 가진 사람들까지를 위한 것입니다. 다양한 목적을 달성하기 위해 이미지를 수정하는 법을 배우게 됩니다. **180** 참가자들에게는 전혀 다른 종류의 네 가지 이미지가 제공되며 그것들을

eye-catching, and convincing. With a **178** primary emphasis on marketing, this workshop is ideal for those in the advertisement business as it teaches both technical and theoretical knowledge.

The class is limited to twenty-five participants. Seats are available on a first come, first serve basis. **179-2** All reservations are final and may not be refunded in case of cancelation. Cost is $120 per person. Group rates are available starting at five attendees. Please contact 222-5934 for more information about this.

더 매력적이고 눈길을 끌며 설득력 있게 만들기 위해 각각을 수정하는 과정을 단계별로 익히게 됩니다. 마케팅에 **178** 주된 역점을 두고 있는 이번 워크숍은 기술과 이론적 지식을 모두 가르치기 때문에 광고업계 종사자들에게 매우 적합합니다.

강의는 참석자 25명으로 제한됩니다. 좌석은 선착순으로 이용 가능합니다. **179-2** 모든 예약은 변경할 수 없으며 취소시 환불이 되지 않을 수도 있습니다. 비용은 일인당 120달러입니다. 단체 요금은 참석자 다섯 명부터 적용됩니다. 이에 관해 더 자세한 사항은 222-5934번으로 연락하십시오.

어휘| beginner 초보자 intermediate 중급의; 중급자 achieve 이루다 walk A through B (단계별로 차례차례) A에게 B를 보여주다 step-by-step 단계적인 eye-catching 눈길을 끄는 convincing 설득력 있는 emphasis on ~에 대한 역점[강조] theoretical 이론의 final 변경할 수 없는, 최종의 in case of ~이 발생할 경우에

---

176 What is the purpose of the e-mail?
(A) To suggest changing a job requirement
(B) To promote an upcoming product line
(C) To request budget information
(D) To provide feedback about a workshop

이메일의 목적은?
직무 자격 요건 변경을 제안하기 위해
곧 나올 신제품을 홍보하기 위해
예산 관련 정보를 요청하기 위해
워크숍에 관한 의견을 제공하기 위해

해설| 글의 목적▶ 첫 번째 지문의 단서 **176** 에서 I was wondering 이하를 통해 바로 이메일의 목적을 나타내고 있다. 할당된 자금의 규모와 자금 수령 방법에 관해 묻고 있는데, 여기서 fund는 부서에 할당된 예산을 뜻하므로 정답은 (C).
패러프레이징| 단서 funds → **정답** budget

---

177 According to the e-mail, what will the marketing department do soon?
(A) Hire more qualified workers
(B) Run a workshop series
(C) Increase its advertising budget
(D) Launch a marketing campaign

이메일에 따르면, 마케팅 부서가 조만간 하게 될 일은?
자격 있는 직원을 더 채용하기
일련의 워크숍 주최하기
광고 예산 늘리기
마케팅 캠페인 시작하기

해설| 세부 내용▶ 첫 번째 지문인 이메일 끝부분에서 이메일 발신자가 마케팅 부장임을 알 수 있다. 또한 이메일 중간의 단서 **177** 의 we plan to start 이하에서 신제품 광고 작업을 시작할 거라고 했으므로 두 단서를 조합하면 정답은 (D).
패러프레이징| 단서 start working on the advertisements → **정답** Launch a marketing campaign

---

178 In the flyer, the word "primary" in paragraph 1, line 5, is closest in meaning to
(A) initial
(B) temporary
(C) main
(D) simple

전단지에서, 첫째 단락 다섯 번째 줄의 "primary"와 의미상 가장 가까운 단어는?
처음의
일시적인
주된
간단한

해설| 동의어 찾기▶ 두 번째 지문에서 primary emphasis on은 '~에 주된 역점'이라는 뜻으로 여기서 primary는 '주된, 주요한'이라는 뜻으로 쓰이고 있다. 따라서 역시 '주된, 주요한'이란 뜻을 가진 (C)가 정답이다.
오답| (A) primary에 '최초의'라는 뜻도 있음을 이용한 오답.

179 What has Mr. Lincoln misunderstood about the workshop?
(A) Its group rates
(B) Its class size limit
(C) Its cancelation policy
(D) Its registration process

링컨 씨가 워크숍에 대해 잘못 알고 있는 것은?
단체 요금
강의 규모 제한
취소 규정
등록 과정

해설| **두 지문 연계/추론 ▶** 이메일의 단서 **179-1**에서 링컨 씨는 일단 예약을 하고 예산이 충분하지 않으면 나중에 취소하면 된다고 했는데, 전단지의 단서 **179-2**에서 모든 예약은 변경할 수 없으며 취소시 환불이 안될 수도 있다고 했다. 따라서 취소 규정에 대해 잘못 알고 있음을 추론할 수 있으므로 정답은 (C).

오답| (A) 이메일에서 신입 직원 6명이 모두 참석하면 할인을 받을 수 있다는 내용과 전단지의 단체 요금이 5명부터 적용된다는 내용이 부합. (B) 이메일에서 좌석이 한정되어 있다는 내용과 전단지의 강의 참석자가 25명으로 제한된다는 내용이 부합. (D) 등록 과정에 대한 언급은 없으므로 링컨 씨가 잘못 알고 있는지 여부를 확인할 수 없다.

---

180 What is suggested about Ms. Goryl in the flyer?
(A) She has only basic image editing skills.
(B) She will help students edit some pictures.
(C) She requested a minimum of twenty-five students.
(D) She works for an advertising firm.

전단지에서 고릴 씨에 대해 암시된 것은?
기초적인 이미지 편집 실력만 가지고 있다.
학생들이 사진 편집하는 것을 도와 줄 것이다.
최소 25명의 학생들을 요구했다.
광고 회사에서 일한다.

어휘| basic 기초적인

해설| **추론 ▶** 전단지의 단서 **180**에서 고릴 씨는 워크숍 강사임을 확인할 수 있고, 워크숍 참가자들에게 몇 장의 사진들을 주고 그것들을 편집하는 과정을 단계별로 익히게 한다고 했으므로 정답은 (B).

패러프레이징| **단서** participants / four images → **정답** students / some pictures

---

181-185

Reah Ring Park and Its Controversies

By Vincent Benjamin

Trinity, April 22—**181** Reah Ring Park, a park that circles around Reah Lake, is finally open to the public. The park covers a one-kilometer-wide ring around the body of water and includes a bike path, a walkway, and several rest areas.

Construction had been delayed several times due to unexpected issues, mostly related to **182** the quality of the soil, which makes it difficult to build a solid foundation. The park's opening had also been delayed after a bridge over a small stream was deemed unsafe in a safety inspection and had to be rebuilt. The city's decision to reject proposed plans to include a playground for children sparked further controversy. "After careful analysis of the environment, we have concluded that building a playground would be too costly due to environmental factors," explained Mayor Peter Garrett. Nevertheless, **184-2 185-2** city council member Veronica McDonnell, who first suggested building a playground, continued to search for a contractor. And she may have found one in Loyden Co.'s Linda Joyce. At a recent town hall meeting, Ms. McDonnell claimed that, "Ms. Joyce has inspected the area, and she believes that she could design something that would be feasible on a small budget."

리아 링 파크와 그에 관한 논란

빈센트 벤자민 작성

트리니티, 4월 22일—**181** **리아 호수를 둘러싸고 있는 공원인 리아 링 파크가 마침내 일반에 공개된다.** 이 공원은 호수 주변의 1km 너비의 고리 모양 지역에 걸쳐 있으며 자전거 도로와 산책로, 몇 군데의 쉼터를 포함한다.

공사는 예상치 못한 문제로 인해 몇 차례 지연되었는데, 주로 **182** 견고한 토대를 만들기 어렵게 하는 토양의 질과 관련된 것이었다. 작은 개천 위에 놓인 다리가 안전 점검에서 위험하다고 판정되어 재공사를 해야 했던 이후로 공원 개장 역시 연기되었었다. 어린이들을 위한 놀이터를 포함하자는 계획안을 시에서 거부하기로 결정함에 따라 추가적인 논란이 일어났다. "환경을 면밀히 분석한 결과, 환경적 요인들로 인해 놀이터 건설에 비용이 너무 많이 들 거라는 결론을 내렸습니다."라고 피터 가렛 시장은 설명했다. 그럼에도 불구하고, **184-2 185-2** 놀이터 건설을 처음으로 제안했던 베로니카 맥도넬 시의원은 계속해서 건설 도급업체를 물색했었다. 그리고 그녀는 로이든 사의 린다 조이스 씨를

Despite these drawbacks, the project was finally completed and the park opened its doors on April 20, welcoming hundreds of visitors on its first day. So far, the park has gotten great reviews from visitors who all seem pleased with the results.

적격자로 생각했을 것이다. 최근의 시 회의에서, 맥도넬 씨는 "조이스 씨가 그 지역을 점검했고, 그녀는 적은 예산에 맞춰 실현 가능성 있는 무언가를 설계할 수 있을 거라고 생각한다"고 주장했다.

이런 문제점들에도 불구하고, 이 프로젝트는 마침내 완료되었고 공원은 4월 20일에 개장하여 첫 날 수백 명의 방문객들을 맞았다. 지금까지 공원은 결과물에 만족하는 것으로 보이는 모든 방문객들로부터 아주 좋은 평가를 받고 있다.

어휘| controversy 논란 circle around ~을 둘러싸다 body of water (바다·호수 등의) 수역 solid 견고한 foundation 토대, 기초 deem ~로 여기다 safety inspection 안전 점검 spark 촉발시키다 analysis 분석 costly 비용이 많이 드는 nevertheless 그럼에도 불구하고 drawback 문제점, 결점

Letter to the Editor

Trinity News Daily
77 Park Avenue
Trinity, PA 19636

Dear *Trinity News Daily*,

I was one of the first visitors to Reah Ring Park on Monday, and I was quite surprised by the article that you published about it. **183** I think you've included some misleading information about how the park was received. There are several negative comments on the forums that complain about the lack of parking, and most importantly, the lack of facilities for children. **184-1** The project proposed by city council member Veronica McDonnell was rejected for no good reason. It is well-known that there are funds left over from the construction that would be sufficient to go ahead with the project. **185-1** I recommend you interview the contractor that Ms. Donnell mentioned to the mayor at the last town hall meeting. I believe we would gain more insightful information from hearing a different point of view.

Sincerely,

Jarrod Kline

독자 투고

트리니티 뉴스 데일리
파크 가 77번지
19636 펜실베니아 주, 트리니티

〈트리니티 뉴스 데일리〉 담당자께,

저는 월요일에 리아 링 파크의 첫 방문객들 중 한 명이었는데, 그에 관해 귀사에서 게재한 기사를 보고 무척 놀랐습니다. **183** 공원의 평가에 대해 잘못된 정보를 포함하고 있었다고 생각합니다. 인터넷 게시판에는 주차 공간 부족과, 무엇보다도 어린이들을 위한 시설 부족에 대해 불만을 제기하는 부정적인 의견들이 몇 개 있습니다. **184-1** 베로니카 맥도넬 시의원이 제안한 프로젝트는 정당한 이유 없이 거부되었습니다. 그 프로젝트를 추진하기에 충분한 자금이 건설 프로젝트에서 남아 있다는 것은 잘 알려진 사실입니다. **185-1** 귀사에서 맥도넬 씨가 지난번 시 회의에서 시장에게 언급했던 도급업자를 인터뷰할 것을 권해드립니다. 다른 견해를 들어봄으로써 더 통찰력 있는 정보를 얻을 수 있을 것이라고 생각합니다.

재러드 클라인 드림

어휘| misleading 오도하는, 오해의 소지가 있는 forum (온라인상의) 토론 게시판 for no good reason 정당한 이유 없이 go ahead with ~을 추진하다 gain 얻다 insightful 통찰력 있는 point of view 견해, 관점

181 What is the purpose of the article?
(A) To explain a delay in construction
(B) To detail some safety precautions
(C) To announce a park's opening
(D) To encourage donations for a project

기사의 목적은?
공사 지연을 설명하기 위해
안전 수칙을 상세히 알리기 위해
공원 개장을 알리기 위해
프로젝트를 위한 기부를 장려하기 위해

해설| **글의 목적▶** 정보 전달을 목적으로 하는 기사의 핵심 내용은 대개 첫 문장에서 언급된다. 핵심 내용을 먼저 말하고 그에 관한 보충 설명이 이어지는 구조이므로, 첫 문장인 단서 **181**의 공원이 일반에 공개된다는 것(open to the public)이 기사의 핵심 내용임을 알 수 있다. 따라서 정답은 (C).

오답| (A) 공사 지연에 대한 내용이 나오지만, 부분적인 내용일 뿐 기사의 핵심 내용은 아니므로 오답.

패러프레이징| **단서** a park ~ is finally open to the public → **정답** a park's opening

---

182 What is suggested about Reah Ring Park?
리아 링 파크에 대해 암시된 것은?
(A) It is built on unstable ground.
불안정한 토대 위에 건설되었다.
(B) It was entirely funded by donations.
전적으로 기부금에 의해 자금 조달을 받았다.
(C) It is mainly targeted at young children.
어린이들을 주된 대상으로 했다.
(D) It is closed indefinitely due to safety issues.
안전 문제 때문에 무기한 폐장되었다.

어휘| unstable 불안정한 entirely 전적으로 mainly 주로 indefinitely 무기한으로

해설| **추론▶** 첫 번째 지문인 기사의 단서 **182**에서 토양 때문에 견고한 토대를 만들기 어려웠다고 했으므로 정답은 (A).

오답| (C) 어린이를 위한 놀이터 건설이 거부되었다는 기사 내용과 상반되므로 오답.

패러프레이징| **단서** difficult to build a solid foundation → **정답** built on unstable ground

---

183 What does Mr. Kline say is inaccurate in the article?
클라인 씨가 기사에서 잘못되었다고 말한 것은?
(A) The information concerning security
안전에 관한 정보
(B) The names of the people involved
관계자들의 이름
(C) The listing of available facilities
이용할 수 있는 시설 목록
(D) The description of the public response
대중의 반응에 대한 서술

어휘| concerning ~에 관한

해설| **세부 내용▶** 클라인 씨는 두 번째 지문인 편지의 단서 **183**에서 공원에 대한 대중의 평가에 대해 잘못된 정보가 기사에 포함되어 있다고 했으므로 정답은 (D).

패러프레이징| **단서** how the park was received → **정답** the public response

---

184 What opinion does Mr. Kline express?
클라인 씨가 표명한 의견은?
(A) That the playground should have been approved
놀이터는 승인되었어야 했다.
(B) That safety procedures have not been followed
안전 수칙을 따르지 않았다.
(C) That more town hall meetings should be held
더 많은 시 회의가 열려야 한다.
(D) That a budget should be increased
예산을 늘려야 한다.

해설| **두 지문 연계/세부 내용▶** 클라인 씨는 편지의 단서 **184-1**에서 맥도넬 시의원의 제안이 정당한 이유 없이 거부되었다고 했는데, 첫 번째 지문인 기사의 단서 **184-2**에서 맥도넬 시의원이 놀이터 건설을 처음 제안한 사람임을 알 수 있다. 따라서 클라인 씨는 놀이터를 건설하자는 의견에 찬성하는 입장임을 알 수 있으므로, 정답은 (A).

---

185 Who does Mr. Kline suggest the *Trinity News Daily* interview?
클라인 씨가 〈트리니티 뉴스 데일리〉 지에게 인터뷰하라고 제안한 사람은?
(A) Mr. Benjamin
벤자민 씨
(B) Mr. Garrett
가렛 씨
(C) Ms. McDonnell
맥도넬 씨
(D) Ms. Joyce
조이스 씨

해설| **두 지문 연계/세부 내용▶** 클라인 씨는 편지 끝부분의 단서 **185-1**에서 맥도넬 씨가 시 회의에서 언급했던 도급업자를 인터뷰하라고 제안하고 있는데, 기사의 단서 **185-2**에서 이 도급업자가 린다 조이스 씨임을 알 수 있으므로 정답은 (D).

https://greenfieldscommunity.com/events

| HOME | ABOUT | **EVENTS** | NEWS | CONTACT |

Greenfields Technology Convention

Attention job seekers!

Learn about the various careers that exist in technology and **186** land a job in a field you love! At the Greenfields Technology Convention (GTC), **187A** **187C** you will have the chance to meet real professionals, including employers, who will be collecting résumés and giving out business cards. This is a networking opportunity you can't afford to miss. In addition, **187D** a series of presentations by experts in tech will provide insight into the requirements and expectations of several growing technological areas. See the program below.

190-2 Cybersecurity	Saturday, June 8, 10:30 A.M. to 12:00 P.M.
Big Data	Saturday, June 8, 2:00 P.M. to 4:00 P.M.
Graphic Design	Sunday, June 9, 11:00 A.M. to 12:15 P.M.
Robotics	Sunday, June 9, 1:00 P.M to 2:15 P.M.

| 홈 | 소개 | **행사** | 소식 | 연락처 |

그린필즈 기술 총회

구직자 여러분께 알립니다!

기술 분야에 있는 여러 직업들에 대해 알아보고 여러분이 좋아하는 분야의 일자리를 **186** 얻으세요! 그린필즈 기술 총회(GTC)에서, **187A** 여러분은 **187C** 실제 전문가들을 만날 기회를 갖게 되며, 그 중에는 이력서를 받고 명함을 나눠 줄 고용주들도 있습니다. 이것은 인맥을 쌓을 수 있는, 놓칠 수 없는 기회입니다. 게다가 **187D** 기술 분야 전문가들이 하는 일련의 발표에서는 몇몇 성장하고 있는 기술 분야에서의 자격 요건 및 기대에 대한 통찰력을 제공해 줄 것입니다. 아래 프로그램을 참고하세요.

190-2 사이버보안
6월 8일 토요일 오전 10:30부터 오후 12:00
빅 데이터
6월 8일 토요일 오후 2:00부터 오후 4:00
그래픽 디자인
6월 9일 일요일 오전 11:00부터 오후 12:15
로봇공학
6월 9일 일요일 오후 1:00부터 오후 2:15

어휘 | job seeker 구직자 professional 전문가; 전문적인 give out 나눠주다 business card 명함 networking 인맥 형성 insight 통찰력 expectation 기대 cybersecurity 사이버보안 robotics 로봇공학

---

189 To: Joe Glax <joeglax@byaincorporated.com>
From: Linda Planter <lindaplanter@byaincorporated.com>
Subject: Chris's Promotion Party
Date: May 30

Hi Joe,

I got the message about Chris's promotion party on Saturday. **189** I know you need an exact head count by tomorrow, so I want to tell you about my situation. Unfortunately, I will be at the Greenfields Technology Convention on that day. **190-1** I can't miss it since I'm giving a presentation. **188-1** I reserved a return ticket for Sunday morning already. However, I can easily cancel it and make a new reservation. Then, **190-1** I could leave on the first train after my presentation Saturday and **188-1** be at Cander Station around 2:30. I can take a taxi from the station and be at the party venue around 3 P.M., which means I'd still miss lunch. Is it okay for me to arrive late at the party?

Let me know what you think.

189 수신: 조 글랙스
<joeglax@byaincorporated.com>
발신: 린다 플랜터
<lindaplanter@byaincorporated.com>
제목: 크리스의 승진 기념 파티
날짜: 5월 30일

안녕하세요. 조 씨,

토요일에 있을 크리스의 승진 기념 파티에 관한 메시지를 받았어요. **189** 내일까지 정확한 인원 수가 필요하실 거라는 걸 알기에, 제 상황에 대해 알려 드리고 싶어요. 안타깝게도, 저는 그날 그린필즈 기술 총회에 참석할 예정이에요. **190-1** 제가 발표를 할 거라서 빠질 수가 없어요. **188-1** 이미 일요일 오전에 돌아오는 표를 예약했어요. 하지만 간단히 취소하고 새로 예약을 할 수 있어요. 그러면 **190-1** 토요일 제 발표 후에 첫 기차로 출발해서 **188-1** 2시 30분쯤에 캔더 역에 도착할 수 있을 거예요. 역에서 택시를 타면 오후 3시경에는 파티 장소에 도착할 수

Cheers,
Linda Planter

있는데, 그래도 점심식사에는 여전히 참석할 수 없을 것 같네요. 제가 파티에 늦게 도착해도 괜찮을까요?

어떻게 생각하는지 알려 주세요.

린다 플랜터 드림

어휘| head count 인원수

https://perextrains.com/schedule					주말 기차 시간표

Weekend Train Schedule
Greenfields-Cander Route

그린필즈–캔더 노선

Train Number	Departure Station	Destination	Departure Time	Arrival Time
188-2 884	Greenfields	Cander	10:30 A.M.	12:30 P.M.
624	Greenfields	Cander	12:30 P.M.	2:30 P.M.
197	Cander	Greenfields	10:30 A.M.	12:30 P.M.
499	Cander	Greenfields	2:40 P.M.	4:40 P.M.

열차 번호	출발역	도착지	출발 시간	도착 시간
188-2 884	그린필즈	캔더	오전 10:30	오후 12:30
624	그린필즈	캔더	오후 12:30	오후 2:30
197	캔더	그린필즈	오전 10:30	오후 12:30
499	캔더	그린필즈	오후 2:40	오후 4:40

어휘| route 노선 departure 출발 arrival 도착

186 On the first Web page, the word "land" in paragraph 1, line 1, is closest in meaning to
(A) arrive
(B) reject
(C) offer
(D) acquire

첫 번째 웹페이지에서, 첫째 단락 첫 번째 줄의 "land"와 의미상 가장 가까운 단어는?
도착하다
거부하다
제의하다
얻다

해설| 동의어 찾기▶ 첫 번째 지문의 land a job은 '일자리를 얻다'라는 뜻으로, 여기서 land는 '차지하다, 획득하다'라는 뜻으로 쓰이고 있다. 따라서 '얻다, 획득하다'라는 뜻의 (D)가 의미상 유사하다.
오답| (A) land의 '도착하다, 착륙하다'라는 뜻을 이용한 오답.

187 What is NOT something participants can do at the Greenfield Technology Convention?
(A) Meet business contacts
(B) Try new technological equipment
(C) Interact with professionals
(D) Attend lectures by experts

참가자들이 그린필즈 기술 총회에서 할 수 있는 일이 아닌 것은?
업계의 사람들 만나기
새로운 기술 장비 시험해 보기
전문가들과 교류하기
전문가들의 강의에 참석하기

어휘| contact (도움을 줄 수 있는) 아는 사람 interact 소통[교류]하다
해설| 내용 일치/사실 확인▶ 첫 번째 지문의 단서 **187A**의 전문가나 고용주를 만나 인맥을 쌓을 수 있는 기회(networking opportunity)라는 내용이 선택지에서 business contacts로 표현되었고, 단서 **187C**의 진정한 전문가들과 만날 기회(chance to meet real professionals)가 선택지에서 interact with professionals로 표현 되었다. 단서 **187D**의 전문가들의 발표(presentations by experts)는 선택지에서 lecture by experts로 패러프레이징 되었다. 따라서 언급되지 않은 (B)가 정답.

188 Which train did Ms. Planter reserve a ticket for originally?
(A) Train 884
(B) Train 624
(C) Train 197
(D) Train 499

플랜터 씨가 원래 예약한 기차편은?
884번 열차
624번 열차
197번 열차
499번 열차

어휘 | originally 원래

해설 | **두 지문 연계 문제/세부 내용** ▶ 이메일의 단서 **188-1**에서 플랜터 씨는 원래 일요일 오전의 표를 예약했다고 했으며 최종 도착역은 캔더 역임을 알 수 있다. 기차 시간표의 단서 **188-2**에서 오전에 캔더 역으로 출발하는 기차는 884번 열차이므로 정답은 (A).

---

189 Who most likely is Mr. Glax?
(A) A software developer
(B) A train station worker
(C) An event organizer
(D) An employee benefits advisor

글랙스 씨의 신분은?
소프트웨어 개발자
기차역 직원
행사 담당자
직원 복지 상담사

어휘 | employee benefit 직원 복리후생[복지] advisor 상담사

해설 | **세부 내용** ▶ 단서 **189**에서 글랙스 씨는 이메일의 수신자임을 먼저 확인한다. 글랙스 씨가 승진 기념 파티에 관한 메시지를 보낸 사람이고, 인원수 체크를 해야 하는 것으로 보아 파티 준비를 맡고 있음을 알 수 있다. 따라서 정답은 (C).

---

190 In what field does Ms. Planter most likely work?
(A) Cybersecurity
(B) Big data
(C) Graphic design
(D) Robotics

플랜터 씨가 종사할 것 같은 분야는?
사이버보안
빅 데이터
그래픽 디자인
로봇공학

해설 | **두 지문 연계/세부 내용** ▶ 이메일의 단서 **190-1**에서 플랜터 씨는 자신이 총회의 발표자라고 했다. 또한 토요일에 있을 자신의 발표 후에 바로 기차를 타면 2시 30분까지 캔더역에 도착한다고 했으므로, 첫 번째 지문의 프로그램 일정표를 살펴보아야 한다. 첫 번째 지문의 단서 **190-2**에서 토요일에 진행되는 두 개의 프로그램 중, 2시 30분 이전에 끝나는 것은 Cybersecurity이다. 따라서 플랜터 씨가 사이버보안과 관련한 일에 종사함을 추론할 수 있다. 정답은 (A).

191-195

Wishing Well Resort Diving Week Event

It's time for this year's Diving Week! Relax at Wishing Well Resort while staying active and learning new skills. For one week, June 2 to June 8, we are partnering with Aronnax Diving to offer you great deals on unforgettable undersea adventures. Join us on any or all of the following:

Monday: reef dive 1
Tuesday: reef dive 2
Wednesday: night dive
195-1 Thursday: wreck dive

Guests staying at the Wishing Well Resort for one or more nights that week will receive **191A** a 10 percent discount on all of these dives. During Diving Week, all guests **191D** get to use the Wishing Well pool for free. In addition, to help you have enough energy for your adventures, **191B** the breakfast buffet is complimentary for the whole week!

For specific rates and reservations, call 555-2957.

위싱 웰 리조트 다이빙 주간 행사

올해의 다이빙 주간이 돌아왔습니다! 위싱 웰 리조트에서 쉬면서 활기를 갖고 새로운 기술을 배워 보세요. 6월 2일부터 6월 8일까지, 일주일 동안 아로낙스 다이빙 사와 제휴하여 잊을 수 없는 해저 모험을 저렴한 가격에 제공합니다. 다음 중에서 어느 것이든 혹은 전부 다 저희와 함께하십시오.

월요일: 암초 다이빙 1
화요일: 암초 다이빙 2
수요일: 야간 다이빙
195-1 목요일: 난파선 다이빙

그 주에 1박 이상 위싱 웰 리조트에 머무시는 투숙객들은 **191A** 위 다이빙 모두에 대해 **10% 할인을 받게 됩니다.** 다이빙 주간 동안, 모든 투숙객들은 **191D** **무료로 위싱 웰 수영장을 이용할 수 있습니다.** 또한 모험을 위해 충분한 에너지를 갖도록 해 드리기 위해, **191B** **조식 뷔페가 일주일 내내 무료입니다.**

구체적인 요금이나 예약을 원하시면, 555-2957번으로 전화 주세요.

어휘 | partner with ～와 협력[제휴]하다 a great deal on ～에 대해 저렴한 가격 unforgettable 잊을 수 없는 undersea 해저의 reef 암초 wreck 난파선 complimentary 무료의 specific 구체적인

From: Aronnax Diving <frank.elser@aronnaxdiving.com>
To: Wishing Well Resort <pdenzel@wishingwellresorts.com>
Subject: Invoice
Date: June 15
Attachment: Invoice

Dear Ms. Denzel,

Attached is the invoice for the Diving Week of June 2 to June 8. It includes $415.00 for the person who decided to get certified. This rate was **192** cleared by the resort staff manager on duty at the time.

I also wanted to point out that many people came to us asking to join the night dive, but **193-1** we had already reached the limit of the number of people, so we had to turn a lot of people down. If you choose to have this promotion again next year, **194** consider scheduling an additional night dive instead of the second reef one, which didn't have a lot of demand. I think we could easily fill up a second night excursion.

Thank you for your business,

194 Frank Elser
Diving Instructor, Aronnax Diving

발신: 아로낙스 다이빙 〈frank.elser@aronnaxdiving.com〉
수신: 위싱 웰 리조트 〈pdenzel@wishingwellresorts.com〉
제목: 명세서
날짜: 6월 15일
첨부파일: 명세서

덴젤 씨께,

6월 2일부터 6월 8일까지의 다이빙 주간의 명세서를 첨부했습니다. 여기에는 자격증을 따기로 한 분에 대한 415달러가 포함되어 있습니다. 이 요금은 당시에 근무 중이던 리조트 직원 매니저가 **192** 승인한 것입니다.

또 많은 분들이 저희에게 와서 야간 다이빙에 참가할 수 있는지 물어보셨는데, **193-1** 이미 정원에 도달해서 많은 이들을 돌려보낼 수밖에 없었다는 점을 알려 드리고자 합니다. 내년에도 이 홍보 행사를 하기로 정하신다면, 수요가 많지 않은 **194** 두 번째 암초 다이빙 대신 야간 다이빙을 추가로 일정에 넣는 것을 고려해 보시기 바랍니다. 두 번째 야간 활동 정원은 쉽게 채울 수 있을 것 같습니다.

거래에 감사드립니다.

194 아로낙스 다이빙 사, 다이빙 강사
프랭크 엘서 드림

어휘 | invoice 명세서, 송장 get certified 자격증을 따다 clear 승인하다 on duty 근무 중인 turn down 거절하다 schedule 일정에 넣다 excursion 체험활동, 짧은 여행

Aronnax Diving Invoice

Bill to: Wishing Well Resort

	Price	Number of Participants	Number of Instructors
Reef Dive 1	$180.00	14	2
Reef Dive 2	$180.00	8	1
193-2 Night Dive	$200.00	15	3
195-2 Wreck Dive	$185.00	17	4
Certification	$415.00	1	2

아로낙스 다이빙 명세서

청구 대상: 위싱 웰 리조트

	가격	참가 인원	강사 인원
암초 다이빙 1	180달러	14	2
암초 다이빙 2	180달러	8	1
193-2 야간 다이빙	200달러	**15**	3
195-2 난파선 다이빙	185달러	17	**4**
자격증	415달러	1	2

어휘 | certification 자격증, 증명

191 According to the advertisement, what is NOT offered during Diving Week?
(A) Reduced prices on dives
(B) Free breakfast
(C) Complimentary nights
(D) Access to the pool

광고에 따르면, 다이빙 주간 동안 제공되지 않는 것은?
다이빙 요금 할인
무료 조식
무료 숙박
수영장 이용 권한

해설 | **내용 일치/사실 확인 ▶** 첫 번째 지문인 광고에서 다이빙 주간에 대한 정보를 찾을 수 있다. 단서 **191A**에서 10% 할인(10 percent discount)이 선택지의 reduced prices로 패러프레이징되었고, 단서 **191B**의 조식 뷔페가 무료(breakfast buffet is complimentary)라는 내용이 선택지의 free breakfast로 바꾸어 표현되었다. 단서 **191D**의 수영장 이용이 무료(use the Wishing Well pool for free)라는 내용은 선택지에서 수영장 이용 권한(access to the pool)으로 바꾸어 표현되었다. 따라서 언급되지 않은 (C)가 정답.

192 In the e-mail, the word "cleared" in paragraph 1, line 2, is closest in meaning to
(A) approved
(B) experienced
(C) refunded
(D) requested

이메일에서, 첫째 단락 두 번째 줄의 "cleared"와 의미상 가장 가까운 단어는?
승인하다
경험하다
환불하다
요청하다

해설 | **동의어 찾기 ▶** 지문에서 cleared by the resort staff manager는 '리조트 직원 매니저에 의해 승인되었다'라는 뜻으로, 여기서 clear는 '승인하다'라는 뜻이다. 따라서 정답은 (A).

193 What is suggested about the night dive?
(A) It could include only fifteen people.
(B) It was not as popular as the reef dives.
(C) It was available only to certified divers.
(D) It had to be canceled at the last minute.

야간 다이빙에 대해 암시된 것은?
15명만 수용할 수 있다.
암초 다이빙만큼 인기 있지 않다.
자격증을 가진 다이버들만 할 수 있다.
막판에 취소될 수밖에 없었다.

해설 | **두 지문 연계/추론 ▶** 이메일의 단서 **193-1**에서 야간 다이빙은 이미 정원이 찼다고 했는데, 명세서의 단서 **193-2**에는 야간 다이빙 참가 인원은 15명으로 나와 있다. 따라서 야간 다이빙의 정원이 15명임을 알 수 있으므로 정답은 (A).
오답 | (B) 이메일에서 수요가 많지 않은 암초 다이빙 2 대신 야간 다이빙을 일정에 넣을 것을 제안하고 있는 것과 상반된 내용이므로 오답.

194 What does Mr. Elser recommend?
(A) Offering certifications
(B) Increasing the limit per dive
(C) Reducing room prices
(D) Substituting an excursion

엘서 씨가 권하는 것은?
자격증 제공하기
다이빙당 제한 인원 늘리기
객실 요금 내리기
활동 대체하기

어휘 | substitute 대체[대신]하다
해설 | **세부 내용 ▶** 두 번째 지문 마지막 부분의 단서 **194**에서 엘서 씨는 이메일 발신자이며 아로낙스 다이빙 사의 강사임을 먼저 확인한다. 이메일 본문 내의 단서 **194**에서 엘서 씨는 두 번째 암초 다이빙 대신 야간 다이빙을 일정에 넣을 것을 제안하고 있는데, 이는 다른 체험활동으로 대체하라는 제안이므로 정답은 (D).
패러프레이징 | **단서** scheduling an additional night dive instead of the second reef one → **정답** Substituting an excursion

195 How many instructors went diving on Thursday?
(A) 1
(B) 2
(C) 3
(D) 4

목요일에 다이빙을 하러 가는 강사의 수는?
1명
2명
3명
4명

해설 | **두 지문 연계/세부 내용 ▶** 광고의 단서 **195-1**에서 목요일에는 난파선 다이빙(wreck dive)이 있음을 알 수 있는데, 명세서의 단서 **195-2**에서 난파선 다이빙에 참가하는 강사 인원이 4명이라고 나와 있으므로 정답은 (D).

196-200

Job opening: Library Assistant

The Treasure Cove Library is looking to hire a library assistant to work at the front desk. **200-2** Candidates must have prior experience working in a public library and have great people skills. **196** The job entails greeting library patrons, renewing library accounts, checking items in and out, putting away books, and taking overdue fines among various other tasks. This is a part-time job with flexible hours, but the library assistant must work twenty hours a week and on at least one weekend day. To apply, please send a résumé and cover letter to Sophie Travia at stravia@tclibrary.org by September 10.

채용 공고: 도서관 보조직원

트레저 코브 도서관에서는 안내 데스크에서 일할 도서관 보조직원을 채용하려고 합니다. **200-2** 지원자는 이전에 공공 도서관에서 일한 경험이 있어야 하며 대인관계 능력이 뛰어나야 합니다. **196** 요구되는 업무는 도서관 이용객 맞이하기, 도서관 이용계정 갱신하기, 물품 반납 및 대출하기, 도서 정리하기, 연체료 수납하기 등의 다양한 업무들입니다. 이것은 근무시간이 자유로운 시간제 일자리이지만, 도서관 보조직원은 일주일에 24시간과 적어도 주말 하루를 근무해야 합니다. 지원하려면, 9월 10일까지 stravia@tclibrary.org로 소피 트라비아에게 이력서와 자기 소개서를 보내 주십시오.

어휘 | assistant 보조원, 조수   prior 이전의   people skill 대인관계 능력   entail 수반하다   check in (빌린 것을) 반납하다   check out 대여[대출]하다   put away 치우다, 정리하다   overdue fine 연체료(윤 late fee)

To: Sophie Travia <stravia@tclibrary.org>
From: Matthew Hunter <matthunter@forevermail.com>
Date: September 9
Subject: Application for Library Assistant
Attachment: résumé, cover letter

Dear Ms. Travia,

I wish to apply for the position of Library Assistant at Treasure Cove.

Although I have not worked in a library before, **197** I have extensive experience in customer service. As such, I believe that I would excel at serving patrons and ensuring that all of their requests are fulfilled. Moreover, **199-2** I am currently pursuing a master's degree in library science. I am already halfway through my degree, and as I keep progressing, I will continue to gain knowledge that will be useful on the job.

I've attached my résumé and a cover letter with further details about my experience and background.

Sincerely,
Matthew Hunter

수신: 소피 트라비아 <stravia@tclibrary.org>
발신: 매튜 헌터 <matthunter@forevermail.com>
날짜: 9월 9일
제목: 도서관 보조직원 지원
첨부파일: 이력서, 자기 소개서

트라비아 씨께,

저는 트레저 코브의 도서관 보조직원 자리에 지원하고자 합니다.

전에 도서관에서 일한 적은 없지만, **197** 고객 서비스에 있어서는 폭넓은 경험을 가지고 있습니다. 그래서 이용객들을 응대하고, 이용객의 모든 요구사항을 확실히 충족시키는 일에 뛰어날 것이라고 생각합니다. 또한, **199-2** 저는 현재 도서관학 석사 학위를 밟고 있습니다. 이미 학위 과정 절반을 마쳤으며, 계속 진행하고 있으므로 그 일에 유용할 지식을 계속 쌓아가게 될 것입니다.

제 경험과 배경에 대해 더 자세히 알려 드리기 위해 이력서와 자기 소개서를 첨부했습니다.

매튜 헌터 드림

어휘 | extensive 폭넓은   excel 뛰어나다   fulfill 충족시키다   pursue 종사하다, 수행하다   master's degree 석사 학위   progress 진행하다, 앞으로 나아가다

To: Circulation Staff<circulation@tclibrary.org>
From: Sophie Travia <stravia@tclibrary.org>
Subject: Library Assistant Position
Date: September 11

Hi all,

We didn't get many candidates for the library assistant job. **198** I recommend loosening our requirements so that we can find at least five interviewees. For example, Matthew Hunter does not have all of the qualifications that we listed. However, he might still be suitable for the job. He has never worked in a library, but **199-1** his current situation suggests that he is familiar with the environment and that he would be able to adapt quickly.

On the other hand, **200-1** Ms. McCawley has all of the necessary qualifications, but she is not able to work on Saturdays or Sundays. It would be difficult for us to rearrange the schedule to accommodate her. Thus, I think we might have to find someone else to interview instead of her.

I look forward to hearing your suggestions.

Regards,

Sophie Travia
Head of Library Circulation

수신: 대출계 직원
〈circulation@tclibrary.org〉
발신: 소피 트라비아
〈stravia@tclibrary.org〉
제목: 도서관 보조직원 자리
날짜: 9월 11일

안녕하세요, 여러분,

도서관 보조직원 자리에 지원자가 많지 않았습니다. 최소한 다섯 명의 면접 대상자를 찾을 수 있도록 **198** 자격 요건을 완화할 것을 제안합니다. 예를 들어, 매튜 헌터 씨는 우리가 열거한 자격 요건을 모두 가지고 있지 않습니다. 하지만 그가 이 자리에 적합할 수도 있습니다. 그는 도서관에서 일한 적은 없지만, **199-1** 현재 상황으로 보아 근무환경에 익숙하며, 빠르게 적응할 수 있을 것으로 짐작됩니다.

반면에, **200-1** 맥콜리 씨는 모든 필요한 자격 요건을 갖추고 있지만, 그녀는 토요일과 일요일에는 일을 할 수 없습니다. 우리가 그녀에게 맞춰 일정을 재조정하는 것은 어려울 것입니다. 그래서 그녀 대신 면접을 할 다른 사람을 찾아야 할 것 같습니다.

여러분의 의견을 듣고 싶습니다.

도서관 대출계 계장
소피 트라비아 드림

어휘| circulation (도서) 대출, 유통   loosen 완화하다   interviewee 면접 대상자   be familiar with ~을 잘 알고 있다   adapt 적응하다   rearrange 재조정하다

---

196 According to the advertisement, what is a duty of the library assistant?
(A) Purchasing books
(B) Collecting money
(C) Repairing items
(D) Creating accounts

광고에 따르면, 도서관 보조직원의 업무는?
도서 구입하기
돈 수납하기
물품 수리하기
계정 만들기

해설| **세부 내용▶** 첫 번째 지문인 구인광고의 단서 **196** 에서 해당 일자리의 업무에 대한 내용을 찾을 수 있다. The job entails 이하에 맡게 될 업무가 열거되고 있는데, 그중에 연체료 받기에 해당하는 (B)가 정답.
패러프레이징| **단서** taking overdue fines → **정답** Collecting money

---

197 What does Mr. Hunter think his biggest strength is?
(A) His background in finance
(B) His in-depth knowledge
(C) His ability to work long hours
(D) His people skills

헌터 씨가 자신의 가장 큰 장점이라고 생각하는 것은?
경제 분야 배경지식
깊이 있는 지식
장시간 근무 가능함
대인관계 능력

어휘| in-depth 심도 있는

해설| **세부 내용▶** 헌터 씨는 이메일의 단서 **197**에서 자신이 폭넓은 고객서비스 경험을 가지고 있어서 고객 응대에 뛰어날 것이라고 했는데, 이는 대인관계 능력이 뛰어나다는 것이므로 정답은 (D).

오답| (B) I will continue to gain knowledge는 앞으로 지식을 쌓아가게 된다는 뜻이지 현재 깊이 있는 지식이 있다는 말은 아니므로 오답.

패러프레이징| 단서 excel at serving patrons → 정답 people skills

198 What is the purpose of the second e-mail?
두 번째 이메일의 목적은?
(A) To recommend offering a job to a candidate
지원자에게 일자리를 제안하자고 권하기 위해
(B) To reject an incomplete application package
미비한 지원서류를 거부하기 위해
(C) To suggest making hiring criteria more flexible
채용 기준을 더 유연하게 하자고 제안하기 위해
(D) To explain the necessary qualifications for a position
일자리에 필요한 자격 요건을 설명하기 위해

어휘| incomplete 불완전한 criterion (판단) 기준 (*pl.* criteria)

해설| **글의 목적▶** 이메일의 단서 **198**에서 지원자가 많지 않으니, 지원자의 자격 요건을 완화하자고 제안하고 있으므로 정답은 (C).

패러프레이징| 단서 recommend loosening our requirements → 정답 suggest making hiring criteria more flexible

199 What does Ms. Travia think makes Mr. Hunter suitable for the job?
헌터 씨가 일자리에 적합하다고 트라비아 씨가 생각하는 이유는?
(A) His relevant field of study
관련 분야의 학업
(B) His extensive work experience
폭넓은 업무 경험
(C) His ideal financial situation
이상적인 재정 상황
(D) His outgoing personality
활발한 성격

어휘| relevant 관련 있는 outgoing 외향적인

해설| **두 지문 연계/세부 내용▶** 두 번째 이메일의 단서 **199-1**에서 트라비아 씨는 헌터 씨의 현재 상황으로 보아 그가 근무환경에 익숙해서 일자리에 적합할 수도 있다고 말하고 있다. 첫 번째 이메일에서 이에 부합하는 헌터 씨의 상황을 찾아보면 단서 **199-2**에서 그가 현재 도서관학 석사 학위 과정을 밟고 있다고 했으므로 정답은 (A).

오답| (B) 도서관에서 일한 적이 없다는 내용과 상반되므로 오답. (D) 대인관계 능력이 뛰어나다는 것은 헌터 씨의 의견으로 트라비아 씨가 생각하는 이유는 아니므로 오답.

200 What is implied about Ms. McCawley?
맥콜리 씨에 대해 암시된 것은?
(A) She is looking for a full-time job.
정규직 일자리를 찾고 있다.
(B) She was already interviewed by Ms. Travia.
이미 트라비아 씨에게 면접을 보았다.
(C) She has worked in a public library before.
전에 공공 도서관에서 일한 적이 있다.
(D) She is applying for a master's degree in library science.
도서관학 석사 과정에 지원할 것이다.

해설| **두 지문 연계/세부 내용▶** 질문에 나온 맥콜리 씨는 두 번째 이메일에서 찾을 수 있는데, 단서 **200-1**에서 맥콜리 씨가 필요한 자격 요건을 모두 갖춘 지원자라고 했다. 구인 광고의 단서 **200-2**에서 지원자는 자격 요건으로 이전에 공공 도서관에서 일한 경험이 있어야 한다고 명시하고 있으므로 맥콜리 씨는 전에 공공 도서관에서 일한 경험이 있다는 것을 추론할 수 있다. 따라서 정답은 (C).

오답| (B) 지원자 면접은 아직 시작하지 않은 상황이므로 오답.

패러프레이징| 단서 have prior experience working in a public library → 정답 has worked in a public library before

토마토
BASIC
RC